THE PROFESSIONAL SYMPHONY ORCHESTRA IN THE UNITED STATES

by

George Seltzer

The Scarecrow Press, Inc.

Metuchen, N.J.   1975

Library of Congress Cataloging in Publication Data
Main entry under title:

The Professional symphony orchestra in the United States.

    Bibliography: p.
    Includes index.
    1. Symphony orchestras--United States. I. Seltzer,
George Albert, 1924-
ML1211.P76   785'.06'61   75-19271
ISBN 0-8108-0855-2

Printed in the United States of America

PREFACE

The important orchestral composers, performers, musicologists, critics, sociologists, economists and lay music lovers whose contributions follow all have at least one common bond--their active involvement with the "greatest musical instrument of Western culture." According to the American Symphony Orchestra League, this country supports well over 1000 symphony orchestras, probably more than half the world's total. When we consider the number of performing musicians, their lay boards of directors (along with the various committees drawn from their communities), their professional business organizations, and their vast audience, we find an impressive number of the American population directly and actively concerned with this musical instrument.

Although there are many excellent books about the orchestra (in generic terms), individual orchestras, conducting and conductors, orchestral performers, orchestral performance and orchestral music, the "whole animal" has not yet been viewed within the covers of a single volume by the multitude of experts in the varied disciplines involved.

Obviously, the broad spectrum of this complex phenomenon we call the professional symphony orchestra cannot be treated comprehensively here. In fact, the purpose of this anthology is to expose the skeleton of the "whole animal" with the hope that the reader will be enticed to add more of the anatomy.

To help achieve this goal, I have adapted a format which clusters expert opinion around a broad general topic in each chapter. For example, a member of an orchestra board of directors may desire expert information about the role (and art) of the conductor. Chapter II ("The Conductor--The Ultimate Autocrat in a Democratic World") contains widely varied views and opinions (and a concise history) of this topic. The selected bibliography at the end of the book is intended to present additional sources of information for this and all other topics in the text. The structure of this book also should aid, for example, the conductor (or student of conducting) to learn more about the professional musician (Chapter III), and the critic to know more about some of the factors involved in "Making the Program" (Chapter V).

In dealing with an institution as complex as the professional symphony orchestra, I have been unable to completely segregate and isolate one general topic from another; of course, this is as it should be. Ultimately, the conductors, performers, listeners, programs, management and funding form an interrelationship as inextricable as is the triumvirate of composer-performer-listener, in terms of the function of the orchestra itself. Articles such as "Philharmonicsville (pop. 106)," by Donal Henahan in Chapter III ("The Orchestral Musicians"), might just as well have been placed in Chapter I ("The Orchestra"). "The Career Experience of the Symphony Musician," by David L. Westby in Chapter VI ("The Business of Music Making"), could appropriately be in Chapter III. Many other articles were candidates for dual or even triple placement.

I owe many thanks for the valuable advice and guidance freely offered over many months by Mr. Benjamin S. Dunham, Director of Publications for the American Symphony Orchestra League. His help has been of the utmost importance. I am also obliged to the following individuals for their many courtesies during the more than three years that preceded the publication of this volume: Dr. John Druesedow, former Music Librarian, Miami University; Mr. Eugene V. Frey, President, Cincinnati Musicians Association; Ms. Jacqi Hallowell of Dick Moore and Associates, New York; Mr. Ronald Herder, former Editor-in-Chief, G. Schirmer, Inc.; Ms. Gail Stockholm, Music Critic of The Cincinnati Enquirer; Ms. Helen Thompson, former manager, The New York Philharmonic; and Ms. Annemarie F. Woletz, Assistant Editor, International Musician.

Although I am thankful for all the assistance given me, the responsibility for the shortcomings of this book is mine. I sincerely hope the reader who finds I have neglected an area of interest or an expert whose opinion would be of value will communicate this deficiency. The professional symphony orchestra in the United States is a vital institution of Western culture. I would like to do all I can to make available the expertise to keep this institution viable.

George Seltzer
Oxford, Ohio
June 1974

CONTENTS

v

IV. THE AUDIENCE: THE MUSIC CONSUMERS

V. THE MUSIC THE ORCHESTRA MAKES

VI.   THE BUSINESS OF MUSIC MAKING: ORGANIZATIONAL, ECONOMIC AND SOCIOLOGICAL ASPECTS

Chapter I

THE ORCHESTRA:
Its European Beginnings and Its
Development in the United States

Introduction. The symphony orchestra in the 20th century is a complex organism. From its heterogeneous beginnings in the 16th century through its gradual standardization and overblown opulence to
the development of individualistic characteristics it is a fascinating
tale, intertwined with parallel developments in the art of musical
composition and orchestration, the mechanical and technical improvement of musical instruments, and the sociological and economic
changes in the Western world.

In this chapter, Adam Carse, the noted British musicologist, details
the historical development of the orchestra through the 18th century.
The French composer, Hector Berlioz, continues with telling comments about the orchestra of the 19th century in Europe.   John H.
Mueller, the American sociologist, brings us information about the
beginnings of the symphony orchestra and its role in the United
States.   Author-critic Joseph Wechsberg, music educator Raymond
Kendall, and conductor Leopold Stokowski tell us more about the 20th-
century professional symphony orchestra.   Finally, Oscar Levant,
pianist and musical raconteur, discusses some of the interactions of
orchestra personnel, conductors and soloists.

HOW IT ALL BEGAN*

Adam Carse

        The story of the orchestra and of orchestration may be said
to begin when, modal vocal polyphony having reached its culmination
in the 16th century, educated musicians began to turn their attention
to the composition of music designed specifically for stringed, wind,
and keyboard instruments in combination, and in particular to the

---

*From The History of Orchestration, by Adam Carse; New York:
Dover Publications, Inc., 1935, 1964.   Reprinted through the permission of the publisher.

embryonic forms of opera, oratoria, and ballet, which, accompanied
by primitive and unorganized orchestras, then began to take shape
and to absorb much of the energy which musicians had hitherto expended almost exclusively on the composition of ecclesiastical and
secular vocal music--the mass, motet, and madrigal.

The birth of the orchestra is thus connascent with the creation of secular instrumental music as a cultured form of the art, and
largely arises out of the transition from modal polyphony to monody.
It coincides with the inception of purely instrumental music for bowed
string instruments, of dramatic music, and with the beginning of the
gradual obsolescence of the viol type rendered inevitable by the greater suitability and practical superiority of the newly invented violins;
also with the beginning of the gradual rejection of plucked string instruments as a medium for the expression of serious music.

The evolution divides itself broadly into two periods, the first
ending soon after the middle of the 18th century with the death of
the two great masters of harmonic polyphony, Bach and Handel; the
second beginning with the rise of modern orchestration in the hands
of Haydn and Mozart.   The transition is chronologically spanned by
the work of Gluck and a group of secondary composers of which perhaps the best remembered are Philipp Emanuel Bach and Hasse.

Intimately and inseparably connected with the history of orchestration are: progress in the art and technique of musical composition; improvements in the construction of musical instruments, both
of which are again associated with the growth of instrumental technique.

Influences not without considerable effect on the subject are
those arising out of the circumstances and conditions under which
composers carried on their work, also the positions occupied socially and geographically by the men who made musical history.   One
may instance, for example, the small public reached by Bach's
music during his lifetime and for long after his death; the comparative isolation and limited influence of Purcell; the obscurity of Schubert's life; or more favorable conditions such as the position and opportunities of Lulli at the court of Louis XIV of France; the cosmopolitan activities of Handel; the advantages enjoyed by Haydn as an
orchestral composer under princely patronage; or the quick diffusion
of his orchestral music by the socially gifted and much-travelled
Mendelssohn.

Other influences are those arising from the political and national histories of European countries and dynasties during the last
three centuries; commercial conditions in so far as they concern the
music printing and publishing trade, and the manufacture of musical
instruments; also from the enterprise of operatic, dramatic, and
concert-giving institutions.   The tastes and tendencies of society and
public in various countries at various times, the patronage of musical
art by royalty, nobility, or wealth, and the different systems of musical education which have been in vogue; all those have reacted directly

on general musical history, and not indirectly on the evolution of
orchestration.

Rapid and easy communication between countries, and facilities for the quick diffusion of orchestral music by means of printed
scores and parts are conditions which did not prevail during the 17th
and 18th centuries; thus, progress made even by prominent composers in one country did not necessarily spread to other musical centers with the same rapidity as at present, or during the 19th century.
Indeed, considering the comparative isolation of some composers,
and the fact that much of their music remained in manuscript during
their lifetimes, the wonder is that progress was so general as it
proved to be.   Little if any of Bach's, Mozart's or Schubert's orchestral music was published while they lived; both Bach and Schubert remained to be practically rediscovered by later generations,
while others wrote in and for one country, in some cases forming
musical backwaters which could not communicate any considerable
impetus to the main stream of general progress.

The same applies to orchestral, and in particular to wind instruments and the improvements to their mechanism which have
transformed them from crude signals of the chase, the field, or the
fair, to the highly organized artistic media of the modern concert-
room or theatre.   Thus, the clarinet, "invented" circa 1690, does
not appear as a regular constituent of the orchestra till quite a
hundred years later; trombones, known and used long before orchestration can be said to have begun, do not permanently join the orchestral body till the 19th century; and valves as applied to brass
instruments, from their inception early in the same century took
quite fifty years to come into anything approaching general use.

The diffusion of orchestral music before the 19th century depended largely on the circulation of manuscript copies of scores and
parts, or the personal travels of composers carrying with them their
manuscripts.   A visit to a particular musical center would result in
the composition of some work written and orchestrated to suit the
resources of a particular theatre or concert orchestra; thus, Mozart
wrote "Prague" and "Paris" symphonies, masses for Salzburg,
operas for Milan, Munich, Prague, and Vienna; similarly, Haydn
wrote a large number of works for the orchestra maintained by his
employer, Prince Esterházy, six symphonies for Paris, and 12 for
London.   Lengthy residence in one locality produced works designed
for the orchestral combination to which the composer had access;
Lulli and Bach wrote each for their own resources respectively at
Paris and Leipzig; Handel for the opera at Hamburg, Hannover, for
Italy or England according to where he settled for the time being;
Gluck wrote for Vienna or Paris, and so on.   Parts are even occasionally added to or deleted from scores when a work was transferred from one center to another where the orchestra differed in
constitution.   Further, there is abundant evidence that composers
often adapted their orchestration to suit even individual players, and
would contrive an exceptional part for a conspicuously good player,
and allot insignificant matter to inferior players, or would write no

part at all for instruments which in particular orchestras were not available or their players incompetent.

All these conditions unite in producing a more or less unstable selection of instruments in the scores of composers who wrote before the time when increased facilities for the wider circulation of orchestral music caused them to orchestrate for the musical world generally, and to score their works for standard combinations of instruments which they could rely on finding at all centers where orchestral music was seriously cultivated. The change takes place about the close of the 18th century, before which time composers vary their orchestration to suit particular orchestras, and after which orchestras, when varying at all, are adjusted to suit particular scores.

Easier communication between countries, increased production and circulation of printed scores and parts, the establishment of more numerous and larger orchestras, and changing conditions which encouraged a more free exchange of music, caused during the 19th century a gradual decentralization and more rapid spread of influences which make for progress, till, as at the present time, the effect of one successful composer's work may easily make a universal impression in the course of a few years. The innovation of one man now quickly becomes the common property of all, the only essential being that his work should be generally accepted and admired. As soon as Wagner's music became popular his orchestration colored the work of all but the very conservative, while Berlioz, whose work has never had more than sporadic success, for all his innovations, progressiveness, and specialization in orchestral effect, has exerted little real influence on the art. A single effect can now exercise a worldwide influence in a few years; it may have to wait on public taste for success, but once having achieved popularity it soon becomes absorbed into the current orchestral language of all composers, whether they are in sympathy with the style of music in which the effect had its origin or not.

For convenience and clearness a survey of progress in orchestration must be divided into periods which, however, should not be conceived as showing clearly defined demarcation of time, nor do they admit of rigid classification. The evolution is always gradual, albeit uneven, but nevertheless continuous and generally progressive.

Going hand in hand, it is impossible to completely separate orchestration per se from the advance of musical art, the technique of composition, the mechanical development of orchestral instruments, or the concurrent growth of instrumental technique; but as far as is possible, the matter will be treated more as concomitant with instrumental technique and construction than with the more generally familiar history of the art and technique of musical composition, and with a leaning to the practical rather than to the aesthetic point of view.

A broad division into two periods has already been made, the first starting with the appearance of the violin type and witnessing the gradual formation of the string orchestra which, well established by the end of the 17th century, has remained unaltered ever since.

Conterminous with the first period is the use of keyboard instruments and lutes in the orchestra in order to supply harmony, and played from the figured-bass part which is found in all scores of the period. This feature is so universal and characteristic of all orchestral writing from the early attempts near the end of the 16th century till the advent of Haydn and Mozart that it might appropriately be labelled "the period of basso continuo." The use and selection of wind instruments during this period lacks organization, stability, and good balance, and remains unsettled till near the middle of the 18th century, when the beginning of what eventually developed into the so-called "classical" orchestra of Haydn and Mozart is seen to be in process of crystallization.

The first period covers the transition from modal polyphony to monody, and culminates in the harmonic polyphony of Bach and Handel; it sees the creation and establishment of opera and oratorio, the instrumental suite, and other forms ambiguously called overture, symphony, and concerto, and precedes the classical sonata form, symphony, and solo concerto. The aria with da capo is a child of this constructive period which in its early stages also witnesses the popularity of masques, ballets and intermezzi. The growth of the string orchestra of violin type hastens the devitalization of music for plucked string instruments--the lute, theorbo, and many kindred varieties--it seals the doom of tablature notation, frets on the fingerboards of bowed string instruments, the five- or six-stringed tuning of viols in fourths and a third, and only allows the occasional use of sympathetically stringed instruments such as the viola d'amore. This period sees the triumph of the transverse flute over the flûte-à-bec, recorder, and flageolet; the transformation from shawm and bombard to oboe and bassoon; the disappearance of the old wooden cornetti and the elevation of the hunting horn into the orchestral horn.

The second period is marked by the expulsion from the orchestra of the basso continuo played on a keyboard instrument. This leaves to the string orchestra the responsibility of supplying the main harmonic structure, of which it had been fully capable for at least three-quarters of a century, and, if it deprives the orchestra of one broad change of color, does away with an incongruity of blend. At the same time an organized and better balanced woodwind section becomes established, consisting of pairs of flutes, oboes, clarinets, and bassoons, clarinets being the last comers. Melodically and harmonically independent of one another, these two main groups form a two-part body with an additional group of horns, trumpets, and drums, which, however, owing to the imperfections of the instruments are unable to supply independent harmony or melody, and this is the improved but hardly fully grown

orchestra which Haydn and Mozart hand over to their great successor, Beethoven.

The early years of the 19th century see an increase in the
number of horns and the occasional use of trombones--long in common use for Church music--in symphonic scores, but the most
pregnant change which the orchestra is yet to undergo is the result
of the invention and application of lengthening valves to horns and
trumpets during the first half of the century, which with the growing use of trombones, transforms the orchestra into a three-part
body of string, woodwind and brass, each group harmonically and
melodically independent, self-contained, chromatic in nature and,
with the drums, constituting the ordinary full orchestra of today.

A steady increase in the number of players to each string
part disturbs to some extent the accepted principles of balance between the three groups, and from the early days of Wagner and
Berlioz, there is an increasing tendency to add wind instruments
of allied nature differing principally in dimensions to the already
established wind groups, but except for the introduction of bass
tuba and harps, the orchestra of late Beethoven and Weber remains the nucleus of all modern combinations, and has sufficed as
a medium of expression for most of the finest conceptions in orchestral language by the great writers of the late 19th century.

The greater appreciation of the use of tone color, of blend,
and of dramatic fitness, is a feature of orchestration which developed and expanded rapidly from the time of Weber onwards,
leaving the formality and traditional stiffness of Haydn's, Mozart's
and Beethoven's orchestral manner far behind, but which as yet has
not rendered the orchestration of those masters too out-of-date and
old-fashioned in feeling to give pleasure and satisfaction to present-
day audiences.

This second broad division in the evolution of orchestration
accompanies the development of musical art through the periods
usually dubbed "classical," "romantic," and "modern"; it covers
two reforms of opera inaugurated by Gluck and Wagner, the creation and higher development of modern symphony, solo concerto and
concert overture, the inception of symphonic poem and program
music generally, and still follows the art into its present-day rami-
fications--"atmospheric," "futuristic," and what not.

However much the growth of the orchestra has been the toy
of circumstances, conditions, or the mechanical or technical development of instruments, the real driving force behind such evolution is after all the insistently growing demand of musical art for
fit means of expression. The impelling power of a constantly ad-
vancing art has always carried with it the realization of better and
more worthy means of expressing itself, and with the demand, the
man, the instrument, and the opportunity have always been forthcoming.

THE ORCHESTRA IN THE XVIII CENTURY*

Adam Carse

When we narrow down our view of 18th-century music and musicians, and focus our attention only on the orchestras and orchestral music of that period, some of our present-day conceptions must be modified, and others must be abandoned altogether.

An orchestra as we know it now, and an orchestra as it was known then, are not quite the same thing. We know it as a fully grown thing; they were witnessing its growth. Disregarding small bodies of players, or any which for various reasons are incomplete, the orchestra of today has a constitution which has long been stabilized and standardized. The main body is a combination of three self-contained groups of instruments, namely, the bowed-string group, the woodwind and the brass groups. The main body is supplemented by a less essential fringe of percussion and plucked-string instruments, and a few outgrowths in the woodwind and brass groups are added or withdrawn without materially altering the general constitution of these sections. At no time in the 18th century would that definition have held good. During that period the main body of the orchestra was still in the process of formation. The foundation or base on which it was built up consisted of one or more keyboard or chordal instruments; to that was added a more or less complete bowed-string group, a small and rather variable woodwind group which was barely harmonically self-supporting, and on occasion a small brass group which could not provide its own harmony. By the end of the century the original basis, the keyboard and chordal instruments, had been almost entirely discarded; the bowed-string group had taken their place as the foundation of the body; the woodwind group had become harmonically self-contained, and the brass group was still growing and remained as yet harmonically incomplete. For the greater part of the century, however, the keyboard and chordal instruments formed the center around which the other groups grew and played, and from which the whole was largely controlled.

When looking back on the orchestras of the 18th century it is important to keep in mind the essential part played by the keyboard and chordal instruments, and to realize how much composers relied on these instruments to supply the harmony for their music. We must imagine the composers conceiving their music in melodic outline for bowed-string instruments against a harmonic background built up on an all-important general or universal bass part, the basso continuo.

We must not expect to find in the 18th century, especially in the earlier part, that clear distinction which we now make

*From The Orchestra in the XVIII Century, by Adam Carse; Cambridge, Eng. : W. Heffer, 1940. Reprinted by permission of W. Heffer & Sons Ltd.

between chamber music and orchestral music; indeed, it is rather difficult to draw the line between a small orchestra in the 18th century and a party of chamber-music players. The old German writers make a clear distinction between church music, opera, and chamber music, but by the latter term they mean both orchestral music and what we now call chamber music. To them, chamber music was the instrumental music of a court, which was played in the chamber or private apartment of a sovereign or ruling prince. The musicians attached to a court were <u>Kammermusiker</u>.

One of the things that must be completely cut out of the picture of the 18th century orchestra is our conception of the orchestral conductor. The time-beating, interpretative orchestral conductor did not exist. It should be understood that the word "conductor" was applied to the musician who was in charge of a performance, but that orchestras were not controlled by a time-beating conductor.

All 18th-century musicians were executants. There were none who were merely directors of performance, and none who were only composers of music. It was left to the 19th century to bring into being conductors and composers of music who did not combine these activities with actual playing on an instrument or singing. Most composers were instrumentalists, very often competent on both a keyboard and a bowed-string instrument, and not a few cases of composer-vocalists occur. Virtuosi, of course, specialized each in their particular line, but never so exclusively nor to the extent that they do nowadays. Practical musicianship was expected of all performers, but somewhat less of Italian vocalists. Just as all composers were executants, so nearly all executants were composers. There was hardly an instrumental soloist that didn't write and play his own solos. The travelling virtuoso carried about with him a bundle of his own concertos and sonatas, and he was reckoned a poor musician who couldn't compose his own repertoire.

The repertoire of German court orchestras consisted largely of works by its own <u>Kapellmeister</u>, and the operas produced in one place were generally the work of one or two composers who were on the spot and directed the performance of their own work. Hasse composed most of the operas produced at Dresden while he was <u>Kapellmeister</u> to the King of Poland, and Jommelli supplied the bulk of those at Stuttgart when he was in charge of the Duke of Würtemberg's musical establishment. Even though the opera was not entirely a court affair, as for example, in Italy, Paris or London, the works produced were those of composers who were settled in these places, either permanently or temporarily, and wrote for the resources of the particular theatre. They were, or became for the time being, local composers. At the Opéra in Paris, for example, of the 105 operas and ballets produced between 1700 and 1750, all were by French, or, one might even say, by Parisian composers, except three by the German-born Jean Batistin (Johann Baptist Stuck). On the whole, it might be said that, during the greater part of the 18th century, the performance of a musical work

was generally associated with the composer's presence at the place
where it was played, and that as far as possible he was the interpreter of his own music.

The clear distinction which has since grown up between
"music" and "light music" hardly existed in the 18th century. The
most distinguished of musicians composed and took part in the performance of dance music, outdoor music and music played during
meals. Court orchestras were at the same time the equivalents
of the modern concert orchestra, the theatre orchestra, the dance
band, the restaurant band and the open-air promenade band. The
same composers wrote the music for all of them. They were not
divided into sheep and goats, highbrows and lowbrows, composers
of art music and trade music. A composer didn't lose caste when
his music became popular; in fact, he gained prestige thereby, and
tried to make it popular. Secular music was intended to entertain
and please; the 18th-century composer knew better than to try to
educate his audience; he aimed at pleasing them. Mozart's letters
make it very clear that he was constantly striving to write in such
a manner as would please his listeners locally, in Italy, in Paris,
in Munich or Vienna, or wherever he went. Handel was not trying
to educate his London audiences; he was trying to please them;
and we may be sure that Haydn would not have kept his job in the
Esterházy household for so long if he had always written above the
head of the prince. We cannot picture an 18th-century Italian opera
audience, the ruling prince of a German state, the Paris aristocracy, the "quality" or "haut ton" of 18th-century London being
taught musical appreciation by any composer. They would soon
have sent about his business anyone who had tried to do so. The
18th-century composer who claimed that he was writing for future
generations would have been considered a lunatic; he wrote for the
present, and didn't set himself to make the "classics" of the future.

In the 18th century the orchestra was only part, and not the
most important part of a musical organization. It existed at first
rather as an adjunct to vocal or solo music; as an accompanying
medium which supported the voices in church music and opera, or
the instrumental soloist in the concerto. By the end of the century, however, the orchestra had gained sufficient independence and
importance to be in a position to begin to challenge the supremacy
of the vocal element which had hitherto been the dominating power
in music.

For the greater part of the century the opera overture was
nothing more than a preliminary to the main effort; something
which could be talked through while the audience was settling down
to listen to the performance they had come to hear. In spite of
the efforts of Gluck to make the overture an integral part of the
drama, and notwithstanding the fine overtures of Mozart towards
the end of the century, most of them, and especially those by
Italian composers, were carelessly and hastily put together.

When, about the middle of the century, the overture,

detached from its opera, became the starting point and model for
the concert symphony, the status of the orchestra began to improve
a little.   The hundreds of symphonies which were printed during
the second half of the century are evidence enough of a growing interest in purely orchestral music as such, and beginning to free
itself from a position which had kept it always more or less in
subjection to vocal music.   Symphonies were then played at every
concert; generally two or three at each concert.   But the programs
of those days show the place of honor still allotted to the vocal or
the instrumental solo.   The symphony would always begin and end
the concert, or the two halves of the program, but the aria, the
duet, the quartet, the choral excerpt or the concerto still occupied
the central positions right up to the end of the century.

The musical literature of the 18th century has to be fine-
combed in order to find references to the playing of an orchestra.
The searching historian must read page after page about the singing of the vocalists and the playing of the violinist or the flautist,
and then be truly grateful if he is thrown a word about the orchestra.   There is so much that those authors could have told us about
their orchestras; but they didn't.   They were writing for the readers of their own time, and what they wrote about makes it very
clear that it was the individual rather than the corporate performance that interested their public.   The singing of a choir or the
playing of an orchestra were to them small matters compared with
the excellence of this singer's shake or the extent of that singer's
compass.

THE ORCHESTRA*

Hector Berlioz (1803-1869)

The orchestra may be considered as a large instrument
capable of uttering at once or successively a multitude of sounds
of different kinds; and of which the power is mediocre or colossal
according to whether it employs the whole or a part only of the
executive means belonging to modern music, and according to
whether those means are well or ill chosen and placed in acoustic
conditions more or less favorable.

The performers of all kinds whose assemblage constitutes it
thus seem to be its strings, its tubes, its pipes, its planes of
wood or metal; machines, intelligent it is true, but subject to the
action of an immense keyboard, played upon by the conductor under
the direction of the composer.

It seems to me impossible to indicate how fine orchestral

*From A Treatise on Modern Instrumentation and Orchestration, by
Hector Berlioz (tr. by Mary Cowden Clark).   London: Novello and
Co. , 1858.

effects are to be found; this faculty--developed doubtless by practice and rational observation--is like the faculties of melody, of expression, and even of harmony, and belongs to the number of those precious gifts which the musician-poet, the inspired inventor, must receive from nature herself. But certainly it is easy to demonstrate, in a manner almost exact, the art of making orchestras fit to give a faithful rendering of compositions of all shapes and dimensions. Theatrical orchestras and concert orchestras should be distinguished one from the other. The former in certain respects, are generally inferior to the latter.

The place occupied by the musicians, their disposal on a horizontal plane or on an inclined plane, in an enclosed space with three sides, or in the very center of a room, with reverberators formed by hard bodies fit for sending back the sound, or soft bodies which absorb and interrupt the vibrations, and which are more or less near the performers, are points of great importance. Reverberators are indispensable; they are to be found variously situated in all enclosed spaces. The nearer they are to the point whence the sounds proceed, the more potent is their influence.

This is why there is no such thing as music in the open air. The most enormous orchestra placed in the middle of an extensive garden open on all sides--like that of the Tuileries--would produce no effect. The reverberation from the palace walls even, were it placed against them, is insufficient; the sound instantaneously losing itself on all the other sides.   An orchestra of a thousand wind instruments, with a chorus of two thousand voices, placed in a plain, would not have a twentieth part of the musical action that an ordinary orchestra of eighty players with a chorus of a hundred voices would have if well disposed in the concert room at the Conservatoire.   The brilliant effect produced by military bands in the streets of great towns comes in support of this statement, which it seems to contradict.   But the music is not then in the open air.   The walls of high houses skirting the streets right and left, avenues of trees, the fronts of grand palaces, neighboring monuments, all serve as reverberators; the sound revolves and circulates freely in the circumscribed space thus surrounding it, before escaping by the points left open.   But let the military band, pursuing its march and continuing to play, leave the large street for a plain devoid of trees and habitations, the diffusion of its sounds is immediate, the orchestra vanishes, there is no more music.

The best way of disposing the performers, in a room with dimensions proportioned to their number, is to raise them one above another by a series of steps, arranged in such a way that each row may send out its sounds to the hearer without any intermediate obstacle.

All well-organized concert orchestras should be thus arranged in steps.   If the orchestra be erected in a theatre, the stage should be completely closed in at the back, at the sides both right and left, and above, by an enclosure of wooden planks.

If, on the contrary, it be erected in a room dedicated to the purpose, or in a church where it occupies one of the extremities, and if, as it frequently happens in such cases, the back of this space be formed of massive building which reflects with too much force and hardness the sound of the instruments placed against it, the force of the reverberation--and consequently the too great resounding--may easily be mitigated by hanging up a certain number of draperies, and by bringing together at this point such bodies as will break the motion of the waves of sound.

Owing to the construction of our theatres, and to the exigencies of dramatic representation, this amphitheatrical disposal is not possible for orchestras intended for the performance of operas. The instrumentalists brought together in lyric theatres, in the lowest central point of the building, before the footlights, and on a horizontal plane, are deprived of the majority of the advantages resulting from the arrangement I have just indicated for a concert orchestra.   Hence, what lost effects there are, what unperceived delicate gradations in opera bands, in spite of the most admirable execution!   The difference is such that composers are almost compelled to bear it in mind and not to instrument their dramatic scores quite in the same way as symphonies, masses, or oratorios, intended for concert rooms and churches.

Opera orchestras were always formerly composed of a number of stringed instruments proportioned to the mass of other instruments; but this has not been the case for many years.   A comic opera orchestra in which there were only two flutes, two hautboys, two clarinets, two horns, two bassoons, rarely two trumpets, and hardly ever any kettledrums, was balanced then with nine first violins, eight second violins, six violas, seven violoncellos, and six double basses; but as four horns, three trombones, two trumpets, a long drum, and cymbals figure there nowadays, without the number of stringed instruments having been increased, the balance is destroyed, the violins are scarcely to be heard, and the result of the whole is detestable.   The orchestra of the Grand-Opéra, where they are, besides the wind instruments already named, two cornets-à-pistons and an ophicléide, the instruments of percussion, and sometimes six or eight harps--is not balanced either with 12 first violins, 11 second violins, eight violas, ten violoncellos, and eight double-basses; it should have at least 15 first violins, 14 second violins, ten violas, and 12 violoncellos, the extra instruments being left unused in those pieces where the accompaniments are very soft.

The proportions of a comic opera orchestra would suffice for a concert orchestra intended for the performance of Haydn's and Mozart's symphonies.   A larger number of stringed instruments would even be, sometimes, too much for the delicate effects which these masters have usually assigned to the flutes, hautboys, and bassoons.

For Beethoven's symphonies, Weber's overtures, and modern compositions conceived in the grand and impassioned style, there

needs, on the contrary, the mass of violins, violas, and basses
which I have just indicated for the grand opera.

But the finest concert orchestra, for a room scarcely larger
than that of the Conservatoire--the most complete, the richest in
gradations and varieties of tone, the most majestic, the most powerful, and at the same time the most soft and smooth--would be an
orchestra thus composed:

21 first violins	2 hautboys	3 trombones (1
20 second violins	1 English horn	alto, 2 tenor
18 violas	2 clarinets	or 3 tenor
8 first cellos	1 corno di bassetto	1 great bass
7 second cellos	(or a bass clarinet)	trombone
10 double basses	4 bassoons	1 ophieléide in
4 harps	4 horns w/ cylinders	B♭ (or a bass-
2 piccolos	2 trumpets w/ cylinders	tuba)
2 flutes	2 cornets-à-pistons	2 pairs, kettle-
		drums (4
		drummers)
		1 long drum
		1 pair, cymbals

If a choral composition were to be executed, such an orchestra
would require 46 first and second sopranos, 40 first and second
tenors, and 40 first and second basses.

By doubling or tripling this mass of performers, in the
same proportions and in the same order, a magnificent festival orchestra might doubtless be obtained. But it is erroneous to believe that all orchestras should be constituted according to a system based on the predominance of stringed instruments; very admirable results may be obtained from a contrary plan. The
stringed instruments--too weak to prevail over masses of clarinets
and brass instruments--then serve as a harmonious link with the
thrilling sounds of the wind instruments; softening their brilliancy
in some cases, and animating their effect in others, by means of
the tremolo, which, by blending with them, renders musical even
the roll of the drums.

Common sense tells the composer--unless he be compelled
to a different course by any particular form of orchestra--that he
should combine his mass of performers according to the style and
character of the work he brings forth, and according to the nature
of the principal effects which the subject demands. Thus, in a
requiem, and in order to deliver musically the grand images of
this hymn of the dead, I have employed four small orchestras of
brass instruments (trumpets, trombones, cornets, and ophicléides),
placed apart from each other, at the four corners of the main orchestra, formed of an imposing body of stringed instruments, of
all the other wind instruments doubled and tripled, and of ten
drummers playing on eight pairs of kettledrums tuned in different
keys. It is quite certain that the particular effects obtained by this
novel form of orchestra were absolutely unattainable by any other.

Here we have an opportunity to remark upon the importance of the various points of procedure of the sounds. Certain parts of an orchestra are intended by the composer to interrogate and answer each other; this intention can only be made manifest and of fine effect by causing the groups between which the dialogue occurs to be placed at a sufficient distance from one another. The composer should, therefore, in his score, indicate for them the disposition which he judges proper.

The drums, long drums, cymbals, and kettledrums, if employed to strike certain rhythms all at once--after the common mode of proceeding--may remain together; but if they have to execute an interlocutory rhythm, of which one fragment is struck by the long drums and cymbals, and the other by the kettledrums and drums, there is no doubt the effect will be made incomparably better, finer, and more interesting, by placing the two masses of instruments of percussion at the extremities of the orchestra, and consequently at a sufficient distance from one another. The constant uniformity of the executive masses is one of the great obstacles to the production of sterling and really new works; it besets composers more from old custom, routine, laziness, and want of reflection than from motives of economy--motives unfortunately all too important, in France especially, where music is so far from forming a part of the moral being of the nation, where the government does everything for theatres, and nothing at all for music properly so called, where capitalists are ready to give 50,000f. and more for a great master's painting, because that represents an intrinsic value, yet would not lay out 50f. to render feasible, once a year, some solemnity worthy of a nation like ours, and fitted to display the very numerous musical resources which it truly possesses without the capability of making them of use.

It would nevertheless be curious to try for once, in a composition written ad hoc, the simultaneous employment of all the musical forces which might be gathered together in Paris. Supposing that a master had these at his disposal, in a vast space adapted for the purpose by an architect who should be well versed in acoustics and a good musician, he ought, before writing, to determine with precision the plan and arrangement of his immense orchestra and then keep them always present in his mind while writing. It is obvious that it would be of the highest importance in the employment of so enormous a musical mass to take into account the distance or the nearness of the different groups which compose it. This condition is one of the most essential to deriving the utmost advantage from it, and in calculating with certainty the scope of its effects. Until now, at festivals, merely the ordinary orchestra and chorus have been heard, quadrupled or quintupled in their several parts according to the greater or lesser number of the performers; but in the case proposed it would be quite another affair and the composer who should attempt exhibiting all the prodigious and innumerable resources of such an instrument, would assuredly have to achieve an entirely new task.

Here, then, is how--with time, care, and the necessary out-
lay--it could be effected in Paris. The disposal of the groups
would remain at the will, and subject to the particular intentions,
of the composer; the instruments of percussion, which exercise an
irresistible influence on the rhythm, and which always lag when
they are far from the conductor, should be placed sufficiently near
him to be able instantaneously and strictly to obey the slightest
variations of movement and measure:

120	violins, divided into two, three, or four parts
40	violas, divided or not into firsts and seconds, of which 10 at least should be ready to play, when needed, the viole d'amore
45	violoncellos, divided or not into firsts and seconds
18	double basses with 3 strings, tuned in fifths (G, D, A)
15	other double basses with 4 strings, tuned in fourths (E, A, D, G)
4	octo basses
6	large flutes
4	third flutes in E♭ (improperly called in F)
2	octave piccolos
2	piccolos in D♭ (improperly called in E♭)
6	hautboys
6	English horns
5	saxophones
4	bassons-quinte
12	bassoons
4	small clarinets in E♭
8	clarinets in C, or B♭, or A
3	bass clarinets in B♭
6	horns (6 with pistons)
8	trumpets
6	cornets à pistons
4	alto trombones
6	tenor trombones
2	great bass trombones
1	ophicleide in C
2	ophicleides in B♭
2	bass tubas
30	harps
30	pianofortes
1	very low Organ, provided with stops of at least 16 feet
8	pairs, kettle drums (10 drummers)
6	drums
3	long drums
4	pairs, cymbals
6	triangles
6	sets of bells
12	pairs, ancient cymbals (in different keys)
2	very low great bells
2	gongs
4	pavillons chinois
467	instrumentalists total

     40   child sopranos (firsts and seconds)
    100   women sopranos (firsts and seconds).
    100   tenors (firsts and seconds).
    120   basses (firsts and seconds)
    360   chorus singers total

It will be perceived that in this aggregate of 827 performers the chorus singers do not predominate; even considering this, there would be much difficulty in collecting in Paris 360 voices of any excellence--so little is the study of singing at present cultivated or advanced.

It would evidently be necessary to adopt a style of extraordinary breadth each time the entire mass is put in action; reserving the delicate effects, the light and rapid movements, for small bands which the author could easily arrange, and make them discourse together in the midst of this musical multitude.

Beside the radiant colors which this myriad of different tone-qualities would give out at every moment, unheard-of harmonic effects would be deduced from them.

From the division of the 120 violins into eight or ten parts, aided by the 40 violas, in their high notes, the angelic aerial accent, and the pianissimo tint.

From the division of the violoncellos and double basses below in slow movements, the melancholy religious accent, and the mezzo forte tint.

From the union, in a small band, of the very low notes of the clarinet family, the gloomy accent, and the forte and mezzo forte tints.

From the union, in a small band, of the low notes of the hautboys, English horns, and bassons-quinte, mingled with the low notes of the large flutes, the religiously mournful accent, and the piano tint.

From the union, in a small band, of the low notes of the ophicléides, bass tuba, and horns, mingled with the pedals of the tenor trombones, with the lowest notes of the bass trombones, and of the 16-feet stop (open flute) of the organ, profoundly grave, religious, and calm accents, and the piano tint.

From the union, in a small band, of the highest notes of the small clarinets, flutes, and piccolos, the shrill accent, and the forte tint.

From the union, in a small band, of the horns, trumpets, cornets, trombones, and ophicléides, a pompous and brilliant accent, and the forte tint.

From the union, in a large band, of the 30 harps with the entire mass of bowed instruments playing pizzicato, and thus forming together another gigantic harp with 934 strings, graceful, brilliant, and voluptuous accents, in all tints, and gradations.

From the union of the 30 pianofortes with the six sets of bells, the 12 pairs of ancient cymbals, the six triangles (which might be tuned, like the ancient cymbals, in different keys), and the four pavillons chinois, constituting a metallic orchestra or percussions, joyous and brilliant accents, and the mezzo forte tint.

From the union of the eight pairs of kettledrums with the six drums and the three long drums, forming a small orchestra of percussion, and almost exclusively rhythmical, the menacing accent, in all tints.

From the mixture of the two gongs, the two bells, and the three large cymbals, with certain chords of trombones, the lugubrious and sinister accent, in the mezzo forte tint.

How can I enumerate all the harmonic aspects under which each of these different groups, associated with other groups either sympathetic or antipathetic with them, would appear!

There might be grand duets between the band of wind instruments and the stringed band; between one of these two bands and the chorus; or between the chorus and the harps and pianofortes only.

A grand trio between the chorus in unison and in octave, the wind instruments in unison and in octave, and the violins, violas, and violoncellos also in unison and in octave.

This trio might be accompanied by a rhythmical form designed by all the instruments of percussion, the double basses, the harps, and the pianofortes.

A simple chorus, double or triple, without accompaniment.

An air for violins, violas, and violoncellos together, or for wooden wind instruments together, or for brass instruments together, accompanied by a vocal band.

An air for sopranos, or tenors, or basses, or all the voices in octave, accompanied by an instrumental band.

A small choir singing, accompanied by the large choir, and by some instruments.

A small band playing, accompanied by the large orchestra, and by some voices.

A grand deep melody, executed by all the bowed bases; and

accompanied above by the violins divided, and the harps and pianofortes.

A grand deep melody, executed by all the wind basses and
the organ; and accompanied above by the flutes, hautboys, clarinets,
and the violins divided.

Etcetera, etcetera, etcetera.

The system of rehearsals requisite for this colossal orchestra cannot be doubtful; it is that which must be adopted whenever
there is an intention to get up a work of grand dimensions, the
plan of which is complex, and certain parts or the whole of which
offer difficulties in performance; it is the system of partial rehearsals.   This is how the conductor will have to proceed in his
analytical operation.

I take for granted that he knows thoroughly, and in its min-
utest details, the score which he is about to have performed.   He
will first appoint two sub-conductors, who should--marking the
beats of the bar in the general rehearsals--keep their eyes continually upon him, in order to communicate the movement to the
masses too far removed from the center.   He will then select rehearsers for each of the vocal and instrumental groups.

He will first make them rehearse themselves, that they may
be well instructed in the way in which they will have to direct the
portion of study allotted to them.

The first rehearser will rehearse separately the first sopranos, then the seconds, and then the firsts and seconds together.

The second rehearser will practice in the same way the
first and second tenors.

The third rehearser will do the same by the basses.   After
which, three choirs, each composed of a third of the total mass,
will be formed; and then lastly, the whole chorus will be practiced
together.

As an accompaniment to these choral studies, either an organ, or a pianoforte may be used, assisted by a few wind instruments, violins and basses.

The sub-conductors and the orchestral rehearsers will practice separately in the same way:

First.   The first and second violins separately; then all the
violins together.

Second.   The violas, violoncellos, and double basses separately; then all together.

Third.   The entire mass of bowed instruments.

Fourth.   The harps alone.

Fifth.   The pianofortes alone.

Sixth.   The harps and pianofortes together.

Seventh.   The wooden wind instruments alone.

Eighth.   The brass wind instruments alone.

Ninth.   All the wind instruments together.

Tenth.   The instruments of percussion alone, particularly teaching the kettledrummers to tune their kettledrums well.

Eleventh.   The instruments of percussion joined with the wind instruments.

Twelfth.   Lastly, the whole vocal and instrumental mass united, under the direction of the conductor himself.

This method of proceeding will have the result of securing, first, an excellence of execution that never could be obtained under the old system of collective study; and next, of requiring from each performer but four rehearsals at most.   It should not be forgotten to have a profusion of tuning forks of exact pitch among the members of the orchestra; it is the sole means by which the accurate tuning of this crowd of instruments of such various nature and temperament can be ensured.

Vulgar prejudice stigmatizes large orchestras as noisy: but if they be well-constituted, well-practiced, and well-conducted; if they perform sterling music, they should be called powerful; and certainly, there is no more dissimilarity than between these two expressions.   A trumpety little vaudeville orchestra may be noisy, while a large body of musicians properly employed may be of extreme softness and should produce--even in their loudest effects-- the most beautiful sounds.   Three ill-placed trombones will seem noisy, insufferable; and the instant after, in the same room, 12 trombones will strike the public by their noble and powerful harmony.

Moreover, unisons acquire real value only when multiplied beyond a certain number.   Thus, four violinists of first-rate skill playing together the same part will produce but a very poor--even detestable--effect; while 15 violinists of ordinary talent might be excellent.   This is why small orchestras--whatever the merit of the performers who compose them--have so little effect and consequently so little value.

But in the thousand combinations practicable with the vast

orchestra we have just described would dwell a wealth of harmony,
a variety of tone qualities, a succession of contrasts, which can be
compared to nothing hitherto achieved in Art; and above all, an incalculable melodic, expressive, and rhythmical power, a penetrating
force of unparalleled strength, a prodigious sensitivity for gradations in aggregate and in detail. Its repose would be as majestic
as the slumber of the ocean; its agitations would recall the tempests
of the tropics; its explosions, the outbursts of volcanos; therein
would be heard the plaints, the murmurs, the mysterious sounds of
primeval forests; the clamors, the prayers, the songs of triumph
or of mourning of a people with expansive souls, ardent hearts, and
fiery passions; its silence would inspire awe by its solemnity; and
organizations the most rebellious would shudder to behind its
crescendo spread roaringly--like a stupendous conflagration!

THE EVOLUTION OF
THE AMERICAN SYMPHONY ORCHESTRA*

John H. Mueller

The modern American symphony orchestras, which display
so many similarities in their professional and economic organization, are obviously a culmination of a long series of experimental
progenitors.   Out of this struggle for mere survival, as well as
the lure of professional excellence, there has evolved a form of
symphonic organization that appears to have adapted itself moderately well to our current [1951] social order; but which will, by
the same token, undoubtedly undergo further developmental muta-
tions in the future.

In comparison with European music, the beginnings of the
American orchestra were pathetically meager.   For in this country
there were no luxurious courts and castles which could sustain a
Haydn, nor a landed nobility which could pension a Beethoven, nor
yet the rich tradition in which whole nations take pride, and are
thereby automatically impelled to nurture the arts and set standards
for emulation.   Still awaited in the United States were the counterparts of their European forebears; the philanthropic amateurs who
were to deliver such a decisive impetus to the development of music
a half century later, and the financiers and captains of industry
who would seize upon the symphony orchestra to proclaim their
civic pride.

Without such royal or industrial patronage, the early American (as well as English) orchestras were thrown upon their own resources.   The Graupner "orchestra," of Boston, the earliest essay

---

*From The American Symphony Orchestra, by John H. Mueller.
Bloomington: Indiana University Press, 1951.   Copyright 1951 by
Indiana University Press.   Reprinted by permission.

in "permanent" orchestral organization, today would hardly merit
the name.   A German who had migrated to London and played under Haydn in 1971-92, Gottlieb Graupner subsequently emigrated to
Charleston and finally settled in Boston where, as teacher of oboe,
flute, and violin and as proprietor of a publishing house, he established himself as the musical factotum in that city of 25,000 inhabitants.   Not only did he inspire the founding of the Handel and
Haydn Society, but he also gathered together a dozen musicians to
play the symphonies of Gyrowetz and Haydn, and to study such other scores as were available in the incipiently cultured Boston of
that day.   His enterprise has gained for him from some historians
the hackneyed but appreciative title of "father of the American Orchestra. "

        Every other city also sprouted its musical organizations,
even though the cultural soil might have been more stony than that
of the precocious East.   Philadelphia, Cincinnati, St. Louis, San
Francisco, and other communities, as they attained a modicum of
wealth and leisure, and attracted German and French immigrants,
cultivated the Muses.   If the beginnings were usually modest, casual, and ephemeral, they still were harbingers of greater things to
come.

        At mid-century, there appeared from across the waters a
source of energy that fertilized the American symphonic movement
and accelerated its maturation.   In 1848, as a precipitation from
the German revolution of that year, a score of impecunious but
competent musicians banded themselves together for a concert tour
of America.   Having gained their initial and greatest success in
Boston, this Germania Orchestra responded to a demand from cities
as far west as St. Louis, played the Beethoven symphonies together
with an assortment of more or less serious music, and inculcated
for the first time some appreciation for reasonably dexterous performance of the classics.   The members of this group, however,
soon became aware of the melancholy truth that traveling orchestras, then as now, were not necessarily profitable enterprises.
At their dissolution in 1854, they scattered from Boston to Chicago,
thereby continuing the work of fructifying American musical culture
to its everlasting benefit.   One of these members, Carl Bergmann,
cellist and conductor, soon became the conductor of the New York
Philharmonic.   Bergmann was an ardent disciple of Wagner and
Liszt, and according to Theodore Thomas, with whom he was associated for many years, he was "the first man in this country who
gave proper rendering of Beethoven ... and the first real conductor
to give us an insight of our great composers" [Musical Courier,
April 29, 1891].

        More sensational, but less durable in influence, was the
French conductor, Louis Antoine Jullien, showman extraordinary,
who brought his orchestra of European artists, including many of
the most prominent instrumentalists, to the United States in 1853-
54.   This orchestra was augmented by an American contingent to
100 players, with whom he presented nightly concerts in New York

for a period of two months. After nine months' sojourn, during
which he conducted two hundred concerts and toured the country
from Boston to New Orleans, the irrepressible Jullien instituted the
first of America's "jumbo" concerts--later to take the name of
"festival"--in New York in June, 1854. This "Grand Musical Congress," which was made up of 1500 instrumentalists and 16 choral
societies, performed selections from the great oratorios as well
as symphonic numbers. The less sophisticated of the 20,000 members of the audience satiated their appetite on this occasion with
one of the Jullienesque "descriptive pieces," specially written for
the occasion, the "Fireman's Quadrille."

Jullien may have been a musical demagogue, for he was
never unmindful of the psychological effect of such extramusical
trappings, the jewelled baton and spotless white gloves for a
Beethoven rendition, or the frenetic gestures for his many quad-
rilles. But he was definitely not a humbug, as was alleged by some
snobbish observers. He received extravagant notices, even in the
best press, for his serious achievements: "His fiddles all bowed
together ... he was painstaking and energetic in rehearsals ... he
attained a pianissimo, while the New York Philharmonic could not
even achieve a piano, much less a pianissimo." He explored the
means of reaching the masses, which the austere New York Philharmonic never dreamed of and the dignified Germania barely attempted. While crude megalomania never again reached such
heights, it was by no means inconspicuous in the monster festivals
of Damrosch, Thomas, or Patrick Gilmore the bandmaster, while
the personal career of the virtuoso conductor down to the present
day is never quite devoid of a subtle touch of it, intent on sending
the music on its way more effectively.

In the local contingent of the Jullien orchestra was an 18-
year-old violinist, Theodore Thomas, who absorbed his first impressions of disciplined rehearsals, and who was to continue the
sowing so that a later generation might reap. Theodore Thomas
was the first modern conductor to fulfill completely the promise of
symphonic ideals. During the middle years of his pioneering career, this indomitable spirit launched, or participated in, three distinct experiments in symphonic organization, the third of which was
destined to become the standard one. The Thomas biography is
the evolutionary history of the American symphony orchestra.

As his first venture, in 1863, he founded his own organization, a permanent and fully employed body of men, presented in
popular concerts in the famous Central Park Garden, Seventh
Avenue near 58th Street, and in serious concerts in Steinway Hall
on 14th Street. It was this well-disciplined band, held together
with minor interruptions for about twenty-five years with modest
material assistance from William Steinway and other friends, that
imparted the first genuine and substantial impetus to the establishment of sound symphonic standards outside New York City. Essentially it was the product of Thomas' own financial and artistic responsibility, whose exciting history of alternating frustration and

success has been repeatedly told [see Charles E. Russell, The American Orchestra and Theodore Thomas, Garden City, N.Y.: Doubleday, Page, 1922]. Although it has been averred that the New York Philharmonic stimulated the organization of orchestras in other cities of the United States [H. E. Krehbiel, The Philharmonic Society of New York, New York: Novello, Ewer, 1892, p. 7], this is an overstatement. It was the migratory Thomas, with the Thomas orchestra, that whetted the appetite for disciplined performance in Boston, Philadelphia, Cincinnati, and Chicago.

After a second undertaking--the direction of the New York Philharmonic Society (1879-91)--Thomas finally achieved the fulfillment of his dream in the Chicago Orchestra (1891) supported by philanthropic subsidy.

This, Thomas' third type of organizational experiment, bears pointed testimony to the tenacity of his purpose and the eminence of his ideals. Even this persistence would have availed little had it not been supported by resolute philanthropic forces, whose patience was fortified by the powerful stimulant of civic pride and the fierce determination of a frontier city to crash the company of the cultivated East.

In addition to the cooperative system of the New York Philharmonic and the private enterprise of Theodore Thomas, there appeared a variation of the philanthropic systems of administration that is today practically obsolete. This was the personal philanthropy practiced by such persons as Edward Bok in Philadelphia, William Clark in Los Angeles, Clarence Mackay, and H. H. Flagler in New York, but which attained its consummate perfection in the Boston Orchestra, the creation of Henry Higginson, the Boston financier. The first orchestra to profit from an almost unlimited philanthropy, it was modelled on the court troupes of Europe, and was established, owned, and administered by one man who looked upon and treated his musicians as his salaried employees. It differed from its European prototype, however, in two significant respects. First, it was in no sense functionally a private orchestra but was administered solely in the interest of public performance; second, it was dominated by an aesthetic idealism which entrusted the musical director with complete and autonomous jurisdiction, unrestrained by any economic, political, or personal consideration. Never has the theory of "artistic supremacy" been more perfectly implemented. It set the pattern of things to come. If detailed features have been altered, the general principle of philanthropic support, which permits a certain autonomy to an aesthetic standard, is now well accepted in orchestral administration.

The story of this long and gradual evolution is best told in the histories of the individual major orchestras.

THE FUNCTION OF THE ORCHESTRA
IN COMMUNITY AND NATION*

John H. Mueller

The symphony concert is not exclusively, nor in one sense primarily, a musical event. For, so complex and inseparable are human interests, that every social occurrence is a blended experience of varied and simultaneous motives. A concert is comparable, perhaps, to a dinner party, where the interest in food may be subordinated to business contacts, social prestige, ceremonial display, or mere convivial association. No hostess would be flattered to be assured merely that the food was nutritious, nor even that it was tastily served; for such an affair has well-accepted ramifications into many other avenues of social intercourse. A symphony concert is similarly a pluralistic event, which may supply an outlet for fashion, prestige, civic pride, heightened national consciousness, as well as musical delight. It is therefore no disparagement, but a psychological and sociological truth, that music is often secondary to nonmusical considerations.

Since music, too, is laden with these derivative functions, which vary considerably in character and proportion from person to person, the quality and meaning of "enjoyment" of a concert displays a wide range of variation in different epochs. When, for example, we reflect on the strenuous content of our recent and contemporary symphony programs, the awe in which the masterpieces are held, the reluctance with which the audience pits its taste and judgment against that of the critic and conductor, and the frankly tentative and reserved judgments of the critics themselves, it is difficult for the modern patron to realize that in the classic period, often called the "golden age," music was generally considered a matter of sheer pleasure, a forthright delectation of the senses, without any pretense of satisfactions of a more edifying nature. It is quite evident from Mozart's letters that he contemplated very little beyond the pleasure of the moment and harbored no conceit about the sacredness of his scores. In 1787 he writes of his having attended a ball where

> I saw with the greatest pleasure all these people flying
> about with such delight to the music of my Figaro trans-
> formed into quadrilles and waltzes; for here nothing is
> talked about but Figaro, nothing played but Figaro, nothing
> whistled or sung but Figaro, no opera as crowded as Fig-
> aro--very flattering to me certainly.

His solicitous father shared this desire for instantaneous success, counseling him "to imitate the natural and popular style which

*From The American Symphony Orchestra, by John H. Mueller. Bloomington: Indiana University Press, 1951. Copyright 1951 by Indiana University Press. Reprinted by permission. Footnotes appear at the end of the selection.

everyone easily understands. " As if in reply to this recipe for success, the devoted son reassures his father at the time of the rehearsals of Idomeneo in Munich: "As for what is called popular taste, do not be uneasy, for in my opera there is music for every class, except the long-eared. " In speaking of his concertos, he almost apologizes for the esoteric passages:

> These concertos are a happy medium between what is too easy and what is too difficult; they are very brilliant, pleasing to the ear, natural without being vapid. There are passages here and there from which connoisseurs alone can derive satisfaction, but these passages are written in such a way that the less learned cannot fail to be pleased, though without knowing why. [1]

Charles Burney, a scholar and friend of artists, statesmen, and musicians (including Handel and Haydn), writing his monumental history of music during the same period, voices the same straightforward and mundane conception, characteristic of the period of The Enlightenment: "Music is an innocent luxury unnecessary, indeed, to our existence, but a great improvement and gratification of the sense of hearing. "[2]

Although much of Mozart's music is still played and enjoyed today, his guileless conception of its function has suffered eclipse, for the typical aesthetician of the romantic 19th century (descended, however, from 18th-century antecedents) held in scorn the theory that music is made merely for pleasure. In fact, it need not even be beautiful. In reviewing Sibelius' Second Symphony, the late Richard Aldrich, then of the New York Times, expressed that notion as follows:

> There is absolutely nothing in this symphony that is written to please the ear as many wish to be pleased. There is much that sounds chaotic and disordered; but it is evident to the listener who can take a larger measure of it, that it is all very definitely related, the coherent expression of a consistent idea. It is not too much to say that this Second Symphony of Sibelius is one of the strongest compositions in the symphonic form that have been heard in a considerable period. [3]

Such a sanction for what was then cerebral cacophony would have been inconceivable to Haydn, Mozart, Beethoven, and their contemporaries. Mozart, Handel, and Bach had great difficulty in producing music in sufficient volume and at a rate to satisfy the honest appetite for novelty on the part of their audiences, while today a novelty is something the modern audience is expected to endure for the sake of possible habituation and future delight. To explain this complete reversal in the conception of the psychological function of the repertoire, in the criterion of aesthetic judgment, and in the relation between the artist and his public, one must examine the intervening period: the 19th century and its Romantic revolt.

The shift is largely attributable to the complete sociological metamorphosis of the audience and of the social status of the musician. During the previous century, the pre-Napoleonic era, the musician had been an employee, who performed a skilled service according to contractual obligations--analogous to the 20th-century staff musicians in a radio or motion picture studio, allowing, of course, for the divergent requirements of the period and the much greater sense of social stratification than now prevails. His secular audience consisted primarily of the nobility, many of whom were themselves adequate performers, and who sometimes arrogated to themselves the privilege of joining the orchestra. Some even utilized their leisure moments for composing. In fact, as late as 1905 Breitkopf und Härtel published a catalogue of compositions by German royalty, including Kaiser Wilhelm--which serves to recall the piquant warning attributed to Brahms that "one should never criticize the compositions of royalty, for you never know who may have written them. "

Composers were craftsmen who composed to order and who, like the architect, the portrait painter and the cook, expected their work to be appreciated forthwith. It would not have occurred to Bach, Mozart, Haydn, and the other Kapellmeisters of the day to ignore the interest of the current generation by writing Zukunftsmusik, nor could they have had the temerity to expect their socially superior patrons to sit through repeated hearings of a suite or symphony on the chance that they or their descendants might possibly enjoy it at some future time. The liveried Haydn admitted that he experimented, but such experimentation was mild and inoffensive, and therefore tolerated and even enjoyed by the prince whom he was paid to serve.

By the turn of the 18th century, a social and political transformation had occurred with rather dramatic suddenness, as historical events go. In the history of music this consisted in the catastrophic bankruptcy, and consequent decline in power, of the musician's two richest employers: the church and the court. To gratify those who feel that they must pinpoint evolving historical events, one may suggest that it was the bombardment of Vienna in 1809, sheltering at once the aged Haydn, the middle-aged Beethoven, and the 12-year-old Schubert, which actually and symbolically gave the coup de grâce to the feudal era and marked the transition from the old order to the new. The musician lost his job and became a free-lance composer and an itinerant performer, with all the risks appertaining thereto.

His audience was no longer the closed group of cultivated nobles and their leisurely satellites, before whom the composer was honored to display his accomplishments. Instead, the 19th-century performer now served the emerging middleclass audience, the third estate, in a commercialized concert to which anyone had access who was able and willing to pay the price of admission. In this new pecuniary social order, the bourgeois audience was not sophisticated, nor well-schooled; but it was ready to be impressed by the virtuosity and the eccentricities of a Paganini, a Liszt, and a host of other virtuosi who mushroomed from that soil.   Instead, therefore, of an attitude of reverence and awe on the part of the musician toward his noble audience, it was now the audience which sat in bewilderment before the musician.   The artist, in fact, held his audience-- his new patrons--in disdain for its crude and undeveloped aesthetic tastes.   In art the customer was never right.   The mass of anonymous urbanites, newly hatched under the wings of the industrial revolution, issued from office and shop, from banks and colleges, from the professions and public services.   Occupied, as they were, full time in gaining a livelihood from the new competitive world, they were by no means a leisure class, they felt keenly their inadequacies in the arts, and acquired a veritable inferiority complex in their presence.   They suffer from this debilitating affliction to this very day.   They eagerly emulated the standards of the decaying, but still glamorous, aristocracy by cultivating and supporting the arts, and stood ready to be instructed.

Now, if the audience generated by the bourgeois social revolution thus drew away from the artist, the artist on his part also drew away from the audience.   Being no longer in the immediate employ of a master whom he was being paid to serve, he developed a sense of autonomy and self-expression in standards of composition as well as in interpretation and execution.   The artist even erected an ivory tower where he could commune with his aesthetic conscience and protect himself from any insinuation of being responsible to the audience.

The evolutionary development of the musical arts abetted the artist in his new independence.   Orchestral instruments were being improved, orchestras were being enlarged, and composition was becoming more difficult and esoteric.   Beethoven's orchestral scores looked "so black" that they literally sounded the death-knell of the amateur player-cooks who had infested the mixed ensembles during the courtly era.   Music was now becoming a learned profession which a lifetime was too short to master.   Art was really long, and time fleeting.   Liszt and Mendelssohn contributed enormously to the enhancement of the prestige of the once lowly profession. As a consequence of these social and technical revolutions, the artistic gap between audience and musician, which had been negligible a generation or two before, was now widening; and the evident explanation was to be sought not only in musical terms, but still more significantly in terms of the social, economic, political, and technological changes unfolding during that period.   It is only against such a social background that the problems of the contemporary "heavy" repertoire can be comprehended.

Synchronized with these social changes, philosophers, as is their wont and function, were drafting a system of thought designed to rationalize and buttress these overt historical trends, which were rendering music incomprehensible even to an intelligent audience. By an evolution too complex to rehearse at this point, music was elevated to the most exalted position among the arts; and in its

unfettered creativeness, it approximated "pure spirit," universal
and absolute Truth. Because of its mystical and supernatural
characteristic, it possessed the power to exert a spiritual and
ethical influence upon its auditors superior to that of any other
medium. Such neo-Platonic doctrines of Hegel and Schopenhauer
inevitably placed the great musician in a position of ethical leadership, conferred a certain sacrosanct validity on his "inspiration,"
and elevated him into the realms of near-infallibility. Music, the
most exalted art, was not only a reflection of ultimate ideas and
sentiments, but was actually a form of thinking in tones--an abstract, subtle, and direct communication superior to crude verbal
symbols, independent of the physical actualities of the world, and
therefore a "universal" language. The inspiration of the artist
was thus of higher validity than the uninstructed taste of otherwise
intelligent people. This was the ideology propagated by such philosophers as Schopenhauer, whose concepts dominated his disciple,
Richard Wagner.

This dogma of artistic supremacy was imported to the United
States from Germany in the baggage of musicians and conductors,
and has set the standards for the musical repertoire to this very
day. Indeed, in this country, where vertical mobility was much
more rapid than in Europe, where class relations were elastic,
where wealth was easier to come by, and the middle class musically unsophisticated, the musical gap was probably still wider than
in the old country. Precisely because of this, the conductors assumed, and were given, greater latitude and freedom in America
than in Europe. The programs in Boston and Chicago were much
more radical--or "progressive"--than they ever were in London,
Vienna, Leipzig, and Berlin, both in relation to the maturity of
the audience and in absolute terms, as far as the latter can be
measured.

The musical interpreters, Bergmann, Theodore Thomas,
Gustav Mahler, Gericke, and the rest pressed the last ounce of
vindication out of the mystical ideologies which upheld the didactic
mission of music, and translated this conviction into an unrelenting
policy, in the face of an indifferent, and even antagonistic, public.
It is quite irrelevant whether it was Bergmann, Theodore Thomas,
or Wagner himself--the essential remark has been attributed to all
three--who replied to the protest, that they "do not like Wagner,"
with the determined resolve: "Then we will play him until they
do. "4 The significant thing is that, consonant with the Romantic
philosophy with which they were imbued, such a retort was symp-
tomatic of a policy which nearly all symphony conductors relentlessly pursued. If Theodore Thomas seemed to be the most fervent
missionary of them all, it was partly because, in those days, there
was more proselytizing to be done. To him, a symphony program
was a stern, humorless "sermon in tones. " The function of a concert was not relaxation, but "what our overworked business and
professional men most need in America is an elevating mental reaction which is not amusement. " He was convinced that music was
a "powerful character building force" which, "by its uplifting

influence" would transport one to a "higher plane. "5   The music
journals of the day regularly carried long articles on the beneficent
effect of music on personal character and national welfare.   This
identity between Beauty and Virtue was an old axiom dating to the
Greeks, who were alleged to have brought this union to perfection.
It was, of course, an abiding faith rather than an empirically derived discovery.   But precisely because it was a mystic faith, it
was more tenaciously and uncritically adhered to than if the generalization had been obtained from prolonged and painstaking empirical
studies of human behavior.

The musical leaders were warmly supported in their ethical
and didactic mode of thought and practice by critics, painters, authors, poets, and even psychologists.   Henry T. Finck, critic and
early Wagner biographer, knew of

> no other art that so vividly arouses the unselfish feeling,
> the desire for sympathetic communion ... one of the
> most important moral functions of music, that of weaning
> people from low and demoralizing pleasures ... the best
> way to eradicate savage impulses....

> ... If such performances of both sacred and secular mu-
> sic were more frequent, we should have less drunken-
> ness, less wife-beating, less spending of winter gains,
> less winter pauperism. 6

There seemed to be no area of human conduct which might not be
susceptible to aesthetic influences.   Western civilization itself was
big with possibilities if the aesthetic front could be maintained un-
broken.   A biographer of Theodore Thomas wrote in 1927:

> When before have we been aware of any such force at
> work on such a scale among us?   Suppose it [the sym-
> phony orchestra program] to keep on for another genera-
> tion, gathering head.   It might produce in this country
> the greatest change ever known....   Two generations of
> it might change the whole American character; it might
> in the end scourge us of materialism.   Is this fantastic?
> Not if what we believe about the power and the ethics of
> art has any foundation. 7

Somewhat more vague, but in exactly the same vein, spoke John S.
Dwight, the influential Boston critic, musical editor, and New England transcendentalist, who opined that "good music must have
some intimate connection with the social destiny of man. "8

William James, the philosopher-psychologist, warned that
musical indulgence, however, could be overdone, by lapsing into an
"inert sentimental condition" and thereby defeat the very ethical
purpose of the arts.   He therefore advised

> never to suffer one's self to have an emotion at a concert

without expressing it afterward in some active way. Let
the expression be the least thing in the world--speaking
genially to one's aunt, or giving up one's seat in the
horsecar if nothing more heroic offers--but let it not fail
to take place. [9]

Hanslick, too, deprecated the overzealous educational policies of
the conductors. When, in 1880, Bülow closed a Beethoven cycle
with a double performance of the Ninth, the famous critic deplored
the "vigorous faith with which he propagated the Beethoven gospel
by baptizing the converts, as it were, with a fire hose. "[10]

In the 19th century, this general exaltation of the arts drew
much of its strength from the deficiencies of the industrial era.
Social critics like John Ruskin, William Morris, Walter Pater in
England, and Ralph Waldo Emerson in America--each in his own
way--were revolted by the misery and ugliness attendant on the
growing pains of the new industrialism, and had a supercilious
scorn for material science, which for them was the root of these
evils. Said Emerson in his Conduct of Life:

Geologies, chemistries, astronomies, seem to make us
wise, but they leave us where they found us.... All our
science lacks the human side.... Science hates the name
of love and moral purpose.... Beauty is the form under
which the intellect prefers to study the world. All high
Beauty has a moral element in it.

It is not at all obvious, nor even probable, that the industrial philanthropists, who liquidated the deficits incurred by Theodore Thomas, Gericke, Mahler, and Stokowski, necessarily shared
these mystical convictions with the crusading conductors whom they
sponsored. Some were indeed musical and philosophical dilettantes,
while many of them were downright metaphysical illiterates and
calculating businessmen to whom the ethical import of the Beethoven Third probably did not make much sense. However, in the
meantime, the orchestra, with its conductor and esoteric programs,
had achieved a certain prestige and glamour. Like fine churches,
public buildings, and parks, it soon became an element in the complete apparatus of civic life which focused not unwelcome attention
upon the community, and consequently deserved support. Such
"tycoon" pride was characteristically expressed by the orator of the
occasion at the dedication of Orchestra Hall, December 14, 1904:

Chicago has been the most public spirited city in the
world. We are proud of our rapid growth in wealth and
population, but we are not satisfied with the merely industrial growth of our city--we demand something more
and something better. We look through the dust and
smoke of Chicago as she is, to see the fair and noble
form of our city as she will be, a center of influence,
intellectual and artistic as well as industrial, a school
for the nation, as Pericles declared Athens was the
school for Greece. [11]

Intercity rivalry was a constant factor that stimulated audience, management, and conductors. Even the idealistic Thomas used this motif on his rebellious constituents in defense of his uncompromising stand on program construction:

> The announcement of a symphony on the program was enough to keep many people from the concert. . . . When fault was found with the severity of the programs I would say: Do you wish our program to be inferior in standard to those of the Boston Orchestra? 'No' was the answer. . . . [12]

That an orchestra had merit as an investment that would redound to the economic benefit of a city was a frequent theme. It was agreed, however, that a city's musical life serves as an enticement to visitors and settlers, and the tours of the orchestra are considered favorable publicity. In one instance, the orchestra was declared to be a force in "helping to sell shoes" for the greatest shoe center in the country. [13]

There are many who are neither sensitive to the supposed ethical overtones of a symphony, nor concerned with the commercial potentialities of a fine civic orchestra, but whose private social ambitions are gratified by indulgence in such an honorific enterprise. These impulses manifest themselves in diverse ways: maintenance of boxes or other preferred locations in the auditorium; program listing as patron; socially exclusive erudition on matters artistic; all the subtle satisfactions accruing from the wide range of contact and intimacy with a fashionable concern, from the occasional ticket purchaser to the confidential relation with conductor and steering members of the board, with all its invidious prestige. The concert-hall box has now all but disappeared in the relentless democratization of audience and patrons. But it once reflected the highly prized prerequisite of the social elite. The private corridor and the anteroom, which conferred a sense of aloof distinction, translated the symphony and opera into a social ritual more highly regarded than the aesthetic relaxation derived from the actual music, which, in fact, was often sacrificed.

Musical politics may run very deep, and orchestras have at times been a "football of society." With motives something less than sublime, various groups have often rallied around rival conductors, thus literally splitting the resources of the community to the detriment of higher values. On occasion, however, such competition has had its salutary moments. Witness the case of the prolonged feud between the followers of Damrosch and Thomas in New York, during which two orchestras challenged each other for supremacy. But in other less inspiring circumstances, two orchestras have been supported when nourishment was insufficient for one. That pioneer period has, in general, passed. Though factions will always exist, funds are not nowadays so plentiful as to permit the luxury of such wasteful competition.

Since 1893, when Walter Damrosch first organized them,
many of the responsibilities for carrying on orchestral affairs have
fallen to the ladies, whose efforts have proven indispensable to the
solvency of the harassed orchestral institution. Largely for the
benefit of the fashionable world, the matinee concerts (usually Friday afternoon) are maintained. Originally instituted by the New
York Philharmonic as a public rehearsal which would offer bargain
rates to students, musicians, or others who might wish to hear
repeated performances,[14] these matinee programs have long since
graduated into more or less exclusive afternoon affairs, constituting an integral part of the winter social season. In Boston and
Philadelphia, where this "Friday Spell" exerts its full potency,
this particular division of the audience into two segments has been
profitable, for the house is sold out. However, in other cities,
for various reasons, the Friday patronage, though involving a
similar principle, has for some time been hardly sufficient in
volume to persuade the management that the retention of the traditional weekday matinee was practicable. History may be repeating
itself, for the economic aristocracy today, analogously to the feudal
aristocracy of 150 years ago, is declining in power and is relaxing
its control over our artistic institutions. Musically this may mean
a popularization of the repertoire and a significant alteration in the
role played by the orchestra in its community relations.

There remains another function of music in general, and the
orchestra and opera in particular, which has never struck such
deep roots in the United States as it has in Europe: its contribution to national solidarity. The urge to integrate the various aspects of national life--religion, politics, family, industry, and the
arts--is not an exhibition of any virtue or perversity inherent in
man or nation. It is, sociologically speaking, induced by conditions of stress, national emergency, and tension, and does not
flourish in times of peace, plenty, and repose. If this totalitarian
phenomenon prevailed during the 19th and 20th centuries in Europe,
it is because Europe, unlike the United States, experienced an
abundance of tension and relatively little repose. Nations are not
"patriotic" when there is nothing to be patriotic about. Patriotism
is rather a defense reaction, to protect the charished values which
are threatened, or thought to be threatened. If nationalism became
the prevailing idea in the 19th century, it was not because of the
vague, spontaneous, and unconditioned promptings of a "romantic
impulse," but it stemmed rather from a definite crisis in the affairs of nations. Prussia suffered a humiliating defeat by Napoleon,
Poland was dismembered by three powerful neighbors, Bohemia
felt itself oppressed by the Hapsburgs, Norway was uncomfortably
yoked to Sweden, and Finland to Russia. Although some of these
culture groups were not to realize their nationalistic yearnings until
1918, their internal cultural cohesion was maintained throughout the
preceding decades. This overwhelming preoccupation with their
cultural autonomy is manifested in their musical preferences in
creation and performance, as well as their political policies.

The usual European conception of musical nationalism is that

of the folksong, in the largest sense, which becomes the basis of
the more sophisticated forms in song, symphony, and opera. This
conception was, indeed, a critical symptom of the growing national
consciousness, for folksongs--the musical expression of the indigenous folk--could be despised only so long as royalty and nobility set the standard of taste. With that power destroyed, the center
of gravity of economic, political, and aesthetic interests veered to
the middle class, and to the rural regions which had previously
been held in serfdom.

In addition to the important folksongs and folktunes, nationalism manifested itself symptomatically in subject matter of song and
opera (e. g. Glinka, Weber); in the use of national dances (Smetana);
in the revival of forgotten music and musicians from their historical past (Rameau, Bach, Purcell); in the pressure to perform native
and contemporary works (Russia, France, Germany); the purging of
foreign music and musicians (Germany, United States in World War
I); and in the fabrication of an ideology which defines music as an
emanation of the national spirit, or an economic class (Germany,
Soviet Union).

If the United States has never been infected with the chauvin-
istic virus as severely as has Europe, it has at least not escaped
exposure. For the United States is a mosaic of polyglot expatriates
who have no common and glorious past that could be revived to flatter provincial pride. As a nation almost without a "history" in the
venerable sense of the word, a nation that has never experienced a
serious external crisis, there simply do not exist the first essentials for a good nationalistic debauch.

Two minor symptoms of nationalism did subsequently put in
their appearance in the United States: the purging of German music
during World War I, which has been a matter of apology ever since;
and the inauguration of a kind of "protective tariff" for American
works. But the wave of sentiment to "buy American" has never
reached a high crest among the populace, and it remains today, as
yesterday, the expression of small and interested pressure groups.
It must be said, therefore, that the orchestral institutions and their
repertoire are not, in the United States, a function of national solidarity. For the average consumer, they have remained essentially
"above the battle. "

1.   Emily Anderson, tr. and ed. Mozart's Letters. London:
      Macmillan, 1938. Letters of Jan. 14, 1878; Nov. 1, 1777;
      Sept. 26, 1781.

2.   Charles Burney. A General History of Music. New York:
      Harcourt, Brace, 1935. Vol. I, p. 21.

3.   Richard Aldrich. Concert Life in New York, 1902-23. New
      York: Putnam, 1941. p. 314.

4. George Upton, ed. Theodore Thomas. Chicago: A. C. Mc-
    Clurg, 1905. Vol. I, p. 235. H. T. Finck. Richard
    Wagner and His Works. New York: Scribner's, 1907.
    Vol. II, p. 511. R. Osgood Mason. Sketches and Im-
    pressions: Musical, Theatrical and Social. New York:
    London: Putnam's Sons, 1887. p. 199-200. Ernest
    Newman. Richard Wagner. New York: Knopf, 1937.
    Vol. II, p. 115.

5. Upton, op. cit., vol. I, p. 251.

6. Henry T. Finck. "Music and Morals," in Chopin and Other
    Essays. New York: Scribner's, 1910. pp. 143-182.

7. Charles E. Russell. The American Orchestra and Theodore
    Thomas. Garden City, N.Y.: Doubleday, Page, 1927.
    p. vii.

8. George W. Cooke. John Sullivan Dwight. Boston: Small,
    Maynard, 1898. pp. 147, 151-152. "Introductory State-
    ments," Dwight's Journal of Music, Vol. I, no. 1. (Ap-
    ril 10, 1852).

9. William James. Psychology. New York: Henry Holt, 1890.
    Vol. I, pp. 126ff.

10. Eduard Hanslick. Concerte, Componisten, und Virtuosen,
    2. Aufl. Berlin: 1886. p. 312.

11. Upton, op. cit., Vol. I, p. 289. Reginald Nettel. The Or-
    chestra in England, A Social History. London: Cape,
    1946. p. 103.

12. Upton, op. cit., vol. I, p. 104.

13. Remark attributed to Rudolph Ganz, conductor of the St. Louis
    Symphony Orchestra, November 1925.

14. In the prospectus of the New York Philharmonic for 1870-71,
    we read significantly: "Inasmuch as compositions in that
    class can seldom be fully appreciated when heard but once,
    the society has, for many years, made the rehearsals pre-
    ceding each concert open to the public. Scale for admis-
    sion: First Rehearsal and Second Rehearsal, 50 cents;
    Third Rehearsal, $1, Regular Concert, $2."

THE CLEVELAND ORCHESTRA*

Joseph Wechsberg

It is generally agreed that the leading symphony orchestras
in this country today are the Boston Symphony, the Chicago Symphony Orchestra, the Cleveland Orchestra, the New York Philharmonic, and the Philadelphia Orchestra. Over the past fifteen years,
critics and audiences in both America and Europe have tended to
agree that the Cleveland Orchestra, which was founded in 1918 and
is the youngest of the five, has become the peer of the four older
ones and is perhaps in some respects their superior. "There are
many first-class orchestras in the United States, and among them
the Cleveland Orchestra is phenomenal," said Aram Khatchaturian,
the composer. "Among the great orchestras of the world the
Cleveland ... is probably the most efficient symphonic body of
them all," the London Times wrote in 1965. "The Cleveland Orchestra is at this time unequalled," the music critic of the Boston
Globe wrote in 1966, and he went on to explain, "It is because of
its unanimity as an orchestra even more than for its surpassing
virtuosity in other ways that I would call the Cleveland Orchestra
uniquely great." After the Cleveland Orchestra's performances at
the Edinburgh Festival not long ago, Sir Neville Cardus wrote in
the Guardian, "No other orchestra so good is to be found in the
United States." "Many friends of music consider the orchestra the
best in the world, and George Szell the best of all musical directors," wrote the music critic of Hamburg's Bild Zeitung.

The question of why a particular orchestra plays the way
it does has fascinated me since my childhood, when I started to
study the violin. Over the years, I have learned that there is no
easy answer. Others have reached the same conclusion. In The
Cleveland Orchestra, a book that the music critic Robert C. Marsh
published in 1967 as "a birthday present to a remarkable orchestra
on its fiftieth anniversary," Marsh wrote that although "little skill
is required to discover that the Cleveland Orchestra is a great ensemble ... it is somewhat more difficult to explain why this orchestra plays the way it does." Obviously, there are things that
cannot be entirely explained. An orchestra's collective personality
can be sensed and described, but it is ultimately as difficult to
analyze as any other personality. Not long ago, in an attempt to
find an answer to the somewhat easier question of how an orchestra
works, I went out to Cleveland--not because the Cleveland Orchestra is typical but because Szell, who has been the Cleveland's musical director since 1946, and whom I have known for thirty-five
years, is said to have molded the ensemble there into "the world's
greatest hundred-man string quartet." To me, a lifelong string-
quartet player, it thus seemed that the Cleveland Orchestra might
afford some clues to the understanding of orchestras in general.

---

*Copyright 1970 by The New Yorker Magazine, Inc.   Reprinted by
permission of Paul R. Reynolds, Inc. , 599 Fifth Avenue, New
York, N.Y. 10017.

Every great orchestra has its own sound, distinguishable
from that of any other great orchestra.   In terms of physics,
sound consists of vibrations varying in frequency and amplitude, and
music is the arrangement of such vibrations, within a certain span
of time, in a definite rhythm.   Musically speaking, matters are
more complicated.   A great orchestra's sound has been compared
to a celebrated singer's timbre, but this is putting the matter too
strongly; it is easier to distinguish, say, Caruso from Gigli,
Bjoerling, or Corelli than to distinguish the Cleveland from the
Philadelphia, the Vienna Philharmonic, or the Berlin Philharmonic.
Basically, the so-called Cleveland sound is a homogeneous, chamber-music sound--a classically noble string tone perfectly blended
with singing woodwinds and exquisitely clear brasses.   Szell has
so forcefully emphasized lucid phrasing and clear articulation that
these have become second nature for his orchestra.   Contributing
to them are exact balances within and among the sections, a deeply
ingrained sense of rhythm, and concentration upon the long line of
the music, which rises through points of tension to a final climax
and release.   There seems to be a unified approach by the hundred
and six members of the orchestra and their conductor to the performance of each particular work of music.   Szell himself doesn't
particularly like to discuss the Cleveland sound.   He maintains that
a great orchestra should have no sound of its own, and that the
qualities of the ensemble should grow out of the style and the manner in which each work has been written.   During a concert, Szell
says, the orchestra may switch from a "Mozart sound" to a
"Brahms sound" to a "Debussy sound. "   Szell thinks of Mozart,
Brahms, and Debussy as individuals.   The re-creation of their
music must faithfully represent their ideas.   It must be done with
style, taste, and a sense of spontaneity and enthusiasm.   Szell is
pleased when people tell him that no two performances of the same
work by the Cleveland Orchestra are alike.   They must not be, he
says.   Great music is a living art, and its performance must never
become soulless and mechanical.

The Cleveland sound is quite different from the sound of
the Philadelphia Orchestra, which is lush, warm, and rhapsodic--
perhaps because Eugene Ormandy, who has been the orchestra's
musical director for the past thirty-four years, was once himself
a "rhapsodic" violinist.   The Berlin sound reflects the dynamic
personality of Herbert von Karajan, the musical director of the
Berlin Philharmonic--beautiful strings, lean woodwinds, and precise
brasses.   The Viennese sound is characterized by singing, sweet
strings and mellow brasses that convey to nostalgic listeners the
magic of the Vienna Woods; warmth and sensuousness are more
highly valued on the blue Danube than transparency and precision.
In most cases, an orchestra's distinctive sound is probably the
reflection of its permanent conductor's personality, as in the cases
of Szell, Ormandy, and Karajan, and only rarely of a local tradition, as in Vienna.   The Cleveland sound was unquestionably created by Szell, even though he conceives of sound not as an end in
itself but as "a means of expression, with the ultimate purpose of
communicating each composer's special message. "   The Cleveland

players themselves attribute their orchestra's sound to their long association with Szell and their ability to produce the sort of music he demands. They are aware that their sound sometimes seems "clipped." "Maybe our sound is so clear and perfect that something of the soul gets lost," one player said to me. Another disagreed slightly, saying, "Szell's approach to the music is analytical rather than emotional. He teaches us to seek the meaning behind the notes." A third called the Cleveland "rather a sober orchestra, more work than fun." I soon gathered that Szell's severe sense of responsibility toward music and his austere self-disciple don't encourage frivolity.

Some conductors don't try to get close to the mystery of sound, while for others sound becomes a fetish, and may ruin their orchestras' taste and style. A first-rate conductor may evoke good sound from a minor orchestra; a bad conductor can easily ruin the sound of a first-rate orchestra. In Philadelphia, beauty of sound was developed under Leopold Stokowski and Ormandy to the point where it became part of the orchestra's style, but purists feel that the lush Philadelphia sound is inappropriate for the performance of works by such classical composers as Mozart and Beethoven. Great conductors can perform miracles with sound. When Stokowski rehearsed the Cleveland Orchestra a few years ago, Louis Lane, the orchestra's associate conductor, watched the Maestro, and he told me later that it took Stokowski only a few minutes to evoke from the orchestra the rich, unmistakable "Stokowski sound." "I studied him carefully, trying to get to the bottom of the miracle," Lane said. "Stokowski had seated the orchestra differently--the first violins and violas on his left side, the second violins on his right side, the cellos and double basses behind the woodwinds, and the brass in the rear." The woodwinds, the brasses, and the percussion instruments almost always remain in the rear, but seating arrangements for the string sections vary. The European arrangement seats the first violins at the left of the conductor and the second violins at his right; the violas face him, and the cellos are to the right, with the double basses behind them. The American arrangement places the first and second violins to the left of the conductor and the violas to his right, with the cellos facing him, or he may have the cellos on his right and the violas facing him. Many leading European orchestras have now adopted one of the American versions. "Stokowski has a way of shaping sound as a sculptor shapes his material," Lane went on. "With a few strong, almost hypnotic gestures, he created full, warm, sensuous sound. The musicians didn't understand what they were doing. They did it instinctively, producing exactly the sort of sound Stokowski wanted. The spiccato disappeared as though by magic and became détaché. Suddenly, the orchestra's sound was richer, darker, juicier in its quality. Yet the whole time Stokowski never said a word. It was incredible!"

A great many members of the Cleveland Orchestra have long been as puzzled as Lane about a conductor's ability to produce his own type of sound from an orchestra, and have tried to analyze

it. In 1965, when Pierre Boulez, then the conductor of the Süd-
westfunk Orchestra in Baden-Baden, first went to Cleveland, it
took him only five minutes to get the orchestra to play Debussy
as Debussy is played in France--in a style that is subtle and
suave, transparent and clean. During the Cleveland Orchestra's
European tour in the summer of 1967, Herbert von Karajan conducted two performances of Prokofieff's Fifth Symphony. Those
players who had previously performed the Prokofieff Fifth under
Szell still talk about the amazing transformation that occurred when
Karajan started to rehearse the orchestra. Almost instantly, the
orchestra switched from a "Szell sound" to a "Karajan sound,"
with its long, legato lines, its lyrical beauty, its sense of the
dramatic, and its feeling for impressionistic effect.

    "Karajan spoke very little," one player told me. "His
gestures indicated what he wanted--gentle sound and sometimes
sensuous sound, different from Szell's lean, sinewy sound. Karajan toned down the cellos. Once, he cautioned the cymbal player
against making a clamorous sound. At the beginning of the last
movement, he conducted more slowly and tenderly than Szell. He
indicated that he wanted us to round off the edges. It wasn't--
well, it wasn't such a struggle as under Szell. Karajan seemed
to look at the music from the outside going in, while Szell seems
to be inside the music, looking out. Incidentally, after our return
from Europe we played the Prokofieff Fifth under Szell in Cleveland. We adjusted ourselves at once to Szell's subtle detail and
played it completely Szell's way. " Karajan kept his eyes open
during the rehearsals, but he had them closed during the performance, as is his custom, which slightly unnerved some members of
the Cleveland Orchestra. They are used to eloquent signals from
Szell, who often indicates increased accents or corrects tonal balance with an expressive glance. A wind player said, "I kept telling myself that Karajan knew the music and that he knew where
everybody was sitting. Just the same, I wished that he would look
at me at certain moments. " A first violinist said, "He asked less
of us than Szell does--he didn't make us work so hard. He seemed
more concerned with beautiful expression and artistic effect than
with clarity of texture and the artistic truth. "

    The Cleveland Orchestra's ability to create the sound de-
manded by different conductors is, of course, a great tribute to
its musicians' flexibility. "They have great respect for good music and good musicians," I was told by Michael Charry, who came
to Cleveland in 1961 as an apprentice conductor and is now one of
the Cleveland Orchestra's two assistant conductors. "Once, I
studied Prokofieff's 'The Love for Three Oranges' with the orchestra. Neither the musicians nor I knew the work, and we studied it
together, doing everything from scratch. I was able to impress
my own personality upon them. They were extremely flexible, and
they carried out my ideas. An orchestra of this calibre knows so
many things. I didn't have to tell them how to play Prokofieff--
they know his music and the style in which it is to be performed.
Afterward, we worked on 'Gianni Schicchi, ' and the players

immediately shifted from the lean, precise sound of Prokofieff to the luscious Italian sound of Puccini. Such things are taken for granted in this orchestra. When Karajan or Boulez told one section to do a certain thing in a certain way, the other sections automatically picked up the conductor's intentions. The Cleveland players enjoy responding this way to a conductor when they respect him. "

Orchestral conducting has evolved, over the past hundred and fifty years, into an important part of a performance. After the strict, foursquare time-beaters of the post-classical era, Wagner and his fellow-conductors introduced a flamboyant style of conducting. This approach soon degenerated into mannerism and excess; according to Szell, the great conductors toward the end of the nineteenth century "interpreted the composer subjectively to the point of arbitrariness. " Mahler and, after him, Toscanini introduced a much needed corrective, each considering himself "the advocate and servant of the composer. " Then, under Willem Mengelberg, Sir Thomas Beecham, Bruno Walter, and Wilhelm Furtwängler in Europe, and Toscanini, Stokowski, and Serge Koussevitzky in America, the great orchestras became virtuoso symphonic instruments on which the star conductors performed as an eminent violinist performs on his Stradivari. They established high standards of orchestral playing, but their strong personalities did not permit real self-effacement. And this situation prevailed. The great showman conductor, the flamboyant artist whose name appears on the recording album in larger letters than the name of the composer, now dominates orchestral music.

A performance has two main components--interpretation and execution. The conductor's musically correct interpretation of a composition is not always matched by a faultless performance, and the virtuoso execution of a work remains an artistic failure if the conductor is unable to interpret and communicate the spirit of the music. It is no accident that some of the most famous conductors today are more successful when they conduct an extravagant, exciting work by Ravel, Mahler, or Stravinsky than when they present a symphony by Haydn, Mozart, or Schubert, in which everything depends on what Szell calls "the artistic truth. " These conductors may bring out every little musical detail with admirable clarity but lose the general line of the music. Orchestra musicians are more concerned with exactness of execution than with the spirit of the musical interpretation. By contrast, Toscanini, during his last years with the N. B. C. Symphony, was sometimes lenient about rhythmical detail and tolerant of the weaknesses of his less distinguished players, but his interpretations were always characterized by clarity and balance, and by integrity, ardor, and power as well.

A great orchestra instinctively forms its collective judgment of an unfamiliar conductor even before he raises his baton. Several members of the Cleveland Orchestra told me that they begin to "feel" a conductor as he walks toward the podium. But there is no mystery about the players' ability to size up a conductor quickly

and accurately--his knowledge and competence, his technique and
experience.   A conductor may fool the audience and the critics,
but he can never fool the hundred highly skilled artists facing him.
They sense immediately whether the conductor knows the music
thoroughly or only superficially.   They are not deluded if he stops
them at certain trouble spots during rehearsal to point out mistakes; it may be obvious that he prepared these interruptions beforehand and studied his lines.   What does impress them is an interruption at a seemingly easy spot which achieves a marked improvement.

The Cleveland Orchestra's attitude toward conductors is rather unusual.   Orchestra players know a hundred ways of sabotag-
ing or betraying a conductor they dislike or scorn.   Very often,
musicians get a morbid pleasure out of seeing a bad conductor expose himself to their collective derision.   But every member of
the Cleveland Orchestra subscribes to Szell's dogma "We are all in
the service of music. "   One player says, "We are always interested in the music and ready to give a competent conductor what
he wants if he can hold the attention of the whole orchestra all the
way to the rear. "   Brass players, who sit in the rear, have their
difficulties with a conductor who speaks poor English or talks softly.   "One tries to catch his words, but after a while one loses interest and gives up, " a trumpeter says.   "Of course, he may hold
our attention without saying anything. "   The best conductors speak
with their eyes and their hands.

Good orchestra players prefer conductors with a clear eco-
nomical baton technique to those who turn conducting into a ballet
performance.   "The conductor should conduct the orchestra, not
the audience, " they say.   A player cares less about the conduct-
or's personality than about good leadership.   What he expects from
the conductor is not only musical erudition but a clear beat.   "They
want a maximum of explanation with a minimum of words, " Szell
says.   Garrulous conductors who lecture on the music are much
disliked, but Szell does explain his reasons for doing something in
a particular way.   One player says, "In many orchestras, the musicians are resigned to doing certain things a certain way--don't
ask, just do it.   Not here.   We are always told why we should do
it a certain way--there is always a musical reason.   Musicians
elsewhere have heard horror stories about our rehearsals, and
about Szell, so when they join us they are often surprised and
thrilled. "

Recently, I arranged to attend some rehearsals of the Cleveland Orchestra.   Szell had suggested that I plan to arrive at Severance Hall in Cleveland in time for a Tuesday rehearsal, at 10
A. M. , and added, "Why don't you come an hour early?"   In Cleveland, the regular weekly concerts are played on Thursday and
Saturday nights, and rehearsals generally take place on Monday and
Tuesday mornings, Wednesday morning and afternoon, and Thursday morning.   (Experienced conductors plan every minute of their
allotted rehearsal time.   The Cleveland Orchestra's rehearsal

schedule is worked out four months in advance so that the musicians will know exactly which pieces of music are going to be rehearsed and how much time will be given to each.) As I walked in through the rear entrance shortly after nine that Tuesday morning, I heard horn and trumpet players practicing; the members of the brass and woodwind sections were warming up in the locker room. Upstairs, the beautiful hall was dim and deserted. Two bulbs spread a pale light over the empty chairs and music stands on the stage. At the rear of the stage one player, a woman, was tuning her harp.

I joined Szell in his private office, where he was comfortably surrounded by framed pictures of famous artists with affectionate or respectful dedications, framed decorations from various governments, and glass-encased photostats of musical manuscripts. There was a couch in the room, but no piano; he has one in a larger room upstairs, which is officially known as the conductor's studio. On his desk when I went in were the scores of the works on that week's program: two of Mozart's Marches for Orchestra, in D major (K. 335) and C major (K. 408); Frank Martin's Concerto for Cello and Orchestra; and Richard Strauss's "Don Quixote." Szell, who was wearing casual shoes, dark trousers, a longsleeved dark-gray wool polo shirt, and a black sweater, was sitting behind the desk giving some instructions to Mrs. Margaret Gloves, his longtime special assistant. Among other things, he asked her to have a platform for the cello soloist placed on the stage, because he was going to start the rehearsal with "Don Quixote." Mrs. Gloves nodded, laid the morning mail on his desk, and went out.

"We had a rough runthrough yesterday, without Pierre Fournier, the soloist," Szell said after we greeted each other. "He arrived from Geneva only last night. He did 'Don Quixote' with us in 1951, '52, '56, and '57, and again in 1960, when we recorded the work, and I'm happy to have him doing it with us again. I love 'Don Quixote.' There is more human warmth and compassion in it than in any of Strauss's other symphonic works. And besides that, it displays the whole range of his musical imagination and his virtuoso orchestra technique. There was nothing Strauss could not do."

From the guest soloist's room, next door, came the sound of a cello being played beautifully; Fournier was getting ready. I left Szell and walked to the concert hall and sat down in the middle of the tenth row. Half a dozen people were there, and most of them had orchestra scores. On the stage, the oboist was warming up and adjusting his pitch, and in the rear the timpanist was tuning his kettledrums. Gradually, the other musicians, most of them in shirtsleeves or pullovers, drifted in and took their chairs. A few minutes before ten, everybody was seated, and Rafael Druian, the concertmaster (he is now with the School of Music at the California Institute of the Arts), came on-stage and raised his arm. The noise ceased, the oboe player sounded an A, and the musicians

began to tune their instruments. The string sections did their tuning first, and after them the woodwinds and the brass players. At
one minute before ten, the sounds died down, and Fournier came
in, escorted by Szell. Fournier shook hands with Druian and some
other players nearby, sat down on the soloist's platform, and tuned
his cello. Szell waited patiently, and then, when Fournier had
finished tuning, rapped the stand with his baton and told the musicians they were going to play the whole piece. He looked at Fournier, who nodded assent. Szell lifted both arms in a commanding
gesture and gave the upbeat to the flutes and oboes, and the orchestra began to play the Introduction of "Don Quixote."

I was lucky to be in Cleveland when "Don Quixote" was on
the program. The Strauss tone poem is a demanding work that
provides a real test for an orchestra and conductor. A noted
Viennese musicologist named Richard Specht, who was a friend of
Strauss, wrote that "Don Quixote" is "one of the least understood
works of the Master ... owing to the fact that a finished performance is extremely difficult to accomplish, and any other must be
misleading with regard to the spirit and fullness of the musical
fantasy of this work." Strauss indicated his intention when he sub-
titled the work "Fantastic Variations on a Theme of Knightly Character." Specht considered the variations "the most comprehensive
form which a tone-poet could give when painting the picture of
Don Quixote." Using Wagner's leitmotiv method, Strauss created
associations with musical phrases and figures and used these with
incomparable mastery throughout the work's theme and ten variations, framed by the Introduction and the Finale. Over the past
three and a half centuries, more than fifty composers have been
attracted to Cervantes's Don Quixote de la Mancha, but it remained for Strauss, in 1897, to give the work what is generally
regarded as its ultimate musical interpretation. "For wit, humor,
pathos and humanism, there is nothing like it in the whole library
of music," the late English critic Ernest Newman wrote in the
London Times. "Certainly, to anyone who knows Strauss's music
to 'Don Quixote,' Cervantes is henceforth inconceivable without it;
the story itself, indeed, has not half the humor and the profound
sadness which is infused into it by Strauss." In forty minutes of
music, Strauss brings the noble and tragic figure of the knight
vividly to life. The various instruments, artfully contrasted and
blended, speak almost like singers; in fact, "Don Quixote" has
been called "an opera without voices." It is an extremely difficult
work, demanding virtuoso technique from the individual players and
the complete integration of the whole orchestra. Only a great conductor is able to blend the small, colorful pieces into the large
tonal mosaic and to bring alive the character of the idealistic ec-
centric who fights and dies for his lost causes.

After a few bars, I forgot that this was a rehearsal. To
me, the term "orchestra rehearsal" had always conjured up a
scene of slack playing and casual attitudes, of musicians going re-
luctantly through the motions, looking bored, chatting, and making
life hard for the conductor. But there was nothing casual about

this rehearsal. No one looked bored, and there was none of the kidding and horseplay that musicians often inject into a dull rehearsal. The players sat on the edges of their chairs, and they played with a happy intensity that reminded me of a successful performance by a string quartet. Everybody played as though this were an important concert, and the players obviously enjoyed making the music. Later, Szell said to me, "The Cleveland Orchestra plays seven concerts a week and admits the public to the final two. We do some of our best playing during rehearsals."

The first rehearsal I heard in Cleveland must have been one of the great ones, being more finished than some concert performances of "Don Quixote" I have heard. During a few solo passages, Fournier smiled at the men around him, who were supporting him beautifully. At the end of the third variation, after a particularly difficult passage that is played by the solo cello and the concertmaster, Fournier and Druian exchanged a happy glance, and Szell, too, smiled. After the Finale, a moving part that Fournier played with great simplicity, Szell conducted the final bars and held up both hands for several seconds after the last pianissimo chord had died away. Then he put down his baton, applauded, and bowed to Fournier in a gesture of old-fashioned grace. The entire orchestra joined Szell in an ovation for Fournier, who was obviously touched by this tribute from his fellow-artists.

Szell then said that, after an intermission, the players were going to work on certain passages, and asked them "to take the cue from the music." The players nodded. One of them later explained to me, "Taking the cue from the music means that you don't play the phrase mechanically but concentrate on its particular quality and its relation to the musical line, considering the phrase as a part of the musical statement. It means in practice that you play the phrase with special feeling, and that the last note will possibly be a hairbreadth later than anticipated. If the man playing the next phrase didn't listen and take his cue from the music, he might be too early."

A few players had questions for Szell, and three of them came up to him with their parts. Szell explained the problems in a few words; he seemed to know more about each part, and the instrument it was written for, than the player himself. Throughout the rehearsal, there was little discussion of technical matters, because the members of the Cleveland Orchestra are expected to work these out for themselves. Moreover, Szell relies on his section leaders to help all the musicians develop clarity of intonation and homogeneity in phrasing. Yet in rehearsal he listens to every instrumental part and instantly judges whether a man must be reminded of an error or will later correct it for himself. Before a rehearsal, the basic elements of the interpretation have been prepared. The music has been annotated with Szell's interpretive markings. The musicians know the style of the composer and how to re-create it, and they have practiced their parts at home. Thus, the quality of rehearsals in Cleveland is extremely high.

During intermission, I saw Szell in the corridor. He
seemed to be in a benevolent mood, and not at all the tyrant he is
often made out to be.

"Now you've heard how we make music in Cleveland," he
said. "'Don Quixote' is a challenge. Many orchestra soloists are
required to play little snatches and small bits of music, and the
whole thing must be put together carefully to get real meaning and
continuity. It's not yet what it must be, but this is only Tuesday."

I observed that I had been surprised by the musicians' cooperation during the rehearsal.

"They are fine musicians, and they love to play good music," Szell said. "During our last European tour, the orchestra
was split by a serious labor dispute. There were two factions,
and there was the possibility of a strike. But when they were
playing, all these things were forgotten, and they were happy.
That is one secret of this orchestra. The other, as you may have
noticed, is that there are no weak spots. All the sections are
perfectly balanced."

After the rehearsal, I went to see Druian, the concertmaster. A graduate of the Curtis Institute of Music, in Philadelphia,
Druian is a noted soloist. From 1949 to 1960, he was concertmaster of the Minneapolis Symphony, and in 1960, when he was in
his late thirties, he was hired by Szell. At Severance Hall, the
concertmaster enjoys the privilege of a small private study, down
the corridor from the conductor's room, and it was there that I
found Druian. He was practicing the difficult solo-violin passage
in the Introduction of "Don Quixote." He motioned to me to come
in, and when he had finished the passage he showed me his violin--
the Nightingale Stradivari, which owes its name to its tonal character. Alfred Hill, the great London violin-maker, called it "an
admirable specimen." Stradivari made it in 1717, when he was
seventy-three--during his Golden Period, from 1711 to 1720. The
back of Druian's violin is maple cut on the slab, and the varnish
has a lovely reddish color. Druian put the violin in its case, and
I asked him about his works as concertmaster.

"In England, the concertmaster is called the leader," he
said. "Some of us visibly lead our section, but a concertmaster
can never assert leadership without having the support of the men.
You must make them do what you want them to do. Also, you
must lead them and remain with them at the same time. In some
orchestras, the concertmaster visibly and audibly leads the attack,
and the section players follow him, but Szell hates that--considers
it in poor taste. Unlike the soloist, who is always ahead of the
ensemble and may do what he wants--within the limits of taste and
style, of course--the concertmaster is bound by the ensemble. If
I played my part independently, slightly ahead of the first-violin
section, I would break up the ensemble. The concertmaster's job
is to provide the necessary courage for what the men have to do,

but he should never push them.   The job is a matter of instinct--
almost a sixth sense.

"Some concertmasters act as a buffer between the orchestra
and the conductor.   I won't do it.   Our men are highly skilled
professionals.   They need no buffer, and they can work out their
problems on their own.   During a rehearsal--but never during a
performance--I may give them some signs.   Holding up the bow
means 'Play softer. '   Or I may turn around and tell them not to
rush.   The men know they have to play differently, depending on
whether the orchestra plays alone or accompanies a soloist during
a concerto.   While the orchestra plays alone--in the beginning of
the Beethoven or Brahms Violin Concerto, for instance--the orchestra performs with its collective musical personality.   But the moment the soloist comes in we instinctively get out of his way.   A
great soloist, in turn, engages in a kind of give-and-take with an
accompanying orchestra.   He always listens to the orchestra while
he is playing his solo part.   He knows the passages where the orchestra may have trouble following him, and he is ready to make
subtle adjustments.   When we play the syncopations in the last
movement of the Tchaikovsky Violin Concerto, say, an expert soloist will play with us, not on his own. "

The concertmaster's job, Druian went on, differs under different conductors.   As a rule, after studying his part carefully,
the concertmaster organizes things both for himself and for the
conductor; after discussing fingering and bowing problems with the
conductor, he marks a master part for the other section leaders
and the orchestra's librarian.   (For the Cleveland, Szell himself
carefully annotated the scores for many years, indicating not only
subtle degrees of dynamics and phrasing but also the exact bowings
for the strings, and he sometimes delegated the bowings to Druian.)   The concertmaster also copes with periodic outbreaks of
"malignant anonymitis, " a sickness well known in the string sections of most major orchestras.   It never affects the woodwinds,
the brass, or the percussion players, all of whom play individual
parts instead of playing in sections.   Every oboist or horn player
has an occasional solo passage in a symphony, and such passages
give him artistic satisfaction of a kind that a second-violin player
on the fourth or fifth stand never experiences.   A section player
is almost never called upon to play a solo passage; instead, he
plays a second-violin passage with fifteen other second-violin players.   In the early Haydn and Mozart symphonies, he may have to
play whole pages of repeated eighth notes.   Anonymitis, a state of
despair caused by a permanent lack of professional recognition, is
in part the result of ignorance on the part of the audience.   Many
listeners believe that the players in the rear do not play as well as
the ones in front.   The contrary is often true.   Able conductors
like well-balanced string sections, and often put exceptional players
in the rear, to support less experienced players.   But to be sitting
at a front stand gives a player status inside the orchestra, and
even in the community.   Another name for the violinists' affliction,
Druian said, is Heifetz disease.   Parents, uncles, and teachers

may tell the budding violinist, "Someday you're going to be another Heifetz." Teachers are the worst offenders in this respect, turning a gifted pupil's ambitions to their own ends; the next-best thing to being another Heifetz, after all, is to be the teacher of a Heifetz. A good teacher knows that the number of potential Heifetzes is extremely small, and that many would-be Heifetzes wind up eventually in the second-violin section of a symphony orchestra.

Another problem that Druian had to cope with involved a more specific recognition of status, in the form of a player merit system introduced by Szell. (Some orchestras work on a seniority system.) Under Szell's merit system, everybody has a chance of becoming a first-chair man. A young section player may work hard and audition for the first chair in the second-violin section, say, but if a man from outside also auditions, and plays better, the outsider will get the first chair. Druian then had to console the disappointed player. "Success under such conditions can be a matter of lucky timing, but it is more often a matter of ability," Druian told me. "The man now sitting next to me in the orchestra started a few years ago at the end of the first-violin section. He wanted to move ahead, and he built his career constructively. In a great orchestra, there is always room at the top."

I asked Druian how he felt about playing under different conductors.

"An orchestra musician must have his own artistic convictions," he said. "But his job is to translate the conductor's ideas into sound. It's easy as long as one's own artistic convictions don't clash with those of the conductor. It's no problem to play for Szell, whom all the members of the orchestra admire--even those who may not like him. It's also relatively easy when we play under somebody whose musical ideas we respect, though they may be quite different from Szell's. The conductor must know what he's doing and be forceful enough to tell us how to do it, and then we'll do it. These things are fundamental. We'll do what an able conductor wants us to do. Individually, each of us may disagree with him, but as an ensemble we'll play beautifully under him."

When the orchestra has to play under an indifferent conductor or a bad one, it's a different story, Druian went on. "We play for ourselves then, and unless the conductor is stupid, he doesn't interfere," he said. "Then I become the leader, and the men follow me, even though not all of them can see me. Under those circumstances, an experienced orchestra musician 'feels' me, because he plays more with his ears than with his eyes. In an orchestra, it is always more important to listen than to watch. Ideally, each man in the orchestra should know the entire score-- all the parts. I instinctively listen to the others while I listen to myself, and I do this constantly. When I was a student in Philadelphia, we used to play string quartets sitting back to back, so we couldn't see each other. We had to listen to each other very carefully in order to carry on the flow of the music."

Druian shrugged. "Unfortunately, once in a while we get a conductor who is stupid but thinks he is great. For a while, we try our best, but when he does nothing to help us to maintain our artistic standards we have to admit defeat. Then the malcontents who are in every orchestra take over--at last they have their chance to get even with 'the enemy. ' Years ago, we half killed ourselves trying to please a conductor whose beat we couldn't understand; maybe he couldn't understand it himself. Instead of trying to coöperate with us, he became furious. 'What's the matter with you? ' he said. 'My beat is perfect. ' Everyone roared with laughter. He was done for. There was chaos. Under Szell, integrity and integration have become a musical way of life with us. Many of us were able musicians when we came here but have become finished artists under his guidance. Last season, he asked me whether I wanted to record four Mozart sonatas for violin and piano with him. I told him I would be delighted. Szell is a great pianist, and many of us regret that he doesn't play the piano more often. Nothing more was said about the recording plan, but I heard that during his summer vacation, in Switzerland, Szell had a piano sent up from Zurich to his hotel room in Crans-sur-Sierre, and practiced there. Then, just before we left for the European tour, Szell and I met one morning at the Columbia recording studios. We hardly rehearsed. We just played the four sonatas, one after another, from beginning to end, and that was the recording. Szell listened to the playback and O. K. 'd it. He plays Mozart perfectly--with clarity and style and a kind of transparent beauty, and never a wrong idea. "

Druian said that although Szell plays none of the instruments in the orchestra, he is thoroughly familiar with the technical problems of each one, and knows what every player can and cannot do. Druian would rather discuss intricate problems of violin playing with Szell than with another violinist. "If I were to discuss the same problem with Szell and with Isaac Stern, I would get different answers, " he told me. "To Szell, the violin means one thing, and to Stern another. Although Szell is not a string player, he has an intimate knowledge of bowing technique, and he is more detached and less hidebound than any violinist could be. "

'Oboists, clarinettists, and bassoonists are entirely dependent upon a short-lived vegetable matter of merciless capriciousness, with which, however, when it behaves, are wrought perhaps the most tender and expressive sounds in all wind music, " the British musicologist Anthony Baines wrote in the book Woodwind Instruments and Their History. Two forms of the "short-lived vegetable matter, " better known as reed, are used. Clarinettists and saxophonists play with a single reed; oboists and bassoonists use a double reed. Most symphonic players make their own reeds. "I have to make my reeds myself, " John Mack, the Cleveland Orchestra's principal oboe, told me. 'No one else can make a reed to suit me. Only a reed I make gives me correct pitch and intonation. "

The orchestra depends on Mack and his reed for its correct pitch. Through long trial and error, it has been established that the oboe is the most reliable instrument in the orchestra from which to take the pitch, because it is influenced less by climate and temperature than any of the others. Nevertheless, it is the most delicate and complicated of the woodwinds, and oboe players have more trouble with their reeds than other woodwind players have. Reeds are made from a special kind of cane, which grows near the town of Fréjus, in the South of France. The cane is harvested between December and February. Formerly, it used to be stripped and put in storage for about two years, but nowadays it is sometimes sold soon after the harvest, and oboists complain bitterly. Oboists are obsessed by reeds, and spend much of their nights sitting up and making new ones. The oboist first selects a strip of cane, then doubles it over and ties it tightly to a small conical brass tube called the staple. Finally, the fold is cut and the two remaining ends are scraped to the thinness of paper, to provide the vibrating tip. When the tip of the reed is pressed between the player's lips, the edges touch, closing the air passage. Changing lip tension alters the curvature and shape of the reed, and of the puffs of air that the lips generate, to produce varied vibrations. The reed transfers the vibrations to the air inside the instrument. Only a minute stream of air is needed, so the player's lungs must be capable of a constant restraint. Moreover, even a trace of moisture may choke the tiny orifice. The life and the quality of the tone, though, depend on the fineness and elasticity of the reed. A very fine reed gives the oboist flexibility in pitch and the plaintive, bittersweet sound for which the oboe is admired. When Mack plays a lot, a reed may last only two or three days. Reeds are an unending source of anxiety to him, and he always carries a few of them around in a small case.

"A bassoon player needs more time than other reed players to make a reed, but after it's broken in he may be able to use it for weeks and weeks," Mack told me. "I've never used a reed for more than two weeks. The reed gives you not only pitch and intonation but also the quality of your tone and quickness of response, and the ability to pass easily from low to high notes. The higher up you go, the better your reed must be. And the oboe presents other problems. Because the bore of the oboe is only a little more than an eighth of an inch at the top, the instrument responds to changes of altitude. The air at higher altitudes, being less dense, vibrates faster, and it makes the reed heavier. On our last European tour, we played in Salzburg and in Lucerne, both of which are fourteen hundred feet, and then we went to Edinburgh, which is near sea level, and there I broke three reeds in succession. You've heard the saying 'You don't have to be crazy to play the oboe, but it helps.' Actually, there is something to it. Originally, the oboe was an outdoor instrument, and it was important to play it loud, and playing it so loud caused the oboist to go mad."

Unlike string instruments, which are just about the same all over the world, different models of most of the woodwinds and the

brass instruments exist, creating different nuances of sound. American wind players have the chance to listen to all sorts of wind instruments, and can select the ones most responsive to their way of
playing. Many of the Cleveland's woodwind players use French instruments, but they play them in a different manner from the
French, who produce a slighter and more nasal tone. The Cleveland woodwinds have a mellow, round tone by comparison.

Mack practices a great deal. "I don't practice just the
notes I have to play," he said. "The notes are relatively easy.
I give a lot of thought to what I want to do with those notes. All
of us in this orchestra do. This is the most difficult part of the
craft. Years ago, a member of our section joined another famous
orchestra in the East. The next time I saw him, he said he was
living the life of Riley, because all that mattered was that he
should play well during the concerts. It's not that way here. In
our section, everybody is constantly trying to do better. "

Robert Marcellus, the Cleveland Orchestra's principal clarinet, is convinced that an orchestra musician can be successful only
if he really loves to play in a symphonic ensemble. "Playing in
an orchestra is my life," Marcellus told me during my visit to
Cleveland. "I suppose there are some people in the string section
who failed to become soloists and consider playing in an orchestra
a sort of substitute profession. This attitude doesn't exist among
the wind players. All of us are here because this is what we want
to do more than anything else. I could make more money teaching
at a conservatory, and perhaps I would have more security. But I
wouldn't be happy. This orchestra takes great pride in its achievements. We are respected by our peers, the members of other
great orchestras; in fact, some of those peers have called the
Cleveland the orchestras' orchestra. That's more important to us
than applause. And our pride gives us an esprit de corps. I do
sympathize with our string players, though. It isn't rewarding to
have to play in a section all one's life. During my military service, I played for three years in the Air Force Band, in Washington, D. C. , in a section of five clarinets, all playing identical
parts. It was terrible. Here, each of the clarinettists plays a
different, solo part. Naturally, we are not true soloists, in the
sense that a great violinist or a pianist is. Instead, we have the
satisfaction that comes from being part of a fine orchestra and
playing the magnificent repertory of symphonic music. "

Marcellus, a native of Omaha, began his musical studies
on the piano, and took up the clarinet when he was eleven. He
joined the Cleveland Orchestra in 1953, when he was twenty-five.
"I came to Cleveland with more talent and skill than style or experience," he told me. Szell's habit of holding four or five rehearsals for a concert pleased him from the start, he said, and
he went on, "Szell taught me to re-create and sustain a musical
line. The orchestra player needs the conductor's impulse. Even
when we are happy and well integrated, the impulse from the
podium makes all the difference between merely playing the notes

and recreating the very spirit of the music. With a superior impulse, we can give a superior performance. All of a sudden, the orchestra doesn't sound just good--it sounds great. Part of it is our own skill, no doubt. Part is the inspiration of the moment, which we're getting from the great conductor. He knows what we can do, he uses our skill, he enables us to sound great. It's often said that orchestra musicians become cold-blooded, cynical, blasé. Not the musicians in this orchestra. Most of us have a total commitment to the music. I remember an evening in Carnegie Hall, during a performance of Mozart's 'Jupiter' Symphony. There are no clarinets in the score, and I went up to the balcony to listen. I sensed the rapport from the stage, and suddenly I had a moment of overpowering exhilaration. I belonged to this group, I was part of it. I was happy. "

Marcellus is proud of his work, but because he is a first-rate orchestra musician he willingly surrenders part of his artistic personality to a conductor he admires. "If I respect a conductor, I'll go all the way to do what he wants from me," he said. "Szell has a consummate knowledge of the music he conducts. I know that I am just one of a hundred and six. Sitting in the orchestra, I could never get the entire picture, even if I were the world's most gifted player and knew the score note by note. And since I can never hear the integrated whole, the sum of the efforts of the hundred and six players, it is my job to play my part as well as I can. Only the conductor can hear the whole. He must be able to hear six or sixty-six or a hundred and six voices and blend them into music. I've seen good instrumentalists improve considerably after coming here. They learned to sustain a melodic line, and showed greater maturity. Everybody knows that Szell is a terrifying authoritarian of the old school, but they also know that he is an artist of terrific ability. Years ago, some of our first-chair men rehearsed the Beethoven septet for violin, viola, cello, double bass, clarinet, bassoon, and horn. All of us were fine instrumentalists and accomplished musicians, but after two rehearsals we had a sense of impending disaster. Each of us played his own part correctly, but what we played together wasn't Beethoven's music. Szell must have heard about it, because he asked us whether we'd mind if he attended our next rehearsal. He listened quietly, never said a word. Afterward, he told us a few things-- some specific orientations that conveyed a sense of structure. I remember that Szell and the seven of us talked together for a while, and then we played the music once more. Suddenly we were no longer seven individuals but a septet. All the parts fell into place, and there was the line of music that we had been unable to re-create. "

The orchestra musician must often do things that go against his musical education, forcing himself to unlearn something he was once taught, Marcellus told me. "You may have studied with a famous teacher--but he was thinking of the instrument rather than of the future instrumentalist's duty to the ensemble," he said. "I'm often asked by young players what is expected of a member

of the Cleveland Orchestra. First, he must have technical skill--
it's taken for granted that he'll know his instrument. Second, he
must respond both to the music and to the conductor. And, third,
he must be able to listen--not only to the orchestra and to himself
but also to the line of the music. " Marcellus nodded thoughtfully
and added, "I think that's what we do so well here--listen. "

Szell has said that the most sensitive ensemble playing
comes when "a hundred and six men are playing, each of them
listening, so far as is possible, to the hundred and five others,
and trying to make music together the way a string quartet does. "
Few members of the Cleveland Orchestra listen as intently to the
hundred and five other voices as does Cloyd Duff, a tall, athletic
Ohioan who studied at the Curtis Institute of Music and has been
the orchestra's timpani player since 1942. Duff is the principal
of the percussion section, which consists of five men, playing
various drums, the cymbals, the triangle, the glockenspiel, the
castanets, and other instruments. In "Don Quixote," one man
plays the tambourine. In the seventh variation, when the knight
and Sancho Panza believe themselves to be flying through the air,
another plays the wind machine--a cloth-covered cylinder turned by
a handle. The cloth is in contact with wooden slats, and as the
handle is turned faster the pitch of the windlike noise rises and the
volume increases. Gershwin's "An American in Paris" calls for
two automobile horns, and Erik Satie's "Parade" for a typewriter.

It may seem that life is never dull for the percussion players, but, because composers use them sparingly, they must listen
and count silently for longer stretches of time than the other members of the orchestra. Duff handles three kettledrums of different
sizes, the largest of which gives the lowest notes. He tunes his
kettledrums whenever the whole orchestra is playing fortissimo,
and at the same time he keeps counting. Counting has become
second nature to him, he told me. He counts subconsciously. He
counts even when he is listening to an orchestra on the radio or
on records at home. When he is playing, he does not rely on the
conductor's cue but uses it merely as a double check. Even in a
symphony that gives him little to do, he does not relax and just
listen to the other sections. Instead, he counts relentlessly.
'Nothing must distract my alertness," he said. "As long as I let
my reflexes do the counting, I feel safe. "

The timpani--which produce notes, whereas many other percussion instruments produce sounds of indefinite pitch--are said to
have originated in Arabia; in any event, they have been standard
orchestra instruments since the beginning of the eighteenth century.
Bach and Handel and their successors used two timpani, tuned to
the tonic and the dominant. Octave tuning for the timpani was
probably invented by Beethoven in his last two symphonies; in the
Ninth Symphony, the timpani player becomes a soloist.

Duff told me he had always wanted to play the timpani. He
took up the drum at the age of six, and has never stopped playing

it. "You have to be an extrovert and a man of some courage to play the timpani, " he said. "You also need perfect pitch, a strong sense of rhythm, and good muscular coordination. " Duff sits on a small platform in the rear of the orchestra, from which he can see everybody around him. He always sits on the edge of his chair, even if he doesn't have to play for the next hundred bars.

"When you think you know the music so well that you can afford to sit back and relax and wait for your cue, you are in trouble, " he said. "Under Szell, I've learned to think of a rest as a special kind of silent sound. Our orchestra is trained to react very fast and with great precision. We are not given as much leeway as other orchestras. We don't go in for long, sweeping notes. The Cleveland Orchestra is known for clarity, precision, and inner voicing, because that's the way Szell wants the music performed. Few conductors take such trouble today. Many are satisfied to perform the score and miss the deeper meaning behind the notes. I'm sure that if we were to play without a conductor, we would play in the style in which Szell trained us for over twenty years. Here, everybody instinctively seeks out the music behind the notes. This way of playing is ingrained in our orchestra. "

In the Cleveland Orchestra, the musicians often rehearse the standard works of the repertory--works they have played for many years and could almost play by heart. "When we rehearse Beethoven's Fifth Symphony, my initial reaction is 'Oh gosh, again! '" Duff told me. But after the first few bars I am caught up in the spirit of the music. Good music always does that to a good musician; only bad music is a bore. But I know good musicians who wouldn't want to play in our orchestra. They wouldn't be temperamentally suited to it. You have to have exceptional artistic discipline to become a successful member of this group. You have to have your own standards and adhere to them--then you have a sense of personal accomplishment. I suppose we are artistic-minded, whereas some orchestras are commercial-minded. I know musicians who tell me, 'It's ridiculous to make so much fuss about a little detail, ' but we not only become accustomed to it--we like it. Szell considers the orchestra an extension of himself, and so do we--we seem to react with him. He no longer drills the orchestra; he coördinates it, watches it, and criticizes it. This attitude creates self-discipline and a sense of spontaneity, and it puts you in the right frame of mind to rehearse Beethoven's Fifth Symphony for the hundredth time. A musician who didn't accept group discipline, and who didn't believe in the virtues of clarity and exactness, would be of no use here. I may be as casual as I like offstage, but I must always be alert when I play. On the other hand, I must never become tense and stiff, because that would ruin my tone quality. "

Even a kettledrum player, I learned, modifies his sound to the conductor's wishes. Under Karajan, Duff told me, he found himself unaccountably playing "with less sharpness and with longer

lines" than under Szell. There was clarity, but it was "external
rather than internal clarity. " He explained, "You don't change the
level of your exactness, but you do mold yourself in a different
way. You adjust yourself to the conductor's spoken or indicated
demands, like a painter changing the subtle nuances of a certain
color. "

Arthur H. Benade, a nuclear physicist and professor of
physics at Case Western Reserve University, in Cleveland, writes
in "Horns, Strings and Harmony, " "I know of one major orchestra
in which the French-horn section once had a standing agreement:
they would go out and drink champagne after any public performance in which none of them burbled or otherwise missed a note.
Sad to say, these men never got their fill of champagne!" The
French horn is an incredibly difficult instrument. A slightly conical tube curled around itself and opening into a wide bell, it would
be twelve feet long if it were uncoiled. The player, blowing
through compressed lips, makes the air inside the tube vibrate,
and the vibrations must travel a long way. The speed of vibration
of the lips affects the speed of vibration of the air column, thus
determining the pitch of the note.

"The brass player 'makes' the note, and his lips can do
some very complicated things to the physics of musical brasses,
not all of them understood scientifically, " writes Benade. The
The French horn is probably the most unpredictable instrument in
the orchestra. Brass players have trouble sustaining a note for a
long time. To produce a nasal tone, the player inserts his hand
in the bell and blows hard in a way that would ordinarily produce a
note a semitone lower. Almost anything can happen with a French
horn, and even the most accomplished horn player is unable to explain why. Years ago, the Cleveland Orchestra was performing
the Brahms Second Symphony, the first movement of which includes
a solo passage for French horn. There was a sudden, terrible
silence where the horn passage was supposed to be. Szell calmly
continued to beat time, and went on with the symphony. Afterward,
Myron Bloom, the orchestra's principal horn player, came to Szell
to apologize.

"What happened?" Szell asked.

"I don't know, " Bloom said, still shaken.   "I just don't
know.   The instrument wouldn't speak. "

"Well, don't get upset about it, " Szell said.

Bloom, a native of Cleveland, studied at the Eastman and
the Juilliard Schools of Music, and is considered one of the great
horn players in the country. But he still cannot explain what went
wrong that night.   "In my younger years, I would break out in a
cold sweat when the horn wouldn't play, " he told me.   "Now I'm
more adjusted to it. To play the horn, one must be in perfect
physical and mental condition. It's not merely a matter of lip

control or strength of breath. The instrument is so complicated that it takes perfect coördination to master it. A sleepless night, a fight with your wife, slight indigestion, some bad news--any little thing may cause a momentary lack of coördination, and then it happens. To remain in top condition, daily practice is absolutely necessary. On tours, I always worry when I can't practice every day. Physical exercise is important, too. In Cleveland, I go to the Y. M. C. A. four times a week for a workout. "

"The brass in general, by nature laggard, come in with as much precision as the woodwinds," Paul Henry Lang, the noted musicologist, wrote about the Cleveland Orchestra. Szell has molded the brass section into a miracle of homogeneity. "When I joined the orchestra, I didn't think that fourteen members of the brass section could be trained to breathe collectively, but I've since learned that with discipline it can be done," says Martin Morris, one of the orchestra's five French-horn players.

Szell calls his brass section's skill "the result of relentless admonition and intolerance of any imprecision. " The French-horn players play American instruments of the same type, they use the same type of mouthpiece, and they have had similar training. By playing with each other and listening to each other, they have come to have the chamber-music approach of the strings and the woodwinds. They know instinctively how to lift a note and attack the next phrase.

Unlike the trombone and the trumpet, which are quite alike in tone color, the French horn at its best has an "unbrassy" sound, and therefore sometimes joins the woodwinds in quintets. The modern French horn, with valves, was introduced only around the middle of the nineteenth century; before that the horn could produce only the notes of the harmonic series. The horn player uses a mouthpiece that is narrow and deep. Unlike a trumpet player, whose instrument has a wide, shallow mouthpiece that produces an incisive tone and makes the player feel reasonably sure of hitting the desired harmonic, the horn player can never be sure. But if his professional life is always tense, he has the satisfaction of playing the instrument with the most expressive solo voice in the orchestra and the most romantic of all brass instruments. "A horn player's professional life is shorter than a violinist's, " I was told by Morris, who played the violin before he took up the French horn. "With some luck, a string player may work beyond the retirement age of sixty, but a brass player suffers from nervous tension, high blood pressure, overexertion, lack of breath control, and trouble with his lips and teeth. If I lose my teeth, I could go back to playing the violin in a section, but I would certainly miss the chance of playing on my own. "

The Cleveland's brass players are sometimes astonished by their own performance. "During a concert, you are often preoccupied with details and have no time to notice how the whole thing sounds, " Morris said. "But afterward, when you hear the recording or the playback of a broadcast, you wonder how it was possible to do it together so well, and you're filled with a tremendous sense of satisfaction. At such moments, you don't mind the ordeals ahead of you. I believe that that satisfaction is the main reason we love to play together. Many of us would very likely play together even if we got almost no money for it. There is an exhilaration that comes when you sit in a fine concert hall, anywhere on earth, and fill it with magnificent music. That's the bonus of playing with a great orchestra."

All orchestral markings are merely indications, and give the players a great deal of leeway. ("Composers write intentions and sometimes pious hopes rather than executions," Szell says.) Exactly how loud is forte, how soft is piano, and what is the difference between mezzo forte and mezzo piano? When a composer indicates rubato, which allows the player additional freedom of expression, where does freedom degenerate into distortion? In the eighteenth and the early nineteenth centuries, composers didn't write elaborate directions in their scores, because they were close to the musicians and could always tell them how they wanted their music played. A musician playing under Haydn, Mozart, or Beethoven and not sure how a certain nuance was expected to sound had only to ask the composer. Wagner started a new trend when he wrote in his scores not the desired effect but the manner of playing required from the player, and Mahler and Strauss put exact markings in their scores. Yet Strauss also wrote in the score of "Don Quixote" such instructions as "Even faster" and "With knightly gallantry" and "Slowing down toward the end," thereby creating problems of taste and musicality that weigh heavily on the conductor's artistic conscience. Every musician knows that metronomic markings are of limited use. The free flow of the musical line cannot be controlled by a mechanical device. It's up to the conductor to secure the all-important nuances.

Exactly what happens at the beginning of Beethoven's Fifth Symphony, when the conductor gives his preparatory beat and the entire orchestra comes in, by what seems a miracle of simultaneity, with its ta-ta-ta-tah? Exactly when does it come in? Under the late Wilhelm Furtwängler, a great musician with an erratic beat, members of the Berlin Philharmonic used to say, "We come in when the conductor's downbeat reaches the second button of his white vest." Whatever the truth of that, the players all came in beautifully, at the same instant. The conductor must indicate the exact tempo with his preliminary upbeat. "It is a general rule that the conductor gives one extra beat, strictly in tempo, before the music actually begins.... It is equivalent to lifting the bow in the string instruments and to taking a breath in the winds," the conductor Max Rudolf writes in his book The Grammar of Conducting.

Not all orchestras react to the conductor in the same way. In fact, each orchestra has its own method of attack. Some orchestras play during the downbeat or near its end. The Cleveland

Orchestra comes in "a tiny little bit after the beat," Szell says.
The Berlin Philharmonic is rather late, coming in only after the
downbeat. The Boston Symphony under Koussevitzky was known
for its late attack. Koussevitzky would shake his arm at them,
and nobody would play. Some people claimed that at a mysterious
moment Richard Bourgin, the concertmaster, would give an almost
imperceptible nod and they would all come in at the same moment.
But one must not underestimate Koussevitzky's contribution. Lane,
the Cleveland Orchestra's associate conductor, remembers attending the rehearsal of a student orchestra in Tanglewood under a
poor conductor which Koussevitzky also attended. The conductor
tried to get the players started on the first movement of Beethoven's Second Symphony, which begins with a thirty-second note followed by a longer note that is sustained at the discretion of the
conductor--a situation in which it is impossible to indicate the
tempo by an upbeat. The conductor made a half-hearted sign with
his baton, and no one understood it. The players came in at different times, and there was confusion. The conductor, flushing,
tried again, and the confusion only grew worse. He just couldn't
get the orchestra started. Then Koussevitzky said, shaking his
head, "What's the matter with you? It's so simple." He stepped
up in front of the orchestra, lifted his arms, and let them fall in
a powerful gesture, and the players all came in with absolute precision. "He had an imperious will, and he was able to communicate his command," says Lane.

"At the beginning of Beethoven's Fifth, Szell gives his downbeat and somehow we all come in at the same time," says Hyman
Schandler, a member of the second-violin section, who has played
in the Cleveland Orchestra for forty-three years. Schandler is
able to judge the conductor's problem from both the player's and
the conductor's viewpoint, since he is the conductor of the Cleveland Women's Orchestra.

I asked Schandler what he meant by that "somehow."

"I never tried to analyze how it is that we begin in unison,"
he said, looking uncomfortable. "It's partly that we've worked together so many years and are so well integrated, and that we listen
to each other until we feel one another. That still doesn't explain
how Szell slowly turns his right hand down for a slow, soft entrance and we all come in together a certain fraction of a second
later. When two people have been married for many years, they
begin to think alike. Maybe the orchestra is a sort of super-mar-
riage. Some conductors give us a furtive downbeat, as if it were
a secret between the conductor and the orchestra. Szell doesn't
do that, but neither does he try to give us a physically unmistakable downbeat--he isn't conducting for the audience. When we are
supposed to come in on a sforzando, he signals the accent with his
eyes one beat earlier, and then we come in all together, since we
are prepared. When you think of a hundred and six players doing
it, with absolute precision, it staggers the imagination. Yet I
don't think it's a matter of intuition; in fact, I don't think there's

any mystery about it.   It is a sudden occurrence, but it is the result of hard work and playing together for years.   When we violins
play a pizzicato with the woodwinds, which happens frequently in
Brahms, it wouldn't do for us to come in with the conductor's beat;
we would be too early.   We've got to listen to the wind sound and
then we come in.   The acoustics of Severance Hall were changed
in 1958, and we couldn't hear one another for a while after that--
we had to learn to listen all over again.   We second violins couldn't
hear the violas at all until we found a new way of listening.
You've got to learn to listen in different acoustical situations, just
as you've got to learn how to follow different conductors.   Stokowski, for instance, insists that we play on the beat.   Young players
who join the orchestra have a lot to learn.   This year, we have
several new ones, and we older men watch their integration carefully.   It may take them four weeks to get integrated, or it may
take them a whole season.   If a man hasn't integrated by his second
season, he'll probably leave.   But in most cases the new player's
reflexes get faster, and he acquires the exact timing that our orchestra is known for.   He learns to play phrases rather than single
notes.   He learns to watch the conductor instinctively before approaching a change of tempo, a ritardando or accelerando.   He
watches the conductor's beat and his eyes.   And he learns to read
the material.   The well-printed parts of older symphonies present
no problem, but some modern works are played from imperfectly
copied manuscripts.   The parts contain accidentals and sudden
changes in metre, and there may be outlandish intervals--and those
are only some of the problems.   But there are joys, too.   In a
Bruckner symphony, the full orchestra plays a divine pianissimo
after a fortissimo--a beautiful, soft sound made by a hundred and
six people.   It sends a chill down my back.   Or when we second
violins come in during the overture to 'The Bartered Bride,' all
of us playing like one player.   After we played that overture in
Carnegie Hall, a friend of mine from the New York Philharmonic
said, 'I've never heard a second-violin section like it. '''

     Since the artistic temperament presents a great many prob-
lems, it is not surprising that a famous symphony orchestra should
employ someone to avert temperamental chaos.   In the Cleveland,
the man concerned with the players' emotional and vocational problems is Olin Trogdon, a double-bass player, who was appointed the
orchestra's personnel manager a few years ago and has now given
up playing in the orchestra.   Trogdon, a tall, outgoing man, sits
in the personnel manager's office backstage, trying to repair hurt
feelings and calm jealousies.   Who should sit next to the first
cellist--the second-best section player or the weakest?   Which violinist enjoys higher status in the orchestra--the one at the second
stand of the second-violin section or the one at the last stand of
the first-violin section?   When only sixty members of the orchestra
are assigned to make a recording, quite a few of the remaining
forty-six want to know why they weren't chosen.   Every large orchestra has such status problems.   But a player's status is determined, ultimately, by the orchestra's musical director, who is
more concerned with the balance of its sections and the excellence

of the orchestra as a whole than he is with the emotions of the
players. The role that Trogdon plays is that of the orchestra's
father confessor. He advises the players about their personal
problems, their financial troubles, and their vocational illnesses.
Violin players suffer from cramps in their arms, double-bass players from rheumatism in their shoulders, wind and brass players
from troubles with their lips and teeth. Some people come to him
because it helps them just to talk about their problems. Others,
too shy to talk about what really bothers them, come in to talk
about practically anything else; Trogdon understands what they are
doing, and often manages to help them. His position is delicate:
he needs to have the confidence of both the players and the management, for he must help the men relax so they can play the music well. "There are men who have few friends in the orchestra,"
he told me. "Others have friends in their section--especially the
string players, who experience common disappointments. On tours,
the brass players seem to stick together, and there is a fraternity
of wind players who worry about their reeds. Common pressures
and a common outlook often work to form friendships. But there
are friendships across all sections, too. Every society has small
groups, but I try to prevent the formation of cliques, which so often make life difficult in other orchestras. When a player gets
angry, I talk to him, so he won't stay angry. As long as one can
talk to people, one can prevent chaos. "

     The attitude of the players toward the orchestra suggests
that Trogdon does his job well. "Even when we have disputes and
are not happy, we play well for Szell," a member of the second-
violin section told me. "We do it out of respect for him, and perhaps out of fear. "

     A viola player said, "There is often a lingering discontent
in our section, but then there will come an evening in New York
when the viola section wins the respect of the audience and of players from other orchestras, and that soothes our hurt egos. In
another important orchestra I've played in, there was a lot of professionalism. Here we have a lot of idealism. In New York, our
men rush out to buy the reviews after a concert, and they talk
about it for hours. "

     They also talk about money. When the Cleveland Orchestra
returned from its first great international success, the European
tour in the spring of 1957, the players' annual wages were below
the average paid by the four other major American orchestras.
Since then, the Cleveland has come to be called one of the world's
greatest orchestras, and, perhaps not unreasonably, its players feel
that they ought to be paid accordingly. Last year [1969], the minimum weekly salary, which most section players got, was two hundred and forty dollars. It is now two hundred and fifty-five, and
a contract for September is still under negotiation. Some wind
players may get as much as four hundred dollars, and the string
players tend to complain that the discrepancy is too large. It's
simply a question of supply and demand, however; there are more
violinists than oboists available.

A big symphony orchestra is an economic monstrosity.
Fund-raisers for the Cleveland Orchestra are often asked why it
needs so much money "when Severance Hall is often sold out. " In
an average week, there are two concerts, which means a total of
forty-one hundred and eight tickets sold, at an average of five dollars a ticket. The orchestra thus takes in twenty thousand dollars,
but there are a hundred and six players, and the average weekly
salary is three hundred and ten dollars--a weekly payroll of thirty-
three thousand dollars. The payroll alone, then, is thirteen thousand dollars more than the box-office receipts, and there are conductors' and solists' fees, staff wages, the cost of the hall's upkeep, and so on. "Before the orchestra plays a note, we are
thirty thousand dollars a week in the red, " says A. Beverly Barks-
dale, its general manager. "The whole business is of necessity a
deficit operation. "

During my visit to Cleveland, several orchestra members
suggested that I sit on the stage among the players during the final
rehearsal of "Don Quixote, " on Thursday morning. "It might give
you the musicians' frog's-eye view of the conductor, " a cello player said. "And on Thursday night, from the auditorium, you'll have
the bird's-eye view of the whole orchestra. " A trumpeter said I
would do well to stay close to the brass and percussion, in the
rear, where the orchestral balance is upside down. "It will be interesting not so much for what you hear as for what you can't
hear, " he said. "It will help you understand a few of the practical
problems players face. " When I told Szell about the suggestion
that I sit at the rear of the stage for the final rehearsal, he said
he thought it was a good idea. Accordingly, a few minutes before
ten on Thursday, I took a chair between Duff, the timpanist, and
Emil Sholle, who is recognized as a master of the cymbals. A
third member of the percussion section, Richard Weiner, was shaking the tambourine and trying out the wind machine. No one paid
any attention to me. The atmosphere was tense and businesslike.
Three trumpeters in front of me were practicing the difficult staccato passage in the Introduction, which they play together. Duff
was tuning his kettledrums, bending down and putting his left ear
close to the drumskins, and he didn't seem to be bothered by the
trumpets' fortissimo.

Druian walked to his place and signalled the oboist for an A.
A few seconds later, Trogdon escorted Fournier and Szell to the
front of the stage, and then went to the far side and took his place
among the double-bass players. Szell greeted the orchestra,
opened the score of "Don Quixote" (though he knows the work by
heart, he uses the score in rehearsal to provide reference points),
and quietly explained a few matters. The orchestra listened in
silence, and a few men made pencil markings in their parts as he
asked for "long, sustained notes" at No. 13; reminded the horns
"to play as pianissimo as possible" at No. 17; and turned to the
first violins, sang a few bars of a phrase, and said, "Start near
the middle of the bow, so it can bounce. " A wind player asked a
question, and Szell said, "Mezzo piano would be better than mezzo
forte. When one sees the 'f' sign, one is always tempted to play

louder. " The wind player nodded and made a note on his part.
Szell then asked the woodwinds "to get a little more involved" before No. 19.   To the three trombones, in the rear, he said, "Make
that entrance we talked about yesterday very soft.   It should be a
completely impassive piano. "

There was some last-minute tuning, and then there was a
silence filled with concentration.   Everybody looked up at Szell,
who raised his arms.   The communication between him and the orchestra was almost palpable.   After a couple of tense moments,
Szell indicated the tempo.   The flutes and oboes began the D-major
motif, and the violins came in with the theme of the gallant, er-
rant knight.   From where I sat, I could hardly hear the grazioso
violin passages.   Even the virtuoso figurations of the solo violin
were almost inaudible.   The balance of the orchestra sound seemed
completely reversed, and sometimes the sound seemed to bounce
off the rear wall of the stage.   But the trumpets played their staccato passage with virtuosity, and the pieces of the musical mosaic
were apparently falling into the right places.   Although the music
sounded unfamiliar from where I sat, I could tell that Szell was
shaping the continuity and the line of the work, using his baton and
his eyes.   Sometimes he seemed to lengthen the value of a tone
almost imperceptibly by making a soothing gesture with his left
hand, and, again, his eyes gave a particular section advance notice
for a sudden sforzando.   His gestures and commands were unmis-
takable--clear and powerful, almost hypnotic.   One had to follow
them.

The subtle colors of Strauss's great tone painting began to
emerge, but I was still confused by the imbalance of the sound.
At one point, the first trombone player, who sat in front of me,
came in exactly with the solo violin, and I wondered how he could
do it.   In the second variation, the woodwinds and muted brasses,
playing a succession of minor seconds in flutter-tonguing, produced
a startlingly realistic imitation of the army of sheep bleating, and
I recalled that Strauss's biographer Norman Del Mar wrote of this
effect, "[His] onomatopoeic representation ... is one of the best-
known features of the tone poem. "

I began to notice little things.   The trombone players had
small bottles of oil under their chairs.   In the percussion section,
Weiner stepped behind the triangle and stood there, counting rests
by beating time with his foot.   In the third variation, during the
Don's description of the fairyland that he and Sancho Panza must
conquer, Weiner played a few notes on the triangle and then sat
down again.   The three trumpet players in front of me seemed less
tense now.   After bringing off another difficult passage in virtuoso
style, they nodded to each other happily.   The trombones came in
with short, staccato thrusts--too early, I thought, but Szell went
on, so they must have been right.   Several times, too, when the
orchestra played sustained notes, some sections came in earlier
than others.   To be exact, some sections seemed, from where I
sat, to come in earlier.   I hadn't learned to listen as a player

listens to an orchestra. It was fascinating to hear the continuing
thread of the musical line woven by groups of instruments.
Szell's beat has been called precise and angular, but there was nothing
angular about the music; it was beautiful and smooth and round.
Szell's movements seemed caressing, delicate, almost baroque.

In the sixth variation, Weiner handled the tambourine, and
in the seventh he turned the handle of the wind machine to produce
an eerie, windlike noise. During that variations, when Don Quixote
and Sancho Panza imagine they are flying through the air, their
themes are raised four octaves, but a low D sustained by the timpanist and contrabassoonist reminds the listener that they have
never left solid ground. In "Don Quixote," the orchestra always
tells the truth.

Duff had been busy producing a constant drum roll during
the flying episode. Now he was again tuning his kettledrums. He
touched a drumskin lightly with the fourth finger of his right hand
and then changed its pitch. At No. 75, Szell stopped the orchestra
and asked the woodwinds to be "a little less heavy." They tried
twice. He shook his head. The third time, he was evidently
satisfied, for he called out "That was nice now!" without stopping
again.

When Fournier began to play the Finale, Szell at one point
put his left forefinger warningly to his lips, and then stretched his
left hand, palm down, above the orchestra, as though reminding
the players not to interfere during the immensely moving solo melody, the beautiful resolution in calm harmony, and the Don's melancholy transfiguration in death. Fournier played with great simplicity toward the end, making the death of Don Quixote a deeply emotional experience. "The composer bids him a fond farewell," as
Klaus G. Roy says in his program notes, "in six grateful and
touching measures."

After the last bar, Szell held his left hand up, to prevent
any talk, and said, "Could you try for more pianissimo in the last
two bars? This is full orchestra but still pianissimo." The full
orchestra played the last two bars once more, with a beautiful,
warm sound, and very pianissimo. Szell nodded to indicate his
satisfaction and gave the sign for the intermission.

Everybody relaxed. Duff stepped down from his small platform. "Such lovely sound! Such wonderful music!" he said, shaking his head in wonderment, as though he had played "Don Quixote"
for the first time. "What a genius Strauss was!"

Lane joined us as we walked off the stage. "What Szell
does so beautifully with 'Don Quixote' is something that can't be
marked in the score," he said. "He gives each phrase the character that suits it exactly, and at the same time he keeps the flow
of the music as a whole. If you were to beat time with him, you
would soon be lost. He makes small ritardandi and accelerandi

that you don't even notice. And Fournier plays his part superbly--
with no trace of sentimentality. "

Backstage, we met William Hebert, who plays the piccolo,
and Lane complimented him on "that passage. " I asked what passage it was, and Lane explained, "After the Introduction, in the
exposition of the Sancho Panza themes, the piccolo and the solo
viola play a fast, difficult phrase together. Abraham Skernick,
who plays the solo viola, hears the piccolo but cannot see Hebert.
And Hebert neither sees nor hears Skernick. During all the rehearsals, the phrase has come off precisely in unison. No one
talks about it. This is one of the many mysteries of orchestra
playing that are taken for granted, and noticed only when they
don't come off. "

Hebert showed me the phrase in his part--very delicate,
with figurations in sixteenth and thirty-second notes. "Usually,
we play it a few times together in the locker room before we come
up here, " he said. "Practicing it makes us feel safer. Then we
both watch the conductor carefully. The viola can hear me, so he
makes the adjustment. It's tricky, because if it's not done right
everybody will notice it. It's hard to be discreet on the piccolo,
the highest instrument in the orchestra. 'Don Quixote' is especially difficult for me, because it's not only high but soft. The piccolo
has a tendency to become flat when you play soft, and I play several times with the clarinet, which has a tendency to get sharp
when one is playing soft. " Hebert shrugged, and added, "You've
got to balance your intonation. If you know what the other man is
doing, you adjust yourself to him, and he, in turn, adjusts himself
to you. It's give-and-take--a matter of listening, skill, and flexibility, and of carefully studying not only your part but the parts of
those who are playing with you. "

Hebert excused himself, and Lane looked after him as
he walked away. "There are not many orchestras in which the
players get involved so painstakingly and carry their sense of responsibility to such lengths, " he said.

In the corridor, we met Fournier. He looked happy. "I
love this piece, " he said. "Every time I play it, the music seems
to get better. Years ago, when Szell and I happened to be at the
Suvretta House, in St. Moritz, we worked together on the Finale.
I've recorded it both under him and under Karajan, and in both
cases it was a memorable experience. I wish, though, that I could
play it every year with this great orchestra and under Szell, who
makes the music so warm and full of compassion. "

Backstage that night, the musicians--the men in tailcoats and
white ties, and the women in long black dresses--were a somewhat
unfamiliar sight, since I had become used to seeing them dressed
for rehearsals. Several men stood by the door leading to the stage
and looked out into the auditorium. It was almost eight-thirty, but
quite a few seats in the front rows were empty, and a viola player

said that they would probably remain empty, even though the entire
Thursday-night subscription series was sold out and there were always a few people at the box office before a concert hoping to buy
a ticket that was returned. "These subscribers won't come, but
they won't call Severance Hall and let other people use their tickets," he said, looking disgusted.

In the program, I knew, there is always a notice reading,
"Subscribers who are unable to use their tickets for any concert
are urged to telephone the locations to the box office so that the
seats may be resold for the benefit of the Orchestra Maintenance
Fund. With both the Thursday and Saturday concerts sold out, demand for any available tickets is greater than ever.... The value
of the turned-in tickets is income-tax deductible as a contribution."

A woodwind player complained about the lukewarm attitude
of the listeners on Thursday nights. I gathered that Thursday was
the night in Cleveland, when the orchestra performed for a socially
prominent but rather uninterested audience. He said that the same
program usually got a much warmer reception on Saturday night.

A violinist agreed. "We love to perform on tour, either in
Europe or in New York and along the Eastern seaboard, because
we're appreciated and cheered," he said. "And then we come
home and nobody seems to care."

"People's enthusiasm seems to taper off from east to west
in this country," the viola player said. "The best audiences are
in New York and the worst in the Middle West. In the Middle
West, the people applaud after the concert, and the orchestra and
the conductor take a bow. Then everybody gets up and applauds
again, and the orchestra takes a second bow. And that's it--every-
body files out. The second applause was a substitute for prolonged
applause."

A bell rang, and the players filed onstage, took their seats,
and began to tune their instruments. I walked upstairs and joined
Mrs. Szell in her box, from which I was going to hear the concert. The rear rows below and the boxes and balconies were
crowded, but in the front rows there were still some gaping holes.

"Only in Cleveland will you see empty seats when the Cleveland Orchestra performs," Mrs. Szell said. "Naturally, some
people who live far away have trouble getting to the hall in bad
weather, but why not let other people have their tickets? Too
many Clevelanders take their orchestra and George for granted.
When we played in Tiflis, people crowded all the aisles and sat
on the floor in front of the orchestra, and in some seats there were
two people."

The tuning subsided, and Szell came onstage. He was
greeted by much less applause than he had received in New York,
Salzburg, or Vienna when I heard him conduct the orchestra there.

The rarely performed Mozart Marches for Orchestra, from
K. 335 and K. 408, showed Szell and the orchestra at their best.
The music was as clear and fresh as spring water, with just the
right tempos, dynamic nuances, and tonal shadings. Then came
Frank Martin's Cello Concerto, which I thought showed musical
taste and erudition but had rather weak thematic material, making
the music seem dry and academic. This was the American première of the work, and Fournier and the orchestra played it beautifully.

I wondered how "Don Quixote" would sound to me now, from
the box. I had enjoyed it at the first rehearsal I attended, on
Tuesday morning, and since I had heard it several more times, I
felt that I almost knew the complicated music by heart. Now, as
Szell unfolded the great tone painting, I realized how much he and
the orchestra had achieved in the past few days. Perhaps the performance lacked some of the happy spontaneity that I had admired
on Tuesday, but it was close to perfection. I could hear all the
voices in Szell's translucent reading, and once again I admired the
virtuosity of the players in all the sections and, at the same time,
the magnificent integration of the orchestra into one instrument.
Although the attack of the trombones had seemed puzzling to me
this morning, it now seemed perfect; their entrance was not de-
layed, not early, but just right. And the many solo phrases never
broke the flow of the musical line; the melodic thread went on and
on. The climax of the performance was the Finale, which Fournier
played beautifully. It made me think of the death of the noble
knight, never of the cello part's technical difficulties.

When Szell lowered his arms after the two final pianissimo
bars, there was a long moment of silence. It was a far greater
tribute to the composer, and to the performers, than a sudden
burst of applause would have been. Clearly, many people were
deeply moved. I was moved, and I was also surprised that I had
been able to enjoy the performance so much--that the rehearsals
had not taken the bloom off the music. I mentioned this to Mrs.
Szell, and she said, "Yes, but this music is very beautiful, and
very close to George's heart. "

Downstairs, people began to file out.

In the corridor that leads from the stage to the rooms of
the conductor, the soloist, and the concertmaster, Fournier stood
talking with a violinist. The two men looked both exhausted and
elated.

Fournier said, "I'm so glad we'll do it once more, on Saturday. We'll do it exactly as we did it tonight. Nothing must be
different. "

We were joined by Szell and Lane. "This is a real red-
letter evening, " Mrs. Szell whispered to me. "George looks almost pleased tonight. "

"C'était très, très beau," Fournier said, touching Szell's arm.   "Merci."

Szell smiled and put his arms around Fournier.   "Yes," he said.   "We've built a cathedral out of pebbles."

THE MANY-SPLENDORED SOUND
OF CALIFORNIA*

Raymond Kendall

In March of 1853, just three years after Congress approved statehood for California, a traveling Hungarian violinist, Miska Hauser, wrote to his brother in Vienna: "The city (San Francisco) is full of concertizing artists and all of the larger halls have long since been engaged, so I was forced to take a small theater for my first concert."

In 1865, Los Angeles had no daily newspaper, no railroad to other centers of civilization, no Protestant church, no theater or concert hall.   In fact, until the Sante Fe Railroad laid its tracks to Los Angeles in 1885, the city was still a small, sleepy town clustered around the Plaza Church.   With the railroad came Emma Albert's English Opera Company, bringing a repertoire including Mignon and Lucia, and within ten years Los Angeles had four concert halls, an oratorio society, and an organ factory!   Between 1880 and 1891, seven colleges and universities came into being in Southern California.   USC awarded its first bachelor of music degree in 1885.   The state normal school (later UCLA) had its first music instructor by 1883, while Occidental College, Pomona, La Verne, Whittier, and Throop University (now Caltech) all gave some emphasis to music.   Los Angeles Conservatory of Music and the Arts opened its doors in 1884.

In the years since World War II, cultural institutions throughout the United States have burgeoned in size and influence. Nowhere has the growth been so dramatic as in California, even though the desire to inaugurate symphony orchestras and opera companies has often outdistanced a firm financial footing.   Only San Francisco and Los Angeles have "major" symphony orchestras--if by the latter is meant the capacity to offer 34 to 45 weeks of symphony concerts per year.   San Francisco's longer musical tradition assured its orchestra a more consistent audience and a finer habitat (the War Memorial Opera House, which it shares with the San Francisco Opera Company) than that enjoyed until the very recent past by the Los Angeles Philharmonic.

*From Saturday Review, Sept. 23, 1967.   Copyright 1967 by Saturday Review Co.   Reprinted by permission.

Walter Henry Rothwell, Artur Rodzinski, Otto Klemperer, and Alfred Wallenstein were the principal conductors of the Los Angeles Philharmonic Orchestra before the brief tenure of Eduard Van Beinum and the appointment of the orchestra's present musical director, Zubin Mehta. Relationships between Mehta and his orchestra are built upon mutual respect. Problems: Mehta's dazzling talents lure him all over the world, often at the expense of much-needed time to make his maximum impact upon the orchestra at home; also, his insistence upon conducting all orchestral and most concerto repertoire from memory tends to limit his repertoire, particularly of contemporary works. But his current tours with the orchestra to the East Coast last spring and to Europe and the Middle East this fall underline Mehta's oft-expressed commitment to Los Angeles for the next few years. His continued association with Los Angeles augurs well for its continued growth. Under the leadership of Gerhard Samuel, the Oakland Symphony has the best continuity of leadership, the most varied repertoire; it also happens to play very decently.

California breeds symphony orchestras with the same abundance as its citrus and cotton crops. [In 1967], there were 25 [1975: 65 -ed.] or more orchestras in California alone. A few, such as in Long Beach, Pasadena, and Sacramento, are basically training orchestras, with resident music teachers and advanced students grouped around a core of required professionals. These orchestras fulfill a valid function, since they prepare for, feed into, and complement the full-time professional orchestra. But problems arise when a community with the concert-giving potential of only six to 12 concerts a season insists on having its own orchestra, named for its own community. Overhead costs, the difficulty of enlisting the services of a qualified full-time conductor. the shortage or absence of adequate concert halls--all these tend to force the employment of a full roster of professional musicians, impose the necessity of minimum rehearsals, often force changes in personnel between rehearsal and concert as well as from concert to concert. What justification can there be for paying prorata costs of $8000 to $12,000 for a concert by a pick-up orchestra, well though it may play (and some play very well), when the Los Angeles Philharmonic or the San Francisco Symphony can be engaged on a "runout" basis for roughly half the cost?

Conclusion: There will eventually be many full-time symphony orchestras in California. But en route to this happy state, the major orchestras should first be used year round, and, in the process of encouraging the formation of new orchestras, several communities may need to combine their symphonic lust--and their buying power--until each can enjoy the luxury of its own all-professional orchestra.

WHAT IS THE AMERICAN SYMPHONY?*

Leopold Stokowski

The American Symphony Orchestra is composed mainly of young men and young women of enormous talent. There are many of these great talents in and around New York and it is fortunate how well the music schools are developing them.

About six years ago I began to receive many letters from young players saying, "I have graduated from a music school; I am ready and wish to enter the musical life of my country but I cannot find the opportunity." I received so many of these letters that I began to think I should do something about this. So I began to give auditions to players of all the instruments in the orchestra. It was not difficult to do because I already knew some of these young players and I said to them, "Whenever you have friends who really have talent and really love music and really love their instrument, give them my telephone number and then, if they call, we will arrange for an audition." From then on it has enlarged enormously. Every afternoon I give four auditions: at 3:00, 3:30, 4:00 and 4:30. I put two hours apart every day for these auditions and some days I hear four wonderful players. Of course, some other days only three or two are outstanding, but every day someone with great talent comes out of the four and we then put that person on our waiting list.

The orchestra now is composed of about 120 players but we have a waiting list for every instrument and cannot put all those good players in the orchestra because it is already full. However, when a vacancy occurs then I look in my book. In this book I keep details of the auditions so I know exactly all the qualities, and even the weaknesses, of all the players. Then we choose somebody and engage him or her.

This happens rather often because other orchestras come and steal our players. We are delighted. We should be angry but we're not: we're delighted because that means we can give opportunity to another player who may have been waiting a long time for that opportunity.

The motto of the orchestra is: "Every rehearsal must be better than the last. Every concert must be better than the last. We must never be satisfied because upwards in quality is without limit." What can be done is limitless, particularly with the modern orchestra because the modern orchestra is extremely complex.

*From the Music Journal, vol. 26 (May 1968). Reprinted by permission of the publisher. After the resignation of Leopold Stokowski in 1972, the American Symphony Orchestra reorganized as the nation's only self-governing professional orchestra.

To have a good relation between individual players and other individual players, or groups with other groups; to have that which we call ensemble--that is difficult. That is why we are trying, every concert and every rehearsal, to do better than the last.

Naturally, all our players are Union musicians. We have players from Japan and China and Korea, and sometimes they have just arrived in America and they do not yet belong to the Union. But the Union has been very kind and understanding about the difficulties of these young players coming from another country and they have co-operated with us in a splendid way.

Every orchestral concert given in the cities throughout the United States is given at a loss. There is always a deficit. When automobile manufacturers make a fine car, they do it for a profit. We give concerts, not for a profit because there is no profit in giving orchestral concerts; there is always a loss. But we are fortunate in having, back of the American Symphony Orchestra, men and women who realize the importance of culture for the United States and for this City of New York. They are supporting us financially with great generosity.

There is in New York the new Madison Square Garden. Inside of that is the Felt Forum, a concert hall where we have been giving symphony concerts and also popular concerts. The difficulty there has been to make the acoustics good. The acoustics have been greatly improved, but there is still more to do, and I am hoping it will be done so that we will then have a third concert hall in New York City--because we need a third. The reason is that orchestras, choruses, ballet companies, solo players and singers, and operatic companies from all over the world come to New York. New York is now the center of world culture so we need those three halls.

In the Felt Forum where we give symphony concerts and the popular concerts, they have made the prices of the tickets low in the hope that families, father and mother and children, will all come together to listen to the music. This happened when we gave the concerts and I noticed many children there, quite evidently in a family group.

The American Symphony Orchestra gives four kinds of concerts now: the regular symphony concerts for adults; another series of concerts for teenagers; still another series of concerts for children younger than teen-agers; and a fourth series of concerts for very small children about ages 5, 6, 7 and 8. We try to plan our programs in relation to the audience, so that the youthful audience will enjoy the music and become music lovers, and perhaps later be part of our audience for the adult concerts.

MUSIC IN ASPIC*

Oscar Levant

It has frequently been remarked, and with truth, that a conductor embarking on a debut in New York is confronted with the
most critical audience in the world; save that this should be
amended to read--at his first rehearsal. Long before a symphonic
conductor appears before an audience to impress his qualities on
the listeners, critical and otherwise, he has already made the impression that eventually determines the extent of his success or
failure--on the members of the orchestra, whose attitude toward
any new conductor may be epitomized as "a hundred men and a
louse."

Contrary to the general opinion, a good ambitious orchestra
can do more to ruin a conductor than it can to make him. One of
the smuggest, most cohesive groups in American music, with the
greatest threat of power, is the New York Philharmonic Symphony
Orchestra; and it is followed closely by the Philadelphia Orchestra.

It is perhaps a corollary that the opinion of an orchestral
musician about a conductor or a piece of new music is quite invalid. So many factors of self-interest are concerned that the
purely musical values involved in the judgment of each are beyond
the players' objective appraisal.

So far as it concerns a conductor, it may be remarked that
an orchestra of the de luxe type mentioned above develops in time
a collective identity derived from its strongest personalities. This
remains constant except in the presence of the most strong-willed
conductors. The strings of the Philharmonic, for example, amount
to some thirty two Piastros, deriving their style and mannerisms
from their concertmaster. There is no trace in their playing of
what might be called a "Barbirolli style." Nevertheless, when this
same string section was conducted by Toscanini it did not possess
this thick, rich Russian overwash--it had a leanness and strength
directly induced by him.

Essentially the question is one of domination--whether the
conductor dominates the orchestra, or the orchestra dominates the
conductor. Utter control of a performance, to the point at which
ninety or a hundred players become not merely a cohesive group
but the single-minded extension of one personality, is a rare talent
among musicians--possessed, among conductors now active in America, primarily by Koussevitzky, Stokowski and Toscanini.

I have found, in my varied experience as a conductor, soloist

with orchestra and ordinary listener, that there is a general mis-
use of power all round, depending in whose hands it happens to repose in any given instance. The orchestra which finds that it has
at its mercy a conductor--whom it may dislike for any reason from
lack of musicianship to mere unsociability--is frequently as ruthless
in its use of power as the conductor who exercises authority merely
because he does not fancy a violinist's complexion or the way he
sits while playing.

Pundits may talk of a conductor's "authority," his "beat"
and his "knowledge of scores," but actual control of an orchestra
is most frequently founded on the less gaudy basis of economics.
When an orchestra is aware that the conductor has in his inside
pocket a contract for next season and the one after that, carrying
with it the power to rearrange the personnel "for the best interests
of the orchestra"--in other words, to hire and to fire--its attitude
is apt to be somewhat more respectful than if he is merely an in-
terloper to be tolerated for a brief guest engagement.

When Stokowski spent his memorable and brief guest engagement with the Philharmonic some years ago (as part of the famous
exchange in which Toscanini conducted the Philadelphia Orchestra)
he certainly did not leave his "authority," "beat" and "knowledge of
scores" in the green room with his topcoat. But no one who recalls the occurrence will forget the playing of the Philharmonic
which led Stokowski to describe the two weeks as one of the unhap-
piest experiences of his life.

To be sure, he made the initial mistake of asking the orchestra to learn, for the first time in its history, Stravinsky's
"Sacre du Printemps," a work not previously in its repertory.
This exertion, coupled with the orchestra's desire--at that time--
to have Toscanini emerge as victor in the competition, induced a
state of extreme resentment and internal opposition. This attitude
was encouraged to no small extent by Stokowski's request, on beginning the rehearsal, for "one-hundred-per-cent co-operation."
As one member of the orchestra says, "Well, you know, after all--
a hundred-per-cent co-operation ... " as though to say, "Who does
he think he is, anyway?"

He also indicated his preference for absolute silence from
the men when he was giving instructions to a particular choir or
soloist. This was in effect an open invitation for whispers and
privately exchanged jokes. When one of the bass players had the
effrontery to smile during a Stokowskian monologue he was summarily banished from the rehearsal. Expecting contriteness, Stokowski
was astounded to hear him say, "Thank you--I haven't had a Thursday evening off all winter." This witticism evoked a giggle from a
rear desk cellist, who was promptly directed to join his colleague
in exile.

Plainly, neither of these occurrences would have happened
in Philadelphia, where Stokowski exacts his "one hundred per cent

co-operation" not merely by will power, his beautiful hands and ex-
quisite gestures, but, more pertinently, through the players' knowledge that dismissal from a rehearsal is not for a day or a week,
but for all time.

It is hardly surprising, therefore, that present-day orchestral players in the more prominent ensembles have become almost
as great prima donnas as the "glamour boys" of music whom they
derisively decorate with that epithet. There is the charming and
somewhat pathos-tinged experience of Bruno Walter's during one of
his first guest appearances with the Philharmonic. Innocent and
unwarned, he had endured for several rehearsals and the first pair
of concerts the mannerisms of Alfred Wallenstein, the orchestra's
brilliant first cellist, whose gaze was everywhere--on the music, in
the hall, up at the ceiling--but not on Walter. Since the first cellist sits almost within baton's length of the conductor, his idiosyn-
crasy could hardly be overlooked.

At last, Walter invited him to a conference and said, "Tell
me, Mr. Wallenstein, what is your ambition?"

The cellist replied that he someday hoped to be a conductor.

"Well," said the conductor, with his sweet and patient smile,
"I only hope you don't have Wallenstein in front of you. "

In the relationship of conductor and orchestra much depends
of course on the first meeting. As a human equation, it has much
the same atmosphere as the meeting of the principals in a prear-
ranged Hungarian wedding, with the bride and groom thoroughly
aware that they are fated to make common cause whether they are
enamored of each other or not. These are not marriages made in
heaven; they are made mostly in the office of Mr. Arthur Judson.

The methods of approach by the conductor vary as widely as
the literary tempers of Dale Carnegie's How to Win Friends and Influence People and Adolf Hitler's Mein Kampf. To this mating the
orchestra brings suspicion, skepticism and mistrust in equal proportions. Unconsciously every conductor feels this and has developed a personal technique for breasting this psychological Maginot
Line. With the less secure, the approach is invariably based on
talk--a tribute to the magnificent musicianship of the band, a small
disquisition on its splendid traditions (in whose future the conductor
implies he hopes to play a part) and a sigh of anticipation for the
pleasure the conductor expects to derive from playing on "this
superb instrument. " An appeal is made to the co-operative spirit
of the men, together with an apostrophe to "what beautiful music
we can make together. " This is further known as the Clifford
Odets or Gary Cooper-Madeleine Carroll approach, with the orchestra inclined to regard the conductor's part in the making of the
beautiful music as perhaps an act of supererogation.

Violently opposed to this is approach II, the martinet or

"knock-this-off-if-you-dare" type, in which the baton is, symbolically, a chip on the shoulder.   Such a conductor invariably enters
unexpectedly (thus immediately placing the orchestra at a disadvantage) clothed in a black half smock buttoned to the chin, providing
a perfect stage setting for the indispensable Il Duce frown.   No
word of greeting is exchanged; a curt rap of the stick and a brisk
command: "Beethoven. "   This the orchestra is expected to interpret to mean the symphony of the program.   Further communication
by word is withheld until the first mistake, no matter how slight.
This provides the opportunity for which the conductor has been
waiting to address a negative greeting to his co-workers, in which
are mingled supercilious endearment and patronizing contempt.

    Falling somewhere between these two is approach III--the
good-fellow or Uriah Heep type.   The conductor walks in calmly,
clothed in a smile, shakes hands with the concertmaster, taps
gently for attention and addresses the orchestra as "Gentlemen. "
A harmless, well-prepared joke follows, leading up to the suggestion that since they are going to be together for weeks and months
it would be best to develop a "Just call me Al" entente cordial.
Sometimes this flowers into a "mingling-with-the-help" manner:
the conductor cultivates a program of socio-musical escapades with
members of the orchestra, invites them to his home for chamber-
music evenings and sponsors Christmas parties for the children of
the musicians.   His purpose is to efface the social (and monetary)
disparities between conductor and players, to give them an illusion
of fraternal equality, to cultivate the impression that he is "just
one of the boys. "   This usually endures only for the first season,
after which the chrysalis is discarded, and he emerges from the
cocoon to try his wings as a martinet.

    More to be pitied than censured is the nervous, irritable
type, generally hired for only two weeks in the middle of the season and secretly convinced that the orchestra is out to get him.
His problem is to conduct a Blitzkrieg against an audience for which
the permanent conductor has just directed every surefire work in
the standard repertory.   He is much in the position of a batter who
steps to the plate after the previous man has hit a home run with
the bases full.   Entering with hasty, energetic steps, he mounts
the podium in a leap, snaps his fingers with brittle impatience and
says, "Three measures before letter C. "   Before the musicians
have a chance to open their scores or raise their instruments his
right arm is describing arcs and angles.   Naturally confusion en-
sues, and he is apt to smite his forehead in despair and expostu-
late, "I won't have it, I won't have it, I won't have it! "

    In such circumstances the musicians are likely to reply,
"Take your time, buddy. "

    A recent development in the post-Toscanini period is the
fabulous memory type.   He is shrewd enough to realize that an
orchestra is no longer impressed with a musician who uses a
score for rehearsals and conducts only his concerts from memory,

so he scorns the use of a score in his rehearsals also. He has memorized not only the notes and tempo indications, but also the numbers of the pages, the lettered subdivisions of the movements and even the accent marks in the bassoon part.

It is part of orchestral folk legend that one such virtuoso, intent upon impressing the orchestra with his memory, planted several errors in obscure places. In the midst of a furious tutti he stopped the orchestra, singled out the third horn player and said, "Third horn, I heard you play a C. It should be a C-sharp."

The horn player responded with proper contempt, "Some jackass wrote in a C natural, but I know the piece backward, so I played it C-sharp as it should be."

Unquestionably the most pathetic of all conductorial types is the man who has risen from the ranks, who frequently combines in his indeterminate manner some elements of all these approaches. As a former member of the orchestra which he is now conducting, he is subconsciously aware that the musicians are only waiting for the end of the rehearsal to get off together and discuss his failings as he has discussed with them, innumerable times in the past, those of the conductors he has played under himself. His method of generating authority cannot adhere to any of the stereotyped categories, since his case is a special one in which he first has to convince himself of his authority before he can transmit it to the players. Another accessible pitfall is eclecticism, the risk of reproducing the effects or mannerisms of some distinguished predecessor, thereupon permitting the members of the orchestra to say that he got this bar from so-and-so, that bar from another so-and-so.

A conductor should reconcile himself to the realization that regardless of his approach or temperament the eventual result is the same--the orchestra will hate him. This is true--hold your breath--even of Toscanini.

When Willem Mengelberg first exercised his virile vocabulary and exciting personality on the men of the Philharmonic early in the 1920's their enthusiasm for the new conductor mounted quickly from eager acceptance to blind idolatry. Perhaps there was an influence in the fact that his predecessor had been Josef Stransky.

This devotion endured for several seasons until a dark cloud, in the form of Arturo Toscanini, appeared on the horizon. For some time the loyalty of the Mengelberg faction in the orchestra resisted the defection of the Toscanini cohorts, until it became apparent from the actions of the board and the public that the Mengelberg tenure was approaching its end. In the words of one of the players, "The boys knew there was a new boss coming in."--and Mengelberg was gleefully sabotaged. There was perhaps no organized plan, but, somehow, an orchestra which had played the first symphony of Beethoven times without number disagreed on the

necessity for a repeat after the trio of the minuet. With the woodwinds espousing one opinion and the strings another, the helpless
conductor found himself engulfed in dissonance.

In his turn, Toscanini passed through much the same cycle
of endearment, questioning and resentment. There was rarely a
cavil with his sincerity or extraordinary equipment, but his insistence on quality eventually won him the characterization which orchestral musicians apply to any intense and insatiable workman--
"slave driver. " This reached open rebellion during his last season, in the preparation of "Iberia" for an all-Debussy program at
one of his final concerts. Contrary to the legend that Toscanini is
unswervingly faithful to the smallest detail of a composer's conception, he felt that a horn passage in the coda required reinforcement
by a trumpet and directed the incomparable Harry Glantz, first-
chair man of that section, to play with the horns. Moreover, he
specified that the addition be played forte. (Subsequently Glantz
has given me many versions, one of which was that Reiner had introduced these changes in the parts previously.)

There was an unconscious reluctance on the musician's part,
since he was accustomed to the sound of the original scoring, to
play the note aggressively, and his forte was hardly more than a
mezzo piano. Toscanini interrupted the rehearsal and launched into
a diatribe against Glantz, whose playing he had on many occasions
praised. Angrily Glantz replied, "The trouble with you is you
don't know how to handle men. "

Such forthright opposition was unknown to Toscanini, and he
stormily demanded an apology, whereupon Glantz walked out.

Unpredictably, the reaction in the orchestra was not sympathetic to Glantz. There was no feeling that he had been unjusti-
fied in his action, but they condemned the action on the eve of Toscanini's farewell from the orchestra. Shortly before, in the preparation of an all-Wagner program, the strings had resented Toscanini's demands for individual playing of a complex passage, impossible to play accurately, man by man, at any time, and sheer
absurdity in their season-end state of nervous fatigue. They had
discussed the possibilities of a strike, but agreed, as in the case
of Glantz, that the time to take action was the year before--when
Toscanini still had a power of dismissal over his men.

The difficulty between the two men was resolved by their
mutual admiration--the fine musician for the peerless conductor,
the demanding conductor for the irreplaceable musician. Through
the mediation of Van Praag, manager of the orchestra personnel,
an armistice was effected--without apology--for the duration of the
concert. At its conclusion Glantz's magnificent performance won
him a forgiving kiss on the cheek from the maestro.

Though it is commonly believed that a Toscanini performance
is the highest reward a composer may expect for creating a work,

it is an experience that sometimes has its embarrassing consequences. There was the time several years ago at a Philharmonic
rehearsal when Ernest Schelling was present as soloist in the preparation of his "Impressions of an Artist's Life" for piano and orchestra. According to his custom, Toscanini was conducting without score while Schelling, the composer, had the music propped
up on the rack before him.

The rehearsal progressed without incident for some minutes,
then Toscanini, listening to Schelling expound a solo passage against
a light orchestral background, suddenly rapped his stick imperiously
on the stand beside him and called to Schelling, "What are you
playing there?"

Schelling looked up in surprise and repeated the measures
he had just played.

"No, no," said Toscanini.   "Let me see the score."

He raised the score close to his eyes in the legendary way,
peering intently at the page.   Suddenly he looked up.   "Just as I
thought," he said.   "You were playing wrong."

Schelling confirmed this astounding dictum by returning to
the piano and playing a minutely different form of the passage he
had just delivered.   As he said afterward, he had always played it
that way, never bothering to check it against the notes he had
originally written.

Another example of Toscanini's remarkable musical faculties
was the remark he made to Bernard Wagenaar, Dutch-American
composer, after studying his first symphony for a performance of
several years ago.   Toscanini brought it back with him on a return
trip from Europe, studying the score on the boat wholly by sight.
When Wagenaar went to greet him at his hotel the day he arrived
Toscanini congratulated him on the work but added, "There are
several places which don't 'sound'"--a revelation that his memori-
zation of the score included the ability to hear the actual timbres
of the orchestra.   The rehearsals revealed precisely the flaws in
the texture of the scoring that he had predicted.   This incident is
in strong contrast to the opinion of others, who contend that only an
actual playing will show the weaknesses of an orchestration.   As a
footnote to this it might be added that the dissonant conclusion of
the first movement left Toscanini unsatisfied, and he insisted on
adding a pure C-major chord to the composer's final page.

It is history, however, that one eminent contemporary felt
otherwise than flattered by Toscanini's treatment of his music.
This was the late Maurice Ravel, who was honored by a performance
of his "Bolero" in Paris during the Philharmonic's European trip.
It was an initial irritation for Ravel that no tickets had been sent
to him, and he made his way into the crowded hall with great difficulty, to discover that Toscanini's tempo for "Bolero" was

unforgivably fast. Ravel added audible, unscored verbal comments
from his box as the work progressed, in a mounting crescendo
that paralleled the surge of the music. This monotone of invective
brought a storm of shushing from the intent Parisians, to whom
Ravel was not a world-famous composer but merely an ill-man-
nered listener.

The performance completed, Ravel descended angrily upon
the green room to deliver his annoyance with the performance in
person to the maestro. With voluble gestures and insistent pounding of his feet, he delineated the impossibility of dancing a "bolero," his or anyone else's, at such a pace. There was the charm
of novelty in this experience for Toscanini, since only a composer
of Ravel's stature could be thus indifferent to the maestro's reaction.

Despite this unprecedented experience Toscanini continued to
conduct "Bolero," content, perhaps, to regard its unparalleled opportunity for orchestral virtuosity as compensation for the bad
manners of the composer. After several brilliant performances
with the Philharmonic, in which he had been delighted by the meticulous playing of the orchestra's percussion section, he summoned
its members to his room and expressed his particular pleasure
with the snare drummer, Schmehl, whose superb pianissimo and
imperceptible crescendo excelled anything in his experience.

A large florid man with the muscularity of a heavy-weight
wrestler and a speech compounded equally of Brooklynese and
Hemingway, Schmehl replied casually, "Tanks, boss--glad you feel
that way about me. "

The praise apparently aroused Schmehl to the difficulty of
his task and a consciousness of how well he had accomplished it,
for at the next repetition of "Bolero" he was swept by panic, beginning his opening solo at a rapidly increasing forte. A contortion
of rage suffused Toscanini's face, and he muttered imprecations.
Schmehl's partner sought to retrieve the sticks and play the solo
himself, but the drummer was too nervous to understand the request. The fury of Toscanini with Schmehl transmitted itself to
the rest of the orchestra, a trombone exploded a blast instead of a
tone at the climax of his solo, and the performance moved swiftly
into confusion.

When the final chord had been reached Toscanini stalked
from the stage without a glance at the audience and rushed to his
room, crying, "Where is Schmehl? I want Schmehl! Send me
Schmehl! "

The culprit finally appeared, to be greeted by a torrent of
"Stupido ... Shame ... You play no more for me! " All this to the
man he had recently decorated with garlands of praise.

Truculently Schmehl accepted the abuse with the patience

born of forty years' experience in orchestral playing and, waiting
his opportunity, finally said, "You don't like my work? Get yourself another boy. " Nevertheless, it cost him his post in the orchestra for one misgauged pianissimo.

There might have been a similar outcome for another impasse at a Philharmonic rehearsal had not the player shrewdly
adapted himself to one of Toscanini's few limitations. The problem
arose in the rehearsing of Berlioz' "Queen Mab" scherzo (in the
"Romeo and Juliet" music). This contains an effect scored for
antique cymbals, the tiny equivalents of the familiar large cymbals.
Toscanini demanded that the rapid tinkling of the instruments be
mathematically precise and metronomically exact, the rhythm sharply articulated.

One after another the percussion players took their turns at
attempting to meet Toscanini's requirements, only to find that the
task of rustling the two tiny disks together at the proper speed and
with the desired clarity defied any technique with which they were
acquainted. They were all waved impatiently aside until Sam
Borodkin, virtuoso of the gong, tam-tam, bass drum and glockenspiel, pushed his way to the stand and said he'd like to try.

The orchestra began, and Borodkin stood poised with the
small cymbals (each no larger than a silver dollar) in his hands.
When his entrance approached Borodkin bent over the stand in an
attitude of extreme attentiveness, meanwhile substituting a metal
triangle stick for the cymbal in his right hand. Then, with his
hands barely visible over the top of the stand, he beat out the
rhythm perfectly.

Toscanini dropped his baton and called out, "Bravo, Borodkin, bravo"--being unable to penetrate the deception with his weak
vision. No doubt if he could have seen that far he would have
found some reason to be displeased with the results.

It is such arbitrary and unpredictable attitudes that exhaust
the patience of men who feel that their status, tried and approved,
entitles them to better treatment. In this genre there is the classic
experience of the violinist Mischel ("Mike") Gussikoff, who was engaged as concertmaster of the Philadelphia Orchestra after Stokowski personally scouted his playing of the solo violin part of Strauss's
"Ein Heldenleben" with the St. Louis Symphony. When the orchestra assembled to begin its season Gussikoff took his place at the
first desk but noticed that Stokowski did not shake hands with him,
greet him by name or even nod.

This situation endured not only for the first rehearsal, but
through the week's concerts and for all of the next month. Eventually Gussikoff began to worry about this silent relationship with
Stokowski and sought to identify it with possible flaws in his playing. He could not find any that justified such mute indictment, and
in final desperation he sought out Stokowski during a train trip from

a New York concert and said, "Please, Dr. Stokowski, I have done something to displease you?"

"No," said the conductor.

"You don't like the way I play my solos?"

"I have no complaint," said Stokowski.

"Then why," questioned Gussikoff, "why don't you say something to me?"

"When I say something," answered Stokowski, "that will be the time to worry."

Baffled by this negative endorsement, Gussikoff withdrew and shortly afterwards found himself a position with another orchestra.

It is possible that Gussikoff reacted with particular sensitivity because he had been reared in the prewar Russian Symphony Orchestra, under the genial guidance of Modest Altschuler. This was the orchestra that was a veritable training school for concertmasters, producing, among others, Frederic Fradkin (of the Boston Symphony), Maxmilian Pilzer (of the Philharmonic), Ilya Skolnik (of the Detroit Symphony), Louis Edlin (of the National Orchestral Association), and the conductors Nikolai Sokoloff and Nat Finston (of the movies). It was this orchestra that introduced many of the finest scores by Scriabin, Rachmaninoff and Stravinsky (his first symphony and "L'Oiseau de Feu" particularly outraging the Krehbiels and Fincks) to New York long before the established orchestras were aware of their existence.

An ardent propagandist for such works, Altschuler also delighted in expounding his conceptions of the scores with illustrated lectures. Attempting to elicit a more soulful solo from his oboist in a rehearsal of "Scheherazade," he stopped and said, "Here is the princess (pointing to the concertmaster, who plays the overfamous violin cadenza) and you are making love to her." Then, studying the pimpled complexion of the violinist, he added, "I'm sorry I can't do better."

Life in this orchestra was much like attendance at a private university. Such men as Harry Glantz, the admired first trumpet of the Philharmonic, had their early training in the German school of playing almost wholly revised under Altschuler's guidance. When the orchestra toured--as it frequently did--the travels resembled a mass picnic, with baskets of native delicacies ranging from salamis to cheeses carted along as sustenance against the barbaric foods to be found inland.

Such an organization could not fail to produce its quota of legend, of which several stories concerned a typical tour during which two Russian violinists, desk mates in the orchestra, who also traveled together, and shared a hotel room wherever the orchestra played, were met with the query by the clerk: "Do you want a room with bath?"

They looked at each other blankly until one could finally find the words to say, "Who wants a bath? We're only going to be here a week."

When they had disposed of their belongings and come down to the hotel dining room most of their colleagues had already eaten. Seeing one still left in the room, they sauntered over and inquired, "What's good? What did you have to eat?"

The friend replied, "I had the chicken potpie. Very tasty."

When the waiter appeared they both placed orders for the chicken pie. "I'm sorry," he replied. "We're all out of it."

The articulate one studied the menu for a moment and then said, "All right, then bring me the deep-dish applie pie."

It was in this orchestra, its scattered survivors of today claim, that there originated the fable that has since been attributed to every musical organization that gives outdoor concerts, from the Philharmonic Orchestra to the Goldman Band. They were playing the "Leonore No. 3" overture of Beethoven during a summer engagement, and the first trumpeter had stolen from his place to give the off-stage fanfare heralding the approach of the Minister of Justice.

Retreating an appropriate distance from the orchestra stand, he raised his instrument, waited for the cue and was just about to blow when a park policeman rushed up and bellowed, "You can't do that here! Don't you know there's a concert going on?"

Regardless of their respect for a conductor's musicianship or their admiration for his interpretative gifts, an orchestra is as frequently made uncomfortably aware of his feet of clay as they are of his head in the clouds. Several seasons ago, according to legend, the men of the Philadelphia Orchestra were baffled by Stokowski's desire to conduct, at one of his final rehearsals of the regular season, Strauss's "Blue Danube" waltz. It was not scheduled to be played at any remaining concert of the year, and the conductor's meticulous preparation of the score, his insistence on this effect and that phrasing, could only be interpreted as a whim.

The incident had passed from their minds by the time they reassembled to play their summer series of concerts at Robin Hood Dell, of which the first was conducted by a guest. Following the intermission the chairman appeared before the audience, thanked the listeners for their attendance and added, "Perhaps you have not noticed that we have among us tonight a distinguished guest--our

beloved Dr. Stokowski. I know you would be delighted to have him
conduct something for us this evening. "

Stokowski resisted the flattery with gestures of unassuming
modesty, listened to the applause and finally indicated that he was
powerless to deny the audience its wish. He mounted the stage
and suggested that the librarian distribute the parts of "The Blue
Danube. "

Occasionally, and at widely separated intervals, a musician
will give forth an opinion based not only on his reaction to a given
situation, but summing up in sparse phrases his reaction to a conductor's whole personality. When such an incident occurs it is
preserved not merely for its succinctness but also for its assertive-
ness, enduring as part of the folk legend of orchestral players.

A famous incident of that nature involved, by coincidence,
two musicians almost miraculously opposed in size, type and tem-
perament--the six-foot-four Otto Klemperer, probably the tallest
conductor extant, and the barely five-foot Bruno Labate, diminutive
oboe virtuoso of the Philharmonic Symphony Orchestra. It is traditional that orchestral conductors follow one of two practices in their
rehearsals of standard works. Generically, conductors of the German school will begin a work, say Beethoven's "Eroica, " and play
it methodically from beginning to end, indicating as they progress
their preferences in dynamics, accents and phrasings. Others,
particularly English and French conductors, in order to expedite
rehearsals during a brief guest engagement, will assume that an
experienced orchestra is competent to deal with the large aspects
of such a work without measure-by-measure supervision and merely
rehearse those sections in which their ideas are personal--perhaps
in the development or at the beginning of the recapitulation.

It is a trait of the thoroughgoing Klemperer to espouse both
methods, beginning with the scattered-intensive and progressing
thereafter to the over-all-intensive. This treatment he frequently
interrupts, in the preparation of a Beethoven work, with discourses,
say, on the metronome of Beethoven's time and the state of the
composer's relations with his nephew Karl when the work was written, with perhaps even a monologue on the alterations of pitch in
the hundred years since.

Having completed such a discourse on one occasion, he
turned to Ravel's "Le Tombeau de Couperin" and proceeded to dis-
sect it, page by page, with particular attention to a rather difficult
oboe phrase. Four times, five times, he asked to hear it, and
even at the sixth playing he was not satisfied. Disregarding the
difficulty an oboist has in controlling his breath for long stretches
and the inevitable tiring of the player's lips, he asked for it again,
pausing for a brief footnote on Ravel's use of the oboe before he
raised his baton.

Labate peered over his stand at the mountainous conductor

and pronounced the undying words, "Mr. Klemps', you talka too much. "

There was, of course, the inevitable demand for an apology. The indispensable Van Praag was taxed to the utmost of his considerable ingenuity in dealing with such situations. Perhaps Labate's outspokenness was based on the realization that motivated him when a co-worker, aghast at his ability to play perfectly any solo, no matter how complicated or unfamiliar, under the tension of concert conditions, asked him, "Don't you _ever_ get nervous?"

To which Labate answered with the assertion, "Wit' seventfive tousanda dollar in the bank, I no get nervous. "

Such conflicts of personality are not limited to the common relationship of conductors and the men they conduct. When a soloist of individual temperament is preparing a concerto for performance, the conflict of personality is not limited to the conductor and the members of the orchestra, but sometimes becomes three sided.

When Toscanini was engaged in his Brahms cycle with the Philharmonic several seasons ago the soloist for the B-flat concerto was the late Ossip Gabrilowitsch. They came to the rehearsal with a remarkable disparity of experiences in relation to the work: Gabrilowitsch having played it with glory in every important musical center of the world and attained a highly personal and intimate understanding of its contents, Toscanini having never had the necessity to conduct it in public even once before. Nevertheless, Toscanini confronted the orchestra and the soloist with a firm, characteristically inflexible conception of its tempo, its nuances, its phrasing, in which Gabrilowitsch's preferences were hardly considered and of course not respected. When the bewildered soloist found himself approaching the work anew, almost recasting his whole conception, he sought to reason Toscanini to an understanding of his viewpoint. In this he was thoroughly unsuccessful. He gave up the crusade in despair, and the performance was canceled.

As recently as last winter the Philharmonic was party to another conflict of soloist and conductor when Artur Schnabel rehearsed the "Emperor" concerto of Beethoven with John Barbirolli. There was a substantial agreement between the two men on the main details of the performance, but as the rehearsals progressed it was apparent that the orchestra was being influenced by two conductors. Schnabel, as he played, not only nodded his approval of this orchestral soloist's phrasing of a certain passage or his admiration for the tone of another man, but he also extended a warning hand toward the orchestra when it produced more tone than he thought necessary and finally singled out the flutist John Amans for an admonishing,

"Too loud--too loud. "

Barbirolli had no choice but to stop the orchestra and suggest to Schnabel that the soloist's desires should be expressed to him and not to the orchestra; that, after all, he was the conductor, and his authority was in jeopardy. Perhaps the conductor would have been more tolerant if his most celebrated excellence--his talent for directing accompaniments--was not, by implication, being questioned.

Musically, Schnabel's action was more appropriate to an operatic tenor than it was to the pianist widely admired as one of the most "scholarly" and musicianly interpreters of his specialty, Beethoven, now before the public. From the orchestra's standpoint Schnabel's behavior was wholly irrelevant and unethical and merely made them twice as eager to respect Barbirolli's wishes, if only as a condemnation of Schnabel's presumption.

As anyone who has had contact with orchestral players is aware, they are not occupationally allergic to authority save when it is misused. A professional, well-routined orchestra such as the Philharmonic or the Philadelphia can give a competent performance of a standard score regardless of who is directing it (as last summer's example of the Philharmonic under His Honor Fiorello H. LaGuardia testifies), but this is a procedure to be embraced only in an extremity. It is only when all efforts to comprehend the wishes of a conductor have failed that the players accept the responsibility for the performance as their own and, largely speaking, disregard the conductor.

This does not mean that a conductor must necessarily have what is called a "good stick" or a mastery of any other of the conventional approaches to conducting to qualify for an orchestra's approval. A "good stick"--that is, a well-defined, clearly outlined beat--can certainly be an asset, but it is by no means indispensable from the standpoint of the orchestral player. What is indispensable is the conductor's power to convey sound musicianship, an unaffected sympathy for the music he chooses to conduct.

Georges Enesco, the Rumanian composer and conductor, is a guest welcomed by any orchestra, even though his movements and gestures are an animated contradiction of everything pedagogues of "baton technique" have ever written. He never asks an orchestra to do anything which contradicts the players' feeling of what the music signifies or what the printed notes of the score actually mean in plain musical language. Moreover, as a kind of musicianly virtuoso (both of the violin and piano) and as a composer whose music is unassailably genuine, he has the advantage of an unspoken and an affectionate communication with the men he conducts. To his credit he does not pretend to omniscience. When a certain progression of programs with the Philharmonic decreed that he conduct the Brahms fourth symphony two seasons ago he disavowed intensive rehearsals with the simple statement to the orchestra, "Gentlemen, you know the work better than I do. "

Both the compliment and the attitude endeared themselves so much to the orchestra that they literally forgot themselves in a mass effort to justify his statement--and, as one of those who heard the performance, I can testify that they delivered one of the most powerful and integrated interpretations of the score that New York has experienced in seasons.

Another conductor widely admired by musicians is Sir Thomas Beecham, who has unaccountably escaped a mass popularity in this country. With orchestral players his jovial hearty un-neurotic approach to music is as welcome as it is uncommon. It is the contradiction of the mystical approach of the Mengelbergs and Furtwänglers, embodying, toward the men with whom he works, something of an Empire-attitude. The wide range of his interests-- from Mozart to Balakirev and Delius to Purcell--is a testimony not only to his intellectual open-mindedness but also to the happy circumstance that made him the son of a multimillionaire.

Devoid of the success-or-failure frenzy in his approach to music, he addresses himself to conducting with the casual but thoroughgoing enjoyment of an epicure ordering a meal at a very fine restaurant, indifferent to the cost and uninterested in the opinions of those about him. He conducted English music when the most popular English composers were Arthur Sullivan and Handel (an English possession by annexation) and continues to do so today, when the most popular English composers are Reginald Forsyth and Ray Noble. Like most conductors, he fancies himself a wit; but in distinction to all others, his jokes are invariably good.

There are few conductors who impress an orchestra (also composers) at first contact as strongly as does Fritz Reiner, whose knowledge of everything pertaining to the mechanical performance of music is, briefly, unparalleled. He has evolved a personal sign language which leads an orchestra through the most complex scores of Strauss or Stravinsky with the case and sureness of a tightrope walker who performs a backward somersault blindfolded. Whenever the complexity of the scoring is a sufficient challenge to his skill Reiner will subdivide beats, flash successive cues to remote sections of the orchestra with either hand and meanwhile indicate the pianissimo, in which he takes such great delight, by a bodily movement that totals by a kind of physical mathematics to the exact effect on the printed page. His ear is so acute, not only for intonation but also for dynamics, that he can detect a wrong bowing when his back is turned to the section from which it emanates.

Together with these faculties is a facility for terrifying inferior orchestras unequaled among conductors of the present day. His technique in this sphere is no less sophisticated than it is in his conducting. A mere series of facial expressions can shade his degrees of contempt for a nervous oboist or a fright-palsied violinist as artfully as he fades an orchestra from mezzo piano

to pianissimo. His passion for the least audible of possible sounds
has created among violinists a new form of occupational ailment
known as Reiner-paralysis. When he is sufficiently challenged by
an operatic score, such as Der Rosenkavalier, or by the collaboration with a fine soloist, to marshal all his virtuosity, he can
achieve fabulous results. The reaction he induces from the orchestras he has conducted runs the full gamut of all emotions but
deep affection.

Discussion of this conductor leads one inevitably to Pierre
Monteux, who may be described as a more amiable Reiner. An
invincible master of the orchestra and everything that pertains to
it, he has the experience and knowledge of even the more obscure
orchestral instruments which permit him to advise a virtuoso of the
bassoon how to better his fingering and breath control for a difficult passage. He is the pedagogue par excellence of orchestral
playing, administering his advice in a firm, friendly way that may
be classified as a blend of Parisian precision and Munich gemütlichkeit.

His service to music as an art and a history has been almost greater than that of any other contemporary conductor, for
he performed virtually all of the pre-war "modern" works--includ-
ing Stravinsky's "Le Sacre du Printemps"--when such sponsorship
required as much physical courage as intellectual ability. Even
today every conductor who performs the "Sacre" (including Stravinsky) consciously or unconsciously imitates Monteux. Orchestral
players are invariably ecstatic about his beat, his precision, his
clarity, but are vague on his Beethoven and Brahms, saying that
they forget how it was. I recall a stunning performance by him of
a Handel concerto grosso with the NBC orchestra, while--believe it
or not--waiting for him to play "La Valse." One may say of Monteux that he can charm, delight, instruct or cajole orchestral musicians but lacks the aggressiveness to inspire awe.

Awe, however, is the word for Otto Klemperer, known to
his intimates as "Doctor" Klemperer. Before I present his qualities as a conductor I would like to lay the unfounded rumor that it
was he who introduced Gilbert and Sullivan's works to Düsseldorf.
I have a special affection for the good doctor based on his chrono-
logical rejection of my compositions with a passionate sincerity
that first impressed me immeasurably and then ripened into love.
I go for the good doctor. In proportion to his monumental stature
is a room-filling voice, an incontrovertible sincerity, a hearty contempt for any humor except the most serious. His prodigious capacity for work, his exuberant vitality and his extraordinary instinct
for sponsoring worthwhile new music (during his last season with
the Philharmonic he introduced three such outstanding scores as
Berg's "Lulu" suite, the Hindemith symphony "Mathis der Maler,"
and the Janáček symphony) are all bars to his ready acceptance
by orchestral players. He demands of musicians the same inexorable, ruthless regime (in attitude, playing and mere platform behavior) that he imposes on himself. As one member of the

Philharmonic Symphony expressed himself after a rehearsal, "Two hours with Klemperer is like two hours in church. "

The pontifical attitude was a strong factor also in the personality of Walter Damrosch, about whose conducting I have a certain reluctance to speak though I cannot think of any good reason for being reluctant. Perhaps it was because his regime at the head of the New York Symphony contained more than a strong hint of the feudal system. The orchestra was, in fact, virtually a Damrosch possession, founded by father Leopold Damrosch, expiring while a Damrosch still conducted it. It has been more than hinted that Harry Harkness Flagler, who discharged its deficit for many years, would have continued to support it had Damrosch been willing to step aside for some stronger opponent to Toscanini and the Philharmonic. Could it be possible that Damrosch preferred to have the orchestra disbanded rather than to permit its continuance under other direction? In any case, as a sentimental gesture he presented each member of the orchestra with a pair of cuff links at the final concert.

Georges Barrere, the peerless flautist of the orchestra and a brilliant wit, contemplated his gift and remarked sadly, "First he takes the shirt off our backs and then he gives us cuff links. "

During his years as an active (the word is comparative) conductor Damrosch sponsored what might be called an inverted virtuosity. Some conductors display their mastery by playing everything faster than it should be, but with Damrosch it took the form of beginning everything slower than anybody else and then getting progressively slower. He reached the zenith of his career against the imposing competition of Josef Stransky, whom a member of his orchestra once threatened with the words, "If you bawl me out again I'll follow your beat. "

Musicians may differ in their opinions of the preceding conductors, but of Toscanini, Koussevitzky and Stokowski the orchestras of New York, Boston and Philadelphia have one universal emotion--no matter how intensely they resent the effort these men require of them, they invariably look forward with expectancy to their return. Playing for a lesser, more pleasant man may have its compensations in mental ease and physical relaxation, yet these orchestras are not unlike the married man who welcomes occasional philandering but is nevertheless unhappy except in the familiar, if undemanding, routine of his home.

Contrary to the common legend, Koussevitzky does read a score--not very well. Aside from his musical personality, Koussevitzky is altogether more a legend to the outside world than an actuality. Though his is the only non-union orchestra in the country, it is in effect a closed shop so far as the emanation of gossip is concerned. He is unparalleled in the performance of Russian music, whether it is by Moussorgsky, Rimsky-Korsakoff, Strauss, Wagner or Aaron Copland. He is also an enthusiast for Mahler and C. P. E. Bach, which, for a conductor of Russian background, is almost as astonishing as his mastery of the double bass.

Few reports leak out of the Kremlinlike secrecy which surrounds the preparation of his programs, but his players have an internal pride in their status as members of the orchestra--unquestionably the finest in the world--even if they resent the manner in which his miracles are wrought. An inquiry about his rehearsals invariably produces the same enigmatic smile, but no information and less satisfaction.

Over a similar period, however, no conductor in America has produced so many valid new works, both domestic and foreign. It is significant that he has conducted no other orchestra than his own in America, which may be an expression of affection for his own men or a silent criticism of other orchestras. (Or is it because his orchestra is not unionized?) No matter how unpleasant his mannerisms may be in certain classical scores, there is invariably one work on his program so magnificently played that the memory of all others is effaced.

As a surmise, one might guess that Toscanini would find the Koussevitzky treatment of the classics extremely distasteful and artificial, so different is it from his own. Paradoxically, however, the end result is frequently the same. There is the same insistence on purity of sound, blending of choirs, effacement of blemishes and personality of phrasing. Many orchestral players consider Toscanini cruel, inflexible and even petty, citing his inclination to find fault with musicians for no other reason than a dislike of their facial characteristics or the way they sit while playing. One such unfortunate, a violinist, was the invariable target of his criticism because of his mottled complexion. During a visit by the orchestra to another city someone in the violin section made a false entrance, and Toscanini in a rage, placed the blame squarely on his bête noire--even though the musician had remained in New York, ill. I know of no man, however, who does not consider him the greatest conductor, qua conductor, with whom he has ever played.

It is an amazing reputation that he has built up on the basis of a really remarkable small range of interests, which merely underlines his superiority to other men in most of the works he conducts. Russian music, save for the Frenchified Ravel version of Moussorgsky's "Pictures from an Exposition," is a closed book to him; French music, save for certain isolated works by Ravel and Debussy, is equally outside his ken (there was evidence of this in the adverse reaction in the Parisian press to his conducting of "Bolero" and Dukas's "L'Apprenti Sorcier"); leaving English and American music, which he rarely conducts, and German and Italian music.

Despite his magnificently vital and invigorating playing of Beethoven, Wagner, Brahms and Haydn, it is incontestable that they were recognized as composers of merit before Toscanini "revealed" them and have a fair chance of survival when he has retired.   It is a fallacy to assume that clarity and the most meticulous fidelity to a composer's indications are the open sesame to a complete projection of a musical work. Sibelius, for example, rescored and altered his fifth symphony three times before arriving at a satisfactory expression of his purpose.   Texture and the most painstaking exposition of it are not necessarily the unfailing road to the heart of a work.   In his sponsorship of this approach Toscanini, in some circumstances, is inclined to give a composer too much credit.

Musicians are by no means agreed that his Debussy is beyond criticism--the tonal haze that envelopes some of his finest passages is too often denied by Toscanini's all-revealing clarity and tonal balancing.   In the same way his Strauss (save for "Tod und Verklärung" and "Don Juan") is often X-rayed rather than recreated, the story-telling element subordinated to his obsession for literal statement.

He has done so little contemporary music that his preferences, except among the Italians, can hardly be discussed.   He has sponsored no controversial music of merit in his twelve years as a symphonic conductor in New York, invariably choosing contemporary works for which someone else has done the pioneering.   No program of his has ever shown the names of such outstanding contemporaries as Bartók, Hindemith and Schoenberg, and the only Stravinsky he conducts are the "Firebird" and "Petrouchka" suites, each as safe as Mendelssohn's "Calm Sea and Prosperous Voyage. "   He would have done more for American music had he played none at all, for the works he has played are neither representative nor deserving of such sponsorship.   In the one field of contemporary music--the Italian--which he has investigated with any thoroughness, he has avoided the works of the two most adventurous men, Malipiero and Casella, preferring those of the pretty-pretty or "sweeter-than-sweet" school.

Nevertheless, he has every physical and temperamental attribute of the complete conductor, including an indomitable authority, a tenacious and communicative vitality, a brilliant rhythmic sense and an infallible ear.   He even possesses the resource of a burning wit, as may be testified by his imperious remark to a violinist who spent every slight pause in a rehearsal tuning his instrument: "It's not the A that counts, but the B. "   Despite the captious comments above, Toscanini remains the "infallible conductor. "

I have also the recollection of a conductor--prominent in the days before the animated cartoon reached its zenith--who was the veritable enchantress of the orchestral world.   (I use the feminine gender aesthetically.)   I miss the tumult he created both with the orchestra and the press.   Physically he had a considerable resemblance to the contemporary Hollywood figure known as Leopold

Stokowski, but the latter is obviously an impostor, taking advantage of this resemblance. A musical Lawrence of Arabia, one scarcely knew from whence the authentic Stokowski came or what his background (prior to the Cincinnati Symphony days) was. Suddenly he emerged in full flower, bringing to orchestral conducting a quality which personalized it almost as completely as Dhiagileff did the Russian Ballet. Essentially, he had tremendous merit as a creative conductor, not alone in his treatment of music but also in his approach to the mere physical properties of conducting.

I would like to have been present, if I could have my choice of all moments in musical history, when Stokowski suddenly became conscious of his beautiful hands. That must have been a moment. Like stout Cortez on a peak in Darien (I know it was Balboa) he saw before him a limitless expanse, a whole uncharted sea that might be subjected to his influence, free from the encumbrance of a baton.

Then came the period of conducting "Scheherazade" from behind a screen, while the mystic shapes of the Color Organ played on it; of reseating the cellos (a musical adaptation of the Notre Dame shift, Knute Rockne then being prominent) to his right; of doing away with the lights on the stage because they distracted the audience, and then beaming an overhead spotlight directly on his tawny mane as he conducted; of the Javanese gongs, the Indian Temple Bells, the Chinese scales; of lecturing his audiences for not applauding a modern work, though it was not clear whether the lecture was based on a sincere admiration for the composer or on an unslakable lust for publicity.

As a gesture to abolish class distinctions in the first violin section he did away with the institution of concertmaster, thereby creating sixteen prima donnas in place of the one he had before. Nevertheless, when he allowed each of them to bow as they might, without regard for the tradition of uniformity observed by virtually all other orchestras, the results, for him and the audience, were excellent. In a later period came the passion for arranging, for making gorgeous tone poems out of Bach's organ pieces, of a Palestrina chorus, of a Buxtehude toccata. But the incomparably polished and iridescent playing of the orchestra--as slick, colorful and vibrant as the audience it attracted--virtually put Bach, for the first time, on the Hit Parade. It is quite possible that if he had not become sated with music (and success) he eventually would have conducted the orchestra blindfolded, with his left arm tied behind his back.

He created, in the Philadelphia Orchestra of the mid-twenties, an instrument that demonstrated in its exquisitely sensual sound, its urbane virtuosity, how well a hundred men could be made to play together. But, possibly surfeited with this accomplishment, he became the dandy of orchestral conductors, a veritable musical Lucius Beebe, wearing his scores like so many changes of attire.

There finally came the period when his vagaries were infinitely more exciting and arousing than the correct traditionalism of the lesser "scholarly" conductors. But when his vagaries became successful--no doubt to his subconscious disgust--he found himself at an impasse. They had germinated the embryo of a new tradition with which--because it had become fixed and static--he was no longer in sympathy. This left him an unwritten character out of Huxley's Point Counterpoint, with his original ennui. The only vagary left to him was to give up conducting.

At this moment, however, his return to the Philadelphia Orchestra is certain, for which I am fervently grateful. This certainty may be contradicted by the last minute arrival of a fascinating script, however.

There are a million lights in a million Philadelphia windows for him.

Hurry home, Leo, all is forgiven.

Chapter II

THE CONDUCTOR:
The Ultimate Autocrat
in a Democratic World

Introduction. In these days of the virtuoso, internationally-known conductor, it is hard to believe that "there were not always conductors!" Musicologist Adam Carse traces this comparatively short and very important musical development as an introduction to statements by some of the great conductors of this century on various aspects of the art (i. e. , Eugene Ormandy, Charles Munch, Sir Adrian Boult, William Steinberg, Gunther Schuller and Leopold Stokowski). Knowledgeable musicians and critics such as Harold C. Schonberg, Michael Caracappa and Paul Hume add "profiles" on still other important conductors. The chapter concludes with an orchestral performer's view. Obviously, not all conductors are loved and respected.

A SHORT HISTORY OF CONDUCTING*

Adam Carse

The art of conducting, as it is understood at the present time, is little more than a century old; time-beating, however, has been practiced by musicians, for the purpose of keeping voices and choirs together, for several centuries, and is much older than any form of organized orchestra.

Evidence that time-beating was practiced even as early as during the Middle Ages may be found in altar pieces, miniatures, and other pictorial representations of musical performances, in which a leader is usually depicted with a hand raised as if in the act of beating time. One of the earliest of these is a miniature which shows the Minnesinger Heinrich von Meissen (1260-1308) seated on a dais in front of which is a group of singers and players on instruments. In his left hand he holds a longish stick, and the index finger of his right hand is extended in a manner which suggests that he is marking time with that hand.

If pictorial evidence as to the prevalence of time-beating at such a remote period of musical history is a little vague and unsatisfying, the writings by musical theorists of the 17th century are quite clear and convincing; these prove beyond question that the singing of choral voices, especially when two or more choirs or groups of singers and instrumentalists were acting together, was commonly synchronized by means of either visual or audible time-beats. From similar sources information may also be gleaned as to the various methods of marking the beats: visual time-beats were made with the hand, a finger, a stick or baton, a roll of paper, a cloth or handkerchief, or, in one case (Caspar Printz, 1696) a handkerchief tied to the end of a stick; audible time-beats are described as having been made by stamping on the floor with the foot or with a stick; a peculiar method mentioned by Daniel Speer (1687) is that in which the time-beater hammered on an organ bench with a key.

All these devices, it should be understood, were used in connection with the rendering of ecclesiastical choral music, and by the organist-composers who occupied the most important and influential positions in the world of music up to the time when the further development of an independent instrumental style of music began to create a class of musician whose work was no longer devoted entirely to the service of the Church.

From the evidence of these early theorists it would seem that only two sorts of beat were known--namely, a down- and an up-beat. Only time groups of two or three beats were recognized (there was no provision for a group or bar of four beats), and in order to provide for a group of three beats the down-beat was made to last twice as long as the up-beat.

In his preface to some psalms for four choirs published in 1612, Viadana, an Italian Church composer who has been credited with the invention of the term basso continuo, gives some particulars regarding the duties of a time-beater when more than one choir are employed: he is to take up his position by the first choir, and from the basso continuo of the organist is to indicate the time and so convey it to the choir; when the other choirs are to join in, he is to turn his face towards them, and by raising both hands give them the signal for their entries. Praetorius (1571-1621) also has left some directions as to the management of several choirs: each choir should be provided with a time-beater, whose sole duty it is to watch the principal time-beater, and to convey the beat of the latter to his own particular group of singers and players. An excellent representation of 17th-century time-beaters may be seen in the frontispiece of Praetorius' Theatrum Instrumentorum (1620); this shows very clearly three groups of vocalists and instrumentalists, each in charge of a time-beater, two of which are using the left hand to mark the time, while holding the music-book in the right hand.

The above, drawn from early 17th-century sources, could be amplified, but must suffice to show that it was considered desirable that a time-beating conductor should control the performance of music played and sung by groups or choirs at a time when written music was not even regularly barred, and almost before a style of music which could be considered at all orchestral, as distinguished from vocal, had become firmly established.

Audible time-beating appears to have been freely tolerated during the 17th and part of the 18th centuries: in Paris it seems to have been regularly employed for the purpose of controlling performances of ballet and opera from the time of Lulli (1633-1687) until even after the middle of the 18th century. The story that Lulli died from the effect of a wound on his foot, accidentally inflicted with his "baton" while "conducting," may or may not be true: if true, it points to the use of a heavy stick, and seems as if it were thumped heavily on the floor. From the complaints of later writers one cannot but accept it as a fact that some such distressing method of time-beating actually prevailed at the Paris Opera even as late as the time when Rousseau compiled his famous Dictionary of Music, published in 1768. Rousseau mentions a gros baton de bois as the implement which so interfered with his enjoyment of the music, and another critic, Baron Grimm, writing in 1753, dubs the conductor at the Paris Opera a "woodchopper" (Holtzhacker). This inartistic method of keeping time also earned the condemnation of the one-time famous North German musician Mattheson (1681-1764), who put it quite neatly when he supposes that choirmasters who mark time audibly with their feet are doing so only because they are more clever with their feet than with their heads.

Early in the 18th century it seems to have been felt that some improvement on the simple method of beating time, which employed only a down- and an up-beat, was due. New and distinct plans for indicating three and four beats in a bar are shown in some diagrams, dated 1706, by an Italian named Tevo. According to his plan, a bar of four beats was shown by giving two consecutive down-beats followed by two consecutive up-beats; for a triple bar the plan was one down-beat followed by two up-beats. This method appears to have become more or less standardized in Italy by the middle of the 18th century, and is described by Rousseau in his Dictionary as being the Italian method, whereas in France (according to the same authority) only the first and last beats of a bar were respectively down and up, any intermediate beats being made either to the right or to the left, much as they are at the present time. The Italian method evidently prevailed in England at a later date, for Dr. Busby in his Dictionary of Music (1786) states that English musicians followed the Italian custom; his words on time-beating are as follows: "Beating the time is that motion of the hand or foot used by the performers themselves, or some person presiding over the concert, to specify, mark, and regulate the measure of the movements. If the time be common, or equal, the beating is also equal: two down and two up, or one down and one up; if the time be triple, or unequal, the beating is also unequal: two down and one up. " The reference to the foot rather suggests that audible time-beating was still tolerated in England at that time.

The present-day method of beating time appears to have originated in France early in the 18th century, and was distinguished from the more commonly used Italian method in that motions to the right and left side were used for all except the first and last beats of a bar. As early as 1702 a Frenchman named Saint-Lambert advocated a scheme of beats for two, three, and four in a bar; his methods for two and three in a bar are identical with the present-day usage, and for four in a bar differed only in that the second and third beats were in reversed directions:

Some few years later (1709) another Frenchman, Montéclair, illustrated what is practically the present-day method, thus:

From the works of other French musicians which appeared during the course of the 18th century it is quite clear that the now standard methods of beating two, three, and four in a bar were well established in France long before the baton was used, as it is now, to direct all manner of musical performances. The following by Choquet [Choquel] (1782) is just another way of showing the same plans:

B		C			D	
			B		B	C
A						
		A			A	

If it is impossible to say just when the Italian began to give way to the French method, there can be little doubt that when, early in the 19th century, baton-conducting began to be generally employed for all purposes, the French method of beating time was universally adopted.

Although time-beating was a recognized means of keeping performers together during the 17th and 18th centuries, it should be remembered that it was employed only for the rendering of church and choral music, and not for purely orchestral music, nor for opera, except at Paris, where audible time-beating prevailed. The orchestral conductor, like the purely orchestral concert, was as yet an unknown thing.   Yet, during the course of the 18th century, the earlier forms of purely orchestral music--concerti, suites, and symphonies--were quickly developing and forming a class of instrumental music which began to seriously challenge the

supremacy of the older vocal forms.   A means of directing these
orchestral works without any time-beating had in the meantime
established itself, and consisted of a sort of dual control under the
direction of a so-called "conductor" who played on a keyboard instrument, and a violinist-leader who gave the tempo and kept the
orchestra together by means of motions of his head and body while
still playing the violin.   Thus, secular music was controlled by the
joint efforts of a "conductor" and leader who played on their instruments, while sacred choral music was in the hands of organists or
choirmasters who beat time with their hands.   The following from
Koch's Musikalisches Lexikon (1802) puts the situation very clearly:
"In Church music the Kapellmeister beats time ... but in opera he
plays the figured bass from the score. "

        Particulars of how 18th-century opera and orchestral pieces
were thus "conducted" from the cembalo or piano in conjunction with
the efforts of a violinist-leader or Konzertmeister are fairly abundant in the musical literature of the period.

        All full scores, from early in the 17th till towards the end
of the 18th century, were provided with a figured-bass part, which
usually occupied the lowest stave of the score.   The piano or
cembalo player, who was called the "conductor, " sat at the instrument playing the bass part continuously, and adding such harmonies
as were dictated by the figuring; he kept a general lookout over the
whole performance, giving a note here and there, filling up thin
places in the orchestration, helping out and playing the part of any
performers who went astray or missed their entries.   His function
was partly to give harmonic stability to the thin orchestration of the
period, and partly to supply accidental omissions on the part of the
performers.   In the 1813 edition of Busby's Dictionary of Music the
following appears under the article "Score": "It is highly requisite
to the conductor of any performance, in order to his knowing whether each performer follows his part, and to enable him to supply
any accidental omission with the pianoforte or organ, at which he
presides. "

        Several 18th-century writers have detailed the duties not only
of the piano-conductor but also of the violinist-leader.   All make it
quite clear that there was no time-beating except that which the
leader was able to give by motions of his head, his violin, or his
foot.   As a time-giver the leader was more important and probably
shouldered more responsibility for the rendering than the piano-
conductor.   He was seated higher than the rest of the players, and
was supposed to act as a sort of link between the piano-conductor
and the orchestra.   Busby outlines the duties of a violinist-leader
thus: "A performer who in a concert takes the principal violin,
receives the time and style of the several movements from the
conductor, and communicates them to the rest of the band.   The
leader, after the conductor, holds the most important station in the
orchestra.   It is to him that the other performers look for direction in the execution of the music, and it is on his steadiness, skill
and judgment, and the attention of the band to his motion, manner

and expression, that the concinnity, truth, and forces of effect, do in a great measure depend. " All concur in allotting great responsibility to the violinist-leader, who, in spite of his being only a second-in-command under the piano-conductor, had clearly more to do with the actual playing and ensemble of the orchestra than the figure-head who sat with the score in front of him at the piano. It was the leader who had to start the orchestra playing, who had to steady them by movements of his head, violin, or body, who had to guide them at any change of tempo or pilot them through rallentandos, and who had to re-start them after a pause.

During the second half of the 18th century the violinist-leader grew in importance, while the piano-conductor gradually became less and less essential. The fuller orchestration of the period of Haydn and Mozart required less harmonic support from the piano, and the larger orchestras could not be so easily swayed by chords played on that instrument. With the eventual disappearance of the figured-bass part from the score began the gradual extinction of the function of the piano-conductor. The instrument relapsed into the position of being little more than a music desk, and its player became an unnecessary and useless figurehead.

The period of dual control of the concert and opera orchestra was followed by an intermediate period during which the violinist-conductor became the sole leading spirit. Amongst such were Gluck, Graun, Stamitz, Cannabich, Dittersdorf, and a host of others who stood up in front of the orchestra, violin in hand, and by their playing and bodily movements urged their followers along, just as their successors did with the baton instead of with violin and bow. The race of violinist-conductors died hard; the last stage previous to the advent of the baton-conductor was one in which the violin bow was actually used as a baton. Habeneck (1781-1849), the famous violinist-conductor of the Paris Conservatoire concerts, was one of the last of a type which lingered even after baton-conducting had become the firmly established method of directing all sorts of choral, orchestral, and operatic performances.

The first quarter of the 19th century, the period of Beethoven, Schubert, and Weber, saw the birth of conducting as we now understand the word. The conductor who stood up in front of the orchestra without any instrument, with only a small stick or a roll of paper in his hand with which he marked the beats of the bar, was actually a further growth of the violinist-conductor; in short, the bow was exchanged for the baton. Continued growth in the size of orchestras and choirs, the development of a more complex orchestration, and the higher standard of execution demanded by the scores of the period, all called out for a leader and guide whose entire attention should be devoted to the control of a larger and more complicated machine. It is enlightening to know that in 1807 one Gottfried Weber, theorist and critic, wrote in favor of silent conducting with a baton as if he were advocating something quite novel, and as if he were prepared to encounter opposition. Before the mid-century was reached the baton had triumphed; orchestras,

choirs, and opera were universally directed as they now are, and
a new type of musician began to come into existence--namely, the
specialist-conductor.

The pioneers of the baton were Reichardt, Anselm Weber,
and Spontini at Berlin, Carl Maria von Weber at Dresden, Mendelssohn at Leipzig, and Spohr at Frankfort and Cassel. Paris and
Vienna lagged behind, remaining true to the old style of violinist-
conductors such as Habeneck and Schuppanzigh, while London
had to wait till 1820 for its first taste of the new style. Spohr's
description in his own Autobiography of how he introduced the baton
at the Philharmonic Society has often been quoted, but is worth repeating:

> It was at that time still the custom then that when sym-
> phonies and overtures were performed, the pianist had
> the score before him, not exactly to conduct from it, but
> only to read after and to play with the orchestra at
> pleasure, which, when it was heard, had a very bad ef-
> fect. The real conductor was the first violin, who gave
> the tempi, and now and then, when the orchestra began
> to falter, gave the beat with the bow of his violin. So
> numerous an orchestra, standing so far apart from each
> other as that of the Philharmonic, could not possibly go
> exactly together, and in spite of the excellence of the in-
> dividual members, the ensemble was much worse than we
> are accustomed to in Germany. I had, therefore, re-
> solved when my turn came to direct, to make an attempt
> to remedy this defective system. Fortunately at the
> morning rehearsal on the day when I was to conduct the
> concert, Mr. Ries took the place at the piano, and he
> readily assented to give up the score to me and to re-
> main wholly excluded from all participation in the per-
> formance. I then took my stand with the score at a
> separate music-desk in front of the orchestra, drew my
> directing baton from my coat pocket and gave the signal
> to begin. Quite alarmed at such a novel procedure, some
> of the directors would have protested against it; but when
> I besought them to grant me at least one trial, they be-
> came pacified. The symphonies and overtures that were
> to be rehearsed were well known to me, and in Germany
> I had already directed at their performance. I therefore
> could not only give the tempi in a very decisive manner,
> but indicated also to the wind instruments and horns all
> their entries, which ensured to them a confidence such
> as hitherto they had not known there. I also took the
> liberty, when the execution did not satisfy me, to stop,
> and in a very polite but earnest manner to remark upon
> the manner of execution, which remarks Mr. Ries at my
> request interpreted to the orchestra. Incited thereby to
> more than usual attention, and conducted with certainty
> by the visible manner of giving the time, they played with
> a spirit and a correctness such as till then they had never

been heard to play with. Surprised and inspired by this
result, the orchestra, immediately after the first part of
the symphony, expressed aloud its collective assent to
the new mode of conducting, and thereby overruled all
further opposition on the part of the directors. In the
vocal pieces also, the conducting of which I assumed at
the request of Mr. Ries, particularly in the recitative,
the leading with the baton, after I had explained the
meaning of my movements, was completely successful,
and the singers repeatedly expressed to me their satisfaction for the precision with which the orchestra now
followed them.

... The triumph of the baton as a time-giver was decisive,
and no one was seen any more seated at the piano during the
performance of symphonies and overtures.

In the same year (1820) Spohr wrote of the Italian Opera at
Paris as follows:

I became confirmed but the more strongly in my opinion,
that a theatrical orchestra, however excellent it may be,
on account of the great distance of the extreme ends,
should not be conducted otherwise than by a continual
beating of the time, and, that to mark the time constantly
by motions of the body, and the violin, like Mr. Grasset
does, is of no use.

By the middle of last century conducting with the baton had
developed the beginnings of a technique of its own. Gassner's
Dirigent und Ripienist (1844), Berlioz' exposition of the theory of
conducting at the end of his well-know book on Instrumentation
(1848), the articles "Taktschlagen" and "Capellmeister" in the
Koch-Dommer Musikalisches Lexikon (1865), Wagner's Über das
Dirigiren (1869), and Deldevez' L'Art du Chef d'Orchestre (1878),
all bear witness to the growth of a branch of musicianship which
was rapidly assuming a separate existence, and was producing musicians who specialized in conducting only.

Very largely owing to the complexity of Wagner's scores
and the growing popularity of his music, still more exacting demands were made on the technical skill of conductors during the
last half of the 19th century; specialization was carried still further, and added to the necessity for a considerable technical equipment was a demand that conductors should also stand out as interpreters of music. The names of such as Liszt and Bülow, followed
by a succession of Wagner specialists such as Richter, Levi, Mahler, Schuch, Seidl, and Mottl, introduce an era in which conducting
had grown far beyond the confines of mere technical skill, and had
developed what might well be called a virtuosity of its own. At
this stage the personality of a conductor, the individuality of his
readings, and his own interpretation of the music he directed,
began to count for more than technical correctness. He was no

longer only a time-beater, a mere technician; he was an artist playing on an orchestra as a virtuoso instrumentalist plays on his instrument.

The names of such as Nikisch, Weingartner, Lamoureux, Colonne, Mancinelli, and Safonof [Safonov] are only a few of a famous generation who were the immediate predecessors of the present race of star conductors. What they did for conducting is the equivalent of what Liszt and Tausig did for piano playing, and of what Joachim and Sarasate did for violin playing.

Within one hundred years orchestral conducting has grown from what can have been little more than mechanical time-beating to a highly complex art which requires such musical and personal qualities as are only rarely found combined in the same person. In addition to technical ability, experience, and sound musicianship, a conductor is now expected to show a personality which will colour every work he touches. His insight and sympathies must be comprehensive enough to enable him to deal with music in a variety of styles ranging from early 18th-century simplicity to 20th-century complexity. He may be sensational, or he may be restrained and dignified, but he must never be dull and uninteresting.

It is well said of conductors that they should be born, not made; the student of these pages, however, will do well to realize that if conductors are born, they are never born ready-made.

THE ART OF CONDUCTING*

Eugene Ormandy

The art of conducting, one of the most complex and demanding activities in the realm of music, comprises both the visual public performance and the constant application of technique. Although they are inseparable in performance, they can be analyzed in the light of the unique problems which each presents. Similarly, the conductor himself functions on three levels, each dependent upon the other, all culminating in the performance itself.

Personal Study. On the first level, his period of study, the conductor prepares himself both technically and artistically. On this level he must be musician, historian, stylist, orchestrator, and listener. He must study the score so that he "hears" it in his mind. As he does this he evaluates the music and makes a beginning toward balancing the many strands of musical line. He must understand the historical context in which a particular work is conceived, and bring to bear upon the growing interpretive edifice

*Reprinted from Encyclopedia International, copyright 1973, by special permission of the publisher, Grolier Incorporated.

a thorough knowledge of the stylistic requirements inherent in the work. To study such a masterwork as Beethoven's "Eroica" Symphony without some knowledge of the composer's response to the ideals of the French Revolution and Napoleon's unique political position in 1806 is to study music in a vacuum. Needless to say, it was not created in a vacuum. Among the elements of stylistic validity are tempi and dynamics. A Mozart allegro differs by far from a Tchaikovsky allegro. Similarly, a forte in Haydn is an entirely different matter from a Wagner forte.

A thorough knowledge of the orchestral colors and timbres enables the studying conductor to "hear" the orchestral sound while he studies. When conducting older composers he must sometimes compensate for the technical inadequacies of the times by delicately rewriting certain passages in terms of today's more complete orchestras and more highly skilled players. Present-day performances of such works as the Fifth Symphony of Beethoven, the Great C Major Symphony of Schubert, the symphonies, of Schumann, to mention but a few, are rarely given without many instrumental changes. Even so "pure" a conductor as Toscanini did not deny the composer the benefit of today's heightened instrumental resources.

Finally, while he studies, the conductor must "listen" objectively to the work, pacing its progress, spacing its climaxes, deriving a general aural concept of the musical architecture, and evaluating its merit as it will be heard by the public. He must recall Richard Strauss's dictum: "Remember that you are making music not for your own pleasure but for the joy of your listeners."

Rehearsal. The second level upon which the conductor functions is the rehearsal, in which he prepares the orchestra both technically and artistically. It is on this level that he acts as a guide to the orchestra, building up in their minds a concept of the work parallel to his own, for the eventual public performance requires an enlightened and sensitive orchestra playing not "under" a conductor, but rather "with" him.

During the rehearsals he must clarify all problems of metrics and tempi, elucidating his own pacing of the work. He must temper all dynamic markings so that the instrumental "sound" is balanced in all its components. The older composers always wrote the same dynamics vertically (for each simultaneous part, straight down the page) in their scores. It was only composer-conductors like Mahler or Wagner, who realized the pitfalls of dynamics incautiously marked.

As he rehearses, the conductor, surrounded by the physical sound of the work, checks his own concept of the music, comparing it with the actual music. In those particular instances where the two do not fit, he must alter one or the other. It is essential that the two, the concept and the actuality, run amicably along. In addition there are instances, such as the lengthy oboe solo in

Strauss's "Don Juan," where the prudent conductor who is fortunate enough to possess a highly sensitive oboe player permits him to "have his head," acting almost as an accompanist rather than a leader.

Performance. It is in performance that the conductor operates upon the highest and most demanding level. Here the work is finished technically; the orchestra is fully prepared for all of its demands; the conductor, his study and preparation behind him, now immerses himself in the music, identifying himself with it both emotionally and mentally. But it is at this crucial time that the most difficult function of the conductor comes into full play. He must, while identifying himself with the music, keep a constant watch upon the progress of the work, allowing a portion of his analytical mind to constantly evaluate the sound and pace of the performance. He must be prepared to instantaneously make any adjustments, large or small, in the actual performance required for the fullest realization of his inner concept. Many factors make this necessary: a different hall, a player's momentary inattention, the effect of several thousand persons upon the acoustics, even the understandable enthusiasm of performance which might affect the tempo. At such a moment the conductor meets his greatest challenge, for the progress of the work must not suffer in the slightest; there must be no detectable "hitch." At such moments the experience of a conductor tells, for the young conductor new to such emergencies, tends to do one thing at a time. Music does not permit this, for it flows in time, and all adjustments must be superimposed upon the uninterrupted continuum.

In the extent to which he succeeds on any and all of these levels lies the measure of the conductor's merit both as a musician and as an artist. In his study he can separate the art from the technique, but in performance he must strive fully and constantly for a total artistic experience. Otherwise he can never fulfill his high calling: recreating the reality of the work itself.

REHEARSING*

Charles Munch

When you arrive at the hall for your morning rehearsal at five minutes to ten, do not open the door marked "Stage Entrance" right away. Stop for a moment and listen to the formless and undisciplined sounds emerging from the musicians' room. The violinists are tuning up, playing scales or passages from concertos. The winds are all exercising hard too, bringing up the temperature

*Chapter 6 of I Am a Conductor, by Charles Munch; New York: Oxford University Press, 1955. Copyright 1955 by Charles Munch. Reprinted by permission of Oxford University Press, Inc.

of their instruments in order to be in tune.   They are like athletes
scattered around a stadium, stretching and warming up before the
game.

   This atmosphere of musical anarchy is as exciting to a conductor as the smell of fresh printer's ink to a journalist or the
bouquet of a rare wine to a chevalier du tastevin.   Little by little
calm returns.   The concert master performs his first task, to tune
the instruments to the A he has taken from the first oboe.   It is a
custom of the greatest importance, observed throughout the world.

   The orchestra must be made to give the impression of playing in tune although absolute accuracy in this is beyond the realm
of possibility.   One orchestra may play more or less nearly in tune
than another--which makes an enormous difference.   Aside from the
mechanical limitations of the instruments and the human limitations
of the players, notes actually become different when they belong to
different keys.   On the piano G-sharp and A-flat are the same, but
for the orchestra G-sharp in the key of E major and A-flat in the
key of F minor are two very different things.   A better approximation of just intonation can often be obtained if you explain to the
orchestra what is happening harmonically.

                        *   *   *

   There you are in your place on stage.   Before you sit a
hundred men who hold in their hands instruments created for the
purpose of making sounds of various kinds.

   The orchestra is not a docile or mechanical instrument.   It
is a social body, a collection of human beings.   It has a psychology
and reflexes.   It can be guided but it must not be offended.   First
you must silence them.

   I remember the conductor of an amateur orchestra in Stras-
bourg who hung a big bell from his stand.   Before beginning to rehearse he used to ring it furiously to let his presence be known.
Happily, those days are gone, together with the cudgel blows of the
baton nervously beating the measure on the back of the stand.

   This was a vestige of the means employed by conductors of
long ago, the remains of the method invented in the 17th century
by Lulli--the first true conductor in the modern sense--who used
a big heavy stick and introduced the authoritarian mannerisms so
dear to many of his successors.   Didn't he once break his violin
over the head of a recalcitrant musician?   Recalcitrant musicians
are still to be found but one no longer breaks violins over their
heads.   This over-energetic measure helps neither performance nor
discipline.

                        *   *   *

   How is the orchestra arranged on the stage?

First of all, the acoustical qualities of the hall must be taken into account. This is a precaution that is often neglected but is nevertheless very important. I remember a concert at the Paris Opera at which I died a thousand deaths because despite the imposing array of forces we used, all the music rose to the stage flies. The entire mass of three hundred choral singers standing behind the orchestra seemed to have been struck dumb.

I usually arrange the strings with first and second violins together at my left, cellos upstage and violas downstage at my right. In this way the violas, whose importance is often undervalued, are brought out more and are heard better.

The loud voices of the orchestra, the trumpets and trombones, may be relegated to a place on the side. I put them on a slant so that their bells will not point directly into the hall. The woodwinds are in two rows in the center of the stage, with the four first-players as close together as possible. The horns curve behind them. The percussion is at the back on the left and the basses on the right, good neighbors of the cellos.

This topography is the one that seems to me to give the best results, the greatest coherence and the finest balance.

*   *   *

The sole purpose of the rehearsal is work--and what a mistake to believe that it is only for the orchestra and not for the conductor. No soloist would dream of appearing in public without practicing on his instrument and the orchestra is the conductor's instrument. I have heard some illustrious conductors claim that they never make mistakes. When something goes wrong it is never their fault, lucky fellows. I take the opposite position.

If a horn player or some other wind player misses a note because his lips are tired, the conductor obviously can do nothing about it. But an accident of that kind is unimportant. It is quite improper to fly into a rage on account of such a peccadillo and to look daggers at the guilty man, already sorry enough himself for his squawk. But of course it is a matter of principle that a conductor can let nothing go by, no faulty entry, no wrong note. He must stop and play the questionable passage over again as many times as he finds necessary--even though musicians generally do not like to.

*   *   *

What attitude should the conductor take toward the musicians to obtain the best results?

Let him not make long speeches to them. Musicians come to play, not to listen to lectures. Say what you must in as few words as possible. Experienced professionals hate to be given lessons. Let them retain some sense of responsibility. Never discourage them. Restore the confidence of those who are in trouble. Do not make much of their errors. Correct them without embarrassing them before their comrades.

Do you distrust the musicians' judgment? They are quick to discover the true quality of their conductor. Richard Strauss's father, a famous horn player, once came right out and said, "Remember this, you conductors. We watch you step up on the podium and open your score. Before you pick up your baton, we know if it is you or we who will be master." In the same vein, there is the story of a cynical musician who, when asked what a famous guest conductor's program was to be, answered, "I don't know what he's going to conduct but we are playing Beethoven's Fifth."

There is no question about it. Musicians know right away if you have the authority to be their leader, if you are 'somebody.' Authority emanates from a strong personality. In his wonderful book, The Art of Conducting, Wagner wrote, "Only orchestra musicians have the capacity to judge good and bad conducting." He made no mistake.

*   *   *

With new works the first rehearsal is devoted to a plain reading, to discover the inevitable mistakes in the music and to acquaint the musicians with the technical difficulties that face them. It is like showing the obstacles to the thoroughbred before the race.

There are many passages in the orchestral literature that are easy to conduct but hard to play. With a particularly problematic work it is often profitable to have sectional rehearsals first, the winds at one time and the strings another. Give the musicians a chance to figure out what the notes are and do not bother with expression. At the next rehearsal of the whole orchestra everything will have been deciphered and all the parts will fall into their proper places. Classical works obviously do not need this kind of preparation.

*   *   *

What is there to say about tempos?

Gluck said, "Just a bit too fast or a bit too slow and all is lost." A presto is obviously not an andante nor an adagio nor an allegro. All music has its own inner pace that belongs to it as branches belong to a tree. To want to change it for another or even to modify it would be criminal. I often think of the reply of a great master, if I may tell another story, who when asked about a proper tempo for a certain classical work, said, "If you don't know what tempo to take, don't take any!"

You do not feel music the same way every day. Fritz

Kreisler used to tell a story about a performance of the Brahms concerto under the composer's direction. Once, late in life, Brahms attacked the finale at a dizzying speed, much faster than usual. Kreisler stopped and protested but Brahms said, "Why not, my dear friend? My pulse is faster than usual today." What a wonderful excuse. It is too bad that only musicians as great as Brahms can use it. The rest of us must plan as much as possible before going on stage--even the pulse rate.

A critic once reproached Richard Strauss, who was an incomparable conductor, for having conducted the finale of a Mozart symphony too fast. Strauss said, "These gentlemen of the press seem to have a direct wire to Olympus."

Is there a simple rule by which the one true tempo may be discovered? I do not think so but Kreisler has laid down this general principle: "Where the notes are few and large in value, don't slow down the beat. Where there are many short notes, take your time." If you follow this, you will at least approach the truth.

There are obviously many problems here. We are not machines, happily. We can make mistakes. It happens to everyone. But if you interpret music as you feel it, with ardor and faith, with all your heart and with complete conviction, I am certain that even if the critics attack you, God will forgive you.

*   *   *

The proper dynamic nuances are easy to obtain if you indicate them clearly and precisely with your stick. Piano and diminuendo are always somewhat more difficult to obtain than forte and crescendo.

The essentials to get from the musicians are respect for the exact value of each note, "singing" tone, and elimination of all elements that are out of the style of the piece--and without theorizing. Musicians are generally not intellectuals. Address yourself to their feelings to get them into the spirit of a piece. They will understand immediately.

The problem of balancing sounds of different weights deserves special attention. Every element must be properly placed in musical relief. The principal voices must be brought forward without suppressing the rest. You must be able to prevent the brasses from covering the strings and make any single instrument emerge from a tutti. The sounds play about you like waves and you must put each one in its proper place. This is difficult for you because what you hear on the stage often gives a poor impression of how the music sounds in the hall. You must sometimes descend from your pedestal and take a seat in the last row to listen, just as you look at a picture from a distance.

*   *   *

It goes without saying that all this takes time and that not all orchestras work at the same pace. With the best of them it is a good idea not to over-rehearse. You must have confidence in the musicians' receptivity and spontaneity.

A mediocre orchestra requires more attention and care but I for one have never disdained any orchestra. I find it interesting to work with some of the less finished groups. Their good will and enthusiasm often more than compensate for their lack of technical attainment. I have many happy memories of conducting orchestras of young musicians and provincial semi-professional orchestras.

*   *   *

I still want to take up here three special situations where experience is helpful.

The first: Playing a new work. If it can be arranged, the composer's presence at rehearsals is of the greatest value. If he has a thorough knowledge of conducting, perhaps the composer himself can best realize the intentions of the work.

The second: Accompanying a soloist. A feeling of friendly cooperation between conductor and soloist is of the greatest importance, but such a feeling is not always easy to achieve. There are times when everything can be arranged amicably, but in case of incompatibility do you follow a soloist who is going against your wishes? I think the conductor cannot do otherwise. If he tries to slow down or hurry up a soloist he risks a catastrophe.

When Goethe was director of the theater at Weimar he once had to arbitrate a dispute between one of his opera singers and an excellent conductor. He ruled in favor of the singer and the conductor was dismissed. It would be better if the directors, even when they are men like Goethe, would not interfere.

When you are accompanying, it is not enough that you hear the soloist's every note or that you understand the singer's every word. Can the audience hear and understand? The singer's diction is your responsibility. The public has a right to understand the words. You cannot expect it to know by heart all the lines in a scene from a Wagner opera.

The third: Recording. This is becoming a separate profession. It supposes close cooperation between the conductor and the technicians, who are not necessarily musicians. At recording sessions you will find yourself repeating passages over and over again and very profitably, for the playing back of what has just been recorded lets you hear exactly what you have done and shows you what you can improve.

*   *   *

In music more than anywhere else, our deeds pursue us.
We should never forget that it is for us to please those who listen.

PERFORMANCE*

Adrian Boult

The great day has come, and we are keyed up for the ordeal. I am sometimes asked what happens if I go to a concert
feeling that I want to do a Beethoven symphony, and I find a
Tchaikovsky on the program. My reply is that that kind of attitude
is the privilege of the amateur; the professional has several days
before (much longer if it is something involving fresh preparation)
begun to condition himself for a performance of a Tchaikovsky symphony. He has thought through it on waking in the early morning,
he has planned his rehearsal when sitting in the Underground, and
he has pictured the orchestra waiting for rehearsal in the hall while
standing in a bus queue. Is he nervous? Of course he is; if I
hear an artist saying that he is never nervous, I know at once he
is one of those technically slick people whose performance will
move no one at all except his relations. Or possibly he is like a
friend of mine who suffered acutely and was persuaded to take a
very useful homoeopathic remedy before a concert, with this lamentable result: "My dear, I can never take it again; I found myself positively revelling in playing wrong notes!" Nerves are sent
to stimulate us to do more than our best, and must be welcomed,
and harnessed to help our work whether at a concert or before an
athletic ordeal.

How else do we prepare ourselves? I for one found it a
great mistake to give way to the feeling we all have--that food is
impossible before a concert. My experience is that if I starve before a concert (as one naturally wants to) I shall be so hungry by
half time that I shall be worn out and useless by the end of the
program. I find, too, that it is most harmful to get to the hall
too early; artists' rooms are poisonous places--their wallpapers
exude noxious thoughts. I still often walk to concerts if the distance is reasonable, and I time myself to get there not too long
beforehand; sometimes I go out again if I have got there too soon.
I have sometimes been amused at the consternation in the faces of
members of the audience when they meet their conductor walking
rapidly away from the hall only a few minutes before the start of
the concert.

We have discussed the method of preparation and the pros

*From Thoughts on Conducting, by Adrian Boult; London: Phoenix
House/Dent, 1963. Used by permission of the publisher.

and cons for the generation of tension at rehearsals; I repeat that
I prefer the cooler method, gradually warming up (provided rehearsals are plentiful), so that the peak of excitement is just reached,
but not passed, when the audience is in the hall and the performance begins.

One stands in the doorway looking out on the orchestra, and
hoping that one can get to the desk without knocking down half the
players on the way.   It all looks a very long way off, and I often
have to repress a strong urge to run at full speed in order to get
there--or perhaps to run harder still in the other direction.   But
that, as we saw, is the privilege of the amateur.   Some brave
spirits manage to walk on to the platform carrying their sticks, but
my advice is to leave the stick on the desk, and not to pick it up
until everything is ready for the music.   Sticks have a very shaky
habit before the music begins.   So we try to stand absolutely still,
looking round at our forces to see that they are all there and "sitting comfortably" while that wonderful sound of diminuendo comes
from the audience to convey that they too are feeling a growing expectation, and the first silence invites us to start.   Now we can
give up all our rehearsal cares; we shall hear all we need to hear,
but our task has become that of engine driver; we supply the motive
power, keeping our eye on the track with an occasional thought for
danger signals, yet mainly possessed with the relentless flow of
the sound to its climax and thence to its inevitable close.

There is a great variety in the tempo set by different conductors, not only of the music, but of the concert itself.   I am an
impatient person.   I hate the breaks between the acts of a play,
and I feel strongly the link (even when musically it is undiscernible)
between the movements of a concerto or symphony.   I know it is
necessary, but when a violinist after closing a movement in, say,
E flat major, plunges us into the D and A tuning fifth, I always
feel like breaking my stick over his head.   It is the custom for
some conductors to leave the platform after every item--I can't
think why.   Of course we should go to meet a soloist, but otherwise I see no reason for going and coming any more than for a
recitalist to go away between the items of his program.

Some conductors, who seem to enjoy dawdling through their
programs, apparently take an opposite view where the length of the
music itself is concerned; they cut every repeat they can find, even
sometimes in scherzos and trios.   It is perhaps arguable that in a
Mozart serenade (which may have been meant to be played while
the archbishop was having supper) the repeats are formally and
thoughtlessly put in to fill the time up, but this is not the case
with his symphonies--indeed, I now find that both repeats in the
last movements of the last three symphonies are essential if those
movements are to stand up to balance their great first movements.
I have always found the symphonies something of a tadpole, and
only recently has this most obvious reason dawned on me.   Bruno
Walter agreed heartily when I said I wanted to hear those repeats.
It seems to be especially in the orchestral world that this omission

is so often practiced. In quartets and sonatas they seemed to be
played much more often.   Of course movements vary in this necessity; for instance, in the "Eroica" I feel neutral about it--
though Kleiber's recent record is published in full; but in works
like the Fifth of Beethoven and the Third of Brahms I feel the
movement almost headless without it.

        I am afraid we still hear the expression "seeing a conductor"
used even in educated circles.   Do people really spend their money
in the hope of seeing a ballet or peepshow?   If so, why not go to
the ballet straightaway (they are better trained for this than we
are)?   Are such people disappointed when a man stands still and
uses his stick continuously and his elbows rarely?   It takes all
sorts to make a world.   Seriously, I sometimes feel that conductors
are insulting skilled orchestral colleagues not only in the way they
speak at rehearsals, but by their behavior at concerts, dotting
every i and crossing every t, giving them credit for no sense or
artistry, and never allowing the music to move, as it were, in its
own way and sweep on to its goal.   I know some of my colleagues
occasionally talk about "my Brahms" and "your Mozart."   Can't
they see that the finest praise they can get is not "What a fine
performance," but something like: "I thought I knew and loved the
work, but tonight it sounded even greater than I imagined it"?

                    THE FUNCTION OF A CONDUCTOR*

                            William Steinberg

        After nearly four decades of conducting symphony and opera
performances around the world, I have come to the irrevocable
conclusion that there is absolutely no function in the entire realm
of the performing arts as universally misunderstood as that of the
conductor.   The irrationality of conducting is primarily attributable
to the fact that the conductor, in performing his podium duties,
never does things by himself.   On the contrary, he is continuously
concerned with getting other people to do them.   And the chief contradiction implicit in his work is that, while the motive of his own
responsibility is eliminated altogether, he is nevertheless always
held responsible for the doings of others and thus virtually forced
into a false position in relation both to the music he interprets and
the audience for which he interprets it.

        How does one become a conductor in the first place?   Aside
from any question of musical ability, which may manifest itself in
a wide variety of forms, there is the matter of a call or summons,
an inescapable compulsion, something one follows blindly and unquestioningly, as though to avoid a collision of natural forces.

*From the Music Journal, vol. 26 (April 1968).   Reprinted by per-
mission of the publisher.

Then there is the question of character. To be a conductor, one must be a born leader--but a leader who understands the responsibilities of leadership and is never for a moment deluded with a sense of absolute power or infallibility and who has the objectivity to withstand the blind hero worship with which amateur listeners may sometimes envelop him.

Assuming one has the conductorial "call" and the properly tempered qualities of leadership, how does he go about developing what is nowadays everywhere called "baton technique"--a term which, to me, has always seemed to be something of a misnomer, since technique is a matter of manual dexterity and manual dexterity per se is of little or no use to the conductor confronted by a live orchestra. Technique, as we know it, is something which originates in the brain and, in the case of vocal or instrumental technique, it is something that can eventually be achieved through solitary training. Conducting, on the other hand, is more a means to an end than an end itself, and obviously one cannot conduct for himself alone. Conducting in front of a mirror or empty chairs to the accompaniment of a phonograph record is meaningless, since in effect, one does not learn to lead, but to follow. Conducting, alas, can be learned only from conducting, and if there is any manual dexterity or technique involved, one must have the response of living players to determine its effectiveness.

To provide a living orchestra for the would-be conductor to practice on at any given time may be prohibitive in cost or impossible in terms of manpower availability in many parts of the United States, although today there exist a number of schools and workshops where training orchestras can substitute to some extent for the innumerable theatres throughout Europe in which the tyro conductor gains his first practical experience. Yet, when faced for the first time by the fully professional orchestra, whose mentality is altogether different from that of any training group, the young conductor often encounters psychological difficulties which make him realize with a jolt that his manual abilities, however admirably cultivated, are hardly sufficient to make him really understood.

There are, of course, many distinguished colleagues of mine who insist that the so-called "diagram" beat is the conductor's principal tool for welding together 50-to-100 diverse musical personalities into a single responsive instrument. My own experience and observation is that the men and women in an orchestra just couldn't care less what kind of diagram is beaten before their noses. Above all else, professional players want to play well (in my long experience I have never encountered an orchestra which really wanted to play badly!) and all they demand from their conductor is a method which will help them to play as well as they possibly can. I have seen conductors who haven't the faintest notion about diagrams, and who may be downright clumsy in their use of their hands, achieve exciting musical results by means of which they are virtually unaware. And, conversely, I have heard some of the most boring performances of my listening experience at the hands of conductors meticulously schooled in the use of the baton. All of which goes to prove that the successful conductor is the one who develops his own method of expressing himself, and that it is the power of his own personality which is his strongest means of commanding his orchestra.

On the other hand, I would certainly not want to give the impression that the conductor's personality should be allowed to ride roughshod to the extent of interpreting each piece of music in a totally personalized and arbitrary fashion. On the contrary, it is important for a conductor to have a keen awareness of style, to realize that each work has its own style conditioned by the time in which it was written, the temperament of its composer, performance technique, et cetera. The conductor develops his feeling for style by studying the different periods of creativity and their prevailing performance techniques in history books, then filtering this accumulated book knowledge through the sieve of his own intuition. His book study will enable him to distinguish between the variety of styles and to analyze the organic structure of the music he wishes to perform, but he must be careful that his preoccupation with the actual technicalities of conducting does not hinder him from re-creating the styles and revealing the structure to his listeners. (It is interesting to note that, where orchestras have played without conductors altogether, their performances, while evidencing great technical perfection, lack the spiritual image of the music, which can only be achieved by the governing mind of the conductor weaving together threads of structure and style.)

But if it is the incontestable duty of the conductor to perform a masterpiece of music literally, it must also be incontrovertibly clear that the written letter of the score does not necessarily indicate the ultimate meaning of the music. It was Mozart who pointed out that the most important part of music is not contained in the notes. This becomes a more and more debatable point in the face of today's everwidening diversity of opinions. Constantly we are asked about a piece of music: "What does it really mean?" "What is its true significance?" By whom can such questions properly be answered? Only by one who has the integrity and modesty to hide himself from the eyes of a crowd waiting to be entertained or provoked and who, having allowed his own virtues of character and spirit to be distilled by intuition and inspiration, is capable of making the music speak for itself.

CONDUCTING REVISITED*

Gunther Schuller

The problems relating to the conducting of contemporary music are, as might be expected, as varied and unpredictable as contemporary music itself. An unprecedented plethora of compositional schools, techniques, conceptions, and philosophies dominate the current scene, and it is, therefore, very difficult to generalize either about the compositional problems themselves or the performance and conductorial problems raised by them. The art of conducting is presently being subjected to some rather fundamental reevaluations, and in a few instances new compositional approaches have radically changed conducting techniques or indeed eliminated them altogether.

However, leaving aside these extremes for the moment, if we compare conducting problems relating to contemporary music-- which now, in 1964, ought no longer to include works composed in the first decades of our century--with those relating to eighteenth- and nineteenth-century music, we discover that there are certain crucial differences in conductorial requirements. These are in some respects differences in kind, but more frequently differences in degree.

By that I mean that the conductor of a contemporary piece is trying to do essentially the same thing as the conductor of a 19th-century work: to express the music with clarity, to shape it into that form which the composer indicates in the score, and to capture the essence of that composer's expression and style. Certain specific compositional techniques or styles will, of course, require rather specifically different conducting techniques, not to speak of a different musical orientation. But at the most fundamental level the conductor's job is still to provide a rhythmic frame of reference (through his beat) and a visual representation of the music's content (through the expression in his beat). On a purely technical level this would apply, for example, whether a given work made use of serial techniques or neo-Classic or freely atonal principles of organization.

But what has changed in the performance of contemporary music is the degree of involvement and participation--I am tempted to say physical participation--required of the conductor.

In order to substantiate this point, we must first be very clear about certain fundamental differences between most 20th-century music and the music of previous eras. A great deal has been said and written about the alleged increase of dissonance in contemporary music and the increased complexity of its rhythms, as

*From The Conductor's Art, by Carl Bamberger (editor); New York: McGraw-Hill, 1965. Copyright 1965 by McGraw-Hill, Inc. Used by permission of McGraw-Hill Book Co.

if these were the only and primary problems for the listener and
performer. But what really has complicated the performer's and
listener's task are the radical changes in the continuity of most
new music, i. e. , its higher degree of variability and contrast.
Not only does contemporary music involve a greater range of technical possibilities (instrumental registers, dynamic levels, timbral
variety, rhythmic complexity, textural density, etc.), but the new
forms of continuity involve a much greater rate of change and contrast in these respects. Whereas in earlier music it was highly
unlikely that contrasts--other than in dynamic levels--would disrupt
the even flow of a given phrase or theme (or indeed sometimes an
entire movement), today one can almost expect the opposite. A
single measure or a single musical idea may in itself involve a
maximum degree of contrast in some or all of the above characteristics. And, of course, the progression from measure to measure
or from one musical idea to another may also be marked by constant contrast and change. In a Mozart, Beethoven, or Brahms
symphony we can reasonably expect a phrase to end more or less
with the same instruments, the same number of instruments, more
or less within the same range, and in the same meter and rhythm
as it started.

In the music of our own time obviously no such guarantees
can be made. Any one of a number of factors--singly or jointly--
may serve to disrupt the continuity: changes of meter, of tempo,
fragmentation of texture, use of extreme registers, of large intervals, of contrasting sonorities, and so on.

This new kind of continuity obviously requires a much higher
degree of involvement on the part of the conductor. Purely statistically, there is more to control, more to shape, and at a greater
rate of change. This does not yet take into account the fact that
new music is, of necessity, less familiar to the performers, in
terms of both specific compositions and general stylistic conceptions. Therefore on that account too, a contemporary work will
require much more conductorial guidance.

It would appear that the points I have thus far raised should
be self-evident. But unfortunately the majority of performances of
new music offer no such evidence. Whether from a lack of knowledge of the specific composition involved or from a failure to understand these basic conducting requisites, too many conductors
still conduct our new music as if it were shaped in eight-bar phrases
and easy symmetrical patterns.

In this connection, it is time that several myths were disposed of once and for all. These center around the notion that the
best conductor is one who uses a minimum of motion and physical
energy. Any number of theories and half-truths are constantly in-
voked to perpetuate this idea; and conductors are fond of quoting
stories associated, for example, with Richard Strauss, who by all
accounts had an absolute phobia of sweating while on the podium,
and who prided himself on the dryness of his armpits after a performance.

My point is not to question the quality of Strauss' conducting, which was indeed great, and altogether exceptional. Nor do I wish to imply that this approach is totally invalid. I am simply saying that in most instances it is not applicable in contemporary music.

It is not only entirely possible but highly desirable to conduct a Mozart symphony, for example, with a minimum of physical motion. Such a work to a large extent plays itself, and the conductor--once he has rehearsed any unsatisfactory details--merely guides and shapes the performance in its over-all form and expression. This is possible, obviously, because both the work and the style are familiar.

But if we move to a "contemporary" work by, let us say, Webern or Schoenberg or Babbitt or Nono, we are facing a totally different set of compositional and performance criteria. Performances of such works by conductors of the "no-sweat" school are with few exceptions disastrous. At worst they suffer from a complete lack of control over structural details, and at best from lack of emotional involvement with the work. And in many cases this approach may simply be a suave camouflage for an inadequate knowledge of the score. I have also seen conductors, who pride themselves on their clean technique and a beat which is near the point of invisibility, resort of necessity to a large vigorous baton technique when faced with a contemporary piece. But at least these gentlemen allowed their innermost instincts--instincts of musical self-preservation, one might say--to supersede baton mannerisms and a bogus visual elegance.

It is, of course, not a question of either large or small beats, which is primarily a matter of conductors' personal styles. And I am certainly not advocating various forms of over-conducting (excessively large baton motions, incessant subdivision of the beat, etc.). I am simply suggesting that baton techniques must be related to the music they serve, and that contemporary music is apt to make entirely different demands in this regard.

It seems to me that the primary areas in which a greater conductorial control is required are those of "cues" and "dynamics." In music where continuity is characterized by fragmentation and multilinear polyphony each individual orchestral part consists by definition of short phrase fragments, sometimes--as in certain Klangfarben structures--even of single notes. Beyond that, orchestral writing of the 20th century in general is characterized by a greater independence of each instrumental part, a chamber music conception first initiated in the works of Mahler and Schoenberg. All this, coupled with the player's unfamiliarity with new music, necessitates a much greater cueing ability and knowledge of the score on the conductor's part.

Similarly, highly contrasting dynamics--sometimes several in one measure, or indeed several dynamics simultaneously--must be clearly delineated by the conductor. In such music the average "common-denominator" beat, usable in earlier music, no longer can do the job. The scale of reference has simply been narrowed down. Whereas the conductor in earlier music might have had to change course in baton movements only at the beginning of a phrase of a thematic unit, he now--in extreme cases--may have to do so every beat.

In respect both to cues and dynamics, one might assume that, if a piece is sufficiently rehearsed--this is in itself usually a big if--the players might on their own initiative deliver all entrances and proper dynamics. In practice, however, even the most experienced orchestral players will play with more conviction and expressivity if their cues and dynamic levels are confirmed by the conductor's beat. The conductor, after all, is presumably the one performer who, by virtue of knowing the score, understands the multiple relationships of all the parts to each other, something the individual player usually does not. Nor can the player be expected to know this in unfamiliar music. Actually, orchestral musicians are trained to give what the conductor demands. But if the conductor demands nothing, the player--with very few exceptions--will take the path of least resistance, and give nothing beyond the most matter-of-fact rendition of the notes on the page.

There are types of music which, once they are carefully rehearsed, can be left more or less to perform themselves. But even the most painstaking rehearsal procedures in contemporary music offer no guarantees for subsequent concert performances. Aside from the complexity of the musical relationships the sheer energy and concentration required of the player in negotiating all the extremes of contrast and technical problems need constant substantiation on the part of the conductor. Anything less will result in the blandness and inaccuracies we usually get in performances of new music.

Another area in which conducting conceptions and techniques need to be focused more precisely is style. Again the great proliferation of techniques and styles in our century is at the root of the problem. For I doubt if such stylistic opposites as Brahms and Wagner or Mozart and Beethoven require different conceptions of baton technique. But Schoenberg and middle-period Stravinsky do; and so does Webern and, beyond that, such distinctive composers as Boulez and Babbitt and Xenakis.

It is always difficult to divorce technique from conception, but the specific compositional techniques involved in the works of the three last-named composers and the conducting conceptions required to realize them are so different as to constitute differences in technique. Certain kinds of texture, continuity, and expressive content determine the specifics of these styles, and in turn require variegated conducting styles. This does not even take into account the radically different techniques required in the works of the aleatory and "interminacy" schools. Common to these is a beat

which is no longer a sine qua non of conducting, either because the
beat as an integrating unit has been supplanted by larger time se-
quences (such as intervals of fifteen seconds, for example, which
are visualized by the "conductor" in the manner of the hands of a
clock), or because conducting is assumed to mean the delineation
not of beats or metric units, but solely of actual sonic events (such
as indicating only the initial attack of a sustained musical event
and not the beats following it). This latter technique, which would
seem to have far-reaching consequences since the conductor no
longer conducts the rhythmic scaffold underlying a work, but instead the actual impulses that characterize the musical continuity--
in other words, not the beat but the actual music--such a technique
obviously places a much greater responsibility on the conductor.
And it involves once again the reflexive capacities of conductor and
performer, thus restoring a vital sense of spontaneity and urgency
which, as a basic ingredient, is sorely lacking in much concert
music.

To be sure, one aspect of conducting has not changed: the
role played by the ear. The ear is still the final controlling ar-
biter, and in contemporary music, perhaps more than any other,
no amount of baton dexterity can make up for deficiencies in either
the ear or the mind. This is not to imply that one needs to know
a Schoenberg score better than one by Mozart. It is simply to say
that the Schoenberg score is apt to be more complex than the one
by Mozart, and there is thus, purely statistically, more to learn
and more detail to control. There is probably also a great deal of
unfamiliar territory to explore, and--in turn--to transmit lucidly to
the player. This cannot be done without an awareness of the compositional techniques involved, a thorough knowledge of the structural outlines which define the work, and a total immersion in the
expressive essentials of that work's style.

It will be noted that this is in essence no more and no less
than what was always required, and these qualities still mark the
highest achievements in the art of conducting. But the demands
made by the music have multiplied; and the conductor's art, if it is
to continue to serve the music, must reflect these increased demands.

ARTURO TOSCANINI*

Harold C. Schonberg

And then came Arturo Toscanini.

---

*From The Great Conductors, by Harold C. Schonberg; New York:
Simon & Schuster, 1967. Copyright 1967 by Harold C. Schonberg.
Reprinted by permission of Simon and Schuster.

Toscanini was the pivotal conductor of his period: the strongest influence, the one who marks the final transition from the Wagner style to 20th-century objectivity. He became the greatest single force on contemporary conducting. "Whatever you may think about his interpretation of a specific work," George Szell has written, "that he changed the whole concept of conducting and that he rectified many, many arbitrary procedures of a generation of conductors before him, is now authentic history. That at the same time he has served as a not too useful model for a generation of conductors who were so fascinated that they were unable to follow him with some sort of discrimination is equally true." Elsewhere Szell points out the major characteristic of Toscanini: that he "wiped out the arbitrariness of the postromantic interpreters. He did away with the meretricious tricks and the thick encrustation of the interpretive nuances that had been piling up for decades. "

The point is that Toscanini followed the progression of such as Muck, Strauss and Weingartner to become a highly objective conductor and the greatest of all the literalists. His literalism manifested itself in many ways, and it was something that went far beyond merely observing in a faithful manner the printed notes and the composers' expression markings. It was a total revulsion against the Austro-German tradition, against the Wagnerian concept of fluctuation of tempo. Even more: Toscanini represented a musical objectivity as intense in its way as the subjectivity of Wagner, Bülow and Mahler. Where they kept putting themselves into the music, using the score as a vehicle for self-expression, Toscanini was equally determined to keep himself out of the score.

He had read a great deal about stylistic problems, and he had come to the conclusion that there was no conclusion. He said that it was futile to try to achieve an "authentic" style. Instruments had changed, pitch had changed, concepts had changed, and Beethoven would hardly recognize a 20th-century performance of his music. Thus the only thing--the only thing--a musician has is the notes, and those he must observe as honestly and scrupulously as possible. And not only must he observe the notes, but he must keep a steady rhythmic flow, avoiding the heaving and hauling that characterized the rhythms and tempos that in a previous age had been used in the name of "expression. " Conductors like Furtwängler who (according to Toscanini) were constantly overinterpreting in the name of "style" aroused his scorn and derision. No. Here are the notes. To interpret them a conductor has to rely on musicianship, taste, and instinct for what the composer wanted. "The tradition, " Toscanini stormed, "is to be found only in one place--in the music! " Thus Toscanini's comment about the "Eroica" Symphony, which he uttered in 1926: "Some say this is Napoleon, some Hitler, some Mussolini. For me it is simply allegro con brio. " Several years later, Willem Mengelberg deigned to give Toscanini advice on conducting. Toscanini, who had a low opinion of him to begin with, was enraged. "Talk, talk, talk, that was Mengelberg, " he later said. "Once he came to me and told me at great length the proper German way to conduct the Coriolanus

Overture. He had got it, he said quite seriously, from a conductor who supposedly had got it straight from Beethoven. Bah! I told him I got it straight from Beethoven himself, from the score. "

Most conductors with this point of view would normally develop into dispassionate, super-objective time beaters. And, indeed, Toscanini was accused of being exactly that in his early years, just as Josef Hofmann was being called a cold pianist because he refused to bend the rhythm and distort the shape the way pianists of the Liszt school used to do. Giulio Ricordi kept attacking Toscanini in the Gazzetta Musicale, charging him with rigidity of execution, mathematical accuracy and lack of poetry. Ricordi said that Toscanini's conducting of Falstaff resembled that of a "mastadonic mechanical piano. " Later on, Ricordi changed his mind, as did virtually everybody else. Once he had conquered the world, Toscanini for decades seemed immune to criticism. He was considered a miracle, a force of nature. "What is the secret of Toscanini?" the London Times wanted to know in 1926. "That he is the greatest of conductors, most of us are agreed. " A French musician swore that Toscanini's looks were not on the musicians but on the sound itself. "He looks at the sound. " There was a mystique about this potent figure, and not until the last years of his life did a new school of criticism dare to question it.

The fact that Toscanini did not develop into a sterile technician was a tribute to a patrician musical mind. Literalist though he was, he also knew that music must sing and expand; and despite his own tenets he was perfectly capable of modifying a score, or getting his own personality into his interpretations. Discussing a certain passage with the American conductor Milton Katims, the Old Man (so he was called in those years) reached for a metronome. "Here, this must be absolutely rhythmically precise. " He started the metronome and played the passage on the piano. After a few bars, Toscanini was ahead. He uttered his famous "Bah! " He shut off the metronome. "One is not a machine. Music must breathe. " And Toscanini did everything in his power to make music breathe, even to the point of altering the instrumentation if that were needed. A literalist he may have been, but not a blind purist. His phrases were long and aristocratic, his climaxes stupendous, his handling of melodic elements gracious and lyric. Above all, the feature that marked his conducting was intensity. There was a tensile quality that no other conductor could match, and even light music suddenly sounded sinewy and powerful when Toscanini conducted. His tempos were supposed to be fast, and sometimes they were. But often they merely sounded fast because everything was so perfectly regulated. Instrumentalists know this. A perfectly adjusted scale or run, at a moderate tempo, sounds faster than a scrambled scale or run that in reality may be half again as fast.

In dispensing with the Wagner-Bülow-Nikisch approach to conducting, in discarding the entire romantic style and going straight to the score, in insisting that everything be played exactly as written, in abolishing excess tempo fluctuation, in demanding that orchestras play in tune (most orchestras, even great ones, were careless about intonation even after the turn of the century), Toscanini vitalized interpretation and performance practice. He even did away with the favorite expressive device of the romantics, the string portamento, or slide. Listen to almost any pre-1920 orchestral recording, and there will be a slide between the two important melodic notes of a slow phrase. Even so fine a conductor as Weingartner was not immune, and in his 1913 recording of the "Pathétique" excerpt, something like this can be heard from the violins:

where the space between the A and the D is filled with a long, deliberate swoop. The mannerism (at least, today it is considered a mannerism; then it was standard performance practice) can be heard in all early recordings in those of Beecham Stransky, Nikisch, Stock, everybody. Obviously the device was used automatically by violinists in orchestras, and the purpose was to emphasize the key note of the phrase. But not Toscanini's violinists, and his first recordings, in 1921, are devoid of the portamento.

So pure was Toscanini's approach, so heroically did he dispense with the "tradition" of generations, and so forceful was his ability to put his ideas across (no conductor in history before Toscanini demanded and got such unearthly precision and such a wide range of dynamics from an orchestra) that his interpretations came as something new and revolutionary. The standard analogy compared him with a restorer cleaning great paintings that had never really been seen in their original colors by modern viewers. Ernest Newman heard Toscanini conduct Tristan und Isolde in Bayreuth in 1931. Now, Newman was the world's greatest Wagner authority and, of course, he had the opera by heart. "I thought," Newman wrote, "I knew that work from end to end and from outside to inside; but I was amazed to find, here and there, a passage coming on me like a dagger stroke." Newman looked up the passages in the score. "Then I found that all, or practically all, he had done was to play the notes just as Wagner directs them to be played." Toscanini always had the ability to balance musical lines so that every relationship was heard, and this kind of fluoroscopic conducting was something he had to a greater degree than anybody else.

The story about Toscanini's impromptu debut in South America is too well known to bear repetition. The correct date, supplied by Walter Toscanini, is June 30, 1886. (It is an interesting coincidence that Mancinelli's debut almost exactly paralleled Toscanini's. Like Toscanini, Mancinelli was a cellist in an orchestra and was suddenly called to the podium in an emergency. The opera was the same--Aïda.) For almost seventy years after his debut in Rio de Janeiro Toscanini was active as a conductor. At twenty-one

he was well launched on his career, though for a long time he was
not very well known outside of Italy except by reputation.   The first
mention of his name in an American publication seems to have been
in the Detroit Song Journal of February 1, 1896.   A correspondent
sent a report from Turin: "What a wonderful chef d'orchestre Toscanini is! ... How sure, how calm he is; the best leader in Italy,
and the only one in Italy capable of conducting Wagner's music in
such a grand manner.   And, think of it, he conducts everything
from memory!"

      In his own country, Toscanini rapidly became the big man,
conducting the Italian premiers of Pelléas et Mélisande, Euryanthe,
Eugene Onegin, Götterdämmerung, Siegfried and the world premiers
of Pagliacci in 1892 and La Bohème in 1896.   Puccini had wanted
Nikisch but had to settle for Toscanini, then director of the Teatro
Regic in Turin.   Soon Puccini was convinced that he had the right
man.   "Extraordinary!   Highly intelligent!"   For years the two men
had an uneasy on-again, off-again friendship.

      Around the turn of the century, Toscanini began to conduct
the symphonic repertoire.   But opera remained his chief occupation.   At La Scala, where he took over in 1895, Toscanini was admired by many, and also attacked by some for his "rigidity" and
his despotism.   His departure was characteristic.   At the last
night of the 1902-1903 season Giovanni Zenatello was singing the
tenor lead in Un Ballo in Maschera, and the audience yelled for an
encore of an aria.   Toscanini refused, and the audience would not
let the opera continue.   So Toscanini walked out after the second
act and remained away for four years.   Wherever he went, he had
to have complete authority.

      In 1908 he came to the Metropolitan Opera with its new gen-
eral manager, Giulio Gatti-Casazza, and remained for seven seasons.   It did not take Toscanini long to make an impact.   He arrived with an enormous reputation, made an impression that fully
lived up to his reputation, and the Boston Transcript wrote about
"this modest man" who "is the most heroic figure in grand opera
throughout the world.   His supremacy is indisputable."   Immediately a legend began to be built.   At first the papers said he could
conduct sixty operas without a score.   Soon this figure was expanded
to 150, then 160.   Stories were written about his memory, and
Wolf-Ferrari was quoted as saying, "It seems strange, somehow,
to think that he knows my opera [Le Donne Curiose] by heart when
I myself don't."   Through his seven seasons at the Metropolitan
Opera, Toscanini conducted twenty-nine operas; and, unlike most
Italian conductors, he was overwhelming in Wagner and French
operas.   He also conducted some concerts, including a famous
evening in 1913 when Beethoven's Ninth Symphony was the featured
work.

      His rupture with the Metropolitan Opera has never been fully
explained.   Gatti-Casazza in his memoirs is reticent, saying merely that he, Gatti, did his utmost to retain the great conductor.

Walter Toscanini says that his father was dissatisfied with rehearsal conditions and penny-pinching economies. The New York Times of September 30, 1915, said that the Metropolitan Opera was prepared to make every concession, "but they reasonably expected him to adapt himself--principal lever though he might be--to the occasional necessities of a great operating machine. " Musical America went more thoroughly into the case:

> Some say, frankly, that while they admire his genius and consider him perhaps the greatest opera conductor in the world today, they would not particularly miss him, for the reason that his great talent and mastery of stage effect were offset by his frightful irritability and his habit of perpetually abusing the artists, the chorus and the orchestra during rehearsals, and never losing an opportunity of hurling invective at poor Gatti-Casazza, whenever he saw him, whether on the stage or in the wings. The result, they said, was that by the end of the season half the company was in a state of nervous collapse.

In any event, Toscanini left the house in one of his typical rages, and he never returned. Nor was he reconciled with Gatti-Casazza until many years had passed. Later the Metropolitan Opera made every effort to lure him back. But Toscanini was one who never forgot or forgave. "I will conduct on the ashes of the Metropolitan, " he snarled.

During World War I Toscanini, who was in Italy, conducted relatively little. He returned to La Scala in 1921 and soon got into trouble with the Fascist government. In 1926 he walked out of La Scala when ordered to conduct Giovinezza, the Fascist anthem. Because the world premiere of Turandot was in the offing, Mussolini bent to Toscanini's wishes. That year, 1926, was also the one in which Toscanini first conducted the New York Philharmonic; and the following year he was co-conductor with Mengelberg. With the merger in 1928 of the New York Philharmonic and the New York Symphony, Toscanini was named principal conductor. Those members of the new orchestra who had never played under Toscanini were petrified with fright at the prospect. Winthrop Sargeant, later a prominent music critic, went from the violin section of the New York Symphony to the Philharmonic, and has written some amusing recollections of the event. The newcomers would point out Toscanini's scowling picture on the Carnegie Hall billboards to their children and warn them if they were not good, Toscanini would get them. When Toscanini finally arrived, the musicians did unprecedented things, such as taking their parts home and practicing them. Toscanini, says Sargeant, had the ability above all other conductors to make every performance and rehearsal "a continuous psychology of crisis. " Toscanini was merely being Toscanini. "Each movement of a symphony became an emergency which demanded every ounce of energy and concentration if it was not to end in an overwhelming catastrophe. Each performance was played as though our very lives depended on its

perfection.... Beyond all technique there was a residue of mysterious personal power that lay outside ordinary comprehension. "

In the meantime, Toscanini was breaking with his own country. Anti-fascist, anti-Nazi, he once remarked that in life he was
a democrat, in music an aristocrat. He refused to conduct in Italy
after 1931 and at Bayreuth after 1933. He left Salzburg when the
Nazis took over, saying, among other things, that he would not associate himself with Furtwängler and the others who had worked for
Hitler.

At the end of the 1935-36 season he left the New York Philharmonic, and apparently the career of the sixty-nine-year-old conductor was over. But in 1937 he returned to the United States as
head of the NBC Symphony Orchestra, the group specifically created
for him by the National Broadcasting Company. Among the by-
products of his programming with that orchestra were the inclusion
of concert versions of several of the operas with which he was so
long associated, and which two generations of Americans had not
heard him conduct--La Bohème, Fidelio, La Traviata, Otello, Falstaff, Aïda. A long series of phonograph recordings was another
by-product.

It was during those NBC years that the Toscanini legend grew
to proportions that dwarfed anything that had gone before. The Old
Man was wonderful newspaper copy, though he never sought publicity
and, indeed, shunned it. He seems to have been genuinely modest--
knowing his own worth, of course, but interested only in his search
for musical perfection. Everything else was secondary, as it always had been. He lived only for music, the only thing he really
knew. As Adrian Boult has said, "He had nothing else to think of
but music. I never heard him talk of anything else. Bruno Walter
could discuss the latest play or novel, but not Toscanini. "

At his rehearsals he continued to operate as before, maintaining his psychology of crisis. His battle cry, says Samuel Antek, one of the string players in the NBC Symphony, was "Cantare!
Sostenere! " Sing! Sustain! 'No conductor could create such a
feeling of ecstasy, " Antek says. Toscanini's relatively simple,
classic beat, controlled and disciplined, pulled music from the
players. (His baton, it can be learned from the August 1941 issue
of Music Trades, was 18 5/8 inches long, with a heavy shaft, a
cork grip 4 1/2 inches long and about 5/16 inches in diameter.)
His baton movements were generally between shoulder and waist,
and his most characteristic pose was one with legs apart, body
swaying a little, left hand over his heart in heavy vibration during
lyric passages (former string players have a tendency to do this).
When the music was dramatic and strongly rhythmic, Toscanini's
beat became shorter (the mark of a good conductor; the wider a
beat, the slower the response from an orchestra).

Toscanini always conducted from memory. His eyesight was
too poor for a score to be of any use to him during a performance.

But he could see, and correct, the slightest bow movement of a
bass some thirty feet away.   He worked like a demon and expected
everybody else to do the same.   If things did not go his way he
went into a tantrum, one of his famous tantrums.   His rages were
legendary.   "It was among the most horrifying sounds I have ever
heard," Antek says, "and seemed to come from his entrails.   He
would almost double up, his mouth opened wide, his face red, as
if on the verge of an apoplectic fit.   Then a raucous blast of un-
believable volume would blare forth."   Unknown to Toscanini, the
Victor engineers kept an open microphone on many of his rehearsals, and struck off acetate recordings of the more interesting ones
for a fortunate few.   On some of these discs Toscanini can be heard
in full eruption, and the sounds are positively Vesuvian.   The discs
also give an idea of his demands, of his insistence on clarity, of
the number of times he could repeat a phrase to get a tiny point--
an oboe staccato, say--to his satisfaction.

     To Toscanini there were no short cuts.   Nor was there any
such thing as evasion.   Saul Goodman, the timpanist of the New
York Philharmonic, points out that Toscanini's insistence on hearing every note, and every note in exact time and tune, led to higher standards of orchestral playing throughout the world.   Every
score contains certain awkward things that players had always
glided over, either because conductors did not notice the evasion
or were sympathetic with the players' plight.   Not Toscanini.   His
musicians had to play the notes as written.   At first there were
great howls from instrumentalists, who had to devise new fingerings and new ways of blowing.   But eventually, under Toscanini,
the unplayable became playable.

     When things did not go the way his vision wanted them to
go, Toscanini suffered, really suffered.   A sloppy phrase, a careless note, an awkward entrance--these were enough to ruin his disposition for a week.   Such mistakes did not happen very often in a
Toscanini orchestra.   Players under his baton took special pains,
partly from actual fear, partly from pride.   Good musicians will
invariably make an extra effort when faced with a conductor for
whom they have respect.   Toscanini may have been disliked, and
even hated, by some of his players, but they played for him as
they played for no other conductor.   Always at a Toscanini concert
the audience could be sure of the whiplash attacks and releases,
the incredibly perfect ensemble, the horizontal rather than vertical
approach to music (that is, to Toscanini, counterpoint--the balance
of line against line--was more important than harmony), the clarity, the force, the tensile rhythms that were Toscanini's special
contribution.

     Toward the end of his career he began to encounter criti-
cism.   A new generation of critics was active, and they were looking for more from a conductor than Toscanini could supply.   His
repertoire came under heavy attack, nor was his musical philosophy
immune.   Toscanini conducted very few contemporary works; and
those he did conduct were mostly ephemera.   Nobody queried

Toscanini's amazing ability to get results from an orchestra; but, some critics asked, was the result worthwhile? Virgil Thomson, one of the doubters, wondered:

> When he conducts any work ... he knows the score and gives it as careful, as polished a reading as if his whole life depended on that single work.... His culture may be elementary, but his ear is true. He makes music out of anything. And the music that he makes is the plainest, the most straightforward music now available in public performance. There is little of historical evocation in it and even less of deliberate emotional appeal. It is purely arbitrary, just ordered sound and little else. There even isn't much Toscanini in it. For in spite of his high temperament, this musician is strangely lacking in personality. That is why, I believe, he has based his interpretative routine on as literal as possible an adherence to the musical texts.... He will not loom large, I imagine, in the history books of the future because he has mostly remained on the side lines of the creative struggle.... His involvement with the formation of our century's musical style, with the encouragement of the contemporary expression in music, with the living composers, in short, whose work will one day constitute the story of music in our time, has been less than that of any of today's orchestral great.

Thomson, as a composer and one of the leaders of the then avant-garde, was of course bothered by Toscanini's lack of involvement with contemporary music. But certainly Toscanini's record in that respect was not any worse than that of some of his contemporaries--Bruno Walter, Felix Weingartner, or Sir Thomas Beecham, for instance. Few conductors on reaching old age interest themselves in new music, and that applies even to such conductors as Otto Klemperer, who in the middle 1920s was associated with the avant-garde. As a young man, Toscanini had fought the good fight, taking up the cause of Wagner, Puccini and Debussy. In any case, conductors can, pace Thomson, live in the history books for other things than being propagandists for modern music; and Thomson's statement that Toscanini had little influence on the century's musical style is nothing more than wishful thinking. The fact is that Toscanini, who had no pupils as such and few protégés--his most promising one, Guido Cantelli, died in an airplane crash at the age of thirty-six--was the greatest influence on conducting in his time, and did more to crystallize a kind of literalism adopted by all musicians than anybody else. As such, Toscanini does indeed have a place in the history books. Almost every young conductor tried to imitate him, refusing to use a score in public, trying to achieve the Toscanini kind of linear independence, adopting a literal approach, avoiding romanticism. The world seemed full of little Toscaninis, all of whom were trying vainly to achieve the impossible. What often resulted was literalism carried to absurdity; movement without vision; music in which

technique was more important than communication. None of this
was Toscanini's wish, but that was what happened. A few of the
younger conductors were able to survive, but not many. To a
large extent, the 1960s are still in the Toscanini dominance; his
influence remains strongly felt.

The Old Man's last concert was heartbreaking. It took place
on April 4, 1954. About a week previously, on his eighty-seventh
birthday, he had sent a letter of resignation to NBC. During the
broadcast, Toscanini--he of the infallible memory--had perhaps the
only mental blackout of his life. Radio listeners heard the Bac-
chanale from Tannhäuser slow up and threaten to disintegrate.
There was a pause, and, shockingly, the strains of the Brahms
First filled the air. What had happened was that Toscanini virtually stopped beating time, standing with a vacant look on his face.
Frank Miller, the first cellist, tried to give the cues. In the control room there was panic; and Cantelli, it is said, told the engineers to cut Toscanini off and put on the Brahms recording. Within some thirty seconds or so, Toscanini recovered, and the Bac-
chanale went back on the air. The broadcast over, Toscanini went
back to his dressing room and, in effect, passed into history. He
died three years later.

LEONARD BERNSTEIN*

Harold C. Schonberg

And where were the American conductors all this time?

They were building up toward Leonard Bernstein. There
were, to be sure, a handful of American conductors in the pre-
Bernstein era. Indeed, one can go back to Ureli Corelli Hill, the
New York violinist who was a founder and first president of the
New York Philharmonic. Hill conducted the orchestra for a while.
Frank van der Stucken, by virtue of being born in Texas, could
technically be classified as an American conductor, though he really
was a Theodore Thomas in reverse. Where Thomas came here as
a child from Germany, and was American-trained, van der Stucken
was taken to Antwerp as a child and was German-trained; and
while he was active for many years in American musical affairs,
as conductor of the Cincinnati Symphony and (for a short time) of
the New York Philharmonic, he preferred Germany and spent the
last twenty years of his life there.

Shortly after the turn of the century the American composer-
conductor Henry Hadley received some attention. He conducted in

*From The Great Conductors, by Harold C. Schonberg; New York:
Simon & Schuster, 1967. Copyright 1967 by Harold C. Schonberg.
Reprinted by permission of Simon and Schuster.

Seattle, San Francisco and New York, did much to promote contemporary music and, in 1934, founded the Berkshire Music Festival.
He was a respected figure, but his conducting never made much of
an impression. There was Leon Barzin, who came to the United
States from Antwerp at the age of two, became first violist of the
New York Philharmonic and in 1930 was appointed conductor of the
National Orchestral Association. This was a training orchestra of
young musicians, and its "graduates" entered the ranks of orchestras all over the United States. There was Alfred Wallenstein,
who deserted his companions in the cello section of the New York
Philharmonic to concentrate on conducting. He had a radio program for many years, in which he had the courage to present such
esoteric items as all of the Mozart piano concertos and untold numbers of Bach cantatas. In 1943 he became conductor of the Los
Angeles Philharmonic and remained there until 1956. Still another
deserter from an orchestra was Milton Katims, the first violist of
the NBC Symphony, who took over the Seattle Symphony in 1954.
Howard Mitchell in Washington, D. C. , Izler Solomon in Indianapolis and Robert Whitney in Louisville are American-trained conductors. Whitney, thanks to a Rockefeller Foundation grant, has
probably conducted more world premieres than any living conductor.
More recently, a group of American youngsters is beginning to attract international attention, especially Thomas Schippers and Lorin
Maazel.

     When Serge Koussevitzky established the Berkshire Music
Center in 1940, he gathered unto himself some of the most gifted
young musicians in America. Thor Johnson was one; he later became conductor of the Cincinnati Symphony. Walter Hendl was
another, and he went away to become musical director of the Dallas Symphony. Lukas Foss (Berlin-born) was another of Koussevitzky's bright young men, and he has become conductor of the
Buffalo Symphony in addition to being one of the leaders of the
avant-garde.

     But none of Koussevitzky's cadets "made it" the way Leon-
ard Bernstein has. Bernstein became famous overnight and has
remained famous--a controversial figure, a showman, a romantic,
a glamour boy not fully accepted by his peers, disliked by many
critics in America and Europe throughout much of his career, yet
the most important conductor--by far--that the United States has
produced. The only native-born conductor to be musical director
of a major American orchestra, he has captured the imagination of
the public to a degree unprecedented in history. He has been accepted as the Renaissance Man: conductor, composer of serious
music, composer of successful Broadway musicals, pianist, educator, writer, poet, television personality. He symbolizes music
to the Americans, and it has been said of him that nobody loves
him but the public. This was a remark that had some validity up
to the middle 1960s, when he suddenly took Europe by storm, creating a sensation conducting Falstaff in Vienna and Mahler in London. Even in New York some of the critics began to discuss his
work in respectful terms instead of looking upon him as a

perpetual Wunderkind: "the Peter Pan of music," as the New York
Times said in 1960.

     In many respects that is what Bernstein has been--a perpet-
ual Wunderkind. But from the beginning he had the kind of hyp-
notism that Nikisch exerted, plus the glamour of the young Stokowski. Unknown until November 14, 1943--he was 25 years old then--
he stepped before the New York Philharmonic, where he was assistant conductor, and led a concert for the indisposed Bruno Walter. His career from that point took off in some kind of weird,
jet-propelled, missile-like ascent. His physical appearance had
something to do with making him a public idol. As a young man
he described himself as looking like "a well-built dope fiend," and
he retained that intense look: part visionary, part oozing with sex,
part filled with a suppressed nervousness. Above all, he managed
to give the impression of eternal youth, and that was still true
when he was almost fifty.

     He came in with the television age, and that too contributed
to his fame. His educational broadcasts, infinitely more sophisticated and infinitely less condescending than Walter Damrosch's used
to be, carried his words and his work to millions of people, all of
whom regarded him as omniscient in matters musical. He brought
to the television public a potent mixture. On the one hand he was
glamorous, romantic-looking, a "long-haired musician" who delved
into the mysteries of Beethoven and modern music. On the other
hand he was boyish, he used slang, had an urban American background, had gone to college (Harvard, '39), liked jazz. No wonder
he achieved an identification with the American psyche. Millions
of words were written about him. No greater-publicized figure
than Bernstein ever appeared on the American musical scene.

     That was one of his problems. Many thought he came up
too fast, and for years he had to fight to overcome the suspicion,
actual hostility--and jealousy, too--created among many professionals by his fantastic success at so early an age. Too much attention was paid to him; and professionals, who know only too well
how a career can be built by publicity, have a tendency to look
with suspicion on a big publicity buildup. So do many intellectuals.
Bernstein was popular, was written up in mass magazines--ergo,
there had to be something wrong with him. A man of supreme
confidence in himself, Bernstein stepped on toes and made enemies;
and there could be no denying that some of his extracurricular
activities caused a great deal of unfavorable talk: his lofty pronouncements, the kiss he gave to Jacqueline Kennedy on television,
even his flamboyant clothes. He was described as having a pre-
Copernican ego, i. e., seeing the whole world revolve around him.
Some critics believed he would never grow up. Irving Kolodin,
writing in 1964, summed up a prevalent critical feeling: "Of the
promise he had twenty years ago as a conductor, the judgment from
this bench would have to be that it has spread wider but it has not
penetrated more deeply.... Most of the time ... one gets the feeling that he gets by on facility, quickness of mind, instinct, and

that age-old endowment called chutzpah. " Chutzpah is a Yiddish
word, and it has been applied more than once to Bernstein.   It
means, roughly, gall, or nerve.   A teen-age boy murders his
parents and then pleads for clemency on the grounds that he is an
orphan.   That is chutzpah.   Kolodin concluded that if Bernstein
would only put his mind to it, he could be a conductor of the first
rank.   "But, " wrote Kolodin,

> there is equally little doubt that he is not temperamentally
> constituted to decide on such a function.   It doesn't ab-
> sorb him sufficiently, interest him enough, reward him
> adequately, to sacrifice other things at which he may be
> less adept, but which tempt him irresistibly.   There
> comes a time, inevitably, of boredom, in which all sorts
> of other impulses--theatrical, verbal, creative--come to
> dominate him.

Kolodin's words were prophetic.   In 1966 Bernstein announced that he would leave the New York Philharmonic at the end
of the 1968-69 season.   He gave as a reason his compulsion to
compose.   The Philharmonic named him "Laureate Conductor" for
life.

Bernstein himself has never disabused anybody about the
breadth of his desires.   Shortly before his appointment to the New
York Philharmonic in 1958 he proclaimed the diversity of his tastes:

> I don't want to give in and settle for some specialty.   I
> don't want to spend the rest of my life, as Toscanini did,
> studying and restudying, say, fifty pieces of music.   It
> would bore me to death.   I want to conduct.   I want to
> play the piano.   I want to write music for Broadway and
> Hollywood.   I want to write symphonic music.   I want to
> keep on trying to be, in the full sense of that wonderful
> word, a musician.   I also want to teach.   I want to
> write books and poetry.   And I think I can, and still do
> justice to them all.

He has tried.   After studying at Harvard and the Curtis Institute of Music (piano with Isabelle Vengerova, conducting with
Reiner), he went to Tanglewood and became Koussevitzky's pet at
the Berkshire Music Center.   Rodzinski engaged him as assistant
conductor with the New York Philharmonic for the 1943-44 season.
When Bernstein substituted for Walter at that famous concert, it
was front-page news.   Bernstein was invited to the Philharmonic as
guest conductor several seasons thereafter.   In the meantime he
composed the successful musical On the Town, which was an expanded version of a ballet he had written for Jerome Robbins.
From 1945 to 1948 he conducted the New York City Center Orchestra.   His three seasons there are fondly remembered as examples
of about the most stimulating symphonic concerts New York has
ever had.   Audiences heard major works of the major 20th-century
composers, plus complete novelties, plus some of the standard

repertoire. Bernstein was young and vital; his audiences were
young and enthusiastic. There was a special air of excitement at
these concerts; the atmosphere crackled like the rhythms in a
Stravinsky ballet. Bernstein spoke the language of his young orchestra and his young audience.

After resigning because of a budget cut, Bernstein did much
guest conducting. He also composed two other successful Broadway
musicals and one that did not last long--Candide. The bouncing
Candide Overture, however, has made its way into the American
symphonic repertoire, and is the only Bernstein work to do so.
His serious music has not been accepted by other conductors, and
is kept alive mainly through Bernstein's own performances. In
1958 Bernstein took over the New York Philharmonic, inheriting a
sullen orchestra and a badly disciplined one. Within a season the
orchestra began to thrive. There were mutters about the "show-
business approach" that Bernstein represented, but there was no
disputing its success. Concerts were sold out. The orchestra
played with enthusiasm. In Bernstein the players found a consid-
erate conductor with a clean-cut technique and a first-class ear.
Some members of the orchestra, especially the older men, mum-
bled about Toscanini and Mengelberg doing things differently. But
Bernstein made the Philharmonic a happy orchestra. An economic
situation, to which players are always sensitive, entered into the
picture. Bernstein proved to be a good provider. With his advent
came longer seasons (culminating in a contract that called for full
employment), added revenue from television and records, and other
emoluments. As one member of the orchestra said at the time,
"It's a positive honeymoon! As long as Lenny treats us good,
we'll treat him good. " It should be pointed out that as the years
progressed, familiarity did not breed contempt. The musicians of
the Philharmonic, a temperamental collection of prima donnas who
have worked under every great conductor, are all but unanimous
in proclaiming Bernstein's gifts. They think he is a superlative
technician, they admire his ear and his musicianship, they claim
that rhythmically he is the equal of any living conductor. Some
of the musicians have less regard for the way Bernstein approaches
the 18th- and 19th-century repertoire; but that, they say, has
nothing to do with his natural gifts.

As a young conductor, Bernstein was identified with the moderns, although he never had much sympathy for dodecaphonic music.
His performances of the classics through Brahms have never been
fully accepted. Where his ideas about Stravinsky, Strauss and
Bartók can be brilliant and sure-footed, his ideas about earlier
music have impressed many as mannered and wayward. How much
his podium mannerisms have colored critical thought is hard to
say. Probably a great deal. Bernstein is the most choreographic
of all contemporary conductors. He is a specialist in the clenched
fist, the hip swivel, the pelvic thrust, the levitation effect that
makes him hover in the air in defiance of the laws of gravity, the
uppercut, the haymaker. These wild motions juxtaposed against a
Beethoven symphony convince many that there is more to the

choreography than to the music. But even listening to Bernstein on records, where choreography is not a factor, illustrates a kind of musical approach much different from that of today's predominantly literal conductors.

For Bernstein is essentially a throwback, a romantic. He employs considerable fluctuation of tempo, often slows down for second subjects, underlines melodies, is constantly using a full palette of expressive devices that are generally scorned today. Virgil Thomson believed that Bernstein, a child of the 20th century, was uncomfortable in a 19th-century repertoire and thus had to counterfeit an emotion he did not really feel. And, indeed, there always has been something calculated about Bernstein's romanticisms. Authentic exponents of a romantic tradition--Walter, Furtwängler--almost never broke a musical line. They always kept the shape of a phrase. Bernstein, on the other hand, often does break the line. He also can, in such music as the second movement of Mahler's Second Symphony, wallow in sentimentality. A good part of this excess may have come from his impulse as an educator, as the man who explains music to the multitude. A natural pedagogue and a high-pressure musical salesman, he can be the exponent of the Big Sell as a conductor. Until recently he had a tendency to reduce his audiences to a common denominator; to play down to them, consciously or unconsciously. He seemed to think that unless he made a big thing out of a specific passage, audiences would miss the point. Look (he would in effect say), now comes the second subject of the exposition! I will have to make it clear to you that this is the second subject of the exposition! And so in his eagerness to emphasize the point, he would slow up to make sure everybody understood the difference between first and second subject. Generally the result was uncomfortably obvious and even vulgar. Similarly, in the second movement of the Mahler, Bernstein would seem to be rationalizing somewhat as follows: "I have to make them realize this is Viennese Gemütlichkeit. I will do it by slowing up and then phrasing the theme with great tenderness. I will make a Luftpause here and a rubato there. " The intentions may have been good. But the playing sounded cute, over-expressive, artificial.

In recent years there have been signs of a change. Bernstein took a sabbatical during the 1964-65 season, and when he returned to the Philharmonic it was with a new kind of confidence. The choreography was still present--that is a permanent part of Bernstein--but there also was greater reliance on the taste of the audience, a more direct approach to music, less of the obsessive exhibitionism that had so marred his work. He also began to think more and more about opera conducting. Bernstein had come to opera relatively late in his career. American-trained musicians have little opportunity to gain experience in an opera house--the route of every Austro-German conductor. Bernstein had always been around the theatre, however, and his performances at La Scala, the Metropolitan Opera and the Vienna Staatsoper had whetted his appetite. He always has had a dramatic flair, and it could be that the great part of his career is before him. Bernstein and opera would appear made for each other.

SKROWACZEWSKI:
THE UNPRONOUNCEABLE CONDUCTOR*

Michael Caracappa

The name at first is unpronounceable. But like football heroes of Polish ancestry whose unpronounceable names become household words from coast to coast, Stanislaw Skrowaczewski (pronounced "Skro-vo-chev-ski") makes his name not only more digestible to concertgoers each year, but the name has stamped him for some time as one of our first-rate conductors.

"What is amazing is that Americans, especially Americans, do very well with my name," he told me the other day, "or I suspect that maybe they spend hours or minutes learning how to pronounce it. Anyway, my name seems to give more trouble in countries like France and Italy."

The mark of a truly distinguished maestro, of course, is judged by his ability to interpret; to communicate and project; to keep the box-office people happy; to be able to extract every ounce of the razor-sharp virtuosity of his men, and by the way he handles himself as Commander-in-Chief of all that transpires on stage.

That Stanislaw Skrowaczewski was blessed with these attributes must have impressed the late George Szell who met him in Warsaw during the Cleveland's European tour in the spring of 1957, not long after Skrowaczewski had become the Warsaw Philharmonic's conductor. What Szell saw of Skrowaczewski's podium technique intrigued him, and he promptly invited him to make his American debut with the Cleveland. The Hungarian-born Szell must have seen in the Pole a model of himself, for critics here later wrote that Skrowaczewski also reminded them of the older man's temperament, style of conducting, and his uncanny ability to make his demands known to his musicians.

When Skrowaczewski made his American debut with the Cleveland on Dec. 4, 1958, he was given a standing ovation. The Christian Science Monitor, for instance, reported that "his keen musicianship was enthusiastically recognized not only by the audience but by the members of the orchestra as well. When someone said to him, 'You certainly made them sing,' Skrowaczewski replied, 'Oh no, it was they who made me sing!'"

*From the Music Journal, vol. 30, no. 1 (Jan. 1972). Reprinted by permission of the publisher.

Like Szell, Skrowaczewski is more conscious of the orchestra playing under him than of the audience in the hall. A champion of modern music, his programs at first were thought to be too bold. But there was unanimous opinion that he had made audiences sit up and take notice of the Minneapolis Symphony (now the Minnesota Symphony) as one of the finest orchestras in the world.

Skrowaczewski, whom I was interviewing at the Essex House in New York, unequivocally agrees with Pierre Boulez that today's orchestras would benefit from exotic instruments. "Absolutely," he replied in an accent still very Continental. "Such instruments could be utilized in the performance of medieval music as well as the music that followed. Adding exotic instruments would give performances a new glow, a wider scope; orchestras should have more flexibility and personality, and play more new but good music, if we are to enlarge our audience. Do you know that there are libraries in Europe with much unprinted and unknown music--some of it 300-400 years old--and that much of it has great merit? Why not bring these compositions before the public and embellish them with new sounds, which might help to expand our tired repertoire."

Skrowaczewski's achievements as a composer do not seem to have turned his head, despite the fact that he has received many awards and prizes. He speaks almost disparagingly about his four symphonies, several orchestral suites, four string quartets, a cantata, six piano sonatas, sonatas for violin and piano, a ballet, [an English] horn concerto, works for the voice and music for Polish films. His [English] horn concerto, which, by the way, is his most recent work, prompted the New York Times to write:

"All are agreed that concertos for this instrument are as rare as fish with fur. When Thomas Stacy, the English-horn player of the Minnesota, started to play, there was much interest in the exotic sounds of the instrument--at least, Skrowaczewski fully exploited those--and the soloist solved all problems with such ease of technique, so unfaltering a lip, such innate musicality, that he swept all before him."

Needless to say, there was tumultuous applause for soloist and composer. Skrowaczewski regrets that his schedule doesn't permit him to do much composing these days. "I think a composer should always be turning [out] fresh music, and unless it's very, very bad the public should have an opportunity to hear it. As you know, modern music fascinates me and I do try to introduce new works each season. Wouldn't it be wonderful if from time to time we could feature a series consisting only of music never performed before? Just think of what encouragement this would be to our young composers!"

I was particularly curious how he approaches Beethoven, Debussy, Wagner and Bartók--composers of different styles--on the same program.

"Well, it's quite easy, I think, once you start to conduct a certain composer whose style you know thoroughly. First of all, you're the interpreter and your entire wisdom of interpretation must conform to the composer's intentions. What is of paramount importance is that the conductor and the orchestra must be flexible, ready to change style from one piece to the next. Unfortunately, very few good orchestras today can switch immediately from Bach to Mahler to Sibelius to Tchaikovsky. Most of them have a hard time of it, and the conductor--like the skipper of a boat--must be able to steer them through some tricky waters. "

In the 11 years as the Minnesota's music director, Stanislaw Skrowaczewski has taken the orchestra to all corners of the globe--and, of course, I shouldn't hold it against him that his schedule doesn't permit him to appear in New York, my native city, often enough to suit me. Rather, I prefer to count instead the musical richness that he has brought to us; a high proportion of his programs extraordinary by any international standards--and many of them matchless. That Skrowaczewski's star becomes brighter is enhanced by reports reaching me that more and more soloists are increasingly anxious to appear on his programs.

On Jan. 11, 1970, the conductor made his debut at the Met in Mozart's Magic Flute, and his complete control of the stage and pit made it a memorable evening. I was rather taken aback, though, when he confided that, while he would like to continue with more operatic work if his schedule permits. "I would never do Puccini. I don't care for it. " This came as a bit of a bombshell, for I thought that Puccini was every conductor's favorite. I was reminded of the old adage: "One man's meat may be another man's poison. "

Born in Lwow, Poland, on Oct. 3, 1923, the son of a brain surgeon, Skrowaczewski studied violin, piano and composition as a lad in the local conservatory. At 8, he wrote his first symphony and overture, which were performed that year by the Lwow Philharmonic. By about 1945, after having studied at various Polish conservatories, he received diplomas in philosophy and in composition and conducting. Subsidized by a fellowship from the French Government, he went to Paris in 1947 to study composition with Nadia Boulanger and conducting with Paul Kletzki, after which he was frequently called on to appear as guest-conductor in Europe. Miss Boulanger once said of her former pupil: "He is an artist of the highest rank. "

As for musical fads, Skrowaczewski feels that each cycle runs about two years. "Musicians, for example, may favor a certain composer for about that time and then turn to someone else. Certainly, we are all entitled to our likes and dislikes. A composer may be 'in' because of his personality, recordings and high-powered publicity, but then quite suddenly he is dropped. I recall not too long ago when Bach and Vivaldi were 'in' and young people were flocking to the concerts. Later, the harpsichord was 'in' and such concerts drew large crowds.   In the 20's and 30's, violin recitals were the big thing.   Since then, pianists dominate the scene.   Do you recall when Debussy and Ravel were constantly programed?   Alas, they now seem to be relegated to the shelf. What I'm trying to say is that musical fads change like the weather. "

Concerning a shortage of string players--a problem that has plagued conductors during the last 15 years--the maestro pointed out that the situation had eased a bit about two years ago.   "It seems that since then the music schools are turning out young graduates who are better qualified than they had been previously. Most of my colleagues agree that the schools were drumming them out too fast and the kids weren't quite ready to meet high professional standards. "

Casually attired in a gray checkered sports jacket and maroon turtle-neck sweater, Skrowaczewski made these remarks at his hotel as he was preparing to return to Minneapolis to work out the details of Mahler's Das Klagende Lied for orchestra, soloists and chorus, which includes a recently uncovered movement and which he will introduce in New York and other cities this season. As he was talking, I thought back to a concert of his I had heard not too long ago when during the intermission I overheard a young thing say to her escort: 'Skrowaczewski may not have much sex appeal, but I find him irresistible just the same.... "

Sex appeal or not, Skrowaczewski is a slim, engaging man and fluent in several languages.   His English is excellent, although a subtle thought may occasionally demand a difficult word that is likely to come out in German, French or Italian as well as in his native Polish.   He is all attention as he listens to a question or comment.   One can see the moment of reflection as he ponders a reply.   Then he leans forward to emphasize his answer and shows his intense concern with the subject.   His eyes are a shade of blue that even dark, horn-rimmed glasses cannot hide and every gesture of head and hands betrays a kind of smooth-flowing physical vitality.

Formerly a sports-car buff, he also won prizes in professional skiing competitions.   He married Krystyna Jarosz, a romance philologist on September 6, 1956.   They had met on a skiing vacation in the Carpathian Mountains.   "I kept falling down and he kept picking me up, " she once recalled.   They have three children.   Skrowaczewski has made it a habit most of his life to be picking up things--like the rich blessings that have come to us through a man whose baton has made the earth a better place for us.

SOLTI AND CHICAGO:
A MUSICAL ROMANCE*

(Time Staff)

The idealized symphonic conductor has Leonard Bernstein's
flair, Herbert von Karajan's grace and Zubin Mehta's youth. But
when the directors of the Chicago Symphony Orchestra cast around
for a conductor to save their troubled orchestra in 1968, they
threw out all the stereotypes and selected a man who looked, according to one Chicago musician, like a "tennis player or short-
stop or golfer" on the podium.   He was also bald and aging. Looks
aside, Sir Georg Solti and the Chicago Symphony were made for
each other.   Together they are producing some of the world's most
exciting music.

In the relatively brief span of four seasons, Solti (pronounced
Sholtee) has brought the Chicago back to the preeminence of its days
under Fritz Reiner (1953-1963).   The Solti sound, not the sound of
trouble, is the talk of the music world.   Indeed there has not been
such excitement about a marriage of conductor and orchestra in the
U.S. since the golden days of the 1930s when Toscanini led the
New York Philharmonic, Stokowski the Philadelphia and Koussevitzky the Boston.   In recent years, only George Szell and the Cleveland Orchestra have approached the august virtuosity, combustible
power and quartet-like intimacy that Solti has established with the
Chicago Symphony.   The advent of Solti in Chicago, as he himself
puts it with characteristic bluntness, "was like awakening the sleep-
ing princess."   At age 60, Solti may be forgiven for depicting himself as Prince Charming for the simple reason that almost everyone
agrees with him.

Hosannas.   Until his arrival the Chicago, heavy with German tradition, was known as a great orchestra that only rarely
gave a great performance.   Now it is an ensemble that Solti can
(as he did two seasons ago) take into such musical bastions as
Vienna, Berlin and Hamburg, and win standing ovations from the
public and hosannas from the stuffiest critics.   The money for that
European tour was raised largely by Symphony Board Chairman
Louis Sudler, as part of a campaign to publicize the board's selection of Solti.   That choice was made, says Sudler, a Chicago re-
altor, on the basis of "just what a good businessman would do.
First you get the best possible product, then you let the world know
that you have the best possible product."   The first dividend was a
homecoming parade in 1971, arranged for the entire orchestra.   It
was enthusiastically promoted by Mayor Richard Daley, with Solti
riding high and proud in a lead car--and not all that common in
Chicago, folks actually carrying violins in their violin cases.

*Reprinted by permission from Time, the weekly newsmagazine,
May 7, 1973.   Copyright 1973 by Time Inc.

Then the money--lack of which had put the orchestra on a disaster alert prior to Solti's arrival--began to come in. Annual donations by individuals rose dramatically from $425,919 in 1968 to $1,607,846 last year, corporate contributions from $60,000 in 1966 to $500,000. As a result, the orchestra's endowment fund is now comfortably at a level of $7 million, and last year's deficit was a mere $74,000, lowest since the pre-crisis year of 1963. Last week, the city's music lovers were crammed excitedly into Orchestra Hall for Solti's concert performance of Act III of Wagner's Die Götterdämmerung.

They witnessed a true musical event. Tenor Jess Thomas died magnificently as Siegfried, and the audience could almost feel the flames as Soprano Helga Dernesch submitted herself to Brünnhilde's immolation. It was a remarkable performance, a fitting finish to Solti's successful spring stint in Chicago. If Chicagoans needed any reminder, the spirited and darkly dramatic rendition of Götterdämmerung demonstrated anew that there is not an opera house orchestra anywhere that can match the Chicago under Solti.

Solti's love for the orchestra, and its for him, is obvious. "It's a marvelous thing to be musically happily married," he says. "I am and I know. I'm a romantic type of musician, and this is a romantic orchestra. That is our secret: at a time when everybody is doing exactly the opposite, we are unafraid to be romantic. "

Romantic for Solti means a predominance of German and Austrian music (ranging all the way from Haydn to Wagner, Mahler and Strauss), plus an orchestral tone that is big and red-blooded but not as luxuriant, say, as the Philadelphia Orchestra under Eugene Ormandy. As much as he relishes the Sequoia-like majesty of the Chicago's brass section, and its evergreen forest of strings, Solti is equally partial to the meadowed tranquillity of the woodwinds. The delicate lyricism he conjures up between oboe and English horn in the pastoral movement of Berlioz's "Symphonie Fantastique" would be welcome at a chamber music recital. Yet for all his romantic predilections, Solti expertly manipulates the arcane configurations of such moderns as Arnold Schoenberg and Elliott Carter.

Solti is an orchestral architect much in the Toscanini mold. He is not one to pause sentimentally over a favorite melody or chord. The long line is everything. Such basic tools as rhythm and dynamic shading are used to sculpt breathtaking new shapes. His phrasing is at times so tight that it often seems the music is moving more quickly than it actually is. "The things that intrigue me are how to make forms clear," he says, "how to hold a movement together, or if I am conducting opera, how to build an act or a scene. " These are traits that produce masterfully cohesive performances of old masters like Wagner, or such Angst-prone postromantics as Mahler and Bruckner. It was Mahler's craggy Fifth Symphony that gave Solti and the Chicago Symphony the first chance

to demonstrate their extraordinary combined talents to New York
audiences.   So stunningly powerful was their 1970 performance in
Carnegie Hall that the Manhattanites yelled, stomped and cheered
for 20 minutes: it might have gone on all night had not Solti led
the concertmaster offstage with one grateful but resolute wave.

Such ovations have become familiar to Solti throughout the
U. S. and Europe.   In addition to conducting the Chicago Symphony
for twelve weeks this season, he devoted ten weeks to the Orchestre de Paris (he also serves as its music director).   A month ago,
at the 700-seat Opéra Louis XV at the Versailles Palace, he led
an exquisitely wrought performance of Mozart's Marriage of Figaro
by the Paris Opéra (he serves as that company's music adviser).
In London, which he calls home these days, Solti regularly guest-
conducts the London Philharmonic for a month each year.

Starburst.   In virtually every musical capital of the world,
the sight of Solti conducting is a familiar one.   It is quite a spectacle: head down, baton held high, tails flying, he seems to spring
from the wings.   The leap to the podium is agile and sure; the
bow to the audience curt, formal and, in the European tradition,
from the waist, with the heels brought together in something just
this side of a click.   At this point, a Stokowski would spin showily
and attack immediately.   Not Solti.   He turns thoughtfully, spreads
his feet and shoots slitty glances around to make sure all is ready.
Then, with a slashing, totally unexpected paroxysm involving every
part of his body, he gives the downbeat.   Throughout the performance, Solti's body language is dramatically explicit.   The violins
are brought in with huge lefthanded scoops to the floor.   The
trumpets are cued by the riveting spear of an arm and index finger.
A starburst of fingers summons the crash of the cymbals.   Moments of lyrical romance come with the left hand cradled near the
heart, the right hand beating coronas of love high above.   Passages
of staccato brilliance are paced by chopping up and down with both
arms.   A furious backhand indicates a sforzando attack; a hand
moving slowly across his mouth implores the players to give him
a soft sound.

His gestures may at times seem overlarge, but they are no
mere sideshow to titillate the audience.   Solti is all business on
the podium, his energies totally focused on the orchestra.   He
eschews any useless movement.   A purring passage that does not
have any tricky entrances usually finds Solti barely conducting at
all.   Says Chicago Oboeist Ray Still, "When everything is going
fine, he doesn't interfere with the orchestra by going into a lot of
acrobatics to make the audience think it's his struggling which is
producing such fine music. "

Often, though, his hours on the podium are indeed a strug-
gle--in unexpected ways.   The years of conducting with arms carried high in tension, or head held tilted back to watch his performers on operatic nights, have produced extensive muscle damage to
Solti's shoulders and neck.   If he sometimes does a spectacular

180° leap from the violins way off on the left to the double basses on the right, it is because he has to. "I can not move my head more than a few inches to the left or right without turning my body," he says. There are other problems too. Solti was flailing away so furiously during a recording session of Parsifal last year that he stabbed himself in the left hand with his baton and had to be rushed to a hospital to have the point removed.

On the podium, Solti defies a current vogue: he regularly conducts from a score. That any number of young and not-so-young conductors think they must conduct from memory, he blames on Toscanini: "Why did Toscanini conduct from memory? Because he was nearsighted. Of course, he had that fabulous memory, but that wasn't really why he never used a score. Today we have an entire generation of young conductors who think they must conduct from memory--all because Toscanini was nearsighted. It is total lunacy."

Such commonsensical candidness has endeared Solti to musicians; that endearment goes a long way toward explaining his success. Without the loyalty and respect of his musicians, no conductor can long preside over an orchestra--much less produce great music. Musicians are notoriously independent, as the old saw about the French flutist demonstrates. Ordered by a conductor to play in a certain style, the musician said: "Very well, I'll play it his way at rehearsal, but just wait till the concert. After all, mon ami, it's my flute." With Solti, it is different. Says Orchestre de Paris Flutist Michel Debost: "I may not like his music making, but I play it the way he wants because I can't resist him." Apart from his candor, orchestras respond to Solti partly because of his personal combination of warmth and frost, partly because of his seemingly endless store of energy and intensity. "With Solti there's always this momentum going," says Jay Friedman, principal trombonist of the Chicago. "The architecture of a piece of music always comes across. Even in very slow passages you're never standing still. I think it's because something metaphysical happens. The music he makes seems to transcend what he does physically." So much so, notes one Chicago woodwind player, that "during rehearsals Solti gets so worked up, the motion is so violent, that his navel is almost always exposed."

If Solti has a weakness it is that as a colorist he prefers primary hues to the shades in between. The delicate pastels of French impressionists like Debussy and Ravel simply seem to be beyond him. Yet one can never rule out any possibility with Solti-- even his becoming a master of the tender brush stroke. The Beethoven represented by his new recording with the Chicago of the Ninth Symphony (London) is significantly deeper and technically nearer perfection than the Beethoven he recorded more than ten years ago with the Vienna Philharmonic. [In May 1973] London issues his Parsifal. Serene, mystical, glowingly colored and, by the way, the slowest in stereo, it is a pantheonic accomplishment he could not have matched a decade ago.

Solti today has a depth, a broader grasp and surer hand
than ever.   Still intense and energetic by any standards, he nonetheless is mellower, more at ease.   Birgit Nilsson, the supreme
Wagnerian soprano, notes: "In his early days he was so energetic,
so impulsive.   He built one climax on top of another.   You felt
like you were going to explode.   Now he knows how to relax. "

No two musicians ever look at a conductor in exactly the
same way.   Where Friedman sees the metaphysical and Nilsson a
mellower Solti, Flutist Debost sees the diabolical: "There is
something of the wolf or the Hun about Solti.   As he conducts, his
eyes turn into cracks, his ears become pointed, and you can sort
of imagine him riding a horse bareback across the steppes. "

That sort of fancy is based on the knowledge that Solti is a
native of Hungary, the land of Magyars.   He comes from a family
of bakers who had lived in the small Hungarian village of Balatön-
fokájar since the 16th century.   His father Mores left the village
in search of opportunities in the grain business and then real estate ('both with very little success, " his son recalls); he set himself up in Budapest, where Gyuri (the diminutive of the Hungarian
version of George) Solti was born October 21, 1912.

At the age of five or six, it was discovered that Gyuri had
absolute pitch.   That prompted his teachers to send word home
that the boy ought to have music lessons.   Mores and Momma
Theres scraped together enough money for an old piano, and Gyuri
went at it with his typically fierce intensity.   "I was--and am--a
very determined little fellow, " says Solti.   By the time he was
twelve, the prodigy was giving recitals.   At 13 he enrolled in the
Franz Liszt Academy, Hungary's leading college of music, where
he studied with Ernst von Dohnányi and Béla Bartók.   The latter
would eventually become one of the century's leading composers,
and Solti one of his major interpreters.

Dirty Jobs.   As a prodigy of the piano, says Solti, "it was
absolutely logical that I should become a pianist. "   Instead, at age
18 he went to work at the Budapest State Opera to become a conductor.   Why?   'I can only say that deep in your heart, if you are
a sensitive person, you know what your strength is.   And I knew
mine was conducting. "

Deep in his heart was where the conducting was to stay for
some time.   For much of the next decade, he worked in the opera
house doing "all the dirty jobs, " coaching singers, positioning
scenery, accompanying the nonorchestral stage rehearsals.   Solti
got his first big break in Budapest on March 11, 1938, when he
was allowed to conduct Mozart's The Marriage of Figaro.   The
first act went well, Solti recalls, but with the start of the second
act, the singers started making mistakes while the audience grew
raucously restless.   To his relief Solti later learned that his conducting was not the cause: word had reached the audience that
Hitler was on his way into Vienna, only 130 miles away.

A Jew, Solti fled to Switzerland in 1939 and lived out the war there, boning up on his piano, winning first prize in the Concours International at Geneva, and developing a reputation as both soloist and chamber-music player. In 1945, then 33, desperately in search of an opportunity to conduct, Solti got word that Pianist Edward Kilenyi, an American who had studied in Budapest back in the 1920s (and whom Solti had got to know then), was the music-control officer for the U.S. occupation forces in Bavaria. Solti shot off a letter to Kilenyi and ended up with the job of music director of the Munich State Opera. Though his experience was practically nonexistent for such a position, there were few other conductors around who could pass the Allies' denazification screening. As head of a major European opera house, Solti had exactly one work in his conducting repertory--the 1938 Figaro. No one in Munich knew that except Solti and, as he recalls now, "I took great care to conceal my rather limited repertory. It was not for several years that Munich began to discover that I was conducting everything for the first time. "

By 1948 Solti was guest-conducting in Italy and Vienna. Two years later he conducted the London Philharmonic, and in 1952 he moved from Munich to become general music director of the Frankfurt Opera. He had nine good years there (44 new productions), but in terms of his international career, it was records that brought him prominence. His 1957 recording of Wagner's Die Walküre with Kirsten Flagsted, Set Svanholm and the Vienna Philharmonic, was so successful that it prompted English Decca (London Records in the U.S.) to engage him to embark upon the complete Ring cycle, a prodigious undertaking that was not completed until 1965.

Outraged. Though Solti first visited the U.S. in 1953 to conduct the San Francisco Opera, it was not until 1960 that he was offered an American orchestra. The experience was a disaster. Solti was hired by the Los Angeles Philharmonic as chief conductor, only to learn that a young conductor from India named Zubin Mehta had been chosen as his assistant--without his consent. Solti quit. Nothing against Mehta, says Solti, but a matter of principle. "If I had given in on this one point, it would never have been the same. I wasn't happy then at all, no, not a bit. But today I am grateful. Because if I'd stayed on at Los Angeles, I wouldn't have Chicago, and where would I be then? "

His humiliation was considerably soothed by his ascendancy to the directorship of England's Royal Opera at Covent Garden in 1961. Still something of a diamond in the rough, the Generalmusik-direktor of the Munich and Frankfurt operas had trouble adjusting to the British predilection for requesting rather than demanding. Recalls John Culshaw, producer of the Solti Ring cycle: "With such a bundle of energy who drives himself so hard, you either give him total loyalty or you can't stand him. " Among those who could not stand him at first were the members of the chorus, outraged that he refused to meet their delegates for discussions of working conditions. The audiences were at times as difficult.

They would treat Solti to an occasional heckle and boo, and one night during Der Rosenkavalier a cabbage plunked down on the stage with the inscription: "Solti must go. "

Solti did not go. In fact, it quickly became clear that he was not quite the ogre his Germanic brusqueness suggested. The musicians soon realized his remarkable talents and total dedication. They fondly began collecting "Soltiisms" that result from his frenzied blend of Hungarian, German and English. Examples: "Dis is it as ve vould never did it. " To signify that the chorus was a bit muddy: "Here we have ze swimming. " Running up to compliment a stand-in singer on his performance, he cried: "Congratulations, I thought it would be twice as bad. "

Under Solti, Covent Garden had its most dynamic presence since the days of Sir Thomas Beecham in the 1930s. Aside from Karajan at Vienna, no other opera house was headed by a musician of Solti's caliber. When he took over, Solti proclaimed that "I have only one desire: to make Covent Garden the best opera house in the world. " By the time he left in 1971, he had almost succeeded, and there was no one to dispute his right to the knighthood bestowed by the Queen a year later, shortly after he had become a British citizen.

Throughout his tour at Covent Garden, Solti was taking on polish--largely due to his first wife Hedi whom he had met during the war in Switzerland. Hedi was formal, proper, acutely aware of class structure; once they were situated in London, she began seeing to it that Solti mingled with the right titles. Friends recall the day that Solti was to have tea in a lordly London home. Hedi had spent all day rehearsing him on the fine points of an English tea. Except, that is, for the sugar tongs: Solti squeezed them too tightly, and his sugar cube popped into the breast pocket of Covent Garden's administrator, the late Sir David Webster.

Hedi managed him, mothered him--and watched their marriage fall apart. "We were still young when we married, and we just grew in different ways, " says Solti today. Whatever the reason, Solti was soon known as the possessor of a wandering eye. All the old jokes about the casting couch were dragged out. There was gossip that he gave his paramours a white fur coat--and that there was an exorbitant number of white-coated women around London.

His eye finally settled in 1964 when, at 52, he met and fell in love with Valerie Pitts, 27, a reporter sent to interview him for BBC-TV. They lived together for two years ("It was a violent affair, " understates Solti) until Hedi and Valerie's husband James Sargant, a theater executive, obtained divorces in 1966. Solti and Valerie married the next year. Hedi now is married to Patrick O'Shea, a landowner in Ireland.

Hedi had begun the taming of the Magyar and Valerie now

completed the process.   When he was in one of his intense moods,
relaxed, unassuming Valerie went her own sweet way, and that,
surprisingly, unwound him.   She never debunked him, and, more
important, never inflated him.   In short, says Solti's American
Manager Ann Colbert, "Valerie took him off the pedestal."   The
aura of happy domesticity sits well on Solti these days.   He has
even been known to end an evening's rehearsal early to go home
and tuck his first child, Daughter Gabrielle, now 3, into bed.

        Though spectacular on the podium, he is just plain Georg in
real life.   Where Karajan tools around in a flashy sports car, Solti
drives a Volvo sedan.   Where Bernstein emerges from a concert
in a flowing cape, Solti strolls out in a faded turtleneck.   He prefers mineral water to wine, and his daily drink is usually a Scotch
just after the concert and before his late-night supper; he never
eats before conducting.

        Night life for him means his concert, or a small meal and
game of bridge with friends.   He abhors the violence on American
TV--but is consumed by the violence of English football.   When in
London he can regularly be found watching soccer on the BBC.

        He also watches the stock market.   That is not surprising,
considering his wealth.   Solti's combined earnings from concerts
and recordings now probably exceed a quarter-million dollars a
year.   Royalties from his disks, spurred by the popularity of his
Ring and Mahler cycles, have risen drastically in the past several
years; he is comforted by the knowledge that if anything happened
to him ("Look, I am 60 after all"), future royalties would certainly
assure his young family a good income for at least the next 15
years.   Yet signs of wealth are extremely hard to detect in his
life-style.   When they come, extravagances are usually a $50
clock for Gabrielle, or the $1,000 phone bill he racks up each
month when on tour, partly for business but partly also to hear
his daughter say "Da da."

        Solti talks regularly of slowing down.   He notes that Gabri-
elle will be five in 1975 and ready for a stable home and school
life.   Also, he and Valerie are expecting a second child this
month.   Like fatherhood, though, Solti's biggest successes have
come late in life and, while mellower now, he is going as hard
today as he did as a handyman at the Budapest opera 40 years
ago.   This week he brings the Chicago into New York for two sold-
out concerts at Carnegie Hall, then on to Texas, Arizona, New
Mexico and California.   In July he will be back in the pit at Covent
Garden conducting Bizet's Carmen.   He will stay on in London to
record Mozart's Cosí fan tutte and Puccini's La Bohème; then after
a month's vacation he will return to Chicago for concerts, and begin recording more Beethoven symphonies.   On it goes.   His engagements already run into 1977.   Perhaps then he will be ready
to slow down, but no one is betting on it.   After all, notes a
friend, Toscanini is one of Solti's heroes--and he conducted until
he was 87.

DO JET-SET CONDUCTORS
LOWER QUALITY?*

Paul Hume

When Seiji Ozawa was busy explaining to the members of
the San Francisco Orchestra, of which he is music director, just
how he was going to continue in that post and at the same time
take the same position with the Boston Symphony, he said, among
other things:

"I don't have to work in the old style when the musical director stays with one orchestra completely for 20-25 weeks.
Times have changed because of jets, and the audience needs more
variety onstage. "

I wonder.

Take a look at the orchestras of this country which are now
regarded as the greatest in the world, those of Boston, Chicago,
New York, Philadelphia and, with a large question mark over its
head, Cleveland.

Boston's greatness, begun by such geniuses as Nikisch,
Muck, and Monteux, reached its finest heights during the 25-year
tenure of Serge Koussevitsky. During those years, Koussy, dis-
daining the many offers that constantly poured in on him from all
over the world to guest conduct, made it a rule to spend all of his
time with his great Bostonians and, in turn, to limit sharply the
number of guest conductors invited to lead from his podium.

In Chicago, the orchestra begun by Theodore Thomas in
1891, lived out its first 50 years with only two conductors:
Thomas and his successor, Frederick Stock, who raised the orchestra to superb heights by working with it practically exclusively
for 37 years.

Or take the Philadelphia Orchestra where Eugene Ormandy
will, during the coming season, equal Stock's record for longevity
as a conductor and at the same time stretch to 60 the number of
years during which that peerless orchestra has been led chiefly by
two men: Ormandy, and his famed predecessor, Leopold Stokowski.

Cleveland's case is much like that of Boston. Profiting
from the leadership of Rodzinski for 10 years, it developed, in the
quarter-century that George Szell was its head, into an ensemble
that some called the greatest in the world.

---

*From The Washington Post, April 30, 1972. Reprinted by per-
mission of the publisher.

Of the five great American orchestras, the New York Philharmonic is the one which has consistently engaged more guest conductors, has enjoyed periods of greatness at times when men such as Toscanini and Bernstein made it their principal business, and suffered severe lapses in years when it was led by a steady procession of too many less-gifted guests in too short a time.

There is a corollary to the Philharmonic's history that is worth noting, especially in view of a comment by Georg Solti last week when he was discussing the whole business of guest conductors. "It is not that guest conductors are bad for an orchestra," he said, "but only that it is bad for an orchestra to have bad guests."

Thus it is true that some years the Philharmonic, sharing its platform with Toscanini and those whom he invited, did not fall into bad habits when those guests were men such as Mengelberg, Furtwängler, Beecham, Reiner, Krauss, Kleiber, Stokowski, Walter and Klemperer, all of whom appeared with the orchestra during Toscanini's great decade from 1925 to 1935.

Such great leaders were able to visit New York because in those days the European orchestras which they regularly led did not make heavy demands on their time. But today, as everyone notes who discusses any aspect of the international music scene, the jet airplane has changed things.

But Solti posed the question that is still the central one, a question that Ozawa, naturally, did not face. Solti asked, "Where are the good conductors these days?" He is looking only for a man good enough to fill a month's absence now facing Chicago by the decision of Carlo Maria Giulini to conduct there one month instead of two.

Ozawa's comment was "Times have changed because of jets, and the audience needs more variety on stage." That argument does not seem to hold water if you ask the audience who listened raptly to the music produced by Szell, Ormandy, Solti, Koussevitsky, or Reiner, men who stayed with their orchestras long enough and closely enough to give them not only singular greatness but also a musical personality strong enough that each orchestra had its own identity, style and sound that could be identified as coming from Cleveland, Philadelphia, Boston, or Chicago.

This is an invaluable and inseparable part of an orchestra's greatness. Otherwise, we would not hear any difference in listening to Orchestra X or Y, and music would become in a disturbing way de-personalized.

Solti was emphatic at one point when he said of our orchestras that there were more than the five great ones. "I could name 10 more that are on a very high level." He did not offer to specify which ones he had in mind, but they would probably come from some 10 of these: Los Angeles, Pittsburgh, Detroit, Minnesota, Washington, San Francisco, Cincinnati, Houston, St. Louis, Baltimore, Miami, or Buffalo, for each one of which there are advocates willing to rank them with the "big five. "

What Ozawa did not say, but what is nevertheless demonstrably true, alas, is that the jet plane enables conductors to fly all over the orchestral world conducting the same small repertoire in each city they visit.

The greater problem for orchestras seeking musical greatness is that unless a conductor with a real genius for teaching an orchestra greatness in technique and style--and many conductors lack this completely--will come stay with the players until, like Koussevitsky and Stock and Ormandy and Bernstein, he knows not only the players' names but their personalities, their problems and their strengths, he will not be able to improve their playing, their morale, or their sense of a unique ensemble.

Even the great orchestras of Chicago, Boston and New York have known times of sheer musical disaster when their boards of directors turned them over, always for wildly ridiculous reasons, to conductors who were infinitely small in their inability to bring forth greatness. This is unfair to both audiences and players alike. It is a danger measurably increased by the jet age and the prevalence of inferior guest conductors. Washington's orchestra has felt its nearness too much in the past two seasons and its progress has been slowed down.

True greatness is today much nearer to the National Symphony than it has ever been before. With its new hall, its new conductor and manager, and a board of directors more enlightened and effective than those of the past, the orchestra should be able to find the way to that stature which has so long evaded it. Those orchestras which possess it have shown a pattern that still seems the one sure way.

ORCHESTRAL TONE*

Leopold Stokowski

Without Tone there would be no Music, because Tone is just as essential to music as Color is to Painting. The palette of a painter can have a full range of basic colors, and a master painter can combine these into unending combinations and contrasts of blended colors. The same is true of the modern orchestra, where the variety and contrast of tone color is endless. It is true that some players and some conductors believe there is only one kind

*From Symphony, February 1951.

of "good" tone, and one kind of "bad" tone. But I believe there are several kinds of "bad" tone, and hundreds of kinds of "good" tone. The problem for the orchestral player is to find the appropriate kind of tone for each style of music, and for each phrase that he plays. The appropriate tone for Mozart is unsuitable for Brahms. They can both be "good" tone, but totally different. Even the same composer will need different kinds of tone as his creative powers unfold. For example, the early symphonies of Mozart require a pure, transparent, light tone--the later symphonies (after he was influenced by the Mannheim School) need a more brilliant, sunny, exuberant tone--the last symphonies, and above all the "Requiem," require a deeper tone to express the great depth of feeling in these masterpieces. Particularly in the "Requiem," the "Dies Irae" and "Rex Tremendae" need a profound, heavy, menacing tone, utterly different from early Mozart.

How to draw from the instrument these many different kinds of tone? The answer to this question is extremely complex, because every player is different, and every instrument is different. Certain basic principles concerning tone, which I shall mention later, will always govern all the different kinds of tone, but each player will find his own way to be master of the full range of tone, in accordance with his mental and psychological personality, and according to the possibilities of his instrument. For example, all violins are different. Of all the hundreds of good violins in the world, no two are alike. All bows are different--their elasticity, lightness, firmness, responsiveness, vary--so that no two are alike. In playing Bach's music, it must be remembered that he used the pre-Tourte bow, probably the Tartini or Corelli type. Bach played a Stainer violin, and the bow he used was probably more adapted to polyphonic music and the playing on three (or even four) strings at a time than the Tourte bow. In Bach's time the flute, oboe, English horn (Bach orchestrated for a kind of alto oboe called Taille, or Oboe da Caccia, which had about the same range as our modern English horn, but was very different in tone quality), bassoon, horn (corno da caccia), trumpet (clarin), were all different in tone quality from our instruments of today, so that when we play his music with our modern instruments it sounds quite different from the way he heard it. Not only are our modern instruments different in tone from those for which the great masters conceived their music, but most modern instruments vary when played by different players. For example, all oboe players produce a different tone, even when playing on the same make of instrument. The same is true of flute, English horn, clarinet, bass clarinet, bassoon and contrabassoon players. The same is true, although perhaps to a slightly lesser extent, of all horn, trumpet, trombone, and tuba players. The reason is that all players are physically and psychologically different. Wind players differ in the formation of the lips and in the control of the muscles governing the lips and the lungs. String players differ in their left hand technique, and particularly in their control of the bow through the muscles and nerves of the bow arm, wrist, hand, and fingers. Even more important is the fact that all players vary in their mental attitude toward music, in their emotional response, and in their control over their nervous systems. These variations are caused by the differences in their musical and general education, in their environment and experiences as little children, and in all the characteristics they inherit from their ancestors.

Because of all the fundamental differences in players, personalities, no standardized rules will fit all players, but certain qualities are essential. First, the player must love music, and be devoted to and enthusiastic about his instrument. No technical skill or professional experience can take the place of love of music. Second, he must enjoy drawing a beautiful tone from his instrument, and varying that tone with a thousand gradations of tone color, according to the style of the music he is playing. Third, he must be sensitive to the poetic mood of all kinds of music.

Strings

For symphonic music, opera, radio, recording, and chamber music, the kind of tone that is suitable, and the technical resources that are necessary, are in many ways different. For symphonic music, violins, violas, and cellos need a wide range of tone-color, including brilliant, dark, metallic, velvety, transparent, solid, light and floating tone, heavy and thick, intense with quick narrow vibrato, relaxed with scarcely any vibrato, extremely soft but carrying, richly warm and sunny. These are only a few of the tone colors the immense range of symphonic music requires. The double basses have many tonal problems. One of the greatest is to produce enough depth to the fundamental tone being played. As everyone knows, each tone that is played by any instrument is a composite tone, composed of the fundamental tone (which is the note that is written in the part) and of the harmonics which sound above this fundamental tone. The fundamental tones of the double bass are sometimes weak in relation to the harmonics, so that actually we hear more of the harmonics than the fundamental. Good players who have good instruments know how to penetrate down into the fundamental tone, so that it is louder than any of the harmonics above it.

Woodwinds

Flutes need a full rich tone in the low register when they have an important solo passage, and the accompanying instruments are thickly or heavily orchestrated. But some solo passages in the lower register need a soft floating tone, that is like a mysterious whisper. Sometimes composers write for a pianissimo tone in in the extremely high register. Because the composer does not fully understand the nature of the instrument, he asks for something in this case that is almost humanly impossible. An approximation is all that can be achieved, even by the greatest flute players. The alto flute should not be over-blown, and yet should have

great fullness of tone.   Composers sometimes accompany an alto
flute solo so thickly that its tone is submerged by the orchestration.   Some scores ask for a pianissimo in the lowest register of
the oboe.   This is against the nature of the instrument.   The result is that the tones stand out, and do not blend with the other instruments that are playing pianissimo at the same time.   The nostalgic, romantic, melancholy tone of the English horn should be
strongly differentiated from the oboe tone.   Personally, I like
vibrato in both these instruments, but that is a matter of individual
preference.   The clarinet has a rich range of tone colors--deep
and somber in the low register, with magical delicacy in the middle ("break" or "throat") register when played pianissimo--brilliant
yet full and round in the high register--expressive in the medium
high register.   The bass clarinet and bassoon need a delicate pressure on the reed so that it vibrates freely--when the pressure is
too tense and the muscles are rigid, the tone becomes choked and
its full beauty is lessened.   In my opinion, the pressure should be
just enough that the reed vibrates.   More pressure prevents the
reed from vibrating freely, and makes the tone less full.   The
lowest tones of the contrabassoon are often a problem for two reasons.   (1) The vibrations of the reed are so slow that the listener
hears them separately.   The result is that the reed noise is sometimes louder than the musical tone.   (2) The harmonics often
sound louder than the fundamental tone so that a true depth of tone
is not achieved.   The high register of the contrabassoon can be
very beautiful in the hands of a good player, and has been neglected
by composers.   It is very different in character from the corresponding tones (in pitch) of the bassoon.   In my opinion, certain
bold passages with strong, savage accents would sound better
played by a double bass Sarrusophone in C or B flat.

Brass

The horn has an endless range of tone color--romantic,
rustic, heroic, mellow, metallic, cuivré, dreamily soft, assertive,
velvety, sinister and threatening (when stopped with the hand and
the breath pressure increased), distant and mysterious when muted
and played pianissimo, in other fortissimo passages triumphant and
jubilant.   According to the character of the music played, the
trumpet can have many tone colors--extremely brilliant and cutting
(the French type of trumpet best produces this tone), heroic and
martial, soft and full (the B Flat Flügelhorn, the same size as the
trumpet, but with a wider bore, best produces this).   The tone of
the muted trumpet is an important addition to the orchestral palette.   Of the many kinds of mutes, one will give a metallic,
razor-edge, sarcastic tone when played with intense wind pressure
--another a distant, mysterious timbre, as if coming from a
dream-world, when played pianissimo--others a voluptuous, warm
color.   There are endless developments possible to mutes with
players who have imagination.   The trombones have three major
colors, extremely brilliant (French type)--more mellow (German
type), muted, with many degrees and variations between.   Theo-
retically, the tuba is supposed to be the bass of the trombone

section, but its tone character is quite different.   The tuba is a
most important instrument in the orchestra because, in the hands
of a good player, its deep fundamental tones are full, and give a
firm foundation to the tutti of the orchestra.   In piano and mezzo
forte passages, its quality makes a better bass to the horn section
than it does to the trombones, in my opinion.   The modern orchestra needs a fourth trombone with valves, made of light metals,
built in F or low C.   This would give a true bass to the trombones
and trumpets, forming a unified, brilliant, brass choir.   The
Kontrabassposaune of Wagner's Nibelungenring was too heavy and
cumbersome.

Percussion

Timpani have immense tonal possibilities.   There is no reason why the lower range cannot extend down to low C, and the upper range can easily reach "middle C," so that two octaves are
possible instead of the one of Beethoven's time.   The tonal possibilities with these two octaves are limitless, but the player must
be a poet with soaring imagination.   Few composers understand
the potentialities of Timpani, so that the part put before the player
looks dry and mechanical.   The player must be sensitive to everything that is sounding from the whole orchestra, in order to adjust
his part to the total expression of the whole orchestra.   This
ranges from a mute, sobbing murmer (as in Wagner's Götterdämmerung) to the thunderous cataclysm in the finale of Brahms'
First Symphony.   By the use of different sticks and heads, by mut-
ing with various materials or with the hand, by striking different
parts of the head, hundreds of qualities of sound are possible to
Timpani.   It all depends on the player.   A wealth of tonal possibilities are also endless from the bass drum, castagnettes, Celeste,
chimes, cymbals, Glockenspiel, marimbaphone, snare drum, tambourine, tam tam, tenor drum, triangle, vibraharp, xylophone.
All these instruments need intensive study on the part of composer
and player to discover their full possibilities.

Other Instruments

The harp is often written for as if it were a piano.   But the
true nature of the harp is quite different.   It can do many things
that are impossible for the piano.   One of the most beautiful is the
sound of harmonics.   These should be clear, bell-like, and ring-
ing, so that the string vibrates freely in two exact halves.   The
sound of the harp glissando can be magical.   Plucking the strings
close to the sounding board gives another tone color appropriate to
certain kinds of music.

Other instruments that I personally would like to see a regular part of the modern orchestra are the saxophones and euphonium
or baritone.   Bizet, Delibes, D'Indy, Hindemith, Saint-Saëns, and
Strauss have already orchestrated for saxophones.   It would greatly
add to the tonal variety of the orchestra to have three or four
saxophones.   Their pianissimo is most beautiful, with a tender

quality that blends perfectly with woodwinds, horns or strings.
The fortissimo of the saxophone has a biting edge that would greatly add to brutal and savage accents that are the character of some
music. The euphonium in the hands of a fine player has a most
beautiful tone. For soft, broad expressive melodies it would be a
valuable addition to the modern orchestra. In full passages it
combines well with the cellos. At other times, if it plays an octave higher than the tuba, it gives a firm foundation to the bass
outline.

I have mentioned a few of the tonal possibilities of the modern orchestra. But most of them cannot be described with words.
Only by experiment in the rehearsal can the exact tone color, appropriate to each phrase or tonal mass, be achieved. Some orchestras have little tonal variety--they are like an engraving. Others have endless tonal possibilities, like the painting of a great
artist. Everyone has the right to his preference regarding these
two types of orchestra. Tone is important because it is the basic
material of music. But it is only the means to a great end--the
expression through music of the myriads of subtle complexities of
the human heart.

AN ORCHESTRAL PERFORMER
VIEWS THE CONDUCTOR*

X. X.

Dear Editor (Woodwind Magazine):

For many years I have been playing around with the idea of
writing an article in defense of the orchestral musician. Since I
am not a writer and since I am dependent for my family's livelihood
on my job with the-----orchestra, I have not taken the opportunity.
However, the following letter should amply express my viewpoint
and I ask that you please delete my name and my orchestral affiliation should you print this letter in your Letters to the Editor
column. Since I intend to retire within the next four years and
teach full time, I think my views should be of great assistance to
young aspiring orchestra musicians, and encourage my fellow orchestra musicians in the bearing of their cross.

I pride myself on being a fairly good musician. I know my
instrument and feel that there is no conceit involved when I say
that I am a good judge of the adequacy of my playing. Yet, through

---

*From Woodwind Magazine, March 1940. Reprinted by permission
of Ralph Lorr, Publisher. This letter to the editor was written and
signed by "one of the leading woodwind orchestra men in the country," whose wish that neither his name nor affiliation be printed
was respected.

twenty years of orchestral work I have been abused, tormented,
taught, scolded, sworn at, and once even threatened with physical
violence by a collection of conductors who knew as little about my
instrument as the proprietor of a turkish bath. In my locality, it
has been the habit of critics to praise the conductor for good performances, and to upbraid the orchestra for bad ones.

    We orchestra men have lost our identity. Perhaps it's a
good thing, but to a great extent it implies that we are beholden to
the conductor. No arguments are tolerated, no discussions as to
the correctness of a certain rhythm as opposed to another. We
live in a totalitarian state in which buck passing has reached the
state of an art.

    As a case in point, many years ago I played under a con-
ductor who somewhere had heard that the only way you could
achieve a pianissimo or a good forte was by changing your reed
to one of a different strength. He insisted that the musicians
change their reeds whenever the dynamic marks changed. They
were compelled to hold reeds behind their ears and play at changing reeds. We ignored him, but had to pretend we were playing
the game. When told that this was a stupid and unfeasible practice, he literally frothed at the mouth. The story may be amusing, but it is deadly serious. This particular conductor simply
didn't know the first thing about woodwind instruments, and the
abuse handed out by him in connection with pet theories was sufficient to make life absolutely miserable. Yet, the local critics,
the so called connoisseurs, and amateurs hailed him as producing
one of the finest woodwind sections the orchestra had ever had.

    Another type of conductor I have worked with is the memory
expert who takes the score home and supposedly memorizes it.
He comes to the rehearsal unprepared and spends five times the
amount of time necessary on the score so that he can commit it to
memory. When he gets lost on some rhythmic change, he hasn't
the decency to start over again without saying anything, but he has
to pick on somebody to make it legitimate. This type of conductor
never really knows the scores he's working with, and yet again,
any mistakes are laid at the feet of the orchestral musician. The
musician has no defense. He is not surrounded by the aura of
glamour that protects the conductor. The whole business of conducting from memory is stupid and tedious. It is certainly wise
for the conductor to know his score, but the requirements applying
to musicians apply as well to the conductor--even though to those
in the know, the baton never makes a mistake. I can remember
clearly that the musicians often will try to help the conductors.
In one case, they went so far as to put an extra thump at the end
of the Jupiter Symphony, but since he insisted on two extra ones,
he was left holding the bag.

    There is the pianissimo expert, of course, who when he
sees a pp in the score, insists that nobody past the tenth row
should hear it. The demands of this type of conductor go beyond

the bounds of physical possibility and nevertheless they are legiti-
mized on the grounds of academic soundness.

What actually is the crucial point? The fact remains that
we, the instrumentalists in any symphony orchestra, are supposed
to know how to do three things when we are hired: we should be
able to read music, play our instruments adequately--and know our
instruments technically well enough as to be able to arrive at some
theoretical musical conclusions. The employment of a conductor
is far different from this. The golden haired geniuses of our time
are inadequate musicians. They are skeleton figureheads made up
out of bits of theory, bits of practice, fragments of past experience and hearsay, and enormous delusions of grandeur. The cry-
babies all over the country who maintain that there isn't a decent
orchestra left in the land today are way off base. There are thousands of good orchestral musicians who must tolerate the most
amateurish, the most unfounded, absurd, intolerant, egocentric
postures of absolute dictators who haven't even had the decency to
learn their trade thoroughly.

There are some awfully [intolerable], foul tongued musicians
playing in orchestras today, but they are in a [small] minority to the
men who can and do respect a serious and adequate conductor when
he comes along. We have spent years, large amounts of money, a
good deal of sweat and heartache learning our trades. Few conductors can claim the same. The great American orchestras are
ready and waiting when the adequately trained conductors appear.
Unfortunately few have to date.

Who is basically at fault? Partially the musicians for having tolerated this condition so long. But there is little we can do
about it. The public can do a great deal, the teachers of conductors even more. I think your articles on reeds, and on technical
phases of various woodwind instruments should be made required
reading for the white-haired boys. In a good number of cases, I
doubt very much whether they know of the difficulties that exist in
finding and making a good reed--invariably not the bad reed, but
the bad instrumentalist is so-calledly at fault.

Best wishes to your fine magazine. Very truly yours,

X. X.

Chapter III

THE ORCHESTRAL MUSICIANS:
The Music Makers

Introduction. Perhaps a better title for this chapter might be, "What's it like to be an orchestral musician?" Of course, the experts who can answer this question are the orchestra members themselves. Except for the comments of Virgil Thomson (a composer), Donal Henahan and Herbert Kupferberg (critics) and Charles Munch (a conductor), all the answers are supplied by men who are or have been members of 20th-century professional symphony orchestras. There are different problems, attitudes and skills discussed here from the various points of view of the different instrumentalists concerned. Here, then, is a composite view of life in the orchestra.

WHAT IT FEELS LIKE TO BE A MUSICIAN*

Virgil Thomson

Every profession is a secret society. The musical profession is more secret than most, on account of the nature of music itself. No other field of human activity is quite so hermetic, so isolated. Literature is made out of words, which are ethnic values and which everybody in a given ethnic group understands. Painting and sculpture deal with recognizable images that all who have eyes can see. Architecture makes perfectly good sense to anybody who has ever built a chicken coop or lived in a house. Scholarship, science, and philosophy, which are verbalizations of general ideas, are practiced humbly by all, the highest achievements of these being for the most part verifiable objectively by anyone with access to facts. As for politics, religion, government, and sexuality, every loafer in a pub or club has his opinions, his passions, his inalienable orientation about them. Even the classical ballet is not very different from any other stylized muscular spectacle, be that diving or tennis or bull-fighting or horse-racing or simply a military parade.

*Chapter 1 from The State of Music, 2d ed. rev. , by Virgil Thomson. Copyright 1939, 1962 by Virgil Thomson. Reprinted by permission of Random House, Inc.

Among the great techniques, music is all by itself, an auditory thing, the only purely auditory thing there is. It is comprehensible only to persons who can remember sounds. Trained or untrained in the practice of the art, these persons are correctly called "musical. " And their common faculty gives them access to a secret civilization completely impenetrable by outsiders.

The professional caste that administers this civilization is proud, dogmatic, insular. It divides up the rest of the world into possible customers and non-customers, or rather into two kinds of customers, the music-employers and the music-consumers, beyond whom lies a no man 's land wherein dwells everyone else. In no man 's land takes place one 's private life with friends and lovers, relatives, neighbors. Here live your childhood playmates, your enemies of the classroom, the soldiers of your regiment, your chums, girl-friends, wives, throw-aways, and the horrid little family next door.

Private human life is anything but dull. On the contrary, it is far too interesting. The troublesome thing about it is that it has no real conventions, makes no inner sense. Anything can happen. It is mysterious, unpredictable, unrehearsable. Professional life is not mysterious at all. The whole music world understands music. Any musician can give to another a comprehensible rendition of practically any piece. If there is anything either of them doesn 't understand, there are always plenty of people they can consult about it.

The profession rules are extremely simple. In the unwritten popular vein, or folk-style, anything goes. If a piece is written out and signed, then all the musician has to do is to execute the written notes clearly, accurately, and unhesitating at such a speed and with such variations of force as are demanded by the composer 's indications, good common sense, and the limitations of the instrument. Inability to do this satisfactorily can be corrected by instruction and practice. The aim of instruction and practice is to enable the musician to play fast and slow and loud and soft in any known rhythm, whether of the pulsating or of the measured kind, without any non-deliberate obscurity, and without any involuntary violation of the conventions of tonal "beauty" current in his particular branch of the art. The musician so prepared is master of his trade; and there are few emergencies in professional life that he cannot handle, if he still likes music.

Private life, on the other hand, is beset by a thousand insoluble crises, from unrequited love to colds in the head. Nobody, literally nobody, knows how to avoid any of them. The Christian religion itself can only counsel patience and long-suffering. It is like a nightmare of being forced to execute at sight a score much too difficult for one 's training on an instrument nobody knows how to tune and before a public that isn 't listening anyway.

Yet plain private life has to be lived every day. Year after

year we stalk an uncharted jungle with our colleagues and our co-
citizens. We fight with them for food and love and power, defend-
ing ourselves as we can, attacking when we must. The description
of all that is the story-teller's job. I would not and could not
compete. From the musical enclosure or stockade, all that really
counts is the easy game near by, the habitual music-consumer.

Sometimes a consumer is musically literate to the point of
executing string quartets in the home. Sometimes he can't read a
note. He is still a consumer if he likes music. And he likes music if he has visceral reactions to auditory stimuli.

Muscular reactions to such stimuli do not make a music-
lover. Almost anybody can learn to waltz, or to march to a drum.
My father and his mother before him were what used to be called
"tone-deaf. " They never sang or whistled or paid any attention to
musical noises. The four to six hours a day piano practice that I
did for some years in my father's house never fazed either of
them. They would read or sleep while it was going on as easily
as I read or sleep on a railway train. Their rhythmic sense,
however, was intact and quite well-developed. They could even
recognize a common ditty or hymn-tune, provided they knew the
words, by the prosodic patterns of its longs and shorts. I do not
doubt that intensive drilling could have developed their musical
prowess to more elaborate achievements. Knowing their lives as
I do, I doubt if either of them would have had a better life for
having wasted time on an enterprise for which he had no real gift.

The music-consumer is a different animal, and commerce
with him is profitable. We provide him with music; he responds
with applause, criticism, and money. All are useful. When Miss
Gertrude Stein remarked that "artists don't need criticism; all they
need is praise, " she was most certainly thinking about the solitary
arts, to which she was especially sensitive, namely, easel-painting
and printed poetry. The collaborative arts cannot exist without
criticism. Trial and error is their modus operandi, whether the
thing designed for execution is a railway-station, a library, a
"symphonic poem, " a dictionary, an airplane for transatlantic
flights, or a tragedy for public performance.

Consumer-criticism and consumer-applause of music, as of
architecture, are often more perspicacious than professional criticism and applause. What one must never forget about them is
that the consumer is not a professional. He is an amateur. He
makes up in enthusiasm what he lacks of professional authority.
His comprehension is intuitive, perfidious, female, stubborn, seldom to be trusted, never to be despised. He has violent loves
and rather less violent hatreds. He is too unsure for hatred,
leaves that mostly to the professionals. But he does get pretty
upset sometimes by music he doesn't understand.

On the whole he is a nice man. He is the waves around
our island. And if any musician likes to think of himself as a

granite rock against which the sea of public acclaim dashes itself in vain, let him do so.   That is a common fantasy.   It is a false image of the truth, nevertheless, to group all the people who like listening to music into a composite character, a hydra-headed monster, known as The Public.   The Public doesn't exist save as a statistical concept.   A given hall- or theaterful of people has its personality, of course, and its own bodily temperature, as every performer knows; but such an audience is just like any other friend to whom one plays a piece.   A performance is a flirtation, its aim seduction.   The granite-rock pose is a flirting device, nothing more.   The artist who is really indifferent to an audience loses that audience.

While I was growing up in Kansas City, the consumers I came in contact with were very much as I describe them here. Later, when I went to college, I encountered a special variety, the intellectual music-fancier.   This is a species of customer who talks about esthetics all the time, mostly the esthetics of visual art.   He views modern music as a tail to the kite of modern painting, and modern painting as a manifestation of the Modern Spirit. This is all very mystical, as you can see.   Also quite false. There is no Modern Spirit.   There are only some modern techniques.   If it were otherwise, the market prices of music and painting and poetry would not be so disparate as they are.

The intellectual music-fancier is useful as an advertising medium, because he circulates among advance-guard consumers. He is psychologically dangerous to musicians, however, because he insists on lecturing them about taste.   He assumes to himself, from no technical vantage point, a knowledge of musical right and wrong; and he is pretty sacerdotal about dispensing that knowledge. He is not even a professional critic, responsible to some publication with a known intellectual or advertising policy.   He is likely to have some connection with the buying or selling of pictures. He is a snob in so far as he is trying to get something without paying for it, climbing at our expense.   And his climb is very much at our expense if we allow him to practice his psychological black magic on us, his deadly-upas-tree role, in the form either of positive criticism or of a too-impressive negation.   On the whole, he is not as nice a man as the less intellectual consumer; and he must be handled very firmly indeed.

In dealing with employers, professional solidarity, lots of good will, and no small amount of straight human forbearance are necessary.   Musicians back-stage quarrel a good deal among themselves.   They practically always present a united front to the management.   It isn't that one dislikes the management especially, or disapproves of his existence.   He is simply a foreigner.   On the job to be done, he just doesn't speak our language.

Verbal communication about music is impossible except among musicians.   Even among them there is no proper language. There is only technical jargon plus gesture.   The layman knows

neither convention. He cannot gesture about another man's trade,
because a trade's sign language is even more esoteric than its jargon. If he knows a little of either, communication merely becomes more difficult, because both jargon and sign language have
one meaning for the outside world, a dictionary meaning if you
like, and five hundred meanings for the insider, hardly one of
which is ever the supposed meaning. The musician and his employer are like an Englishman and an American, or like a Spaniard
and an Argentine. They think they are differing over principles
and disliking each other intensely, when they are really not communicating at all. For what they speak, instead of being one language with different accents, as is commonly supposed, is really
two languages with the same vocabulary. The grammar is the
same grammar and the words are the same words, but the meanings are not the same meanings. The plain literal meanings of
words like pie, lamb, and raspberry are different enough between
America and the British Isles. For an inhabitant of either country
even to suspect what the other fellow means by general words like
gratitude, love, loyalty, revenge, and politeness requires years of
foreign residence.

So it is between us and our non-musical collaborators.
Preachers and theatrical directors, for instance, will practically
always ask you to play faster when they mean louder; and they get
into frightful tempers at what they think is a too-loud background
for a prayer or soliloquy. Nine times out of ten the musician is
playing just this side of inaudibility and is killing the effect not by
playing noisily but by playing espressivo. He thinks an expressive
scene needs an expressive accompaniment. It rarely occurs to
him, unless told, to play senza espressione. He doesn't mind
playing so when told, because the senza espressione is a legitimate, though rarish, musical effect. It just doesn't occur to him
usually.

It is impossible, however, for a layman to ask a musician
to play without expression. He can demand a little less agony
when the player gets clean out of hand, but that is as far as he
can think technically. Even if he knows the term senza espressione, he imagines it to mean "in a brutal or mechanical manner,"
which it doesn't. To musicians it means "without varying noticeably the established rhythm or the dynamic level." It is far from
a brutal or mechanical effect. It is a very refined effect, particularly useful for throwing into relief the expressive nature of whatever it accompanies.

Film-directors are particularly upsetting to the musician,
because, dealing with photography as they do, they live in constant
fear lest music, the stronger medium, should take over the show.
At the same time, they want it to sustain the show whenever the
show shows signs of falling apart. They expect you, wherever the
story is unconvincing or the continuity frankly bad, to deceive the
audience by turning on a lot of insincere hullabaloo. Now insin-
cerity on the part of actors and interpreters is more or less all

right, but insincere authorship leads to no good end. Theater people and musicians all know this. Film people do not seem to.
For all the skill and passion that have gone into the making of
movies, the films are still a second-rate art form, like mural
painting, because they try to convince us of characters and moti-
vations that their own authors do not believe in, and because they
refuse a loyal co-operation with music, their chief aid, choosing
naively to use the more powerful medium as whitewash to cover up
the structural defects of the weaker. It takes lots of tact and persistence to pull off a creditable job in such an industry.

The most successful users of music are the concert organizers. They confine themselves to saying yes and no. The workman never has much trouble with an employer who knows what he
doesn't want. On the contrary, negation simplifies everything; and
one can then proceed by elimination. What gives a musician the
jitters is positive criticism, being told in advance what the result
should sound like. Such talk sterilizes him by bringing in emotive
considerations (the layman's language lending more moral-value
connotation to technical words than the workman's language does)
at a moment when successful solution of the problem in hand, that
of speaking to an audience expressively (though not necessarily con
espressione), demands that he keep all moral values and taste-con-
notations out of his mind.

I am trying to tell in this roundabout way what it feels like
to be a musician. Mostly it is a feeling of being different from
everybody but other musicians and of inhabiting with these a closed
world. This world functions interiorly like a republic of letters.
Exteriorly it is a secret society, and its members practice a mystery. The mystery is no mystery to us, of course; and any outsider is free to participate if he can. Only he never can. Because
music-listening and music-using are oriented toward different goals
from music-making, and hence nobody really knows anything about
music-making except music-makers. Everybody else is just neighbors or customers, and the music world is a tight little island entirely surrounded by them all.

THE MUSICIAN'S LIFE*

Charles Munch

I want to speak here of the lot of the modest and anonymous
orchestra musicians who are sometimes more talented than the
famous soloists they accompany. It is proper to pay them homage,

*From Chapter 8 of I Am a Conductor, by Charles Munch; New
York: Oxford University Press, 1955. Copyright 1955 by Charles
Munch. Reprinted by permission of Oxford University Press,
Inc.

for what would a conductor be without them? After all, it is they
who play--not the conductor and not the manager.

*   *   *

In most parts of the world the musical profession is badly
organized. Musicians must trust to luck or to their skill in business. Talent is not always the first consideration of organizers
of orchestras. They are more often concerned with budgets than
art. When they have recruited a few good first-desk players, they
consider their work well done and are then satisfied with just filling up the rest of the chairs on the stage. Their methods resem-
ble those of the buccaneers of old who filled out the complement of
their crews without being too particular about seamanship.

*   *   *

How to become an orchestra musician?

Conservatory students are endowed with great ambition.
They dream of world-wide fame and the careers they will make as
soloists. You must have known these dreams yourself to understand the orchestra musician's psychology, to measure the disenchantment of a prize pupil who finds himself one fine day in possession of a handsome diploma but with no opportunity to be heard.
Recital giving is expensive and the impresarios do not line up to
come running with contracts when you ring.

Happily, musicians do not always join orchestras out of dis-
illusion, though often out of necessity. The taste for it comes
later. At least I hope it does.

Most conservatories have now been induced to supplement
their instruction by forming student orchestras in which their pupils
may acquire at least the spirit that is indispensable in a properly
integrated orchestra. Though they may still dream of independent
careers, the young musicians learn among their comrades to love
music as it should be loved--unselfishly. They learn that there is
a loftiness in the profession of the orchestral musician and treasure
its memory even if they abandon it.

*   *   *

The daily existence of an orchestral musician presents difficulties that only the love of music makes endurable.

In some cases, playing violin or clarinet in one of the regular Paris Sunday concert series is almost a philanthropic act. I
am thinking of specific cases. The musicians band together to give
one or sometimes two concerts a week. At the end of the year
they share the profits. When the members of one of the best orchestras in Paris divided their infinitesimal profits among themselves after a recent full season of rehearsals and concerts, each

one had earned the equivalent of $1.45 per service. They had played three rehearsals and at least one concert every week of the season for about $6.00 per week. The disproportion between time spent in carefully preparing the pleasures of Parisian music lovers and the gain received is painfully evident and sadly eloquent.

Such orchestras continue to exist because they are business centers and hiring halls. During rehearsal intermissions, the fifteen minutes reserved to the cigarette, the musicians often find their other engagements that are financially more rewarding.

Among orchestral musicians there are the more privileged who belong to the national opera and radio orchestras. They are fortunate in that they receive regular salaries and are allowed to combine their official positions with occasional engagements. They make records, play for films, in churches, in the homes of the wealthy.

But all this adds up to a working day of 18 hours almost without interruption. Such a musician's daily schedule accounts for every minute in the day. And music is counted among the 'liberal' professions!

The lure of a big income is not the motivating force behind this feverish activity. The mere necessities of life, food, lodging, and clothes, are as important to musicians as to everyone else. In the vast majority of cases musicians cannot afford a moment's respite if they are to make ends meet.

Always working or on the run, that is the musician's lot. Never to be sure of the next day, never to have the security of a regular salary that can calm the shooting pains of anxiety in the struggle for his daily bread--is there any other priesthood that demands so much of its priests?

And then when can he find time to practice by himself? Playing in an orchestra, playing no matter how many concerts does not replace the valuable hours of work that a musician should have in the solitude of his studio--hours essential to staying on top. And when shall he find the no less necessary time for relaxing his nerves and refreshing his spirits?

Consideration is not often enough given to their physical labors. They work like galley slaves but like slaves intoxicated by the fresh sea air.

In addition, it is not generally understood how hard the work itself is. The public cannot imagine what exhausting toil it is for the brasses, for example, to play a Wagner opera. For the rest of the orchestra, even for the strings, it is killing to play five hours at a stretch.

To earn as many fees as possible becomes an obsession. I

think it miraculous that under the circumstances musicians still
keep their enthusiasm, their faith in music, and their love of their
profession.

A few years ago I toured the entire United States with the
Orchestre National de la Radiodiffusion Française (the French National Radio Orchestra). We had great successes wherever we
want. It is a wonderful orchestra and is still talked about. But
it is not generally known under what conditions we made that trip.
First, we traveled by bus. Then after 300 miles on the road, always too hot or too cold and always dirty, we arrived somewhere
or other, tired out and usually behind schedule. The musicians,
men and women too (and the women's courage thoroughout the trip
was altogether admirable), often had to play without even a chance
to change from their traveling clothes or to restore their spirits
with a cup of coffee. Those of us who made that tour will never
forget the kindness of the good people of Montreal who, hearing of
our miseries and knowing that we had arrived hungry and thirsty,
immediately ordered fifty roast chickens for an after-concert supper. The concert was a good one, the chickens delicious.

                        *   *   *

In all the conservatories of both the old world and the new,
little notices appear on the bulletin boards at the end of every
school year announcing auditions in one orchestra or another for a
viola player or a second bassoon or bass drum. But it is heartbreaking to admit that all the orchestras in the world--in Paris
they can be counted on the fingers of one hand and in New York
there is practically only one--cannot provide places for all the
qualified musicians turned out by the schools and conservatories
every year.

Remarkable talents go to waste. Some take refuge in small
towns where they establish themselves as teachers. Others form
the nuclei of impoverished provincial orchestras whose membership
consists chiefly of amateurs. Smaller cities in the United States
recruit musicians for their part-time orchestras by offering them
employment in factories and stores. In France how many simply
beat the pavements of Paris looking for work. On a fine spring
day there not long ago I saw a crowd of unemployed musicians on
the street where a documentary film was being made, hoping to be
engaged to play in a little street band.

Many musicians not at first so inclined end up playing jazz--
and they are not the farthest from their goal. Too many are obliged to abandon the art they love. I was once driven to a concert
at the Salle Pleyel in Paris by a taxi driver who told me that he
was a first-prize winner at the Conservatory. And it is to France
that all the world comes looking for musicians who will maintain
the quality of the greatest orchestras.

I have conducted all over the world. I have found French

musicians everywhere, especially French oboists, who are as much in demand as the greatest wines of Burgundy and Bordeaux. The world is not enough aware of the great human richness that France exports.

And everywhere I have admired the spirit and the high ideals of the great orchestras. Each has its own character, its own color, and its own special quality. But the musicians always know that they are only individual cells of a larger body. They know that they are completely dependent on one another and they place all their talent at the service of the musical collective of which each is but a part. They teach us an important lesson in human solidarity. It is an honor to conduct them.

Sometimes the head of an orchestra section comes forward from the ranks to play a concerto. His comrades never fail to give him the best support and to applaud him without any reservation or any suspicion of jealousy. But a true orchestra musician does not dream of making solo playing his career. Outside of the orchestra, he is probably more inclined to chamber music and may well spend his rare free evenings playing quartets or trios with his colleagues. I know many world-famous ensembles of this kind that are made up of musicians who are still also members of orchestras and who consider the foundation of their musical lives to be still within this great family, which they will never abandon.

*   *   *

Next time you go to a concert, look at the orchestra on stage before the conductor's entrance. You probably cannot connect any of the names in the program book with the faces you see, but they deserve your respect and admiration just the same--and just as much as the famous virtuosi who prefer their glorious isolation to the splendid anonymity of the orchestra.

PHILHARMONICSVILLE (pop. 106)*

Donal Henahan

The [New York] Philharmonic is a political group, a complex little city-state that one of its keener internal observers characterizes as "a small town. " Philharmonicsville, N. Y. (pop. 106; principal industry, classical music) is, in fact, the paradigmatic small town, with its gossips and idealists, its clubs and cliques, its precinct captains and its activists, its joiners and its fence-sitters, its cranks and village wits.

Demographically, it is an odd town, perhaps: 88.68 per cent of its residents are married; 100 per cent have college degrees or the equivalent; the age range is 22 to 65 (average age, 52); 99.1 per cent are white; 98.02 per cent are male. Eighty-three of the members were born in the United States (more than half of those in New York City), and only four are natives of Southern states (two from Texas, one each from Maryland and Tennessee). Eight are from Pennsylvania, five from Poland, six from New Jersey, four from Ohio, three from Austria. Joseph Bernstein, second assistant concertmaster, was born in Bessarabia; Paul Clement, a cellist, in Belgium. Carlos Piantini, a violinist, is from the Dominican Republic, and Carlo Renzulli, also a violinist, is of Italian birth.

However, despite its cosmopolitan cast, Philharmonicsville is more nearly homogeneous than any modern town. Like all great orchestras and small towns, it is inbred and sometimes contemptuous of outside opinion. To consult with a Philharmonic musician about the music of the last 20 years can be like listening to a mandarin's opinion of the barbarians who live beyond the Great Wall.

Without anyone's willing it, an orchestra bends to its common purpose (some would say flattens) all the diverse human types that enter it. There comes to be a recognizable symphony orchestra personality, an orchestra level of talent, an orchestra temperament. Like any walled city, the orchestra demands of its inhabitants submission to authority and unquestioning response to a leader. Not that the demands are invariably met, of course, humans being humans.

Paul Hindemith, the composer who himself did much successful conducting late in life, advanced the seriocomic theory that the modern orchestra with its heroic conductor exists largely to gratify the baser instincts of its audience: to the concert-going public "the display of overt despotism, the demonstration of some refined and stylized form of oppression seems to be imperative." Orchestra men, he observed, live under a system that subjects them to "a man who with the consent of human society exercises a power which we would look upon as cruelty if we saw it applied to dogs or horses."

It is no wonder then that every orchestra, squirming under the system's inherent tyranny, contains its share of men constantly plotting to escape over the wall. Some want, in fact, to escape into conducting, and do. Among the Philharmonic's baton-wielding hopefuls are Larry Newland, a violist, and Carlos Piantini. The latter, a 12-year veteran of the orchestra, led his Philharmonic colleagues (under another, free-lancing, name) in a highly acclaimed performance of Verdi's "Requiem" at Philharmonic Hall. Such an experience could make an orchestra man look rather sharply at the efforts of a visiting star of the podium.

Most Philharmonic musicians these days, however, seem reasonably content with the system.   And why not?   This season, in the third year of a three-year contract, the Philharmonic will pay its lowliest member a minimum of $270 a week plus a $1000 yearly guarantee against recordings.   Since the orchestra now is employed 52 weeks a year, including a six-week vacation this season, that means no man earns less than $15,040, and under a gradation system spelled out in the union contract, many are paid up to $40 a week more than the minimum.   Pay scales of first-desk men and section leaders (who often must play solo parts) are closely held secrets, but the cream of orchestral soloists in American orchestras is reputed to earn $40,000 and more.   [Since this article was written in 1969, pay schedules have improved considerably.]

To a day laborer, or a small-town physician, the hours might look good, too: Under their contract (Local 802, American Federation of Musicians) the men play eight "services" a week, "service" being a flexible term meaning either a concert (two to two and a half hours, usually) or a rehearsal (two and a half hours).   James Chambers, the orchestra's new personnel manager, who had been the solo horn since joining the Philharmonic in 1946, says "about 80 per cent" of the musicians also find time to do some teaching.

During the season, a Philharmonic man's typical orchestral week looks like this:

Monday - Rehearsal, 10 to 12:30; concert at 7:30

Tuesday - Day off unless there is a recording session

Wednesday - Rehearsals, 10 to 12:30 and 1:30 to 4:00

Thursday - Pay day (checks given out at morning rehearsal); rehearsal, 10 to 12:30, with possibility of up to a half hour of overtime if program needs it; concert, 8:30

Friday - Morning free unless there is a Young People's concert; concert, 2:00

Saturday - Morning free unless there is children's concert or rehearsal for pop program; concert, 8:30

Sunday - Day off (this is inviolate)

That adds up to 20 hours a week at most, says Chambers, "but they are 20 hard, concentrated, tense hours. "

The 48-year-old Chambers is generally regarded in the orchestra as "one of the new school" of personnel managers, and some musicians hope he can help break out-dated but ingrained practices.   As liaison between men and management, and as the

administrator who hires all substitutes, sits on many audition pan-
els, and mediates all union problems, the personnel manager is
one of the most powerful figures in an orchestra. Even though he
is constantly "between two cymbals," in Chamber's words, he could
be a potent force for change. "However, he didn't get to be personnel manager by rocking any boats," comments one musician
wryly.

Joachim Fishberg, who joined the orchestra in 1924 and resigned last season, freely admits that there are Philharmonic veterans "who couldn't get up at Town Hall and give a good solo recital." That, he contends, does not keep them from being top-
drawer orchestra craftsmen.

But such subtleties, Fishberg adds, are for orchestra men
to judge without outside aid. Audition formalities, he feels, often
are a waste of time. He has an easy solution: "Let them sit next
to me for a week. I'll tell you if they are orchestra men or not."
Fishberg was the last active member of an orchestral family that
at one time counted six members in the Philharmonic as well as
other members in the N. B. C. Symphony and the Philadelphia Orchestra. Without casting doubt on the truly astonishing breadth
and depth of the clan's talent, it is possible to imagine nepotism at
work in similar situations. Lowly ranked members of many American orchestras often remark with amused cynicism if not resentment about the long-established practice of letting section heads
bring in their pupils when openings occur.

The orchestral soloist is presumed to be one of the best
men in the world at his job, and therefore will inevitably attract
the better pupils. In some instances, he will also know how to
teach. Even the glossy multi-million-dollar conservatories and
music schools are not trusted by some orchestra men to produce
really polished players. "A talented kid and a great teacher face
to face in an attic" is the best music school, in the Emersonian
view of David Nadien, the concertmaster. At the new Juilliard
School in Lincoln Center, Nadien believes, "they are more concerned with the lushness of their building and equipment than with
teaching." Nadien, incidentally, is not one of the eight to ten
soloists or first-desk men currently on the Juilliard faculty.

Since it is orchestra man's lore that good old players produce good young students, it is no surprise to find in spite of
[Philharmonic Managing Director] Carlos du Pré Moseley's efforts
to scan the country's talent for new men, that much of the Philharmonic roster is made up of former students of first-desk players. Although Moseley insists that favoritism to soloists' pupils
is against current Philharmonic policy, no orchestral tradition is
more deeply imbedded. James Chambers, as personnel manager,
no longer will be sitting in the orchestra ("It's not easy to keep
up your embouchure [stiff lip] when you don't play the horn regularly"), but a 22-year-old student of his, John Cerminaro, has
worked as an extra with the Philharmonic and moves into the regular horn section this fall [1969].

Cerminaro's leap from school to Philharmonic is a rare instance of a Philharmonic man's being engaged without a great deal of previous orchestral experience. Saul Goodman, the principal timpanist, made a similar jump: while in high school in 1926 he heard Alfred Friese play the timpani at a Philharmonic concert, and went right backstage and asked to be his student. Shortly afterward, at age 19, Goodman became head of the Philharmonic's percussion section. Goodman, who owns a timpani-building shop, teaches at Juilliard and has students in many top American orchestras. In fact, all three present members of the Philharmonic's percussion section are former Saul Goodman students at Juilliard.

Normally, nowadays, there are two stages for a candidate. If he survives a preliminary audition, at which he may be ruled out of contention after anywhere from five to fifteen minutes of playing works of his own choice and others thrown at him on the spot by his judges, he is heard without fail by the top man. "And the Philharmonic Society always takes the music director's word," Moseley says. "There has never been a veto."

Only a few skeptical members of the orchestra find serious fault with the current system of selection. Sanford Allen [the first black member of the Philharmonic] says that in such a vaguely defined situation "nobody is responsible for anything--the buck isn't just passed, it disappears." He calls it a "shell game, essentially."

Most of its members, though, feel not a whole lot is really wrong with the Philharmonic. No job is ideal, of course, and if they had their way the musicians would arrange working conditions, for instance, so they would not have to arrive back in New York from an out-of-town concert after midnight and then have to rehearse or play the next morning, or dress four to a trailer while on tour. The wages and the pensions could be higher. Some militants would like a clear say in selecting guest and permanent conductors. But, even though changes--particularly of the latter, more radical, sort--are not likely to come overnight, changes in the Philharmonic do come. They may crawl, but they come.

Orin O'Brien, who is 34, pretty and single, joined the orchestra in 1966 as its first woman regular (she was recently followed by cellist Evangeline Benedetti). To Miss O'Brien the Philharmonic management seems "unusually sensitive to the musicians' problems--Moseley was a pianist, after all." And she believes that all sorts of discrimination are "fading fast" in the orchestra. "I frankly feel we girls are doing pretty darn well. I don't feel there is any war going on."

Miss O'Brien teaches, and this term has eight students at the Manhattan School of Music, where she recently was appointed to the faculty. Like many Philharmonic regulars, she lives within an easy stroll of Lincoln Center, in a three-room West Side apartment. "That makes it nice for a double-bass player. You just stick a wheel under it and roll it to work."

Miss O'Brien keeps four double basses at the moment, three at home ("There's none in the bathroom, which is nice") and one at Philharmonic Hall. She came to the Philharmonic after 10 years with the New York City Ballet orchestra and opera experience as a substitute at the Metropolitan. "I enjoyed doing opera, although it's harder than symphony work" (opera hours are far more taxing; for instance, a performance of Die Götterdämmerung may stretch over five hours, or twice the average symphony concert length). "I also liked doing free-lance--you meet so many interesting men--and playing in small ensembles."

Miss O'Brien is happy about the [Pierre] Boulez appointment [as Music Director] because, among other things, he likes to break up an orchestra into smaller units for chamber-sized works. "Right now the use of the symphony orchestra is not as exciting as it could be. Lennie [Leonard Bernstein] did a lot, of course, a lot of new things. I enjoyed Lennie so much. Everything he did, he made you like it. Never a dull moment." But Bernstein's stepping down as head of the orchestra, she says, has started the musicians worrying about the financial future: "The first thing the orchestra felt when it heard Lennie was leaving was, there goes the recording work."

David Nadien, who is starting his fourth season with the Philharmonic, is another who can walk to work. Formerly he made an excellent living as a free-lance musician, but now he insists there is no time for anything but orchestra work and "a little private teaching." His schedule includes 10 to 15 "very advanced" students ("About 18 hours a week, maybe--I don't punch clocks with students"), as well as three or four hours a day of working out on his instrument to stay in shape--"perhaps more if I have a concerto appearance coming up." As concertmaster, he says, his responsibility "is threefold that of anyone else in the orchestra." Nadien, married and 43 years old, is one of the few players hired in recent years who did not go through a Philharmonic audition. "I didn't exactly audition. Bernstein knew of me, and said he wished to hear me, so I played for him privately."

Like an increasing number of Philharmonic musicians, Nadien is a native New Yorker (born in Brooklyn, as were such other first-chair men as Stanley Drucker, the clarinetist, and William Lincer, the violist). The Philharmonic is now, in fact as well as name, a New York institution, with 43 natives on the current roster.

Historically, it had a long period of Germanic influence, when conductors such as Gustav Mahler, Adolf Neuendorff and Anton Seidl were in charge. After the merger of the New York Philharmonic with the New York Symphony in 1928, there came an Italian period, from the appointment of Toscanini to his resignation in 1936. The influence of Toscanini, in particular, is still reflected in the roster, which contains a remarkable number of Italian names.

But, as indicated, European-born musicians have been largely supplanted by native New Yorkers.   Among soloists alone, there
are six New Yorkers, in addition to Nadien, Lincer and Drucker:
Frank Gulino, assistant concertmaster; Leopold Rybb, principal
second violin; Saul Goodman, Timpani; Bert Bial, contrabassoon;
Edward Herman Jr. , trombone, and Myor Rosen, harp.   Outland-
ers among the soloists include Lorne Monroe, cello, from Winni-
peg; Robert Brennand, bass, from England; Englebert Brenner,
English horn, from Vienna.   Other front-line men come from
Philadelphia (Joseph Singer, horn); Portland, Me. (William Vac-
chiano, trumpet); Cleveland (Julius Baker, flute); Malden, Mass.
(Morris Gomberg, oboe); Paterson, N. J. (Stephen Freeman, bass
clarinet), and Rochester, N. Y. (Manuel Zegler, bassoon).

Many Philharmonic members, no matter what their origins,
choose an outlander status.   Walter Rosenberger, one of the percussion crew, lives in Tenafly, N. J. , and gladly commutes.   Now
50 years old, he played in the Pittsburgh Symphony under Fritz
Reiner during the forties, and did a few turns with the original
Sauter-Finnegan jazz band.   "I played as a Philharmonic sub before
going into the Army," he says, "and when I got out in 1946 I
joined the orchestra without an audition."   The Philharmonic is "a
pretty nice life now" to Rosenberger, "better than in the old days--
although I liked it then, too.   What with the seasonal sort of work,
you could be off more."

A cheery, scoutmasterly type who heads the percussion department at Mannes College, Rosenberger kids himself as a lawn-
tending suburbanite.   He is a member in good standing of the orchestra's hearts-playing group and doesn't mind cross-country jet
trips because "you can go coast-to-coast now on one hearts game."
There also is a strong poker contingent, some pinochlers and some
chess nuts.   Others in the hearts club are Bert Bial, William Carboni, Morris Lang and Enrico DiCecco.   Bill Carboni also is an
instrument builder and repairman, and takes his kit of tools along
on tours, just in case.   If a tuning pin on a cello sticks or someone drops a violin, Dr. Carboni is there to operate.

Rosenberger confesses he is a plate-passing deacon of his
Presbyterian Church in Tenafly ("I don't know if I should mention
that--I'll be kidded about it").   "My wife and I are president of
the parent-teacher association.   They wanted me to be president of
the Pony League, too, but I said I couldn't afford the time."

It probably would be difficult to be an enemy of the amiable
Walter Rosenberger, and in his view "the orchestra men get along
pretty well together."   In the percussion department, he says, you
had better get along well because there is so much tightly choreo-
graphed rushing from instrument to instrument during a performance.   "But there's none of that stuff you get in some orchestras,
where you run to the xylophone and find somebody has left sticks
strewn all over it."

Long-standing feuds, kept alive by the men's necessity of working so closely together that they can hear one another breathe, are not unknown in orchestras. In one Big Five organization, solo clarinet and solo oboe, forced to sit side by side day in and day out, have not spoken to one another in years.

The Philharmonic phalanx, in fact, has traditionally been drawn up not against its own but against outsiders, among whom have been counted not a few famous conductors. When the fiery controversialist Artur Rodzinsky took command of the Philharmonic in 1943, his first move was to fire 14 musicians whom he thought incompetent. Philharmonic tacticians maneuvered adroitly for four years, and finally won. Rodzinsky resigned in 1947.

The weapons available to the orchestra in a feud with a conductor are many and they are mighty. The classic story is about the orchestra (not the Philharmonic, surely) that decided to haze a new conductor during the rehearsal and find out exactly what he knew. Little by little things went awry--a slightly wrong note in the cellos, a drunken glissando by a tuba, notes switched from one instrument to another. The conductor grew increasingly suspicious that something was wrong. At last, when the more playful members had succeeded in virtually recomposing the score under rehearsal, there came a great thud on the bass drum. The maestro, pushed too far, put down his baton and asked, "Now, who did that?"

A less obvious method of testing a conductor is to have a soloist play his part, say, a third higher than written, and wait for the baton to rap for a halt. In its time, the Philharmonic has used all the orchestra guerrilla's devices, and invented a few itself. To the present writing, the Philharmonic retains, in fact, its reputation as a "tough" orchestra, although that is disputed by its more sensitive players. Proud, yes, and not easy on musical fakers, they protest, but perfectly willing and able to be welded into a great ensemble by an able, serious conductor.

It is the men and women of the Philharmonic themselves, however, who decide on conductorial abilities, and no glamour or publicity will help the poor soul who does not win their confidence. The most recently publicized incident (not necessarily the most recent) came last season when the outspoken Indian maestro, Zubin Mehta, sounded off about the Philharmonic.

Mehta said, or was quoted as saying in a magazine, that he and many other conductors felt the Philharmonic was a graveyard: "A lot of us think, why not send our worst enemy to the New York Philharmonic and finish him off once and for all?" The Philharmonic's truth squad reacted immediately. The brash Indian was forced to appear before the union and apologize, and soon thereafter the management decided that his scheduled debut with the orchestra could be deferred indefinitely. If you call that "tough," all right; the Philharmonic musicians call it being proud.

Staying proud is easier nowadays than it was in the mass-dismissal era of Rodzinski, not to mention earlier times when a Toscanini or a Mahler ruled his orchestra like a Bismarck. Around 1909, the Philharmonic was, in Mahler's view, "a typical American orchestra--untalented and phlegmatic," and he waved aloft constantly the threat of summary dismissal. Dismissals now are so rare that Frank Milburn is not able to recall offhand an instance during his decade with the orchestra. Under the union contract a musician must pass a two-season probation, but getting rid of him after that is harder than getting a dishonest man out of the United States Senate. There must be a long, complicated process involving election of a Dismissal Review Committee of his colleagues; Byzantine interchanges among committee, management and union, and ultimate placing of the dispute before an outside arbitrator whose decision is binding. Moreover, before a man can be let out he must be notified at least by February 15 of the year in question. The day is past when a conductor could stalk into rehearsal after a fight with his wife, point an imperious finger at the solo piccolo and bawl: "You there, Kunstmorder, you're fired! Out!"

The orchestra man's life is more stable now, and it is from those stormier past times that much of the Philharmonic musician's reputation dates. Still, it is a devilish image that survives, one that even the relatively harmonious Bernstein decade has not quite exorcised.

Back in 1943, Virgil Thomson wrote that the Philharmonic "has had too many riders. It has been whipped and spurred for 40 years by guest conductors and by famous virtuosos with small sense of responsibility about the orchestra's future or about its relation to our community's culture. It has become erratic, temperamental, undependable, and in every way difficult to handle."

Although Leonard Bernstein functioned more as the "famous virtuoso" than as the orchestral good housekeeper during his 10 years, the stability brought by his popular success and the financial balm that it rubbed over the orchestra's wounds brought the Philharmonic to a better technical and temperamental state than it had enjoyed since Thomson's evaluation 26 years ago. It was to keep matters from reverting to an elder state, no doubt, that the Philharmonic management chose Cleveland's George Szell as its musical adviser for the next two seasons.

The 72-year-old Szell [Died July 30, 1970] is unrivaled today in the respect he commands among orchestral musicians. Many dislike him enthusiastically, as they hated Fritz Reiner and others of the taut-ship school of conducting, but no player disputes his mastery of the orchestra or his ability to make it sound great in the chrome-plated, hyper-precise style of his own Cleveland Orchestra. At the moment, Szell's Clevelanders are accounted by many critics as the "best" American orchestra (whatever "best" may mean in the musical art). The Philharmonic is regarded as a

more erratic group, full of superb musicians who can be worked
up to an occasional inspired performance. Critics in some European cities, Vienna among them, prefer this, and are repelled by
machine-tooled perfection. The Bernstein style emphasized the
occasional "wow" performance, in line with Philharmonic tradition,
rather than predictable excellence..

To most critics' ears, the Philharmonic has not in recent
years developed a characteristic "sound," such as the chamber-
music definition and precision of the Cleveland, or the famously
opulent string tone of the Philadelphia. (The latter was so palpable and identifiable to Virgil Thomson that in a review he once
narrowed its tone color down to "pinky beige.") Today, like the
Chicago Symphony since the time of Fritz Reiner, the Philharmonic
is a symphonic chameleon, capable of taking on any color or character its conductor--if he is skilled enough--wants it to adopt.

But if the Philharmonic has not an easily identifiable, com-
mercially marketable tonal character to offer, it inherits from the
Bernstein decade other and more interesting traits. Under Bernstein the Philharmonic has done as much as or more than any orchestra to keep the priceless Western symphonic tradition alive
while many musical institutions either tacitly or openly are accepting museum status.

The Philharmonic has developed into a band of quick sight-
readers, able to put together and perform extremely difficult pieces
on short rehearsal. Sometimes a piece by a Stockhausen or a
Babbitt strains its abilities (and perhaps some musicians' patience
with the avant-garde) past the breaking point, but the amount of
new music played by the Philharmonic in the last 10 years is impressive. The musicians, at any rate, reject the commonly expressed notion that the symphony orchestra may be a dying dino-
saur. "I guess Bernstein said something like that, but Lennie
likes to astound people," says one Philharmonic member. "There'll
be a Philharmonic long after people have forgotten he said that."

David Nadien gets upset at the very suggestion: "We've
done more than our share for new music. No, the orchestra is
not dying. An electronic synthesizer is born dead, but real music
can only be made by live people. Why, saying the orchestra is
dying is like saying the human being is dying."

Nadien believes program-makers should go back to concentrating on "lovely, warm music that sends people home singing,"
and for him there isn't much of that to be found after Prokofiev,
or possibly Shostakovich. Miss O'Brien voices the consensus:
"It's ridiculous. The Metropolitan Museum isn't doomed just because it shows old pictures." Like most of the players, she could
accept gracefully the orchestra as a repository for great art rather
than as a testing ground for novelties, though she also adds:
"There is no more expert group than the Philharmonic at the service of today's composer."

Sanford Allen, in the minority here, too, finds much of what the modern symphony orchestra plays to be beside any point. "I've played a lot of rock in recording sessions," he says, "and much of it is closer to reality than the system we are trying to exist under." A concert manager who knows many Philharmonic men contends that even getting off the orchestral treadmill to the extent of playing chamber music is looked on with mistrust: "There's a hostile attitude toward the chamber music players," and too much tendency to act like plumbers or firemen rather than serious musicians. "Just drop backstage at Philharmonic Hall sometime and see the poker players in action," he snorts. That case may be overstated, but there is no question that a frustrated orchestra man serving out his time can have his musical instincts ground out of him by the routine of playing tiresome old pieces or meaningless new ones.

Some years ago in a Yale lecture the composer Paul Hindemith drew the following picture of a musician condemned to triviality by the modern orchestral system: "I concentrated on the triangle player. Here he was, a grown-up man, wife and three children waiting for him at home, a man perhaps owning one of the greatest stamp collections in the country and being Exalted Potentate of his Shrine; in short, a man of highest social repute. Now he meekly counted his rests and once in a while elicited some tinkles from his triangular bread basket, an activity which in this case absorbed about as much mental exertion as the unlacing of a shoe, but was backed by five years of conservatory instruction, a bachelor's degree, auditions and victories over competitors. Of course, we know the difference between good and bad triangulists ... but one refuses to see in the sporadic triangle tinkling the ultimate purpose of a human being's earthly existence."

What Hindemith complains about here, in a rather heavy-handed bit of satire, is the orchestra's tendency to put music into an institutional trance from which musicians themselves are unable or unwilling to break out. Each man is necessarily a cog, and the interworking enterprise can often amount to the sublimest moments that Western art has imagined, but for the cog itself the suspicion that the machine may be running meaninglessly most of the time could squeeze all real music out of him.

It is therefore the next musical director's loftiest mission to keep the symphony orchestra from lapsing into the mumbling institutionalism of most opera houses and other museums; to keep the orchestra and its repertory from turning into a petrified forest. It may not be possible, of course--the historical cards are not all his to play--but if any musical director can do it, it will be one who remembers what Leonard Bernstein wanted, as much as what he achieved, and who can encourage the Philharmonic's deep musical instincts. If Pierre Boulez is such a man he can not only keep the orchestra alive but write some of the brightest pages in its history.

THE AMERICAN PLAYER*

Herbert Kupferberg

That orchestras are made up of people is a fact sometimes overlooked by musical commentators and historians, not to mention an occasional conductor. They are people linked by a common interest which also happens to be their profession, but they also are motivated by the same goals and purposes as others--making a living, raising a family, staying healthy, pursuing happiness.

Orchestras embody a tremendous ethnic variety. Music has always been a melting pot, and few groupings of 100 persons represent as great an admixture of racial stocks and religious backgrounds as a typical symphony orchestra. And yet the make-up of a group like the Philadelphia Orchestra has been undergoing a tremendous change in the post-World War II era, and its end is not yet in sight. It is becoming, in a word, Americanized.

The typical musician of the late 19th century was foreignborn and trained; indeed, in some cases he even retained his foreign citizenship. The Philadelphia Orchestra that Leopold Stokowski inherited in 1912 was almost entirely German by birth and schooling. So was the Chicago Symphony of Theodore Thomas and Frederick Stock. The Boston Symphony always had a high proportion of French players. Hungarians contributed heavily to a generation of symphonic musicians in America; when Eugene Ormandy was engaged for the Capitol Theater Orchestra it was conducted by Erno Rapee, a fellow Hungarian, and he found a good many other compatriots playing there. The violin was the traditional instrument handed to the children of Jewish families in Czarist Russia, and many of these young "fiddlers on the roof" eventually made their way to American symphony orchestras. Italians followed a similar path. The influx of foreign artists was at its height during the era of unrestricted immigration into the United States, but in the years immediately before and after World War II musicians were numerous among the refugees who found haven in this country.

But perhaps for the last twenty years, and certainly for the last ten, the Americanization of the symphony orchestra has been proceeding at a rapid pace. This process is but one facet of the slow but steady growth of musical culture in this country. High school bands and orchestras--particularly the former--are discovering incipient wind instrumentalists throughout the land. Good string players are far less common; no one has yet devised a quick and easy method of learning the violin, and the only time to begin is in early childhood. But surprising numbers of brass and

---

*From Those Fabulous Philadelphians, by Herbert Kupferberg; New York: Scribner's, 1969. Copyright 1969 by Herbert Kupferberg. Reprinted by permission of Charles Scribner's Sons.

woodwind players don't really get started until their early teens,
and public high school bands are turning out some first-rate musicians.

Certainly their products are playing an increasing role in
the make-up of the Philadelphia Orchestra.   Trombonist Tyrone
Brueninger began playing the baritone horn in elementary school,
switched to the trombone at Upper Perkiomen High School in
Pennsylvania, auditioned for the U. S. Army Band where he passed
the musical test but flunked the physical, and stepped into the
Philadelphia Orchestra at the age of 28.   Tuba player Abe Tor-
chinsky first became acquainted with his massive instrument when
he joined a neighborhood band as a boy in Philadelphia.   Bass
trombonist Robert Harper, one of the orchestra's two players of
American Indian descent (the other being cellist Samuel Mayes),
became a musician at the age of 12 in school in Quincy, Massachusetts, trying various instruments and finally settling on the trombone.   Ferdinand Maresh played violin as a child; his high school
teacher needed a double-bass player, switched him to the instrument, never thinking he was training a budding Philadelphian.   The
paths to a great orchestra do not always lie through a traditional
conservatory.

Some authorities, such as Sol Schoenbach, former first bassoon of the orchestra and now head of the Settlement Music School
in Philadelphia, believe that the next great wave of orchestral musicians is going to be Negro.   The Philadelphia has already had
two Negro players in the category of "extra musicians"--that is,
instrumentalists who are employed on a more or less regular basis
when the orchestra has to be augmented for special concerts or
when there is a temporary vacancy owing to an illness or death in
the ranks.

But whatever the color, race or religion of its players,
there is scarcely any doubt that within a relatively few years the
Philadelphia Orchestra will be virtually 100 per cent American-born
and trained, and the probability is that while the great conservatories such as Curtis will supply many players, more and more are
going to get their basic training in public schools.

What kind of young player is coming into the orchestra these
days and is likely to continue doing so in the immediate future?   A
typical example might be that of a cellist named Lloyd Smith, who
was born in 1942 and joined the orchestra in 1967, playing at the
last stand of his section.   In appearance, at least, Smith resembles
a young lawyer or business man rather than presenting the traditional image of a musician; he is married, has a young child, lives
in nearby Bryn Athyn, builds model trains for a hobby, and except
when he gets onto the stage with a cello between his knees is in-
distinguishable from the mass of middle-class, suburban humanity
of which he is a part.

Like many of today's newer players, Lloyd Smith is a

mid-Westerner, born in Cleveland and raised in Indianapolis, where he attended Arsenal Technical High School. After stabs at the piano and violin he settled on the cello as his preferred instrument, and played it in his school orchestra. He spent a full year in academic work as an undergraduate at Columbia University before deciding to shift to Curtis Institute and a full-time musical career.

While still a first-year man with the Philadelphia Orchestra, Smith had an experience which illustrates vividly the twin pulls on a modern musician--the responsibilities of being a family man and the challenges of being a performing artist. The conflict came about in June, 1968, when, just at the time his wife Rheta was expecting their first child, he was invited to appear as soloist in Dvořák's Cello Concerto in B minor in several summer concerts with the Indianapolis Symphony at Garfield Park in Indianapolis. No father wants to miss the arrival of his first-born; no orchestral musician wants to miss the chance of stepping forth as a soloist. Rheta Smith was not only an expectant mother but an understanding musician; she had been an oboist in the Pittsburgh Symphony when she met Lloyd. She told her husband to take care of Dvořák while she took care of the baby. Eugene Ormandy was equally co-operative: he gave the young cellist a week off to appear in Indianapolis as soloist.

And so the concerts went on. Smith was able to rush back to Philadelphia between appearances to greet a baby boy a few hours after his birth, and then to return ecstatically for his final performance in the park. The management even announced the birth to the crowd just before the concert began. Then, to provide a soggy anticlimax to the whole hectic weekend, a cloudburst hit the park at the fourth measure of the concerto, scattering the audience, the orchestra, and the still somewhat bewildered new parent.

Not all of Lloyd Smith's weekends are like that. But he, like thousands of other musicians--and their wives--have found that earning one's living playing in a symphony orchestra in the United States today makes for a life that is exciting and rewarding, exhausting and frustrating. But for all its tensions and pressures, not many of them would exchange their careers for any other.

PEOPLE AND PROBLEMS*

Herbert Kupferberg

The fact that a certain trumpeter can't eat sauerkraut because it destroys his lip control, or that many a violinist has to

*From Those Fabulous Philadelphians, by Herbert Kupferberg; New York: Scribner's, 1969. Copyright 1969 by Herbert Kupferberg. Reprinted by permission of Charles Scribner's Sons.

contend with tennis elbow or chin rash, or that a particular cellist has an aversion to the cellist at the next stand may seem like purely personal problems, but they have their effect upon the proper interpretation of a symphony by Mozart or Beethoven who, it should be remembered, had troubles of their own.

Physical fitness is a basic matter to an orchestra musician. An office worker can drag himself through a day with a bad headache; a physician usually ignores his own head cold; there are newspaper men who contend they are at their best after a night on the town. But an orchestral musician who plays at less than peak condition endangers not only his own performance but that of the orchestra. "You don't go out on a binge the night before a concert," says trumpeter Gil Johnson. "Most players place a great value on their general physical condition. It affects their breathing, their diaphragm control, their co-ordination, their alertness." Many musicians watch their pre-concert diets carefully (sauerkraut is only the beginning of a long list of spicy foods that trouble brass players), and a good many work regularly at physical conditioning. A visit to the YMHA gymnasium at Broad and Pine Streets near the Academy of Music is likely to find a number of surprising spectacles: bassoonist Bernard Garfield and bassist Gilbert Eney running laps around a track, violinist Irvin Rosen briskly punching a bag, cellist William Saputelli lying on his back pushing up a metal bar with his feet. The Friday matinee audience never saw them like that.

Not only must a successful musician be conscious of his own state of mind and body, he must also keep an eye on his neighbor's. The problem that office and industrial workers have of adjusting to one another's personalities and idiosyncracies is multiplied a hundred-fold in the human interplay of an orchestra. The ultimate objective of an orchestra's activity--the performance of music--depends upon 100 people working together in absolute and literal harmony. To withdraw or to sulk, to soldier on the job or to offer anything less than one's best, is fatal.

And yet abrasive elements are always present. Playing music is grueling and exacting work, and the better one is at it, the more demanding are the standards he is likely to set himself to meet. Playing music in close proximity to others poses special problems: in an ordinary office it's always possible to change the location of one's desk, to decamp to a corner where the light is better, to move away from the loud-mouth who's always using the phone, to take up a position with a better view of the steno pool. But a bassoonist is stuck with his fellow bassoonists and the rest of the woodwinds; a first violinist must sit with the first violins and a second with the seconds; the cymbal player has to rub shoulders with the timpanist.

In this tightly confined world in which a player spends his entire working days (and nights), personalities can grate and viewpoints clash. A great deal of attention is necessarily paid to such

matters as compatability of stand partners.   Most of the instrumentalists in an orchestra line up, like Noah's animals, in pairs,
two players to one stand.   The musicians on the inside, that is,
away from the audience, gets to turn the pages, which most players say they do not regard as an onerous chore, however it may
seem to an onlooker.

Adjusting to one's immediate neighbor both musically and
personally is essential, since musicians see their stand partners
almost as much as their wives, and find them much more inescapable.   "Even the positioning of the music stand can become a
major issue," says violist Gabe Braverman, who for years has
worked in close association with his partner Leonard Mogill.
Braverman says that stand partners often develop musical ideas
and interests together.   Since they work from the same sheet of
music they have to see to it that bowing indications, accents and
other markings are clearly distinguishable.   "In our orchestra,"
Braverman adds, "the pencil and eraser are very busy."   Seeing
to it that the music is in good order and on the stands for each
concert is the responsibility of librarian Jesse C. Taynton, a
former double-bass player.

If working with a stand partner involves one of the basic
personality adjustments a player may have to make, taking his
place as a member of a section is another.   A cellist may not
automatically love or admire every other member of the cello section, but he has no other choice than to work with him closely.
Markings of bowing and phrasing are worked out by the section
head, usually in cooperation with the conductor, and passed back
through the section; here, as in so many other aspects of orchestral playing, individuality has to be sacrificed, although any conductor who knows his trade will listen carefully to an objection or
suggestion even from the last desk.   Sometimes string players
have difficulty in hearing themselves as they play in their sections.
"We're listening to the other players, too," explains Lloyd Smith,
"and your own sound always doesn't come through.   You can't tell
by looking at the fingerboard or the bow, either; you have to listen.   That's what makes it difficult to play well in an orchestra as
compared to chamber or solo music."   Section loyalties are sharp
in the Philadelphia Orchestra; a bass player, for example, insists
that "man for man, we have the finest basses in the country."
The Philadelphia strings in general regard themselves as second to
none.   Says Francis de Pasquale, cellist who recently collected his
Swiss watch for 25 years of service: "There's a shortage of string
players in the United States--until the Philadelphia Orchestra an-
nounces an audition.   Then a hundred show up."

An orchestra as a unit must also have its own esprit de
corps, and probably the Philadelphia works together as cohesively
and amicably as any large musical organization in the country.
There seems little division along racial or religious lines, which
has not always been the case in American orchestras.   Double-bass
player Carl Torello recalls: "There was a time in Boston when if

you didn't speak Parisian French, you were just about out. There was a Bohemian group in Chicago that operated the same way. Man, they had sharp elbows." Says trumpeter Samuel Krauss: "We have the most homogeneous group in the world."

Despite the closeness of working relationships among the players--or perhaps because of it--differences in personality, opinions and outside interests have a way of making themselves felt once the performances are over. "When the stick comes down for a concert," says first flutist Murray Panitz, "nobody thinks of individuals. But when it's not playing, an orchestra is like any large group of people. There are cliques and groupings, feuds and friendships. Some people you're really friendly with; others you just nod to." Since approximately half the orchestra attended the Curtis Institute there are a good number of friendships that date back to student days. Union affairs also serve some members as a rallying point; as in most locals there are both militants and moderates, and the differences between them sometimes become acrimonious. Actually, the musicians in the orchestra have found it desirable to form a kind of union within a union, for although all belong to Local 77, American Federation of Musicians, they have established, with the consent of the local, an orchestra committee (headed by violinist Ernest Goldstein, who succeeded bass player Neil Courtney in 1968), which conducts most of their collective bargaining and grievance affairs directly with the orchestra association.

If there is one point upon which orchestral musicians differ from most other mortals it is in the intensity with which their job becomes part of their daily lives. A few years back there was a delightful anecdote about the wealthy Texan who flew his private plane to New York to hear his compatriot Van Cliburn play on his triumphal return from Moscow. Lost in the big city, the Texan accosted a bearded old rabbi who happened to be passing by and asked him how he could get to Carnegie Hall. The sage looked him up and down from his ten-gallon hat to his spurred boots, and replied: "Practice, practice, practice."

Exactly the same path leads to the Academy of Music, and the members of the Philadelphia Orchestra never cease following it. Not that every fiddler goes home every night and works over every part of every piece of the following weekend's programs; that's what rehearsals are for. But when musicians have an unfamiliar composition coming up or an especially difficult one, they will not hesitate to take their work home with them. And when, for any reason, there is even a slight lag in concert or rehearsal schedules, they will take out their instruments on their own just to stay in trim. Many, indeed, practice literally every day of their lives. There's an old saying that you can recognize a musician's house by two things: it looks slightly run down, and there's always music coming out of it.

ON PERFORMING*

Josef Marx

Playing an instrument and performing music are two entirely different processes. Playing an instrument, problematical as it may be, involves one man's functioning--his ingenuity in relating physiological activity with a sound-producing mechanism evolved by social usage. Lessons of anatomy, psychology, good common sense, tradition and hard work may help us all in attaining a skill with which to dazzle the uninitiated and to astound the adept. Mastery of an instrument can serve only two useful purposes for the practitioner: the economic one of holding down an orchestral job in order to feed the player and the artistic one of harnessing the player's personal intensities--his dynamics--for purely musical ends. This is accomplished by putting instrumental skill into the service of performing music.

Performing music is the creative element in the life of the instrumentalist. In earlier times, the composer and the performer were one and the same person and the creative act of composing was simultaneous with the actuality of the performance. Through a period when composing and performing were practiced by the same person but no longer necessarily simultaneously, we have reached a phase in which the composer specializes in creation only--in which, in fact, the composer has earned himself a reputation for his inability to perform with excellence upon an instrument--and a separate class of instrumentalists dedicated to the sole task of performing. This split between composing and performing has invested the instrumentalist with a function of great responsibility. He must make audible to the listener the now soundless creation of the composer.

Many players of instruments take it for granted that mere instrumental skill is sufficient to do justice to the music they perform: the belief is indeed widespread that proper instrumentalism is synonymous with performance. This cannot be true if we take music at all seriously. The dynamic values inherent in creation must always exceed those called upon for performance. The creative artist is a person driven by intensities of unique vastness which tend to propel him into a dangerous misrelation to the surrounding society, unless--given the concomitant talents necessary for artistic creation--he pits them against problems of form rather than man, and abstraction rather than reality. This accounts for the cosmic content of his ideas as manifest in his work and the characteristic sweep which propels his melos across the changing fashions of future generations.

The performer, although his very talent raises him above the dynamics of the surrounding average, is nevertheless a more

*From Woodwind Magazine, September 1954.   Reprinted by permission of Ralph Lorr, Publisher.

earthly organism, more human, more temporary, and more perishable. His intensities are more immediate and more easily manageable in terms of reality. To make things more difficult, his instrument obeys most effectively when handled in a gentle, relaxed, and loose manner. Rameau already emphasized that the harpsichord functions most properly if the fingers of the player are attached to his hand as loosely as the two buttons of a cufflink are held together by a little chain. Our instruments, especially in this era of bel-canto-sound-at-all cost do not lend themselves to rough and explosive treatment.

The performer's task begins with his realization of this discrepancy. It is his business to rearrange the intensities of the work he is performing so that they will adapt themselves on one hand to the exigencies of optimum instrumental manipulation and on the other to the limitations of time and space as well as tone and taste of the specific occasion on which he steps before his audience. A particular phrase may have taken the composer a week to compose, or a year. It embodies all of the experience of his life, it may represent the distillate of his culture. The performer has fifteen seconds and a few strings or feet of air-column within which to express these imponderables. The zaniest fiddling of Paganini or pianistic pounding of Horowitz may be satanic, but it can never be as monumental as are, let us say, the first eight bars of the C Minor Violin Sonata of Beethoven. Nothing that a performer can do by means of immediate expression can equal the phenomenon of the human mind at its greatest as revealed through a Bach, a Mozart, or a Beethoven. The performer's problem-- and this is where the creative element of his art enters--is to rearrange the balance of the intensities in such a way that he can present within the limited means and time at his disposal the total dynamic relationships which are characteristic of the work he is performing. This is the true meaning of the word "interpretation" when used in relation to music.

Such an approach to performing is not taught in our music schools. It must grow within the player out of his own resources either instinctively or through the effort of his intellect. In both cases it presupposes a deep involvement with music without which the playing of an instrument is meaningless. Instinctless or thoughtless approaches to interpretation likewise are meaningless because they represent only the narcissistic elements of the performer's nature and do not relate to the intensities held captive in every composed musical phrase.

The performer's stock-in-trade, face to face with so great a problem, must even be greater than just flawless instrumentalism, artistic instinct, and thoughtfulness, and a personal dynamism beyond that of the ordinary mortal. He must also be a magician, the master of illusion: illusion of time and illusion of space. He must have his audience hear what is not really there and believe what is not really true. The word magic may antagonize the denizen of the scientific age but, as used here, it is not so elusive an element as it may at first seem. It derives from the powerful urge of the performer to

communicate with people. This urge was basic with the composer-
performer of the past. In the subsequent splitting of the composing and performing functions into two individuals, the composer not
only lost his ability to perform, but the performer also lost the
ability to compose, a deposition which severely injured his feelings
of belonging within the confines of his art. Furthermore, because
of the mechanical aspect of the instruments of the machine-age,
mastery of the instrument as a complex precision tool has assumed
such great importance that the element of communication is all too
frequently left dormant in the player. The development of orchestral
playing likewise has done much to suppress this erstwhile primary
function of the instrumentalist. The orchestral player plays for
the conductor and not for his audience. In the opera and pit orchestra he is not even seen and only half listened to, and in radio
and film he does not relate even indirectly to people but plays
anonymously for the machine. All feeling of communication atro-
phies under such conditions. Its natural reward is never achieved,
and the indirect recompense of financial remuneration never sufficiently satisfies. The non-communicating musician lives in a constant state of vague discomfort and frustration.

It is up to the individual to find his own way out. Our
musical society is sterile because in America music is a business
and not an art. Money comes to music by way of the advertising
account or as a tax exemption in the form of charity. Commerce,
by means of the most up-to-date advertising methods, teaches the
audience what to like so that in turn it can sell plentifully the
soulless commodity which it can produce. The musician, not being of a thinking turn of mind, gets lost in the maze. He tries to
be valuable by becoming as much of a well-functioning machine as
his psyche permits, but since commercial trends change faster
than it takes to learn to master an instrument he is soon outdated
and useless and a new generation fresh from the commercial training school displaces him when he should be in his best years. In
his ripe maturity the successful instrumentalist of the machine-
age is a disgruntled, useless, often indigent man, hating his calling and constantly fearing for his livelihood.

The player, in order not to be caught in a pattern which
holds so little reward for him over the span of his life, should begin by developing his desire for communication. He should go
forth to find his audience as an individual, using all of his gifts of
instrumentalism, instinct, intelligence, and intensity. He should
learn not to lose himself in the cult of his instrument but to give
of himself by means of it. If he is truly talented, then he will not
remain merely a player, a flute or cello in the black book of a
contractor, but he will become a performer, a person, uninter-
changeable, with a respected place in a society of his own choosing.

ENTRANCE EXAM*

Harry Ellis Dickson

How does one become a member of the Boston Symphony
Orchestra? It isn't easy. First, there must be a vacancy, which,
in an orchestra like the Boston Symphony does not occur too often.
And when a vacancy does occur, there are usually at least two
dozen applicants. Unlike any other profession or business, references, diplomas, or degrees don't count. You have to audition
and conductors are cynical. "Let's hear you play!" is their motto. Of course there are exceptions. Our fine violist, Eugene
Lehner, was engaged by Serge Koussevitzky solely on Lehner's
reputation as a member of the famous Kolisch String Quartet, a
quartet which played together for 13 years, playing from memory
the entire chamber-music literature including contemporary works.
Lehner signed his contract without playing a note for Koussevitzky.

Auditions are usually horrible affairs. I vividly remember
my own inquisition. Koussevitzky was seated in the center, a group
of solemn pallbearers all around him. These were the section
leaders of the orchestra, who were there to advise Koussey, but
whose advice he rarely took. After I had played a concerto (Arthur Fiedler was my piano accompanist) I was given the inevitable
sight-reading test. First there was an easy slow movement from
a Mozart symphony, evidently to test my sense of phrasing and
ability to heed the dynamics. Then came a more difficult movement from a Brahms symphony, then a Richard Strauss tone poem,
then some Stravinsky. And then Dr. Koussevitzky asked the librarian to bring a symphony by Taneyev, of whom I had never even
heard. While I was struggling with it, Koussevitzky kept looking
at the other members of the jury with a fiendish glee. "Very
good!" he exclaimed. "You have never played dat?" And I knew
he was making fun of me. He said, "Thank you!" and I packed up
my violin, going home to commit suicide. An hour later, however,
the manager called to tell me my contract would be ready in a day
or so.

Whenever a vacancy occurs in the B.S.O., our personnel
manager advertises the fact in all the trade journals. Then, after
applications have been received, a date is set for auditions. While
Charles Munch was the director of the orchestra, he instituted a
system designed to be as fair as possible to all and this system is
still used today. Each applicant plays behind a curtain on the stage
of Symphony Hall, unknown and unseen by the jury, made up of
players of the orchestra. Each contestant has a number and his
or her name is known only to the personnel manager. From whatever number of contestants three or four are invited to play again,

*From Gentlemen, More Dolce Please!, by Harry Ellis Dickson;
Boston: Beacon Press, 1969. Copyright 1969 by Harry Ellis Dickson. Reprinted by permission of Beacon Press.

this time with the conductor joining the jury.   If the jury cannot agree, it is the conductor who decides.   This system of unseen contestants probably accounts for the fact that we now have four women members of the orchestra.   No one knew they were women except the personnel manager, who had wisely and fairly asked them to remove their high-heeled shoes before walking onto the stage!

Years ago, before the present system was established, we needed a new first clarinetist and auditions were held not only in Boston, but also in New York.   Munch and a jury of first players were seated in Carnegie Hall to listen to a number of clarinetists. Each came on stage in a state of nervousness, some more nervous than others, went through his ordeal, and left.   One of the applicants was Gino Cioffi, an excellent clarinetist who had played under many famous conductors and who was certain that the Boston Symphony needed him more than he needed it.   Cioffi came to the center of the stage, clarinet in hand, and said, "Good morning, gentlemen, what do ya wanna hear?"

Munch asked, "What have you prepared?"

"Anything you want--concerto, symphony, opera--anything!"

Munch asked, "Do you play the Mozart Concerto?"

"Ma sure!" answered Cioffi.   And at this point he beckoned to his pianist and they gave a brilliant performance of the first movement.   Finishing with a flourish, Cioffi walked to the edge of the stage and said, "Pretty good, uh?"

Munch turned to Richard Burgin, our concertmaster, and said, "Such confidence!   We must have this man!" and Cioffi is still with us.

Sometimes chance plays a role in the manner in which a musician enters the orchestra.   For instance, one of our percussion players came into the orchestra without meaning to.   Some years ago when our tympanist retired, a number of applicants from all over the country came to play for the job.   One of these, a tympanist from New York, played as one of his audition pieces a composition for solo tympani accompanied by various other percussion instruments, having brought with him, at his own expense, a young man to play these instruments.   The tympanist did not get the job, but the young man so impressed Mr. Munch and the jury that he was engaged on the spot.   There is now an unwritten law among all percussion players: "When you audition for a job, go alone!"

The system of orchestra auditions is, in the opinion of many, not a perfect one; many factors, impossible to ascertain at an audition, go into the making of a good orchestral player--his ensemble ability, his sense of rhythm when playing with the whole

orchestra, his ability to follow the conductor, his rapport with fellow players, and his sense of dynamics.   (It takes a long time for
an inexperienced player to learn to play without hearing himself.)
For these reasons a new player in the Boston Symphony is accepted
on a one-year probationary basis, during which time the conductor
can judge all of his qualities not immediately apparent at an audition.   Not even all good soloists are good orchestra musicians.
Once the great Fritz Kreisler sat in on a Boston Symphony rehearsal at the last desk of second violins and later admitted, "I was
lost immediately!"

THE BUSINESS OF AUDITIONS*

Daniel Bonade

One of the greatest farces of our profession, and I am sure
many musicians will agree with me, is the way auditions are held
to fill vacancies for woodwind players in our symphony orchestras.
Here are some of the facts: conductors often leave the choosing
of musicians to a manager or a favorite string player who has only
the faintest idea of how a woodwind instrument should sound.   Conductors will place very difficult technical passages from obscure
symphonies and operas before a young player trying for his first
job--music that most seasoned players in major symphonies would
have to practice a week in order to play well.

I know of one conductor who carries orchestra study books
of obscure Strauss operas to auditions.   It was not long ago that
another conductor was advertising for part-time musicians; one of
the qualifications required was that the applicant should be able to
read the works of Richard Strauss at sight!   Such nonsense.

Such conductors do not pay the slightest attention to a player's phrasing of the "easy" oboe and clarinet passages in Schubert's "Unfinished," or the flute solo in Brahms' Fourth Symphony.
I know of one instance when a first clarinet was engaged for one
of our symphonies after having played the cadenzas from "Le Coq
d'or" twice.   The conductor did not take the trouble to determine
how well the player could phrase a simple solo like the one in the
Tannhäuser overture correctly.   Of course, the player was released the following year.   Added to the general abuses already
mentioned are the recommendations by a "friend of a friend," etc.
These, then, are some of the prevalent abuses at auditions today.
If conductors would approach an audition with the intention of testing the player's abilities in all kinds of orchestral playing, rather
than how well he can "noodle," we should not have the wholesale
changes in personnel that occur so often in most orchestras.   Such
changes are only a confession that the conductor did not have the

---

*From Symphony, June 1949.

critical ability to select the type of musicians he wanted in the
first place.

     <u>The Cure</u>. The cure for this sort of nonsense is not diffi-
cult. It is a method of auditioning already used by some few of
our symphony orchestras. The conductor should not be accompanied by the manager, assistant conductor, or triangle player,
but by two or three of the first men--musicians who know the real
requirements for players of each instrument--who act in an advisory capacity. The test should include one or two well-known
cadenzas, such as those in "Scheherezade"; slow passages from
popular works to examine the player's phrasing ability; some delicate staccato passages; and finally, some well-known technically
difficult passages. That is all that is required if the examiners
know their business.

     A player needs a prodigious technique to get a job. Once
he has it, 90 per cent of his energy is required to phrase well--
not for technique. Although one should have a good technique, a
beautiful tone and fine phrasing is far more important. When was
the time when a fine conductor wanted to change a player because
he thought he could get another with a finer quality of tone!

     Sur ce, à bientôt!

THE CONCERTMASTER'S JOB*

Michel Piastro

     One evening, a few years ago, during the concert of a visit-
ing orchestra at Carnegie Hall, I noticed some ragged string playing in the Brahms First Symphony. At the moment I paid little
attention to the cause since I wished to enjoy the music and not
dwell upon technical details. However, after the concert I joined
the concertmaster for a snack at a nearby restaurant and asked
him, "Why do your strings fight among themselves?"

     He smiled. "You are right. Why do we? Because we
have a very stubborn first cellist."

     That was the difficulty--the first cellist would not cooperate
with the rest of the string section. The incident is an illustration
of where the main task of the concertmaster begins: to coordinate
not only the playing of the violins, but of the entire string section.

     A good concertmaster does not have an easy task. In addi-
tion to the necessary musical qualifications, he must have qualities
of leadership--which implies a good deal of diplomacy. If there

*From <u>Symphony</u>, November 1948.

are 18 violins in the section, there are certain to be 18--or more --different opinions as to how any particular passage should be played.

It is easy for the concertmaster to settle a dispute by dictating the answer, but it does not always solve the difficulty. There are problems of bowing and fingering that can be solved in a number of ways, yet, there usually seems to be a particular way which solves the difficulty best. Experience has taught me that it is necessary to be sensitive and react quickly to suggestions offered by members of the section. One will usually find that there are those among the section whose particular abilities solve certain kinds of playing problems, while the talents of others contribute more effectively to the solution of other problems. It is assumed that the concertmaster should be the best equipped in the section; it is also true that on each specific problem there is usually a member in the section who has as good an answer, and sometimes a better one, than the concertmaster.

A few years ago the orchestra in which I was playing was rehearsing a unison passage for the strings. The intonation was faulty. The conductor could not stand it--nor could we. He turned to the double basses and chose a very fine player on the third stand to play alone. The first note the bass player played sounded flat. The conductor lectured upon the vice of playing out of tune, blaming bass players in general and that bass player in particular for the offense. But the man was not to be cowed. He stated emphatically that it was not he nor the double basses were at fault, but the rest of the strings, particularly the violins.

Since the statement was made in front of the whole orchestra, it could not very well be ignored, and the subsequent check-up revealed that the bass player was correct. We should have been much better off if closer attention had been paid to the pitch of the basses.

In passing, it should be said that violinists are castigated by woodwind, brass, harp, and tympani players. They accuse us of playing sharp--and they are usually right. I have never been able to understand why we violinists invariably turn the peg up, not down, when we adjust our instruments. There is nothing intentional or even rational about it; certainly no devilish delight in tormenting other players. Perhaps it is a conditioned reflex, such as slipping the right arm in the sleeve first when putting on a jacket. The theory that I hold, but which I confess I cannot prove, is that the lower strings maintain their pitch better because they play the fundamental tones, whereas we violinists play in the overtone register where the tendency to play higher and higher is much more difficult to resist.

The problem of coordinating the playing of the violins alone is complex. For example, in many passages in the music of composers such as Haydn and Mozart, it is necessary that the same

fingerings be used.   If one person were to play a passage on the
D string and another on the A, the music would lose its character.
It is absolutely necessary that not only the same bowings should be
used but also the same strings, particularly in old music.   In this
respect it is always a particular joy to listen to the Boston Symphony whose strings have developed this particular technique to a
fine art.

"Ah yes!" my critics say, "But what about Stokowski?"
Stokowski knows how to draw a rich and beautiful tone from strings,
there can be no doubt about that.   He knows that some members
of the string section have a good tone at the top of the bow as well
as at the bottom.   Mr. Stokowski's emphasis is on tone and his
free-bowing (no two bows changing at the same time) is part of that
concept.   Personally, I prefer the whole section to play literally
like one huge instrument.   Stokowski's technique of free-bowing
requires Stokowski's conception of tone painting.

A technique that is developing rapidly is that of virtuoso
bowings.   Today, the average string player in our orchestras is
far superior to the player of 25 years ago.   Better teachers, orchestras, conductors, schools, and a greater appreciation of good
playing by audiences have all been contributing factors.   Most orchestral string players have had virtuoso training with the concert
stage in mind.   They played the Beethoven and Brahms Concertos
with technical proficiency before graduating from music school.
But most of them found, to their sorrow, that the concert stage
was closed to them, and turned to orchestral playing for a livelihood.   The result is that we have remarkably good string sections
today.   Conductors are taking advantage of this and are experimenting in advanced bowing techniques with highly satisfactory results.

Not so many years ago Toscanini was conducting a rehearsal
of Schubert's C Major Symphony.   He took the last movement at an
exceedingly fast tempo with the result that the quarter and eighth
note figure in the violins was not clean in the soft sections.   The
Maestro was, of course, displeased.   I asked him if he would consider playing the triplets saltando.

"We can try," said the Maestro with a twinkle in his eye.

And we did with results that were noticeably good.   It has
now become the custom in a number of orchestras to play that particular passage that way.   The opening of the Allegro of Weber's
'Oberon Overture" is another example of the same technique.   One
could cite dozens of examples which demonstrate the progress that
has been made during the past few years in the development of orchestral string technique.

It is gratifying to note these accomplishments, and we can
be justifiably proud of them.   We now have a number of orchestras
throughout the country of a better quality than was general in the

largest orchestras of 25 years ago.   We cannot be complacent,
though, when we know that 25 years from now musicians will surely be discussing us, with the added advantage of listening to our
recordings.   I believe we would not be flattered were we to hear
their criticism, but then--that's progress.

THE ORCHESTRA VIOLINIST*

Carl Flesch

And now we come to that member of the musical confrater-
nity who is most important to the cultivation of music in general--
the orchestra violinist.   His significance increases in the same degree as the old traditional form of publicly cultivated music, defined by the term recital (individual concert), falls into decay.   As
a result those originally trained for the solo profession are being
crowded into the orchestra career in an increasingly intensive manner, and the orchestras themselves are provided with human material more and more perfected.   Yet to the solo player who remains
faithful to his special branch, some time spent in the orchestra,
although only as a temporary measure, offers an uncommonly valuable means of extending his musical horizon.   Joachim, Ysaye,
Thomson, Thibaud, Capet, the Writer and many others were active
in the orchestra for years.   The belief, generally current, that
playing in the orchestra is injurious to the maintenance of the virtues of the soloist is erroneous.   The violinist who handles his orchestra part with the same care that he does a violin solo will experience no injurious results as a consequence of his orchestral
activities.   The one, however, who holds his violin perpendicularly
instead of horizontally (in order to save himself the trouble of raising his upper right arm when playing on the lower strings), who is
careless with regard to how he sits, or draws his bow, and does
not interest himself in what the conductor has to say, in short,
who lets himself go in every respect, will soon find that his art is
subjected to that baneful influence which every occupation carried
out without inner participancy exerts.

Exactly as in the state, where the middle classes, together
with the farmer who tills the soil, represent the most valuable,
because the most permanent kernel of the entire body social, around
which the upper and lower circles crystallize, so the plane on
which the orchestra musician and, in particular, the orchestra violinist stands, above all determines the general level of the musical-
reproductive art of any land.   The performance of the most gravid
works is in their hands.   The general contemporary level of violin

*From The Art of Violin Playing, book II, by Carl Flesch (tr. by
Frederick H. Martens); New York: Carl Fischer, 1930.   Copyright
1930 by Carl Fischer, Inc., New York; copyright renewed.   Used
by permission of Carl Fischer, Inc.

playing, therefore, depends only secondarily on the quality and quantity of the soloist, whose purely musical influence, naturally, must in itself be limited in view of the relative paucity of the material available for performance. The artistic qualities of the orchestra musician, on the other hand, not alone determine the quality of the collective performances, but, in first instance, have a stimulating or discouraging effect upon the development of the composer. The latter, again, by the new tasks which he sets the orchestra musician, compels him to develop effort which, in itself, motives the further development of the whole orchestral body. The famous violin figure in the rhythmically displaced scale-sequences in Beethoven's third "Leonore" Overture, in its day undoubtedly caused a general shaking of heads among its performers. And how much more so the counter-bass recitative in the Ninth Symphony, the artificial harmonics of Queen Mab, in Berlioz's "Romeo et Juliette" (appearing only a short time after Paganini had introduced them in violin technique), the violin passages in the Tannhäuser Overture, or in the "Magic Fire Music" from Die Walküre! Wagner surely would not have expected the orchestra violinist of his day to play such passages, had he not been convinced that the latter was able to adapt his technical ability to even higher demands within an appreciable period of time. This reciprocal influence of creator and orchestra musician is determinative for the importance which the latter has in the development of musical art as a whole. Hence it is only natural that this present work is addressed to him too, because, up to a certain point, his course of study is identical with that of the soloist. Only the lack of certain qualities indispensably necessary for a solo career, or the bitter demands of the everyday struggle for existence have compelled him to bid his ideals farewell with a heavy heart, and to make orchestra playing his chief occupation.

Like the wind-instrument players and the doublebasses, whom the concert hall hardly ever offers any solo opportunities, we also have a certain class of string players who have taken up the study of their instrument with the intention of exploiting it only in the orchestra. The following considerations do not, of course, apply to them. They address themselves only to those orchestra violinists who, in the start, looked forward to a concert career to crown their studies.

The tragedy of the orchestra violinist's career is, that his activity from the very first is equivalent to a renunciation, that it does not represent a beginning supported by joyous hopes, but in most cases forms the close of a period of painful disappointments and hopes destroyed. Nearly every orchestra violinist, once upon a time, has dreamed of becoming a celebrated soloist. Had his teacher not confirmed him in this supposition, he might, perhaps, betimes have taken up some other profession. An orchestra violinist of this type, therefore, will and must always be discontented with his lot. To what degree this wrangling with fate is justified we shall now investigate more in detail.

Above all, the activities developed in a symphonic orchestra should not be confused with those of a theatre musician.   While the orchestra player, in the bright light of the concert-platform, visible to the auditor, has his share in contributing to the success of the whole, the theatre musician, unknown to the public, drags on his anonymous existence in a pit.   Between himself and what goes on upon the stage there is no direct connection--this last is only established by the conductor.   Hence the theatre musician, as a rule, takes far less interest in the art-work to be performed than does the member of a symphony orchestra.   For in opera the attention of the auditors, in the main, is concentrated upon the stage action, and upon the vocal cast; whereas in the concerthall the orchestra as a whole, with its conductor at its head, is the focal point of interest.   The artistic and personal satisfaction of the individual, therefore, is incomparably greater in the symphony orchestra.   When an orchestra alternately cultivates both activities, the musician regards the symphonic concert as a species of consolation prize for his theatrical work.

The orchestra violinist was encouraged by his teacher to take up the study of recital pieces of every kind, which confirmed him in the conviction that later he would be called upon to perform them as a soloist.   Since his teacher could not help but know that there were several thousand representatives of the more humbly estimated activities for every one soloist, we cannot summarily dismiss the accusation that he was guilty of a certain amount of misguidance, of a certain misrepresentation of fact.   Yet the teacher, for his part, may offer the excuse that the pupil can only be induced to make the sacrifice of a wearisome technical training by the mirage of the honors which await him, and that his latent desire for perfection is aroused only when the goal of his ambition beckons from afar.   Besides, the contemporary orchestral repertoire, whose technical demands yield but little to those of the concert repertoire, calls for the identical preliminary training.   As a matter of fact, at the completion of their respective studies, there will seldom be found any essential difference between the future soloist and the coming orchestral musician with regard to their technical equipment.   Not until later does the gulf between the two widen, owing to the instrumental advance, as well as, above all, to the inner maturing of the player destined for the concert-stage, until finally the life of each runs into an entirely different channel.   Therefore, if the frequent failure of any explanation given the student, from an ethical standpoint is not altogether free from criticism, at least one cannot, be it only from the practical point of view, reproach the teacher because, first of all, it is his duty to provide our orchestras with a serviceable growth of new wood.

So we find our man sitting in the orchestra--let us take for granted among the violins.   On the credit side of his ledger we might set down: the advancement of his musical abilities; the broadening of his musical horizon as a result of making the acquaintance of numerous tonal creations hitherto unknown to him; the

inner satisfaction he experiences after the performance of certain
works of which he is especially fond; and, finally, the conscious-
ness--not to be underestimated--of having done his duty. True,
the external honors, with which the world consoles the soloist for
his lack of posthumous fame, are here entirely missing. And the
material compensation which is the reward of his toil is rather that
of an artisan than of an artist. Yet an undertaking which is to
function without a deficit can afford no greater wage than that which
is at present customary in Europe. In order to equalize to some
degree the tremendous gap between the orchestra musician's services and the pay he receives for them, the willingness of wealthy
patrons of art (whom, nowadays, one encounters especially in the
United States) to make financial sacrifices is essential. And yet
all this still does not afford a sufficient explanation for the growing
discontent of the orchestra musician with his fate: I am convinced
that his mental embitterment originates first and foremost in a
certain psychic bondage.

The member of an orchestra, to be useful, aside from those
instrumental and musical qualifications to be taken for granted in
his case, must, in addition, be able to comply with the following
demands: the entire renunciation of his personality, of his artistic
convictions, of his individual trends of taste; complete subordination
to the will of the conductor, who forces him to accept his own
human and artistic qualities--hence the denial of his own ego, the
compulsory acceptance of an alien individuality. The essential
signs of his usefulness, therefore, are a certain enslavement and
negation of his proper will, a selfless waiving of every personal
stirring of emotion on his part. A collaborator who attempted to
force through his own artistic and human independence would soon
have to be removed from the orchestra as unfit. The player who
is to be of use must follow every agogic and dynamic nuance prescribed by the conductor in the air, no matter how much it may
go against the grain. Indeed, often enough unsympathetic fingerings, bowings and bow-divisions are prescribed for him. From
the standpoint of the collective result to be gained, this entering
into details is surely necessary, yet many an orchestra musician
suffers greatly thereby. Instinctively the comparison with the military drill obtrudes itself, yet with the difference that the orchestra
musician must remain a subordinate his whole life long, and must
obey blindly. So long as his superior is an artist, from whom he
cannot withold respect, to whose superiority he must bow, and who
treats him humanely, so long is he ready to subordinate himself to
the conductor's power of suggestion. Yet woe to both participants
when the superior is not recognized as standing on a higher level,
when he is not sympathetic as a human being, when he does not
seem to be an artist of the first class! An abyss will then open
between conductor and musician in whose depths the leader's intentions will vanish without a trace. The musician in such case
girds himself in an armor wrought of contempt and indifference,
one against whose impenetrability the leader's most obvious signals,
his most violent outpourings of emotion rebound as would an Indian
arrow from a modern concrete fortress. What a tragi-comedy does

not such a duel represent, the contradiction between the yard-long movements of the conductor's baton, and the inch-long ones of the passively resisting violinist's bow!   His bitter smile, mingling irony and contempt, speaks volumes when one of the conductor's remarks betrays his incapacity or when he even holds the orchestra responsible for some error he himself has committed.   To this must also be added the extraordinary nervous tension and irritability due to overlong rehearsals and too frequent interruptions. It is true that there exists a type of conductor, unfortunately very sparsely represented, under whose guidance the musician is less conscious of a feeling of dependence, because he is conceded a minimum of artistic freedom and individual expression.   A conductor of this sort, at the appropriate moment, allows him to throw himself into his work heart and soul, in accordance with his own feelings, instead of muzzling his personal sentiment, and thus secures for himself an enthusiastic collaborator who, inversely, may become the source of fruitful stimulus to the conductor himself.

In the rare cases when the writer on music has paid any attention to the orchestra musician, his efforts have always taken the form of suggestions for the improvement of the latter's material situation.   No one, thus far, has paid very much attention to the nature of his psychic condition.   Yet even the highest wage can never compensate for the inner distress which clings to the whole profession.   Hence the conductors should try in every way to reconcile the orchestra musician, in some degree, to his fate.   Yet the conductor only very rarely occupies the right position vis-à-vis his subordinates.   He hardly ever tries to consider their position with sympathy.   A multitude of seemingly incidental details, of which the conductor himself is not conscious, but which goad the orchestra musician daily and hourly, and drive him into a frenzy, are the true causes of many conflicts between the two parties, conflicts whose real reasons are never made public.   I am convinced that the results achieved by the conductor depend as much on his inner relation to the orchestra member as on his musical qualities. †   Here, however, we meet with the strange phenomenon that conductors, whose honest intentions with regard to the art-work cannot be questioned, intentionally suppress any purely human feeling where the individual member of the orchestra is concerned. The orchestra musician to them represents no more than a tool, a negligible quantity barely good enough to adorn art's altar as a beast of sacrifice.

How much more favorable, in most cases, would not the relations between orchestras and their conductors become, if the latter would only adopt certain principles of conduct, not difficult of realization, for example:

The conductor should appear promptly at the time fixed for rehearsal.   He should know the works to be performed thoroughly, and have carefully prepared them in advance.   (The orchestra musician does not like to have the conductor study a work for the

first time with the orchestra.) He must be entirely at home in the
technique of the string instruments, so that he does not make himself the laughing-stock of the orchestra by remarks which display
his ignorance.   Incidentally, let him not hesitate to admit an error, and not first attempt to blame the orchestra for it.   An experienced orchestra musician is nobody's fool.   The conductor
should speak neither too loudly nor too softly.   Those who make
a practice of screaming are hated by the orchestra.   Let him be
sparing in his comments.   The more technical they are, the less
the poetical comparison is drawn upon, the more effective they
will be.   At half-past nine in the morning the orchestra musician
is not in a mood for poetry.   There is nothing to which he is
more responsive, and for which he is more grateful, than the saving of time where he is concerned.   The conductor should be firm
--but not harsh; energetic yet not impolite.   Every conductor has
his scapegoat, whom he prefers to hold accountable for any mistake occurring in the instrumental division to which he may belong
--in most cases solely because his eye, when he raises it from
the score, ever and again happens to fall on the same orchestra
musician.   He should make an effort to address his criticism
where it rightly applies.   Some conductors indulge in the bad habit
of expressing their displeasure at unfortunate occurrences in the
orchestra during a public performance, by violent stamping of the
foot or even by insulting cat-calls.   In this category there also belongs the uninterrupted staring at a guilty wretch, whose nervousness, in consequence, is increased to the highest pitch.   Nothing
reacts more unfavorably upon the relation between conductor and
orchestra, as well as upon the quality of the performance itself,
than this want of self-control, especially when it becomes a habit.
When a phrase presented by one of the windplayers does not please
him, he should not have it repeated ad infinitum, for the orchestra
musician in question, as well as his colleagues, become increasingly nervous in consequence.   It is better if he summon the musician to him in his study after the performance, and there convey
his wishes to him in confidence.   He must compel himself to enter
into more intimate human relations with his people.   They will reward his interest with a doubled devotion.   And he should lose no
opportunity of breaking a lance for the material improvement of the
orchestra musicians' position.   This is his duty; for they sacrifice
their all to him and aid him to gain honor and glory.

     The concertmaster in the orchestra is regarded as a con-
necting link between the professional soloist and the orchestra violinist.   He must unite in himself the best qualities of both, and
must be able to exchange roles without effort and to step from the
chiaro-oscuro of the orchestral tutti into the radiant light of solo
violin playing without previous preparation.   The ability of metamorphosis essential to this end is not to be underestimated, and
there is many a famous soloist who would make a sad fiasco at
the concertmaster's stand in the orchestra.   The courage of the
concert violinist in daring the crowd is not in the same category
with the daring required for the attack of the responsible leader of
the first violins, when he is called upon to save the situation at

critical moments by his presence of mind and his reckless taking
hold of things. Violinists deficient in the power of personal suggestion, it is true, but who otherwise possess all the external
qualifications of a soloist, are best suited for this dual activity,
and feel most at home in it. Hence the education of an efficient
tribe of concertmasters is one of the most important tasks de-
volving upon the teaching body.

†Nikisch was able to carry out all his intentions in a flawless manner with his orchestra body, because his musicians regarded him,
not as an official superior, but as a friend more highly placed.
Gustav Mahler, on the other hand, though inwardly one of nature's
noblemen, was so hated in consequence of his contempt for the
wind- and string-playing individuals of the Vienna Hofoper orchestra, which he conducted for ten years, that his friends often feared
he would be assaulted. And in Paris, Lamoureux, who was inhuman enough to place nothing but stools at the disposal of his
string-players (for four-hour rehearsals and for two-and-a-half-
hour performances), in spite of the pioneer work which he did for
the musical life of the French capital, was justly reckoned among
the most hated of all conductors.

THE GOOD ORCHESTRA VIOLINIST*

Sol Babitz

The elements that go toward making a good orchestra violinist are complex and not often understood. Many fine violinists
make poor orchestra material while many players of ordinary skill
make outstanding orchestra men. To be sure, orchestral ability
is a special gift which some possess in greater abundance than
others, but every player can train himself to improve this ability.
Of course this training requires determination, a factor which will
be lacking if the player thinks that he is too good for the orchestra
and that he should be a soloist.

Because many violinists are trained for solo playing, orchestra work is often a disappointment. Resentment at this "let-
down" is shown by a psychological let-down. The player in such a
case is not only a failure as a soloist but is not good as an orchestra player either.

Suppression of Individual Expression

The basic skill in orchestra section playing, apart from accurate note reading and following the beat, lies in knowing how to

*From The International Musician, March 1956. Reprinted by per-
mission.

suppress individual expression for the sake of the group effect.   In
sport, this is known as team play, namely, giving up a chance to
shine as an individual so that the group as a whole may benefit.
In this category are such elements as following group bowings,
blending of tone and adjusting of intonation for the sake of the total
effect, as well as being an excellent reader and follower of the
beat.

In symphonic music there is apt to be an abundance of
ritardandos, holds, accelerandos and other unexpected changes in
rhythm and tempo.   The good player will follow the conductor with
fair accuracy, even at a first reading.   The "independent" player
will discover these changes only after they occur, and I have found
that such players usually complain about the conductor's incompetence.

Problems of Location

When the player is located at a desk which is far removed
from the conductor, there is the additional problem of trying to
watch the notes and the distant beat at the same time.   Many players who are accustomed to sitting near the conductor find that,
when moved to the rear, it is much more difficult to follow the
beat.   On the other hand, sitting close to the conductor has some
disadvantages such as being more exposed and not having a group
of players in front to follow.   No matter where he is located, the
good orchestral player will avoid "noodling" to show how talented
he is, and will try to stop playing immediately when the conductor
requests silence.   This latter trait is a good one to cultivate not
only because it speeds up the rehearsal, but also because it helps
to conserve energy.

Respect for the Conductor

The individual has no control over his opinion of the conductor, and if he does not respect him he will be incapable of doing his best.   If enough members of the orchestra share this low
opinion of the conductor, the orchestra simply will not sound good.
This is the sole explanation of why the same orchestra will sound
good for one conductor and bad for another.

How does an orchestra sense that a conductor is incompetent?   There are many obvious signs with respect to the beat, cues
and such.   Ingolf Dahl once told me that he could tell a good conductor from a bad one at a rehearsal simply by the way in which
the conductor stopped the group.   If during this stop the conductor
made a suggestion which caused the passage to sound immediately
different this was a sign that the conductor had an ear.   If after
the suggestion the passage sounded the same, this showed that the
conductor merely stopped the orchestra for an imaginary reason.

However, no matter how poor the conductor, no orchestra
really wants to play badly: and it takes a lot of nonsense on the
podium to produce a really bad sound.

Individual Contributions to the Group

Although he must suppress his individuality to help the group, there are cases, particularly when a good player is playing in an inferior orchestra, in which the individual must stick out somewhat for the sake of the group. If the music calls for a crescendo and he hears that those around him are not paying any attention to the crescendo sign, the good orchestral player will produce an exaggerated crescendo in order to compensate for this lack in the group. If the music calls for a sudden pianissimo while those around him are continuing to play loud, the good player will stop his sound altogether (while moving his bow) so that by subtracting his tone entirely he will do more toward helping the soft effect than he could do by merely playing softly. If the section is running ahead of the beat or dragging, he will through one or two exaggerated accents on the beat try to call attention to the error. When it is time for an entrance after a long rest and he senses that the group is hesitant to enter, the good player will lift his violin conspicuously to give the cue rather than enter alone without warning.

PROBLEMS OF CELLO PLAYING*

Frank Miller

Strings, bridge, sound-post, rosin, hair, bow--worrying about these fundamental parts of a cello has grayed the hair and creased the forehead of many cellists. It has been written truly that "Ignorance is bliss. " I envy the blissful cellist who plays his instrument without knowing whether his strings are too high or too low above the fingerboard.

The layman does not realize that in the summer the belly and back of a cello (or of any other of the string instruments) expand, thereby raising the height of the strings. The performer must then use added pressure merely to bring the string down to the fingerboard before a note can be played. The added height causes a harder or rougher sound, and the increased pressure makes the playing more difficult. Result--the performer carts his cello to the repair shop to have a lower bridge made. In winter the opposite holds true. The wood contracts, the strings are lowered--one is afraid to press the bow too hard for fear the strings will rattle against the fingerboard, and pizzicato becomes hazardous for the same reason.

Many a cellist has received conductorial frowns for the ugly sound from pizzicato, simply because his bridge was too low. The

*From Symphony, February 1949. There have been innovations in manufacturing strings since this was written, the most notable being the steel-braided core for all-metal strings.

player once more carts his cello to the repair shop to have a higher bridge made.   The cellist who owns a particularly flat-bellied
instrument is fortunate, for it is likely to vary but little with the
change of seasons--although even he is not entirely free from
bridge trouble.

It is said that Casals carried a bag full of bridges, and
just before going out on the stage to play a recital, would change
the bridge.   It is also well known that Alfred Wallenstein nearly
drove the repair men crazy making so many bridges for him.   I
might add that I was also once classified in this category.

During many years of experimentation I have tried, among
other things, a gadget for raising and lowering the fingerboard in
order to keep from changing bridges--also a bridge with a screw
attachment in the legs to raise or low the height.   Now I have two
bridges--one for summer and one for winter--and when my steel
strings cut too far into the bridge, I have ebony inserts glued into
the notches.

Types of Strings

Strings are the source of unceasing misery for the sensitive
string player.   In the old days the cello was a genuine bass instrument.   That is, the cello parts generally doubled the bass, sounding an octave higher.   This can readily be seen in the symphonies
of Haydn, Mozart, and Beethoven, and in the early chamber works
of these composers.   Along came Bernhard Romberg (1767-1841),
a fine concert cellist with a new conception of the instrument, to
whom we owe one of the greatest periods of evolution in cello
playing.   He is generally credited with having invented the use of
the left hand thumb, and his ten cello concertos are concerned
mainly with the development of the thumb as an extra finger, and
with the ability to perform on the cello in the violin range.   Romberg thus showed composers the value of the cello as a solo instrument, and from that time our string troubles were to begin.

Cellists of the 18th century played on four plain gut strings.
During the 19th century progress was made.   First, someone invented a wire covering for the two lower strings.   Then pure silver
was used to wrap the gut core.   Finally, around 1930, aluminum
was used to wrap the gut D string.   Other metals such as bronze
alloy, even gold, were tried in rapid succession for the D, G,
and C strings.

Concert cellists found that the combination of the plain gut
A string and the aluminum covered "D" did not produce perfect
fifths after the newness of the strings wore off.   The aluminum
"D" was inclined to remain true while the plain gut "A" rose in
pitch.   To one whose fingers perspired as profusely as mine, the
playing of a fifth with that string combination resulted in a good
minor sixth.   I was constantly juggling my left hand, trying for a
perfect fifth, without success.

Finally a European, Dr. Thomastik, invented all-wire
strings for cello, viola, violin, and even for bass.
For many
years prior to their invention I had been trying every make of
string--plain gut, gut with aluminum, alloy, bronze and silver
wrappings, and chromium and silver wrappings on wire cores. I
had even tried banjo, guitar, and harp strings, and the bass G
string for the cello "C. " There were countless days when my living room floor was literally covered with strings. They haunted
my sleep, coming alive as slithering snakes.

The Answer

Thomastik's steel strings (chromium or silver wrapping on
wire for the "A, " and chromium wrapped wire D, G, and C) at
last gave me a measure of relief.

At this time I was first cellist of the Minneapolis Symphony.
For two years, 1938 to 1940, I used all four Thomastik steel
strings--and I remember that performances of the Dvořák cello
concerto with the Minneapolis and the Brahms double concerto during my first season with the NBC Symphony, were some of the best
playing I have ever done--which I attributed to the relief from
string trouble.

In the spring of 1940, with a performance of the Boccherini
concerto with the NBC a week away, the gadgets covering the
bridge notches for the four steel strings began to bother me.

While playing chamber music one evening, I tried a colleague's instrument, a beautiful Tecler, on which he still used the
gut A string. It sounded so good that the next day I ripped off my
steel strings and reverted to the plain gut A and D, and to a wire-
wrapped gut G and C. Of course there was difficulty in accustom-
ing myself to the sound of plain gut, and to their thickness which,
compared to the thinness of steel strings, felt like ropes under my
fingers.

However, the Boccherini concerto went well, and again I
attributed it to the string combination. For the two ensuing years
I used the gut "A" and an aluminum covered gut "D, " changing
the "D" to plain gut for concertos. (My perspiring fingers seem
allergic to sliding on aluminum, and a fifth was next to impossible.) But the drawback was in having to replace the gut "A"
every three days--perspiration acid literally wore out the string
that quickly.

Some two years later, just before a performance of Don
Quixote under Fritz Reiner, I put on a new gut "A, " for I could
not trust the old one (two days old). The new string kept losing
pitch, as all new guts will, and I had to tune continuously. During a tutti passage I frightened Reiner by stepping behind a screen
at the side of the stage in order to tune. (Mr. Reiner thought I
had broken it.) My trouble with harmonics on the "A" during that
performance was a nightmare.

That settled the gut "A" for me for all time.   Since then I
have used the Super-Sensitive steel "A" and "D," and the Kaplan
pure silver wrapped gut "G" and "C. "

Incidentally, I use no rubber in the notches under the "A"
and "D," and even after an hour of working on a new steel string
the Super-Sensitives have a very fine quality and do not give that
banjo "twang. "   After years of experimenting I find the tone is
freer without the rubbers, and that the rubbers tend to dampen the
sound on the lower strings.

The Sound-Post

One often hears that the bass-bar is the heart of the instrument.   Wrong, I say the sound-post is the heart.   Remove your
sound-post some time and try to play.   It will sound as if you had
ten mutes on the bridge.   Replace the sound post, and presto,
your instrument is again a cello, violin, or viola.

That little inconspicuous stick, six to seven inches long, and
not quite half an inch wide (in a cello), makes a world of difference in the sound of a string instrument.   Although there is a
more or less definite "spot" for placing the soundpost, I have found,
upon experimenting, that every instrument needs individual adjust-
ment--so that very often there is considerable leeway for the
sound-post "spot. "

Having taught cellists from the 48 states, Canada, Mexico
and many other places, I have had the opportunity to examine many
different ideas on the placement of the sound-post.   At times the
location of the post on some youngster's cello has amazed me.
Yet the sound of the instrument was not too bad, and in trying to
adjust the post in such a case, the tone was not much improved.
I have even tried two sound posts in my cello, but found the second
made no difference in sound, and added hazards, such as causing
a rattle and sudden unwanted vibration.

Bass-Bar

The bass-bar should be left entirely to an expert.   The top
of the cello must be removed in order to replace the bass-bar, and
if your repair man has done an expert job, the bass-bar is good
for at least 25 years.   The only advice I can offer is that in a
narrow cello it should be placed close to the edge of the "F" hole.
I also like the ends of the bass-bar to be shaved quite thin.

Bows

Almost any rosin is good enough for all playing, but having
had trouble with it in different climates, I have tried all the rosins
on the market.

The difficulty here is generally with the bow hair.   During

the war the hair was especially bad, and no amount of rosin really
helped. What matters particularly is to have your bow repaired
expertly. A bad rehairing can cause the finest bow to play badly;
and if too much hair is put on one side of a bow, it will curve the
stick in the opposite direction. Many an expensive bow has been
damaged by bad rehairing, and more than one bow has been broken
for the same reason. Repairmen must be careful not to injure the
frog of the bow when removing and inserting hair. Many a frog
has thus received cracks.

My own bow, in constant use for 14 years, has weakened
from the continuous pressure and strain. For three years I have
tried, without success, to find another to suit my individual needs.
It is more difficult than to find another cello.

However, whether or not one has a fine instrument and bow,
and despite any of the problems presented in this article, one's
playing will be judged by musicianship above everything else.
Pablo Casals, our great master of the cello, has proven this point
beyond doubt. Technicians come and technicians go, but great musicianship lives on.

FRENCH BOW vs. GERMAN BOW*

Murray Grodner

Modern society seems to pressure man into choosing sides,
making clear cut decisions and voting either straight "Democratic"
or "Republican," regardless of the individual qualifications of each
candidate or issues. It seems so necessary for man to "belong,"
to become part of, to be in one camp or another, and this is not
wrong if it is not at the expense of giving up one's honest individual
evaluation of issues. How broad are our investigations of both
sides of an issue before our decisions are reached? Are the op-
posing sides in an issue really as extreme in character as are
virtue and vice or as hot and cold? Must one side always be
wrong and the other right? If this is so, then how can we explain
in our own profession, the many schools of bowing which have
brought forth fine performers? How do we explain the many
schools of scale fingers which are adopted by different teachers?
Must we also choose sides here or is it not possible to have convictions that allow a devotion to one side but also recognition of
the seemingly worthwhile principles of the other schools? I have
chosen this prologue to introduce what I feel has been the fallacy
in the underlying attitudes causing the present situation of French
vs. German bow.

*From American String Teacher, vol. 15, no. 3 (summer 1965).
Reprinted by permission of the American String Teachers Association.

I pose some questions for those who have chosen to champion either the French or German bow and for those who will be tempted to do so in the future.   Are you a bass player?   Have you studied both schools of bowing long enough to be informed as to the differences in manipulation?   Have you studied with qualified instructors of the double bass?   Have you taught both schools of bowing?   Have you observed outstanding performers representing both schools of bowing?   Have you seen enough of the world's leading orchestras to know where the different schools are predominant and why?   Have you evaluated the quality of the bass sections in these orchestras?   If your background is not fairly complete in these areas are you really qualified to make a valid judgment?

At this point, I will inject a story of the experience of one of my students who auditioned for a double bass opening in one of our country's fine orchestras.   After being told he was the leading contender for the position, one of the auditioning committee who was not a double bassist, asked my student if he would switch to the French bow if he was given the job?   The fact that he was the only one who auditioned with the German bow, and proved to be the most qualified, did not remove cause for concern from the mind of the questioner.   He only knew that my student represented the "opposite camp" and that there had to be something wrong even though he couldn't hear it.   My student did get the job and is one of the most respected members of this bass section.   He has not yet switched to French bow, now six years later.

The above story typifies the type of thinking that concerns me.   Did the man on the auditioning committee have justification by virtue of background and experience to ask his question, or had he little more than prejudice and hearsay to back up his convictions?

So to all who must make a decision and place their feet firmly in one camp or another, to all who have already made a decision, and to those that are just interested in what facts I have to offer I submit the following testimony as to my experience in the "Battle of the Bows. "

I have spent 10 years in the teaching of French bow and 18 years in the teaching of German bow.   Included in my performing experience is membership in the N. B. C. Symphony under Arturo Toscanini, the Pittsburgh Symphony under Fritz Reiner and just last year during my leave of absence, the Danish National Radio Symphony Orchestra.   I have been a performer for 24 years and last year during my sabbatical leave, I consulted with the leading performers and teachers of the double bass in western Europe.

It is my feeling that the trend toward French bow is one mostly influenced by the prejudices of non-bass players in the string sections who do not accept the validity of a bow that doesn't look enough like the one the rest of the string section uses.   As similar as the French bow may be to the violin and cello bow, its requirements of physical manipulation and positioning are in many

ways vastly different and yet in many ways not dissimilar. On the
other hand as dissimilar as French and German bows appear to be
physically and in manipulation, they are really quite closely related in bowing motions and leverage. The major difference is in
the manner in which fingers contact the bow. There is however
even a similarity in finger motion on both bows. Perhaps the
most significant difference is that the thumb is the most obvious
finger that transmits pressure on the German bow whereas the index finger does the same for the French bow. Remember however
that both the thumb and index finger are flexible and strong. Both
are necessary in writing with a pencil and both are essential in
using either bow.

         In Germany almost all double bassists play with the German
bow.   The Berlin Philharmonic certainly has an excellent bass section.   In France, all double bassists play French bow and the Orchestra Nationale has a fine bass section.   In Vienna the situation
is much the same as in Germany.   In the Philadelphia Orchestra
bassists all play French bow and here we have an excellent sounding bass section.   Gary Kerr is one of the world's great double
bassists and he plays German bow.   In Italy I heard perhaps an
equally outstanding young bassist and he played French bow.   Finally, my experience with my students has pointed toward the same
reality.   I have had excellent results with both French and German
bow students who had talent and practiced.   I have not found a general reason for switching them to one bow or another.   Both
schools of bowing have their strong and weak points and both make
a significant contribution to the art of double bass playing.   If you
observe and truly listen to fine performers from both schools of
bowing, you will have a difficult time making an unnecessary decision as to which is superior.

         To finish this dissertation I will tell you a true story of an
experience I had with the late Dr. Fritz Reiner, conductor of the
Chicago Symphony. [His offer to me] was without audition because he
knew me as a member of the Pittsburgh Symphony when he was
conductor, he said "By the way, I forget, do you play French or
German bow?" "German," I said wondering if he had fallen victim
to choosing "camps." "Good," he said, "Now I will have half
French and half German bow players in the bass section." These
are truly the words of a wise man.

                    THE CHANGING WORLD OF STRINGS*

                            Henri Temianka

         Much has changed in the world of string playing during the
past generation.   Every concert violinist of consequence in the 19th
century, all those whose names have remained alive in the annals

*From The Instrumentalist, August 1970.   Reprinted by permission
of the Instrumentalist Co.

of history, were composers of no mean accomplishment. To this
day we play the concertos and caprices of Paganini, the concertos
of Ernst, Vieuxtemps and Wieniawski, the Spanish dances of Sarasate. The history of violinist-composers goes back to the very
beginning of violinistic history with Corelli, Tartini, Vivaldi, etc.
This magnificent tradition continued until the time of Fritz Kreisler, whose enchanting concert encores, such as the "Caprice Vien-
nois" and the "Tambourin Chinois," are still in the repertoire of
every self-respecting violinist.

Then, suddenly, everything came to a grinding halt. Actually, even during Kreisler's lifetime, there were indications that
something had changed. Whereas Paganini felt completely unin-
hibited about playing entire programs of his own compositions,
Kreisler went into hiding. He programmed and published his miniature masterpieces under the names of other composers, usually
little-known ones who had been long dead. That unquestionable
masterpiece, the "Preludium and Allegro," was credited for years
to "Pugnani, arranged by Kreisler." Kreisler's acquaintance with
forgotten dead composers was impressive. Martini, Francoeur,
and a host of others ghosted for him. Or to be more precise, he
ghosted for them, giving them almost all the credit while doing all
the work.

The deception worked beautifully until 1935 when Olin
Downes, of the New York Times, tried to trace the origin of the
so-called Pugnani and engaged in some research. To his amaze-
ment he could find nothing, whereupon he contacted Kreisler, who
finally spilled the beans and admitted that he was the guilty party.

One would have thought that the world would hail him for
this newly revealed facet of his genius, as well as for his modesty.
For Kreisler, as a young man, had feared that the critics might
consider him immodest if too many of his compositions appeared
on his programs under his own name. But if there is one thing
music critics hate, it is to be exposed as less than infallible.
Here they had listened to Kreisler's own compositions for twenty
and thirty years, and praised them to the skies as 18th- and 19th-
century gems. Now the critics trotted out their pitchforks and
watercannons and mounted an attack, the fury of which reached its
apex in an article by the redoubtable Ernest Newman in the London
Times. Kreisler, as gentle and kindly a man as I have ever encountered, was equal to the occasion. His reply, published in the
Times, referred to Newman as that "musician by the grace of
Grove's dictionary," which has become one of my favorite expressions.

Now let us look at the leading violinists who have emerged
since the days of Kreisler, some of them already barely remembered, others at the height of their fame today: Huberman,
Szigeti, Thibaud, Oistrakh, Stern, Menuhin, Francescatti, Milstein,
Spivakovsky. A few of them may have made some transcriptions,
but if any of them are composers in their own right, I am not
aware of it.

I almost overlooked one major exception, Georges Enesco, the remarkable Rumanian contemporary of Kreisler, who was equally at home on the violin, the piano, as a conductor, and last not least as a composer, some of whose works, such as the "First Rumanian Rhapsody," are among the most popular in the orchestral repertoire today. With his death in 1955, followed by Kreisler's in 1962, the last of the major composer-violinists disappeared from the scene.

Composer/ Performer--What Happened?

What accounts for this total collapse of the art of composition among the concert violinists of our time? One can speculate on the subject from now to doomsday without reaching a valid conclusion. Nonetheless, being human, I am tempted to speculate. For one thing, I surmise, overspecialization is at fault. Regardless of the tales of Paganini's and Liszt's extraordinary virtuosity and search for perfection, they were the exceptions rather than the rule. We know that Clement, a Viennese violinist, actually sight-read the Beethoven "Violin Concerto" at the first performance. We also know that as a result of his monstrous treatment of this masterpiece the "Violin Concerto" was never again performed during Beethoven's lifetime. We also have an account, in one of Mozart's own letters, of a performance of one of Mozart's Divertimenti for Strings, in which he light-heartedly mentions that the second violin lost his way for about a half dozen bars during a performance, but ultimately rejoined his partners. Again, the performance was a rough and ready exercise in sight-reading, or practically so.

There is another important element not to be overlooked. A century ago performers were not expected to play from memory. When Mendelssohn played a concerto with orchestra in London and discovered that he had forgotten his music, he placed another piece of music in front of him on the stand, so as not to be discovered playing from memory.

How vastly the situation has changed! Today it has become a matter of life and death for every performer to memorize everything he plays, including sonatas for violin and piano. Conductors are the greatest fanatics of all on this subject. Even if they don't know or understand the music, they memorize the number of bars in the piece and simply count while beating.

Monumental Memories--Here's How

There is a famous story about the conductor who conducted the most hair-raisingly complex modern scores from memory. He had one peculiarity that simply baffled the orchestra players. Every so often he would pull up his left sleeve and look at something concealed underneath. Impossible to find out what it was.

One day the conductor had a heart seizure and collapsed in

the middle of a concert. Without a thought for the man's condition, the entire orchestra jumped up as one and bore down on his
left sleeve. Pulling it up, they found a slip of paper pasted to his
arm. There was a message on it. It said: "Violins to the left--
cellos to the right. "

Aside from the burden of memorizing, we must bear in
mind one other factor: the enormously expanded literature, and
the fact that every soloist is expected to have a vast repertoire
at his fingertips. David Oistrakh told me that he has 35 violin
concertos ready for performance at any time during the concert
season, and that he plays a total of 45 concertos. Naturally he
also plays the six solo sonatas of Bach, dozens of sonatas for violin and piano, and further dozens of shorter pieces, all of which
he plays from memory.

Concertizing Conductors

Playing a string instrument is unquestionably a more sensitive and difficult job than playing, say, a piano. I can easily
document that statement. Among famous conductors, Bernstein,
Szell, Mitropoulos, Walter, Steinberg and Nikisch, to name but a
few, continued to make major solo appearances as concert pianists
throughout most of their conducting careers. Name me one major
symphony conductor who was able to do as much with a string instrument. The only string players who were able to continue their
dual allegiance were chamber orchestra conductors like Antonio
Janigro, Szymon Goldberg, myself, and, a more recent phenomenon,
Yehudi Menuhin.

Yes, the days of carefree, sloppy sight-reading may be
gone forever. We now live in a mechanical age, an age that is
excessively conscious of mechanical precision. The critics demand mechanical perfection and much of the time they get it. Under such circumstances little time is left for performers to devote
themselves to another craft, that of composition.

There is, of course, the other side of the coin as well.
There are those who, having started out as excellent performers,
found that their real destiny lay in composition and had to make a
choice. Shostakovich is a case in point. Nevertheless, while almost all performers stopped composing, many composers continue
to perform. Hindemith, who freely admitted that he could not
serve two masters well, nonetheless appeared as viola soloist with
orchestras, continuing to appear in public long after real artistic
integrity should have motivated him to put his viola in mothballs.
When I delicately broached the subject, he answered with total
candor: "I need the money in order to compose, and if I am to
compose I can't waste my time practicing the viola. So long as
people engage me I gladly pocket the money. " And so Hindemith
continued to play, confident that he was justified in pursuing any
course that would leave him free to compose.

Ravel, Milhaud, Bartók, Prokofiev, Britten, all concertized as pianists, the first two badly, the others well. Of course, Beethoven, Brahms and Mozart were all concertizing pianists, and Bach reportedly was the greatest organist of all time. How did they manage to find time for concert appearances while continuing to write such incredible amounts of music? It is an unfathomable mystery. Today many composers conduct. From Copland to Stravinsky, they have substantially increased their annual income by guest-conducting all over the world, espousing the Hindemith principle.

Fireworks--Gone Forever?

There are other reasons why the torrent of music composed in the past by performers for their own instruments has dried to a trickle. Public taste has become either more sophisticated or more snobbish. Violinists like Wieniawski, cellists like David Popper, created primarily display pieces for their own use in concert, replete with fireworks and sweet, passionate melodies. The virtuosos of today still sprinkle their programs occasionally with these delectable relics of the past, if they are brave enough to risk the stern frowns of the critics. Pseudo-sophisticated members of the audience look upon the inclusion of such pieces as an expression of condescension on the part of the artist. Under these circumstances it is discouraging for today's performer to compose and perform works of this nature. Well, what should he write? Music in our time has become more and more complex. The performing composers of the 19th century were no great innovators; they did not aspire to the originality of a Debussy or Wagner. They wrote for entertainment and pleasure. After all, the concert performer is an entertainer, albeit in a higher sense than a circus acrobat. The only alternative to entertaining an audience is to bore it, and the performer who does that will not last long.

There is a whole new trend afoot in the field of string playing. During the past generations the bulk of great violinists and cellists emerged from Eastern Europe, Spain, France and Belgium; witness Casals, Heifetz, Thibaud, Vieuxtemps. An astonishing number of them emerged from the Jewish ghettos of Poland and Russia, whether their names were Wieniawski or Mischa Elman. Today, enormous new sources of string talent are opening up in the Far East, primarily Japan and Korea. Participating as a judge in a recent chamber music contest, we of the panel unanimously awarded the first prize to a string quartet of young Japanese virtuosi who played the first quartet of Bartók as I had never heard it played before by the most celebrated quartets in the field.

When I first became aware of this new emergence of Oriental string talent, I had the impression that we were dealing only with mechanical prowess. I was convinced that, lacking the Western tradition and cultural background, they would be slow to catch up with us in depth of musical understanding. How wrong I was! The best of the new Oriental crop of string players perform our

Western classical and contemporary composers with a sensitivity
and depth of understanding that transcends all national boundaries.
If East can understand West so well and so quickly, perhaps there
is still hope for a united humanity in which people can stop mur-
dering each other.   Perhaps the time is at hand for artists to take
a share in the management of the world.   They could hardly do
worse than the politicans.

Orienting Ourselves to the Future

How do I see the future of string playing?   I think more and
more Oriental performers will be in high demand in American and
European orchestras, whose prime concern is to maintain their
artistic standards.   Tokyo alone has six major symphony orchestras.   Compare this to New York or Chicago, each of which has
only one major full-time symphony orchestra.   I think concert
music in the coming years is going to be oriented in the direction
of orchestral, rather than solo, performance.   Solo recitals may
well be on their way out, although only gradually.   Music lovers
with record collections, accustomed to switching at will from one
medium to another, ranging the gamut from Ravi Shankar to Rimsky-Korsakov, and accustomed to listening to varied programs of
good music on radio and occasionally on television, will increasingly want the same variety in the concert hall.   Not variety in the
sense that existed when I started out in my career, when we were
sent out on "celebrity concert tours" in England in the most bewildering combinations; in those days I would find myself thrown
together with a pianist, a singer and perhaps a choir, all on the
same program, none of us knowing what the other fellow was going
to perform.   The resulting program mixture was sickening.   I am
not talking about this kind of variety.   But I think that the success
of this concert programming in the coming decades will depend
largely on the imagination, inventiveness and good taste of program
coordinators whose job it will be to make every concert a meaningful, revitalizing and exciting experience to the audience.

Excited Youth Ends the Crisis

I think that what we refer to as the great string crisis a
decade ago has passed.   Gifted string players are coming out of
the woodwork everywhere.   Last year [1969] I gave a string class
in Minneapolis that was attended by 150 students, and at the ASTA-
MENC in Chicago last March an estimated 1000 listeners attended
a string talk I gave at 8:30 a.m.   I think these are signs of a new
spirit in the world of string playing.   I, for one, am filled with
optimism.

ARTICULATION ON THE FLUTE*

John Wummer

Music is a rich art in which the whole range of human experience and emotion can be expressed.   The principles of musical
art are also applicable to literature, painting, sculpture, architecture, and the many other arts.   As the painter must be able to select the exact color needed, so must the writer be able to use the
correct word and phrase to give life to his thought.   The correct
word--is it timely, opportune, well-timed, timeful, or seasonable?
At times the difference is small, at other times great, but the discriminating artist will use the precise word.   So it is in music.
The artistic player will try to use the precise intensity of tone, to
play with the style that will interpret most effectively the true content of the music to be performed.   It is with this thought in mind
that the following observations on articulation are made.

Generally speaking, articulation has been one of the most
neglected aspects of flute playing.   The standard equipment of the
flutist usually consists of a sharp and a soft attack, and two or
three shades of staccato.   This is to speak only of producing the
tone, not mentioning the many combinations of articulation that only
the most conscientious students will practice.

The most widely used staccato is produced by using the syllable tu.   This syllable is used, for example, in the cadenza of
Schumann's First Symphony.   The Loure or soft attack is important
in such places, for example, as on the last note of a slow movement of a Brahms symphony.

Many flute players of years ago experimented a great deal
in this field.   Some suggested that the tongue should strike the
teeth; others were strongly opposed.   Tulou advocated placing the
tongue to the opening of the lips without allowing it to pass beyond
them, thus producing a short note comparable to a pizzicato on a
string.   There are times when the tongue must change from striking the palate, teeth, or lips.   Indeed, the resources of the instrument are sufficient enough that flutists should set themselves the
task of matching the flexibility of the string bow.

In double tonguing the question arises as to which is the
most suitable vowel for the student.   Some teachers suggest tu-ku;
others suggest ke-ke, ti-ki, etcetera.   With tu-ku, the ku strikes
the palate much farther back than if one uses the ke for the second
syllable.   These considerations also apply to triple tonguing.

Of great benefit, too, will be the attention that a player de-
votes to the various combinations of articulation, which, as mentioned above, are a matter of indifference to the average student.

---

*From Symphony, June 1954.

It is unfortunate that most flutists realize their importance only when actually confronted with a difficult articulation in the orchestra. Among the best available studies are "Exercises" by Taffanel, and "Exercises Chromatiques" by M. Moyse. The latter are the most complete because they are written out in full, and the student is more likely to practise them than when told to continue a pattern without having the notes in front of him. It is interesting to note that Taffanel used about six variations of articulations in the first eight measures of his "Scherzettino. "

It is only possible here only to draw attention to the great variety of articulations that the artist needs and to indicate some of the paths along which one may explore. The flutist will be well repaid for his study in this field by the freedom gained and the deeper understanding of the music acquired in applying his expanded technic.

GUIDE TO A FLEXIBLE OBOE*

Harry Shulman

For years, American musicians have been faced with an almost catastrophic paradox. We have been faced with the radical decision as to whether to follow our own artistic impulses, or yield to the relativism of orchestral life. In the case of the oboe, our fundamental problem has involved tone coloration. In Europe, the problem has been quite simple. The distinction between French, German and English conceptions of desirable sound values is graphically clear. The average French oboist grows up within the limits of a traditional "French sound" and he is both musically and socially conditioned to its use. The same applies to the German and English schools.

In the United States, however, there has never been a specific determination of the most desirable sound. American conductors are so diversified in their tastes and demands that a competent oboist (and any other woodwind instrumentalist, for that matter) is confronted with the problem of satisfying them all at once. In my own experience, I have known innumerable fine oboists who were raised to the pinnacles of glory with one conductor, and rejected as inadequate by others.

Given the reasonable assumption that the legitimate musician, the well trained instrumentalist, is the final determinant as to how he should play and sound, the paradox has arisen in the acceptance of the individual's musical integrity and the demands that he be able to cover the gamut of sound conceptions. Further,

---

*From Woodwind Magazine, vol. 2, no. 10 (June-July 1950). Reprinted by permission of Ralph Lorr, Publisher.

there is no sense in discussing the manufacture of reeds, the development of a specific and well regulated vibrato, or even the
method of so-called sound education without facing the reality of
the situation.   Whereas one teacher, or one conductor will prefer
a dark tone, another will call for a brilliant, thin sound.   What
is true of teachers and conductors, is also true of audience reaction.   The effect of well organized and appealing methods of musical education (radio, motion pictures, etc. ,) has been extraordinary
in the training of the layman.   But his training has been disorgan-
ized.   His conception of instrumental sound is weak and tends to
follow the line of dramatic appeal.

Meanwhile, the oboist is in the middle.   It appears to me
that there is a preeminently practical solution which should make
life easier for the oboist and allow for the exigencies of orchestral
life today.   Beginning with the problem of flexibility, I believe that
a basic, moderately dark sound allows for the greatest possibility
and facility in the change of coloration.   An instrumentalist, ad-
hering to such a sound conception, is capable of playing a brilliant,
thin sound when necessary as well as a heavily dark one.   A
basically thin sound is inadequate where a dark sound is called for.

However, there are also primary aesthetic reasons for such
a sound conception.   Tabuteau, the great Philadelphia oboist as
well as supreme teacher, has demonstrated through his own playing
and that of his school, that this moderately dark and the variable
variable around it is highly adequate to requirements of orchestral
work.   The instrumentalist is supplied with what I might call an
"aesthetic mean," namely, a position in the sound rainbow which
appears to be just right for the manipulation of the demands of a
score.   I am certainly not trying to be dogmatic in the above assertion.   I am fully aware of the principle that one cannot approach
all music from the same tonal point of view.   It is certainly not
necessary to state the truism with reference to the difference in
playing Debussy and Bach.   However, it is certainly wrong to agree
with the extremist viewpoint.   Solo passages in Debussy and Ravel
needn't sound like hysterical cocktatoos.   Nor should passages in
early music be so heavy and gross that the sound resembles the
thickness of tar.

The moderately dark sound possesses the virtue of selective
modification in the sense mentioned above.   The aesthetic realities
of Bach and Debussy fit into a rational and critically selected pattern.

The utilitarian point lies in the fact that with such a sound
conception as the starting point, the variability of conductorial
tastes can be easily handled ... at least more easily than possible
when the basic conception is extreme.   It is possible for the instrumentalist to mold to the demands of different conductors without at the same time sacrificing his tonal base.   It is unnecessary
to retrain to suit the demands of the conductor ... but simply to
modify.

Despite agreement or disagreement with the above, the fact remains that innumerable instrumentalists have objected to the "moderately dark" conception because of so-called technical difficulties in its elicitation. While all the technical problems cannot be gone into in this article, it should be stressed that the sound is the result of two factors, essentially: (1) The correlation between sound imagination and performance; and (2) The conception of the breathing chamber.

The first factor is old hat and needn't be gone into. The second is generally forgotten, or eliminated. The quality of sound production is dependent on the depth of the biological sound chamber. It is of extreme importance that the air column extend down to the diaphragm. Superior control and quality result from the concomitant depth. Witness the case of limitation to the mouth and the inadequacy of sound value.

Other than the above, every professional is aware of the means necessary to create sound quality of this specific type. What should be emphasized and re-emphasized is the fact that there is no need for the difficulties so inherent in the flexible situation of the present orchestral oboist. While preserving his integrity as a musician, he is still capable of conforming to the demands and tastes of the conductor or conductors he works with. Some decision must be made with respect to this problem. This is one method which offers a reasonable solution.

THE ART OF PLAYING
IN AN ORCHESTRA*

Gustave Langenus

The art of playing successfully the clarinet or any other wind instrument in an orchestra cannot be learned in a few months; it takes years. Before entering an orchestra, be it large or small, a player should be equipped with enough musicianship to read tolerably well at sight, have a steadiness of tone, some technic, and be able to phrase neatly. In order to obtain a thorough orchestral routine, it is best to start at the root, which means playing duets with a friend. This is the foundation stone. Later on, some easy solos with piano accompaniment will be found of great help and also where possible, the playing of chamber music. From there on, real orchestral experience begins. It little matters whether the number of musicians consists in an organization from three to a hundred players, the following remarks hold good in all cases,

*From Six Articles for Woodwind Players, by Gustave Langenus; New York: G. Langenus Inc., 1923. Copyright 1923 by Carl Fischer, Inc., New York; copyright renewed. Used by permission of Carl Fischer, Inc.

provided these orchestras play something else besides one-steps.
The first and paramount thought that every individual player must
constantly bear in mind is: "Who is playing the melody, my colleague or I?   If it is my colleague, then I play a secondary part,
in other words, an accompaniment; in consequence, I must subdue
my tone in order to let the melody stand out.   But if, on the contrary, I am playing the melody, then I expect my colleague to
modify his tone quantity, so that I am enabled to play with more
freedom and bring out the melody with greater lucidity. "

This reasoning is of great importance when playing in an
orchestra, many are the musicians who are so absorbed in their
own performance that they cannot possibly pay attention to what is
going on around them.

Another mistake often made by players is to give the expression marks in their parts such as: pianissimo, piano, mezzo-
forte and forte a certain volume of tone as if they had a standard
value of a quarter, two quarters, three quarters or a full pound of
avoirdupois weight.   This is a frequently misapplied quality and is
acceptable only when performing alone in a room; but when playing
in an ensemble, those nuances are unreliable beacons, and must
be treated with caution.   A singer may have a big or small voice,
a colleague may have a big or small tone on his instrument, a
certain hall will reverberate loudly, another very little; in all
these and other cases the player must use his own judgment, and
modify his tone accordingly.   Besides composers have often mis-
judged the nuances they wrote, often marking pp when it should
read f. and vice-versa.

One of the greatest difficulties the orchestral player has to
master is the question of pitch.

Wind instruments are greatly subject to the influence of
temperature.   At 40 degrees Fahrenheit, they are about a quarter
of a tone too flat, and correspondingly sharp at 90 degrees.
Stringed instruments are affected by those temperatures in exactly
the opposite way, for strings contract when it is cold and in consequence sharpen, and the reverse happens when it is warm.
However in winter, an equilibrium is established between these
two positions of the orchestra, by playing in a concert hall where
a normal temperature is maintained, somewhat between 65 and 70
degrees.

Wind instruments are far from being perfectly in tune, notwithstanding the great progress that has been made in their manufacture the last fifty years.   Indeed I doubt they ever will come
near to perfection, unless the compass of each instrument is con-
densed from three to only one octave.   Anyway, we have now with
us the flute, with its lower octave very much inclined to be flat,
and its upper register sharp.   The oboe has the same acoustical
characteristics [as] the flute, but in a much lesser degree.   It is
now the best-tuned instrument of the whole woodwind family, due,

no doubt, to its smaller compass. The bassoon has, to a certain extent, the same characteristics as the oboe, but is much more complicated on account of a greater compass, and it has also many more defective notes.

From the foregoing it is seen that the registers of flute, oboe and bassoon have much in common. The clarinet, on the contrary, acts quite differently; most of its lower notes are slightly sharp. If this were not the case their twelfths would be too flat. Furthermore, all wind instruments have a tendency to sharpen when making a crescendo and to flatten when playing a decrescendo; the clarinet again makes a noteworthy exception to the rule, and contrarily to the other instruments it flattens markedly in a crescendo and sharpens in a decrescendo.

These complexities that beset the instrumentalists are not altogether insurmountable; all of them can be partly remedied. First of all, concert halls should have a normal temperature between 65 and 70 degrees, as already mentioned. This is not always the case, especially when concerts take place in theatres, which are very seldom free from drafts.

Secondly, players should adjust their instruments to the adopted orchestral pitch [A], which in New York consists of 440 double vibrations in a temperature of 65 degrees. In warm weather this can easily be done by lengthening the instrument at the joints, but when the temperature is low then complications arise. The only thing to do, under such circumstances, is to cause the warm breath to flow continually through the instrument before and during the concert. Brass instruments have here an advantage over the other wind instruments, inasmuch as each tone is emitted through the bell part; in other words, the warm breath travels throughout the entire length of the instrument, while on woodwind instruments most of the notes sound from the side holes. Hence, the necessity to warm both upper and lower joints--a precaution often neglected when a number of bar rests are encountered. The most handicapped man in this respect is the clarinetist, who has constantly two instruments to take care of.

Finally, in order to reach that perfection in intonation among woodwind instruments, it is absolutely necessary that the player be not only conversant with the defects and peculiarities of his own instrument, but also with those of his colleagues. Every one should be able to sharpen or flatten his instrument to a certain degree in order to make mutual concessions of pitch as the case may necessitate. This can be done with either lips or factitious fingerings. If there is one among them that has such an inflated idea that his instrument is perfectly in tune, then the whole ensemble must inevitably suffer. In short, good fellowship is essential among the players to obtain that homogeneity of sound.

It is hardly necessary to add that the above observations are not the product of a couple of hours office work, but the result of many years' experience, gained sometimes at much discomfort, and feeling only too well how much I would have appreciated similar remarks from someone fifteen years ago, I gladly dedicate this article to my pupils and to those clarinet players who take their art seriously, hoping they will derive some benefit from it.

AN INTERVIEW WITH SOL SCHOENBACH*

Arthur Hegvik

A. H. Throughout your career you have worked and associated with many of the greatest artists in the music profession. Are there common factors in the lives of these people which could explain their superiority?

S. S. Well, are they really superior? Or are they just fortunate that things have worked out so? Most of the people that I know in symphony orchestras have an almost monomaniacal desire to do just that; others are indifferent to the whole concept. You have to have the psychology. Some people want to be in Benny Goodman's band and others want to be in the Metropolitan Opera-- it depends a great deal on the environment. Mine was the New York Philharmonic, and my teacher, Simon Kovar, made me go through their entire repertoire with him, so everything I knew and appreciated in music was based on what they were playing. Those were the great Toscanini days when every concert was a complete spiritual experience. Where else could I aim?

A. H. Have the environmental factors regarding music changed much since then?

S. S. Tremendously so. When I was a boy the great idols were Jascha Heifetz and Mischa Elman. They were gods. A poor Russian emigrant Jew in the Bronx could buy a violin for a few dollars and if he practiced and worked and struggled long enough and hard enough someday he would be another Heifetz. That was their dream--it was their ticket into the middle class. Now it's different. Tell me, who wants to be a Heifetz today?

A. H. I understand that you became a staff musician for CBS when you were only 17. How did this come about?

S. S. It was an unusual situation. During the depression I played in a kind of relief orchestra which gave some concerts at the Metropolitan Opera. (My parents had been against the bassoon from the very beginning; they much preferred the violin or piano, and this only made me want it more. As it turned out when the

*From The Instrumentalist, October 1969. Reprinted by permission of The Instrumentalist Co.

depression hit I was the only one in the whole family who could make a living. I supported them all, including my brother at Harvard, so they had to revise much of their thinking about the bassoon.) Somebody mentioned they were having auditions over at CBS for a staff bassoon player, so I went over, gave my name, and they called me later to come in and audition. When I got there the manager took me into a studio containing just a stand full of music marked with numbers. (Every bassoon player was given a number, and I think mine was two.) It was all done with microphones--the conductors were downstairs in another room. I just sat there and played. There were solos from Tchaikovsky and from this and that, and there was a pianist who accompanied me--I didn't even know who he was. I finished playing and went home. It was the fairest audition I've had in my life, because nobody ever saw who it was. Later they called and asked if I was "Number Two. " I said, "Yes," and they said, "Report tomorrow, we like your playing. " But when I went in the conductor asked, "Who are you?" When I told him he said, "There must be a mistake. We expected a man, not some child. You might as well play today, but we will have to make other arrangements. " I played like that for years--they never got anybody else.

A. H.   Who were some of your colleagues at CBS?

S. S.   I belonged to the concert unit, which was a marvelous little group of about 25 musicians. These musicians were placed in CBS by Arthur Judson, who had been manager of both the New York Philharmonic and the Philadelphia Orchestra. He had a contract to supply all singers, musicians, and entertainers because CBS didn't want to be bothered with the selection of these people. As a result our orchestra consisted of former members of the two orchestras. For example, our first clarinet was Daniel Bonade. Nick Lucas, the flute player, had been with the New York Philharmonic until Mengelberg took it over. There was Peter Henkelman on oboe (he had played English horn with both orchestras), and so on. There were so many players like that, each one a great star in his own right, and there I sat, 17 years old, honking along.

A. H.   Was this after Bonade had been in Philadelphia?

S. S.   Yes, I played with him for years, and then he left to go to Cleveland. Later the clarinetist was Ralph MacLaine, who became so great in the Philadelphia Orchestra. I learned a lot from these men, because they all had tremendous backgrounds and experience, and they were so diverse in their own training.

A. H.   What was the work itself like?

S. S.   It was the beginning of radio, and I played all the big programs that started up then--everything from jazz with Benny Goodman to symphonies with Howard Barlow. The concert unit would join a jazz unit with Kostelanetz, or with Mark Warnow, whatever the occasion called for--The Lucky Strike Hit Parade with

Johnny Green, background for shows, Gilbert and Sullivan--every-
thing.   Sometimes I played English horn parts, or second clarinet
in B♭ and A, or horn parts--all transposed at sight.   This was
assumed; you did it or else.   Sometimes you'd do it by ear, but
after a while you developed a facility.   Those were very formative
years and anybody who gets a chance to do a lot of work shouldn't
turn it down because it's beneath his dignity.   He should take it
and learn.   We don't have enough practical experience today.

A. H.   How did the change to the Philadelphia Orchestra come
about?

S. S.   The manager wrote me a letter (the bassoonist was
dying).   It sounded like a very far-fetched idea, but I thought,
"Why not try it?"

A. H.   Did you audition?

S. S.   Yes, I had several auditions.   They were very fair.
I played on the Academy stage--they had a book and guided me
through what they wanted.   The conductor was there, and a nucleus
committee from the orchestra, plus a committee from the union.
(The Musician's Union here was very strict, and I had to compete
against all the local players.)

A. H.   Was the audition all on orchestral repertoire?

S. S.   Almost completely; plus some concerto work, like the
Mozart.

A. H.   To most players auditions seem to remain an unsolvable
mystery.

S. S.   I think they're horrible!

A. H.   How would you advise young people to prepare for them?

S. S.   I would say they should prepare the repertoire of the
organization they plan to join.   There is usually not enough preparation to do the thing that you are going to be asked to do, and
that is where an apprenticeship is so helpful.   If a person has an
education which is directly connected with the thing he's going to
do he's going to do it better than if he does things just because
others think it's going to enlarge his mind.   My son [Peter, also
a bassoonist], for example, is getting his Doctorate in Spanish and
Portuguese at Rutgers University.   He never studied Latin.   I was
told as a child to study Latin and Greek--that it would help me--
yet I can't speak Spanish or Portugese.   Many teachers spend a
lot of time with their students on etudes and solo material.   When
the poor chap finally gets into an orchestra he doesn't know how to
start the Marriage of Figaro Overture.

A. H.   What about the criticism leveled at some of our colleges that they don't provide students with the specific skills needed for professional performance?

S.S. Well, every college isn't the same as every other college, and I'm a great believer in having that education. Nowadays there is much more required of a musician, and he needs a thorough understanding of music. Also, university standards have gone up tremendously in the last 25 years--there are now many opportunities for performance--so you can't say anymore that these people are just pecking at it. I've heard orchestras and operas in colleges that are just as good as anything I've heard professionally.

A.H. What was it like when you joined the Philadelphia Orchestra?

S.S. It was the culmination of my musical life. The attention and the care--the attention to detail--that goes on in a symphony orchestra makes everything seem so worthwhile. However, it is a difficult adjustment to make, since they aren't going to take time out to rehearse the entire orchestra just for a new man. Their repertoire was established, so I think I was there years before ever rehearsing a Brahms or Beethoven symphony, or any of the chestnuts that the Philadelphia Orchestra knew inside out--Ormondy and Stokowski certainly weren't going to bore everybody by going through it. I can even remember recording sessions where they did remakes of single sides of records which had been found defective and I suddenly found myself in the midst of a section of Petrouchka. I didn't know what was happening or even where they were beginning, and Stokowski would never tell you where he was going to finish. He would throw up his arms at the end and you'd just better watch it. Those were interesting days.

A.H. Did you have to make many adjustments in your playing?

S.S. When I joined the orchestra I stuck out like a sore thumb. This was the time of the great Tabuteau-Kincaid tradition, and although Bonade had hinted at what was ahead, we never really put it into practice. I had to revise all my ideas on bassoon playing: I played sharp, my reeds were heavy, I couldn't duck in and out of a harmony, I wasn't flexible, and I didn't have a set approach to phrasing. I phrased as I felt, and sometimes I didn't feel well, so I didn't phrase well. Tabuteau and Kincaid, however, had a system of approaching the phrase and of inflections which gave the phrase significance. They didn't actually teach me or tell me what they were doing, but I started to copy what I heard around me because my own playing sounded so ridiculous by comparison. Then I would say to them "I know that you do this and this. Do you do it for this or that reason?" and they would say, "Yes." That's the way I got my education. It's so much better if you can have someone like that for a teacher.

A.H. Who played clarinet then?

S. S. McGinnis; followed by Portnoy, MacLaine, and Gigliotti, the present man--and with all these men I enjoyed great personal friendship and rapport.

A. H. Bonade has produced an unusually high number of our greatest first chair players. Would that be primarily because of his position at Curtis?

S. S. You know, he spent very little time with the Philadelphia Orchestra for the scope of his influence. He was a very dominant character, and his personality made this possible--plus the fact that he was an excellent musician and had complete control over what he was saying at a time when there weren't too many clarinet players who did.

A. H. On the instrument or verbally?

S. S. Both. The situation was very fluid. There were many German and Russian clarinet players around who didn't have a definite school; Italians who wanted to refine their playing, etc. Bonade arrived and had this very definite approach to the clarinet. It was almost overwhelming since the others were still wandering around. He was a very positive personality.

In every school, in every situation, some people emerge because of their basic personality, not just because they have the facts. Of 100 students attending a medical school one will emerge as a great doctor, not because he knows more than the others, but because he can express himself more. Bonade was such a man.

Ironically, he never had much luck as a performer, probably because his personality was too dominant to permit a conductor to supervise him.

A. H. You mean he played it the way he wanted it?

S. S. Eventually--and I suppose conductors don't like that too much. They like to have a little to say.

A. H. What about his sound? What type of sound was it?

S. S. Very pure. Completely lacking in vibrato. Quite lovely and cool and limpid, but it didn't have any vibrato or inner warmth. Quite straight, especially in contrast to many of the Frenchmen of that time who undulated (particularly Langenus, who had a pronounced vibrato).

A. H. And MacLaine? How would you characterize his sound?

S. S. He had the best sound of all (he got that from Hamelin). He used a diaphragm vibrato and double-lip embouchure, and was very much like Wright, the man you hear today with the National Symphony. Wright plays that way, but maybe even better than MacLaine.

A. H. I've always been struck by the diversity and strong individuality of Bonade's products.

S. S. That's true, but there's another factor involved. If you establish your reputation as a superior player and teacher pupils want to come to you. You tend to get the best, and you become even better as a teacher because you're always dealing with the best and the most serious. It becomes a self-sustaining thing. Kincaid used to tell of a lady coming up and saying, "Your students are so wonderful," and he said, "Why not? I only select the best." This is true of Leopold Auer and everyone else. It works both ways--you become good and the good comes to you. Then everybody thinks you're better than you are, but you're never any better than your students, and they're the apostles who carry the word along. I know most of Tabuteau's students, for example, and they say, "This is what Tabuteau said." So we have the Gospel according to Gomberg, and The Gospel according to DeLancie, and The Gospel according to Bloom--and I, who knew Tabuteau intimately, never heard him say any of these things they say he did. Of course it's very possible that he said something quite different to them. The personality of the individual is the biggest single factor in any music-making situation.

SHOULD HORNS VIBRATE?*

Gunther Schuller

With the visit of a French orchestra not too long ago, and a steady flow of imported French recordings becoming available in recent years, the question of the vibrato on the French horn has been brought into general prominence. It has caused considerable discussion among native wind instrumentalists (and not only of the brass variety) and more recently resulted in the airing of the pros and cons of this old controversy on a well known weekly program of record reviews. The problem has been brought into focus further by an increasing number of hornplayers, and incidentally, clarinetists in this country adopting the vibrato, Mr. Reginald Kell's arrival in this country no doubt causing further stimulation.

Since the question of whether to use a vibrato or how much and when is one that concerns all wind players, even if in varying degrees, it is perhaps time that the problem be somewhat clarified.

It seems to me that there is one basic standard by which the whole subject of vibrato can be judged and that is quite obviously its contribution to the truest and stylistically most correct interpretation of a given piece of music. This seems so

*From Woodwind Magazine, vol. 3, no. 7 (March 1951). Reprinted by permission of Ralph Lorr, Publisher.

elementary and for many it will be a superfluous admonition, and
yet, judging from performances, both recorded and live, both here
and abroad, many instrumentalists seem to ignore this simple,
fundamental precept.

At the outset, it must be stated that not much of a case can
be made for the complete, unqualified abolition of the vibrato on
the horn, because, as we well know, in the hands of a sensitive
and discriminating musician, the vibrato can be a tremendous asset, both in giving life to the written music and in adding a certain
individuality to the performance.   But it is at the indiscriminate
use of the vibrato (and this concerns all instruments, whether it
be strings, woodwinds or brass) that this article is directed.

There is no reason why a moderate and intelligent use of
the vibrato should not be adopted on a French horn if the musical
phrase demands it, in the form of emotional warmth or stress at
certain moments, just as a sensitive violinist will not use the
same degree or speed of vibrato throughout a given piece, but will
vary it to suit the intensity or mood desired.   But let me emphasize the moderate use of vibrato, especially on the horn.   Several
years ago, one of our most prominent horn players expounded the
theory to me that, because of the more intense vibrations, longer
air column, and richer sound of the horn, the use of the vibrato
to the degree employed on the oboe or flute, for example, becomes
obnoxious on the horn.   I am not well enough acquainted with the
physics of brass instruments to be able to quote facts and statistics
to back up this opinion and yet it seems to be based on strong
logic.   Any reader better versed in this subject is, of course, invited to render his opinions.

It is well known that many instrumentalists have adopted the
vibrato because the basic tone quality upon which this vibrato is
superimposed is not adequate in itself; therefore they seek superficial ways of improving the sound, deluding themselves into thinking that they have added to the tone quality when actually they have
brought the poor sound more into prominence by projecting it via
the vibrato.   That the sound thus produced is often akin to that of
a hotel-band saxophone would, it seems to me, do little to endear
it further to the listener.

I have heard it argued, not only by instrumentalists, but
also by prominent composers and pedagogues, at present to remain unnamed, that an instrument such as a horn, should adopt
the vibrato if it is being used with another instrument that commonly uses a vibrato ... a violin or a bassoon, let's say.   Aside
from the fact that subjugating one instrument to another is against
all the precepts of chamber music playing (it is rather a question
of complementing one another in a musically equal partnership), it
is sheer nonsense to assume that the satisfactory blend of two instruments will depend on the use of similar vibratos.   A violinist
with a thin scratchy sound and a horn player with a big, fat
sound, will never blend tonally whether they use vibratos or not.

A good blend will be achieved rather through (1) a common, thoroughly integrated musical conception and (2) a similarity or melting together of the basic tone qualities of the instrumentalists. This latter, incidentally, is the basic ingredient in the recipe for first rate woodwind quintet playing.

Another abuse, unfortunately encountered more often than should be the case, is the use of vibrato on the sustained harmony and pedal points that are to be found constantly in the classical symphonies, especially those of Haydn, Mozart and Beethoven. Usually in octaves and found mostly in the horns and trumpets, occasionally in the bassoons, the very immobility of these parts enhances the orchestral texture, and their sustaining character adds to the broadness of the melodic line which they support. That these sustaining passages are not melodic lines requiring emotional expression would seem to be obvious, and that if so played, these relatively unimportant parts interfere with and sometimes cover the real melodic line or contrapuntal design would seem equally obvious. And yet, this indiscriminate use of the vibrato seems to be condoned by many an instrumentalist and conductor.

Very closely related is an equally common abuse found mostly in the woodwind family. In a chord consisting, for example, of double woodwinds and horns, it is not uncommon to hear one flute or one bassoon playing with a vibrato while the other instruments are playing with none, or almost none. This naturally prevents any homogeneous blend of the chord and can have a very disturbing effect upon the listener. It must be remembered that evils like these are at such a point no longer a matter of individual taste. They become a matter of right and wrong, because they prevent the fulfillment of the composer's intentions and this, of course, should be the primary concern of every musician.

To sum up, the moderate position, which would also meet all requirements of the musician playing a repertoire covering a period of about 200 years, would be one based on the very discreet application of the vibrato and would conversely be directed against the continuous, unqualified use of it.

TRUMPET PLAYER--OR ARTIST?*

Harry Glantz

Occasionally, advanced students from various parts of the country will ask me how one achieves a beautiful tone, good articulation, and legato, or how one solves any number of problems concerning similar aspects of trumpet playing. Sometimes definite answers can be given to some of these questions, particularly if

*From Symphony, February 1953.

they involve physical or mechanical problems, but the more advanced the players, the more nebulous become the answers. Beyond a certain point, education must move from the studio into the
outside world.

In my early years I, too, spent hours practicing Arban, but
beyond a certain point the further development of pure technique
becomes unimportant. What does a trumpet player, aspiring to
play in a symphony orchestra, need in the way of technical equipment? He should be able to play his chromatic, major, and minor
scales, and the few well-known exercises based on them; he should
have a good legato, and be able to single, double, and triple
tongue; he should have a good tone and range; and finally, his sense
of rhythm and his reading, etc., should be adequate. We might
say that all this is F.O.B. Graduation Day. It is standard equipment and basically is all that is needed to play in an orchestra.
One player might have a larger tone, another might have a greater
range, etc., but all players have their strong points and weaknesses. In the individual player a balance is gained--a player who
has a slow single tongue usually has a better-than-average double
tongue. (The worst thing a player can do is to become obsessed
with one aspect of playing or his instrument, such as his legato,
articulation, mouth-piece, etc.) Actually "Cappriccio Italien,"
"Pictures at an Exhibition," and Richard Strauss' "Bourgeous
Gentilhomme" are the most difficult symphonic compositions for
trumpet--and there are many, many trumpet players who have
enough technique to play them adequately. Let us take the slow
movement of the Beethoven Violin Concerto, for example. Technically there are thousands of violinists who can play it well, but
why is it a moving experience when played, say, by Heifetz or
Kreisler?

The answer lies in the artistry of the player. Beyond a
certain point, which is relatively easy to reach, technical equipment is secondary. Artistry flows from a person's response to
and appreciation of all phenomena in life, from his sensitivity
which he has developed by study and by listening to and associating
with great artists.

A player can play the call in the "Leonore" Overture No. 3
with the proper content only if he knows that in the opera the call
heralds the arrival of the Governor. A passage in any composition
may be played beautifully in the studio (or in the orchestra), but
if it does not fit into the picture that the conductor is trying to
project, it will have a disturbing effect, and in many cases will
even sound bad, even though the audience and many insufficiently-
trained musicians will not know why. When one aspires to become
an artist, one must concern himself with the music as a whole as
must the conductor or the piano soloist. It is the degree to which
the player can successfully do this--which requires both knowledge
and sensitivity--that determines how fine an artist he is. This is
a viewpoint that is quickly brushed aside by most ambitious young
players because they believe that somewhere there are a couple of

"angles" which they have overlooked, the discovery of which will solve all their problems. Some professional players also regard this viewpoint rather contemptuously, but experience has taught me that the greater the artist, the more he is concerned with such matters.

Therefore, to young players seeking the secret of artistic playing I always give the following advice: Master the technique of your instrument, which many good teachers can help you to do, but then try to project yourself beyond the trumpet part into the soul of the music. If you succeed in doing this, your trumpet playing will also assume the quality of greatness.

ON PLAYING THE TUBA*

William Bell

A few years ago a paragraph appeared in the column entitled "Keeping Up with the World" in Collier's magazine, stating that a violinist can play approximately 1250 notes per minute whereas only 50 notes per minute are possible on the tuba. This is a typical piece of popular misinformation. The good tuba player can easily play half as fast as a violinist. Indeed, with one or two reservations--the main one being that a tuba requires more breath--a tuba can be played as fast as a trumpet. We can double and triple tongue, and play scales equally as fast. And speaking of flexibility, the average tuba player moves over a much greater range than that of the trumpet. That we usually play at an easy pace in performance is due, of course, to the character of the parts written for the instrument--whether or not the composer is aware of the potentialities of the instrument.

In teaching, I do not use tuba studies, but the Arban Cornet Method. Outside of occasional breathing difficulties, it is ideally suited to the tuba or any other brass instrument. Tuba playing has developed a good deal during the last twenty years, and most conductors and composers are behind the times in this respect.

Another prevalent misconception is that the bass tuba is a difficult instrument because it sounds clumsy in certain passages. The bass tuba, it should be remembered, has been in general use only some seventy years, and many of the parts performed on the instrument today were not written for it, but for its predecessors --among them the ophicléide, an instrument with a body somewhat resembling the saxophone. Another factor is that many tuba parts --Berlioz' "Romeo and Juliet" and the Fantastic Symphony, for example--were written for small instruments which bear a closer resemblance to our baritones than to our bass tubas.

---

*From Symphony, January 1950.

Last winter when Charles Munch was rehearsing Roussel's Third Symphony and the first entrance of the tuba arrived, I demonstrated the tone of our American bass tuba. Mr. Munch nearly hit the roof of Carnegie Hall, but by the time he had recovered I was ready with the small F tuba to give him the small tone that I knew he wanted and which is customary in France.

The national and historical background of each composition is a factor which must be taken into account by tuba players and conductors. The title, "Tuba," on the score is only a rough indication of the instrument that is required. It should also be said that tuba players in general have a tendency to play too loud which destroys not only the balance but the quality of tone as well. I use several tubas: a double instrument--bass and tenor tubas combined--for general use and a small F tuba for a small sound.

Musicians have probably noticed that some tubists, when playing passages extending from low to high notes, have to readjust their embouchures when entering the high register, or vice versa. Usually such a player will not have a good tone, and close examination would reveal mouthpiece markings on the lips which testify to a faulty embouchure. And, I am sorry to say, a great many instructors in colleges and other schools teach the totally incorrect embouchure known as the "smiling" method. The principle of this system is that the higher the note, the more one stretches the lips (or smiles); the lower the note, the flabbier the lips.

The tuba player who uses this method cannot sail into the high register easily inasmuch as there is a limit to the stretch of the lips and thus to the high range of the player. The closer the player comes to this limit, the more anemic and poor in quality becomes the tone. The player must therefore stop in the ascending passage and completely change his embouchure. Strictly speaking, he has two embouchures, not one.

The proper formation of the embouchure is to bring the corners of the mouth slightly forward so that they act as anchors and hinges for the lips, and so that the lips form a cushion between the teeth and the mouthpiece. The lip position in the mouthpiece is about even--half upper and half lower--although it can vary as much as 60-40 one way or the other. Further, it is of no great importance whether it is the upper or lower lip which vibrates; equally good results can be obtained from either lip.

The section of the instrument's range to be dealt with first takes in the two octaves approximately from the F on the fourth line downwards to the F below the staff. In this range the pitch is lowered by dropping the jaw, thereby exerting a pull on the lips. In ascending, the procedure is reversed. In the ranges below and above this section, the change in pitch is effected by compression and decompression of the lips.

This method of embouchure control, when mastered, gives

the player full control and flexibility.   When needed, a vibrato can
be made by the movement of the jaw.

Roughly, this is how a tuba player ticks.   But we often
sigh and wish there were more composers who could read the
time.

WAGNERIAN BRASS STYLE*

Maurice Faulkner

Numerous brass specialists have researched the literature
of that verbose composer, Richard Wagner, and those who followed
him, either in conducting his music or in interpreting his words
about his music, in order to learn how to perform his magnificent
brass parts.   The fact that this one man developed and required
new brass tone colors for performances of his later operas is
enough to place him in the "Brass Hall of Fame." whenever and
wherever it should be established.   But Wagner notwithstanding,
his own descriptions of what he intended do not really place the
emphasis where it belongs: namely, on the production of the brass
sound on the particular instrument notated for in the score and
balanced by an astute musician playing that instrument under the
baton of a true Wagner conductor.

The usual German Kapellmeister, when he interprets Wagner, insists on loud blowing rather than a finesse of balance.
Some, whom I have heard, even go so far as to permit the brasses
to dominate an orchestra of one hundred men.   These are moments
when such domination becomes essential to the proper interpretation of the motives and the concepts of the music, but to permit
such domination at practically all brass entrances is to misunder-
stand Wagner and spoil the performance for the true connoisseur,
as well as contribute to the early damaging of the voices on the
stage.

Seldom does an ordinary Kapellmeister earn the opportunity
for conducting at the major opera houses in the world because the
taste and knowledge of proper Wagner playing has become a special
quality for most opera managers these days.   But there were moments in history when the "Blechbläser," as the brasses are called
in German, meant nothing more than loud and obstinate sound, in
certain quarters.   I will never forget a point in my career when I
was expected to overblow the climax of Die Meistersinger Overture
and almost "blacked out" in the process.   Such "windy" brass is
seldom tolerated these days in the finest professional ensembles.
But there is a tendency for such a thing to develop in amateur and

*From The Instrumentalist, September 1969.   Reprinted by permis-
sion of The Instrumentalist Co.

semi-professional performances of Wagner, and brass players must guard against the tensions and stresses which generate under conductors who demand that approach.

The Proper Concept

There is no precise measurement of what is the right or proper concept except the taste of the conductor and the good judgment of the musician.   I have heard fine brass sections of famous ensembles perform superbly in the first act of Götterdämmerung only to falter in the difficult measures of the second act.   Time and again the horns measure up to the demands of the eight horn canonic materials in a Wagnerian masterpiece only to fail the conductor in the last act climaxes.

A brass musician should attempt to understand how his particular motive fits into the fabric of the orchestral accompaniment. This becomes more essential nowadays when the supply of Heldentenors is at an all-time low and their voices need the protection of competent pit performance.   When a brass figure becomes a highlight of the dramatic motion of the music and the stage action, then it must be played in the spirit of its character: a bravura solo will require a refined tongue control, not too far forward so that it doesn't become blatant, and still precise enough to give the essence of the heroic element.   When the motive is more lyrical then the musician must "cuddle it," so to speak, with his tongue so that it becomes suave, velvet in color, and resonant.

Thus a concept of the dramatic materials is essential to the well-trained player.   Many instrumentalists in the opera houses learn these concepts from experience in daily rehearsals under competent conductors who describe what they want and who expect the performers to produce it regardless of the technique needed. I have watched apprentice trumpeters, for instance, sit along with their teachers in the opera pits of European houses during rehearsals, listening and assisting in the climaxes, copying the sounds and the attacks of their mentors.   In the United States, where we have almost no opera houses and only a limited number of opportunities for brass specialists to learn these skills, there are great varieties of sound that pass for Wagnerian style.

The Tone Quality

Basic to the Wagnerian style is the resonant, sonorous tone quality which the composer heard in his mind as he put the music on paper.   Wagner has discussed these concepts in the ten volumes of his prose works, although he has not been able to define the technical skills essential to producing the results.   But above all, he was acquainted with the German and Austrian version of the rotary valve trumpet which provides the musicians in those opera houses and symphony orchestras with the type of tone ingrained in their personalities and traditions.   In these countries, and in most of Eastern Europe, the piston valve trumpets, such as we use, are referred to as "jazz trumpets."

The even scale of the rotary valve trumpets in the Central and Eastern European nations offers finer intonation than that of our piston models and less resistance on certain tones which speak with more body and less nasal color. Engineers will debate this with measurements and oscillograph readings that appear to be the same whatever the type of trumpet. However, all they need to do is compare, in the confines of the opera pit, the two types of instruments in a Wagnerian opera, and their ears will point up the effectiveness of the rotary valves in reproducing the Wagnerian sound in the complex environs of his scores. The same is true also for the music of Richard Strauss, although that is a topic for another article.

The instrument is not the only factor in developing the sonority of the tone. The lips must provide a smooth and full surface for the vibration of the sound. Some instrumentalists achieve this with a round opening that provides more air surface in the vibrating center than does a more tense, thin line.

The air current is also enlarged by a wider opening of the throat so that a broader volume of wind passes into the lip area. Some teachers insist upon the player forming his sound with dark syllables, such as oh and awh. This will color the tones more darkly but it also affects the pitch, and the musician must accommodate that change in order to match his colleagues in the section and throughout the orchestra.

Tongue Style

Most specialists in Wagner brass playing have emphasized a different type of staccato and legato tonguing in order to produce the broad, sonorous tone. I have analyzed a number of major brass sections including those of the Bayreuth Wagner Festival Orchestra, the Munich Opera, Vienna State Opera, Hamburg State Opera, Covent Garden Opera, Metropolitan Opera, Chicago Lyric Opera, Berlin German Opera (in the West), and the East Berlin State Opera. It appears to me in a subjective inventory of these skilled musicians that there are a variety of tongue placements essential to the total gamut of Wagner playing. These placements vary from instrument to instrument: that is, what is first-rate for a trumpet will be too forceful for a French horn, etc. I believe, though, that a competent brass specialist should be able to use the broad end of his tongue against the back of his upper or lower teeth, depending upon his needs, and produce in that fashion a full, warm, heavy attack which will not be blatant, but which will have all of the power necessary and be broad enough to match the powerful broad, string sound.

Furthermore, as the player comes upon accent marks for such a tongued note, instead of driving the tongue more forcefully into the teeth and lips, he would produce a more competent sound by using a breath accent in conjunction with the tongue rather than the hard tongue stroke so commonly used by amateurs and, unfortunately, also by some professionals.

These tongue sounds will vary as the demands and styles of the passages change, but this ability is a basic one that serves many purposes in playing Wagner. Obviously, such a skill would not be very compatible with playing Mozart or Haydn. Nevertheless, some of the finest Germanic Wagnerian playing I have heard has been accomplished with just such tongue concepts on the rotary valve instruments.

Conclusion

Space does not permit me to deal with other vital aspects of Wagner style such as transposition and alternate fingerings, so essential to proper intonation and blending. Also, the breadth of sustaining of tones in one category of playing will vary from act to act in the same opera. For instance, the quarter note with a dot or with a legato mark above it will change its character as the drama changes its intensity. Such notation in a third act climax would require a different set of values from those of the more relaxed earlier acts. The musician must measure these values against the sounds he hears evolving in the strings and woodwinds. One of the best authorities on this sort of playing was the famous Wagnerian conductor, Hermann Scherchen, whose book on conducting was a masterpiece. Unfortunately it has not been reprinted, as far as I know.

The astute section leader and section member of any orchestra or band needs to understand much more than just the requirements of the printed notes in his part. He must bring superb skills to the playing of that part, but those skills must be guided and molded by a knowledge and an understanding of what the total artistic idea is all about.

HARPISTS VERSUS CONDUCTORS*

Carlos Salzedo

It would be unreasonable to expect that all orchestral conductors could know everything about each musical instrument. But, there is one in particular about which they know surprisingly little --the harp.

In the first place, orchestral leaders do not always reckon with the fact that most symphonic and operatic harp parts are to be partly or fundamentally rewritten. Among the great composers, Debussy, Ravel, and Puccini are the only ones whose harp parts are harpistically and intelligently conceived. Two giants, Wagner and Strauss, wrote harp parts just as unplayable as they are useless from the viewpoint of sound. Musicians who are not aware of

---

*From Symphony, January 1952.

these facts may wonder what are the causes of them. This is due
to three principal factors. Prior to the latter part of the 19th
century the carrying power of the harp was very limited. Then,
too, most harpists of the past were bad musicians. As a result,
composers were not attracted to compose for that instrument. It
took the supersensitiveness of Debussy, Ravel and Puccini to sense
the harp, and to give it its proper orchestral function.

In general, conductors approach harpists, or harp problems,
from the wrong end. For instance, when a conductor is about to
audition a harpist, one of his first queries is whether the harpist
is a good sight-reader! This question is unreasonable, and does
not speak well for the conductor. Why is it unreasonable? Two
reasons. The first one refers to composers. As pointed out
above, very few composers wrote playable harp parts; most of
them conceived their harp parts at a piano or in their misinformed
imaginations. Aside from proverbial arpeggios (in which they have
always too many notes), they write passages, more or less pianistic, never realizing that the fingering of the harp is exactly the
opposite of that of the piano. A simple example: on the piano we
finger the C major scale 1-2-3-1-2-3-4-5; on the harp the fingering
is 4-3-2-1-4-3-2-1. How many musicians, conductors included,
know that? (Take a bow, Reader!) Also, on the piano the mixture of black and white keys facilitates hand patterns; certain passages "fall under the fingers. " Nothing like that exists on the
harp: our 47 strings, in spite of having three colors in each octave, have no palpable landmarks and this precludes schemes for
hand patterns. The second reason refers to pedals. As everyone
knows (or am I presuming too much?), we have seven pedals
through which all chromatics are governed; this is a very complicated subject. Of course, there are wizards among harpists, but
those harpists have passed the stage of auditioning. I wish to be
forgiven for quoting my own case in relation to sight-reading: I
have the reputation of being one of the best score readers on the
piano; give me a harp part to sight-read and my reputation might
vanish instantly. I have pulled many of our young colleagues out
of embarrassment by stating this in front of their prospective conductors!

The question of the carrying power of the harp is also
greatly miscalculated by most conductors. During my four years
at the "Met" (where I was imported from Paris by Toscanini) I
came in contact with many conductors. The immortal maestro was
the only conductor imbued with a sense of sonorous evaluation. He
never distorted or nullified the sound of the harp (or of any other
instrument).

Without any thought of mingling internationalism with music,
I have always noticed that Italian, French, Hungarian, English and
Russian conductors have a much better conception of the harp
sound, and a better general understanding of the instrument, than
their Teutonic colleagues.

Conductors are not always consistent. The following anecdote may be edifying. During a rehearsal, one of our eminent
harpists was repeatedly requested by the conductor to play softer,
"more softly, " "even softer. " In truth, she could hardly hear herself play, and from the auditorium I could not hear her at all.
Perplexed by such an unreasonable request, she asked me what to
do. I advised her to play almost inaudibly at the next rehearsal
and then normally loud at the performance. She did, and the conductor did not even look at her! (Such tricks could not be played
on Toscanini--nor would he demand such an unreasonable thing.)

Another typical instance of sonorous miscalculation: a conductor was listening to the rehearsal of his orchestra from the
auditorium. He stopped the assistant conductor and shouted, "More
harp. " My young colleague played louder. After the intermission
the head conductor took charge of the rehearsal. When arriving
at the same passage he stopped and exclaimed, "Too much harp. "
I was in the auditorium and can affirm that the harpist had played
the passage exactly alike both times! Only the conductor did not
seem to realize that a harp twenty feet near by and one 200 feet
away sound different.

The location of the harp section in symphony orchestras is
not always selected beneficially, either for the orchestra or for the
audience. Some conductors put the harps toward the back of the
orchestra. They pretend that the sound blends better with the other instruments. That antiquated theory is on a par with the proverbial German "papier musik"--an interesting dead matter without
sonorous worth. The truth is that, placed way back, the harps
are swamped by whatever instruments are around them. Those
conductors have no regard for instrumental aesthetics; they fail to
realize that the public likes to look at the harps, all the more
when enhanced by our attractive lady harpists. Everything well
considered, the harp section in a symphony orchestra ought to be
at the end of the first row, at the conductor's right.

Tuning is another orchestral problem. Conductors do not
always know that a harp can get out of adjustment without notice,
and that the best harp tuner in the world is powerless whenever a
modulating disk gets out of order; indeed, it puts the whole harp
in an untunable condition. Sometimes, too, depending on extreme
temperature, strings are liable to become false, thereby untunable.
This fortunately happens less frequently since we now use nylon
strings from the top of the harp down to middle C.

The pitch of a harp does not agree consistantly with that of
other instruments; it depends on whether all the woodwinds are
properly warmed. The string players, as everyone knows, love
to tune too high; this does not facilitate matters. It seems that
the only instruments with which the harp is in tuning agreement
are cymbals and triangle! While on this subject, I should like to
tell a personal story. When we were playing Meistersingers at
the "Met, " I would always go for dinner right after the beginning

of the Prelude (if I may confess this now!). Returning from the restaurant in time to play the end of the first act, I had to pull up all my strings a good quarter-tone higher, notwithstanding the fact that all the other instruments were playing around me. Conductors never have difficulty in keeping their batons in tune!

THE PERCUSSION RENAISSANCE*

Robert Ricci

It is a fascinating aspect of human perception that the rhythmic force in music tends to dominate other musical elements such as pitch, timbre, texture and harmony. No doubt because of the implicit immediacy of rhythm, percussion instruments have had a long, important, and varied function in the most diverse cultures.

While the percussion instruments have also had an important function in Western music, they have slowly acquired the role of decoration or emphasis. During the baroque period, for example, Henry Purcell and Jean-Baptiste Lully employed timpani for the first time as a component part of the orchestra, not as devices to be used in their own right as had often been the case in Renaissance courts or in battle. (Gordon B. Peters in his remarkable Treatise on Percussion remarks that it was a supreme honor, in battle, to capture the kettledrums of the enemy!) As soon as specific parts were written out for the percussion, it became clear that their role would be limited and subservient to the overall musical conception.

The classical period, with its inherent precision and economy of style, could not give to the percussion a role of great magnitude. Nor could the romantic era that was to follow do much more in recognizing the potential of percussion, although in the eyes of some composers (e.g., Berlioz, Meyerbeer and Bellini) the role of percussion in the orchestra was considerable.

With the technical improvements achieved in instrument building during the latter part of the 19th century the timpani became more versatile. The pedal made more chromatic passages possible, so that the door was opened for the advent of a new approach to the employment of percussion in its own right, as well as in an expanded role within the orchestra itself. Mahler and Berlioz began to call for a percussion section greatly augmented and more soloistically oriented. Only then was the full color of the percussion ensemble beginning to be explored.

It wasn't until the 20th century that composers began to

---

*From Selmer Bandwagon, no. 62 (1971), published by Selmer Division of the Magnavox Co., copyright 1971. Reprinted by permission.

make full use of the percussion instruments, employing them in fascinating new settings, with virtuoso technique often becoming mandatory. Now the percussion has finally become liberated from the role of occasional support or a splash of color at a point of emphasis or climax. In particular composers have become intrigued by the keyboard percussion such as xylophone, vibraphone, xylomarimba (xylorimba), glockenspiel and the marimba.

Composers can achieve a tremendous variety of effects on these instruments. The xylophone, for example, can provide rapid and facile passage work. It can arpeggiate, or play a more continuous type of running style as in Henry Cowell's "Concerto for Percussion." Yet, in the hands of a composer like Messiaen one finds the same instruments used for very disjunct leaps, grace notes, trills, rolls and glissandi imitating the calls of birds, as in his "Oiseaux Exotiques." For a composer like Stravinsky the instrument becomes harsh and sardonic, as in his "Agon."

When one considers all of the types of beaters available today for use on the xylophone it becomes clear why the instrument can be so versatile:†

Plastic mallets: most "unusual" sound

Hard core mallets: less "bite" than plastic mallets

Wood mallets: "toy-like" effect in the upper register; a good general xylophone sound

Hard rubber mallets: good general sound; not much bite

Medium cord mallets: less "bite" than hard rubber mallets

Soft cord mallets: a good subdued sound, somewhat akin to that of the marimba

Hard yarn mallets: subtle, quiet sound

Soft and medium yarn mallets: more subtle than hard yarn mallets

As one speaks of the keyboard percussion instruments, it seems important to mention the effect that new kinds of music in the twentieth century have had in bringing out unfamiliar potential in these familiar instruments. Among these are the pointillistic style, jazz and its various affiliates in the popular and rock idioms. Jazz has been a stimulus for an instrument such as vibraphone, for example. Great jazz virtuosi such as Milt Jackson, Red Norvo, Gary McFarland and Lionel Hampton have given this instrument a new place in the sun. The fact that it can be played with a motor on or off gives it a shifting capacity not present in other similar instruments. "Serious" composers, among them Alban Berg and Boulez, were quick to pick up the instrument after they became acquainted with it in jazz.

Jazz drumming techniques have been another spur to more creative use of the drum ensemble. It was in the jazz ensembles first that the drummer was allowed to display his technique and skill in extended solos. Gene Krupa's lengthy solo on the Benny Goodman recording of "Sing, Sing, Sing" (1937) is a notable case in point. Jazz drummers since that time are usually afforded similar extended solos. Without this type of background it is unlikely that a piece such as "Echoi" by Lukas Foss, with its extremely demanding percussion part for one performer, ever would have been conceived.

It was the 20th-century composer who took the percussion instruments out of the orchestra, and put them in specialized ensembles so as to feature their unique capabilities. It is generally conceded that Edgard Varèse's "Ionization," which was first performed in the United States in 1933, started the trend toward the employment of the percussion ensemble as a separate entity. Aside from the great variety of instruments and performers required, it incorporated new effects such as the breaking of ginger ale bottles, the rubbing of a resined glove over a snare stick held on the center of a bass drum, and glissandi on the xylophone resonators. The fact that new sounds and new resources for sound were being explored led to many more compositions of this type, in which the overall "effect" was paramount over more traditional methods of organization in music. Composers such as John Cage, Lou Harrison, and Henry Cowell were quick to seize the implications evident in "Ionization."

Carlos Chavez, in his "Toccata" for six percussion players developed an effective piece through the simple contrast between the use of the drums alone for the first movement, tuned percussion (tubular bells, xylophone, glockenspiel) over untuned metals such as cymbal and gongs for the second movement, and drums with some Latin American instruments added for the third movement. And at this point I should mention the tremendous effect the increased knowledge of other cultures has had upon percussion writing. Today one commonly finds instruments such as congo drums, African goblet drums, Chinese drums, Chocolos, tablas, the guiro, maracas, and the Egyptian sistrum, to mention but a few, not uncommon in scores.

For example, in Jean Barraque's "Chant après Chant" alternating groups of players create rapid color and instrumental changes using such diverse instruments as tom-toms, tablas, bongo drums, the snare drums, marimba, glockenspiel, cymbals, Chinese cymbal, and mokubios (an extra large temple block with a deep and mellow sound sometimes called Buddhist slit drums.)

Undoubtedly, the trend toward diversification will increase as time goes on.

This brief historical survey only suggests the reasons why percussion instruments have recently achieved a prominence in our music they had not had in centuries.

†This information on mallets is superbly presented in a valuable
book on percussion by H. Owen Reed and Joel T. Leach entitled
Scoring for Percussion (Englewood Cliffs, N. J. : Prentice-Hall,
1969).

_____

TIPS OF THE TRADE*

Daniel Bonade

Several years ago, a typical heartbreaking conversation took
place in a conductor's dressing room in the middle-west. In this
particular case, the conductor was both a nice guy and a competent
musician. The interview was embarrassing, doubly so because it
concerned the discharge of a musician who was well liked. After
considerable prodding and pleading for the reasons, the conductor
finally told the musician that he was deficient. Technically, the
musician was excellent, but he simply did not know how to phrase.

The musician was incensed. He was accused of the rankest
of crimes ... and one which he refused to confess to. The interview ended heatedly and shortly thereafter word spread that such
and such a conductor was a ... and a ..., etc. It just so happened that in this case the conductor was absolutely right and was
competent enough to realize that nothing could be done about the
situation.

Unfortunately, most cases of this sort are not as cut and
dry. There are literally thousands of reasons why particular musicians do not qualify for orchestral work. This article was written as an introduction. Most professional musicians will toss it
aside as old hat. For many, it is. For many others, it isn't.
There are musicians who have been playing with orchestras off and
on for years who still have not developed a good "orchestral
sense. " While there are hundreds of things to watch for, I will
only mention a few and try and give a perspective which will be
helpful both to students and professionals.

An orchestral musician is made before he even plays in
one. Despite denials from many quarters, I maintain that there
is no reason why a musician who has had adequate "basic training"
cannot walk into his first orchestra job and make the grade successfully. McGinnis started when he was in short pants, knowing
all the ins and outs. His basic training lasted for four or five
years and did the trick.

In the past several years, the standards of our orchestras
have gone up, particularly in terms of basic requirements. Where

_____

*From Woodwind Magazine, September 1950. Reprinted by permis-
sion of Ralph Lorr, Publisher.

the emphasis was placed on technique, it is now decidedly more on phrasing.   Where formerly it was possible to bone up on a specific work, flashy and convincing in nature, now a good audition is based more on ability to phrase and handle the conductor's momentary whims.

There is an old prejudice to the effect that there are two kinds of musicians ... orchestral players and soloists.   This is to my way of thinking, completely false.   The so-called personality requirements of an orchestral player apply as well to the soloist. Their basic training is identical in its tediousness and in its disciplinary requirements.   A certain adjustment is necessary to be able to switch from one to the other, but any competent musician should be able to make the switch.   While what the musician really wants to do determines his choice of a career, any suitably equipped musician should be able to play in an orchestra.   I have seen any number of soloists play in orchestras, quickly adapting themselves to the conductor's requirements.

The problem of technique is also heavily overexaggerated. Anybody can acquire technique.   It is the most mechanical feature of instrumental playing and requires only patience and time.   This is obvious when you take the case of student or amateur orchestras. The same programs are studied for six months and then are played with varying degrees of competence.   But when faced with the problem of playing a different program each week, the best players won't be able to make it.   Even those instrumentalists in amateur orchestras who have a satisfactory technique require considerable time before being able to master a given work.   There are the innumerable little tricks of ensemble work which have to be mastered, such as when to come in, when to go out, etc.   These things are only learned through experience and by imitation.   But they are all secondary to the prime problem of phrasing ... which must be learned and learned methodically.

Basic to orchestral work is the acceptance of the fact that the conductor is the leader, in every sense.   The musician who refuses to accept this fact might as well give up orchestral work. Whether you like him or not, whether he is wrong or right, you cannot lead or dispute.   It is always his prerogative as to how he wants a work played and you must follow.   The problem for the woodwind instrumentalist is a little bit more complex.   The individual woodwinds are actually soloists playing alone, not together in a group, while the violins must go along with the rest of the section.   In addition, the woodwind choir has the problem of matching each other, even though they all have different parts. But superior to all these things is the real dependency on the conductor.   You must do everything in time ... his time, not yours. This is one of the greatest problems for many orchestral men.   A lack of flexibility and inability to respond plasticly to the conductor results in tempo difficulties.

One of the most annoying and difficult jobs in orchestral

playing is the necessity of counting bars rest. There is no point in stressing the importance of counting correctly. It is obvious that a musician cannot rely entirely upon cues from the conductor or upon his ear for the correct bar to make his entrance. However, when the musician is confronted with a large number of bars rest, especially in slow movements, there is a tendency for his mind to wander. Only the utmost concentration can assure him of the correct spot for entrance. Counting each bar mentally, one often has to count all the inner counts of each bar and if there is any tendency to day-dream, the musician will be unable to come in with assurance. The best and most efficient method of counting is actually with the fingers. Be sure of establishing a habit in using this method. Assume that the thumb is always the first bar rest, the index, the second, etc. Your mind is then free to a large extent and you can follow the different motions of the conductor's baton in any rhythm, through fermates and rubatos, without losing the count of the number of bars that have passed.

Another important factor in orchestra playing is the understanding of the correct application of dynamic markings. Each of the woodwinds has certain characteristic qualities in each register. They have a certain level of dynamic spread which composers do not always understand or take into account when writing orchestrally for them. An orchestral pianissimo will be indicated by pp in all the voices in the score. But it is often necessary to deviate from these markings considerably, depending on the importance of the voice played and the quality of the register the music is written in. A low voiced oboe part is difficult to play softly. Hence, if marked piano, it must actually be played pp and a high voiced bassoon part, because of its natural quality, must be played at least mf for a correct balance. Countless examples are available, but an understanding of the relative importance of the voice being played and its natural strength will enable the musician to correctly correlate his voice in the orchestral tapestry with a certain disregard of the composer's markings.

It is well to mark an x or other indication in your part to indicate when this voice is prominent. In playing through large quantities of music, the performer cannot always rely on his memory to recall and spot the small passages that are heard through the orchestral texture but are not solo and hence have no composer's markings to differentiate them from the rest of the part. Every seasoned orchestral musician will recall moments when he suddenly heard himself playing for a moment or two "out in the open" without realizing that the passage would be "open" simply because he had not marked the part with some indication. Tutti playing is somewhat coarser than solo playing and such an emergence can prove embarrassing.

At any rate this brings us to another point about orchestral musicians and orchestral playing. If you can play a solo a hundred times without missing, you may be able to play it well once in the orchestra. Actually, a musician is as good as the solo he plays

the worst. It is then possible to play anything well 75 per cent of
perfection. The most important thing (which some people refuse to
recognize) is consistency. Very good players miss a cadenza now
and then. It doesn't mean a thing because they make it most of
the time. The whole idea of perfection is nonsense and only the
biggest fool of a conductor could possibly expect it. Any musician
plays certain things better than others and his prime function in an
audition or in the orchestra is to make the conductor feel that he
knows his business. Remember ... the biggest thing of all ... the
musician is there to please the conductor, and not vice versa. The
conductor is always right. All he has to say is ... "That's the
way I want it" ... and you do it. Whether you like it or not, this
is the meaning of the orchestral relationship.

To sum up, I want to stress phrasing again, because it is
still the biggest problem today. There are plenty of men who can
play everything fast ... at breakneck speeds which amaze everybody including themselves. But the slow passages ... ah ...
that's where they're caught. Technique can always be acquired,
the little tricks involved in doing an efficient job are only a matter
of time as they are in any job, finesse is learned by imitation ...
but phrasing! ... that's a different story. The phrasing problem
involves the conductorial relationship as well. There are too many
cases in recent history where conductor and soloist battled all season over details of phrasing. There are trillions of tricky little
passages in the repertoire which hit you between the eyes when
you see them for the first time ... and then it's too late. Unless
you were ready for them to begin with, no amount of flash will
save the day. A professional has no time to learn the musical
trade once he hits an orchestra. The stuff has to be there to begin with. You can fool one conductor, two conductors, three conductors ... but someday you run up against the one maestro who
can look right through you, and then ... back to the rockpile.

TIPS OF THE TRADE*

Ralph Lorr

Men and women of the symphony orchestra! Are you secure? Are you successful? Does your conductor listen to your
each and every word? What is the greatest threat to your job,
your home, your security? The new musicians, of course, that
join your orchestra from strange cities like Chicago, New York
and Philadelphia. They are the ones who come charging in with
their new and stupid ideas and of course little orchestra experience.

*From Woodwind Magazine, April 1951. Reprinted by permission
of Ralph Lorr, Publisher.

These people can be very dangerous if not carefully watched. Their contaminating ideas on tone, phrasing, vibrato, etc., are low brow and vulgar. The fact that too many music lovers are taken in by these cheap ideas only gives me greater strength and conviction that we wiser and more experienced old timers must use strong tactics to fight off these foreigners. There are many systems of course, but mine has stood the test of time and is guaranteed (as many of my students will testify). Once you have mastered the Lorr method, nobody ... I repeat ... nobody will be able to rob you of the prestige, the fame, the money, the adoration that comes after years of applying my method.

Let's start with a hypothetical case. You are head of your section. A new man has come in. Regard him as vicious, sly, and tricky from the very beginning. You must never let your guard down and must hasten to beat him to the draw. The first step is subtle, infinitely cunning and sets your foe up for the drop kick that follows. Win his confidence. Treat him like a friend, like your one and only son. Swelter him with sly pats on the head and jovial slaps on the back. Praise his work and make him feel completely comfortable and relaxed. Remember, we must never hesitate or proscrastinate if we are to save the cause of good music ... and our jobs!

After this campaign, which is occasionally expensive, but well worth it, the invader is off guard and the first blow is carefully planned and executed. There are many variations, all of which are successful. The one you use depends on the particular case, because, of course, you must size up your opponent with all the care and skill of an ace psychoanalyst:

1. Subtly and genially suggest to the other members of your section that the new man is ruining the section ... bad intonation, smug attitude, smart alecky, poor rhythm, etc. You can readily supplement this list with a bit of imagination.

2. Suggest to the invader that the orchestra and conductor are terrible. If he says nothing, it surely indicates that he agrees. At the first chance to get the conductor's ear, be sure to enlighten him on the new member's attitude and, of course, thoroughly spread the news throughout the orchestra. It often helps to single out the other first chair men and tell them, "The new man says you play like a dead fish."

3. At your first opportunity, stop the orchestral rehearsal to ask the conductor whether the second man has a ff or pp indication in his part. This invariably convinces the conductor that you are on the ball and causes your colleague to respect you more.

4. If the instrument you play has a natural tendency to play sharp in the lower register and flat in the higher register (or vice-versa), wait for a quiet passage where you are playing in octaves with the second man. Lip down or up, as the case may be,

so that the second man cannot possibly adjust to your pitch. The best effect is secured when it sounds like one of you is a quarter tone off. Be sure to announce in resonant whispers to all about, "Isn't the intonation horrible lately?"

5. Whenever moving passages in unison occur, be sure to play them just a trifle ahead or behind the tempo. This gives a poor ensemble effect and can lead to asking the conductor if he doesn't think the passage would sound better with only one instrument playing it.

6. Confuse your colleague by counting bars rest softly, but audibly, being sure that the count is always wrong. Counting 1, 3, 2, 4, 6, 5, etc., is effective, as is 10, 8, 6, 4, 2, 1, 3, etc. This tactic is especially forcible when playing piano concertos where 30 to 50 bars of rest give the player time to relax. An additional strategy most revealing is to lift the instrument hurriedly to the mouth one bar early in an effort to make the second man enter a bar early with a beautiful tutti forte.

7. When a difficult program is scheduled, be sure to get sick just before the second rehearsal. Your colleague will undoubtedly have the wrong reed for playing the first chair and generally messes the rehearsal up. Everybody is happy to see you limp in the next morning and will appreciate your artistry all the more.

By this time, the enemy is reeling. Now to go ahead with the knockout blow.

8. Carefully bend the keys on your colleague's instrument if he is stupid enough to leave it on the chair during intermissions. This can be accomplished readily if one is alert and the tactic well planned in advance. A quiet movement of the hand during the exit of the instrumentalists is quite sufficient. ONLY USE THIS TACTIC DURING CONCERTS. When the second man returns, he will have to repair his instrument as best as he can in a very few seconds. The resultant squeaks are wonderful to behold. A variation on this is the horsehair treatment. However, this method takes a somewhat more careful preparation. It is 100 per cent effective. Simply place a very short length of horsehair under a closed key in the upper portion of the instrument. The horsehair must not protrude more than $1/4$ to $1/2$ inch from the key in question. The other end of the hair must be placed under the pad so that it projects a bit into the actual hole. The result is a badly leaking pad that is very difficult to locate, and, in addition, makes playing in the lower register almost impossible.

9. Now is the time to announce in no uncertain terms that you will not return the following season unless the management gets rid of your hopeless colleague, as he has ruined the section, disgraced the orchestra, slandered the conductor. The following season you can then install the most mediocre of your students in the

second chair and at the same time do a genuine service for the good of music.

Remember, friends, keep these ideas to yourself and use them only when it appears that the new man actually may develop into a better instrumentalist than you.   We can kid everybody else, but ourselves. Beware of talent.   It must be stifled with the utmost dispatch.   If these methods are not used almost immediately who can tell how long you will be sitting in your first chair.

Chapter IV

THE AUDIENCE:
The Music Consumers

Introduction. Orchestral music would be pointless without the listener.
This important factor in music making, the audience, is viewed by
economists (William J. Baumol and William G. Bowen), professional
market researchers (Eric Marder Assoc., Inc.), performers-con-
ductors (Harry Ellis Dickson and Zubin Mehta), critics (Howard Taubman and Stephan Bornstein), a music educator (Thomas H. Hill) and
an orchestra manager (Helen M. Thompson).

THE AUDIENCE*

William J. Baumol
and William G. Bowen

        The relevance of an analysis of audience characteristics to
a study of the economics of the performing arts may not be immediately apparent. After all, one might argue that, from a purely
pecuniary point of view, the only pertinent factor is box office receipts, and not the identity of the individual who buys the tickets.
If the box office does a sufficiently brisk business, a performing
company's finances will be in satisfactory condition, no matter who
purchases its tickets. Why, then, do we care about the makeup of
the audience?

        In fact, there are many reasons for our concern. First and
perhaps most important, though not from an economic point of
view, we care who attends because we believe participation in an
audience contributes to the welfare of the individual. If the arts
are a "good thing," we must concern ourselves with those who are
deprived of the experience.

        Second, we must know the characteristics of the audience if

we are to evaluate ticket pricing and distribution policies.   The
complaints one hears about high ticket prices discouraging certain
groups of people from attending can be evaluated ultimately only in
terms of audience composition.

A third reason for concern with the nature of the audience
is associated with the issue of government support.   Both the de-
sirability and the political feasibility of government support may
depend, at least in part, on the composition of the audience.

Fourth, even if we consider the performing arts dispassion-
ately as a product and nothing more, effective marketing policy requires that we know something about those who demand the commodity, just as an automobile manufacturer needs to know who buys
his cars.   This information helps the manufacturer to merchandise
his product and to plan his physical facilities: by giving him a
better idea of his future market potential, it enables him to reach
more rational decisions on investment policy and on the size and
direction of his future activities.

Audience data are necessary, too, for a variety of analytical
purposes which arise out of the questions with which we shall deal
in later chapters.   We have already mentioned one such fundamental
question, the effect of ticket prices on audience composition.
Equally significant is the relationship between the make-up of the
audience and the extent of the contributions which the performing
organization can hope to receive.   However, the present chapter is
primarily descriptive; it is essentially a report on who attends performances today, not an examination of the influences which determine attendance or a discussion of the possible effects of policy
changes on the nature of the audience.

Survey Methods

Most of this discussion is based on our own data--on figures
compiled from direct questioning of a sizable sample of audiences
throughout the country--because, by and large, detailed statistics
on the audience for the performing arts throughout the country are
unavailable.   There do exist a number of earlier studies treating
particular sectors of the arts, especially the theater.   We shall
refer to some of these later, but their structure and specialized
character restrict the extent to which they can be related to our
findings.

Some explanation of the nature of our survey and the procedures used in conducting it is necessary.   Our general procedure
involved the use of questionnaires which were distributed to a predetermined sample of the audience (usually 50 per cent) at performances of various kinds, by inserting copies into the programs.
Recipients were requested to complete the forms and return them
to us before they left the hall.   The respondent was asked about
his age, education, occupation, income, distance traveled to the
performance, the amount he spent on tickets, transportation,

restaurant and other expenses associated with his attendance, his frequency of attendance at other types of live performance, his inclination to contribute, and so on. Critical to the success of our survey was the truly extraordinary cooperation we received from the organizations involved. A request for permission to conduct a survey was rarely refused, and once it was granted we were usually offered all possible assistance.

The surveys were conducted from September of 1963 through March of 1965. In order to determine who should be surveyed, we first compiled a roster of professional organizations for each of the art forms, and then developed a sample which, though not random in a technical sense, gave us wide coverage in terms of art form, region and night of the week. In all, we surveyed 153 performances (88 theatrical, 30 orchestral, 8 operatic, 9 dance, 5 chamber music and 13 free open-air performances) and obtained 29,413 usable replies. The distribution of usable responses by art form corresponded closely to the distribution of estimated audience sizes. Only the Broadway audience was relatively under-represented by our survey, and this was deliberate, for we already had a great deal of information about the New York City audience from other sources.

As a direct consequence of the geographic distribution of the nation's professional performing organizations, most of our surveys took place in cities of substantial size. The list includes Los Angeles, San Francisco, Portland (Oregon), Seattle, Oklahoma City, Dallas, Houston, Chicago, Ann Arbor, Minneapolis, Cleveland, Cincinnati, Pittsburgh, Atlanta, Abingdon (Virginia), Washington, Baltimore, Philadelphia, Brooklyn and Boston.

On the average, our response rate--the proportion of persons who returned the questionnaires they had been given--was almost exactly 50 per cent. This rate is high for a survey requesting information about income and other personal matters. Broadway and opera audiences produced the lowest rate of response-- about 25 per cent in each case. While the low rate of return on Broadway is fairly easily accounted for by the special nature of its audience, which will be described later, our results for opera are less easily explained. The response rate is important not just because it affects the number of usable questionnaires, but also because it may have significant implications for the degree of bias in our results. For example, if bachelors were more willing than married men to provide the information requested, the tabulated results of the survey would report a proportion of married people in the audience much smaller than the true figure.

In order to determine whether, in fact, our results were seriously biased, we undertook several tests. In general, the results are reassuring. There were no marked differences in rates of return from various classes of seats; that is, holders of expensive tickets did not reply at a significantly different rate from holders of less expensive tickets. There was a very slight relationship between response rate and median income, with a small increase in rate of response associated with increases in the median income of audiences; and there was also a slight relationship between response rate and proportion of males in professional occupations-- the higher the number of professionals, the higher the number of returns. However, most of these relations were very weak and, in technical terms, did not satisfy the requirements of "statistical significance. " From a more general point of view, what is most comforting is the great consistency of our results. The fact that they show the same pattern at performances differing widely in type and geographic location suggests very strongly that they are not the consequence of accidental biases imparted by the nature of particular audiences.

Characteristics of the Audience: Age

Before presenting the results of our survey we shall comment briefly on one important audience characteristic which, for a variety of reasons, we did not investigate directly--ethnic composition. Several persons experienced in the management of performing organizations emphasized that this is a crucial characteristic. As one commented, musical performances are often in trouble in a city without a large German, Italian or Jewish population. A Jewish holiday can decimate the audience even in a Midwestern city. Several managers noted that Negroes, on the other hand, attend infrequently, even where there is no overt discrimination, except perhaps when Negro themes and performers are presented. Of course, these are only casual observations, and we have no way of substantiating them--let alone any way of separating out the effect on attendance of ethnic characteristics per se from the effect of income.

What does our survey tell us about differences between the typical audience and the population as a whole? A succinct summary of our principal findings is given in Table 1, where we present a composite profile of the audiences at the various art forms, each weighted by estimated attendance in 1963-64, and a corresponding profile for the urban population of the United States as of 1960.

The first thing these data suggest is that the performing arts audience, contrary to what many people believe, seems to be somewhat more heavily male than the population as a whole. Nearly 53 per cent of our respondents were male, whereas only a little more than 48 per cent of the urban population is male. However, this probably should not be taken too seriously. It may simply reflect a male prerogative: if a husband and wife were present and the questionnaire was contained in the wife's program, it is very possible that the husband would have filled it out.

Though the median age for the U. S. population is 8 years below that of the arts audience, this indicates simply that children do not often attend the theater although they are included in the Census. The rest of the data on age indicate that the audience is

(cont. on p. 246)

Table 1. Profile of the U.S. Performing Arts Audience, Compared with the Total Urban Population

	Performing Arts Audience[a]	Urban Population[b] (1960)
Sex		
Male	52.8%	48.4%
Age		
Under 20	6.9%	37.1%
Over 60	9.0	13.1
Median Age	38 yrs.	30.3 yrs.
Occupational Category		
Males:		
Employed Persons:[c]		
Professional	63.0%	12.7%
Teachers	10.3	1.1
Managerial	21.4	12.6
Clerical and Sales	13.0	17.2
Blue Collar	2.6	57.5
Students[d]	13.9	
Females:		
Employed Persons:[c]		
Professional	63.2%	14.0%
Teachers	25.4	5.6
Managerial	7.2	3.9
Clerical	24.9	34.3
Sales	2.8	8.5
Blue Collar	1.9	39.3
Students[d]	15.1	
Housewives[d]	35.2	
Education		
Males (age 25 and over):		
Grade School and Less Than 4 Yrs. High School	2.2%	56.6%
4 Yrs. High School	6.5	22.1
1-3 Yrs. College	12.8	9.8
4 Yrs. College	23.1	6.2
Graduate School	55.4	5.3
Median Category	Grad. work	2 yrs. h.s.
Females (age 25 and over):		
Grade School and Less Than 4 Yrs. High School	2.8%	55.1%
4 Yrs. High School	15.3	28.9
1-3 Yrs. College	23.6	9.5

244

	Performing Arts Audience[a]	Urban Population[b] (1960)
4 Yrs. College	26.7	4.5
Graduate School	31.6	2.0
Median Category	4 yrs. college	3 yrs. h. s.

Income

	Performing Arts Audience	Urban Population
Over $5000	91.3%	64.8%
Over $15,000	39.5	5.4
Over $25,000	17.4	1.5
Median Income	$12,804	$6166

Frequency of Attendance

Average Number of Performances
Attended in Last 12 Months:

	Number
Theater	8.4
Symphony	5.1
Opera	1.7
Dance	1.2
Other Serious Music	2.2

a Based on Twentieth Century Fund audience survey; 24,425 respondents. The figures given here are weighted averages of the results for individual art forms. The weights are based on estimated attendance in 1963-64 and are as follows (on a 100 point scale): Broadway = 38, off-Broadway = 5, regional repertory theater = 9, major orchestras = 38, opera = 6, dance = 4.

b Data from U.S. Census of Population, 1960: Detailed Characteristics, U.S. Summary, Tables 158, 173, 185, 194, 203, 224. A composite profile could have been built for just those cities where we conducted surveys, but some experimentation indicated that this refinement would have made little difference.

c The number of employed persons is the base for the following percentages. The percentage of teachers is a component of the "Professional" category.

d The base for these percentages is the total number of respondents.

FIGURE   1

AGE DISTRIBUTION OF THE U. S. PERFORMING ARTS
AUDIENCE AND OF THE TOTAL URBAN POPULATION

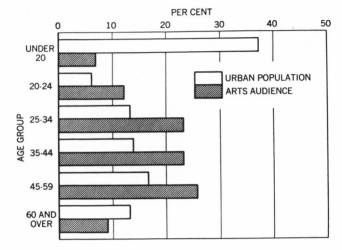

relatively young. This is shown most easily with the aid of Figure 1. In that graph, the dark bars represent the proportion of the audience in different age groups and the light bars the proportion of the urban population as a whole in these age groups. We see that relative to total population the arts audience is greatest in the interval 20 to 24 years of age. Twice as high a percentage of the arts audience (12. 2 per cent) lies in that age interval as is the case for the total urban population (6. 1 per cent). This ratio of 2. 00 is what we call the relative frequency; it is equal to the proportion of the audience within a given category divided by the proportion of the total urban population in that same category. Calculation of such figures for each of our other age group categories shows very clearly that relative frequency declines steadily with age once we get beyond the interval under 20 years of age. These figures tell us that the audience at a typical performance is far younger than the urban population as a whole, and that the older the age group, the smaller is its relative representation in a typical audience. Consequently, older people (those over 60) are the scarcest members of the audience in relation to their numbers in the urban population of the United States. In a word, audiences are young. With the proportion of the nation's population in the younger age brackets growing rather rapidly, this fact may be quite significant.

Two alternative hypotheses can explain the relative youthfulness of the arts audience. If the same age patterns have always characterized the audience, it means that people attend

performances when they are young and then gradually drop out of
the audience as they grow older.   They may become less interested,
or attendance may become more difficult for them, or other interests and responsibilities may keep them from the theater.   The
second hypothesis is more sanguine.   It may be that the performing arts are now attracting a younger audience than ever before.
If young people did not attend very frequently in the past, this
would account for the smaller number of older patrons today, the
absentees never having developed an interest in live performance.
If this is so and younger Americans are attending in far higher relative numbers than they did in the past, then we may be building
a base for a great future expansion.

Unfortunately, because there is so little in the way of comparable survey results for earlier years, we cannot be sure which
of these alternatives applies.   The only source of historical data
known to us is a series of Playbill surveys of the Broadway theater
audience going back to 1955-56.   These data show almost no change
in the age composition of the audience and thus support the view
that the audience is not growing younger.

Occupation, Education and Income

Turning next to the distribution of audiences by occupation,
we see that roughly 15 per cent of all our respondents were students, and that among employed males only 2 to 3 per cent of the
total audience included in the survey was composed of blue collar
workers, as compared to a figure of nearly 60 per cent for the
urban population as a whole.   We conclude that the audience for the
arts is made up preponderantly--indeed, almost entirely--of people from the white collar occupations.   In the typical arts audience
all of the white collar groups are over-represented (in comparison
with the urban population), with two exceptions, clerical and sales
persons.   The degree of over-representation is by no means the
same, however.   Among males there are roughly nine times as
many teachers in the audience as in the urban population of the
United States, and nearly five times as many professionals of all
sorts (see Figure 2).   The arts' share of professionals is also
much greater than their share of managerial personnel.   In general,
the very high proportion of members of the professions in the arts
audience is characteristic of both sexes.   However, the proportion
of teachers in the audience is much higher for men than for women.
As a possible explanation one might surmise that a high rate of
theatergoing is characteristic of teachers at more advanced professional levels, and that female teachers are more heavily distributed
in the lower grades of the schools.

Two numbers not shown on the table or the chart are of interest.   Three per cent of our employed male respondents were
themselves performing artists or performers and 5 per cent of the
females were in this category.   These proportions are surely significantly higher than those for the population as a whole, but the
unavailability of related Census data prevents a direct comparison.

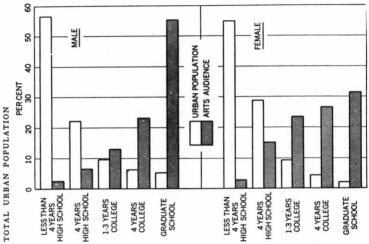

FIGURE 3

EDUCATIONAL ATTAINMENT OF THE U. S.
PERFORMING ARTS AUDIENCE AND OF THE
TOTAL URBAN POPULATION

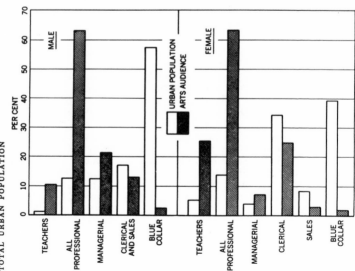

FIGURE 2

OCCUPATIONAL DISTRIBUTION OF THE U. S.
PERFORMING ARTS AUDIENCE AND OF THE
TOTAL URBAN POPULATION

Next we turn to the educational attainment level of the audiences, reported in Table 1 and shown graphically in Figure 3. All of these results refer only to persons 25 years of age and over, in order to avoid the biases introduced by including persons who are still in school. We conclude that the audience is composed of exceedingly well-educated persons. Less than 3 per cent of the males and females did not graduate from high school, as compared to the more than 50 per cent of the U. S. urban population 25 years and over who did not do so. At the other end of the spectrum, over 55 per cent of the males attending performances did some work beyond college--an educational level attained by only 5 per cent of the urban population. Almost one third of the women in the audience did some graduate work, as compared with 2 per cent of the female urban population who did so. In Figure 3 the sharp decline in the length of the light bars as we move from top to bottom means that the proportion of the urban population at each educational level falls very rapidly as the level of educational attainment increases; the reverse is true of the arts audience. [1]

The last socio-economic characteristic reported in Table 1, audience income, is described in more detail in Figure 4. Once more the results are clear-cut and extreme. They show that the median family income among a typical arts audience is roughly twice as high as that for the total urban population. Forty per cent of our arts audience had incomes of $15,000 or more, and 17 per cent had incomes of $25,000 or more. The proportion of the arts audience in the category $15,000 to $24,999 is nearly six times as high as that of the urban population as a whole; and about 11 and a half times as large a proportion of the audience earned over $25,000 as is true of the urban population generally. [2]

Differences in Profiles Among Art Forms

What variations in audience characteristics can be observed when the several art forms are examined separately?

The most remarkable finding is that audiences from art form to art form are very similar. They all show a median age in the middle 30's; over 60 per cent of the audience for each art form consists of people in the professions (and this finding holds for both sexes); all exhibit an extremely high level of education, with 50 per cent of the males having gone to graduate school and 50 per cent of the females having at least completed college; and there is a consistently high level of income, in no case involving a median under $11,000.

Some moderate differences by type of performance are worth pointing out. For instance, there are differences in attendance by sex among art forms. Women tend to predominate in the audiences of symphonies and the dance, whereas men constitute the majority attending the theater, opera and programs of chamber music. There is also a slight difference in age among the various audiences, with symphonies having a higher percentage of persons over

FIGURE   4

INCOME DISTRIBUTION OF THE U. S.
PERFORMING ARTS AUDIENCE AND OF THE
TOTAL URBAN POPULATION

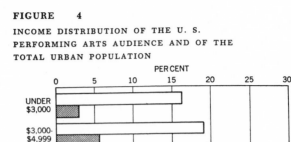

60.   However, we must point out that symphonies, perhaps more
than other art forms, frequently have special young people's concerts, none of which were surveyed by us.   The existence of these
concerts must surely bias our estimate of the age distribution of
symphony audiences, because many of the young people who attend
such special concerts might otherwise have been found in audiences
attending other performances.

As to occupations, we find that a relatively small number
of students attend ballet, opera and the theater, but that chamber
music audiences are heavily peopled by students, teachers and professionals in general.   While the number of blue collar workers
is low for all art forms, the highest proportion is found at the
opera.   This finding could reflect the effect of the culture of Europe, where opera is a popular art form, and may, therefore, report what is primarily an immigrant group.   On the other hand,
because of the small number of operatic organizations surveyed, it
may simply represent the influence of the New York City Opera
with its low admission prices.

The number of blue collar workers remained consistently low
throughout the survey.   Their share of the total male audience

reached 6 per cent in only 5 of our 35 theaters, never reached 5
per cent in any of the 12 major orchestras surveyed, constituted
5 per cent of the audience at the Brooklyn Opera, and 7 to 9 per
cent of the audience for non-contemporary opera at the New York
City Center. In dance, the proportion of blue collar workers was
7 per cent of the total at a performance of the Alvin Ailey Dance
Theatre (a Negro company with a considerable Negro following),
while in three of the other audiences surveyed there were no blue
collar workers. In chamber music audiences the number of blue
collar workers never reached 2 per cent.

Educational level was the most consistent element of all,
with chamber music drawing the most highly educated audience--
over 75 per cent of the males and 52 per cent of the females having attended graduate school.

Incomes also were consistently high, though theater patrons
had an income about $1500 higher, on the average, than members
of the audiences of other art forms. In only 2 of the 35 theaters
surveyed did median audience income fall below $10,000. The
highest median income was not found on Broadway, but at a West
Coast theater, where it was over $18,000. A Broadway theater
did, however, come in a close second. In 29 of our 35 theater
audiences, median income was between $11,000 and $15,000. The
top figure for any single performance was almost certainly higher,
because these figures represent the average of all the surveys
taken at each organization (there was more than one in almost
every case). All 12 major orchestras surveyed showed median
audience incomes above $10,000, the highest being $15,000.
Again, the results varied little; 8 of the 12 exhibited median incomes between $11,000 and $13,000. Audience incomes at dance
and chamber orchestra performances were slightly lower than those
of audiences in general. Two of our five dance surveys reported
median incomes under $10,000. Three of the five chamber group
audiences were in this category, but one of the string quartet audiences had a median income over $16,500.

A distinct pattern emerges from the responses to questions
about frequency of attendance. Theater is shown to be the most
popular art form. With one exception, the patrons at all types of
performance--members of dance, opera or chamber music audi-
ences--indicated that the theater was the art form which they attended most frequently. Even in the exceptional case, the symphony, theater came in a very close second in frequency of attendance; that is to say, members of the symphony audience indicated
that they attended theaters almost as frequently as they went to orchestral concerts.

The New York Audience

We also investigated the audience in New York City by itself.
This enabled us to deal with a constant basic population, one drawn
primarily from a single region. It also permitted us to make a

direct comparison between off-Broadway and Broadway audiences,
casting some light on differences between audiences for more and
for less experimental theater groups.

In general, the off-Broadway audience resembles more
closely that of the other art forms than it does the audience of the
Broadway theater.   On Broadway the age distribution is concentrated in the middle range--comparatively few persons under 20
and over 60 attend.   Similarly, the Broadway theater audience includes fewer members of the professions than does any of the other
art forms in New York, both among males and females.   But even
there, professionals constitute more than 50 per cent of the audience.   Broadway seems to draw a larger proportion of its audience
from among the managerial group than do the other art forms.
More housewives are represented in the Broadway surveys and, incidentally, in the orchestral audiences, than at other art forms.
The educational level is slightly lower on Broadway, though even
there it is remarkably high, with nearly 50 per cent of the men
having done some post-graduate work.   While income levels are
highest in the orchestral audiences, they are not very much higher
than median incomes of attendees on and off Broadway, and the
off-Broadway incomes are surprisingly close to the incomes of the
Broadway audience.   In terms of socio-economic characteristics
there is no evidence to support the notion that off-Broadway attracts
a clientele significantly different from that of any other art form.

The only reasonably comparable series of historical data on
audiences which we have been able to find applies to the New York
theater.   The Playbill survey of the audience for the commercial
theater on Broadway has been conducted for more than a decade,
though at some point there was a change in procedure so that the
data are not strictly comparable. [3]   What is most noteworthy in the
figures for the six years that are usable is how little change in
audience composition has occurred during the decade.   One can
only say that today's audience is about the same as that of a decade
earlier except that it earns more money now than it did then.
Even this is a misleading observation, for incomes per capita in
the United States have also been rising.   Indeed, the figures suggest that in this respect, too, the theater audience has remained
about the same in relation to the rest of the population. [4]   Thus,
if there was a "cultural boom"--a movement toward "mass culture"
--there is little sign of it in the composition of the audience of the
commercial theater.

Audiences Outside New York

Since our investigation of the audience outside New York
City showed the same patterns reported for the New York audience,
a few brief comments on the subject will suffice.   Three differences
stand out.   We found a relatively high proportion of students in the
theater audience outside New York, a group which was comparatively poorly represented on Broadway.   About 21 per cent of the
theater audience was composed of students, as compared with

figures of 8 per cent for Broadway and 11 per cent for off-Broadway.   The same general pattern was evident in the orchestral and operatic audiences.   Members of the professions made up a slightly larger proportion of the audiences outside New York City, and, if anything, the educational level was higher in other parts of the country. Income, however, was slightly higher in New York, though the median outside New York City was over $11,000. Frequency of attendance was somewhat greater inside the city, but not nearly as much greater as one might have expected, given the availability of performance in New York.   Indeed, attendance at chamber music concerts was, if anything, somewhat higher outside the city.

The main point, then, is that the general features of our over-all audience profile are by no means due solely to the characteristics of New York audiences--as a matter of fact many of its most noteworthy elements are even more apparent outside New York City.

The British Audience

Because our results for the United States suggest that the audience of the performing arts comes from such a very limited segment of our population, it is important to ask whether this reflects a peculiarity of the American culture--whether in other countries, with other traditions and other educational systems, the audience represents a broader spectrum of the general public. For this reason (though we did not know our American results at the time) we decided that a few audience surveys should be undertaken in Great Britain, along with other kinds of research to be described later.

When we discussed our plans with British colleagues, they offered two general predictions: first, that our response rate would be lower in Great Britain than in the United States because the Englishman is particularly sensitive to any invasion of privacy; second, that the British audience would indeed be drawn from a wider group because British education places greater emphasis on the humanities and less on the sciences than does education in the United States.   Both conjectures proved to be wrong.

We received a total of 2295 usable responses at seven surveys conducted in the spring of 1965, two at the National Theatre (formerly the Old Vic), one at the Ballet Rambert, one at a performance of the New Philharmonia Orchestra, one at the London Philharmonic Orchestra, one at the London Symphony Orchestra, and one at an operatic performance at Sadler's Wells, all of them in London.   Our over-all response rate was 50.3 per cent, almost exactly the same as the rate for the United States.

The similarity of the British and American results is remarkable. Table 2 provides data for Great Britain analogous to the figures given in Table 1 for the United States.   The precise figures for British audiences should not be taken at face value. They are almost certainly distorted by the unrepresentative weighting of different art forms, a source of error for which we could not correct because of the small number of surveys conducted. Nevertheless, the results once again are very consistent from survey to survey and from art form to art form, and the orders of magnitude of the figures can, therefore, be accepted with considerable confidence. (The only noteworthy difference among British audiences by art form is that the British theater seems to draw its audience from a particularly exclusive group. In our sample the members of theater audiences have higher educational levels and higher incomes and are more frequently in the professional classification than the members of other audiences. The theater also has the highest frequency of attendance, with orchestral performances second.)

All of the special features which characterize the American audience are apparent in the data for Great Britain in Table 2. The same high proportion of professionals was found: among male members of the audience, 60. 5 per cent were in the professional classification in Great Britain and 63 per cent in the United States; for females the figures are 55 per cent in Great Britain and 63 per cent in the United States. There was a somewhat larger representation of blue collar workers (4. 6 per cent in Great Britain and 2. 6 per cent in the United States), but this group still constituted an insignificant part of the total audience; and, as in the United States, the operatic audience contained an unusually high proportion of blue collar workers--nearly 8. 5 per cent of the males were in that category. The educational level of the British audience was extraordinarily high, just as was true of the American audience. Since there is not so well organized a system of postgraduate education in Britain, a direct comparison with the American results is not possible, but the similarly high level of educational attainment is shown by the fact that nearly 50 per cent of the males in the British audience left school at age 20 or over, while this level of education is reached by only 3. 7 per cent of the entire British male population. The British audience, like ours, seems also to be very well off financially. Its median income of nearly £1700 is a little less than twice that of the general public. Incidentally, frequencies of attendance were slightly higher than those in the United States, but their ordering by art form was the same, with theater attended most frequently in both countries, orchestral performances second, opera third and dance last.

Some noteworthy differences were found between British and American audiences. While the American audience was young, the British audience was even younger. The proportion of the American audience aged 20-24 was twice as high as that in the general population, but the British audience proportion was about three and a half times as large. And while the proportion of the American audience aged 60 and over was only 0. 69 per cent of that in the general population, the comparable British audience ratio was less than half as large. Thus Englishmen are even more likely than

(cont. on p. 258)

Americans to attend when they are young, and even less likely to
attend when they are older. An even higher proportion of British
professionals seems to attend the arts than is true in the United
States. In Great Britain the proportion of male professionals in
the audience was over eight times that in the British population,
whereas the corresponding American ratio was about five. There
was also a somewhat higher proportion of clerical-sales occupations represented in the British audience.

The relation between income and attendance differs somewhat for the British and American audiences. Low income groups
are about equally represented in the audiences of both countries.
However, the British lower middle income groups are a little more
heavily represented, while in our country it is the upper income
groups who are relatively more frequent in their attendance.
This, then, is about all that can be said in support of the view
that the British audience represents a broader segment of the
population than does that in the United States. Even here, however, the differences are small.

The Frequent and Infrequent Attenders

It should be clear by now that "the common man" is fairly
uncommon among those who attend live professional performances.
But one may well ask whether he is much better represented
among those who go only very occasionally. To some extent this
turns out to be the case. A breakdown of our data by frequency
of attendance shows that people who are well educated, well-to-do,
and who are engaged in professional occupations constitute a particularly large proportion of those who attend performances frequently. Conversely, those who attend only rarely have lower incomes, are a bit more frequently the blue collar workers and have
a slightly lower level of educational attainment.

Our regional theater surveys show that among males who
attended only once during the year of our survey 59 per cent were
professionals, 8 per cent were blue collar workers, the median
educational level was four years of college, and the audience's
median family income was $9500. But for those who attended at
least 10 other performances that year the corresponding figures
were 67 per cent professional, 3 per cent blue collar, the median
educational level was graduate school and the median annual income
was $14,500. Our data shows that similar differences between
frequent and infrequent attenders hold (but to a smaller degree) for
the major orchestras and (much more markedly) for the Broadway
theater. Moreover, with few exceptions, the relationship between
these variables and frequency of attendance is perfectly regular.
For example, among the audiences of the major orchestras one
observes the following pattern:

Number of Performances Attended Per Year	1	2-5	6-10	over 10
Family Income	$9500	$10,500	$12,500	$13,000

Table 2. Profile of the British Performing Arts Audience, Compared with the British Population

	Performing Arts Audience[a]	Population[b]
Sex		
Male	54. 3%	47. 6%
Age		
Under 20	12. 0%	30. 8%
Over 60	5. 5	16. 6
Median Age	31 yrs.	. . .
Occupational Category		
Males:		
Employed Persons:[c]		
Professional	60. 5%	7. 5%
Teachers	11. 7	
Managerial	19. 1	10. 9
Clerical and Sales	15. 9	12. 7
Blue Collar	4. 6	68. 9
Students[d]	17. 8	
Females:		
Employed Persons:[c]		
Professional	54. 8%	9. 7%
Teachers	22. 8	
Managerial	5. 3	4. 2
Clerical	35. 0	25. 9
Sales	1. 9	11. 4
Blue Collar	3. 0	48. 4
Students[d]	20. 1	
Housewives[d]	16. 2	
Education (school-leaving age)		
Males:		
14 or Under	7. 1%	57. 9%
15	6. 9	20. 2
16	13. 5	9. 3
17, 18, 19	24. 0	5. 9
20 and Over	48. 5	3. 7
Median Category	age 17-19	14 or under

Income

Females:
14 or Under	3. 8%	59. 7%
15	5. 9	19. 2
16	16. 0	9. 2
17, 18, 19	32. 0	6. 8
20 and Over	42. 3	2. 7
Median Category	age 17-19	14 or under
Over £499	96. 1%	78%
Over £1749	47. 3	14. 5
Over £2500	29. 2	5
Median Income	£1676	£990 (est.)

Frequency of Attendance

Average Number of Performances
Attended in Last 12 Months: Number

Theater	10. 2
Symphony	7. 9
Opera	4. 6
Dance	1. 7
Other Serious Music	2. 9

---

a   Based on Twentieth Century Fund audience survey; 2295 responses. Implicit questionnaire weights. No attempt has been made to weight according to attendance at different art forms.

b   Figures obtained from preliminary tables to be included in the 1961 Census volumes, from special tabulations made for us by the Central Statistical Office, and from the Demographic Yearbook of the United Nations.

c   and   d   See notes to Table 1.

Curiously, students are generally better represented among the infrequent attenders, perhaps because their studies or their social activities keep them too busy or because they cannot afford to attend very often, though the availability of reduced rate student tickets may cast doubt on the latter explanation.

On the whole it appears that the group that attends performances very rarely is more similar to the general population in its composition than is the audience as a whole. Yet even the infrequent attender is no "common man." His (median) family income is over $9500, his (median) educational level is at least four years of college, and, if he is an adult, there is a better than even chance that he is engaged in a professional occupation. This is still a highly select group.

The Size of the Arts Audience

The data we have just discussed permit us to estimate the size of the audience for the live performing arts. In 1963-64 approximately 20 million tickets were sold by Broadway, off-Broadway and regional theaters, major and metropolitan orchestras, opera groups and (American) professional dance companies. But since most of the individuals who purchased these tickets attended more than one performance, we can be sure that the number of different persons purchasing tickets was considerably under 20 million. Table 3 summarizes our estimates of the number of different individuals who attended each of these art forms.

How large, then, is the number of Americans attending some type of live performance? That number must be considerably smaller than the total of the corresponding figures for the individual art forms because of the overlap in the audiences for different types of performance. If 50 persons attend only theater, 50 attend only opera and 50 attend both, then the theater and opera will each have 100 patrons even though, in all, only 150 individuals are involved. An intense examination of our data has led us to estimate that (excluding "the road" and summer stock) the audience of the live professional performing arts in the United States totaled 2-1/2 to 3 million persons in 1963-64. We suspect that this figure and the estimates for the individual art forms in Table 3 are a little low since, as any student of survey techniques would affirm, respondents tend, perhaps unconsciously, to exaggerate the frequency with which they attend performances. In addition, the frequency figures are inflated by our inability to remove from them attendance at non-professional performances. If average frequency of attendance is lower than our figures indicate, then the 20 million tickets sold in 1963-64 must have been distributed among a correspondingly larger group of people. Nevertheless, it seems to us quite unlikely that the audience comprises more than 5 million individuals, a figure which would be 4 per cent of all residents of this country 18 years of age and older.

In this chapter we have tried to provide an extensive profile

Table 3.   Average Estimated Attendance, by Art Form

	Average Estimated Attendance	Average Number of Times Attended in Last 12 Months[a]	Number of Individuals Attending (col. 1 ÷ col. 2)
Broadway	7,000,000	4.5	1,555,556
Off-Broadway	900,000	6.5	138,462
Regional Theaters	1,500,000	4.5	333,333
Major Orchestras	6,600,000	4.8	1,375,000
Opera	1,700,000	2.6	653,846
Dance	750,000	2.3	326,087

a   An average weighted inversely by frequency of attendance to
correct for overrepresentation of frequent attenders in our sample (if individual A attends twice as often as B, he is twice as
likely as B to be included in our sample). Specifically, let i
represent any one of our frequency of attendance categories
(once, 2-5, 6-10, over 10), let f, be the average frequency of
attendance for the given art form and category, and let N, be
the number of individuals in the category. Then our weighted
average figure in column 2 is obtained from the expression
$\Sigma f_1 \ (N_1/f_1)/ \Sigma(N_1/f_1)$ or, more simply, $\Sigma N_1/ \Sigma(N_1/f_1)$.

of the audience of the live professional performing arts in the
United States. Two of its features are especially significant.

The first is the remarkable consistency of the composition
of audiences from art form to art form, from city to city and from
one performance to another.

Second, the audience is drawn from an extremely narrow
segment of the American population. In the main, it consists of
persons who are extraordinarily well educated, whose incomes are
very high, who are predominantly in the professions, and who are
in their late youth or early middle age. This finding has important
implications for the nature of whatever growth has occurred in audience demand for the arts. Even if there has been a significant
rise in the size of audiences in recent years, it has certainly not
yet encompassed the general public. If the sociological base of
the audience has in fact expanded, it must surely have been incredibly narrow before the boom got under way. This result indicates also, in a larger sense, that attempts to reach a wider and
more representative audience, to interest the less educated or the
less affluent, have so far had limited effects.

Yet there is also evidence that something can be done to broaden the audience base. As will be shown later, when professional performances are given free of charge or with carefully set low prices, the audience is drawn from a consistently wider cross section of the population. But even here there are no easy and overwhelming victories--in these audiences the number of blue collar workers is almost always under 10 per cent and the number of professionals is always well over 50 per cent; over 50 per cent of the males have completed college; and median incomes are almost always well over $9000. Obviously, much still remains to be done before the professional performing arts can truly be said to belong to the people.

---

1. The only serious disagreement between the results of other surveys and our own relates to the quantitative effect of level of education. While other investigations also report that the audience is very highly educated, their conclusions are not quite as extreme as ours. In general they show a plurality of persons with college degrees rather than a plurality of persons who have attended graduate school. Examples are the Baltimore Symphony audience survey: college graduate 41 per cent, graduate school 21 per cent; the UCLA Theater Group audience survey: college 55 per cent, post-graduate 13 per cent; the 1964 Playbill survey (males): college 50.3 per cent, graduate school 28 per cent; the Guthrie Theater audience survey (males): college graduate 25.4 per cent, post-graduate 45 per cent. These figures suggest that our questionnaires, perhaps because of their length, were answered more readily by highly educated persons. But, despite some disagreement on the magnitudes involved, all of these results confirm fully our qualitative conclusion: that the audience for the arts is very highly educated.

2. Since the income figures for the urban population of the United States are based on the 1960 Census, and income in 1963-1965, when our survey results were obtained, was undoubtedly somewhat higher, the true differential between the income of the audience and that of the general public is a bit smaller than our results suggest. Nevertheless, the differential is so substantial that a correction for this discrepancy would alter our numerical comparisons only slightly.

3. Unfortunately, we have been unable to locate a complete set of survey reports either from Playbill or any of the library theater collections. In fact, we have not seen the original report on the 1955-56 survey; our data for that year had to be reconstructed from figures quoted in an article by Max Frankel in the New York Times (May 20, 1956, Theater Section, p. 1).

4. This can be seen as follows. The median income of the

audience in 1959-60, the first year for which this statistic was calculated, was $9650, whereas the figure for 1963 was $11,011. (As already indicated, the 1964 jump to $16,700 should probably be ascribed to the influx of World's Fair visitors and so is irrelevant for a calculation of the basic trend.) This represents a rise of a little over 14 per cent during the three year period. Now, according to the U.S. Census, median family income in the United States rose about 9.5 per cent over the same time interval. (U.S. Census of Population, 1960: Occupational Characteristics, Final Report PC[2]-7A.) Since incomes of people in the professions have recently been rising more rapidly than those of the population as a whole, one suspects that the incomes of members of the audience of the commercial theater were perhaps just about keeping up with the incomes of others in the same socio-economic classes.

THE PRECARIOUS STATE
OF THE PERFORMING ARTS*

Malcolm G. Scully

Most Americans do not attend live performances of symphonies, ballets, operas, and plays. Those who do are disproportionately rich and well-educated. That profile of a small, relatively elite audience for the performing arts can be drawn from a telephone survey of 6000 people in 12 major cities, designed to find out who attends live performances and why.

The report of the survey, conducted for the Ford Foundation by Eric Marder Associates, Inc., a research organization, is part of the foundation's new study, The Finances of the Performing Arts, released this month.

For the sake of comparison, the 6000 people were also asked about their attendance at movies, Broadway musicals, and jazz, rock, and folk-music concerts.

The survey revealed that 90 per cent of the interviewees had not attended a concert by a professional symphony orchestra in the previous year.

Ninety-six per cent had not seen a live professionally performed opera, 96 per cent had not seen a live, professionally performed ballet, and 84 per cent had not seen a live, professional performance of a play.

*From The Chronicle of Higher Education, vol. 8, no. 40 (August 19, 1974). Copyright 1974 by Editorial Projects for Education, Inc. Reprinted by permission.

WHO ATTENDS?

	Movies	Theater	Musical	Jazz	Symphony	Opera	Ballet
By Income							
Up to $7500	47	7	8	17	4	2	3
$7500 to $15,000	72	14	15	24	8	3	3
$15,000 to $25,000	83	25	28	32	16	6	6
$25,000 and over	83	38	44	36	28	13	13
By Education							
Some high school	57	7	9	20	5	2	2
High school graduates	71	12	15	22	5	2	2
Some college	81	23	25	35	14	6	7
College graduates	81	39	39	31	26	11	13

Source: Eric Marder Associates, Inc.
This table shows the percentage of people with various incomes and levels of education who attended at least one movie or one live presentation of the performing arts during a 12-month period.

By contrast, only 31 per cent had not seen at least one movie in the past year. Seventy-five per cent had not attended at least one jazz, rock, or folk-music concert.

The subjects, also asked about their exposure to the arts on television, indicated that they were far more likely to have seen a performance on TV than in person, although for opera and ballet the percentage of viewers was still quite small.

"The data illustrate how dominant television is," the report said. "Seventy-one per cent of the people saw a movie on television more than once a month, and 41 per cent more than once a week, but only 18 per cent saw a movie in a movie theater more than once a month, and hardly any people saw a live professional performance of a play more than once a month."

The data also provide "striking confirmation" that the people who do attend live performances are well-to-do and well-educated. Among the specifics:

The percentage of people with incomes of $25,000 or more who attended a performance of a symphony in the previous year was seven times greater than the percentage of "attenders" with incomes below $7500.

The percentage of college graduates who attended plays, symphonies, operas, and ballets was five times as large as the percentage of "attenders" who had failed to complete high school.

People with high incomes and more education also were far more likely to attend the "popular" arts--movies, jazz, folk music, and rock concerts.

The percentage of upper-income people attending those performances was twice as large as that of low-income people. The percentage of college graduates attending such performances was one and one-half times as great as the percentage of those who had failed to complete high school.

While the study showed that both income and education were important factors, education was the more important of the two.

"Within each educational group, the percentage attending is only somewhat higher among the high-income people than among the low-income people," the study says. "But within each income group, the percentage attending is much larger among the high-education than among the low-education people. "

The report also includes a warning about assuming that the audience at live performances include only the rich, and the well-educated.

"Even though the rate of attendance among upper-income people is many times that of lower-income people, the audience at any particular performance may contain more lower-income people than upper-income people since there are, of course, far more lower-income people in the population, " the report says.

While the survey does reveal a relatively elite audience for the performing arts, W. McNeil Lowry, vice-president of the arts and humanities division of the Ford Foundation, said he felt the makeup of audiences was changing.

He said more and more blacks and working-class people were attending live performances, even performances of opera and ballet.   The foundation plans to try to determine how much the audience is shifting in future surveys, he said.

The survey revealed these characteristics about the audience:

People tend to fall into various types of attendance categories.   "Opera" people, for instance, "are also highly partial to the symphony, but less partial to the theater. "   "Ballet" people are partial to both the theater and the symphony, but "symphony" people and "theater" people are less partial to any of the other performing arts.

Popular music--jazz, rock, and folk--does not seem to be wooing young people away from the classical arts.

"Young people who attended performances of jazz, rock, or folk music were more likely to attend plays, symphonies, operas, and ballets.... Thus, it would not be fair to say that the young have substituted the popular for the traditional arts, but rather that they are generally more alert, more receptive, and that they are maintaining an interest in the traditional arts in addition to their interest in the popular music," the report says.

"Hardly any of the respondents attended performances alone." Some 2 per cent went alone to the theater, 2 per cent went alone to the opera, 5 per cent went alone to a ballet, and 5 per cent went alone to a symphony. The respondents usually went to performances with "spouses or social friends" rather than with business associates.

While as many as two-thirds of the respondents said they would rather wear casual clothes than "dress-up" garb to opera, ballet, or symphony performances, easing the dress habits for those performances probably would not produce larger audiences.

In fact, the survey revealed, the change might result in a slight reduction, since those who objected to casual dress were more likely to be regular attenders than were those who said they approved of more casual dress.

The symphony, ballet, and opera could gain significant numbers of attenders if their image as "restrained, formal, and aloof" were changed.

To change the imagery, the report suggests that "any advertising for the arts should avoid elite symbols." "Beyond that," it adds, "it might be possible to affect the general feeling in the community by a selective distribution of special tickets, possibly to students, to the underprivileged, or both."

OUR FAITHFUL SUBSCRIBERS*

Harry Ellis Dickson

From the stage of Symphony Hall, as we look out into the audience, the faces of our faithful listeners have become, over the years, as familiar to us as ours to them. Indeed, if the "big hat" isn't in her usual seat on Friday afternoon my partner and I are a bit concerned and look for her eagerly on the following Friday.

Our oldest regular audience is that of Friday afternoon. For this series it is practically impossible to buy tickets.   They have been held in the same family for generations and are handed down from father to son, mother to daughter.   And going to the Friday-afternoon symphony is a religious ritual for all proper Bostonians.

One problem with the Friday-afternoon audiences has never quite been solved, that of early-leavers.   Unlike the distracting habit of opera-goers who habitually miss the first act of every opera, there are a number of Friday-afternoon listeners who have never heard the last movement of most symphonies.   No matter how short the concert is, or how early the time, as soon as the next-to-last movement is over, there is a determined rush for the exit; and some of the ladies are so expert at timing that they are able to make the door just before the last movement begins.   We have already moved up our concert starting time from 2:30 to 2:00, but this has had no discernible effect upon the pathological early-risers.   I wonder if it wouldn't be a good idea to give a series of concerts of only last movements, in order to acquaint our customers with what they have been missing all these years. Or, perhaps we should begin symphonies with the last movement.

There is an apocryphal story about an elderly couple and their son who occupied the same seats for years.   One Friday afternoon the lady occupied her usual seat, but the two seats beside her were vacant.   During the intermission she was asked by a friend why she was alone.   "Oh, " she said, "my husband passed away. "

"And where is your son?" she was asked.

"Well, " she replied, "someone had to go to the funeral. "

Our Friday-afternoon audiences are not inherently boisterous, and sometimes the native reserve of these Back Bay ladies, plus the fact that they are not overly strong to begin with, creates embarrassing situations at the end of a concert, especially when their applause dies down before the conductor or soloist has had time to walk off the stage.   Often we musicians can see them applauding, but can't hear them and sometimes I am tempted to run after the soloist and say, "Please come back for a bow.   They really like you!"   After one of these concerts Jascha Heifetz once said to me, "These Friday-afternoon concerts would be so much more enjoyable if the ladies would only remove their gloves. "

The only time I ever saw the Friday audience in an uproar was when Vladimir Horowitz made his debut with the Boston Symphony.   At that concert the ladies not only removed their gloves, but resorted to pounding their canes on the floor!

Yes, this is a discriminating audience, which, after many years of concert-going, is much less conservative than one would imagine. I have heard heated discussions in the corridors of Symphony Hall by elderly ladies in defense of the music of Bartók and Schoenberg and Webern. (Alas, I have also heard some strange remarks before concerts, like the following: "Agatha, what are they playing today?" "Brahms' Fourth in E Minor." "Oh, I hate minor symphonies, don't you?")

Our Saturday-night audience, second in age and prestige, is quite different from Friday's. It is more earthy, more outspoken, and more bourgeois in its attitude and behavior. It is also not as loyal. One constantly sees new faces (not new subscribers!)--who have been given or sold tickets for a concert that didn't appeal to the regular ticket-holder. This audience is the fussiest of all. They constantly write letters complaining about the programs, especially about "too much modern music." Without a moment's hesitation they will leap from their seats at the conclusion of a new work with which they are completely unfamiliar, even after hearing it, and hasten to deliver to one of us in the corridor an erudite musical denunciation.

My fourth-desk partner, with whom I have been sitting for many years, loves to scan the audience before a concert. He usually comes out a few minutes early and when I have arrived, he files an oral report on where the pretty girls are sitting. For a few years he and I witnessed a real-life cycle take place before our eyes. Each Saturday night a young man would dash in at the last minute before the conductor came on the stage and breathlessly take his seat in the first row just below us, and each week he had with him a different girl, equally breathless as she sat down next to him. We used to watch this man explain the music to his friend after each movement and during the music he would quietly conduct along, sway with the music, and occasionally look knowingly at the girl. I must say the girls seemed very impressed. The young man would also greet us with an approving nod after a piece was finished and the fact that he knew us also seemed to impress the girls. Each week my partner and I would conjecture as to what kind she would be--blonde, brunette, redhead?

Then we suddenly noticed that there was no more variety. The same girl was there with him week after week. We noticed a diamond ring on her left hand and at the same time the young man discontinued his swaying and conducting. At the very first concert of the following season we eagerly awaited our young couple and, sure enough, they both came in, early, and greeted us warmly. This time I noticed, during the overture to "The Marriage of Figaro," that they both wore wedding rings.

After a few months my colleague, who has five children and knows about these things, whispered to me, "She's pregnant." And week after week there was more and more tangible evidence that my colleague was right. Then for a few weeks before the close of that season we noticed different people in those front-row seats. And at the final concert of the season, while we were already

seated on the stage, in walked our young couple, she quite thin
again. He came directly to the stage, took out two cigars, and
handed them to us.   "A boy!" he said.

If the Friday audience is different from the Saturday audience, the Tuesday audience is different from both, and the brand
new Thursday audience is the most different of all.   Let us first
consider the Tuesday-night audience, which is divided into two
series, the old Harvard University Sanders Theatre concerts now
transplanted to Symphony Hall, and the newer Tuesday-night series.
The former audience is still largely college people--faculty and
their families, former teachers and students--also Dr. and Mrs.
Paul Dudley White.   The other Tuesday series seems to be made
up largely of very appreciative, good-listening professional people--
doctors, lawyers, etc.

Of all our formal audiences the newest is usually the most
enthusiastic and our newest audience today is the Thursday audience.   But our most vital, live, and swinging audience is our informal "open rehearsal" audience, who come on eight Thursday
nights.   These audiences are mainly college and high-school youngsters and they are knowledgeable, bright, and enthusiastic.

Even our out-of-town listeners in New York and Providence
have become familiar to us and each year, at the opening concert,
we are in the habit of greeting old friends from the stage.   There
is, however, one "old friend" in the front row at our Providence
concerts whom we try to avoid.   He is quite evidently a would-be
conductor, perhaps a bit frustrated, who comes to the concert
armed with scores and conducts the entire program from his seat.
The reason we try to avoid him is that his "beat" is rather unor-
thodox and he is apt to confuse us if we should inadvertently look
at him.   I remember playing a Tchaikovsky symphony in which
Charles Munch had made a couple of substantial cuts, and at the
Providence performance I watched our friend.   When we made the
first cut he kept on blithely conducting for many bars until he suddenly realized something was wrong.   He began to turn pages back
and forth furiously.   And just as he found the place, we made
another cut.   This time he just couldn't keep up with the orchestra
and when we finished the movement, he was still turning pages,
and perspiring profusely.

HAIL, THE AUDIENCE!*

Howard Taubman

Audiences are the lifeblood of music, as it is practiced today, as it was practiced yesterday, and as it will be practiced

*From Music on My Beat, by Howard Taubman; New York: Simon
& Schuster, 1943.   Copyright 1943 by Howard Taubman.   Reprinted
by permission of Simon and Schuster.

tomorrow. Like the theater, movies, radio, baseball, football,
and murder trials, music thrives because of its audiences. Amateurs play for fun, and so do professionals, and occasionally they
seek to amuse only themselves, but even amateurs are constantly
rounding up people to listen to them.

The paying audiences make possible such professional music
as is purveyed in these United States, and fortunately for the musicians the number of customers has been growing steadily. Among
older people, there may still be a predominance of women over
men in our audiences, for there was a time when it was unmanly
to be fond of music. There is little doubt that the ladies of America have kept alive many of our musical institutions, for better or
for worse. But among the younger generation, the notion that music is sissy has all but gone. The war, with its absorption of
millions of young men into the armed services, may have upset the
equilibrium once more, but only temporarily. When the men return, they will take up where they left off. For music is no longer an ornament for the few; the radio has made it accessible to the
many, and, praise be, the many like it.

Audiences are as diverse as the people of this democracy.
The least important, if not the least amusing, are the musical and
social snobs. They patronize the shows that are regarded, in the
best circles, as the cream of the moment. In New York, for a
time, Toscanini and the New York Philharmonic reigned supreme;
then Stokowski and the Philadelphia Orchestra became fashionable;
later the Boston Symphony Orchestra and Koussevitzky were de
rigueur. In each case the snobs shifted their favors to the orchestra and maestro in fashion. These people also subscribed to the
Metropolitan Opera on the flossy Monday evening, when the best
people usually came. Possibly they derived some pleasure from
music, but, more important, it was the thing to do. They came
to be seen, and to stare at those who had come to be seen.

The great majority of our audiences pay their money because
they want to hear music. You can divide this majority into two
sections: the initiated and uninitated. But general classifications
are merely a short cut to discussion, for among the initiated and
uninitiated there are many variations.

The initiated may be regarded as the people who have experience and judgment in music. They choose their programs and
performers with care; they pay to hear music and performers that
are worth while but not necessarily glamorized. They do not bow
the knee to current idols, nor do they turn away from great musicians just because they happen to be celebrated. They are not
stampeded by rave notices, nor are they turned away by disdain.
They are true connoisseurs. They are wonderful.

The uninitiated are prey to what is popular and puffed up.
They do not discriminate; they accept current standards. If a big
name happens to be a great artist, they hear a great artist. If

the big name is a pretentious phony, they patronize a phony.   They are as likely to have a swell time listening to the phony as to the great artist.   They are the mass buyers in the new mass production of music.   They may not be connoisseurs, but they are wonderful.

Anybody who pays good money to hear music is wonderful, if you ask the trade.   Even audiences of deadheads that turn out to listen to newcomers have their uses; to the particular performers and managers, these audiences are also wonderful.   In a word, all audiences are wonderful.

The public as a whole loves big names.   It is customary to charge this amiable predilection of the paying customer to our vast apparatus of publicity and our habit of glamorizing the virtuoso. American audiences are constantly being castigated for their susceptibility to high-pressuring.   The lofty souls who do the castigating forget that it has been thus for more than a century wherever audiences gather to hear Western music.   Horowitz, Kreisler, Heifetz, Anderson, Flagstad, Toscanini have drawn packed houses wherever they have gone.   In any town on any continent, the situation is about the same.   Moreover, people remain faithful to their heroes and heroines.   For decades they will continue to patronize the same big names.   They will take a chance on a new figure with reluctance.   Only as the newcomer is built into a star and accumulates his own tradition and folklore does he entice the cautious and conservative public.

It is a pleasant parlor game among the high-brows to flail American audiences for lack of discernment.   Some musicians turn up their noses at our tastes and tell us that elsewhere people are more discriminating.   Take it from a man like Horowitz that this high-brown pose is the bunk.   He is quite willing to play Tchaikovsky, if that is what the public likes, and he sees no reason to be patronizing about it.   "Some musicians keep telling us that in Europe audiences have higher tastes," he says.   "Well, I made more money in Germany playing Tchaikovsky than some of the stuffed shirts playing Beethoven and Schubert.   And the German audiences loved Chopin, too--another composer who was not for these high and mighty musicians. "   Does the public like flashy arrangements? "Let them have them.   Didn't Bach, Beethoven, and Brahms make plenty of them?" he wants to know.

Szigeti is another musician who has a good word to say for American audiences.   He recalls that as a famous virtuoso in Europe he was restricted to the top-price circuit.   That meant the big cities--Paris, Berlin, Rome, London, Vienna, and the like.   He once wanted to play in Cracow, the Polish town which has a fine, old tradition of civilization, or had before the Nazis desecrated it. But Cracow was on the lower-priced circuit, and Szigeti's manager would not book him there, admonishing him that if he played Cracow, it would hurt his standing in the bigger cities.   When the violinist came to the United States, he was surprised and gratified to find that small towns considered themselves quite as good as large, that if a community of 15,000 could raise the money to pay for the highest-price musicians, they heard them.

It takes all kinds of people to make an audience. Nearly always there are the late-comers who have a constitutional inability to arrive on time and who think they have a constitutional preroga- tive to climb over everybody else. There are people who have to show themselves off in their finery. There are chatterers and dozers, program rattlers and fidgeters. There are the scholarly folk who bring their scores to concerts and operas; they seldom have enough light to follow their bent and they aim flashlights on printed pages to the vast annoyance of their neighbors.

Among my favorites are the fervid applauders. I don't mean the professional applauders--the claque, relatives, or manager of the artist--but the amateurs who have paid their way and who ex- press themselves by wild beating of the palms. They sometimes set up a terrific clamor, and frequently they cannot contain them- selves until a piece of music is over. At any promising point, at any cadence that sounds like the end, their hands are poised to start beating. No one begrudges them their innocent pleasures, but the place where the insistent applause gets you down--provided you are not the artist on the receiving end--is at song recitals. A scientific observer once kept a stop watch on the time elapsed at a song recital in applause and acknowledgment of applause and com- pared it with the time spent in singing. Fifty per cent more time was devoted to the amenities than to music.

The public is bewildered and bewildering. There are people who want everything fitted into neat compartments and who bother musicians and writers to give them opinions that will arrange them- selves precisely and unquestioningly. They want lists of the world's ten best pianists, singers, violinists, and conductors. Usually they have made bets with their friends on the correct order, and anyone timid enough to suggest that musicians cannot be classified like the best tennis players, the all-America football teams, or the best- dressed women in America is a low, lazy, lying lout.

Some of the simple souls expect musicians, newspapermen, music publishers, or librarians to know the answers to all their questions. They will phone you late at night, while you are work- ing, to sing and whistle a tune and to ask what opera, symphony, movie, musical comedy, or radio show it comes from. Sometimes these tunes seem to stem from the imagination of the whistler on the other end of the phone. A friend of mine in a newspaper office has developed an efficient technique for dealing with these insistent questioners. He tells them, as he hangs up the phone, "I'm only the janitor."

Bewilderment may arise out of too much reading of program notes. Schnabel was once approached by an angry lady after she heard him play a Beethoven piano concerto. "The program notes

said that Beethoven was in love again when he wrote this concerto, "
she cried out indignantly.   "I did not find that love in your interpretation. "

Or people are literal-minded.   Gian-Carlo Menotti wrote
an opera called The Old Maid and the Thief, spoofing spinsters.
At the end of a lecture at a university extension course, he was
confronted by a middle-aged lady, who bawled him out.   "And remember, " she concluded, "not all old maids are lovelorn. "

Or people are just plain befuddled.   At a concert devoted to
the music of Orlando di Lasso, the program clearly indicated that
the composer was born in 1530 and died in 1594.   After one number, the conductor led forth a young man from the ranks of the
chorus to take a bow for his singing of a solo passage.   I heard
an old gentleman whispering to his companion, "Is that the composer? "

Or people want exact information.   A man went to a concert
by a well-known violinist and enjoyed it.   He also liked the review
that one critic wrote about the event.   He wrote the critic a letter,
complimenting him on the review, since it agreed entirely with his
own judgment.   Could the critic tell him, he ended, the precise
location of his seat so that he might compare it with his own?

Or a customer is outraged that Ettore Panizza, conducting a
performance of Mozart's Marriage of Figaro at the Metropolitan
Opera House, permitted a baritone to hold the last quarter note of
an aria for four additional measures.   He writes a threatening
note, signing it Hector Berlioz, Jr. , and saying, "If at the next
performance of Figaro this shameful exhibition is repeated--if at
the next performance the American public is to hear what Mozart
did not write, I shall rise from my seat and in a loud, clear tone
will shout, 'Who has dared to correct Mozart?'"

I hope he does, and I hope I'm there when he does.   Nothing would surprise me in a member of the audience.   There is a
tradition that Americans take their music politely, compared with
the hissing, booing, shouting, and cheering of European, particularly Latin, audiences.   The tradition is based on the fact that
people seem to sit through anything, bad or good, and give it the
same measure of polite approval.   But that describes only a portion of the audience, which holds no strong views and has no
marked reactions to what it hears.   It is certainly not true of a
section of the audience which is increasingly independent in its
judgments and growing bolder in displaying its feelings.   The audiences that have heard Toscanini in recent years have known how to
shout and cheer.   The gatherings at the Berkshire Festival have
been almost as demonstrative as a Latin audience.   The audiences
at the rarefied chamber-music programs know when they are getting value and they can be stiffly indifferent when receiving less.

The people who take their jazz seriously do not hesitate to

state their feelings, and they make quick decisions as to whether an outfit is good or bad.   I am not talking of the exhibitionistic jitterbugs who dance in the aisles for their favorite bands, but of the critical listeners who can relish the music without self-display. These audiences reserve the right to hoot and catcall, if they are not satisfied, and they refuse to be short-changed.   Some time ago Erskine Hawkins and his band arrived at a dance hall in a Midwestern town to find a huge crowd in the street and only three or four people in the hall.   When the band entered, each man was looked over critically, because the young jazz fanciers had been bilked once too often.   Big-name leaders had arrived with make-shift bands.   The youngsters knew the personnel of their favorite bands, and they decided to check up on Hawkins before parting with their money.   Once the word was passed along that the regular outfit was on hand, the boycott was canceled.

Musicians, in all branches of the art, are discovering that they can't get by with lesser stuff in the hinterland, which is a tribute to the growth of a knowing audience.   Springfield, Massachusetts, objected when several visiting orchestras gave programs without a single American work.   The managers of musicians, and the musicians themselves, occasionally receive letters from outraged customers in the so-called sticks.   The big city newspapers receive them too, and we know how keenly people are listening. The comments are cutting, and they do not spare the illustrious. Toscanini's "sense of proportion" is condemned, Stokowski's "virtuoso manipulations" are lambasted, Serkin's "program was hackneyed and the performance something he should be ashamed of. " To one listener Jan Kiepura was simply "Dizzy, " like the pitcher known as Dean; this listener would rather hear "a singer with visual appeal than one with mere vocal perfection. "   A new pianist is damned with faint praise in the press, and an irritated listener argues that the pianist was not entitled to any praise, even faint. When a young conductor objected to the arrangements for the seating of orchestra and audience at a free concert with a WPA orchestra, some of the listeners shouted that they were not interested in him but in Beethoven.

When you are patronizing with this new audience, you get slapped down, and rightly.   In reporting a festival of contemporary music at Yaddo, Saratoga Springs, one year, I noted that five young maids in the audience had squirmed through the serious stuff but had perked up when a work by Robert McBride, written in the jazz idiom, was played.   I soon received a letter that put me in my place.   It said in part:

"At first we did not recognize ourselves as the five young maids at Yaddo, perhaps because we are not accustomed to being described by such nineteenth-century adjectives as 'prim, modest, and well-bred. '   We hope that you will not consider us ill-bred if we describe the conditions under which we squirmed.   Even if you were not the restless man behind us who kept prodding us with sharp kneecaps and practicing well-shod arpeggios on our spinal columns, you must have been near enough to observe how crowded we were. The crowd there in the afternoon seemed almost double that of the morning session; perhaps none of the critics got up in time to hear the morning concert.

"You were near enough, at any rate, to see how we perked up at Bob McBride's 'Wise Apple Five.' It is only fair to tell you that our interest was not evoked by the introductory remarks about jazz, but was only the natural interest of five who have been playing Bob's music from manuscript for three years. "

The letter was signed, "The Five Wise Apples." If the girls had given their names I should have been glad to apologize. Anyhow, dear Apples, those were not my kneecaps.

The days of adulation are by no means over. It is difficult in these times--it was difficult even before the war--to engineer enough enthusiasm to get up marching and chowder clubs in honor of a musician. A generation ago the friends and admirers of Geraldine Farrar could organize the Gerry Flappers and they made quite a to-do at her farewell to opera. More recently a hard-pressed press agent tried to promote an adoration society for Lily Pons, and the idea died in desultory fashion shortly after it was spawned. But you can always get the devotees mad by saying a harsh word, merited or not, about their gods and goddesses, even the dead whom they worshiped long ago.

If you mention the fact that a contralto's figure is plumpish, which it is, though no gentleman should harp on it, you will get a sharp reminder that you are probably no Apollo yourself, and since when are opera singers supposed to look like Hedy Lamarr? A lady who heard that the members of the New York Philharmonic-Symphony, her favorite orchestra, were being handled with ironclad discipline by several guest conductors wrote this heart-rending appeal: "To have players sweat in fear for my enjoyment is equivalent to sweatshop labor in industry. The men who give us such joy, I contend, should love their giving. I'd rather have Barbirolli with any imperfections he may have but with his keen human interest in his work with the men--co-operation rather than slave-driving--than all the conductors who may wring wizardry out of their instruments but wear the men out and warp their souls in the doing! "

If you don't mention the favorites of the devoted, you will hear about that, too. An admirer of Flagstad, saddened by the news that she was not returning to America, wrote to a newspaper, "Even though Miss Flagstad will not be here we can console ourselves by talking and writing about her, so please let's have many stories about her. " A lady who read that Kreisler would not be able to play for many months because of an accident said she consoled herself by playing his records, summing up her thoughts with the observation that "while Heifetz and Menuhin were merely miraculous, Kreisler was superlative. "

There was the chap in Evansville, Indiana, who wrote Szigeti, "Thought you might like to know that there is quite a large group of local Szigeti worshipers who are particularly thrilled that you are finally coming to our city for a concert. I claim to be the original local Szigeti fan. I have traveled several hundred miles to hear you play, twice to Chicago and once to Louisville. My friends say that I remained a bachelor until I found a girl (she's from Buffalo) who admires Szigeti as much as I do. Of course, she had the extra-attractive quality of playing the violin in tune and she is pretty."

Astrid Varnay had her admirers even before her debut at the Metropolitan. They were a group of young girls who had sat with her in the upper reaches of the house to listen to other singers. They knew that she was studying to be a singer, and they were on hand the night she made her surprise debut as Sieglinde, substituting at the last moment for Lotte Lehmann. One of these girls was standing in the lobby near the box office before the show, and she heard a disappointed customer say that he wanted his money back because Lehmann was not singing. She approached the customer and, speaking rapidly and heatedly, urged him to give the young singer a chance. The man was amused and decided to stay. Later he wrote Miss Varnay a note, telling her that he got his money's worth and that he applauded the loyalty of her friend.

If there is any musician who has his legion of hero-worshipers, it is Nelson Eddy, and they are mostly young women. Even before he became the darling of the movie fans, his power was clear. In February, 1934, he gave his first New York recital at Town Hall. He had made a modest career as a radio singer, though he was far from being a star. At that debut recital, the hall was packed, and most of the glamour girls of 1934 were there. The first appearance of the strapping young man with the handsome face and the blond, wavy hair induced a wave of admiration that was palpable to a toughened concertgoer. After the recital, a throng of girls overran the backstage quarters, and the stage manager, a hardened veteran, ducked across to the other side of the stage and stayed there behind the lighting switchboard until the charge of the debutantes was over.

When Eddy became a Hollywood idol, the number and devotion of his admirers multiplied incalculably. Two girls turned up one day at New York's Town Hall to buy tickets for a Nelson Eddy recital eleven months before it was to take place. They were told that tickets for his concert were sold as part of a series. The girls didn't want the series. They threatened a sit-down strike if they did not get the tickets. They had made it a practice to follow Eddy on his journeys. They had traveled to Philadelphia, White Plains, and even to Chicago to hear him sing. They were not to be denied in New York. I am sure that Eddy will agree that audiences are wonderful.

MEHTA VIEWS AUDIENCE BUILDING*

Kimmis Hendrick

"We've been talking about having what might be called an educational concert series," said Zubin Mehta. The Los Angeles Philharmonic's energetic young music director was speaking about the problem that challenges almost all American symphony orchestras these days--the problem of building loyal, supportive audiences.

"If I knew the answer," he said with a boyish laugh that didn't diminish his intense earnestness, "we wouldn't be in trouble. We're all trying."

By "trouble," Mr. Mehta made it plain, he partly meant financial pressure. But he also meant, he indicated, and doubtless more fundamentally, the lack of assurance that audiences are deeply enough involved to guarantee full-scale intellectual, spiritual support for symphony performance. "I don't know of any single American city, except maybe Boston and Philadelphia," observed Mr. Mehta, "that isn't faced with the problem."

Mr. Mehta was in his mid-20's when he became the Philharmonic's seventh permanent director just 10 years ago. The orchestra still had a loyal audience; its support for the Philharmonic had become one of Los Angeles's few traditions. Barely three years later the Philharmonic moved into the Pavilion of the Music Center, which seated 1000 more people than the old downtown concert hall.

It was packed to capacity the first two seasons. The orchestra now never plays to half-empty houses--it draws big crowds. But attitudes have changed and costs have soared. Mr. Mehta's word for what needs to be done these days is "nurture"--to nurture audiences. Hence the educational concert idea.

"I've often been asked to speak more at my concerts," Mr. Mehta said. "But I think half the audience comes to listen to their favorite music and the other half has a little bit of the adventurous spirit. I don't think they want to be taught all the time. Maybe we should do the same program a second night. Yes, I've been talking about doing a Thursday night when we'd play, say a Mahler symphony, and then on Friday night we'd explain it. There could be people who would want to come back and relearn and rethink it."

Wouldn't programming more new works attract people?

"I don't think there's one newspaper in America," said Mr.
Mehta, with a smile, "that says enough contemporary music is being played. And yet when we do play it, nobody comes. We do a
certain amount of evangelistic railroading, let us say, but we find
we are the losers--financially--in the end. "

That doesn't really stop him. He won't, he said, play the
Tchaikovsky Fifth just as a "catalyst" to draw a crowd. If he
plays it, Mr. Mehta stressed, it's because he wants to play it; he
came out strong on "wants. " "It used to be, " he recalled, "that
when we were playing to practically 100 per cent subscription audiences I could use a talented young musician as soloist and play
something new. I could take the risk. Today I have to think
twice. "

He cited as a case of railroading, the three December solo
appearances with the Philharmonic of pianist Rudolf Serkin. "I
wanted to honor him--he plays two concertos. So I could also do
the West Coast premiere of 'Horizon Circled' by Ernst Křenek.
In other words, " said Mr. Mehta, again with his laugh, "I used
Serkin to bring in the people. "

Then he also did the same thing with popular young pianist
André Watts, playing three times in December with the orchestra.
It gave Mr. Mehta the chance to premiere on the West Coast
Roberto Gerhard's Symphony No. 3 for orchestra and electronic
tape. Mr. Watts was scheduled to play the First Liszt Concerto.

"I mean it's terrible to speak this way, " said Mr. Mehta,
looking genuinely distressed, his voice rising. "I wish I could do
the Gerhard--he was very talented--and after that some unknown
Mendelssohn or something. But if I do, the house will be half
empty. "

That it isn't ever empty seems to be due to programming
based on the fact that people love what they know. Everybody
hears the Schubert Seventh another time expectantly, he commented.
Presumably listeners would have the same experience with contemporary works if they had the chance to hear them often.

That's what an educational series might provide, although
saying so, Mr. Mehta used classics as his illustration. "When I
listen to a new Haydn symphony, " he said, "I'm terribly interested
in how the composer has built the piece--and how the conductor
does it. But I don't know how much of the American public actually listens architecturally to a classical composition. "

He seemed to be wondering if they'd care to be shown how.
As Mr. Mehta said, he loves to talk, and the notion of becoming
an instructor of audiences obviously fascinates him.

Sometimes the Philharmonic's public notices the youthfulness
most of all--and the growing youthfulness of the orchestra. It's

natural that a young director would fill vacancies with young instrumentalists.   On the other hand, probably the Los Angeles Philharmonic's widening world reputation is partly due to the maturing artistry of its basic corps of mature musicians.   "We've all matured, " Mr. Mehta has said more than once lately, as though he wanted to pay tribute to both youth and experience.

This season's opening concert got enthusiastic response for the Philharmonic's performance of Mahler's Symphony No. 2.   Mr. Mehta loves to do Mahler--his student days in Vienna immersed him in echoes of Mahler's ascendancy.   He has arranged for Mahler's "Kindertotenlieder" to be presented with mezzo-soprano Yvonne Minton as soloist, under guest conductor Istvan Kertesz. And Mr. Mehta himself will close the season (in April) with tenor Jon Vickers and baritone Dietrich Fischer-Dieskau singing Mahler's Das Lied von der Erde with the orchestra.

Doubtless these will be great crowd-drawers.   But could the Los Angeles Philharmonic, or any American symphony, be surer of support if it were government-subsidized, as orchestras are in Europe?   Mr. Mehta often conducts European symphonies and always, he said, the houses are packed.

"But I would say, " he concluded, "that our situation in the long run is much healthier.   There is a greater public participation because everybody donates.   The people of Europe just buy their seats. " He laughed again.   Nobody supports the Philharmonic just by buying a ticket, Mr. Mehta pointed out; it takes donations too. This, so far as educating audiences goes, remains perennially Los Angeles' lesson number one.

THE RUG CONCERTS*

Stephen Bornstein

Conductor Pierre Boulez strode to the platform, raised his baton, and began to inspire some of the most spirited music ever to flow through the town this June when he presented his most bizarre and enchanting musical event to date, the first series of "Rug Concerts" at New York's Philharmonic Hall.

Night after night for a week, Boulez turned musical phrases into communal life and brought thousands of cheering fans to their feet for encore after encore.   One critic was moved to call the experience "a love affair exploding open.... "

The occasion was one of those rare artistic moments when

---

*From Catalyst; A Quarterly Publication of Affiliate Artists, Inc. , no. 10 (August 1973).   Reprinted by permission of Stephen Bornstein, ed.

all the ingredients are exactly right: an eager audience, a lively program, and most of all an atmosphere of almost perfect friendliness combined to free players to join music and people together in an unrestrained and memorable exchange of virtuosity and joy.

Positioned off the stage and in the center of the hall, the orchestra was literally surrounded by the energy of enthusiastic listeners who followed every note with uncommon devotion until they erupted at the conclusion of each piece into exhilarating ovation.

No one could tell from their looks or behavior that they were the usual concert audience for they most certainly were not. They had come to hear the music and to be together and though their tickets were popularly priced, the big attraction was the removal of seats from the floor and the transformation of all but the galleries of Philharmonic Hall into an intimate indoor park. People spread all over, intermingling and touching, some resting on foam cushions, others comfortably sprawled out on the vast red rug that carpeted the stage and floor.

Above the musicians hung a huge sectional disk focusing attention on the players and spraying raindrops of soft, blue light over the tiered ceiling and walls. When the orchestra played, it was as if the music were being spewed forth from a fountain.

Sold-out houses each evening saw Boulez and the Philharmonic give the performances of the year and treat New Yorkers to the most daring and illuminating classical music experience in recent memory. For two almost uninterrupted hours, people in the hall were spellbound by the music that filled it and you could tell from the way he conducted that Boulez was as thrilled as they were.

Dividing the orchestra into two ensembles--one for symphonic repertory and the other for chamber works--Boulez alternated programs on successive nights and gave the "Rug" series an expansive musical reach that stretched from Haydn and Webern one evening to Purcell and Stravinsky the next.

It was not the first time music had been played in-the-round, or the first time Philharmonic Hall had been cleared of seats, but it was the first time they had been brought together and the results were a rousing and unreserved success. Critics praised everything from the climate in the house to its new acoustics and confirmed Boulez' aim "to create a feeling that we are all--audience, players, and myself--taking part in an act of exploration. "

Only the cost of the concerts presented a predicament. Converting the hall and reduced ticket prices ($3.50 top) were as impressive an expense as they were an attraction. Without independent financing, the "Rug Concerts" could not be included in the regular season, although Carlos Moseley, President of the

Philharmonic, expressed little doubt that they would be repeated.
"We need this kind of patronage, it's as simple as that. "

The "Rug Concerts" violated seemingly sacred traditions
with such artistic profit and personal appeal that Philharmonic Hall
will never be the same.   The overjoyed audiences who found they
could relax, speak and even touch one another knew something
magical had happened, that somber concert life could be changed
for the better.   Perhaps now that the ice has been broken, we can
all look forward to some enticing improvements in the great halls
in which we hear great music.

HISTORY AND PURPOSE OF YOUTH CONCERTS*

Thomas H. Hill
and Helen M. Thompson

Symphony orchestra concerts for youth are not new either to
the educational or orchestral scene.   There is a vast body of experience in presentation of concerts for young people.   Within only
the 20 cities included in this study, at least 5000 symphony concerts for youth have been presented during the last fifty-odd years. †
Prior to this study, however, comprehensive data on youth concert
purposes and practices had not been collected and made available
to orchestras and educators.

Within the 20 cities studied, the earliest symphony concert
for young people (of which there is record) was presented in Cincinnati, Ohio, on the Fourth of July in 1858, by the Philharmonic
Society conducted by Carl Barus, and consisted of music composed
by Mozart, Auber and Rossini, plus some polkas.   An admission
price of 25¢ was charged.

Fifty-three years later (1911) the San Francisco Symphony
played its first youth concert.   The Seattle Symphony followed with
its first student concert in 1912.   Within these 20 cities, however,
the Detroit Symphony was the first orchestra to initiate, in 1914,
regular and continuing youth concerts.

For all practical purposes, then, the study covers the experience amassed by 20 orchestras located in large and small cities
in presentation of some 5000 symphony concerts for young people
during a total of 546 youth-concert-operation-years.

*From The Organization, Administration and Presentation of Sym-
phony Orchestra Youth Concert Activities for Music Education Purposes in Selected Cities, Part I, Summary, by Thomas H. Hill
and Helen M. Thompson for the Office of Education, Bureau of Research; Washington, D. C. : Gov. Printing Office, 1968.

Historical Development

In each city studied, with the possible exceptions of Seattle and Winston-Salem, the orchestra organization took the initiative in organizing and financing symphony concerts for young people. The Seattle development is described as a joint venture between the orchestra and public schools, and the Winston-Salem director of music education served with the orchestra's conductor and manager in planning the first youth concert presented by the Winston-Salem Symphony.

In several cities the director of public school music education or the superintendent of schools was a member of the orchestra's board of directors at the time youth concerts were started and it is impossible to assess the role these educators may have played in encouraging the orchestra association to present youth concerts.

Conductors provided the leadership for establishment of youth concerts in at least 13 of the 20 cities with equal credit given to the orchestra managers in three of those cities. Symphony women's associations apparently were the chief instigators of youth concerts in three cities. The Junior League emerges as the prime motivating agency in two cities.

Pattern Of Development

With rare exceptions youth concerts in each city, regardless of the date initiated, go through a similar pattern of development. The rate at which the different stages of this development take place varies markedly from city to city.

At the outset, each orchestra seems to have relatively simple concepts of youth concerts, focused upon the basic premise that the orchestra has an obligation to play symphony concerts planned especially for the pleasure and cultural development of young people of the area.

The concert is announced, tickets usually are sold, and supplementary funds garnered from some source; the conductor and orchestra prepare and present the program according to the conductor's musical taste and experience; the children attend and the original goal is generally met to the satisfaction of almost everyone involved. This format may continue for several concerts or for several years.

Ultimately, however, there seems to come to almost every orchestra the urge and a felt obligation to widen its community services by making more concerts available to more children. This leads either to greatly increased promotional efforts, and, perhaps, changed programming concepts, or to presentation of concerts during in-school time with involvement of the orchestra in unfamiliar areas of formal elementary and secondary education techniques and principles.

Purposes For Youth Concerts

With the exception of the Cleveland Orchestra, no orchestra (included in this study) had established and clearly articulated the specific purposes for which it is presenting youth concerts. Neither had the orchestras related their choices of concert formats and programming policies to specific goals to be achieved with the specific audiences for which concerts were designed.

When asked to state the reasons why their orchestras are presenting youth concerts, orchestra board members, conductors and managers usually responded with general statements concerning:

(1)   The obligation of the orchestra to provide fine music for the youth in its community;

(2)   The value of developing in youth an awareness of fine music and cultural experiences;

(3)   The need to do all possible to develop among young people those who will become concert-goers and who will assume cultural leadership for the community in the future;

(4)   The need to provide children with the spiritual values inherent in listening to great music.

The Cleveland Orchestra, however, adopted a specific goal and plan for youth concerts some 30 years ago--largely as the result of the initiative of Miss Lillian Baldwin who at that time was an employee of the Cleveland public school system. The plan has given continuity and direction to Cleveland Orchestra youth concerts throughout these many years although various aspects of implementing the plan have undergone change.

The basic purposes of youth concerts in Cleveland were clearly set forth by Miss Baldwin to be those of: (1) providing for children as nearly as possible a normal symphony concert experience through presentation of significant music by the full orchestra in the regular concert hall and by requiring the children to pay at least a token admission fee; and (2) providing pre-concert study for all children through closely coordinated work between the orchestra and the public schools.

The Practice Begets The Purpose

Deliberately adopted or not, the purpose of many youth concerts evolves out of practices followed in their presentation. Analysis of youth concerts covered in this study indicates existence of two general types of student concert developments: (1) educational concerts that are (or, at some time, have been) closely coordinated with the public school music curriculum; and (2) student concerts planned to attract ticket purchasers from the general public and more or less lavishly embellished with special "attactions."

Some orchestras are committed exclusively to either one format or the other. Others present both types of concerts but in separate series and under separate financial plans. A few orchestras attempt to combine both types of concerts within the same series, and a few others have developed concerts that cut across the customary formats of the above two general types.

Purposes and types of concerts presented obviously have some relationship to the sources of financing developed for them. Every conceivable kind of financial plan is found to be operative for the educational concerts (described under 1 above)--from free concerts financed by federal education monies, to concerts for which admission is charged with supplementary funding from public and/or private sources. The "attractions" concerts (described under 2 above) customarily are financed from combinations of ticket sale income and contributions from various sources.

Regardless of the number or type of youth concerts presented, each orchestra organization studied--be it large or small, professional or avocational--subsidizes its youth concert presentations to some extent from its basic operating funds, funds that must be raised annually from concert fees, ticket sales and other earned income, and from contributions to its maintenance fund.

Evaluating Results Of Youth Concerts

The study failed to reveal existence of significant efforts on the part of orchestras to try to devise methods of evaluating results of youth concerts. Perhaps it is impossible for orchestras to devise them, but there is no record of formal, comprehensive efforts to do so.

When orchestra representatives were asked whether or not they had any measurement for the degree to which their purposes in presenting youth concerts were being achieved, the answers came in terms of generalizations, or of personal observations interpreted as success or failure with reference to one specific concert, or a specific group of individuals of which the following statements were typical:

"We've been playing youth concerts for nearly 30 years but still can't sell out our adult subscription series concerts this year."

"I personally know many of our present ticket holders and contributors who became interested in the orchestra as a result of attending youth concerts."

"I notice that we have many more young people and young adults attending regular concerts than used to be the case."

Educators' Concepts Of Youth Concerts

In conjunction with the study, over 1000 teachers, administrators and supervisors expressed their philosophies concerning the purposes of youth concerts. Their principal points may be expressed as follows:

Education in music is a necessary part of the general education of the public school student. As one of man's nobler forms of self-expression, music offers nourishment for the innermost recesses of a person's intellect and emotions.

Attendance at youth concerts can result in:

(1) The fostering of an appreciation for meaningful music of a highly developed nature.

(2) The successful social interaction among students in the audience.

(3) The increasing enjoyment of music.

(4) An increase in voluntary concert attendance.

(5) The stimulation of interest in music as a vocation or a profession.

(6) The opportunity to benefit from the unique qualities of the live performance.

Whereas educators have identified youth concert purposes and goals more specifically than have orchestras, the educational practitioners have not developed a specific methodology to be employed for the purpose of achieving stated goals.

Neither have educators devised methods of measuring the degree to which the stated goals are being reached as related to various teaching techniques used by teachers in conjunction with youth concerts, various types of youth concerts being presented, and diverse operating practices followed by orchestras in conjunction with presentations of youth concerts.

Just as in the case of orchestra representatives, educators' responses to questions relating to measurement of results of youth concerts came chiefly in terms of personal observations of specific situations, such as:

"My students buy many records of the concert music immediately after each youth concert."

"More students in my classes show an interest in taking up an instrument right after a youth concert."

"The music is over the heads of my deprived area students and they get little from the concerts. "

Total evaluation of youth concerts as educational experiences in any of the 20 study cities was non-existent for all practical purposes. Only about 11 per cent of the teachers questioned were aware of any post-concert evaluations being undertaken in their school systems, and the results of even these evaluations would not stand the test if subjected to the rigorous examination given to the results of learning in other subject matter areas.

In Summary

Lofty principles, deep conviction of the worth of fine music, selfless service on behalf of youth, a fierce desire for children to have "the best"--all exist among orchestra organizations and educators in profusion, but the half-century of youth concert presentations have not produced proven methods that are clearly identifiable as the best procedures for making fine music available to young people of this nation or for drawing them into the charmed circle of people who enjoy it.

----

†The 20 cities studied were: Group I--Cities in which the orchestra engages all or a substantial number of the musicians on a full-time basis for all or part of the year.

City and State	Orchestra
Baltimore, Md.	Baltimore Symphony Orchestra
Cincinnati, Ohio	Cincinnati Symphony Orchestra
Cleveland, Ohio	Cleveland Orchestra
Detroit, Mich.	Detroit Symphony Orchestra
Hartford, Conn.	Hartford Symphony Orchestra
New Orleans, La.	New Orleans Philharmonic Symphony Orchestra
Pittsburgh, Pa.	Pittsburgh Symphony Orchestra
Salt Lake City, Utah	Utah Symphony Orchestra
San Francisco, Calif.	San Francisco Symphony Orchestra
Seattle, Wash.	Seattle Symphony Orchestra

Group II--Cities in which the orchestra engages the musicians on a per service basis.

City and State	Orchestra
Chattanooga, Tenn.	Chattanooga Symphony Orchestra
Columbus, Ohio	Columbus Symphony Orchestra
Evansville, Ind.	Evansville Philharmonic Orchestra
New Haven, Conn.	New Haven Symphony Orchestra
Pasadena, Calif.	Pasadena Symphony Orchestra
Providence, R. I.	Rhode Island Philharmonic Orchestra

Sacramento, Calif.	Sacramento Symphony Orchestra
Sarasota, Fla.	Florida West Coast Symphony Orchestra
Spokane, Wash.	Spokane Symphony Orchestra
Winston-Salem, N. C.	Winston-Salem Symphony Orchestra

Chapter V

THE MUSIC THE ORCHESTRA MAKES

Introduction. Given the orchestra, the conductor and the audience in a 20th-century setting, we still need to know what composers (and what compositions) from the past four hundred years will be performed. It seems "programming" is everybody's business (although generally the responsibility of the musical director) and following are opinions of conductors (Charles Munch, Peter Paul Fuchs, Stephen Simon and Milton Katims), economists (William J. Baumol and William G. Bowen), critics (Gail Stockholm and Harris Green) and a man in orchestral management (Benjamin S. Dunham).

MAKING THE PROGRAM*

Charles Munch

The program--the conductor's first pre-concert care and a complicated one with so many different elements to consider.

First there are your personal preferences. Play the music you love but avoid building all your career on two or three programs that may seem to assure success but will surely render no service to the art of music. Do not risk falling into the quicksand of routine. You will be working less hard, which is fatal. There is no reputation that can resist this kind of spreading mediocrity.

Many conductors have "war-horses" that they ride at certain times but if they wish to travel far they must spare their mounts. Others pass themselves off as specialists in some particular piece or in one composer. Such conductors have never inspired anything in me but suspicion.

*   *   *

*From I Am a Conductor, by Charles Munch; New York: Oxford University Press, 1955. Copyright 1955 by Charles Munch. Reprinted by permission of Oxford University Press, Inc.

You must take into account the taste and the wishes of the public--but only up to a certain point. The music, the interpreter, and the public form a tri-partite entity in which each factor is indispensable to the others. Each has its rights and its duties.

The public comes to concerts to hear good performances of beautiful music just as it goes to museums to look at beautiful pictures or statues. It comes to be enriched, instructed, fortified. It does not come to criticize. It comes to take its place in the trinity with the composer and the performer. I am speaking of course of a "good" public, which listens thoughtfully and receptively to good music and good interpreters.

We know that music lovers all over the world want to hear the Beethoven symphonies but we limit the field of our activities and in fact betray our art if we do not show music's many other aspects.

Above all, never attempt to flatter and indulge the public. Do not play a Sibelius symphony for a Finnish audience just because you know they like it. Because they like it, they know it, and knowing it, they will never forgive your attempted flattery if your interpretation is not of the best.

*   *   *

If you make your programs too long, you will weary your audience. Music requires a state of high nervous tension on the part of both listener and performer. Don't overstrain it. A concert should not ordinarily have much more than seventy-five minutes of music if you do not want to hear the rustling of inattention or the noise of seats slamming behind you.

It is difficult to give an example of a typical program. Here is one scheme among many that seem reasonable to me:

1. A classical symphony or a baroque concerto grosso or an overture.
2. A difficult work. This is the place for Berg or Bartók.
3. A big symphony.

First we prepare the terrain and sharpen the receptivity. Then we can try to make the public love music whose tartness may still be disturbing. Finally, the classical, rich and solid, relaxes the atmosphere.

Build the program in such a way as to keep audience attention without a moment's waning. There are two ways to do it. First, select and perform the works in order of increasing tension. Second, give an impression of variety by juxtaposing works of very different periods, styles, or characters.

Consider the orchestra too when you make your program.

Musicians do not have the same instincts, reactions, or habits all over the world.   Where you do not have many rehearsals, it is wise not to play works completely unfamiliar to the orchestra, or, more properly, in a style or spirit totally strange to it.

The first principle is to choose works that suit your temperament and the orchestra's and the public's all at the same time. This is a difficult but necessary condition, although still not enough by itself for a true musical communion.

*   *   *

The custom of putting the soloist, if there is one, at the end of the program has been spreading from the United States.   It is a practice that I do not much favor for it breaks what should be the unity of a concert into two disparate halves.   I do not consider it wise to present the soloist in a kind of side show, for it gives the public the impression that the rest of the concert is really only a framework for the freak.   Nor do I care for the resemblance to the music-hall system in which the time is simply filled in with less brilliant acts until the appearance at the end of the star acrobat everyone has been waiting for.

And incidentally I think that "evenings" and "festivals" of a single composer are very much overdone these days.   It is a program-making formula that I avoid.   I do not like to be classified and labeled.

Music should be treated chivalrously, not put on parade.

*   *   *

There are many other burdens on your conscience at the moment of fixing on a program.   Must you play contemporary music?   I agree with this aphorism of Saint-Saëns: "The two kinds of music are not the contemporary and the other kind but the good and the other." Of course the knowledge that Beethoven's symphonies are good does not require you to measure all others by his.   But having accepted the principle, when you find good contemporary music, can you play it without risk?

This is really no problem.   It is proper to play some at every concert but with moderation, lest the public be discouraged. Nothing does modern music a greater disservice than dissociating it from the rest of the repertoire.   Doing so is an imposition that may not be borne with good will, for it demands a level of awareness, a span of attention, and degree of concentration not to be expected from the general public.   Modern music sometimes discourages even the specialists themselves.   How can the mere amateur set about penetrating its mysteries?   Certain problems of a very general nature do intrigue him and he likes to know where music is going, but that is enough.

The music of our own century interprets the preoccupations and the concerns of the world we live in.   We must play it and listen to it, learn about advanced aesthetic positions, new theories of harmony, and new principles of construction, but this acquaintance is not made instantaneously.

It is certainly necessary to have heard a very large number of works of greater or lesser significance to be able to discover a masterpiece on the day of its birth.   Posterity usually sorts them out for us.

Life goes so quickly these days that it takes a conscious effort to avoid being outdistanced.   If we wish to function as active human beings rather than remain passive spectators, we must present to our audiences what we consider important.

There is only one proper attitude to take toward the music of our own time: be patient, open our hearts, listen without prejudice and without snobbery.   André Gide has said, "Always be on an incline but always be on the way up. "

Young musicians always want to create a movement at any cost and they always want to impose it on others.   They try to do so with ardor and often with insolence, with the expectation of freeing themselves from a past they scorn and disdain, and without the smallest concern for the masters who also sought, struggled, and suffered.

Every creative force has its roots in the past but every composer finds his own language as he works.   Listen to the young Strauss and hear Mendelssohn; Debussy, Massenet; Schoenberg, Wagner; Stravinsky, Rimsky-Korsakov.

Be that as it may, it is our duty to bring out the young composers and to encourage them, while seeking to discover as best we can their true value.   A conductor must be a treasure hunter.   This is a duty he too often neglects but one that may gain him the greatest recognition in his own time.   I for one have had the good fortune to live among such musicians as Roussel, Honegger, Schmitt, Messiaen, Martinu, when they still needed to be played.   In twenty years the list will be much longer for the history of music has no end.   Tomorrow's conductors will not have to envy their elders.   It will be for them to forge the glory of composers still unknown.

*   *   *

A few more problems: You have fallen madly in love with a certain score.   One days its charms seem to have exhausted themselves.   Love flies out the window.   How to react?   The best thing, under these circumstances, is a separation until love is reborn, as it may well be one day.

There are also such things as neglected masterpieces. Take careful note that I do not believe in "forgotten masterpieces," although there are people who make a profession of rediscovering them, people who sift through the musical rubble of centuries past, from which time has already separated the valuables.

But I know works that are greatly respected though they fall just a little short of being true masterpieces. Sometimes a slight abridgment gives them a more favorable shape, just as cutting gives a diamond its full value. The composer may have neglected this essential operation himself. This is a problem to be faced, I think, in the magnificent symphony of Paul Dukas. If no cuts are made, if its present form is respected to the letter, it will disappear forever. I do not think it barbarous to say that everything possible must be done to save it from that undeserved fate.

Another example is the charming symphony Bizet wrote when he was 17 years old. If you play it in its original form, it will seem just too long for its substance. If you make a few little cuts without throwing the form into a new state of unbalance and without sacrificing a single musical element, you sense its real beauties and you possess yet another jewel.

"FREEDOM" OF CHOICE*

Peter Paul Fuchs

Every spring, among the blooming of the lilacs and the reawakening of the birds and butterflies, a fearful task awaits the conductor and music director of a symphony orchestra: he must plan the programs for the following season. Why fearful? Could there be anything more heartwarming than to dig among the scores of great masterworks and to choose which ones to perform? Seemingly not. But what are the realities that surround this ostensibly very blissful occupation?

Let us assume that the board members who have hired our man are generally sensible people, not the kind that make long speeches about "I don't know music, but I know what I like, etc.," and who try to dictate programming policies down to the tiniest detail. No, these people are sensible, and they do not try to dictate either policies or programs. They have assured the conductor repeatedly that they trust his sound judgment as a musician and as a "salesman of culture." "You know what our problems are," the chairman of the board said to him. "We must attract more people to our concerts, or we will be in bad shape financially. Of course,

---

*From The Psychology of Conducting, by Peter Paul Fuchs; New York: MCA Music, 1969. Copyright 1969 by MCA Music, a division of MCA Inc. Reprinted by permission.

we don't want you to lower your standards.   Just make it all nice
and attractive!"

So, with these golden words in his ear, the music director
retires to his study, ready to attack his beautiful library of orchestra scores.   The field is now wide open to let his wishes and desires go rampant.   Or is it?

Not quite.   He takes a quick look at the letters on his desk
that have accumulated during the past few weeks.   First, there is
that letter from Mrs. Q. H. Winterbottom, the widowed heiress of
a sugar fortune (she gave $500 to the Symphony last year).   It is
a nice, friendly letter, and it pays the maestro some beautiful
compliments about the excellent job he is doing for the people of
this city, about how wonderful the orchestra sounds now, etc.   But,
oh, that last paragraph!   "Now, that the time for making next
year's programs is drawing near, I hope you will give a little
thought to us older folks and to our likes and dislikes.   I am sure
there are some people who like that modernistic stuff that you
played last year (Bartók: "Dance Suite"; Hindemith: "Symphony
Mathis"; Copland: "El Salon Mexico"), but why so much of it?
When there is such a wealth of real music to choose from!   Of
course, it is your decision, and I am not trying to influence you.
But how about giving us some of those lovely gems that we have
not heard in a long time, such as the "Marche Slave," or the
"Peer Gynt Suite," or "Clair de lune"?   I know you won't find it
in your heart to turn down a simple request from an old lady...."

Then there is another letter.   This one bears 15 signatures,
and it comes from the headquarters of an organization called Students for Cultural Progress.   "Dear maestro," it says, "we know
that you are a man of our time and sympathize with everything
progressive.   But why have you shown so little eagerness to express this tendency in your symphony programs?   Surely you are
not trying to tell us that the fifty-year-old "Dance Suite" by Bartók
and the stodgy and old-fashioned "Mathis" are your idea of the new
directions in music!   What about the tastes of the culture-minded
young people?   Must they be made to feel that good music is only
what their great-grandfathers liked?   Why not some real contemporaries for a change: Nono, Boulez, Stockhausen, Cage?   Yours
for progress, etc...."

Ugh!   Suppose you ardent youngsters get together with Mrs.
Winterbottom, and I shall take it from there.   But wait--here is
another letter that I haven't even opened.   Oh, again at least a
dozen signatures.   "Dear Mr. Longhair, Our moms and dads keep
complaining that your symphony concerts are not sold out.   You
want to know why?   Because you play all that square junk that no
one wants to listen to.   Man, what a drag!   Have the Monkees appear with your band, and we guarantee they'll be hanging from the
rafters!   You dig?   The Mad, Mad Swingers."

Great--just what I have been waiting for!   But what is this official looking airmail letter? Oh yes, I remember now. It comes from an important nationwide organization. "Dear maestro," it starts. "Have you been fair to the American composer? Truthfully, when was the last time you programmed a piece by Ives, by Barber, by Sessions, by Carter, by Piston?" (Must I really tell them?) "If you don't perform these composers, who will?" A good question. I wonder how Mrs. Winterbottom would answer it.... But what is this exotic-looking envelope with the oriental drawings on it? Ah, from a music publisher. What does he want? "Dear Music Director, it gives us great pleasure to inform you that the performance materials of the works of two of the best known symphonic composers of Eastern Manchuria are now available at a discount rate. We know you will not wish to deprive yourself and your audiences of this unique opportunity." Here is another, also from a publisher. "The newly discovered Symphony in D Minor by Adolphe-Charles Adam has now been made available for performances in a scholarly edition. Please send us your order for this moving and significant work immediately." Here is something personal that I must have overlooked, handwritten: "Dear Maestro: Perhaps you are not aware that our beloved Dean Emeritus, Dr. Jeremiah Jones, wrote a full-length symphony some thirty years ago. It is a pleasing, tuneful work, not modernistic and technically not very difficult. I know your orchestra would enjoy playing it. We, the friends of the composer, feel that it would be a lovely gesture if you performed this work at the occasion of Dr. Jones' eightieth birthday next year, in recognition of all that this outstanding man has done for our cultural community...."

At this moment the conductor's beautiful wife enters the room. "Pardon me, darling. Ah, I see you are making the programs for next year. I am sure you won't forget the little request that the Smiths made the other night: the suite from Swan Lake. After all, the Smiths have been such wonderful friends...."

"Of course, of course. But I think I shall have a glass of wine now, and then go to bed. I can start making the programs tomorrow...."

Different conductors may disagree on how much of the preceding story is truth and how much is fiction. To assuage their doubts, let me say that it is not exactly autobiographical, but also that it is not wholly invented. There is no gainsaying that the conductor of a symphony orchestra is exposed to all kinds of pressures. And if his tendency should be to be a "nice guy," if he should wish to please everybody and comply with all the requests, he will soon realize that he has chosen the wrong profession. The making of enemies is a very natural activity for the music director of a symphonic organization, and if he is bent on survival, he must learn how to make enemies gracefully. This is not to say that he should ignore all the wishes of his "constituents," as it were. Since he is in a public position, he must in some ways please the public. But pleasing the public is not synonymous with having the audience decide what type of music should be played and what type avoided. The audience as such cannot decide, only individual members of the audience. And to be trite about it, what is one man's meat is the other man's poison. Therefore, he should carefully listen to all requests but then make up his own mind as to what it seems best to present.

Invariably the conductor must walk a tightrope. On one side there is the so-called popular taste: the clamor for familiar, easy-to-grasp music. This pleases the majority, for the person who recognizes a piece of music becomes an instant expert, which in turn flatters his vanity. Much of this can be translated into increased ticket sales. On the other side there is the conductor's educational function: he must develop the taste of the audience and also the potentialities of the orchestra. This involves the presentation of music which is not so easy to grasp and not as familiar. He should always strive to offer a sampling of the best in music, both classical and contemporary: music significant enough to preserve his own self-respect and yet not far enough away from the taste of the majority to lose their support.

All this will entail a great many compromises, and some hair-raising decisions must be made. If he bends over backwards in the direction of programs that seem interesting to his own searching mind, he may overtax the receptive faculties of the majority and thereby lose his audience. But if he bends over backwards in the direction of popular taste and keeps repeating the all-too-familiar, he will soon lose the more discriminating members of the audience and gradually the others, too, since an overplaying of even the most cherished works is bound to end in boredom. So he will find himself faced with two alternative methods of losing support, and in between, a slim and precarious possibility of keeping it. To find this possibility and to remain faithful to it is the ever-renewed problem of program making.

To begin with, a great deal depends on the number of concerts in a subscription series. Every conductor finds it comparatively easy to make a good program for one concert: here he can afford to be selfish and present three or four works that will be "down his alley" and that will make him appear in the best possible light. To make programs for a series of 15 or 20 concerts is easy again, for in such an extended cycle there are enough opportunities to have every major composer and every significant musical style represented. The really difficult task is to plan a series of five, seven or ten concerts. In that case one obviously tries for a fairly complete representation of all the trends but often finds the available playing time not sufficient to do so. Important gaps are bound to occur, followed by the inevitable recriminations as to why this or that composer, this or that popular work was ignored.

I do not believe that a music director should go about the task of programming a series with computerized coldness. It is not just a question of representing every important composer and every significant style. The works offered must in some way relate

to the conductor's personality.   If a musician whose forte is impressionistic music should offer a heavily German-oriented series,
with Mozart, Beethoven, Brahms, Mahler and Strauss in the lead,
the result would in all likelihood be unsatisfactory since much of
the music would sound dutiful rather than impassioned.   If, on the
other hand, a man of prevailingly German background, in order to
show his catholic taste and his versatility, decided to offer a great
deal of Ravel, Debussy, Respighi, Delius, Fauré, etc. , it might
not be any better since some of these works would probably be
presented in name but not in spirit.   Of course, it is rather tedious to have a conductor ride his favorite scores to death year after
year--to have the subscribers ask each other during the summer:
"What is it going to be this year, Tchaikovsky's Fifth or Tchaikovsky's Sixth? Strauss' Don Juan or Strauss' Till Eulenspiegel? Ravel's 'Daphnis' or Ravel's 'La Valse'?" He should always attempt
to create variety, and he should also work steadily to improve his
handling of scores that may initially have been foreign to him. But
at the same time he should not forget that all the works he conducts are being presented through the mirror of his own personality, and that therefore it will be to the good of the series to let
his strongest stylistic affinities put a stamp on it.   Even a very
outstanding conductor will occasionally "lay an egg" when he cannot
find a spiritual bridge to the work he conducts.   And no conductor
can afford to offer his audience a basketful of "eggs"!

    This delicate situation can become even more so in the case
of contemporary works.   Some conductors feel very little sympathy
for contemporary music, and so they largely ignore it in their
programming.   Others love it with a passion and will perhaps present more of it than the audience is ready to receive.   But then
there is an ominous third group: musicians who have very little
genuine liking for contemporary music but who feel that it is their
duty to play it.   So they offer a number of modern scores which
they conduct in a businesslike fashion, never really getting involved.
That such performances are likely to be a total loss and will make
no friends for contemporary music need not be explained any further.

    Now to the actual process of program making for the series.
Even if all the pressure groups have been handled in a satisfactory
fashion, the conductor is not likely to start the planning with a
clean slate, for there is always the question of the soloists.   In
many cases they are, as it has been pointed out before, the chief
selling attraction of the series.   Furthermore, good soloists often
line up their engagements quite far ahead of time, and if the organization wishes to obtain the services either of soloists in the
topflight category or of somewhat less expensive ones that are "a
good buy for the money"--to use management terminology--then it
must act quickly and preferably have all its solo contracts signed
by Christmas of the preceding year.   Even at that the choice of
soloists is not a completely free one: it depends on the funds that
have been budgeted for the purpose and on the availability of the
artists themselves.   Since, in the process of negotiating, many

modifications of the original plans and wishes will become necessary, the slate of soloists, as it appears in the final edition of the
printed program, may be quite different from what conductor and
board members had agreed earlier to try for.

Then comes the question of what each artist is to perform.
Here again it is not simply a matter of choosing a concerto at
random and asking the artist to play it. If a pianist has become
famous for his rendition of the Rachmaninoff Third Concerto, it is
unlikely that you will ask him to play the Mozart D Minor instead,
even though it may fit better into your series. Besides that, the
artist himself may express a wish concerning the work he is to
perform, and in that case it will be wise to humor him since most
musicians play best what they really like to play. Sometimes an
otherwise logical choice must be turned down if the work in question had been played too recently on the series. Sometimes for
other reasons: an audience that has not heard Tchaikovsky's Violin
Concerto in six seasons will probably not be happy if the far less
popular Vieuxtemps No. 4 is programmed. And lastly, the conductor will have to organize a certain balance between the various
solo numbers in the series: when there are only five or six subscription concerts in the series, it is decidedly inadvisable to present both piano concertos by Chopin or two violin concertos by
Mozart during the same year.

After the soloists have been engaged and their programs
chosen, the next step, if it has not been taken care of earlier, is
the decision on whether to present a choral work during the series.
In that case arrangements with a chorus and with vocal soloists will
have to be made. It is hard to advise a symphonic organization on
how often it should present major choral works. This will depend
on the availability of a good chorus and also on the taste of the audience. In a series of five to seven concerts, one choral work for
the year will probably be quite sufficient. In fact, it is not at all
certain that under these circumstances a choral work should be offered every year. If the choice is to offer one, it must again be
coordinated with the already established program numbers: with a
pianist being scheduled to play the Brahms B♭ Concerto, and perhaps a violinist having chosen the Brahms Violin Concerto, it would
be somewhat less than judicious to engage a chorus for a performance of the German Requiem.

Then, after all these contingencies have been settled, the
music director is at last ready for the planning of the orchestral
numbers. Symphonies and major symphonic poems will come first,
then overtures and other relatively short numbers. There are many
viewpoints according to which the selection of these numbers can be
organized, and some of them will undoubtedly conflict with each other. Therefore, it seems safest to start with the most important
principle, which is the musical balance of the entire series. No
conductor should feel that the planning of a series should put him
into a straitjacket and that his sense of originality should be stifled.
Just the same, since there is an educational process involved, it is

perhaps wise to establish certain basic principles and not to violate them unless absolutely necessary.

Without wishing to be pontifical about it, I am offering as an example a few principles that I have established for myself in making the programs for a five-concert series (which to all intents and purposes is the shortest series ordinarily encountered). I feel that in such a series there must be as a minimum requirement:

a) a symphony by Beethoven

b) a symphony by Haydn or Mozart

c) one major symphonic work by Brahms--if not a symphony then a piano concerto, the violin concerto, the double concerto or the Haydn Variations.

d) a romantic non-German symphony or symphonic poem (Tchaikovsky, Dvorák, Smetana, Franck)

e) an orchestral work by Debussy, Ravel, Roussel, etc.

f) a symphony from the early Romantic period by Schubert, Schumann or Mendelssohn. If this is impossible, then at least an overture or concerto by one of these composers.

g) a major and established work from the twentieth century by Stravinsky, Hindemith, Bartók, Prokofieff, etc.

h) a local or regional premiere, perhaps a commissioned work.

This list is admittedly far from complete, but at least it is a basis to operate from. I have purposely left some ambiguities, especially in categories in which the conductor's personal taste and inclination may be the decisive factor. These categories include, for instance, Baroque music (works by Bach, Handel, Vivaldi, Corelli, Telemann, etc.), French works of the 19th century (Berlioz, Saint-Saëns, Fauré, Bizet), overtures and excerpts by Wagner, works by Bruckner, Mahler and Strauss, and finally works that do not seem to fit any particular category, such as Mussorgsky's "Pictures," Kodaly's "Hary Janos," Stravinsky's "Firebird" and others of the same type. Also, there are some works in a somewhat lighter vein that can sometimes be included to best advantage in a regular concert series: overtures and waltzes by Johann Strauss, the "Rhapsody in Blue" or the "Concerto in F" by Gershwin, or a "fun" piece like Ibert's "Divertissement."

These are only the minimum requirements. Now the question arises as to how they can best be balanced against each other so that no style will be overweighted. (For instance: having Brahms Fourth, Tchaikovsky's Fifth, Franck's D Minor and Saint Saëns' Symphony with Organ on the same five-concert series would

not be very good programming!) In order to accomplish this, I
have developed a system for myself that has proved most helpful.
I use two sets of tabulations, which are as follows:

Tabulation I

German (or Austrian) works   . . . .
French works   . . . .
American and English works   . . . .
Russian and other Slavic works   . . . .
Works of other national origin   . . . .

Tabulation II

18th Century   . . . .
19th Century   . . . .
20th Century   . . . .

Now I proceed to select the individual scores. If, for instance, I choose Beethoven's Seventh, I put one mark in the German
line of Tabulation I and one in the 19th-century line of Tabulation
II. If I select Bartók's "Concerto for Orchestra," I put one mark
in the line in Tabulation I that says "Works of other national origin," and one in the 20th-century line in Tabulation II. Simultaneously, I list each work chosen in the program of the concert in
which I intend to perform it. After about a dozen works have been
chosen and the proper marks been put in each line, a trend will
have been established. It is easy to tell by then whether the tendency is toward properly balanced programs, or whether there
seems to be too much French or German music, whether there is
perhaps too much emphasis on any one century, and so forth.

Of course this is not to imply that all the lines should be
numerically equal. It stands to reason that the average audience
would not be very happy with a symphonic series if it had as many
works from the eighteenth century as from the nineteenth, or if
the number of Hungarian, Finnish and Latin-American works were
equal to that of the German ones. It must be considered from the
very beginning that there are certain areas, both of period and na-
tionality, which by their very nature will require more emphasis
than others. Conversely, if my listing should show seven Slavic
works and only two French ones, I am safe in suspecting an imbalance which I must try to correct. However, I must always be
careful about not upsetting one tabulation too much while correcting
the other.

Although this procedure is helpful, it is far from foolproof.
It will not work very well if all the Russian works are major symphonies, with only overtures and one symphonic poem on the German side. This is a matter of common sense, and the device is
only offered for basic orientation. Also, decisions must be made
as to which of the selected works should be well known standards
and what others somewhat less familiar. Though it is necessary

to offer a certain number of "chestnuts," this should not be overdone since the excessive popularity of a work may ultimately mili-
tate against it. For instance: it has become difficult to program
Schubert's "Unfinished Symphony" in a regular subscription series,
due to its having been played too much, while the same composer's
great C Major symphony is very familiar but far from hackneyed,
and while his third, fourth and fifth symphonies may be particularly
ingratiating to an audience, due to their relatively offbeat quality.
By the same token, Tchaikovsky's "1812 Overture" has also by now
gone well past the limit of tolerance of the ordinary symphony audience. But this factor should cause no undue concern. There are
many other works that are also "chestnuts"--as for example Beethoven's Fifth, Brahms' First or Tchaikovsky's "Pathétique"--but
that are still gratefully accepted by audiences as the superb masterworks that they are.

      In a medium-sized or small city in the United States, it is
possibly a very sane principle to include one universally familiar
score in each program: this will pacify the "steak-and-potato" kind
of music lover! A music director who follows this routine will find
that he can afford to be much freer and much less tradition-bound
in the choice of the remaining works on each program.

      The choice of contemporary works can be a major headache
for the conductor. It goes without saying that when modern scores
are played, many members of the audience will have to come to
grips with an unfamiliar and perhaps somewhat repellent medium,
and it may take all of the conductor's wisdom to make this encounter a peaceful one. For that reason he must be sure to present
only compositions that he himself strongly believes in, for his own
lack of confiction would transmit itself to the audience in no time.
At the same time, a conductor who thinks he can discharge his obligation to contemporary music by performing Schoenberg's "Verk-
lärte Nacht," Stravinsky's "Firebird," Prokofieff's "Classical Symphony" or Webern's "Passacaglia" will not be fooling anyone. The
pretext that some contemporary composers wrote openly romantic
works during their early years--despite the fact that some of these
works are well worth presenting--will not solve the issue but only
dilute it. There is a great number of more advanced scores that
these and other composers have written which will introduce the
listeners to a modern idiom without needlessly shocking them.
Sometimes it seems that even a mild shock is of a certain thera-
peutic value if it serves to present a fascinating new style to the
audience, such as in Webern's Six Orchestral Pieces, provided that
the work is not too long. In such a case the conductor may further
the cause of contemporary music (and incidentally his own!) by turning to the audience before the piece is played and explaining in a
few simple words the expressive principle and the compositional
method of the score.

      Sometimes an advanced score by a local composer will fare
much better with an audience, for personal reasons, than if the
same work had been written by a total stranger. This again is a

bit of self-deception (though the composer will not mind it!), and it will not solve a problem that must be attacked on a broader basis.

All in all it can be said that no known type of programming will please everyone in the community. But at least we may hope that the number of dissenters and complainers will be small and that the music director, in his program building, will have satisfied his own conscience and a relatively large number of his listeners. For the rest he can only hope that even in the minds of those who are critical of him the good points will outweigh the bad ones. The strongest element in every artistic presentation is convinction, and the conductor who has it to the fullest extent will more easily convince listeners that are indifferent or that are openly opposed to his efforts. He should depend on this for both his classical and his contemporary interpretations. All the offerings, whether controversial or not, must in some way be designed to reach the audience, perhaps not in the sense of immediately causing the reaction of a wild burst of applause, but at least gradually and consistently.

In all probability there is no better guideline for any performing musician than the one given to us by Alban Berg when he said that "we should perform the classics as if they were contemporaries and the contemporaries as if they were classics...."

CONTEMPORARY WORKS:
THE ECONOMICS OF "ADVENTUROUS" PRODUCTIONS*

William J. Baumol
and William G. Bowen

As we have seen, size of audience depends on a variety of considerations, including general economic conditions, the competition of the mass media, promotion and the ease with which tickets can be obtained. The specific production or program offered, however, may have a greater influence on attendance than any of these other factors.

Thanks to cooperative managements, we were able to collect attendance figures for individual operas from the Metropolitan Opera for 1962-63, the New York City Opera for 1961-62 and the fall of 1962, and from Covent Garden for 1957-58 through 1963-64. In addition we obtained some case-study figures from the Chicago Lyric and the Santa Fe Operas. We next compared attendance when contemporary works were being performed with attendance on other occasions. "Contemporary" operas were defined arbitrarily as those

---

*From Performing Arts: The Economic Dilemma, by William J. Baumol and William G. Bowen; New York: Twentieth Century Fund, 1966. Copyright 1966 by The Twentieth Century Fund. Reprinted by permission.

written after World War I, a definition which has the advantage of
objectivity, though "adventurous" is, in at least a few cases, something of a misnomer.

We found that ticket sales at the Metropolitan fell from their
usual 97 per cent to 89 per cent of capacity when a contemporary
work was performed. At the New York City Opera the corresponding decline was from 65 to 39 per cent of capacity, and at Covent
Garden there was an average reduction from 83 to 67 per cent of
capacity. [1] On the basis of our figures it may be estimated that a
single performance of a contemporary opera results in a foregone
revenue loss of nearly $2500 at the Metropolitan, nearly $4000 at
the New York City Opera, and over £400 at Covent Garden. [2] At
the New York City Opera, operating at City Center, we were told
in an interview that the maximum capacity gross was over $11,000,
but contemporary operas usually grossed between $2000 and $5000
per performance, and a $5000 or $6000 gross was considered a
tremendous success.

Nor is this the end of the financial difficulty caused by the
production of such works. In part because contemporary works
are often presented by the company for the first time, and in part
because they are characteristically difficult to perform, they may
require a substantial expenditure on extra rehearsals as well as
associated production costs. And since the piece is usually given
only a few times, these production costs cannot be spread over a
considerable number of showings.

Adventurous works cause similar financial problems in other
art forms. In the theater, "adventurous" is not synonymous with
"contemporary. " True, the "theater of the absurd" and other experimental plays are not generally a blessing to the box office.
But neither are the classics. Apparently the bulk of the theatergoing public wants new plays, but plays which place little strain on
conventional attitudes.

We have few data on this subject pertaining to the theater
generally, but we have figures extending over a ten-year period
(1953-1963) for the Bucks County Playhouse, which, as a matter of
policy, has been putting on several new plays each season. The
new shows ordinarily constitute a little less than one-third of the
theater's offerings. Even though none of these productions was
radically experimental, they did more poorly at the box office than
the tried and true productions in 7 of the 10 years reported. The
difference was small, however--on the order of magnitude of 5 per
cent overall. Cost data for the Bucks County Playhouse for both
types of productions show that running costs for the premieres were
higher in every year, the difference amounting to about 5 to 10 per
cent. Here we see again the double financial pressures besetting
new productions.

Finally, we may look at the orchestral situation. We have
no American data, but excellent British figures were prepared by

the Royal Festival Hall for the Goodman Committee.   In this case
"adventurous" programs are defined most conservatively, as any in
which at least one piece is not part of the standard repertoire.
Even so, adventurous programs reduced attendance by about 20 per
cent of capacity on the average.   Furthermore, this holds for all
orchestras performing at the hall, and for all seating price categories.

While we have no corresponding figures for the United
States, we suspect that the effect on audience size of the inclusion
of a contemporary work on a program is somewhat less drastic
than it is in England.   There are two grounds for this surmise.
First, American orchestras operate closer to capacity, so that at
least some audiences in this country may be forced to purchase
tickets to performances which are partially contemporary if they
wish to hear the orchestra at all.   Second, American orchestras
sell tickets in subscription series, a procedure which has only recently even been proposed for London orchestras.   The practice of
selling subscriptions clearly gives the ticket purchaser less choice--
if a concert containing contemporary works is part of a set of concerts offering more standard works, he can less easily avoid purchasing a ticket to it.   But whether our guess is or is not valid,
the path of the contemporary composition in this country is not
usually smooth.   It is often argued that the repertoire still consists
primarily of revered standard works, and that even those contemporary composers who are played are likely to be represented by
their "safest" and most conservative works--pieces for which they
themselves have little affection.   Like token integration, such token
representation of contemporary pieces in the musical repertoire
conceals a problem instead of solving it.

To be sure, in determining program content a performing
group must take into account the likely economic consequences as
well as its own beliefs about the relative merits of the works it is
considering.   It has been suggested by one manager that any musical organization which does not play new works cannot maintain its
reputation among other musicians.   But an organization which pursued an art-for-art's-sake approach and disregarded the type of
audience response that we have documented might well be committing financial suicide--a fact largely ignored by critics of conservative programing. [3]   On the other hand, if new plays, operas and
musical compositions are not performed, they may not long be
written and the arts will lose their vitality.   The problem, then,
will probably not be solved by the individual organizations; they cannot fairly be criticized for hesitating to embark on a path which
may be catastrophic financially.   Instead, it must be solved by all
organizations together, and ultimately by society itself.   The Ford
Foundation's program of financial assistance for the presentation
of contemporary works may illustrate the type of support required.

---

1.   These are, of course, only averages, and there are exceptions.
The Santa Fe Opera has done well with "Lulu" and several

Stravinsky works, and a contemporary work is sometimes well attended when tickets are sold as part of a subscription series or when an outstanding soloist is involved.

2. These estimates utilized data on capacity gross obtained from the various performing organizations, i. e., figures indicating the total amount that would be earned at a performance if every seat in the house were sold. In these calculations it was assumed that a reduction in attendance would have a proportionate effect on ticket sales in every price category. Where capacity gross varied by night of the week or for any other reason, a weighted average figure was utilized.

3. Though most published criticism of their programing objects to the conservatism of the performing groups, those who dislike contemporary music are also vehement in their criticism. In the course of our audience survey we received a number of unsolicited comments denouncing performances of contemporary music as a blight on the art and an offense to the audience. Another example is provided by an article in a right-wing publication which condemns the sandwiching "between ... acceptable compositions of some outpourings of more or less raucous dissonance," describing this practice as "a violation of cultural freedom." See William H. Chamberlin, "Musical Forced Feeding," The Freeman, June 1965, p. 11. _____

THEY'RE ROCKING THE BOAT IN ROCHESTER*

Gail Stockholm

Samuel Jones, the young new conductor of the Rochester Philharmonic Orchestra, must have some fantastic musical good luck working in his favor--and he'll need every bit of luck he can get, because his creative and unconventional approach to concerts is bound to shake up the more conventional musical community.

So far, Lady Luck (and a generous dose of ability) have been on the conductor's side. His orchestra was rescued from sudden death this year by a large grant. He himself leaped over another stumbling block when he became chief conductor of the same orchestra he worked for as assistant conductor. (In music, as in Presidential politics, the No. 2 man almost never gets the No. 1 spot.) Then too, he's a native American with an inconsequential name like Jones. His orchestra board showed that it wouldn't succumb to the illogical American custom of hiring European conductors.

*From the Cincinnati Enquirer, March 14, 1971, by Gail Stockholm, Music Critic. Reprinted by permission. [Both Samuel Jones and Walter Hendl have since moved, but their innovative efforts in Rochester are of continuing importance.]

Best of all, Jones' appointment as conductor last month
[i. e. , February 1971] is proof that he has succeeded in convincing
part of the musical community in Rochester, N. Y. , of the need to
re-examine our traditional musical environment in order to build
new audiences. He wants to get back to the basic appeal of music
on an emotional and intuitive level, using an approach that stresses
human and universal themes that all generations can identify with.

Since Rochester is the home of the Eastman School of Music,
one of the three great American conservatories founded in the '20s,
it has been the alma mater of a great many music educators and
administrators, and a gathering place for such upright musical citizens as composer Howard Hanson, former director of the school
and still director of the school's Institute of American Music, and
Walter Hendl, present director of the school and former associate
conductor of the Chicago Symphony Orchestra.

The Eastman School was innovative when it was founded fifty
years ago. In order to compete with Boston, Philadelphia and New
York, it tried to offer something more than other music schools
did.   Under Howard Hanson, it came up with an educational philosophy that combined a thorough training in the humanities with technical training in music.   Most schools then stressed technique only.
During his first year in charge at Eastman, Hanson proposed a
concert in cooperation with the Rochester Philharmonic devoted to
works by American composers. At that date, Aaron Copland had
heard his own works performed in the United States only twice.

The concerts grew into an annual American Music Festival
and made Eastman an important center of creative musical activity.
Now, fifty years later, it ranks as "The Establishment" in music.
Yet Walter Hendl, in addition to his post at the school, has just
accepted a post as musical adviser to the Rochester Philharmonic,
which means he and the swinging younger conductor will work together in conducting concerts and planning programs.

This too, is a rather unexpected plus for Jones, as the professional orchestra and Eastman have had a rather tenuous relationship over the years, despite the fact that the school trains many of
the orchestra's players.   In fact, Jones himself has his master's
and doctorate from Eastman.   But his approach to music is far
from academic.

Controversy may be yet to come in the year ahead, for
Jones' work already is shaking up Rochester.   It also is alerting
people to concert music and bringing many young persons and adults
into the concert hall for the first time.

The most flagrant example of the stir he has caused this
season was a concert entitled "Music of Man and Woman. "   The
posters, advertisements and program for the concert featured a
picture of Rodin's famous sculpture, "The Kiss. "   The attendance
for the program was unusually large and much of the overflow

consisted of first-timers at the symphony, who admitted that the
picture and the theme had sparked their curiosity.

Did they see a sexy program? Not really, according to the
local critics. "Sensual, certainly, but not sexy," said George
Kimball of the Times-Union. "A well thought-out program featuring
fine music," said another. "Rodin really packed them in," said a
third, and reported that first-nighters said the music wasn't complicated and communicated its message immediately.

And what was on the program? Teleman's "La Putain"
(The Prostitute), César Franck's "Psyche and Eros," Richard
Strauss' "Don Juan," Tchaikovsky's "Romeo and Juliet," and Arnold
Schoenberg's "Transfigured Night," an atonal account of an uneasy
relationship between a man and his wife and her unborn child.
Easy music? That depends on how you approach it, apparently.

Jones anticipated some static on the Man and Woman concert
and he made the most of it. The program opens with a dramatic
skit of two solid citizens reading the concert notice in their newspaper. It goes like this:

Husband: Hey, Martha, did you see this?

Wife: What, George?

Husband: The Philharmonic is giving a sex concert.

Wife: A sex concert? You mean the Philharmonic, OUR
Philharmonic?

Husband: YOUR Philharmonic. Look at this. I mean, it's
like free love. Wonder who they got to pose for that
picture?

Wife: George, that's the famous statue by Rodin. But it
belongs in an art gallery, not a concert hall.

Husband: It belongs in the trash can, if you ask me....

Than a slide of the Rodin is flashed in front of the audience
and the narrator sweeps them into well-known poems of love, quoting the Bible, Herrick, Greek myths, the musical "West Side
Story" and Schoenberg's inspiration, the poem by Richard Dehmel
translated into English.

Most of Jones' programs make extensive use of multi-media
techniques, introducing dance, theater, art slides, film, pantomime,
comedy--whatever he thinks will get the theme across. This is in
itself nothing new. Concert halls all over the country are trying
the same things.

But what is new is the degree of coordination of the arts

that Jones achieves in his programs. This is where the other programs fall apart at the seams. In the others, the analogies between the arts don't gel. They are too superficial, or sometimes there is no attempt to interrelate film, music and live performers.

It has taken Jones two or three years to write and produce his scripts. As a composer himself, he has a good sense of how to use music to build links between sections of the program.

Only 35 years old, he also is young enough to communicate with the young people and students and to learn what they want and need, a factor that all too often is overlooked by those planning musical programs for communities. One of the secrets of Jones' success is a good communications line to students at the university and a special symphony committee called the Under 30 series which volunteers enthusiastic advance publicity efforts.

"Music of War and Peace" is another theme in Jones' series. Here he took Leon Balada's musical composition "Guernica" and coupled it with slides of the Picasso painting that inspired the composer in the '30s during the Spanish Civil War.

Ned Rorem's "Poems for Peace," a song cycle set to a 15th-century French text, was interspersed for contrast, then another composition on war, Ronald Herder's "Requiem II--Games of Power" for contralto, electronic tape and orchestra, was presented with an accompanying light show. The Herder work was commissioned by Miami University, in Oxford, Ohio.

For a program for school audiences entitled "Space, Time and Music," Jones called on nearby Strasenburgh Planetarium, where technical director John Paris was more than willing to cooperate. It opens with a visual effect showing "Earthrise" (Sunrise from the Moon) and the music of Strauss' "Thus Spake Zarathustra." A slide of Apollo in his chariot introduces Bach's cantata, "The Contest Between Phoebus and Pan." Then the program offers Haydn's Symphony No. 43, "The Mercury Symphony," Beethoven's "Moonlight" Sonata, Holst's "The Planets," and a contemporary work by Henry Brand called "Galaxy 2."

The critic who was present called it "as sensitive and sophisticated a presentation as one could find, an evening that made Leonard Bernstein and the producers of his televised concerts look like 'technological drop-outs.'"

Another hit was "Music of Protest," which besides using humanitarian themes by Bartók, Vaughan Williams and Carl Neilsen even included an antipollution composition of 1911, Charles Ives' "The Ruined River."

Jones often employs local artists, dancers and actors in his programs. He believes in giving young performers a chance to take part in the arts in a professional context. He thinks this is the way to encourage creativity at home.

A jazz history of Western sound in collaboration with the Eastman jazz ensemble is his latest success. Other popular themes are "The Weather in Music, " "Music of the Sea, " "Music for a Great City" and "Black and White, " a civil rights program. Many of these were videotaped by the New York State Education Department, and the orchestra just received a $35,000 grant from the National Endowment to videotape four more for U.S. distribution.

"I hope the series will turn students on to classical music, " Jones said. "My goal is INTENSE communication. The whole purpose of my TV series is to try to reawaken the imaginative and emotional response to music. If these themes, environments and concerns inspired composers to write the music, then why should we look down on people who respond in the same way to music?

"The young today are going back to Nature in a very real sense. They have been so cerebral for so long and now they're beginning to use their eyes and ears. I feel general music education in the schools has a problem. Most kids drop music when they get into high school or else they concentrate only on band or instrumental performance. Appreciation as a listener isn't developed enough, and after all, my life and the life of my orchestra depend upon having a live audience out there listening. "

ROCK AT SYMPHONY*

pro: Stephen Simon

I go to a symphony concert to enjoy myself. I think most people throughout history--especially today--have gone to the theater, the ballet, the opera, and the symphony to be entertained.

Entertainment need not preclude an intellectual experience. I can define a Wagner opera or a Bach Passion as entertainment. I can hear the Penderecki "Threnody" and be moved in a positive way. How exciting it is to come away from the performance of a Brahms symphony with a sense of enjoyment.

con: Milton Katims

Is it a legitimate idea to program rock music and rock groups in combined or joint concerts with symphony orchestras?

In planning the programs of the Seattle Symphony, I have constantly sought new ideas. I have always been interested in adding other dimensions to the customary, tradition-bound evenings with the symphony. These experiments were aimed not only at inspiring continued interest on the part of our regular subscribers, but also at

*From Symphony News, vol. 22, no. 3 (June 1971). Copyright 1971 by the American Symphony Orchestra League. Reprinted by permission.

And how disappointing to hear a less-than-entertaining performance of anything. One almost feels cheated.

If one can accept the premise that the prime purpose of musical performance is to entertain, it becomes clear that concert programming should both guide and serve the tastes of the audience. And because audiences are comprised of persons with varied likes and dislikes, doesn't it follow that our orchestras should perform all kinds of music? There is such a wide choice of good program material today, from the traditional through the avant-garde and on into jazz and rock, that it seems only logical to perform the whole spectrum.

This season in New York City, Leonard Bernstein's "Symphonic Dances from West Side Story" were performed on a subscription concert. The audience ate it up. One critic suggested, at the risk of appearing a "snob," that such a work be relegated to "pops" programs. This attitude, hardly unique, frightens me, because I feel it has the potential to kill the concert field.

The audience at large loves West Side Story. This subscription audience enjoyed the performance. They wanted to be entertained. That's why they came in the first place. Not everything on a symphonic program has to be a great intellectual experience. West Side Story represents an important genre in American music. There is no reason to look down on it.

attracting representatives of the "now" generation.

When we played "Deserts" by Varèse we engaged the Retina Circus to project a light show on a screen above and in front of the orchestra. For William Schuman's "Judith," Yuriko (with minimal stage props) danced in front of the players, separated from them by a scrim. For performances of music inspired by paintings (Mussorgsky, Hindemith, and Gunther Schuller), slides of the appropriate paintings were projected onto screens on both of the side stages in our Opera House. We have "semi-staged" works like Honegger's "Jean d'Arc" and Stravinsky's "Persephone." We have built small sets (placed in front of the orchestra) for performances of Schoenberg's "Erwartung" and Poulenc's 'Le Voix Humaine."

During this past season we commissioned and performed a work for Moog synthesizer and orchestra. And for our performances of Scriabin's "Poem of Ecstasy," a young moviemaker of the Northwest created a film to be shown at the same time. Did this unusual programming succeed in attracting younger people? Very definitely. And many of them returned to hear the orchestra perform the more traditional symphonic literature.

From the foregoing you might think that I would be among the first to want to include rock with symphony. But I don't. Why not? Such a combination might attract hordes of young people to the symphony hall. Yes, but it would be basically dishonest.

Similarly, to suggest that our "commercial" market is anything but serious--to make light of the artistic ability of the arrangers who "stoop" to commercials, television, or pop and rock records--seems to me, in the light of today's market, a snobbish overreaction on the part of the classical establishment. There are many fine creative composers writing and arranging music for a consumers' market. When was the last time you really listened to a cartoon soundtrack or to some of the better commercials that use Baroque concerti or imaginative synthesized sound. The size of the industry itself should attest to its seriousness.

Rock has been changing over the past few years. If you listen carefully to the car radio, you can pick up the artistic difference between AM and FM rock music and hear the influence of folk and jazz. Rock is a developing field, and its creators are seriously pursuing an expanding frame of reference. It is in this context that I support the programming of rock in symphony concerts.

As an example of the kind of rock programming that seems to me artistically worthy and defensible, I offer Little Big Horn, the rock oratorio by Mike Zager and Aram Schefrim whose premiere I recently conducted with the rock group, Ten Wheel Drive, and the American Symphony Orchestra. Mr. Schefrim's text is a kind of narrative commentary from the point of view of the American Indian, drawn from various Indian sources. It serves well as a verbal medium for this

The disparity between rock and symphonic music is far too great to overcome by mere juxtaposition, far too great to achieve any degree of aesthetic validity, far too great to justify the tremendous effort needed to solve problems of sound and balance. Added to these objections is the truism that if you attempt to please too many tastes you inevitably please none.

Symphonic music, by its very nature and as absolute music, stands very firmly on its aesthetic value as art. It does not depend upon any external driving force. Rock, with its powerful lyrics, depends largely on the meaning of words for its effect and value. Instrumental rock is somewhat more subtle, and at first glance would seem to be a form of absolute music. But a close examination of rock shows it to be a form of music that derives most of its meaning not from its value as an independent and self-existing piece of music but from what it can generate in audience energy--audience involvement-- what it can generate in the creation of a mystique.

Great symphonic music has a universality that transcends time and place. Rock is bound to the moment. What is that moment? It's the meaningful expression of a generation, an expression that is topical, a symbol of this generation's alter ego, a symbol of where it's at, a symbol of the look and dress of young people in the 1960's and 1970's. It's an identification with and the expression of a culture. Rock obviously fills a need for this oratorio in the same way that the Passions served Bach and the Old Testament served Handel.

Musically, the 22-minute Little Big Horn divides into five sections: (1) "Omens of Three Rivers," depicting the mood of the Indian camp; (2) "Killing Weather," the mood in Custer's camp with allusions to the General's bid for the Presidency; (3) "Take Me Home," a return to the Indian camp just before the battle; (4) the Battle; and (5) "Buffalo Calf Woman," recollections. The sections shift in mood and tempo, contain harmonic interest, leave plenty of openings for improvisation (Ten Wheel Drive is a jazz-rock group carrying three trumpets, trombone, [wood]wind man, and rhythm with organ) and were well orchestrated by Mike Zager.

The Battle sequence is built on an eight-bar riff over which solos are improvised, including a written out solo for oboe. There is a heavy gospel quality to some of the music, with a chorus responding to vocalist Genya Ravan's verses. To my mind, it all works. If it is any criterion for judgment, all of us--the members of the American Symphony Orchestra, my relatively "straight" chorus, Genya, Ten Wheel, and myself--really enjoyed performing the work.

The audience reaction was very positive. To be honest, they were more "turned on" by the encore, "Eye of the Needle," a Ten Wheel hit record built

generation. But it offers emotional coherence rather than meaningful musical coherence. Lifted out of context, it does not make the same musical sense.

Rock is part of a larger scene. It includes being part of an "in" group, the togetherness of such a group, the religious experience of sharing, the physical contact of joining hands, psychedelic lights, and all the rest. Big rock festivals are not unlike the rituals of primitive tribes, in which the repetitive and rhythmic beat of the drums provides a similar expression of religious feeling. While the tribal ritual is primarily an expression of religious fervor, rock is somewhat more. It is sociological commentary, and criticism of established values. (Nonetheless, total immersion in its full sound does offer rock disciples an escape valve in a complicated world.)

I am well aware of some of the attempts in the recent past to marry symphony and rock. One of the ventures was called by a writer "an unhappy flirtation." I can't help but think of them as shotgun weddings. They have no legitimate basis for a happy marriage because they have so little in common. And the very necessary give/take formula for success is so one-sided. Rock has comparatively little intrinsic musical value to bring to the marriage --that is, little that symphonic music has not long been capable of offering.

What about the other obstacle mentioned earlier? Sound and balance. For its full

on a continuous riff, which included audience participation, singing along with Genya, the chorus, and the symphony--a sound that literally "rocked" Carnegie Hall and brought down the house. But it appealed to a different instinct than Little Big Horn, since "Eye" is a rock tune rather than a concert piece, if you see the distinction.

To judge from the applause at the conclusion of the oratorio, Little Big Horn was liked. Those we spoke with afterwards enjoyed it enough to want to hear it again.

The critical reaction to Little Big Horn astounded me. Some writers thought the lyric banal (not to my mind).   Some thought the gospel quality was out of place in an Indian setting, some thought the work wasn't properly symphonic, or rock, or jazz, or pop, or....

I'm convinced the critics spent so much time trying to pigeonhole the piece that they didn't listen to it. It has all the elements of good musical composition: melody, harmony, rhythm, pace, contrast, a viable text with historical content and value. The performance, under hasty conditions including problems of amplification (which will always accompany works of this kind) was at least serviceable. But if the 2000 persons in attendance enjoyed the work, it didn't score with the hardcore establishment.   Are we so hung-up on traditional categories that if it can't be named, it can't be good?

If there were voices of

effect, and for the total involvement of the listener, rock depends upon being heard at an extremely high decibel level. (A few summers ago, Mrs. Katims and I went to an evening of rock in an arena in San Diego.   I was amazed that the men and women policing the events night after night were able to take that level of sound, until I learned that they all had plugs in their ears.) Bringing this kind of sound into the symphony hall presents all sorts of problems of balance. Unless the natural sounds of the orchestra were also to be amplified (don't think for one moment that this has not been suggested), it would be impossible to achieve any kind of proper balance.

I wonder, as I recall the few efforts to create concertos for jazz band and orchestra (Liebermann and Brubeck), whether similar attempts at writing works for rock groups and orchestra could be any more successful.   Perhaps a composer with an understanding of both styles could introduce elements of rock into a symphonic composition as Ravel introduced elements of jazz into some of his music.

Considering the very basic and relentless 4/4 beat of rock and its harmonically simple structure, I can think only of a composer like Carl Orff and his "Carmina Burana," also quite uncomplicated rhythmically and harmonically, to conceive of the possibility of bringing to a symphonic work some of the facets of rock. But then, almost before the thought is expressed, I find myself reacting negatively.

reasonable dissent, they came from some of the kids, who told us they liked their rock hard and their classics separate. My personal guess is that, were it not for the presence of Ten Wheel Drive on the program (which included works of Copland and Bach and ran 75 minutes without intermission), they would not have attended at all. Because such a work as Little Big Horn was created, it may have opened up new listening areas for the hip and the establishment alike.

One cannot sell the classics to rock audiences. Neither can you sell rock to the classicists. But it seems to me you can say: music has elements common to all styles of composition. In this context, the rock oratorio is a viable form of expression in contemporary times. So enjoy it!

No! Rock has its own very special function. It would be a disservice to expect it to do more than serve as an important and integral part of the ritual of a generation.

On the "Youth" page of the May 2, 1971, Parade magazine, the question is asked, "Is there any future for rock music?" And Harvard student Andy Klein comments, "Somehow the importance of rock and roll in our lives has declined in the last year or two, even for those who were most obsessed. This is partly due to a falling off in the quality of the music and partly to our growing up." So this whole discussion may prove to have been purely academic.

The criterion for the choice of any music that I program is how well it fits into the challenge I face as a conductor and as a musician. That challenge is to inspire, to ignite a spark within the hearts and souls of our listeners. This spark can best be touched off by the profoundest expressions of great composers. Symphony is indeed for the uncommon man!

"MUSEUM" IS NOT A DIRTY WORD*

Harris Green

The present season of unnatural calm that the Philharmonic is sailing through offers an excellent opportunity to consider not only the weather that could descend, once Pierre Boulez takes command as music director in 1971, but those nasty little squalls that the ideologues and perpetrators of contemporary music send whistling through our musical life when they damn the Philharmonic--

*From The New York Times, Sunday, October 5, 1969. Copyright 1969 by The New York Times Company. Reprinted by permission.

and, indeed, every orchestra and opera company--for being "a
museum!"

The use of "museum" as a pejorative is, in itself, a measure of the esthetic void at the heart of contemporary music. To
one who cares, deeply, for the special pleasures that painting and
sculpture afford, the Frick, Metropolitan and selected walls of the
Museum of Modern Art are where one must look instead of to
those Now galleries that transform themselves into a supermarket
or a boutique, a drafting room or a junkyard, merely by displaying the confections and constructions of today. And anyone who
cares, deeply, for the unique pleasure music affords has no choice
but to commune with the mighty dead and to scorn the puny living.
Naturally, "morgue" and "necrophile" are frequent insults in the
intellectually unrewarding handicraft of musical polemics.

To understand how age or the composer's death is supposed
to affect the merit of a symphony or opera, one must realize that
today's musical life is contending with disruptive forces very much
like those now assaulting society. Anarchists are at large in music. A winsome improvisor like John Cage assures us that any
noise he and his equipment care to make is music and urges us to
leave our minds at home when we immerse ourselves in the neo-
Huxleyian sensation bath of his media mix-up, "HPSCHD." (Since
the fad-mad are always with us and their minds are as disposable
as Kleenex, Cage should pack 'em in--for a while.) That computerized charmer, Milton Babbitt, hurled at concertgoers this immortal, and easily answered, query: "Who cares if you listen?"
(Who cares if you compose?) Now that Dr. Babbitt has sent the
audience home, Mr. Moog has taken the next step in the inhuman
logic of Technocracy and dismissed the musicians by designing a
synthesizer, with its shallow or splintery resonance and rigidly im-
personal phrasing. The inevitable technical refinements will still
not make this child of technology replace all instruments in everyone's affection, though the Moog and its kin, when cheaply manufactured, may well replace Cage and the synthesized electronic
wizards.

Every change is an improvement in the Ideology of Progress
--instead of merely change--so "newness" has become what Larry
Austin ... called "a critical concept for the artist," thus cram-
ming the composer into the most procrustean bed he's had
made for him since Cherubini left the Academie. In this era
of stereo tape, live performances are now felt to be anachronistic--
even worse, if given over to putrescent corpses like Mozart and
Beethoven. To our ideologues, the only sign of life in live performing has been the appointment of Pierre Boulez by the Philharmonic. He champions 20th-century composition, you see.

While I am delighted by such renewed faith in the concert's
viability and relevance, to use today's most favored accolades, I
welcome M. Boulez to New York for reasons that have nothing to
do with contemporary music but everything to do with our musical

museums at Lincoln Center and elsewhere. As a critic, I am not the
least concerned with the age of a piece of music. Its merit and how
it's performed are what matter. I have not blamed Beethoven for the
ennui that's been overwhelming me at performances of the "Eroica"
these past years, nor have I written off this work as "stagnant," since
I was well aware that all familiarity could be offset by a great conductor's conscientiously presenting his "Eroica," as Colin Davis showed
last season in a splendid performance with the Philharmonic. What has
been dispiriting, and often enraging, is the low level of artistry in high
places. Our musical "curators" aren't fit to run our museums.

HAVE ORCHESTRAS TURNED THEIR BACKS
ON THE 20th CENTURY?*

Benjamin S. Dunham

This year's Orchestral Program Survey, like the ten before,
was compiled and published by Broadcast Music, Incorporated, in
cooperation with the American Symphony Orchestra League. The
booklet tells such a remarkable story about the viability of symphony orchestras that a minority report may be in order.

Facts and figures from the 1969-1970 concert season have
been tabulated from the reports of 620 American orchestras in four
categories: major (29), metropolitan (63), urban and community
(351), and school and youth-training (177). A total of 26,214 individual performances in 6758 concerts (both figures up markedly
from the previous year) have been analyzed in two major chrono-
logical breakdowns: pre-1900 and 20th century, with a separate
break-out within the 20th-century category for works written after
1940.

It is the opinion of BMI that the figures in this survey indicate an abdication by the symphony orchestras of their responsibilities toward modern contemporary music in general and contemporary American music in particular. According to Oliver Daniel,
vice-president of BMI for concert music administration, "The rut
which programmers have gotten into is still appallingly deep.
Basically our [symphony] programs seem to suffer from an over-
dose of ancestor worship, and about the only consolation one can
take in the situation as it stands is the fact that the condition of
opera is worse."

Irving Lowens, music critic for The Evening Star, Washington, D. C., has written in a column, "I'm afraid that Daniel's pessimistic view is borne out by the statistics with startling clarity.
Subtract the big 'hits' ... and you get a really dismal picture of

*From Symphony News, vol. 22, no. 6 (December 1971). Copyright
1971 by the American Symphony Orchestra League. Reprinted by
permission.

the amount of 20th-century music being performed by American orchestras today."

With these opinions in mind, the general reader is left with the impression that contemporary music plays a minor part in the programming of all symphony orchestras. Visions are called to mind of starving composers scribbling away at full orchestral scores, only to be snubbed at the doors of the nation's concert halls. In some cases, there is no doubt good contemporary music going unperformed. But is the picture as bleak as these critics suggest?

For example, given the popular notion of the symphony orchestra as "merely" a museum, what percentage of all works programmed on symphony concerts would you expect to be written after 1940? Five percent? Ten?

You are wrong. Forty-two percent of all works programmed were written within the last thirty years!

But what if you subtract the big hits, as Mr. Lowens suggests? What if you take away those rip-snorting money-makers by Copland, Bernstein, and Richard Rodgers? What are you left with then? How many other, less popular modern composers are being heard? Here the figures are startling indeed. Nullify the effect of the big hits by giving every composer from Dufay (1400-1474) to Davidovsky (1934-) one equal vote. Now you can see the depth of the commitment of American orchestras to give their contemporaries a fair hearing.

Seventy-nine percent of all composers programmed by symphony orchestras are listed as 20th-century composers, and 61 percent are listed in the post-1940 category. By this standard of measurement our contemporary composers actually dominate the scene.

When you count individual performances of works, the statistics are still pretty heartening. The undeniably popular blockbusters by Beethoven, Tchaikovsky, and the like (1969-1970, remember, was the beginning of the Beethoven centennial) weight the figures more heavily toward the standard repertoire, but 20th-century works held their own with 46 percent of all performances. Twenty-one percent were post-1940. It is interesting that more 20th-century composers than pre-20th-century composers received over 30 performances of their works.

None of these figures reveal a hint of tokenism toward modern music. BMI lists 96 works by American composers given their world premieres by American orchestras during 1969-1970, and the names include America's best-known members of the avant-garde. It is true that there is an unfortunate syndrome working against subsequent performances of world premieres, but it is common knowledge that this is largely the fault of the economics of the situation--and sometimes a reflection of audience interest.

Surely, with these figures in hand, we should not attack symphony orchestras for programming the classics of the repertory, but rather congratulate them for their openness to music of all periods and encourage them to continue their active search for contemporary orchestral scores of real merit. Only in the last few generations has the concertgoing public acquired a taste for the music of the past, for the strange but becoming sonorities of the Baroque and earlier periods, whose music is being rediscovered in symphony concerts and smaller recitals. We lament the eighty-year neglect of the music of Johann Sebastian Bach during the time of Mozart and Beethoven in favor of some now-forgotten contemporary hacks. Could we ever make the same mistake again?

In conclusion to his introduction to the BMI survey, Mr. Daniel says that his company is so depressed with the result of the survey that they will no longer keep track of performances of the standard pre-1900 repertory. "We hardly need a tabulation on the eight-millionth performance of the Beethoven 'Fifth' or the Overture to Don Giovanni. " Such a decision is regrettably short-sighted. If put into effect, how would we know (as we do for 1969-1970) that Anton Webern's "Six Pieces for Orchestra" was heard three times as often as the Overture to Don Giovanni (61 to 20). Or that Bartók's "Concerto for Orchestra" was twice as popular as all the concerti grossi of George Frideric Handel combined?

"With the weight of the past a little less evident, " says Mr. Daniel, "we may have glimpses that will make us less forlorn. " We should all be thankful that orchestras no longer need to be protected in this fashion.

Chapter VI

THE BUSINESS OF MUSIC MAKING:
Organizational, Economic and Sociological Aspects

Introduction. The orchestra world is not a world unto itself. The orchestra is truly an entity functioning as a part of our continually changing society. Management, the musicians union, the individual musician, the lay public and government at all levels are involved in the sociological and economic interrelationships of the orchestra. Budgetary control, job descriptions, working conditions, discrimination, product market and a host of other problems relate to orchestras as well as to other business organizations, and the "nonprofit" category of most orchestras tends to enhance rather than detract from the importance of these concerns.

Sociologists, business managers, critics, musicians and involved laymen offer here some insights into making music with people-- for people.

GOVERNING BOARDS OF SYMPHONY ORCHESTRAS*

Helen M. Thompson

The growth of symphony orchestras in the United States during the last twenty-five years is uniquely American. Never before in any culture or in any nation has there taken place such rapid numerical growth of orchestras, such determined efforts on the part of so many people to establish and maintain organizations devoted to the financial support of symphony orchestras.

The most amazing part of this orchestral development is to be found in the fact that the control of these orchestras, the responsibility for their financing, and guidance of their destinies rests, not in the hands of professionals in the music world, but rather in the hands of laymen. Upon the boards rest the responsibility for

*From "Report of Study on Governing Boards of Symphony Orchestras," by Helen M. Thompson. Copyright 1958 by the American Symphony Orchestra League. Reprinted by permission.

engaging artistic and administrative personnel, for raising and spending the money needed to maintain the orchestra, developing, establishing and enforcing the policies of operation.

Practically all orchestras in the U. S. and Canada (with the exception of the college orchestras) are incorporated as non-profit institutions with full control placed in the hands of lay boards (usually referred to as boards of directors, or boards of trustees) whose members are elected or appointed to their positions by other laymen.

The tremendous amount of time, energy, thought and money contributed voluntarily to America's orchestras by men and women throughout the land is unbelievable--and for the most part, the contributions are made in a spirit of selflessness, for the purpose of enriching the cultural life within each person's home city.

The [American Symphony Orchestra] League has spent many years studying various aspects of orchestra operations in an attempt to isolate those factors which seem to predispose an orchestra toward failure or success--including the influence of the conductor, influence of the manager, the financing methods of the orchestra, the cultural and artistic leadership the orchestra assumes in the community, the orchestra's promotional policies and methods, etc.

Invariably, investigation of these factors leads back to the orchestra's governing board which holds the power to engage personnel, formulate and carry out basic policies of operation.   The story of a successful orchestra is, in reality, the story of an effective orchestra board.   Conversely, the reasons behind an orchestra's lack of success usually are to be found in the existence of an ineffective board of directors.

These things being true the American Symphony Orchestra League, a non-profit service and coordinating organization of U. S. and Canadian orchestras, undertook a study of governing boards of orchestras in the hope of discovering why some boards are effective and others ineffective.   The study is a part of a three year survey of the organization and support of arts organizations made possible through a Rockefeller Foundation grant to the League. The specific purpose of the study was to seek the answers to the following questions:

(1)   Are there specific characteristics which distinguish boards of successful orchestras from boards of unsuccessful orchestras?   If so, what are those characteristics?

(2)   Are there specific characteristics of board members as individuals which distinguish the valuable board member from the ineffective board member?   If so, what are those characteristics?

(3) Are there certain mechanics of board operations which
generally are employed by successful orchestras but which
are not used widely among the unsuccessful orchestras?
If so, what are they?

The orchestras to serve as study subjects were carefully
selected according to the following plan:

(1) Two groups of orchestras were chosen--one group composed of obviously successful orchestras, the other
group composed of orchestras just as obviously unsuccessful. Success or lack thereof was judged on the following points:

(a) Has the orchestra consistently maintained high
artistic standards over a period of time?
(b) Has the orchestra maintained a stable financial
operation over a period of time?
(c) Has the total organization demonstrated continuity,
cohesiveness, leadership and steady growth over
a period of time?
(d) Is the orchestra really serving the cultural needs
of its community?

(2) Within this framework of success or lack thereof, the
additional following qualifications were used in choosing
the orchestras to be included in this study:

(a) Major, metropolitan, and community orchestras
were included. Budgets of the orchestras ranged
from somewhat below $50,000 to several hundred
thousand dollars a year.
(b) Only mature organizations having been in operation
for several years were chosen for the study.

In all, 20 orchestras and approximately 700 board members
were involved in the study. Certain reports were disqualified because of apparent lack of objectivity in the information filed. The
tabulations actually reported in the study were developed from reports involving 14 orchestras whose boards totaled 511 individuals.

Information concerning the board members was gathered
from many sources and cross checked. Inasmuch as the evaluation
of an individual in terms of his or her effectiveness as a board
member was in some measure dependent on opinion and judgment,
great care was taken to disqualify those reports in which the objective data failed to support the subjective data.

Approximately 70 different items of information were gathered for each different board member of each orchestra including
the following:

- Age

- Sex
- Education
- Profession or business affiliation, and level of operation
  such as "policy making," "administrative," etc.
- Position held in the community, such as "old family,"
  "newcomer," etc.
- Sphere in which the board member's influence is significant
  in the community such as: financial circles, own professional circles, education circles, art circles, labor
  circles, political circles, etc.
- Activity in connection with other civic affairs.
- The board member's interest in the arts, such as "casual
  interest," "deep personal interest," "interest as a civic
  asset," etc.
- Information on board member's participation in orchestra
  work including his/her attendance at concerts and board
  meetings, purchase of tickets, personal contributions,
  the specific areas of orchestra work in which the individual is especially valuable to the orchestra, length of
  time having served on the board.

   Every possible precaution was taken to preserve the anonymity of the board members. Code numbers were assigned to each
orchestra. In each locality, individual code numbers were assigned
to the board members. When reports were assembled, an individual could be identified only as "Board Member No. 26 of orchestra No. A-10. "

   A statistical punch card was set up for each board member,
and all data was transferred to the card under a statistical coding
system. The cards were then divided into two groups:

   Group A - Cards of all board members serving with orchestras
             judged to be successful.

   Group B - Cards of all board members serving with orchestras
             judged to be unsuccessful.

By odd chance, the number of board members involved in the
boards of successful orchestras was 255, and the number involved
in boards of unsuccessful orchestras totaled 256--making it very
easy to compare the findings of the two groups. Tabulations of all
the factors under study were then developed separately for Group
A and Group B. Similarities and contrasts between the two groups
were analyzed and conclusions drawn.

   The next step was to study the characteristics of board
members as individuals, and the cards were again divided into two
groups but in a different manner:

   Group C - Cards of all individuals judged to be personally
             effective as orchestra board members regardless
             of whether they were affiliated with successful or
             unsuccessful orchestras.

Group D - Cards of all individuals judged to be personally
ineffective as board members regardless of whether
affiliated with successful or unsuccessful orchestras.

Of the entire 511 board members involved in the 14 successful and
unsuccessful orchestras, 387 individuals were judged to be effective
and valuable as board members.   112 were judged to be ineffective
or "harmless" as board members.   12 were judged to be actually
harmful to their orchestra.

The findings of this study may prove to be disappointing to
many people seeking a magic method whereby an orchestra board
suddenly may be transformed from a group of well-intentioned persons reasonably interested in the orchestra into a closely-knit unit
flushed with missionary zeal and prepared to march forth and do
battle for the orchestra at all costs.

Unfortunately, we found no secret potion which can be administered to boards, no panacea for dealing with the chief sins of
board members--procrastination, aloofness from the orchestra,
half-hearted interest, unawareness of problems and unwillingness to
spend the time and energy required to learn about them.

What we did find, however, is statistical evidence which
supports beliefs long held by people having worked seriously with
symphony orchestras over a period of years--evidence that there
is no easy way for an orchestra board to achieve success.   Boards
have to learn their business and, having learned it, must continue
to improve their techniques and skills and extend their knowledge
and understanding of orchestras.

Managers and conductors must expect to help the boards
learn the intricacies of the orchestra world, and the job must be
done repeatedly as new members are added to the board.   Every
conductor expects to have to repeat over and over again basic instructions for the musicians during rehearsals.   In like manner,
every conductor and every manager can expect to have to repeat
over and over again basic information and philosophies in their
work with boards.   The better the devices employed in this communication between professional and laymen, the more effective
will be the work of the board.

The findings of the study can be summarized as follows:

A.   Boards of successful orchestras really work at the job.
The members raise funds, serve on committees, attend concerts,
attend board meetings and constantly use their finest talents and
community leadership on behalf of the orchestra.   Members of
these boards are members in fact, not just in name.

B.   Boards of successful orchestras have etched out a sound
philosophy of the value of the orchestra as a permanent institution

in the life of the community thereby giving them a proper perspective from which to view policies, plans and proposals for action.

As one person phrased it, "Boards of successful orchestras have gained a sense of the worth and dignity of an institution. " This phrase, the sense of the worth and dignity of an institution, grows in significance as the work of orchestra boards is analyzed and evaluated. Invariably, the work and policies of the successful orchestra reflect an understanding on the part of the board of its own proper relationship to an institution which is committed to public service, financed in considerable measure from funds contributed by the general public and granted special privileges and tax exemptions from the federal government as a result of the institution's claim of serving as a non-profit educational and cultural organization.

These circumstances demand that the board of an orchestra consider itself to be a steward of a permanent community trust, charged with the responsibility of seeing to it that the community's cultural needs are placed ahead of all other considerations in decisions concerning orchestra policies and procedures. The artistic excellence of the orchestra, the soundness of its financial policies, its program of community service and education--these are matters of public concern. Decisions concerning them must emanate from a dedication to community needs and knowledge of orchestral potentials in meeting them rather than from personal preferences, prejudices and loyalties.

Dedication to community needs and a true sense of trusteeship of a permanent institution lead a board to chart the orchestra's course on the basis of long-range planning rather than on a concert-to-concert, season-to-season basis.

C. Boards of successful orchestras are composed of individuals well qualified to serve in a capacity of leadership. Within the successful boards, you will find the top leaders of all phases of community life--the leaders of finance, business and industry; the pace setters and experts in education and the arts; the leadership of the community's social life. This power and influence is absolutely necessary to the success of the orchestra.

D. A high percentage of the members of successful orchestra boards are people who have a strong personal interest in the arts. Apparently, a belief that arts developments (including symphony orchestras) are "good for the community" is not sufficient motivation to spur people on to continued super-charged activity on behalf of the orchestras. People interested in arts activities as civic assets are needed on the board, of course, but the board also must provide itself with a good proportion of members who are personally convinced that the arts are vital to a full life, people who find a glimpse of immortality within an inspired performance of great music, people who know from personal experience that the arts are closely linked to spirituality.

E. There is a close relationship between effective management and effective boards.   What is the relationship between the
effectiveness of an orchestra board and the effectiveness of an orchestra's manager?   In other words, does a board become effective
through the guidance and leadership of a skilled manager?

The study certainly shows a close correlation between the
presence of effective managers and effective orchestra boards.
However, in the last analysis, it is the responsibility of the board
to select, employ and release the orchestra's manager and conductor.   Therefore, it is up to the board to see to it that it provides itself and the orchestra with effective management and artistic leadership, and we cannot exonerate an unsuccessful board with
the explanation that the orchestra's manager fails to produce effective board work.   If the manager is ineffective, it becomes the
board's responsibility to replace the manager.

F.   Another finding of the study has to do with board representation from possible new sources of orchestra financial support.
Constantly, the question is asked "With the yearly increases in orchestra operating costs, where are we going to find the necessary
new sources of financial support?"

There are at least two potential sources which, to date, remain relatively unexplored--support from municipalities and coun-
ties, and support from labor unions.   In all probability, if funds
from either of these sources are to be tapped in a major way,
representatives from governmental bodies and labor organizations
will have to be drawn into the orchestra's activities and controlling
body.   Yet, there is very little representation from governmental
units or labor organizations on the boards of either the successful
or unsuccessful orchestras included in this study.

G.   Board analysis proves valuable to individual orchestras.
One of the unexpected benefits of the study developed in the course
of collecting the data.   It was soon discovered that few orchestra
organizations keep detailed information concerning their governing
bodies.   Mere listings of names and addresses are standard practice.   Boards apparently are seldom analyzed to see whether or
not there is maintained a balance of talents, representation and
strengths which will meet the orchestra's needs.

As the data was being collected for the study, several orchestra organizations began to obtain for the first time a sort of
profile of their own governing boards.   In some cases, it was immediately apparent that reorganization of the board was needed.
This already has taken place among some of the orchestras participating in the study and the progress in terms of increased activity, improved finance, etc. within only a few months as a result of
board reorganizations has been utterly amazing.

Inasmuch as there seems to be great value in an orchestra
making its own analysis of its board, the American Symphony

Orchestra League has prepared extra copies of the forms used in collecting board data. These forms are available without cost to League affiliated organizations and can be obtained by requesting them from the League office.

Within the study we found 99 "Finest Board Members," and from now on in our daydreams of a splendored, perfect orchestra the board will be peopled by these 99 members. (Unfortunately, however, we know them only by code numbers.) Within the total 511 board members, there were 99 (roughly 20 per cent) who proved to be outstanding in all five phases of orchestra work: fund raising, committee work, valued for the good judgment they bring to bear on orchestra affairs, valuable in policy making, and willing and able to use extensive influence on behalf of their orchestras.

Through the use of our statistical cards, we were able to put these 99 board members under the microscope and study their personal attributes and orchestra participation. Again the findings of other sections of the study were borne out. All of the 99 are over 35 years of age; all but four have college educations and 52 have graduate or professional study; 73 have travelled widely; and 61 are members of leading families in their respective communities. None is an "old resident but little known" and only 4 are newcomers to their community.

Of the 99, 62 possess greater than average personal wealth and 12 of the remaining 37 represent corporate wealth; 81 are recognized for their general community leadership; and 91 are active in other civic affairs, with 80 of these currently raising money for other civic and non-profit organizations in addition to their fund raising on behalf of their orchestras.

All 99 are reported to have the "best interests of the orchestra at heart" and all 99 obviously are at work for their orchestras. Only 5 are judged to be motivated in their orchestra work by a desire to enhance personal prestige, and the same 5 are said to be attracted by the glamor surrounding an orchestra. All but 4 contribute personally to the orchestra and one of these four makes a generous gift through his corporation.

Eighty are reported to have a deep personal interest in the arts. Only one is reported to have no personal interest in the arts, but even he feels the arts are a valuable asset for the community; 93 buy season tickets and 65 of them always attend concerts with the remaining 34 attending usually or occasionally; 68 always attend board meetings with the remaining 31 attending usually or occasionally.

It's interesting to study the professional and business connections of these 99 finest board members. Half of them are businessmen--another bit of evidence, if more be needed, of the wonderful contribution business leaders make to the cultural development of our nation. One fourth of them come from the professions

with the legal profession far in the lead.   The remaining one-fourth
includes 18 women community leaders, one professional musician,
and 6 persons who are retired from business affairs or whose financial means relieve them of the necessity of devoting themselves
to business interests or the professions.

MUSINGS ON THE DUTIES
OF THE ORCHESTRA MANAGER*

Helen M. Thompson

         In using the term "orchestra manager" in its fullest sense,
we refer to the chief executive officer of the organization.   His
counterpart in the artistic portion of the work is the conductor.
Each has certain areas of autonomy, but many areas of the work
require harmonious joint effort between conductor and manager.

         Both, of course, are employees of the association, respon-
sible to the board of directors for carrying out the policies adopted
by the board but at the same time responsible for providing the
leadership, vision and information needed to enable the board to
adopt constructive, progressive, sound and practical plans for the
continued development of the organization and the continued expansion of the musical life of the community.

         Viewed within this general framework, the role of the mana-
ger is to do all things possible to see to it that the organization
constantly improves its musical product; that it operates on as
stable a financial basis as is possible; that it carries out its obligation to serve as a community cultural and educational institution--
obligations placed upon it by federal tax laws as well as by the
fact that the organization solicits and accepts contributions from the
general public for the purpose of strengthening the musical assets
of the community.

         Specifically, the manager's overall executive responsibilities
reach into all phases of the work unless the board of directors
adopts an alternate plan.   This does not mean that the manager
necessarily personally carries out these manifold tasks, but customarily he is held responsible for seeing that they are handled in
some manner.   For example:

         1.   Long Range Planning.   Manager and conductor should
provide the association with facts, figures, information on national
and local trends so that the board can adopt constructive long range
goals which will assist in formulating operation and growth plans
for each individual season.

*Reprinted by permission of the American Symphony Orchestra
League (no date).

2.   Fund raising and ticket sale campaigns.   The manager
cannot personally raise the funds and sell the tickets, but he is
responsible (unless otherwise directed by the board of directors)
for all phases of the planning, supervision and execution of the
campaigns, ticket sales plans, special fund raising schemes, etc.
His task is to do all possible to enable the volunteer campaign
workers from the board, women's association and community to
work effectively, efficiently and constructively.

To that end, the manager is responsible for keeping and providing sales and campaign records of all kinds, analysis of the
market for symphony support and ticket sales, promotion and publicity, organization plans for the campaigns, follow-up procedures,
etc.

3.   Budgeting and financial records.   The manager is responsible for guiding the board in drawing up the annual budgets,
providing necessary data on past and anticipated expenditures and
sources of income; for keeping the board informed of the financial
status of the organization throughout the year; for supervising the
bookkeeping methods, so that the operation can be handled efficiently, etc.

4.   Coordination of units of the organization.   The manager
is responsible for knitting together the various units of the organization on behalf of the accepted goals, programs and purposes so
that there is a minimum of duplicated effort.

5.   Promotion and publicity.   The manager is responsible
for the supervision and coordination of all promotion, publicity and
public relations activities so that the total purposes and goals of
the organization are well served.

6.   Technical Activities.   The manager is responsible for
the general supervision of all technical activities having to do with
all phases of the work including such matters as payrolls, working
out details of production and staging problems, work of the librarians, personnel work, etc.

The degree to which the manager personally handles these
tasks, depends on the size of the orchestra's operation.   In fully
professional organizations, various staff members are engaged to
carry out many of these tasks under the general supervision of the
manager.   In smaller organizations, many of these tasks are
handled by volunteers--but the manager remains responsible for
seeing to it that the work is done.

Obviously, it requires a person of almost superhuman dedication, ability and stamina to carry out such a program.   The
amazing thing is that we find just those qualities among the most
successful managers.   It also is obvious that successful managerial
work is greatly dependent on the willingness of the board of directors to view the position of manager as a truly executive position

and to vest the necessary authority in the position to enable the
manager to be a manager.

JOB DESCRIPTIONS:
PERSONNEL MANAGER; ORCHESTRA LIBRARIAN*

Richard H. Wangerin

Generally speaking, the personnel manager provides the lines
of communication between the players and the orchestra management. He sees to it that the musicians meet requirements of attendance, dress, etc. , and he also makes sure that management
carries out its obligations in such matters as adequate stage lighting, temperature control, dressing room facilities, etc. If a work
to be performed calls for additional musicians beyond the orchestra's regular complement, it is usually up to the personnel manager to locate the necessary people and, subject to the conductor's
and manager's approval, make the necessary arrangements with
them. He also helps with details of auditions. The personnel
manager must serve both the orchestra management and the orchestra's musicians, a situation which calls for a considerable degree
of diplomacy and fair-mindedness.

The librarian's responsibilities vary from one orchestra to
another. Librarians of some small orchestras do little more than
distribute music prior to rehearsals and concerts and collect it at
the close. In such cases the job of locating and/or ordering music
is handled by the orchestra's business office. In many situations,
however, the conductor gives the librarian the list of music to be
performed and it is up to the librarian to procure the music in
time for the first rehearsal, see that all the necessary parts are
on hand, insert any markings the conductor may want on the parts,
distribute and collect the parts before and after rehearsals and performances, and be responsible for returning all music, in good
condition, within whatever time limit has been specified. Because
of the cost of music purchases and rentals, there must be an understanding between the librarian and the orchestra manager as to
the librarian's range of authority in committing the orchestra to
these expenses.

*An unpublished letter to the editor, September 9, 1971. Used by
permission of Richard H. Wangerin, McLean, Virginia.

ORGANIZATION AND MANAGEMENT*

Rockefeller Brothers Fund Panel

Whenever performing arts organizations reach the stage of development where permanence is sought, they almost invariably become nonprofit corporations, headed by a board of trustees vested with the responsibility of maintaining and expanding the organization.

This board has certain obvious functions: to determine the larger objectives of the organization, to retain the best available artistic direction and business management, and, having accomplished the latter, to back their judgment when the inevitable conflicts with artists or with elements in the community arise.   In fulfilling these responsibilities, the board has a pressing obligation to make certain the institution has financial stability, for without it there can be little hope of attaining either the long-range or the short-term goals the board may decide upon.

The actual selection of goals is crucial.   Too many arts organizations seem to live from minute to minute or, at best, from year to year.   A careful step-by-step plan, projected over a number of years, is essential to the arts organization, as is the selection of ultimate goals that are realistic in terms of the needs and desires of the community served.   In the selection of intelligent goals the board can be of great assistance to managers and artistic directors, who may be strangers to the community, without intimate knowledge of its tastes or its capacity for artistic growth.   In this connection it should be noted that lofty but impossible goals are easy to proclaim; practical goals, representing the highest level of achievement attainable with available resources, are the products of the most difficult and sustained effort on the part of the board and management--artistic and business.   The story is true of the board members who would have been happy to disband the orchestra on being faced for the first time with a five-year budget based on the plan they themselves had developed.

Goals cannot be the product of snap judgments nor are they likely to result from the deliberations of board members who regard their posts as merely a social honor.   Indeed, as the number and complexity of arts organizations grow, board membership is becoming much more arduous than in decades past.   Yet board recruitment remains much too casual in most organizations.   Meticulous auditioning procedures are used for second violinists, members of the opera chorus, and bit players in the theatre, but people about whom practically nothing is known often are chosen to be trustees.

*Pages 150-171 from The Performing Arts: Problems and Prospects, by a Rockefeller Brothers Fund panel; New York: The Fund, 1965. Copyright 1965 by Rockefeller Brothers Fund, Inc. Reprinted by permission.

Board members should be as carefully screened as performers, and procedures for rotating membership should be considered. The potential for serious and prolonged damage to the organization is as high in the board room as on the stage.

It should also be borne clearly in mind that, with the increase of interest and the base of support for the arts broadening, a board should be more widely representative of the community than is generally true today. There is simple common sense in this principle. Board members informally representing many different publics within a community can be effective mobilizers of audiences and support from new sources. Beyond this, valuable personal skills are added to the board when members are recruited from the arts, from education, from the mass media, labor, and government. Too many boards continue to draw members from a relatively narrow segment of the community. In so doing, they take on the character of a closed club, with disastrous effect on their ability to develop audiences and to appeal for support from the community at large. They also run the risk of a narrow parochialism of outlook that can hinder all planning and growth.

It is particularly important that board members be receptive to change and innovation. Too often the relationship between a board and the artistic director of an arts organization deteriorates into a squabble between traditionalists who "know what they like" and artists who insist on pressing outward against the boundaries of the usual. A certain amount of tension is undoubtedly healthy, but board members will sacrifice some of the strength of their position--and the respect of their artist colleagues--if they do not bring to these discussions of aesthetic questions a degree of knowledgeability and sophistication. We have already noted that a great need in the performing arts is for a higher and higher degree of cooperation between arts organizations. In this context the modern board member must be prepared, on occasion, to sacrifice some of his organization's autonomy for the greater good of his community or his region's cultural development, or, indeed, for its own long-term gain. Again, sophistication and flexibility are needed if board members are to seize these opportunities for growth.

In this country, the artistic leadership has frequently been responsible for the very creation of the organization. Many orchestras were founded on the initiative of a conductor; most dance companies were established solely by the conviction of a choreographer that his works merited performance; the impetus toward permanent professional theatres in recent years has often derived from the men and women who serve as directors. The artistic leaders have even reversed the usual sequence and chosen their boards and business managers to take responsibilities from their overburdened shoulders. Such reversal, however, should not be accepted as changing the respective roles of trustees, manager, and artistic director. The presence of a strong founding personality actually places an extra obligation on the board of directors. An organization has a way of achieving a life of its own, of

extending beyond the interest span or the talents or, perhaps, the
very life of the individual largely responsible for its creation. The
board has a distinct obligation to develop within itself the strength
to carry on after the founder departs and to create machinery to
assure a smooth transition of power when that event occurs. Similarly, the founder-artist has an obligation to his community, even
perhaps to his own place in history, to see that "his" board has
the strength and intelligence to carry on after he leaves.

The Chairman and His Board

Special qualifications for the chairman of a board of trustees
range from ability to conduct a meeting with due regard for Robert's
Rules of Order (a capacity that is not a natural endowment, although
many seem to think it is) to capacity to mediate between his lay
and artistic associates on matters calling for supreme tact and diplomacy. He is the bridge between the management and the board
and between various groups on the board. As the leader of a part-
time avocational group, he must also expect to put in far more
time for the organization than the other trustees generally do.

Serious consideration should be given by the large organizations to the currently almost untried procedure of having a full-time
paid president or chief executive. No industry with a budget comparable in size to those of a growing number of orchestras would
think of operating with voluntary leisure-time leadership. The
chairman must also have good, well-organized help from the board.
Appropriate committee structures necessarily vary from one art to
another, and from one stage of development to another. In all
cases, however, a strong executive committee capable of moving
with dispatch is essential for effective performance. So, too, is
the limitation of committees to those that clearly have an important
role to perform such as finance, development, community service.

The flow of command and control should be clearcut and the
organization and procedures of the board readily understandable and
practical. In theory, the articles of incorporation and the bylaws
of nonprofit arts organizations should be something of a blueprint of
their broad purposes and procedures. But a study of these documents for symphony orchestras discloses that all too often they fail
to provide an adequate or accurate statement of their organization's
purpose.

The Board's Relationship to Management

Governing boards will constantly be faced with problems that
can be solved only by deliberate, systematic, and wholesale delega-
tion of responsibilities. They must therefore depend, to a frightening extent, on the counsel they receive. Success in the extraordinarily complicated field of the performing arts depends on the good
will and mutual trust of all concerned. This derives from thorough
understanding of the common goals to be sought and from mutual
respect for areas of responsibility in the struggle to attain them.

Although effective trustees are bound to work continuously with their artistic directors and business managers, they do not meddle in artistic direction and business management. For them there is profound wisdom in the injunction: Do your best to see that the organization is good, that it is well manned, and that it runs smoothly--but don't try to run it.

As part of its primary responsibility for raising funds and spending them, the board must see that orderly business procedures are maintained and that money is available for maximum efficiency of operation. It should require that management submit periodic financial and progress reports, that sound bookkeeping and accounting procedures be followed, that annual audits be made, and that the organization have maximum financial protection.

Toward their artistic directors and business managers, the trustees have a critical responsibility no less crucial than seeing that they are well selected in the first place and working with them to develop and carry out basic policy: It is the responsibility of backing them up when necessary. All trustees are necessarily involved in the defense of artistic freedom, although this responsibility varies from one performing art to another. It is perhaps a more apparent and complex problem in the theatre, which frequently deals with highly inflammatory matters of morality and ideology. But it may also arise in the symphony orchestra field on the question of how much contemporary music is to be played even when sufficient funds are available. Surely no one should accept trusteeship of any performing arts organization who is not willing, on occasion, to stand embattled in defense of management's freedom to fulfill what it conceives to be its artistic mission. The defense, however, can be both simplified and made more effective by being an expression of a broad and firmly held basic policy rather than a catch-as-catch-can improvisation arising from the immediate issue at hand.

ARTISTIC DIRECTION

The task of selecting an artistic director is perhaps the most critical a board of trustees faces. The artistic director sets the standards of production, and artistic results can be no better than the quality of artistic direction. His duties are many and complicated.

Selection of Artists

Selection of artists is one of the most difficult responsibilities of the artistic director. In this process the director must come to terms with the star system. This question is, of course, closely allied to the question of artistic standards, but it also has economic aspects that cannot be overlooked. To engage a star is obviously to increase operating costs, though increased box office revenue frequently more than offsets these costs.

As a rule--to which, of course, there are notorious excep-
tions--a star's fame rests on superior talent and accomplishment.
Therefore, a star's presence should insure higher quality performance. His presence may also lend cachet to the organization. But
each artistic director must decide whether in the long run the star
system is good for the institution.

Perhaps the most valuable form of stardom toward which an
organization may aspire is that the company in and of itself have
the power to draw the public to it. When this takes place, one
may find that individual stars will be attracted to it too. The New
York City Ballet, to mention but one example, lists all of its dancers in alphabetical order; yet an Erik Bruhn will give up personal
billing for the sake of dancing with a stellar company.

For an arts institution to reach stardom requires time.
Meanwhile, a policy of featuring guest artists, so long as their
salaries do not ruin the budget or destroy the institution's potential
for development on its own merits, may be necessary. But the
artistic director who builds his program around visiting personalities is not giving adequate thought to the final objective--the day
when the organization itself, not the names it hires, will attract
the public.

Maintenance of Artistic Standards

The artistic director--the conductor, the stage director, the
choreographer--through his competence, leadership, and imagination
is the largest single factor in determining the morale and creative
contribution of an artistic enterprise. Save in the orchestra world,
where the conductor is in single artistic control, there must be a
continuous merging and cooperation of talents--the director with the
designer, with the choreographer, with all of those on stage who
have important roles to play. If collaboration fails at any point,
the quality of the entire effort may deteriorate.

But it is the artistic director who is finally responsible for
the quality of performance, so it follows that he must maintain conditions from which high standards derive. What, generally, are
these conditions?

Well-Trained Artists. The capable artistic director can
sometimes weld a coherent musical or theatrical entity out of players with a wide diversity of backgrounds. But not even the finest
can go beyond a certain point with ill-trained talent. The education and experience of the ensemble, individually and as a whole,
are crucial elements in determining standards of performance.

Rehearsal Time. Most critical in the preparation of new
and unfamiliar works, insufficient rehearsal hours can likewise
damage with almost equal force the standard repertory. Few artists ever feel adequately rehearsed, but it is too often true in fact
as well.

Length of Season. Quality thrives on practice and sustained performance. It can scarcely grow in a season that is nothing but a limited engagement or a scattered handful of performances. On the other hand, a full-year contract has drawbacks for many artists who feel that leisure--for contemplation, for study, for work they cannot accomplish during the hectic activity of "the season"--is a necessity for personal growth. As seasons lengthen and rehearsal and performance demands squeeze out "refreshing" activities essential to artistic health, it will be necessary to find a balance between continuity and variety, between holding a group together and providing free time for the individual. Perhaps an adaptation of the academic practice of the sabbatical would prove effective.

Compensation of Performers. Whatever the size of the group or the length of its season, an ill-paid performer is a dissatisfied performer. The size of the pocketbook also affects the adequacy of the instruments orchestral musicians can afford or be provided. This is an important building block in the total structure, especially since the problem may occur just below the level of the finest orchestras. For a musician, capital outlays for some instruments can represent the savings of a lifetime.

Physical Facilities. Many a performance might as well go unheard and unseen as to play in halls so ungrateful to sound and sight that players and audience alike have trouble perceiving a total effect. Other facilities, as they relate to the artists' comfort and convenience--adequate warm-up space for musicians and dancers, well-lighted dressing rooms for actors--can likewise be subtle contributors to the total health of the ensemble.

Audience. Only at its peril does an artistic director ignore his audience's taste. This is a delicate and difficult measurement to make, not unlike the statesman's: How to lead forward, but not too fast. An audience's knowledge and ability to appreciate affects the product. A conductor and his orchestra, a director and his cast, a choreographer and his dancers know perfectly well whether they are liked and understood, and they respond with their best when it is their best that the audience clearly wants and expects.

Each of these conditions is to an extent controllable by trustees and management, artistic and business. Each decision carries a price tag and each requires judgment, knowledge, and taste, in order that proper decisions may be arrived at by all concerned. It is essential, therefore, that artistic and business management work in true partnership, the director respecting the manager's concerns, and vice versa, and the trustees respecting both. Only a smoothly functioning team, in which each of these elements complements the others, can create a strong arts organization.

It would be unrealistic to think that adequate resources for all these objectives are obtainable by all organizations, especially in the early stages of development. It would be foolish, for example, for the conductor of the average community orchestra to

demand from his orchestra a level of performance exceeding the
competence of the musicians.   The real challenge is to strive for
an ever closer balance between the actual and the attainable and to
make measurable progress toward the time when all conditions of
quality can be considered relevant in planning future programs.   If
the artistic standards an organization sets for itself do not rise
steadily upward, neither will quality, and performance will be
doomed to spiritless mediocrity.

MANAGEMENT

Resourceful business and administrative leadership is a necessary element in the successful development of the performing
arts.   This is true of more firmly established organizations like
symphony orchestras as well as it is of those, like repertory
theatre and dance companies, that are in the early stages of growth.
(Indeed, it might be said that until management does enter and take
firm hold, the dance world will remain as inchoate and economically
insecure as it is today.)

Too often the dilettante mentality--belief that all that is
needed for success is talented artists--prevails.   But a good orchestra, a good theatre, a good opera or dance group cannot be
established or run by well-wishing volunteers.

Good business brains and performance are essential to the
successful operation of these organizations, but more than these
are required, for the problems are unique.   Artistic judgments
defying business calculations enter at every step.   In the profit-
seeking business world there are clearcut measures of effectiveness:
the income account and the balance sheet.   For the nonprofit arts
organization there is no such measure.   There are no profits, and
although a diminishing deficit might seem to indicate effective business management, this is not necessarily the case.   It might simply reflect an increasing failure to meet artistic obligations.

What constitutes a good manager in this field?   He has been
described by an authority on the subject as a man "who must be
knowledgeable in the art with which he is concerned, an impresario,
labor negotiator, diplomat, educator, publicity and public relations
expert, politician, skilled businessman, a social sophisticate, a
servant of the community, a tireless leader--becomingly humble
before authority--a teacher, a tyrant, and a continuing student of
the arts. "   It is obvious that artistic knowledge of the field itself
is not the only qualification for a successful manager.   Indeed,
some excellent managers have come from other fields and obtained
their orientation in the arts on the job.

Managers as Skilled Businessmen

Let us examine one or two of these qualifications in detail.
A "skilled businessman" functioning as manager of a performing

arts organization will be expected to exhibit a high degree of analytical ability as well as the mechanical ability to carry out established business routines. With no profit ledger to measure success, other benchmarks must be observed.

Adequate accounting procedures go far beyond the record of
cash intake and outgo and protection against dishonesty. A skilled
manager also possesses the ability to prepare and present systematic reports of business operations that will give to those who are
not masters in this field a broad understanding of the true picture
and assure the board that administration is in accordance with approved policies and budget.

Not only is clearly presented, straightforward financial information important for the board as a guide to administration, it
can also serve to improve relations with contributors--especially
foundations and corporations--all levels of government, and, indeed,
with unions. Too often, hiding facts whose publication would un-
cover an arts organization's sorry financial predicament, or even
reveal unexpected affluence, works to its long-term disadvantage.

Perhaps because of their chronic condition of financial in-
security, arts organizations are notoriously adhesive to long-established methods of conducting business operations. Frequently these
methods are as wasteful and inefficient as they are well intended.
A good manager develops a deeply ingrained impatience with conducting business operations as they have been conducted simply because "that's the way it's always been done. "

Managers as Labor Negotiators

The role of the general manager in the field of labor relations evolves from his responsibility to cope with a wide range of
personnel problems.

While some unions on occasion impose restrictions on arts
organizations, there are also occasions when unions have made life-
saving concessions to encourage and stimulate development. For
example, the American Guild of Musical Artists, whose members
include dancers and singers, has recognized that modern dance has
such a small audience and is so imperfectly established as a way
of life that application of standard union regulations is out of the
question. It has made numerous concessions and in fact sponsored
several talent showcases. It has similarly recognized the problems
of choral singers. The off-Broadway theatre has also benefited
from union cooperation, but as it grows finds the craft unions
tightening their regulations. The stagehands and musicians have
been particularly uncompromising in their dealings with theatrical
managements. In the theatre one finds as well the largest number
of abuses--featherbedding and needless extra charges such as those
for standby musicians who never play.

Symphony orchestras and opera companies also have had

serious union difficulties, widely publicized in recent seasons. The opera is especially vulnerable, since a management like the Metropolitan's must deal with some fourteen separate unions. Wage scale increases and other benefits granted to one union are bound to affect the others as well.

The difficulties in relationships between management and labor in the performing arts are undoubtedly aggravated by the fact that the supply of performers is generally larger than the demand for their services, that the seasonal nature of most organizations in the field often creates intolerable hardships because of intermittent employment and resulting inadequate salaries, and that adequate funds for support of the arts organization are difficult to raise.

It should be clearly understood that these conditions will not be solved by an attitude that assumes the artist should subsidize the arts by working for the lowest possible fee. Nor, on the other hand, is an answer to be found in union practices that are detrimental to the long-run growth of the arts.

The employment provided by a nonprofit organization should not differ in principle from that provided by a commercial operation. Too often, however, unions do not adequately take into account the difference between the transient character of Broadway, for example, where salaries are high to compensate for the temporary nature of employment, and the relatively more permanent character of the season of orchestras or permanent professional theatres. These at least make a commitment for a definite season, no matter how short.

The core of the performing arts--the actor, the musician, the dancer, the singer, the stagehand, the scene painter, the trucker, the press agent, and sometimes even the usher and the ticket taker--is made up of union members. Management in effect is an agent for the performer in collecting money, providing the stage, and creating the audience. Hence, there is a clear demand for mutual responsibility. A constant balance has to be struck between management's drive for quality at a reasonable cost and the union's aim of job security with fair pay for services rendered. If either fails, both suffer.

It is precisely for this reason that there is considerable hope in mechanisms through which management and the unions discuss their problems in a relaxed atmosphere, without the pressure of a strike deadline. To tell employees, when a contract is about to expire, how badly off the employer is has never been a persuasive management tactic. More candor and more contact on a year-round basis would help both sides anticipate issues and achieve greater understanding of their mutual problems.

Arts Management Training

The conduct of labor negotiations is only one of arts

management's many preoccupations.   There are daily crises relating to backstage and front-of-house operation that must be coped with; there are public relations to be maintained, everything from press releases to arranging opening night parties for subscribers. The general manager of an arts organization holds a position that has few counterparts in other fields.   It is of great importance as these organizations proliferate that there be a comparable increase in the number of men and women equipped to supply high-grade managerial skills.

The American Symphony Orchestra League recognized this problem in 1952 when it launched a management training program that has been operating one week a year ever since.   Over sixty persons now employed in managerial positions with orchestras and arts councils have attended the course.   Recognizing that a one-week course could provide little more than orientation, the League moved on to offer an In-Service Management Training Program, aided by grants from the Avalon Foundation and the Martha Baird Rockefeller Fund for Music.   Under these grants five young men have completed their year of training with leading orchestras and now serve as managers of substantial orchestras; two others are currently in training.

In 1961, the Ford Foundation launched a similar inservice program to train managers for arts organizations.   In 1964, the third year of that program, 24 interns were provided with the opportunity to work for one year in an apprentice managerial capacity with outstanding nonprofit professional theatres, opera companies, and symphony orchestras.

Good as these programs may be, it must be recognized that arts administration cannot be left to improvement on such a modest scale, or to trial and error, or to the hope that somehow sufficient information will pass from one person to another.   The steps that have been taken to train a new generation are welcome, but more effort, on a more formal basis, needs to be made--perhaps within the universities.

COOPERATION IN THE ARTS

The strength and efficiency of performing arts organizations rest on the ability of each one to handle its own problems.   Expert assistance from without can, however, be of great value to the individual organization.   There is an evident need for increasing communication in the performing arts both within and among the various fields.   Not only is there a dearth of systematized information on the operations of performing arts organizations, there is still insufficient cooperation among them, despite the promise cooperation holds and despite the advances that have been made.

Arts Councils

The success of cooperative movements in health and welfare has led many community leaders to turn to the arts council idea as a means of stimulating practical cooperation among the arts organizations and focusing community attention on their activities, while at the same time preserving the artistic independence of each institution.

Most of the 100 community arts councils are organized as nonprofit, tax-exempt institutions.   Some accept memberships from individuals, others admit only organizations.   Delegates from the member organizations serve on some councils' boards of directors, while other councils prefer to select their members from the community at large.   Arts councils usually obtain their administrative funds by soliciting contributions and charging nominal dues.   Some that conduct annual united fund-raising campaigns receive a share of the total raised.

There are hazards in the operation of an arts council, largely those of bureaucracy, but these can be avoided if the leadership has sufficient experience and high quality.   Councils provide important services that are often missing or when available are needlessly duplicated by individual organizations: central clerical and promotional services for members, professional leadership for fund raising, publication of periodic calendars of events, advice in scheduling performances, and provision of management counseling services.   Many councils have raised funds for community arts centers and are responsible for their operation.   Approximately thirty councils include arts festivals in their programs.

The Winston-Salem Arts Council and the Saint Paul Council of Arts and Sciences have been in the vanguard of the movement, and their work has set an example for other communities.   One of the former's many successful projects has been its campaign to increase support for the Winston-Salem Symphony Orchestra.   In the 1963-64 season, for example, the membership drive to fill a 2000-seat auditorium produced 2124 season memberships.   The Saint Paul Council has recently completed a $3 million Arts and Science Center for its members and has steadily increased its united fund contributions.   It has also been effective in promoting cooperative ventures among members.   For example, both the Arts Center and the Science Museum, in cooperation with the Philharmonic Society, have given evening programs for students at the Philharmonic's Summer Music Camp.   Informal luncheons scheduled by the Council director every two or three weeks for the professional directors of the six member organizations have been useful in fostering the cooperative spirit.

In 1960, individuals interested in the arts council movement formed a central clearinghouse for arts councils.   Arts Councils of America (formerly Community Arts Councils, Inc.) issues a handbook and periodic bulletins to its members on fund-raising methods, arts calendars, festival promotions, and other cooperative arts projects. The organization also sponsors an annual conference for exchange of information and exposure to expert views on a wide range of artistic and management problems.

A Service Association for Each Art

The diversity of the various performing arts and the differences between the organizations within each field might create impossible complexities for a national "trade association" that attempts to serve all of them. But the need for service can be accomplished by strengthening existing organizations--like the American National Theatre and Academy, the American Symphony Orchestra League, the Central Opera Service, and the Theatre Communications Group--and establishing new ones as necessary.

The American Symphony Orchestra League was founded in 1942. Its purpose is to assist orchestras to strengthen their work, stabilize their financial base, expand their cultural services within their own communities, and reach toward higher artistic standards.

The League sponsors study and training projects for musicians, conductors, managers, and members of orchestral boards and women's associations. It holds an annual convention. It provides an advisory service to its individual members on many problems, including assistance in locating personnel. It publishes a newsletter and special reports on various aspects of orchestra work, including concert attendance, comparative finances, and statistics.

Working expenses for the League are financed largely from membership dues and contributions. In 1963-64, the amount came to approximately $86,000. Funds for special projects and activities are made available to the League by foundations, music organizations, and individuals, and totaled approximately $119,000 in the same year. In addition, the League receives almost $100,000 annually in contributed services. Expenditures for the operations of most other service organizations in the arts are small by comparison.

With the number of performing arts groups increasing all the time, with the strong desire for expansion in already established groups, more effective service organizations could be very useful in each of the performing arts. Given the stringent budgets of most arts groups, it must be assumed that they will need outside support. The institutions that would benefit the most from the strengthening of existing service organizations or the establishment of new ones are the least able to support them financially.

A NATIONAL CENTER FOR INFORMATION

In addition to the encouragement of community arts councils

and national service organizations for the various arts, there is need for a national repository of information, a place to which inquiries about all the performing arts may be directed. Despite the diversity of problems confronting the various arts, it is also evident that there are many common problems as well, and that groups in each field can learn from the experience of the others and that the general public needs to know more about all of them.

First and foremost, a central institution would collect existing information about the operations of professional performing arts organizations and about the activities of all organizations in the arts. Its library should not duplicate existing collections, but complete bibliographies could be prepared on organization, management, and financing. There is also need to collate and analyze new material on a continuing basis in order to make it useful to the organizations and to the general public.

In addition, a bulletin is needed to set forth facts and figures about the activities of various groups as well as special articles about attendance, box office, financing, fund raising, facility construction, organization, and the like. The sponsorship of conferences to extend knowledge about the arts would also be valuable.

Finally, the center might undertake research projects in problems of interest to any or all of the performing arts, although this function would perhaps be more wisely initiated as a second stage in the development of the center.

In all its programs this center would have to cooperate in the closest manner with the national service associations that already exist in order to eliminate duplication of effort. Certain activities would clearly be the responsibility of the service organizations. Technical advice to individual organizations and the operation of an employment service are examples of work it would not undertake.

In summary, the panel believes there is urgent need for an independent national information center that can assume an important and continuing role in the development of the performing arts and urges that every encouragement be given to its establishment.

MANAGING ORCHESTRAS IS A FINE ART TOO*

Martin Mayer

Some years back, an imaginary report from an imaginary time-study engineer circulated among musicians and their friends.

*From Fortune magazine, September 1, 1968. Copyright 1968. Time Inc. Reprinted by permission.

Its author had been shocked by what he saw at a symphony concert:
Sixteen first violins, all doing the same thing, nine double basses
just to swing back and forth on the notes of a single chord. Even
the woodwinds, which looked as though they had individual functions,
often proved on examination to be doubling the notes already being
played by the strings. Many players, especially in the brass and
percussion sections, were idle most of the evening. Worse yet,
much of the music the orchestra played was made up of short repetitive phrases, and sometimes entire sections of a piece were
played all over again. It was no wonder, the time-study man wrote,
that orchestras lost money. He recommended a program of personnel reduction and musical editing that would improve productivity
and enable half as many people to play twice as much music during
a two-hour concert.

Anyone concerned about the business end of the performing
arts risks a plunge into this pit of incomprehension; there really
are people who don't know that art is an economic surplus operation.
A professional symphony orchestra that provides a living for a
hundred-odd people is among the more luxurious artistic institutions: it can no more pay for itself at the box office than a well-
staffed museum can pay its way with admission charges.

There is, however, no reason for its backers to pay for the
additional luxury of weak management. As a Rockefeller Panel Report put it in 1965, "Resourceful business and administrative leadership is a necessary element in the successful development of the
performing arts." And as a number of orchestras have been discovering in recent years, there is all the difference in the world
between an annual deficit of $250,000 and one of $1,250,000. The
rising costs that narrow profit margins in business rapidly widen
the "income gap" in the performing arts, where it is hard both to
control expenses and to predict revenues. Despite rising attendance
and ticket prices over the last five years, most orchestras are in
trouble; and some, especially where the business management has
been weak, are in bad trouble.

A Call for Hercules

The current crisis of the Chicago Symphony is instructive.
Its unrestricted endowment shrank from $6,200,000 in the spring of
1964 to little more than $1 million this spring [1968]--with most of
that almost certain to be lost next year. Between 1964 and 1967
the orchestra's annual operating expenses rose about $1,400,000
(to $3,250,000), while operating income rose only about $600,000
(to $1,551,000). The 1964 operating deficit of $840,000 was more
or less manageable on endowment income, plus a small grant from
the city, plus the sort of fund raising that could be done, as an officer of the symphony puts it, "by a small group of men sitting
around the Chicago Club." The operating deficit of $1,700,000 in
1967 could be managed only by taking $776,000 out of the orches-
tra's endowment.

The four-year period was marked by several changes on the executive committee of the volunteer board of trustees that controls the orchestra, and two changes in the top-level paid management. "The administration of the Chicago Symphony," says its present general manager, John S. Edwards, "doesn't resign or get fired. It disappears, like a Central American government." Edwards, a veteran of more than thirty years in orchestra management and until this year president of the American Symphony Orchestra League, came to Chicago in June, 1967, after 12 years in Pittsburgh. George Szell, conductor of the Cleveland Orchestra and an old friend, warned him about what he would find, saying, "It's like cleaning the Augean stables." Edwards took the job and told Szell, "We'll just find out whether I'm Hercules."

Two contracts were the proximate cause of the troubles. The more damaging was the contract with the musicians' union, signed in 1965, guaranteeing the orchestra players a longer season every year until they achieved a full 52 weeks of pay in 1968-69. (This past season the orchestra still had one week of unpaid leave.) Yearlong employment for musicians was already, clearly, the wave of the future, and the Chicago Symphony management had to bargain under pressure from Mayor Richard J. Daley. But the trustees seem to have signed up without even thinking very hard about finding the added bookings that would justify the added weeks on the payroll.

The second contract was bothersome in a quite different way. In 1965 the symphony's trustees were planning to spend around $2 million to remodel Orchestra Hall; they would dip into endowment funds but later replenish these with the proceeds of a special renovation-fund drive. This plan was put aside, however, after the symphony received an offer of support from Mrs. Arma Wyler, heiress to a fortune from a dehydrated-food business. She agreed to pay the costs of remodeling Orchestra Hall; she would provide $1,950,000--$100,000 of it in 1970, the other $1,850,000 to be paid after her death. In return for these funds, the auditorium was to be renamed Silvain and Arma Wyler Hall, with large gold letters bearing that legend over the lobby doors.

Members of the board of trustees, who had apparently been woolgathering when the contract was originally discussed, were shocked on their arrival for the opening concert of the 1966-67 season to find the large gold letters. They were further shocked by the discovery that, as the contract had been drawn, Mrs. Wyler's legacy could be diminished if an economic downswing should depress the total value of her estate. During the intermission at the opening concert, Louis Sudler, the newly elected president of the board, visited with several influential Chicagoans active in the symphony's affairs. He was strongly urged to get Mrs. Wyler's name off the hall; the fear was that any such prominent recognition of one donor might diminish the enthusiasm of others. Sudler arranged to cancel the contract, but the entire cost of the modernization--it turned out to be close to $3 million--had to be charged

342   THE SYMPHONY ORCHESTRA

against the unrestricted endowment. And there were of course no offsetting funds from any renovation drive.

"When I became a trustee in 1965," Sudler says reflectively, "I didn't--and neither did the board generally--have any sense of impending trouble. Now at least we know what we have to do. We have to double the annual giving, raise endowment, find new markets for our services, and get a profitable recording contract. Meanwhile we're still trying to get down to the bottom, find our base-- the way any corporation in trouble does." Among the shocks Sudler has had to absorb was the revelation that several profit items-- e. g., from past recording contracts--were illusory. The 1966-67 statement of income and expenses carried an income item of about $60,000 from "recording royalties, etc. "; the 1967-68 statement shows a $132,000 "net cost" of recordings.

How to Get By in the Summer

Though nobody else has got into quite such hot water as Chicago, all the major orchestras face problems of the same kind. Of these, the "Big Five" orchestras--New York, Boston, Philadelphia, Chicago, and Cleveland--have or soon will have year-round employment contracts, and at least a dozen others have contracts for 35 weeks or more; meanwhile their local subscription series, the foundation of any such enterprise, run 20 weeks or less. Baltimore, for example, under the contract expiring this year, must maintain its orchestra 36 weeks although its subscription series covers only 16 Wednesday night concerts (eight of which can be paired with a repeat of the same program on Thursday night).

Faced with these longer-term contracts, all of the Big Five have naturally worked hard to nail down as much "summer business" as they can. Chicago is blessed with the separately managed and financed Ravinia Festival just north of the city, which buys the orchestra's services for eight weeks every summer. The Philadelphia Orchestra has the long-established Robin Hood Dell Concerts in July and the newer Saratoga Festival in August. Boston has its famous and flourishing Berkshire Festival at Tanglewood in the summer. The New York Philharmonic has created a May-June series of Promenade concerts, found four corporate and government sponsors for free concerts in the parks, and organized extended tours (last year across Canada, sponsored by the Canadian Government as part of the centennial celebration; this summer to Europe, helped by $150,000 from T.W.A. and $200,000 from the State Department). And the Cleveland Orchestra has invested almost $7 million ("Twice what I would have told you it was going to cost if you had asked me a year ago," says General Manager A. Beverly Barksdale) in the physical plant of the Blossom Music Center, which in mid-July began providing off-season concerts and a summer music school in a wooded setting near the Ohio Turnpike between Cleveland and Akron. "Blossom," says Barksdale, "does have a little bit of pure idealism in it--it bothers me and some others that during our season we play in a small elegant hall, and reach so few people." But its major

purpose, the justification of the financial risk, is to find employment for the nation's largest orchestra--108 men and women who
must be paid all year round.

Years ago the answer to an employment contract longer than
the local season was the tour, which in theory was artistically
stimulating for the men (who got a chance to play before fresh and
enthusiastic audiences in fresh and acoustically different halls) and
financially profitable for the orchestra.   But in the last decade or
so, rising costs of transportation and accommodations have made it
necessary to book an orchestra for six concerts a week on tour,
which often means six moves a week, which is hell on men and
management.   Carlos Moseley, managing director of the New York
Philharmonic, still remembers clearly a week in its 1959 tour of
Europe when the orchestra played Monday in Paris, Tuesday in
Basel, Wednesday in Munich, Thursday in Belgrade, Friday in
Zabreb, and Saturday in Venice--and taped a C. B. S. television show
at the close of the Venice concert.   And whatever artistic enchant-
ment distance may lend is quickly dissipated by the need to play
parts of one program--usually a relatively popular program--over
and over again.

And even at such forced draft, a tour can be financially debilitating.   Costing out its most recent cross-country tour, the New
York Philharmonic found that receipts would have to be $18,750 a
night for the orchestra to break even.   These figures were indeed
met, thanks to the audience appeal of Leonard Bernstein and bookings in big outdoor amphitheatres like the Hollywood Bowl and Den-
ver's Red Rocks.   The Philadelphia Orchestra asks a fee of
$12,500 a night on the road, but is unable to break even on that.
Orchestras of the quality of Detroit and Los Angeles played last
year for as little as $3500 a night to fill out a week's schedule
while on tour.   The Minneapolis Symphony--punished at the traveling
box office by the absence of its regular conductor, who was ill--
actually went out of pocket $10,000 on its eastern tour last winter,
without counting any of the payroll or overhead costs of the orchestra.

The Perils of Four-a-Week

Expansion of the regular home market is obviously what the
orchestras need, but making this policy is much easier than executing it.   Quality considerations dictate a limit both in the size of the
hall and in the number of performances in a week.   A full-time
union orchestra contracts to give eight (sometimes nine) "services"
a week, usually two and a half hours each.   About half of these
services may be devoted to performances and the other half to full
orchestra rehearsals.   Except for pops concerts, or with the reduced standards of summer festivals, orchestral programs of professional quality cannot be prepared in a single rehearsal; if anything of even moderate difficulty is billed, up to four rehearsals
may be required for each program.   And artistic quality suffers if
a program is repeated too often.   Even if the union will go along,
it's hard to play more than four performances a week.

An orchestra on any such schedule will have trouble expanding its market. The great majority of regular-season tickets are
marketed on a subscription basis, e.g., to someone planning to
come every Thursday evening for 14 weeks. Since an orchestra
cannot play the same piece twice for the same audience in the same
season, four separate audiences are required every week. And a
long season will usually mean more than one subscription period
and more than four separate audiences. Very few people love symphony concerts enough to want to go every week--and a long subscription series may cost $200 or more for a pair of tickets.
Short series sell out these days much faster than long series; the
resistance is apt to be especially severe for periods of more than
20 weeks.

The New York Philharmonic has a 32-week subscription season (the nation's longest) at Lincoln Center; it can play more or
less the same program there four times a week and sell out every
night. But the Philharmonic plays for the nation's most sophisticated and affluent audience. No other city could sell as many
tickets as New York does for a 14-week series at $105 for a seat
in the orchestra. Also, New York has been unusually imaginative
in devising subscription combinations; at present there are 12 covering different time spans.

Mrs. Tiffany's Husband Hates Music

Any expansion of the home season, then, begins with an effort to market the product in and around the home territory. Unfortunately, the demand for the product is uneven and variously
motivated; it is affected not only by pure musical interest, but by
ethnic backgrounds, education (in its medicinal "good-for-you"
sense), and social status. "In a lot of families," says Carl Shaver, a former vice president of Grand Union now in business for
himself as a management consultant and fund raiser for orchestras,
"the symphony has been like a religion--it's put in the wife's name.
And it's suspect to a lot of husbands, like the household checking
account." Most of the older orchestras play a regular weekday-
afternoon subscription series for an almost exclusively feminine
audience, which spends the morning shopping and the afternoon listening. When he was conductor of the Philadelphia Orchestra, Leopold Stokowski objected strenuously to these "ladies with bundles,"
and an effort was made to switch the orchestra's afternoon series
in New York to a series of evening concerts. Arthur Judson, then
manager of the Philadelphia Orchestra, kept framed on his wall for
some years thereafter a letter the management received when this
switch was originally announced: "Mrs. Tiffany regrets that she
cannot take her tickets for an evening series, because she cannot
go out alone in the evening and her husband hates music."

The economics of symphony orchestras are heavily affected
by "women's committees"--volunteers who sell subscriptions, raise
funds, and arrange educational events, lunches, teas, parties, and
an annual "orchestra ball" that is in many places a prime social

occasion.   A number of subscriptions are sold entirely on the social importance of the annual opening night, for which everybody dresses up.   No orchestra that benefits by such events wants to risk losing them (in Boston and Philadelphia the charity ball raises more than $150,000 a year), but some thoughtful board members wonder whether the identification of the orchestra with high society may not be counterproductive.   Frank P. Thomas of Indianapolis, whose Burger Chef Systems has made substantial corporate contributions to that city's orchestra ("When you're in the hamburger-joint business, " he explained amiably to a meeting of the American Symphony Orchestra League, "you have to do something to improve your image"), argues that the annual full-dress opening night depresses sales to middle-class families: "Wives see that opening night on TV and they say, 'This place is not for me--I'd be uncomfortable there. '"

Many orchestras make little effort to sell subscriptions to people not already known to members of the women's committees. Shaver says that in one of the cities where he has worked for an orchestra he made a list of the officers and directors of all publicly held corporations and found that the symphony subscription list included names from only one-quarter of the companies.   "The others hadn't even been approached. " Income is also lost, Shaver feels, through "inferior techniques for merchandising single tickets. "

In some cities--Indianapolis, Los Angeles, Milwaukee, New York, Phoenix, Seattle, St. Louis--new audiences have been drawn to symphony concerts by new auditoriums and "cultural centers. " For reasons nobody fully understands, the cultural centers have ordinarily been promoted by political and business leadership rather than by high society, and their socially neutral elegance seems to attract sections of the middle class not previously reached by the arts.   In Los Angeles, to take one major growth situation, paid admissions went from 76,700 in the orchestra's last year at Philharmonic Auditorium to 123,900 in its first year at the new Music Center.   Even where attendance cannot improve, because the new hall has no more capacity than the old one, a new hall permits a large rise in ticket prices and income.

Many orchestras have a tradition of selling concerts to organizations or even individuals, who then supply their own audience. John Edwards hopes to bail out the Chicago Symphony's year-round contract eventually by establishing weeklong orchestra-in-residence arrangements at midwestern universities; the universities, not the symphony, are responsible for ticket sales.   Detroit gives annual concerts for, among others, the University of Detroit and the Lutheran Church.   A few years ago a Negro church brought the services of the Detroit orchestra to launch the career of a young conductor in its congregation; the orchestra now employs the conductor regularly for school concerts in the inner city.   Detroit has also sold a concert to the Master Brewers Association convention. The Rochester Philharmonic sells Kodak eight lunch-time concerts a year, in the company's auditorium; the Cleveland Orchestra plays three concerts in tents at local country clubs; Phoenix plays an annual benefit for the Salvation Army.

The Case for Running Out

To date, however, the easiest way to expand the home season has been to expand the geographical definition of "home. " In what is called a "runout, " the orchestra invades a suburb or nearby city to play the program it has just given in its own hall, and everybody then goes home to sleep in his own bed. Runout series have been arranged to Milwaukee for the Chicago Symphony, Tacoma for Seattle, the west end of its own city for Cleveland, Santa Barbara and San Diego for Los Angeles, Rochester and St. Joseph for Minneapolis. In the West, where the buses fly over flat roads, runouts may be arranged to cities as much as 200 miles away. There is no doubt about their profitability. The added costs of performing the same program one more time are obviously small, and the orchestra can often hope to build a constituency that will contribute money and political support.

Baltimore has dug itself out of what once looked like a hopeless deficit situation largely by concentration on runouts, which now account for 41 of the orchestra's evening engagements (as against only 36, including pops concerts, in the city's own Lyric Theatre). Twelve separately organized symphony societies have been established to sponsor the series of three to five concerts in towns around Baltimore. "Our judgment, " says the orchestra's young general manager, Oleg Lobanov, "is that a fair price for outside concerts, in the halls where we play them, is $2.50 per adult per concert. We take the risks and the net after expenses. " The price suggests a money-losing operation, but the resulting statewide support for the symphony makes possible an annual legislative grant of $125,000--and the new societies are already producing contributors to the annual maintenance drive. Pittsburgh's unprofitable runouts to small towns in the western half of the state are underwritten by Columbia Gas of Pennsylvania.

A Boost from a Brew

Perhaps the most envied of the middling-large orchestras is Seattle's, whose $1,200,000 budget is handsomely supported in several different ways. Nearly 5900 subscriptions are sold for 12 pairs of concerts--"giving us, " says manager Alan Watrous, "the nation's sixth-largest subscription audience, in the nineteenth-largest city"--and the orchestra plays in 17 other cities in the state, 14 of them under the sponsorship of each city's own, independent Seattle Symphony Society. In addition, Olympia Brewing supports a low-priced series in Seattle itself that offers younger and less wealthy audiences the chance to hear the same programs that the subscription audiences will hear, with young artists substituted for the big names who help sell the subscriptions for the more expensive series. Of the orchestra's 163 performances in 1967-68, about three-fifths were for school audiences; these too are well supported. "We get some money from Title III [of the Elementary and Secondary Education Act]," says Watrous airily, not talking about the work that must have gone into the litany, "some city, some county, some school system, some that the children pay for themselves, some from the union's Music Performance Trust Fund. . . . "

Seattle has certain advantages other orchestras do not enjoy. It has only 75 players under annual contract, beefing up as needed for specific programs.   Moreover, because the separately financed and managed local opera company employs the same musicians, the union permits the orchestra to pay its personnel a separate fee for each service rather than a weekly salary, thus relieving the pressure to find employment for the symphony in dry seasons.   Seattle's conductor Milton Katims, as Watrous puts it, "relates beautifully to the community. "   In 1967 the Real Estate Board chose Katims as Seattle's Citizen of the Year.

Several other success stories argue that the soil for symphony can be found anywhere, given the right gardeners.   Good management has helped give Cleveland what is probably the world's finest symphony orchestra (European musicians think it is, though Americans tend to be provincially fearful about praising their own); it has put Minneapolis in a position where it is likely to add a sixth name to the Big Five; it has given Salt Lake City, with a population of around 500,000, one of the dozen best orchestras in the country; it has enabled Detroit, for the first time in its long and mostly discouraging musical history, to come up with a wholly first-rate orchestra.   These wonders have been worked by leadership, mostly by the musical leadership and audience appeal of a conductor, but always with help from intelligent management and well-planned community support.

"Everybody Is the Manager's Boss"

The term "management," as it is applied by symphony orchestras, ordinarily refers to two quite different kinds of people: paid professional administrators, who usually have the title "manager"; and unpaid voluntary chairmen or presidents of boards of trustees, who are usually well-connected local businessmen or lawyers.

The manager's post carries great responsibility and relatively little authority.   "Everybody in town is the manager's boss, " says Helen Thompson, who has run the American Symphony Orchestra League for most of its 26 years.   "Everybody who buys a ticket or gives five dollars.   The minute a man comes on the board he's an expert in what you should do, and if he isn't, his wife is. "

Managers are usually consulted by conductors about programs and soloists.   They must handle negotiations with various unions and with the agents for the soloists.   They must schedule rehearsals, concerts, and runouts with due regard for the teaching and other professional obligations that are often (especially in smaller

orchestras) the musicians' main source of income. Any number of
details must be dealt with exactly, from the floral decorations at
the women's committee lunch to the arrival of rented scores in
time for the musicians to learn unfamiliar works. There are the
people who want to change their seats for next season's subscription series and there are the Birchites opposed to paying good
American money for Communist soloists. At all the larger orchestras the administration of payrolls is a complex chore: although
they operate under a union contract and at a union wage scale, the
orchestras pay most of the men (93 out of 106 in New York) some
amount individually negotiated over scale.

The volunteer presidents from business and the professions
carry different kinds of burdens. Their first responsibility is, of
course, to raise whatever money is needed to cover the deficit.
In palmier days, when seasons ran 20 weeks and the men took jobs
at hotels for the summers, individuals could sponsor an orchestra
as a hobby. A Henry Lee Higginson in Boston, a William Andrews
Clark Jr. in Los Angeles, an Elbert Lawrence Carpenter in Minneapolis would simply write a check for whatever was necessary at the
end of the season. Some of this tradition survives, especially in
the smaller cities, where the income-and-expense statement of the
orchestra balances exactly because at its last meeting the board
passes the hat. But at the larger orchestras the deficits today go
beyond what individuals are likely to contribute every year. C.
Wanton Balis, president of the Philadelphia Orchestra, estimates
that by 1971 it will have an annual "income gap" of a million dollars. Los Angeles is there already; and Chicago is beyond.

It was in expectation of mounting deficits, and of a time lag
before the orchestras could learn to cope with them, that the Ford
Foundation in 1966 granted 61 of the nation's orchestras a total of
$80,200,000. About three-quarters of the grant was marked for
endowment purposes, and was contingent on the success of the orchestras in raising an equal amount (the largest orchestras had to
raise twice as much as the $2 million Ford offered) through their
own endowment drives. The rest was for development purposes--
e.g., to help develop runout programs in places like Baltimore,
Phoenix, and Seattle--and to guarantee that during the endowment
drives the orchestras would not also have to increase their annual
maintenance appeals. In most of the larger cities the Ford grant
has stimulated drives to exceed the required matching funds:
Minneapolis has already raised more than $6 million of a projected
$8 million to put with Ford's $2 million, and Chicago, Philadelphia, and Boston have similarly ambitious intentions.

But unfortunately for the fiscal health of the orchestras, the
magnitude of the new figures floating about has stimulated substantial extra demands from the musicians' union, which has in any
event, like many other unions, lost control over its membership.
The difference between an endowment fund and operating income is
by no means too subtle a matter to be understood by a violinist--
but he can pretend it is.

Corporate Harmony

Increasingly, in recent years, the orchestras have looked to corporations for support. The model in this area, which nobody has been able to copy exactly, is John B. Ford's reorganization of the Detroit Symphony's finances following a horrendous collapse shortly after World War II. Ford went to 30 local companies and asked them each for $10,000 a year--nobody was allowed to contribute more. Today the maximum is not enforced (several companies contribute $30,000), and last year 26 Detroit corporations together put up about $400,000 for the orchestra, which was about 60 percent of the maintenance drive.

Orchestral fund raisers solicit corporations and local governments with arguments of self-interest. Boston and the San Francisco Bay area have demonstrated that an active cultural life helps companies recruit top-level people. In an ad offering a job for a physicist, Honeywell not long ago used a picture of Minneapolis conductor Stanislaw Skrowaczewski. Last spring's West Coast tour by the Utah Symphony was underwritten by the State Industrial Commission, because a previous appearance by the orchestra in New York had stimulated inquiries from business.

Ultimately, a good chunk of the support of symphony orchestras may have to come from tax revenues. It could come in the form of grants, or as payment for services in the form of school concerts and free outdoor concerts, or as a share of contributions to a richer "public television." But for the time being, the burden rests on individuals. Some meet it enthusiastically, in the spirits of Philadelphia's Balis: "The reason for doing all this work is when you sit in the hall and listen--these people are so damned good." Others work more in the pragmatic spirit of an argument that Chicago's Hercules, John Edwards, threw at a rather shocked audience of members of the American Symphony Orchestra League: "Do any of you really believe that a city really needs a symphony orchestra? I mean need--N-E-E-D--a symphony orchestra, in the way that a community needs other things, like social services, bread for the children, and all that sort of thing. The answer is no. If you ask whether a city would be better off or worse off without a symphony, the answer is different: it would be worse off."

Given careful management--and perhaps just a few glamorous new conductors--some such calculations should continue, at least for a while, to provide a strong enough foundation for the nation's orchestras. But in many cities it is going to be a very close call.

RUNNING THE B. S. O.*

Harry Ellis Dickson

It used to be said in Boston that the Cabots spoke only to the
Lowells and the Lowells spoke only to God, but the trustees of the
Boston Symphony Orchestra, until recently, didn't speak to anyone.
This august body, once known as the Protestant Vatican, sat on
Mount Olympus, quietly dispensing its wisdom and managing the affairs of the orchestra. No one ever saw them. No one knew
where or when they met. Their names appeared on every symphony
program to attest the fact that they existed, yet they seemed to be
mythical--until recently when, along with the emergency of the "New
Boston," the trustees of the B. S. O. gradually came out of their
shells and were revealed as real people. There are 19 of them,
plus four trustees emeritus, and they represent a variety of call-
ings--several lawyers, a couple of merchants, a banker, an insurance company executive, a minister, a priest, two publishers, a
judge, a United States Senator, and one woman (the latter, the
charming and able Mrs. James H. Perkins, a recent tradition-shat-
tering addition). Being a trustee of the Boston Symphony Orchestra
is the highest status a Bostonian can attain.

    Henry B. Cabot, until very recently the chairman of the
trustees, is a rare human being, forthright, honest, liberal--and
loved and respected by all of the musicians. This is not the case
with presidents of other orchestras, whose relationship with the
players is, in some instances, one of suspicion and misunderstand-
ing. A New England Yankee whose love of music and musicians is
so great that he devoted a third of his life to the affairs of the orchestra, Henry Cabot served willingly and proudly without a cent of
remuneration. As a matter of fact, he paid handsomely with both
time and money for the privilege. He is urbane, quietly witty, and
enormously modest. Occasionally, he has even been mildly pro-
fane. He was an iconoclast about himself and his fellow trustees.
(Koussevitzky used to call them "trusties.")

    Cabot recently stepped down from his position and handed
over his responsibilities to a fellow Bostonian, Talcott M. Banks.
With characteristic modesty Cabot announced to the members of the
orchestra that his failing memory had been a prime consideration in
his decision to relinquish his office. He remains, however, keenly
interested in the affairs of the orchestra as a trustee emeritus.

    Banks is a distinguished Boston attorney, a good amateur
pianist, longtime lover of music, and a great doer in the musical
affairs of the community. He is a fine gentleman, respected and
loved by all who know him, and there is no reason to doubt that he
will continue in the Boston tradition of sound management.

---

*From Gentlemen, More Dolce Please!, by Harry Ellis Dickson; Bos-
ton: Beacon Press, 1969. Copyright 1969 by Harry Ellis Dickson.
Reprinted by permission of Beacon Press.

In keeping with the spirit of the times the "New Boston"
symphony trustees have an ecumenical face.   Henry Lee Higginson,
indeed, might not recognize a Boston Symphony Board of Trustees
that now harbors in its ranks alongside a Cabot, a Jennings, a
Perkins, and a Noonan, such names as Laughlin, Kennedy, Berko-
witz, and Rabb.

What, then, are the duties and functions of a symphony board
of trustees?   Years ago their duties were quite simple.   They were
expected personally to make up the inevitable deficit at the end of
each year, as Ernest Dane had, which they did without fanfare and
without publicity, keeping these mundane affairs to themselves.   The
Boston Symphony was considered their private club and they were
proud of their ordained heritage in keeping it so.   They chose the
conductor and the manager without asking or expecting outside advice and most of the time they were extraordinarily lucky in their
choices, for the Boston Symphony became known as the greatest
musical organization in the world.   Even today, when so many other
fine orchestras have sprung up in the United States, the Boston Symphony remains pre-eminent.

Conditions, however, have changed.   The day of enormous
fortunes being privately made and spent is gone.   Today's trustees
are not all men of wealth and their original function of giving money
has changed to that of raising money to keep up with the ever increasing costs of maintaining an orchestra.   Although the Boston
Symphony still boasts that it is almost 75 per cent self-supporting,
its over-all annual budget of 5 or 6 million dollars still leaves an
annual deficit of some $500,000.   The private approach has had to
be changed to a public one and a number of years ago an organization called "Friends of the Boston Symphony Orchestra" was formed
for the express purpose of defraying the deficit.   This organization
has grown into one of thousands of music lovers, mainly from
Greater Boston, but with branches in other cities throughout the
country, who contribute each year.   For their generosity they are
rewarded with an annual meeting and concert in Symphony Hall,
plus the privilege of attending numerous events at the Berkshire
Music Center every summer.   In addition, private foundations, like
Ford and Rockefeller, have begun to lend their support.   And it is
not too unreasonable to assume that some day in the future there
will be direct government support for the arts as there has been in
the European countries over the centuries.   Some of us have even
dared to hope that some day we will have in our national government a cabinet Secretary of the Arts, whose function will be to develop the enormous talent that exists in the United States, and to
bring it to the attention and enjoyment of all.

Manager

Being the manager of a symphony orchestra is quite different
from being the manager of a profit-making firm.   If the manager of
an orchestra should show a profit, he would certainly be looked upon
with suspicion.   The nature of a symphony orchestra, as that of an

opera company, where so many are involved in producing the finished product is such that it is impossible to break even, let alone
make a profit.   So it becomes one of the primary duties of a manager to keep costs down while keeping artistic standards up.   The
manager of a symphony orchestra, like a reluctant maiden, has to
learn to say no, and to keep saying it over and over again, especially to the players.

George E. Judd, manager of the orchestra for many years,
was a master of refusal.   He returned to Symphony Hall for a visit
a few years after his retirement and when he was seen in the corridor, four different players approached him and, from force of
habit, they asked him for a raise.   And, from force of habit, he
refused all four!

Judd was a completely dedicated man, whose concern for the
orchestra was almost religious in its fervor.   He was wise, efficient, honestly shrewd, and scrupulously fair in managing the orchestra.   If he sometimes seemed cold and unbending to the players,
he was equally so to himself.   During his many years with the orchestra he never asked for a raise in salary and indeed when the
trustees voted him one, time after time, he always adamantly refused it.   George Judd has been retired from the orchestra for a
number of years, yet he still retains a personal and lively interest
in its affairs and whenever he comes back for a visit he is greeted
like a beloved father.

There are, of course, many duties and problems which beset
a symphony-orchestra manager.   He must make concert schedules,
arrange dates and engage soloists and guest conductors a year in
advance, all with the approval or recommendation of the music director.   Out-of-town concerts must be arranged, transportation
problems solved, negotiations made with out-of-town managers,
etc. , etc.

The manager has also the task of negotiating and arranging
salaries of individual orchestra players; for although the minimum
salary of a player is set, only about one third of the orchestra receives the minimum.   The rest, according to their position in the
orchestra, seniority, and their over-all value, receive above-mini-
mum pay, arrived at by individual bargaining.

Our present manager, Thomas D. Perry, Jr. , is a soft-
spoken, boyish-looking man, whose mild exterior masks an acquired
stubborn toughness.   He is a Yale man who broke the tradition of
Harvard-bred managers for the Boston Symphony.   Although not a
Bostonian by birth or schooling, he has earned the respect and high
regard of even our Harvard-bred trustees.

The Staff

Most people are surprised at how many people it takes to run
the Boston Symphony.   When I joined the orchestra I naively thought

that the B. S. O. consisted of 106 musicians, a conductor, and a
manager. Last year's payroll of the orchestra numbered some five
hundred employees! The second floor of Symphony Hall is a maze
of offices and cubbyholes peopled by librarians, the manager, assistant managers, secretaries, press officers, program editors, a
personnel manager, fund raisers. The Tanglewood complex employs
many additional people, some full-, some part-time. There is of
course an all-year-round caretaker who lives on the grounds and
oversees the physical operation of the grounds and all the various
buildings. The Boston Symphony Orchestra is probably the only
orchestra in the world that owns its own tractors, trucks, and other farm equipment.

The stage manager of the Boston Symphony has always occupied a unique role in the symphony family. He is as much a part
of the orchestra as any player and in some respects is much more
important. If a musician gets ill, he can be replaced by one of his
colleagues, but if the stage manager has to miss a concert, there is
a real crisis. Our stage managers have become an integral part of
every concert. The late Harvey Genereux, who preceded our present stage manager, was more temperamental than any musician
and actually took it upon himself to decide certain musical matters.
For instance, he hated large cymbals and, on out-of-town trips, he
would conveniently forget to pack them, remarking, "The small
cymbals sound just as good. " Before a trip he would always ask,
"Are the big chimes necessary?   Can't you play those notes on the
bells?" Harvey also hated conductors who conducted from memory.
"They give me nervous prostration, " he used to say.   "What if they
forget!" And in many instances he would drag out the conductor's
music stand and place the scores upon it, even if the conductor
didn't want them.   Before each of the concerts for children which
I conduct, he would beg me to use the music, and each time when
I didn't, he would say, "Damn fool!"

Our present stage manager, Alfred Robison, is a six-foot-
five gentle giant, who watches over his brood like a mother hen.
He is completely levelheaded, devoid of temperament, always cheer-
fully optimistic, and he does his job proudly and efficiently.   He
calls the members of the orchestra "my men, " and when the concert goes well and there is great success, he is enormously proud.
Over the years Al has also become a music critic and, by the
second day's rehearsal, will predict which new piece will have success and which will "lay an egg"--and he is usually right.   In the
Pops repertoire his favorite is "Days of Wine and Roses, " and on
the evenings when we play it, he sits quietly backstage humming it
to himself, swaying from side to side, a look of benign happiness
on his face.   On most outside Pops engagements when I am conducting, I try to make sure "Wine and Roses" is included, just for
Al.   So far I have never played it quite the way he thinks it should
go.

Like his predecessor, Al Robison is quite concerned when
conductors conduct without a score.   "Let me put them out anyway, "

he will say, and when I refuse, he mutters to himself, "Smarty pants," and as I walk onto the stage, his last admonition to me is, "Don't blow it, now!"

One of the most unusual and extremely valuable members of the Boston Symphony until his early retirement a few years ago was Rosario Mazzeo. For many years he wore two hats in the orchestra--that of bass clarinetist and personnel manager. "Rosy" was, and still is, a man of many talents. Possessor of an inventive mind, trigger brain, and great imagination, he was not only a fine and sincere musician, but he was also an inventor, expert photographer, writer, ornithologist, and public speaker. It was Mazzeo who devised the present pension plan of the Boston Symphony Orchestra, a plan which has been studied by insurance experts and pronounced eminently sound and which has been adopted by other orchestras in the United States.

When we first played Shostakovich's Fifth Symphony and it was discovered that a low F which Shostakovich wrote for the bass clarinet did not exist on the instrument. Rosy simply devised a new bass clarinet which did include the F. For many years he was dissatisfied with certain clumsy fingerings on the regular clarinet, so he invented a new instrument which simplified these fingerings, and today these instruments are manufactured by the Selmer Company, bearing the name "Mazzeo System." Rosy has among his friends most of the world-famous photographers, and he himself has had numerous exhibitions of his own pictures. Still a comparatively young man, Rosario Mazzeo lives today, in his so-called retirement, with his family in a beautiful rustic home on the side of a mountain in Carmel, California, writing, teaching, bird watching, photographing--all the fruition of a plan made years ago when he joined the Boston Symphony. And some day I hope to join him out there.

Symphony Hall may be a "temple of music," but it is also a plant which requires many people to run it efficiently. On the first floor in back of the box office a suite of rooms houses the treasurer, James Brosnahan, and his staff. Here every day, and some nights, a different kind of music is made, the music of computers making payrolls and paying bills.

The superintendent's office is in the basement just behind the stage door of Symphony Hall, and further back in the basement are the quarters of carpenters, painters, electricians, and maintenance men, all employed full time by the Boston Symphony. In addition there are the occasional workers who are called in for special jobs, like removing all the seats for various purposes--recording sessions, dances, Pops concerts, etc. These men, mostly derelicts from the surrounding saloons and barrooms, are rounded up by some secret grapevine system. Whenever they are needed, usually late at night after a concert, they seem to appear, ready and eager to work for a few hours, sometimes until 2:00 or 3:00 A.M., collect their few dollars, and go back into the night.

The four men in the box office at Symphony Hall are probably the rarest such men in the United States.   They are part of a
profession that prides itself on insulting customers, yet the B. S. O.
box-office staff, headed by Robert Carr, are polite, friendly, and
even helpful.   No dirty looks, no impatient snarls will you get from
behind the bars at the Symphony Hall box office.   Our men are
well-mannered and always scrupulously pleasant.

Before each Boston Symphony concert it has long been the
tradition for the manager or one of his assistants to stand in the
corridor and greet the familiar subscribers, many of them by name.
Back in 1881 when the orchestra began at the old Music Hall one
of the requirements of Henry Lee Higginson was that the musicians
were to greet the customers before the concert and to circulate in
the corridors during intermission, a practice which is followed to a
lesser degree even today, except that we now do it from choice.
One of the pleasant traditions of the Boston Symphony is that of
meeting our friends in the corridors of Symphony Hall during intermission.   Indeed, one of the reasons we dislike the new Philharmonic Hall in New York is the lack of opportunity for meeting people.   The orchestra seems to be barricaded backstage.   During an
intermission at Lincoln Center I once tried to meet a friend in the
corridor and got hopelessly lost.   The music library of the Boston
Symphony Orchestra on the second floor of Symphony Hall is the
busiest and probably most important room in the building.   It is the
nerve center of all musical activity.   Here surrounding our two librarians and their occasional assistants are shelves from floor to
ceiling containing the orchestra's scores.   On the left wall are the
thousands of numbered scores of works performed during the almost
ninety years of the orchestra's existence; and the right wall houses,
in neatly arranged cardboard containers, the players' parts.   All
around the room, in seeming disarray, there are piles of music--
music for next week, music for last week, music just arrived from
the publisher, music about to be shipped back to the publisher, and
music for the current week.   Yet in all this confusion nothing ever
gets lost; the players always find the right music on their stands at
rehearsals and concerts.

Since there are constant additions to the library, much of the
older material--music not often played--has been stored over the
years in another room on the third floor of Symphony Hall directly
above the library.   This "second library" now contains more music
than the regular library.   It has been estimated that the replacement value of all of the B. S. O. 's music would be well over a hundred thousand dollars.

One cannot discuss the B. S. O. library without thinking of the
late Leslie Rogers, librarian from 1912 until he died in 1953.
Rogers had the most infallible musical memory of all time.   It was
he who installed the system of locating in a moment any score or
piece of music.   He even remembered all of the thousands of scores
by number and all kinds of information about each piece.   For instance, if a conductor should ask him about a certain composition,

Leslie Rogers would say, 'Oh, yes. That was first played under
Nikisch in 1892. It has four movements. It takes thirty-six and a
half minutes, needs three flutes and piccolo, two oboes and English
horn, two clarinets and bass clarinet, four horns, two trumpets,
three trombones and tuba, tympani, two harps, and strings. "

Rogers went through all of the scores of music played before
his time and marked in each a record of performance, when and
where, which conductor, and in all subsequent scores he continued
these notations, adding the exact timings of each conductor. This
system has been continued by our present librarian, Victor Alpert.

Rogers carried on voluminous correspondence with composers, and whenever a famous composer came to Symphony Hall,
Rogers would try to talk with him about his music, with the result
that many scores bear observations and admonitions delivered by
the composer to Rogers. For instance, the score of Alexander
Glazunov's arrangement of Chopin's "Military Polonaise" contains
this remark. "'This orchestration is rotten!' says Glazunov, 'I did
it when I was a young man. ' LJR. " We used to make some drastic
cuts in Georges Enesco's "Rumanian Rhapsody" until Rogers showed
them to Enesco on one of his visits to Symphony Hall. Now the
score contains this admonition: "Enesco says no cuts are permis-
sible!--LJR"

Leslie Rogers' dedication to his job was unique. His whole
life revolved around 'his" library. He was at his desk from morning until night, and even at home he worked on library matters.
He was easygoing, slow, thorough, and very talkative. He loved
to reminisce about orchestral incidents, musicians, and composers
and always seemed to have time to talk, no matter how busy he
was. He was a close friend of Arthur Fiedler, who depended
largely on Rogers' advice and musical counsel. Occasionally when
things became quite hectic in the library (their desks faced) and
Leslie would begin one of his interminable stories, Arthur would
say good-naturedly, "Les, start in the middle. " Yet, in spite of
his easygoing ways, in all the years he was at the hall no mishap
ever occurred. The music was always ready for every rehearsal
and concert, the parts were legible and in good order, and all of
the conductors' wishes carried out.

One week in advance of each symphony concert the music is
available in the library for the players to examine and take home to
practice if necessary. Usually the four or five rehearsals for each
program are more than sufficient for each player to learn his part
technically. If, however, a particularly difficult piece is in the
offing for the following week, the player can practice it ahead of
time.

Even though I am a professional musician, I am constantly
amazed at the ability of an orchestra to read through for the first
time a thoroughly complicated and complex piece of music. Of
course, the success of a first reading depends largely on the

conductor, his own mastery of the music, and his technique of conveying his wishes to the orchestra.   One of the many reasons for which I admire Erich Leinsdorf is his ability to do just this.   He comes before an orchestra completely prepared, having worked out ahead of time the difficulties to be encountered.   I remember his preparation for Benjamin Britten's "War Requiem" in its first American performance in Tanglewood.   This is a large and complex work, requiring a good-sized orchestra, a smaller chamber orchestra, a large chorus, a children's choir, and three singers.   Leinsdorf had worked with each group individually before the first general rehearsal and so thoroughly had he prepared every detail that that rehearsal was practically a performance.   He had fitted the parts together like a fine watch.

Some conductors create a great deal of work for the librarians.   In an effort to bring out the salient qualities of a score, and in their never-ending search for proper balance, they constantly "edit" scores, reinforcing here, lessening there, changing chord structures, and driving the librarians to distraction.   It will probably come as a shock to some that most music written before the 20th century is not performed exactly as the composer intended. For instance, in the music of Beethoven and Brahms, and Schubert and Schumann, the winds are almost always doubled, except in the solo passages.   This is done for the sake of balance, to compensate for the larger number of strings used in our present-day orchestras, and our larger concert halls.   Also, some composers, like Schumann, for instance, were not great masters of orchestration, no matter how sublime their music, and conductors, over the years, have taken the liberty of re-orchestrating their scores, always with the intention of better presenting the composer's music.

Guest conductors with the B. S. O. usually send their own material with their own peculiar markings, editings, and bowings. Leopold Stokowski, for example, conducts his own version of Beethoven's Seventh Symphony with myriad changes and Stokowskian peculiarities.   He prides himself on being a nonconformist, indeed boasts of it, and if he did not have his own material, there would be constant pitfalls for the players.   For instance, Stoky makes sudden ritards and holds where you least expect them; he makes changes in articulation; he makes cuts; and he dislikes uniform bowing by the string players.   A friend of mine once asked me after a Stokowski concert if we had had enough rehearsals.   When I asked him the reason for his question, he said, "Well, none of you bowed together!"   I told him that was the way Stoky wanted it.   At this same concert we had played Stokowski's arrangement of Moussorgsky's music from "Boris Godunov," and the music was so badly marked up with penciled additions and corrections it was almost impossible to read.   During his visit with us we played this piece a number of times and each time it was different.   Sometimes his conducting indications bore no resemblance to what was in our parts.   Later he told our librarian he was still, after many years, arranging it and had not yet come to a satisfactory version.

The symphony librarian's work is arduous, exacting, and
time-consuming. The mere job of laying out the parts for each
player and putting them into the right folders for the right concert
consumes a great deal of time. He must work at least a week or
two ahead in preparing for rehearsals and must have the music
ready for each of the one hundred six players to look at ahead of
time.

How does the librarian lay out the music for rehearsals?
On a long table in the library he sets out each part, from left to
right, according to the way it is written in the conductor's score--
the higher instruments first, starting with the piccolo and going
down to the double basses. After he has laid out each part, he
goes on to the next piece, until the program is complete. He then
puts each music pile into its respective folder, the folders are
stacked on a wagon, and on Monday morning the wagon is wheeled
to the stage where the music is distributed to each stand. This
program is rehearsed all week for the regular Friday and Saturday
concerts, then becomes the program for the following Tuesday and
Thursday concerts, while a new program is prepared for the current week.

Each season the Boston Symphony prepares 24 different programs for its regular Friday and Saturday pairs of concerts. These
programs are then repeated at the Tuesday and Thursday series and
on the road trips. The Tanglewood concerts are also made up of
music played in the winter season, with some variations. So the
librarian is responsible for going over some one hundred or more
works each season. The Pops season of nine weeks presents additional, different chores for the librarian. Here the program
changes every night, and there are many more pieces on each concert.

Guest soloists often bring their own material (score and
parts), for each has his own musical wishes about his concerto. A
violinist, for example, who uses a certain kind of bowing to play a
phrase that is then repeated by all the violins in the orchestra
naturally wishes them to bow as he does.

A brand new work, premiered by the Boston Symphony, usually causes a great deal of excitement and extra activity in the library. I remember the first performance of the Samuel Barber
Piano Concerto which was commissioned for the opening of Philharmonic Hall in Lincoln Center. The soloist was the excellent American pianist, John Browning. The orchestra parts arrived in manuscript from the publisher, in good order, except that the last movement was missing, so we rehearsed only the first two movements
until the last movement came. Meanwhile, after each rehearsal
Barber worked in the library with the librarian, correcting mistakes
in the parts, for it seems that no matter how thoroughly a new
work is proofread by the copyist and composer, rehearsals always
disclose wrong notes--especially if the conductor has a keen ear.
Even after a composition has finally been printed (the publisher

usually waits to see what success a piece will have before he decides to print it), there are inevitable overlooked errors.

One of the important duties of a librarian is to examine all new orchestra parts as to their legibility. Occasionally the music is so badly written that it is refused performance until the publisher, or the composer, can supply better parts. It is a maxim among musicians that a clear score produces a clear performance, and vice versa; and a good librarian becomes, in a way, a watchdog for good performances.

Librarians are usually ex-players. Our present head librarian, Victor Alpert, is a fine violist who, occasionally when needed, plays in the orchestra. He is a man of extraordinary good nature and infinite patience who leads a hectic life trying to keep one step ahead of the conductor while acting as nursemaid to the musicians.

WHAT MAKES WOMEN'S ASSOCIATIONS RUN?*

Barbara Tucker

If you carry in your head the condescending image of women symphony volunteers as twittering members of the teacup and doily set, let me separate you from your thoughts. Since 1904, when the first volunteer committee pioneered in Philadelphia, dedicated women have made gargantuan efforts to develop audiences and income for symphony orchestras. Through fund raising, ticket selling, and education, women's committees have demonstrated their passionate belief that orchestras contribute both to the good name and to the cultural health of their communities.

Today we estimate a total of over 300 women's associations in the United States and Canada. There are two organizations of national unity: the Women's Association for Symphony Orchestras (formed in 1937) and our Women's Council of the League created in 1964. The first directly serves only the major orchestra group; however, both seek to solve mutual problems of all orchestras and to strengthen the symphonic cause at every level.

Who were these women activists whose influence in music has been so titanic and what explains their dedication? The female psyche seems convinced that music is thoroughly woven into the fabric of our life. Barbara Weisberger, artistic director of the Pennsylvania Ballet, defines it this way: "Art, more than other textures or dimensions of civilization, is all about human values-- yes, about love and freedom and dignity, but also about form and

*From Symphony News, April-May 1973. Copyright 1973 by the American Symphony Orchestra League. Reprinted by permission.

order, composition and discipline. " Belief in these values may be
why women are so unshakable in their financial and moral support
for cultural activity.   Certainly members of women's associations
have come from affluence, and have been well-educated, intelligent,
talented, and ambitious.   In one sense they might have been the
Germaine Greers and Kate Millets of their time, liberated enough
to devote weeks and months to their activities without trifling over
household details.   It must also be said that their husbands were
equally liberated and indulgent.   There is no doubt that this "caste"
system has affected the nature of symphony women's associations,
but there is also no doubt that the entire community has benefitted
indirectly.

        Things are pretty much the same today, somewhat modulated
perhaps.   There are unhappily many subtle restrictions imposed on
membership in these cultural conglomerates, and I see few real
trends toward democratization.   I still detect the countryclub, social register syndrome at work in many communities, placing the
"average American housewife" outside the pale.   That may be the
way things have to be, but imagine what forces would be unleashed
if symphony guilds went on a "Mother's March for Music" like
Muscular Dystrophy or the Heart and Cancer Funds.   Without sacrificing people-quality, we should consider a change in our organizational metabolism.   Let's seek out and ask all seriously interested
women to join us (in a comfortable structure) and work to improve
the situation of the performing arts through an increased collective
influence.   With over sixty million volunteers for all causes in the
nation, there are rumblings for law changes favoring a more dignified tax status for volunteers.   If generous deductions were allowed for hours donated, we could recruit more women for symphony work among those who are not in a position to forget that
time is money.

        It's been said that if it weren't for our energetic women's
associations, symphony orchestras would not exist, and this may
not be an exaggeration.   The dollar value of these donated women-
hours is incalculable.   No orchestra, even with full Federal support, could afford the exorbitant payroll if volunteer hours were
calculated at minimum wages, or the thousands of stamps, phone
calls, and services that are donated.

        Women's associations have written some stunning chapters in
fund raising.   Without question, symphony women in any given town
are first with the clever ideas and the fresh approaches.   For instance, they did the first big Rotogravure sections in many cities:
they saw dollars in the "designers showcase," and used sports
events to support symphonies--witness the trendy tennis and golf
matches of these past two years.   Profit from an individual project
may be as small as $100, or as much as $75,000 for a big Roto,
with annual amounts contributed in the quarter-millions.   The repertoire of money-making projects is almost inexhaustible: house
tours, antique shows, theater parties, special concerts, lecture
series, geranium sales, art shows, coffee concerts, and parties,

parties, parties.   (One must observe that we've exploited the human desire for social contact.)

Although women have not invaded management, boards of directors, or the artistic bastion to any extent, thousands are engaged in activities that make managers and board presidents look very, very good.   A clever manager will court his ladies with great charm, realizing that this superforce brings the orchestra association money, publicity, and a full house.   It's true that maintenance fund campaigns are usually masterminded by the "big boards," because men have better corporate connections than women and don't shy away from $1000 requests.   However, when a women's committee decides to solicit smaller individual contributions, the dollars extracted can be phenomenal.   I hope women will take greater interest in this extremely important phase of orchestra work. They can if boards take the time to indoctrinate properly.

If any constructive criticism can be made of this frenetic activity, it is this: ladies must take a more business-like view of their procedures.   Some managers worry about Nancy Hanks' P.E.T. Factor (People, Energy, Time) and wonder if certain projects are simply "wheel spinners."   Women's boards should review projects and seek help to train volunteers in sound business principle; hours spent must be equated with profit.   Wouldn't a $20,000 project with $19,000 worth of expenses make any CPA cringe?

Looking at future fund-raising trends, we find some changes already taking place as new life styles evolve.   Although fancy formal balls are still popular, they are quietly being dropped in many towns; not as many young people today want that kind of formality. Social events are more casual in out-of-the-way places (a bank, a boat, a zoo, a public garage ramp) and smart committees can guarantee dollars by pleasing a diverse crowd not bound by the social register.   Fashion shows are also beginning to cloy; instead we find "garage sales" netting $50,000, shows with superstars like Streisand, and relaxed parties with an admissions charge far lower than the old $100-per-couple.   Anyone in symphony work today must realize that the under-40 set refuses to be anything but relaxed.   This fact must affect almost everything we're doing.

That unglamorous responsibility, selling the house, is left pretty much to a selfless group of ladies who tackle the work like generals.   In Detroit, Cincinnati, Rochester, Pittsburgh, Phoenix, Seattle, and Milwaukee (the huge budgets), over 1000 women work on the renewal and new-subscriber campaigns each year, while towns like Huntsville, Green Bay, and Sioux City recruit under 500. Size of community is not the only factor in deciding the size of the effort; the work has to be done, so the women get busy willingly.

Once tickets are sold and fund raising planned, women's associations engage in programs that have social, promotional, and educational importance.   As the official "hostesses" for most orchestras, they plan press parties, receptions, and opening nights.

At the same time they sponsor open rehearsals, purchase musical equipment, work with youth and senior citizens, and commission new works. And, as if the list weren't long enough, women's guilds have been known to hold the conductor's hand, soothe a ruffled musician's brow, pay salaries, establish endowment funds, and deal with unions.

What we've created is miraculous, but we must run faster and faster just to stand still, if our orchestras are to survive rising costs and what might seem like a reordering of the universe. Orchestras have the potential to prevail, but laziness of mind, pat thinking patterns, and passive (almost automatic) attitudes work against us. I feel our symphony world is bogged down by its insularity and, in many communities, its concern for the preservation of the status quo--a delicious pastime. Women, because they have more time and are seriously involved, have a heavy responsibility to adopt forward, positive attitudes and change their philosophy in order to help bring our orchestras through the 20th century.

We must open up our ears and listen to the new sounds. I warn against a too conservative musical taste. Many orchestras stick to safe programming in order to please us. I agree with Boulez: "Music should not be summed up in a few masterpieces and frozen." Painters, dancers, and actors are not restrained by official inflexibility. Classics and masterpieces have their place, but there must be a continual progress toward new directions and new experiences that appeal to a wider taste and audience. Maybe semantics are at fault. The words "good music," "symphonic form," "masterworks," even "classical" itself, all imply a foreknowledge and pre-education rather than an enjoyment of music in all styles for its own sake. Critics, especially, are guilty of turning off audiences (before they can participate in the musical experience) with their excessive erudition.

And what about youth! Do we really know (or care) what they want to hear, or do we impose taste according to our own likes. We've always said, "Educate youth and the audience is assured." If that were true, surely more than five percent of our population should be filling concert hall seats. It might be revealing to assemble a panel of young people and have them tell us what is needed--what it is they like--and ask their advice about the future of music.

Since women are the most powerfully organized cultural bloc in the nation today, they should be influencing other changes as well, in education, in legislation, and in the new "era of professionalism."

As symphony women, we must be aware of what the school boards are up to. The arts are being ruthlessly budgeted out of education. Have you entertained your music supervisors and teachers, or invited your school board to a student concert? How about talking to your school superintendent about a joint effort in

curriculum enrichment, or assisting the Girl Scouts to earn their
Music Badges.   And don't neglect to investigate other forms of
education for conductors, musicians, and art administrators.   We
must also demand better professional programs at the college level,
or we are going to be short of leadership.

Women, too, should be informed about "cultural politics."
Even those of us who once shied away from government support,
assuming that it would dictate local arts policy, today understand
that tax dollars are an indispensable element in financial survival.
While focusing at the local level on your own problems, you must
be aware and active about national legislative matters.   Legislative
bodies need to know how you feel about built-in controls that may
limit artistic growth--special project funding against direct support
funding, for instance.   In order to form opinions on issues like
these, all women's associations should organize committees to keep
themselves abreast of legislative matters.

I've already suggested professional volunteer training.   But
evaluate your entire orchestra operation--attitudes, procedures,
programming, personnel, and your board structure.   Every organization is surfeited with dilettantes, social-climbers, and "cultural
dudes," but we're not in the business of social therapy.   We need
serious minded board members.   Robert Commandy, the San Francisco critic, has told us: "The Boards are still composed almost
exclusively, if not entirely, of individuals who are prominent and
generous patrons.   There is little or no representation of the public and taxpayer at large on Boards, nor of the highly knowledgeable and vitally interested community of professionals in the arts."
I wish to add that there are few of our dynamic women at the policy
level.

Women, with their staggering record of success in supporting
symphony orchestras, should work locally and unite nationally to
play a big part in the next evolutionary stage of arts support.   The
declining birthrate (now below replacement value) is actually stimulating; the population will be slightly older and more sophisticated,
with families smaller.   Transportation, medical services, adult
education, and entertainment will get major attention by 1985.   We
should be planning now to see that orchestras are in a position to
profit from and contribute to these improvements in our life.

We women represent a great nucleus of energetic thought
and can make the difference between public apathy and an expanded
market for musical services.   Our causes have been many--aboli-
tion, temperance, civil rights, anti-war, and suffrage.   Be assured
that the performing arts will continue to have our loyal commitment.

THE AMERICAN SYMPHONY ORCHESTRA LEAGUE*

Benjamin S. Dunham

The American Symphony Orchestra League, founded in 1942 by Mrs. Leta Snow of Kalamazoo, Michigan, is the nonprofit, research, coordinating, and service membership organization of the symphony orchestras of the United States and Canada. Located at Symphony Hill on the grounds of the Wolf Trap Farm Park in Vienna, Virginia, near Washington, D.C., the League maintains a national headquarters with a staff of 13 persons.

Beginning in 1950, when Helen M. Thompson was appointed Executive Secretary, League programs grew rapidly to match the expanding orchestra movement. When Mrs. Thompson left to manage the New York Philharmonic in 1970, the board of directors named as President Richard H. Wangerin, who served until 1973. Mr. Ralph Black was appointed Executive Director in December 1973.

The League was granted a federal charter by the United States Congress in 1962. The Charter (Public Law 87-817) states in Section 3 that it shall be the purpose of the corporation to:

I. Serve as a coordinating, research and educational agency and clearing-house for symphony orchestras in order to help strengthen their work in their local communities;

II. Assist in the formation of new symphony orchestras;

III. Through suitable means, encourage and recognize the work of America's musicians, conductors, and composers; and

IV. Aid the expansion of the musical and cultural life of the United States through suitable educational and service activities.

Symphony orchestra associations hold the voting memberships in the League--one orchestra, one vote. With one or two exceptions, all of the leading symphony orchestras of the U.S. hold membership, as well as hundreds of the smaller city and college orchestras. Individuals (conductors, composers, musicians, orchestra managers, music critics, musicologists, members of orchestra boards, women's associations, etc.), educational institutions, business firms, libraries, civic organizations, etc., hold associate (non-voting) memberships. The League is governed by representatives of member orchestra organizations, elected annually

by the membership at the National Conference.   Total membership
numbers approximately 2000.

The League's basic financing derives from dues and contributions paid by its members.   Membership dues for symphony orchestras are established on a sliding scale according to gross financial operations; the smallest budget orchestras pay dues of $50
annually; the largest $1000.   The League's impressive record of
self-support has elicited additional financing from business firms,
individuals, foundations and agencies for special projects and training programs.

Financial assistance for some of the League's projects has
been received from the Avalon, Ford and Rockefeller Foundations,
Martha Baird Rockefeller Fund for Music, Baldwin Piano Company,
ASCAP, BMI, and other organizations and individuals.

The League's staff and resources are on frequent call to
public and private organizations at national state, regional and community levels.   The League's counsel is sought in arts legislation
and administration, in philanthropic determinations, and in the expansion and extension of the music and arts industry.

Established services available to members include: field
analyses of orchestras; group and individual research and reports
service; liaison with national organizations and agencies; national
conferences; Symphony News (a bimonthly); concert attendance and
and performance data; orchestra management courses; a summer
Institute of Orchestral Studies (a study program for conductors,
composers, and instrumentalists at Orkney Springs, Va.); retirement income plan for conductors and administrative personnel; service memoranda on conducting and managerial openings; statistical
and financial data exchange; Talent Pool for orchestra musicians;
women's association regional workshops; and speakers bureau.

The League's initiatory work in many of these undertakings
has focused attention on needs and has provided research and
demonstrations that encouraged other organizations and foundations
to adapt concepts of manifest consequence to America's cultural
enrichment.

Under the National Endowment for the Arts of the National
Foundation on the Arts and the Humanities, the League has administered federal grants relating to commissions for composers and
technical assistance projects for symphony orchestras, including
field study analyses, consultation services, etc.   Under the Arts
and Humanities Program, U.S. Office of Education, the League
conducted an extensive study of symphony orchestra concerts for
young people.   [This study is reprinted in the present volume beginning on page 279.]   The project was carried out during the 1966-
1967 concert season and was jointly directed by the League and
American University, Washington, D.C.

THE AMERICAN FEDERATION OF MUSICIANS*

American Labor Staff

As a statement of overall findings, any exploration of the activities and aims of the American Federation of Musicians must reveal that the subject matter covers one of the most intriguing and unusual labor organizations in the world.

The planet's largest union of musicians, it's a composite of intriguing subtleties and enormous contrasts. Within its better than 650 locals the compensation to its individual artists ranges from the astronomical to zero. It's a market-place in which there is always room at the top and little at the bottom; one in which talent (and luck), not seniority, are the only keys to the big brass ring; an ever-changing arena where heartaches and frustration are the greater parts of the diet and where the bread of success is tasted by the very few.

It's a union which has practically nothing to say about its people's individual success or failure, for it is the public which ultimately determines who will make it and who will not--a public that worships or ignores with equal intensity and whose affections can no more be managed than the winds. It's a union with an overwhelming majority of members who are able and dedicated artists and who--unhappily--will remain anonymous in an emotional milieu that cries out for recognition; a union in which the triggering factors that catapult an individual into overnight stardom are still among the eternal mysteries; where the life expectancy for major earnings can be turned off as rapidly as it was turned on--a fact of existence that members understand and accept as part of their destiny. It's an extraordinary union because the talent of each artist contains a chemistry of its own.

Ponder this statistic: less than 17 percent of the musicians in the AFM are regularly employed--a fantastic figure, that would decimate most other labor organizations should that ratio ever come to pass. Another 35 percent may be partially or sporadically engaged in the field. Some 40 to 45 percent have not made a penny out of their musicianship for perhaps half a decade or more. Outlandish numbers--these--that make one wonder what must be the elixir that keeps the AFM so very much alive.

Ponder this second statistic: despite the oddities and frustrations inherent in its structure; despite the minimal percentage of opportunity acknowledged as the rule rather than the exception; despite the fact that some 40 percent of the members earn nothing out of their instruments, the Musician's Union--in the face of this multiplicity of negatives--incredibly--is a viable, robust organism

---

*From "Herman David Kenin: Pragmatist with a Soul," American Labor, vol. 3, no. 6 (June 1970), published by Master Communications, Inc., New York.

that not only is not shrinking, but actually has been expanding at a
growth rate of about 6000 new members a year over the past decade
to reach its present total in excess of 300,000--placing it among
the top two dozen Internationals in America today.

Like the bumble bee, which by every engineering calculation
should not be able to fly, The American Federation of Musicians
somehow confounds mathematics--and does.   There are part-time
AFM people whose major earnings are gained as steelworkers,
teachers, scientists, bank tellers and shoe clerks--the canvas is
as all-inclusive as there are job titles.   Of the 302,999 artists
presently in the labor organization, some 50,000 have full-time
schedules in their chosen profession.   About 125,000 are in the
part-time category.   The remainder pay their dues regularly but
make no income out of music at all.

A musician is apparently an individual who wants to be a
part of the musical scene whether he earns a living out of it or not.
In an economy where the dollar is warranted to be king, this is a
remarkable example of a spiritual adhesive, stronger than any deity
money has yet conceived.

THE MUSICIANS' UNION*

John H. Mueller

The origins of the musicians' union in America may be
traced to a small group of German musicians in New York who, in
1860, formed an association jestingly titled the Aschenbrödel Club
[i. e. , Cinderella Club]; "for the cultivation of the art of music . . .
and the relief of such members as shall be unfortunate. " But before many years, a more serious atmosphere prevailed, and its
members incorporated as the Musical Mutual Protective Union.
Meanwhile Baltimore, St. Louis, and other cities established similar clubs, which, in 1886, consolidated as the National League of
Musicians.   Somewhat squeamish about considering themselves
"laborers, " the League resisted the urge to affiliate with the
Knights of Labor and the American Federation of Labor until 1896,
when a small number of Western locals attended the A. F. of L.
convention in Indianapolis and laid the foundation for the American
Federation of Musicians.   The League soon capitulated and all locals
finally entered the Federation.   Its first president was Owen Miller
of St. Louis.   He was succeeded in 1900 by Joseph N. Weber of
Cincinnati.   In 1940 the presidential choice was J. C. Petrillo of
Chicago.

---

*From The American Symphony Orchestra, by John H. Mueller.
Bloomington: Indiana University Press, 1951.   Copyright 1951 by
Indiana University Press.   Reprinted by permission.

The greatest source of competition for orchestra jobs in our undeveloped country up to the time of the first World War were the finished players from Germany and, to a lesser extent, from France and other European countries. It was not until the early eighties that the unions reacted energetically to this hazard, provoked by the members of the traveling bands and orchestras, particularly from Germany, who would often desert their native organization and seek work in the American theatre and concert orchestras. On the occasion of the World's Fair at Philadelphia (1876), Chicago (1893), and St. Louis (1904), as well as in ordinary years, hundreds of musicians of every grade entered this country while American musicians stood by powerless and unemployed. In order to secure well-trained talent, American conductors not only abetted this policy, but actively recruited especially competent players from Europe and imported them on contract for the best positions in their orchestras. To counteract this peril to their security, the American unions at first attempted to invoke the Alien Contract Labor Law enacted by Congress in 1885 for the primary purpose of preventing industrial employers from inducing immigration by making contracts abroad. Since the law, however, expressly exempted professional persons, it was not immediately clear how the musicians' unions could find relief in its provisions. As early as 1885 Theodore Thomas, who had obtained many members for his famous orchestra in Europe, secured an injunction from a Judge Potter against the Musical Mutual Protective Union of New York which was at that time trying to prevent the Belgian Felix Bour, oboist, from taking his place in Thomas' New York orchestra. In 1893, the same union dispatched a protest to President Cleveland on the interpretation of the law which "allowed bands and orchestras to enter this country ... under the flimsy pretext of classing them as artists" [Musical Courier, March 15, 1893]. Even Arthur Nikisch, imported to conduct the Boston orchestra in 1889, and the opera composer Mascagni, who entered this country for a triumphant tour in 1902, were challenged, but merely evoked the expected ruling that they could legally enter to "pursue their calling." Taking no chance of being intercepted, Nikisch slyly landed in Boston after his arrival had been announced for New York.

As a deterrent to this foreign infiltration, the union had recourse to a contrivance of its own: the "six-months rule" concocted in 1882 by the New York local as a countermeasure against the engagement of Schreiner's German orchestra at Long Beach. It withheld union membership, and therefore employment, from a foreigner during the first half-year of residence in this country. However, when candidates for particular vacancies were clearly not available in the United States, the union usually waived this requirement. Such was the case in 1891 when Walter Damrosch, conductor of the New York Symphony Society, imported as his concertmaster the distinguished Russian violinist, Adolf Brodsky. It was this artist who had gained notoriety for his sensational première in Vienna (1882) of the now standard Tchaikowsky Concerto and occasioned one of the choicest examples of Hanslick's vitriolic style. Such a celebrity clearly merited the exemption accorded him.

Although many such instances of administrative tolerance could be cited, the unions could just as easily be aroused to drastic action.   Two years after the Brodsky episode Damrosch, perhaps feeling himself secure, invited the much less famous Danish cellist, Anton Hegner, to take the first chair in the same orchestra.   On Sunday evening December 17, 1893, shortly after his arrival in this country and without observing the "six-months rule," Hegner took his seat on the stage--a signal for the rest of the orchestra to walk off and desert their posts [Musical Courier, Dec. 20, 1893].   Pre-concert negotiations having failed, the union thus made its reply in the form of the first strike in American symphonic history.   The musicians had, of course, acted under union orders.   The chagrined Damrosch could only dismiss the audience with a few tactful and dignified remarks, of which he was always so eminently capable, and retire to the conductor's room.

This episode turned out to be a critical step in the establish-ment of the power of the union.   Although Theodore Thomas had successfully defied the union in 1885 on the principle of restraint of trade, Damrosch had weakened his case by previously recognizing the six-months rule in successfully requesting its suspension in the Brodsky case.   This time, however, the conductor for some reason chose to ignore the rule.   After some weeks of negotiation, during which Hegner had twice illegally appeared with the orchestra, the showdown was set for the Sunday concert in question.   The union had no choice but to follow through with the conventional fines for conductors and players: $20 for the first, and $10 for the second offense.   There followed several days of uncertainty before Dam-rosch conceded defeat and paid the fine.   The players, who had "acted under false assurances of the conductor" received remission of their fines.

There was some speculation that Damrosch after all may have enjoyed the last laugh.   The strike automatically abrogated all contracts, which he then renegotiated on more favorable terms to himself.   Some have even insisted that the whole strategy of the financially hard-pressed conductor was diabolically designed to that very end. †

Again, in 1905, the same Damrosch clashed with the union, and the rebuff assumed the still characteristic pattern.   He was fined a "nominal" amount of $1000 by Joseph N. Weber, president, for importing five French musicians for his recently reorganized orchestra--punitive action which was sustained at the May 1906 convention of the American Federation of Musicians.   Damrosch had proferred the usual claim that America could not supply his needs, while Weber had charged that the conductor had made no honest attempt to determine the availability of the supply in this country.   The offending French musicians were, however, mag-nanimously permitted to join the union since "these men came to this country in good faith and were not responsible for their em-barrassing predicament" [Musical Courier, May 30, 1906].

On the more fundamental issue, the courts had always ruled since 1890 that musicians were "artists" and not laborers, and therefore not under the protection of the Contract Labor Law. In 1902 Alexander Bremer, then president of the New York Musicians Mutual Protective Union, directed another futile protest to President Theodore Roosevelt, in which he again insisted that musicians were "wage earners entitled to the protection of the law as were other wage earners" [--, Dec. 3, 1902]. On the same principle, in 1927, Joseph N. Weber submitted a brief to the United States Department of Labor anent an imported orchestra at the Carleton Hotel, Washington, D. C. [--, Aug. 4, 1927].

The union interpretation really did not seem too inconsistent with the actual fact. Many of these musicians, either through incompetence or lack of broader opportunity, plied their music only as a part-time occupation, and simultaneously held cards as cobblers, stove-molders, saloon keepers, and what-have-you. In fact, Alexander Bremer was himself a minor official in the New York city government and his opponent in the election for the presidency of the M. M. P. U. in 1897 was a boss carpenter and violinist [--, Dec. 15, 1897]. They were a versatile lot in those unspecialized days, and their varied talents undoubtedly dulled their devotion to a single art and facilitated the spread of the pattern of unionization of the "artist" with the artisan. Nor did those who were fortunate enough to gain their entire livelihood in music always scale the exalted heights of artistry, for there is nothing necessarily elevating or divinely inspiring in fiddling, night after night, in the squalid pits of cheap theatres, or in scraping through the popular rounds and dance tunes of the day. Such players quite justifiably felt themselves more akin to the hack worker than to the symphony artist, whose dignity might have inhibited crude protests.

But there were some symphony players who were conscious of a higher tradition, and who often winced a bit when "contemplating the fitness of the Bach and Beethoven interpreters, hod carriers, bricklayers and longshoremen forming a union to strengthen our position, while architects, painters, composers, actors and poets live a life of weary isolation. " They feared that too close an affinity between symphony men and the run-of-the-mine theatre and dance musicians would aid the incompetent in rising, to jeopardize their own position and thereby depress the relative opportunities of the better-class musicians by placing all on one level [Musical Courier, Oct. 7, 1896].

When it was not a question of importations from abroad, the local unions endeavored to protect their jobs from migrations from other cities. Because of the principle of local autonomy in the Federation, union cards are not normally transferable from one local to another. Hence there is always a union-imposed barrier to free migration which constitutes a vexatious restraint to the conductor or local management in strengthening his orchestra by bidding in the national market. Here too, however, amicable agreements are often made for the good of the order, although strife and

friction were common, especially during the period of the founding
of the permanent orchestras a half-century ago.   When Theodore
Thomas was engaged to organize the Chicago orchestra in 1891, he
literally transferred almost his entire New York orchestra of sixty
men to Chicago as the nucleus for the new body.   In retort to union
protests, Thomas insisted: "I shall select my players where I find
them ... New York ... or Europe....   If there are good men in
Chicago I will use them" [Otis, Chicago Symphony (see Bibliography)
p. 30].   Van der Stucken in Cincinnati; Scheel in Philadelphia; Hen-
schel and Gericke in Boston; Gabrilowitsch in Detroit; Rothwell in
Los Angeles--all these conductors encountered this normal, but im-
potent, impulse on the part of the local musician to protect his job
as it came in conflict with the principle of artistic supremacy as
entertained by conductor, civic committee, and guarantors.   On this
front, too, the union lost its battle, for the modern orchestra had
now reached a kind of "industrial stage" in which musical efficiency
was the controlling law, and generally had priority over job security.

The displaced personnel of these early orchestras, and their
public sympathizers, of which there were many, fought grimly and
sometimes "split the community" in their pathetic efforts to protect
the "local boys. "   The usual promise that "all competent musicians
will be retained, " was scant consolation to the mediocre majority.
In extenuation of the demands of the perfectionist, most of the local
orchestras had been mere "sandlot" affairs whose strength lay not
in their musical ideals, but in social and professional companion-
ship.   In the cooperative manner, they usually divided the modest
"take, " which was never considered anything but a pleasant source
of extra income, much less remunerative, but more exhilarating
than the tedious theatre routine and humdrum teaching.   But now
the orchestra was to be organized from above, with the membership, and even the conductor himself, put in the role of salaried
employees.   At last, the conductor could choose his men rather
than the men the conductor.   Although the union has preserved certain safeguards against arbitrary and exploitive tactics, nothing is
now more generally conceded than the essential and responsible
right of the conductor in the selection of personnel.

With the problems of basic employment settled in principle,
there is still the whole area of "working conditions" and their en-
forcement--including wage scales, hours, and the host of details--
which are, of course, subject to continuous negotiation between union and management.

Although it was not until after World War I that negotiations
on salaries and working conditions became momentous, periodic
tiffs between union and orchestral management were not unknown
before that.   Early in 1904, while rehearsing the new and difficult
score of "Symphonia Domestica" under Richard Strauss, who was
then making his first tour of the United States, the members of the
Wetzler orchestra of New York walked off the stage when the contractual rehearsal time had expired.   This episode, which some

have condemned as a rude and inhospitable gesture toward a distinguished foreigner, incidentally could not have befallen anyone with
greater poetic justice, for no musician and composer had achieved
a more deserved reputation for calculated negotiation with musicians
and publishers than the fabulously successful Richard Strauss.

By 1920 the unions were entering into a period of increased
bargaining power, and their demands for revision of salary scales,
stimulated by the postwar inflationary spirals, threatened the very
existence of some of the major orchestras.   This bargaining power
was enhanced by the relative scarcity of musicians during that postwar period.   Not only was the competitive European supply cut off
by more stringent immigration laws, but the fashion for symphony
orchestras was spreading to the Middle West and the Pacific Coast
where newly founded, or reinvigorated, organizations were bidding
for the limited supply of competent players.   During this period of
Coolidge prosperity even moving-picture theatres were adding pit
orchestras of symphonic proportions to the sumptuous décor of
their cinema palaces.   Clearly, it was a propitious time for unions
to press their advantage.   And this they did, to the great distress
of the philanthropists whose economic surpluses, once the rich economic topsoil from which the arts had extracted their nutriment,
were now being washed away by the slow but fatal erosion of the
changing industrial climate.

Whether or not the contending parties fully realized the ruthless drift of events in which they were helplessly dragged along,
there is nothing in the light of contemporary or subsequent developments which would suggest that either side was bluffing.   H. H.
Flagler, the guardian angel of the New York Symphony Society, was
irked by the "continued attempt by hampering restrictions and purely
commercial methods to destroy artistic projects," and warned that
"if the worse element prevails I see but two courses open, (1) to
give up altogether the maintenance of the symphony orchestras, or
(2) to found nonunion orchestras" [Musical Courier, May 5, 1921].
In Chicago in the spring of 1923, the union threatened to strike "in
the fall. "   These ominous soundings subsided only when 'both sides
compromised. "   This was the same orchestral management that,
in 1928, had already notified the musicians that "they were free to
seek employment elsewhere" when the differences were again patched
up.   Orchestras had folded up before.   Cincinnati was dark from
1906 to 1908 when the management, even in those early days, met
with "labor troubles. "

As is usual in a democracy, both sides appealed for aid and
comfort to the public conscience, each presenting its own case in
the best possible light and that of its opponent in the worst.   The
"exorbitant and shortsighted demands of the union" were set off
against the selfless generosity of the philanthropists, whose bene-
factions to society were made difficult, and even impossible, by the
aggressive and myopic "commercial" motives of the players' union.
As for the musician, he in turn considered himself worthy of his
hire.   He had a great investment in his long years of concentrated

study and in the acquisition and maintenance of a costly instrument and delicate skills. The legitimately expected return on this investment was rendered precarious by the brevity of the concert season, the uncertainty of the yearly contracts, and the postwar inflation. All this obviously argued a sympathetic review of the player's plight.

This clash between the imperious demands of rising costs and the dissipation of available philanthropic resources assumed national proportions, and in the minds of some leaders required consultation on a national scale. In February 1924, Clarence H. Mackay, who had recently become chairman of the board of the New York Philharmonic, invited the patrons of about a dozen major orchestras to New York for the specific purpose of discussing the now universally experienced mounting deficits. Many of the leading philanthropists were present: Van Rensselaer (Philadelphia), Hamill (Chicago), Carpenter (Minneapolis), Flagler (New York Symphony), together with Juilliard, Kahn, and Marshall Field, of the host orchestra. The managers, among whom were Judson (of New York and Philadelphia), Mrs. Hughes (Cleveland), Mrs. Caroline Estes Smith (Los Angeles), and others, joined in the deliberations. Some of their plans to reduce deficits had no durable significance, but the informal organization, expanded to meet developing needs, still exists and is convoked annually for the discussion of common problems.

There was one orchestra that did not avail itself of the opportunity to participate in the council on the pending crisis. Boston, which had operated the best of all major orchestras, and the only one on the open-shop principle, apparently felt no need for collaboration and, in fact, might even have pointed up the embarrassing anachronism of its position if it had taken part in the sessions. During all these decades, when union and management were learning to live together to promote their common ends, the Boston orchestra had been able to cultivate a splendid isolation from the inexorable trends.

There were several factors that contributed to the amazing self-reliance of the Boston organization. First, the paternalistic foresight of its owner had provided for a long and profitable season. Not only was the winter season of 24 pairs of concerts then the longest of any in the country, but the famous "pops," founded in 1885, and the Esplanade concerts, beginning in the late twenties, guaranteed to many a member almost full-year employment, and at a high wage scale. The Boston orchestra never stopped playing! Dignified supplementary income from teaching and summer resort contracts was facilitated by the universally acknowledged prestige of the orchestra. Consequently the musicians were somewhat less receptive to alarms of exploitation than they might have been under average circumstances. A large proportion had been imported expressly for membership in this orchestra and so felt a loyalty to it.

Over and above this whole scene, there hovered the ominously possessive philosophy of the guarantor, who, until 1918, assumed full personal responsibility for the economic security of the orchestra, and kept its membership dependent on the pleasure of owner and conductor. This watchfulness against any discontent must have been a powerful deterrent to overt expression of any latent restlessness. When, in 1903, murmurs of revolt became audible, Higginson rendered his usual obbligato in his typical unambiguous manner: "No one will interfere with my orchestra. If there is interference I will abolish it and declare publicly who is at fault and why it was done" [Musical Courier, Nov. 4, 1904]. A much more serious crisis was weathered in 1920 when, as a result of a strike, the orchestral board dismissed the concertmaster and about thirty members of the orchestra in a desperate attempt to halt the inevitable.

But finally, when the scepter had dropped from the hands of the ruler, the orchestra lost its independence through a series of squeeze plays maneuvered by Mr. Petrillo: his refusal to allow Bruno Walter and Carlos Chavez to conduct the nonunion Boston orchestra; his threat to prevent Koussevitzky from accepting invitations from union orchestras; his threat to blacklist the auditoriums where Boston might appear. Most alarming of all was the imminent danger of interference with broadcasting and recording, which would have struck at the very subsistence of the orchestra. Finally, enmeshed in the larger world of affairs, the management could only capitulate in December 1942, after having wrung from Petrillo certain minor concessions.

All symphony orchestras are now fully organized and, in that sense, the union "problem" may be written off as "solved. " Harassed more than ever by deficit financing, management still resents many detailed restrictions imposed on its freedom to act in its own interests, and occasionally accuses the musician of not thinking beyond the tip of his bow. On the other hand, any idealism which the practitioner of the "queen of the arts" may have inherited from the 19th century, and any professional enthusiasm which formerly sustained him in the old cooperative days, must now be tempered by the realities of the competitive age. Although the symphony artist may at times still feel the discomfort of being yoked with the popular musician, they all present as solid a front as do the members of any other union.

†Mrs. Adolph Brodsky, the wife of the concertmaster, places this interpretation on the incident. She asserts that Damrosch deliberately maneuvered the musicians into a strike for the purpose of voiding their contracts, which would then be renewed on easier terms for himself. See Mrs. Adolph Brodsky, Recollections of a Russian Home (2d ed. , London: Sherratt & Hughes, 1914), pp. 187-202.

THE INTERNATIONAL CONFERENCE
OF SYMPHONY AND OPERA MUSICIANS*

Henry Shaw

The International Conference of Symphony and Opera Musicians was formed in 1961, the culmination of a meeting held by the
delegates of 20 United States and Canadian major orchestras. Its
stated purpose was to "promote the welfare of, and make more rewarding the livelihood of the orchestral performer, and enrich the
life of our society. " At the inception of the organization, the majority of the major orchestra musicians enjoyed little better than a
half year of employment and a yearly salary that was close to sub-
sistance level. Of equal seriousness was the fact that very few
orchestras were permitted the right to ratify agreements entered
into by their union representatives. These union-management negotiations traditionally resulted in token salary increases without concerning themselves with the fundamental problems which prevented
symphony orchestra musicians from earning a living wage.

ICSOM, then, undertook the responsibility of addressing itself to the aforementioned problems, along the way affiliating itself
with the American Federation of Musicians, becoming a special
"conference" within the framework of that organization. A yearly
conference was held. Delegates of an ever increasing number of
member orchestras, including now several metropolitan orchestras,
tackled an agenda with the following prime objectives: representation of orchestra committees at the bargaining table and the right
of the general membership to ratify agreements; establishment of a
Strike Fund; 52-week contracts; establishment of meaningful pension
plans; exchange of information on the qualification of conductors and
development of programs within member orchestras in support of
Government financial aid for the Arts.

By 1973 virtually all major orchestras were accorded the
privilege of contract participation, of ratification and in many cases
the choice of legal counsel at the bargaining table. A Strike Fund
had been established and year-round employment was a fact in almost a dozen major orchestras, with others approaching that mile-
stone. A major goal, a yearly living wage was commonplace.
Between 1963 and 1971 the average annual salary of symphony musicians had increased from $4147 to $9893.

The glue that holds the organization together during the playing season is the organization newsletter, Senza Sordino (Italian for
"without mute") which publishes bimonthly and is distributed to
every member as well as to libraries, government agencies, critics,
management personnel and union officials throughout North America.

*Used by permission of the author, member, Cincinnati Symphony
Orchestra, and editor, Senza Sordino, official publication of the
ICSOM.

Bulletins are distributed when quick dissemination of information is
necessary and orchestra contracts are distributed by the ICSOM
Rapid Communication Center in Washington.   The past dozen years
have been significant in that professionals who work for public institutions and non-profit organizations have been forced into a militant
posture to solve their economic problems.   Hospital workers, teachers and symphony musicians fall into this category.   The emergence
and development of ICSOM was the musicians' response to a basic
need for rectification of grievances brought about by years of community complacency.   ICSOM now numbers 38 orchestras and is a
recognized third force which with unions and management promises
to shape the future of the profession and the institution.

MUSIC PERFORMANCE TRUST FUNDS*

MPTF Staff

        Music Performance Trust Funds is a non-profit, public ser-
vice organization created and financed by the Recording Industry under agreements with the American Federation of Musicians.   It is
the largest single sponsor of live music in the world.

        MPTF spends its funds to provide performances of free,
live, instrumental musical programs throughout the United States
(including Puerto Rico and the Virgin Islands) and Canada, on occasions which will contribute to the public knowledge and appreciation
of music in connection with patriotic, educational and public activities.

        In the early 1940's professional musicians found that the
popularity and widespread use of phonograph records posed a threat
to live music performances before live audiences.   To counteract
the decrease in the number of live performances, the American
Federation of Musicians in 1948 made agreements with the producers of phonograph records, electrical transcriptions, and later,
television film producers and distributors to establish the Music
Performance Trust Funds.   A fixed formula of contributions was
established, based on the sales volume of the product.   Disburse-
ment of the funds since its inception has totaled over $100 million.

        All programs sponsored by MPTF must be free and open to
the public so that all may enjoy good, live music.   Typical projects
are performances at schools, hospitals, parks, playgrounds, civic
ceremonies, band concerts, parades, senior citizens' homes, dances
for young people, deprived-area street shows, and performances of
music of particular artistic significance.

---

*Reprinted by permission of Kenneth E. Raine, Trustee, Music
Performance Trust Funds.

Administration

MPTF is administered by a completely independent trustee, appointed by the U. S. Secretary of Labor. The present Trustee, Kenneth E. Raine, was appointed in June 1970. Only the trustee's office can approve projects. No AFM local or agency may commit the trustee without his prior approval.

Generally, the trustee prefers that expenditures should be divided into thirds for: (1) music of cultural or educational intent; (2) music at youth dances, in hospitals and other institutions; and (3) music at band concerts and civic celebrations.

MPTF does not provide welfare benefits to musicians, nor is it intended to serve as an unemployment fund. All performers work for their pay. MPTF pays for the services of union and non-union players at the same rate--the union scale prevailing at the place of performance. Expenses connected with the performances, other than the pay to musicians, are usually paid by co-sponsors who organize or request the performances.

To enlist the assistance of co-sponsors and to reduce administrative costs over the wide territory served by MPTF, recommendations for projects are invited and received from local affiliates of the American Federation of Musicians, and from civic, community, and educational organizations, and each recommendation is individually reviewed and approved by the trustee's staff before the project is authorized.

The funds do not accumulate and, as nearly as possible, are expended in the year following their receipt. Any money allocated but not spent during the year is returned to general funds for allocation in subsequent years. Ninety percent of the available funds are allocated (according to a predetermined formula) to approximately 650 Local areas of the United States, Canada, Puerto Rico and the Virgin Islands. The remaining ten percent, the National Reserve Fund, is spent without reference to local allocation, and is devoted principally to events transcending local significance.

MPTF seeks new programs to support, new co-sponsors to join in its work, new audiences to share in the public benefits it provides.

In the Past

Since 1948, MPTF has allocated and spent over $100 million for live music. About $9 million is currently spent each year for approximately 360,000 separate musical presentations provided free to the public. MPTF presentations cover the musical gamut from chamber music to rock. MPTF has made it possible in the last two decades for literally millions of people to enjoy many thousands of live musical performances without charge. MPTF is the only source of live music in many areas of the United States and Canada.

MPTF disperses about 550,000 individual payments each year to more than 400,000 musicians for their performances. MPTF also gives student awards and honorariums to encourage instrumental proficiency by pupils of high school age; further information can be obtained from local AFM affiliates.

In the Future

Types of performances MPTF will sponsor:

A marching band for a community parade.

A symphony orchestra for a summer night park concert.

A rock group for a teenagers' dance in the school gym.

Music for senior citizens' activities.

Strolling players for patient therapy at veterans and other hospitals.

Professional players for school music appreciation courses.

A jazz group for a block party.

A string quartet for museum or library presentations.

Musical programs at shopping centers, if the public interest is served without commercial advantage.

Entertainment for shut-in convalescents if their welfare is the primary concern.

Country music in a playground.

Musical accompaniment for events of national or local patriotic or community significance.

A basic guideline is that the Trustee will consider a recommendation for a grant for any occasion which will provide education, culture, entertainment or therapy, and where no commercial advantage is served.

This guideline does not automatically rule out private convalescent homes, for although they are managed for a profit, the patients are usually confined to the home, and so the concert must be taken to them, if the performance is free, reasonably open, preferably co-sponsored by the owner, the trustee will consider a recommendation.

Commercial shopping centers, which have become in effect community centers, may also be suitable sites for an MPTF sponsored program, if the performance is not located where some particular commercial tie-in is suggested. The public interest must be served, and if this is the primary consideration the expenditure may be proper.

No solicitation of voluntary contributions may be made at any MPTF performance either at the entrance or exit of the place where the music will be played. No prior payment in cash or in kind may be imposed as a condition of entry. Members of the public who wish to attend must always feel free to enter without embarrassment.

MPTF will pay for religious music, but only when the premises are open to the public without any charge, when the primary purpose of the program is musical, not religious, and is not a part of a religious service. Again, the public must feel free to attend without feeling that the program was created for a special interest group.

A civic symphony, which is composed of a nucleus of union performers augmented by a larger number of performers who are not union members and who participate for love of music, may request recommendations from the trustee for a performance. If the recommendation is approved, the trustee will pay at union scale, for services rendered by the non-union performers. These payments are made in the expectation that the non-union players will contribute what they receive from the trustee to aid the maintenance of the symphony organization. Such organizations applying for funds should be legally established and declared tax-exempt by the state in which they reside.

Performances MPTF Cannot Support

The Trust Agreements do not permit grants-in-aid or contributions directly to any organization. They permit only payments at local union scale to individual instrumental performers for services actually rendered at a public performance to which no admission charge of any kind is made.

MPTF will not pay for incidental music for a business or union meeting, charity drive or fund raising; a picnic or reception to be attended primarily by members of any closed organization such as church, fraternal order, trade organization, or the like. Nor will MPTF pay for music for partisan political rallies or for parties organized to honor or benefit any professional athletic organization.

MPTF will provide music for a dance if it would serve some useful public interest, but not when the musicians perform merely for a social function.

THE SILENT SPRING OF OUR SYMPHONIES*

Amyas Ames

There is more than one way to kill. A lake or a river can
be killed by the outpouring of our wastes; birds--the singing of the
oriole--can be stilled by our enthusiastic use of DDT; we can kill
music by starving our orchestras, leaving our cities dreary places
indeed. We can surround our cities with great traffic interchanges
that cost $25- to $50-million apiece and not realize until it is too
late that, for a fraction of the cost of a small one of these, we
are depriving our people, committing them to lives without music.
The silent spring came inadvertently. In the same way, music and
dance can be stilled without intent.

That the nation's symphony orchestras are in serious trouble
was dramatically demonstrated a few months ago when the presidents of the ninety principal orchestras of this country were invited
to Philharmonic Hall in New York to discuss their plight. Almost
to a man, these busy, public-spirited men from as far away as
Hawaii, California, Texas, Florida, Maine, and Alaska dropped
whatever they were doing and gathered. After two days of discussion, they formed a "Committee-of-the-Whole" and became united
for the first time as a result of desperate crisis. They prepared
testimony to present to Congress; an appeal for support to the National Endowment for the Arts; a request that, as a people, we
support the performing arts of this country so that they may endure.
Here briefly is what they are saying:

When we speak of the nation's symphony orchestras we are
talking about some 1400 different organizations, located in every
state, in practically every city of more than 50,000 people.

We are speaking of a total audience of at least twenty million men, women, and children who attend more than 11,000 concerts a year.

We are speaking of aggregate expenditures totaling nearly
$100-million a year and a veritable army of musicians and sup-
porters--contributors and civic-minded men and women who serve
the symphony. Nearly every member of our Congress has a symphony orchestra of larger or smaller activity "back home."

---

*From Saturday Review, February 28, 1970. Copyright 1970 by Satur-
day Review Co. Reprinted by permission. Although verification of
Mr. Ames' projected figures for these "90 principal American symphony orchestras" is difficult to obtain, the 1974 study, The Finances
of the Performing Arts, sponsored by the Ford Foundation, indicates
that there may be a fivefold increase of outside funds needed by 1980
if the activities of nonprofit orchestras, opera companies, theaters
and dance groups are to be as available to the public then as they were
in the late 1960's.   [See table, p. 382.]

Our symphony orchestras serve their communities in many ways.   They are the center of the musical world in their home communities.   The musicians of these orchestras teach in the schools, colleges, and music institutes.   The truly talented young of the area come to them to learn.   The orchestra musicians organize chamber music ensembles that play throughout their communities.   In some areas, orchestras serve as the sponsoring and financing body for the local opera society (as in San Antonio) or as the parent organization for the local community chorus (as in Cleveland and Chicago, and many smaller cities).   Symphony orchestras sponsor and give financial help to the local youth orchestra in their city.   They search out and give awards, scholarships, and performing opportunities to young soloists and composers in the area.

Many of the orchestras' women's auxiliaries finance youth concerts.   In Charlotte, North Carolina, the women actually have driven school buses in order to enable children to get to concerts.   In Huntsville, Alabama, the symphony women go into the classrooms to help hard-pressed teachers acquaint the children with the music they are about to hear.

Some of our orchestras have taken their concerts to Indian reservations.   They have played in hospitals, in ghettos, even in prisons; they have performed noon-day concerts in industrial plants and morning concerts in shopping centers to make it easier for young mothers with small children to attend.   Other orchestras have organized jazz groups in order to serve varied tastes and interests.   One orchestra presents a series of sacred music concerts each year.   Another piles onto buses, traveling to small, isolated mountain communities, and plays concerts in any kind of building large enough to accommodate the musicians and an audience.

A generation ago, the subscription concert was the main activity of our orchestras.   Now 70 per cent of the orchestras' activities are public service in nature.   Last year, they gave 3500 concerts for children and students, and another 4000 concerts for the general public, in parks and on tours.   Many were educational or special in nature.   They sponsor and present hundreds of small ensembles from the orchestra personnel giving performances in public schools--often in individual classrooms.

So, the orchestras of this country have greatly expanded their public service and educational work, their playing for people, but they have received little help.   Who pays for this new generation of concerts--for the young, in parks, on tours?   The loyal supporters have done so in the past and will continue to bear more than their share, because they love music and want it for themselves and for their children.   But the public service concerts cost money, and inflating costs increase the burden of support beyond what the local loyal supporters can bear.   Without help from government, music--and the performing arts in this country--will wither.

The 90 orchestra presidents analyzed their operating problems, and presented figures to the Congressional committee. The significance of these figures can best be understood by scanning the following table.

90 Principal American Symphony Orchestras

	Total Expenses	Cash Loss
1963	$28,820,500	$ 169,800
1969	66,794,500	5,215,800
1972 (est.)	87,090,000	13,222,000

Looking ahead to the year 1972 [see footnote p. 380], when the Ford Foundation grants that have so helped the orchestras will terminate, these figures show that:

Total Expenses will be up 30 per cent (to $87,090,000). The greater part of the expense of orchestras is the salaries of the musicians. There is every reason why the musician should have his compensation comparable to wages of other sectors of our society, and rising as those wages rise.

Income will be up 20 per cent (to $40,405,000). This figure includes income from tours, recording and broadcasting fees, etc., as well as ticket sales. Ticket prices cannot be raised much, for to do so would mean excluding large segments of the public--higher prices result in lost listeners; the number of seats cannot be increased; the competition from foreign orchestras limits income from record sales. Most important, the orchestras are undertaking many additional public service programs that produce little income. So, income will cover only 46 per cent of operating expenses in 1972. Symphony orchestras are confronted by the same problem that schools and colleges have had to contend with--to raise tuition enough to cover good salaries for educators would close them. And so with symphony orchestras: without new support many orchestras will have to disband.

Contributions will be up only 20 per cent (to $33,463,000). There is clear evidence that the giving by individuals cannot keep up with inflating costs, and may even be sharply restricted by rising prices and changes in the tax laws. Contributions by government are virtually microscopic when compared to either what other countries of the Western world do, or what we do for other interests of our people.

Cash Loss will rise 150 per cent. The present loss of $8,500,000--a cash loss that threatens bankruptcy for some orchestras--is jeopardizing the existence of many orchestras across the country. The loss of an estimated $13,222,000 in 1972 will begin to silence living orchestra music throughout the land.

The bitterness of the fruits of inflation is evident in these figures. Corporations can and do raise prices as wages rise; the government increases taxes to pay the inflating costs for everything it buys. Orchestras cannot raise prices and find the very foundation of their support--the generous giving of individuals--undermined by the effect of rising taxes and prices. Looking ahead to 1972, each of our most famous orchestras will probably have to find some $500,000 of new money in that year alone. That is not their doing, but the act of our society. We can kill them with inflation.

The amount of federal aid so urgently needed to maintain the orchestras' various activities is small indeed when compared to the practices long followed by other governments. Howard Taubman, the distinguished critic-at-large for the New York Times, in his report on symphony orchestras abroad points out that the orchestras of Munich, Berlin, Amsterdam, and the Hague are given annual government subsidies of approximately $1,200,000 each--or more than 75 per cent of their total budgets. The four London orchestras and the Manchester orchestra are supported by government grants of about 20 to 30 per cent of their total budgets.

In Austria, a high government official told Mr. Taubman: "The arts are felt to be a great, perhaps the greatest, adornment of the nation's image--for itself and for the rest of the world. "

And Taubman goes on: "It cannot be too strongly stressed that the main objectives of the subsidies are to keep the orchestras in existence and to insure that their quality will not be diminished. ... One might speculate that there might be no orchestras at all in most countries without [them]--and certainly not distinguished ones. "

The financial comparison between Europe and America is not exact, inasmuch as we operate under different circumstances--but the spirit is largely the same. It is clear that the American orchestras must have government support. They have had remarkable success in finding the funds necessary to keep operating, but a whole new approach and development of a new set of priorities in this country are necessary to make these efforts successful in the future.

The request of orchestra presidents is not that our federal government assume responsibility for 75 per cent of the total operating costs of symphony orchestras as is customary in Europe, nor even for 20 per cent of the costs as is done in England. But rather that our federal government assist the orchestras in an amount less than 10 per cent of the current gross costs of our orchestras' operations--58.5 million, an amount barely equivalent to the costs of one-third of a modern traffic circle.

Furthermore, the orchestra presidents recommend that federal funds should be used to support only those orchestras that

(1) maintain a high level of earnings and local voluntary contributions for annual operations; (2) meet reasonable qualifying standards of operations and management; (3) maintain broad-based programs of cultural and musical services for the general public.

Two hundred years ago, the people of this country fought for independence. Now we fight not only to save our rivers, our lakes, the very air we breath, but also to save our music. This must be part of the drive of the people of this country to enrich the total life of its citizens and to work "toward a reflection of the goodness and grace of the human spirit. " The arts, like nature, are more part of us than we think. Why else would people in twelve hundred cities, in every state of the union, organize and struggle to support symphony orchestras?

It is time to act--to stand up and be counted as a backer of the arts. What we ask is well within the power of our government to give.

Q. WHO SUBSIDIZES THE ARTS IN AMERICA?
A. The Artist.   Q. Who Else?*

R F Illustrated Staff

Some civilizations have been quick to recognize the usefulness of the arts; America has been slow.

Great artists have been produced in America since colonial times. People have expressed their vitality in music, dance, theater, painting, poetry, philosophy and architecture with an irrepressible genius. But it was not until World War II that the country became a self-conscious art-and-artist producer. Overnight--between about 1936 and 1942--America became a haven for some of the most distinguished composers, painters, writers, scientists and thinkers of Europe. These men and women found work in American universities and businesses and, through their influence, a culture which had become American-conscious suddenly became international-conscious. Arnold Schoenberg, the creator of the all-pervasive 12-tone system of music composition, and his contemporary, Paul Hindemith, to name only two, stemmed the tide of American composers who were bent on "being American"--Virgil Thomson and Aaron Copland among others--and changed forever a frontier-style of composing which included jazz and other "folk" elements.

In art and architecture, the Bauhaus School threatened to take over. In theater there was Piscator and the great Max Reinhardt. Only in dance was America strong against a cultural

*From R F Illustrated, vol. 1, no. 2 (February 1973), published by the Rockefeller Foundation. Reprinted by permission.

invasion, for modern dance was an indigenous art form like film
and jazz.   But if American lost its twang, it gained at least a
nascent sense of world culture and along with that a new attitude
toward the arts.   No longer, after the war, was America second
to Europe in anything--except, perhaps, experience.

Then several things happened that were to change America's
view of the arts in an irreversible way.   In the early 50's, civic
leaders in New York began meeting with leaders of the Metropolitan
Opera.   The Opera needed a new home.   Carnegie Hall, the home
of the New York Philharmonic, was threatened with demolition; the
orchestra, too, needed a home.   The solution was to build homes
for both, adjacent to each other, and bring in perhaps the New York
City Center, which had also for some time needed adequate stage
and audience facilities.   In 1956, the Rockefeller Foundation granted
assistance to the new Lincoln Center for the Performing Arts.   The
sensibilities of the times regarding the arts were concisely stated
in the wording of an RF [Rockefeller Foundation] document recom-
mending that a grant of $2.4 million be made toward the acquisition
of a site for the projected performing arts center:

> Characteristic of the performing arts in the United States
> is the proposal that Lincoln Center is to be a non-govern-
> mental venture.   In few other major countries are nation-
> al theaters a private enterprise on citizen initiative.
> Lincoln Center will be a cogent demonstration of the value
> which the people of the United States accord these arts
> and the independence from political control which they
> consider essential.

The prediction that Lincoln Center would be a demonstration
of the value which Americans would accord the arts was quite accurate.   But the sentiment expressed by the Rockefeller Foundation
about the necessity of the arts remaining free from all political
control and therefore continuing to depend for their support on "private enterprise and citizen initiative," could not have been more wrong.

Enter the Foundations

Although several foundations had been active in supporting the
arts intermittently during the 1950's the most significant entry into
the field of arts support was to be the Ford Foundation, which in
1957 announced an exploratory five-year program in the arts to be
funded at $2 million a year--a program which, in its third year,
was increased to $3 million.   Although several other foundations,
including the Rockefeller, were soon to move toward creating programs for support to the arts, none other has begun to match the
dollar amounts given to the arts by Ford.   From 1957 to November
1971, Ford committed a total of $232 million to grants and projects
in the arts.   The Ford Foundation joined with the Rockefeller
Foundation in supporting the initial construction of Lincoln Center.
The growing awareness on the part of these major foundations that
there was a real need for arts support contributed substantially to

the general level of concern about the arts--in general long regarded
by the average man as a field for madmen in which one could expect
only misery and penury in return for a life of single-minded dedication.

The Empire State and the Arts

The next key date in the growth of support for arts was
1960, when Governor Nelson Rockefeller successfully persuaded the
New York State legislature to create a Council on the Arts. Since
the mid-1950's, pressure had been mounting from a number of civic
leaders for an involvement of government in the arts. This was a
hotly debated issue, since, as indicated in the previously cited
docket item, there was some lingering fear of government control
of the arts if there were funding from federal or state sources.
But the people of New York State took the plunge.

The history of the New York State Council on the Arts has
been one of unparalleled importance in this field. The initial budget
in 1960 was $50,000, which grew slightly each year until it reached
almost $18 million in 1970-1971.

The creation of the New York Council had a multiplier effect. Other states and organizations began to press for the formation of their own arts councils, and this was done, although no
state has ever matched New York's record. In 1964 the Rockefeller
Foundation, too, began a program in the arts, and Norman Lloyd,
dean of the Oberlin Conservatory, was named director. This was
the first appointment of a working musician to a directorship in the
arts in a major foundation. Yet, as the 60's waned, the hand-to-
mouth existence of the arts remained depressingly constant.

The National Endowment: Welcome, Big Brother

In 1965 two events profoundly influenced public awareness of the
necessity for greater funding for arts organizations. One was the publishing of the Rockefeller Panel Report, The Performing Arts: Problems and Prospects (McGraw-Hill). The other was the creation by
Congress of the National Endowment for the Arts and Humanities.

The impact of the Panel report, and also a subsequent volume
by Princeton economists William J. Baumol and William G. Bowen,
Performing Arts--The Economic Dilemma (New York: Twentieth Century Fund, 1966), did much to clarify thinking on the economic problems of the arts. These studies offered continuing evidence that arts
organizations could never be expected to make it at the box office, that
arts organizations, in order to be able to offer their unique services
to the public, would always have to operate at deficits, and that the
sources of support for such organizations would have to increase their
giving and multiply in number if existing institutions were not to be
threatened with extinction. The questions raised in this report were
debated in leading articles by critics and artists, in newspaper editori-
als, in lectures and informal discussions which helped to swerve the
arts community away from its former fear of governmental influence.
Now the fear was not that Washington might control or censor the arts
through its support, but that Washington might not fund them.

The National Endowment's funding level began modestly and has increased gradually in response to the demands for support. In 1972 the Arts Endowment made a total of $26,250,000 available in grants to groups, individuals and state arts councils.

The Corporations and the Arts

The two major reports on arts funding which were cited earlier also stressed the need for the business and corporate community to consider its role in this area.   Another study, titled The Corporations and the Arts, by Richard Eels, called for the creation of an organization which would address itself directly to this problem.   This was done in 1967 when David Rockefeller joined with financial and business leaders to form the Business Committee for the Arts.   In 1968, the Rockefeller Foundation made a grant of $200,000 to help this information and service organization set itself up in the business of coaxing business to increase its giving. The record here, of gradual though undramatic increase, given inflationary and other factors, is heartening.

The Arts Go Populist

A recent issue of Giving USA indicated that an all-time high of philanthropic giving--$21 billion in 1971--included a total to the arts of $800 million, an increase over the previous year of $80 million.   In citing the new direction of the arts toward the masses, the report stated, in part:

> The arts are in the midst of a populist movement, which
> means more exposure to the performing arts, more at-
> tendance at museums, and more problems. ...   Philan-
> thropic funds are now easier to acquire for groups which
> show this wide community interest.   The arts have be-
> come relevant. ...   No longer are museums just big
> buildings that awe the visitor.   They are alive with activ-
> ity, sometimes too much, putting a strain on resources.
> Opera companies, symphony orchestras, theater groups
> are traveling to the people, instead of waiting for the
> audiences to come to them.

The $800 million takes into account bequests (about $50 million), individual contributions as reported in income-tax returns (about $500 million), and gifts in kind (about $25 million), plus donations from foundations, state councils, the National Endowment and corporations.   The total amount looms large in terms of support to the arts, but is only 3.9 percent of the total of $21 billion given annually by philanthropic organizations and individuals.

The populist-movement theory received added recognition in the newly created expansion-arts section of the National Endowment, aimed at aiding only community-based arts activities, such as ghetto or rural arts programs.   And the New York Council initiated a special programs division which provided in 1971-72 about $1.5 million in funding and technical aid to ghetto arts projects.

Now that giving is up and the arts are in--i. e. , getting support from new sources--how do they stand? In artistic terms, the arts in this country have never been more vigorous. Since the influx of the European immigrants during the war, the edge has been with us. With very little encouragement, our artists have made America the world's center in theater, painting, music and dance.

That recognition should come so quickly from abroad may have surprised the struggling Americans since America cares so little about her artists' welfare. But it should not have surprised anyone knowledgeable about Europe's long concern over the artist's well-being.

Sweden, with a population of about 7 million, has fewer people than New York City. Yet this small country provides more than $3 million a year just to maintain one opera house in Stockholm, and it supports opera, theater and other arts throughout the country. In West Germany, support to some 120 theaters amounts to $35 million a year. The City of London and the British Arts Council give more than $2 million a year to maintain two London repertory theaters, and in each case other arts are similarly supported. Tables of national expenditures clearly show that the United States spends less on its arts per capita than any major country, including Canada. Now, the argument cited in the Rockefeller Fund, 1956 document, quoted earlier, is being used to the opposite effect--namely, that few other major countries have a national theater supported by "private enterprise on citizen initiative, " and since they don't, why should we?

When Robert O. Anderson stepped down as president of the Business Committee for the Arts this year (Frank Stanton to be his successor) he made some remarks about the already noted increases in giving to the arts from corporate sources: If there is to be a cultural boom, we have only heard the click of the firing pin thus far.

> Clearly our impact [the BCA's] is now a significant one in the field of arts support and yet it has been achieved at a minuscule percentage of the dollar support generated. But the amount contributed by the business community, though increasing rapidly, is still far from the level where it would be a major factor in assuring the stability and breadth of the economic base needed to sustain our artists and arts organizations.

Will America ever grant to the artist the place he deserves in society, a living wage for his work, resource centers in which to work, and ways of sharing his work with others? The dawn of this age may now be upon us. It is certainly not high noon.

The funding of the arts by state and federal legislative bodies is a matter of annual whim. Other industries are given subsidization on planned levels that cannot and do not fluctuate so capriciously.

But while the request to recognize the arts as a labor force may persuade some, the argument strikes the sour note of Babbittry.

Is there no intrinsic merit in the arts which should compel support, or must they be made relevant to a utilitarian society? It is interesting that in attempts to justify increased support, some people outside the field have come up with interesting rationales. J. Irwin Miller, chairman of Cummins Engine Company, Columbus, Indiana, said in addressing a recent meeting of the BCA [Business Committee for the Arts]: "Art is best understood as attempts at human communication at the most intense level. " It is in this newly emerging concept of the arts as "communication" that the arts may win further understanding, which in turn may lead to increased support.

How Much and for What?

A major question remains. If the arts ever do attain the support level they need to flourish--would $2 billion from all sources be sufficient?--will those funds take care of all needs? And what are the needs?

These can be separated into two basic areas of action: start-up costs and maintenance. The general pattern during the past decade has been that the largest amounts have gone to the maintenance area--i. e. , to existing organizations for ongoing activities. For example, the largest single grant in the arts--Ford's $80. 2 million --went to symphony orchestras which did not have to alter their formats (the playing of basically 19th-century music) one iota. In other words, the Ford grant supported a financial and artistic status quo. Similar figures could be shown for ballet and theater. But what of start-up costs, the work by the experimentalists? Who supports the untried approach? And from where comes the eventual enrichment of every art form if not from the creative artist who dares do something new?

There continues to exist, then, a great need for risk capital to help the creative artist move the art along. Just as the GNP depends to some extent on new inventions and developments--television, xerography--for its growth, so the arts depend for their vitality on new ideas. Those ideas come from artists who will need special consideration even if the halcyon days of full support ever do arrive.

If the Rockefeller Fund's total expenditure in the arts since 1964 (about $28 million) were measured only in its dollar value against the combined giving of all sources, it would seem to be relatively unimportant. But considering the track record in terms of the pioneering work of the arts institutions and individual artists that has been carried out with this support, the contribution can be seen to be almost monumental, and certainly far out of proportion to the amounts given. The Rockefeller Foundation ranks second in foundation giving in this field, Ford outstripping it financially. The

Rockefeller Brothers Fund and the A. W. Mellon Foundation are in third and fourth places respectively.

It is crucial that major foundations continue to recognize this need through well defined and adequately funded programs. Since World War II, the arts have come into their own and have moved closer to a central position in our culture. But the cultural boom, if there is to be one, lies ahead.

SUBSIDY UNDER THE AMERICAN SYSTEM*

Hope Stoddard

In practically all of the civilized nations of the world, the United States excepted, symphony orchestras and opera companies are given government support, and this is a tradition of hundreds of years standing. If the United States has no such direct subsidy of music, it does engage in indirect subsidy. That is, through financing tours of musical organizations and individuals abroad, it helps to pay for the upkeep of such organizations and individuals.

These facts, promising as they are in themselves, have so far had little effect on the policy of the United States within its borders. It is time we began to think about what we as a people should do for musicians here at home, those citizens who, like other citizens--plumbers and auto mechanics, teachers and preachers, doctors and lawyers--cue up at cafeterias, ride buses, dig out of snowstorms and put their children through school, but who, unlike most other citizens, are distinguishable not only by the instruments they carry but also by the lines on their foreheads and the harried look in their eyes.

It is the aim of every government to be acutely conscious of the groups making up its population, to be fully aware of the functions of each and their contributions to the general good, and to produce and sustain employment in so far as is possible. Not a government but helps those groups which it believes further the nation's goals.

Our government, for instance, holds farmers to be especially worth looking after. Between 1951 and 1960 annual farm subsidies rose from $905,000,000 to $3,568,000,000. Another group the government helps prodigiously is businessmen. The $525 million deficit in handling business mail sustained by the post office in fiscal 1960 was made up by the government in its aid-to-business program. Other groups coming in for government aid are those engaged in air

**From Subsidy Makes Sense, by Hope Stoddard; published by the American Federation of Musicians, ca. 1966 (reprinted from a series of articles in the Federation's Journal, International Musicians).

navigation and in maritime navigation--the air transportation industry to the extent of $228 million last year and the water transpor-
tation, to the extent of $165 million. War veterans and victims of
sudden disasters--hurricanes, earthquakes, floods--receive special
grants.

Why are these groups singled out for largesse? Because
the life-blood of the nation must be kept circulating healthily--crops
growing in its fields, goods transported coast to coast and abroad,
business running on oiled wheels--no group a drag on the others.

It is a curious paradox that our government, so sensibly-
minded in matters of growing corn, disposing of farm surpluses,
distributing low-priced lunches to school children, improving roads,
sidewalks and postal service, and dispatching speedy aid to hurri-
cane sufferers, should remain blind to that group which gives cultural significance to the nation.

For it is obvious that a nation whose citizens are not kept
in living association with the best in music is not in a healthy
state. Public concerts of the hundreds of amateur orchestras from
coast to coast do not give such contact. For these do not come
under the head of good music professionally performed. How can
they, played as they are by organizations whose members support
themselves precariously by doing unsuitable work during much of
the year, in order to keep themselves available for a three-month
orchestra season? Nor do the dozen or so major symphony orchestras located in key cities suffice to uphold the musicality of the
nation. On such fare musicians as a nation-wide group cannot
thrive; citizens cannot be roused to proper pride in their musical
organizations; a sense of musical life cannot be sustained.

The trend, moreover, is downward. More and more orchestras are switching to evening rehearsals, since the players must
hold daytime jobs outside of the music field; more and more of our
young singers are flocking abroad for experience and job security.
According to recent trade reports, 350 American singers are now
employed full season in Central European opera houses, and their
numbers are increasing.

This represents a curious paradox. For the United States
government has shown again and again that it is aware of the persuasive powers of music and the responsibilities of a country to
stimulate music making. The Voice of America continually beams
musical programs overseas (with no payment to musicians responsible for it, however). Musical scores, sheet music and recordings of American music are made available at 170 United States
information centers abroad. A sum of about $2 million is appro-
priated each year for the President's Special International Cultural
Exchange Program. Annual Congressional appropriations allow for
sending abroad specialists in music, among them, during recent
years, Thor Johnson, Virgil Thomson, Allen Hughes, Howard
Mitchell, Paul Creston, Jesus Maria Sanromá, Malcolm Frager and
Seymour Bernstein.

American dollars have helped restore a number of old European opera houses and music halls which had been damaged by bombings in World War II. At the time we were allotting half a billion dollars of military aid to Turkey, that country established annual appropriations of $350,000 for the Turkish Philharmonic, $750,000 for operas performed, and approximately $3,300,000 to build an opera house in Istanbul.

The inconsistency of this generosity abroad compared with our niggardliness at home was pointed out in a letter to the New York Times by George Szell, conductor of the Cleveland Orchestra. Commenting on an article stating that "With the financial assistance of the United States, Germany is reconstructing the Berlin Philharmonic Building," he comments, "Surely if the money of the United States taxpayers is being used to rebuild the home of the Berlin Philharmonic Orchestra, there cannot be any valid argument against this kind of money being used to help and support our own organizations."

There are evidences that the United States government is becoming aware of its own inconsistencies. It is beginning to realize that musicians who are fanfared abroad also deserve to be cared for at home. The WPA initiating a Federal Music Project in 1935 was the first faint sign of this, even though this project was instituted as an emergency measure, tiding over musicians together with other segments of the jobless for the sake of the nation's economy.

In 1951 came the first real murmurings of concern for musicians for their own sake, with the passage of a bill allowing tax relief to non-profit symphony orchestras and opera companies. Then, in 1956, legislation was passed granting a Congressional Charter to the National Music Council, which was at the time an organization of 45 nationally active musical associations that had a combined individual membership of some 800,000. It had been founded in 1940 for the following purposes: to provide a forum for the free discussion of problems affecting the musical life of the country; to speak with one voice for music; to provide for the interchange of information between the member organizations, and to encourage coordination of effort among these organizations; to organize surveys of fact-finding commissions whenever deemed necessary; to encourage the advancement and appreciation of the art of music; and to foster the highest ethical standards in the musical professions and industries. There are now 53 member organizations (of which the American Federation of Musicians is one), which have a total individual membership of over 1,228,000. General meetings are held twice annually, and the Council's Executive Committee meets six times a year. The Council is the only national musical organization to hold a Congressional Charter.

Then, on September 2, 1958, Congress authorized the National Cultural Center and set aside nine acres along the Potomac for its construction. The law directed President Eisenhower to

appoint a Board of 30 Trustees and an Advisory Committee on the
Arts. The American Federation of Musicians' President Kenin,
one of the members of this board, stated, on receiving the appointment, "I welcome this opportunity to aid in building a national home
for the American living arts, and commend the President and the
Congress for taking this long-needed action. The United States has
been the only major country in the world which does not recognize
and support its native arts and artists in any organized degree.
There is much to be done in this field, and I believe we must work
overtime to correct the previous indifference toward one of America's greatest resources, namely, its musicians, artists, writers,
actors, dancers and poets. By helping them we also help our symphonies, theaters, universities and cultural foundations. "

It may be sensibly argued that a mere building or group of
buildings in Washington, even if dedicated to the arts, can do but
little to spark the idea of general subsidy, especially since the Federal government takes à part in the project only by making the
ground available, while the money for the construction of the facilities must be raised by voluntary contributions.

Still, this act brings with it a new concept of the nation's
capital as a patron, defender and stimulator of the Performing
Arts. It implies recognition of music and musicians as a significant aspect of our society.

It is a beginning.

THE GROWING CORPORATE INVOLVEMENT
IN THE ARTS*

George Gent

If the arts in America are facing a financial crisis, they
are also, like so much else in American society, troubled by success and abundance. The paradox is that as the arts assume an
increasingly important place in the lives of more and more people,
they are pricing themselves out of the market. In the arts, unlike
most enterprises, increased production and more customers do not
necessarily add up to higher profits. Indeed, greater production,
capital investment and larger audiences frequently mean bigger deficits for harried arts managers. While support from individual
patrons and foundations continues at a high level, new sources of
revenue must be generated if the growth of revenue must be generated if the growth of the arts in America is to be anything like
assured.

*From Art News, vol. 72, no. 1 (January 1973). Copyright 1973
by Art News Associates, Inc. , New York. Reprinted by permission.

It was with this in mind that, in 1967, a group of concerned businessmen, headed by David Rockefeller, chairman of the Chase Manhattan Bank and a vice-chairman of the board of trustees of the Museum of Modern Art, established the Business Committee for the Arts, a private, tax-exempt national organization, to serve as a catalyst with four major objectives:

(1)   Obtain necessary research and statistical analysis pertaining to support of the arts, and make the information available to the business community.

(2)   Provide expert counseling for corporations interested in starting or expanding programs related to the arts.

(3)   Develop a nationwide program of public information to keep corporations informed of opportunities for support of the arts and tell the art community what the corporations are doing in the arts.

(4)   Help cultural organizations increase their effectiveness in obtaining support from business and industry and encourage the participation of more businessmen in groups concerned with the arts.

Ninety of the country's major corporation heads were invited to become members of the BCA and to work in their communities to spur financial support, publicity and business expertise for the arts.   There are now 112 members of the committee.

So far three prominent men have served as chairman of the BCA.   The first was C. Douglas Dillon, former Secretary of the Treasury.   He was succeeded by Robert O. Anderson, chairman of the Atlantic-Richfield Corporation in Los Angeles, succeeded in turn last April by Frank Stanton, vice-chairman of the Columbia Broadcasting System.   From the first, the man chosen to head the BCA as president and chief executive officer was Goldwin A. McLellan, a former public-affairs director for the Olin Corporation who currently presides over a small staff and a $300,000 annual budget at the committee's headquarters in New York City.

How successful the BCA has been was detailed by Anderson in his final report to the membership last spring.   He said that corporate philanthropic support for the arts had increased by roughly 160 per cent since 1965--from $22 million to $56 million.

"We believe," he said, "that in large measure this increase results from the BCA's activities.   Millions of dollars in the form of business expense have also been released for the arts as a result of the new climate for arts support created by the BCA.   According to a [BCA] poll taken two years ago, the amount given in the form of business expense equals, and may even exceed, that given as corporate philanthropy.   Therefore we think it reasonable to assume that both categories of giving together now total nearly $100 million annually. "

The BCA's projection is that for 1972 business will have contributed $75 to $80 million in philanthropic gifts to the arts, with an almost equal amount coming in the form of written-off business expenses. Much of the latter comes in the forms of free exhibition space, publicity, fund-raising drives by company executives and donated management expertise.

These important gains must be measured against the general decline in corporate giving to almost all other forms of charity in recent years--a result, most people agree, of the recession. And support for the arts continues to grow, with contributions to museums second only to support of music groups. Why this continued support?

"There are a number of reasons," said McLellan. "For one thing, there is the obvious public-relations benefit accruing to any company that supports an activity of interest to large numbers of people in its community. But the thrust today is more toward social responsibility and sound business considerations."

He noted that government is increasingly taking over the role once played by private philanthropy in the fields of health, education and welfare while, simultaneously, corporations are discovering that the arts are vital to the mental and civic health of the communities they inhabit. There is also the consideration of corporate realism.

"American corporations are only now discovering what European businessmen have always known," McLellan said. "Business is already deeply involved with the arts through product design, packaging, media advertising, public relations, plant architecture and interior design. All of these--and many more examples could be cited--require a conscious concern for art and design."

The arts are also essential to business today, he said, as a means of attracting and retaining highly skilled and educated managerial and professional personnel. He cited a Wharton School of Finance and Commerce study that disclosed that graduate students listed art, music, entertainment and the presence of intellectual stimulation high on the list of requirements for communities to which they planned to move with their families. Many companies, in their campus recruitment, now describe their involvement in the arts.

Another view was voiced by J. Irwin Miller, chairman of the board of the Cummins Engine Company, Inc., of Columbus, Ind., and a member of the BCA board:

"Support for the arts is part of our responsibility to the society which gives us our franchise," according to Miller. "It ought not to fall under the category of non-controversial public relations: business support of the arts is even in a sense shameful if it is prompted only by a desire to enhance the corporate image.

Business should support the arts and work to increase support of the arts by government and citizens because such action is an appropriate response to a peculiar and intense need of these times; because business itself has been enormously enriched by the work and the free inheritance of past generations, and because the only way to discharge this honest debt is to hand over to the future a country and a society truly responsive to the deepest needs of its people. "

A 1970 national survey of corporate support of the arts was done for the BCA by Touche Ross & Co. It provides a statistical profile of the new corporate patrons. It shows, for instance, that the typical arts benefactor is in an occupation other than manufacturing, with supporters coming predominantly from banking, insurance, utilities, wholesale and retail trade, communications and transportation.

It was also learned that a company with local markets is more likely to contribute than one with national markets; that the smallest businesses give at a rate of 40 times that of the largest; that the smaller the company (fewer than 1,000 employees), the larger the gift, whether the criterion be contributions per employee or the company's net income before taxes; and finally that publicly owned companies give more frequently than privately owned, and give more, whether the criterion is rate per employee or net income.

Of the 38 different art forms and organizations listed in the 1970 BCA questionnaire, the two most popular recipients of corporate support were symphony orchestras and museums. The preference for these two is presumed to be, in part, the presence of significantly large numbers of business leaders on their boards of directors (a seeming guarantee of sound management) and the feeling that such organizations are usually solidly embedded in the local social structure.

The original goal of $200 million in annual corporate contributions is nearly in sight and the BCA now hopes to generate the same kind of support that education got from business following World War II and which now amounts to about $325 million annually.

To accomplish this, the BCA hopes for a change in the tax laws that would permit businesses to increase their charity deductions to 10 per cent from the present five per cent. Meanwhile, the BCA plans to offer greater assistance to state and regional arts corporations.

"Six months ago," said McLellan, "we found regional programs were increasing so fast that we decided it would be wiser to channel our efforts into the states, instead of concentrating on the national level as before. We've already started statewide business-arts conferences to share information in North and South

Carolina, Louisiana, Ohio, Indiana, Wisconsin and Pennsylvania.
Local arts groups rarely have the skills or the money to buy
skilled management, so our task will be to help them help themselves. "

     Patrons have rarely been loved by the artists they sup-
ported. Samuel Johnson defined a patron as "one who looks with
unconcern on a man struggling for life in the water, and when he
has reached ground encumbers him with help. " Businessmen have
usually regarded artists as impractical dreamers, if not radicals.
The BCA hopes to change those attitudes. The arts, as they expand and multiply throughout the country, need the financial support and managerial skills of the business community, while businesses must realize its already large debt to the arts and see its
involvement with them as part of an ongoing responsibility to the
larger community. Together they may fashion a new Athens. That
would not surprise the Business Committee for the Arts.

THE CAREER EXPERIENCE
OF THE SYMPHONY MUSICIAN*

David L. Westby

     The situation of the symphony musician in the United States
today is reflective of the somewhat tenuous economic status of
symphonic music as an art form offering meaningful aesthetic experience to a limited public.   The symphony musician is caught
between the potent forces of general public apathy, a management
dominated labor market, and a union that in some ways works
against his best interests.   To these may be added the effects of
a recording industry over which he has little control and which
offers him only short-term rewards while extracting long-term profits.   From the disjunction of his social position as a dependent
craftsman and his idealized self-image as a gifted and highly
skilled artist emerge problems of reconciliation of his social and
aesthetic expectations with the realities of his occupational life.
Strong commitments to the values of art and of his chosen profession, essential to fine performance, are often undermined by
unhappy experiences centering about unmet demands for material
and status rewards, and the felt instability of his position.   Sensing
that others pull the strings that may ultimately affect his destiny,
many a symphony musician experiences a chronic anxiety concerning his life chances: he feels such a situation is inconsistent with

*From Social Forces, vol. 38 (March 1960), published by the Uni-
versity of North Carolina Press, Chapel Hill.   Reprinted by permission. "The data ... were gathered ... in the winter of 1956-
57.   In this paper very little will be said about the conductor.
This is not an oversight. ... "   The author thanks Howard J.
Ehrlich, Norbert F. Wiley and James R. Dove for their assistance.

the image of the musician as the bearer of the highest kind of aesthetic value which he offers for the enrichment of the community.

The purpose of this paper is to describe the career aspirations and career experience of a selected group of symphony musicians (those comprising one major symphony orchestra) in the context of the organization of symphonic music in the United States. The material discussed here is drawn from a larger study centering on the orchestra as a work group. The study was conceived as broadly exploratory in design, and the material presented below will be cast in an interpretive mode. The perspectives gained in this effort will be utilized in the formulation of a study of considerably broader scope, encompassing a number of representative orchestras. Since no comparative materials on other orchestras were gathered in this study many of the formulations to follow must be regarded as provisional and suggestive rather than as pronouncements of finality.

It was originally intended to interview the entire membership of the orchestra, but before this could be accomplished the organization left its resident city on an extended trip. For this reason 16 of the members were never interviewed. Fortunately, just such an eventuality had been anticipated and all the members of the smaller sections (brass, woodwinds, percussion) had been interviewed, and the larger sections (strings) "sampled" in roughly equal proportions.

The initial 6 weeks of the study were spent entirely in mutual familiarization. It was felt that such a period was necessary in view of the nature of the organization. Symphony musicians are an occupational group exhibiting considerable anxiety over their jobs on a number of dimensions, most prominently performance and security. This is especially true in their relations with the conductor, who has relatively unrestricted formal power and dominates the work situation to the extent that he is typically perceived as an imposing threat to artistic integrity and occupational security. Gaining the confidence of the musicians in the interview situation was therefore crucial for the elicitation of unthreatened responses. Also, care was taken throughout the entire study to insure against the researcher becoming associated in any way with any arm of management: no one in any such position was interviewed or contacted for any purpose whatever, other than to gain initial permission to attend concerts and rehearsals. It is felt that whatever loss has ensued from this procedure has been more than compensated for by the richness of the material gathered from the musicians.

The Mobile World

From the perspective of the professional symphony musician, his occupational world may be thought of as an array of symphony orchestras in major cities, each of which is the bearer of a

relatively stable quantum of prestige, and the entire array ranged
on a status hierarchy roughly corresponding to (1) the relative
wage scale, and (2) the length of the "season," the top orchestras
having the highest wages and the longest season. At the top of
this hierarchy stand such organizations as the orchestras of Boston, New York, and Philadelphia, celebrated as the finest in the
world. At the base are found a great proliferation of "civic" and
semi-professional orchestras in which musicians perform for little
or no pay. The playing of symphonic music is for these musicians
an avocation at best, and more often, a form of creative leisure.
In the middle ranges it is possible to distinguish several groupings
on the basis of prestige. Of the orchestra studied 70 members
were asked to rank in order the 10 best symphonies in the United
States. There was remarkable consensus on the order: the orchestras of Boston, New York, and Philadelphia were ranked 1-2-3
by 90 percent of the respondents. Immediately below these, three
more orchestras were grouped, and below these, three more. In
all, 21 orchestras were named but the top 6 were mentioned by 96
percent of the respondents, and the top 10 by 47 percent. The
orchestra upon which this paper is based was one of those immediately below the top three.

It is within this system that demands for material and status
rewards are realized: its structure sets the conditions for the
success of individual musicians. [1] Each orchestra is known and
perceived as the receptacle of rather well-defined status and financial rewards. Since the major symphony orchestras, let us say
the top 15 or 20, are geographically distributed throughout the
country, from Boston to Los Angeles and Minneapolis to New Orleans, realization of career expectations almost invariably means
considerable geographic mobility. No musician who identifies himself as a full-time professional symphony musician can achieve his
occupational aspirations apart from movement up and into orchestras at or near the top rank, depending to a limited extent on the
specific position in the orchestra. There is little ambiguity concerning the jobs that will satisfy his reward and status ambitions.

The prestigious character of the orchestra is not, however,
the sole factor involved in the musician's mobility decisions. For
instance, images of conductors and even of section principals (section leaders, or first chairs) sometimes become significant for
such decisions. A first violin player had this to say: "As far as
symphonies are concerned I'm better off here. I could have gone
to K [names a somewhat more prestigious orchestra] last year on
viola. The salary is a little better than here, but I can't stomach
the conductor." Also values originating outside the orchestra or
the whole system of orchestras (home town, health, etc.) are
sometimes related to musician's mobility decisions, but we need
not concern ourselves with these.

More important than such idiosyncrasies is the fact that,
not only the orchestra as a unit, but also specific positions within
it, are ranged on a scale of status. The principal chairs (in the

case of string sections) and the chairs of "first men" (in the case of winds) top this scale. Incumbents of these positions are paid roughly double the salaries of others (section men). Therefore, within each organization rewards and status are to some extent at least formally available for the fulfillment of mobility demands. The internal status system of the orchestra is by no means unconnected with career-furthering chances of movement through the larger system. Experience gained in such jobs as assistant concertmaster, and to a lesser extent, assistant principal positions, may weigh heavily in conductors' personnel replacement decisions. A man who had played second stand, first violins would probably merit slightly greater consideration than one off the last stand,[2] or one from the second violin section, other things being equal (which they practically never are).

Despite many denials, position in the section is an important source of job satisfaction and status deprivation. Though no systematic evidence is available to demonstrate this point there are a number of considerations that bear immediately upon it. The mere fact that chances for outside jobbing are directly dependent on position injects a purely economic aspect that poorly paid musicians could hardly ignore.[3] Also, if one takes the trouble to observe carefully he may sometimes detect a nonchalantly calculated, subtly surreptitious competition in the edging forward of chairs. And a few violinists in the back of the section confess that being thus displayed before audiences of thousands is a status-effacing experience. But perhaps the best indicator of the status meaning of section position is gleaned through the frequently inventive rationalizations enunciated by status-deprived musicians. Here, a first violinist who was 10th of 16 in the section elaborates on his promotion chances.

Q. Do you expect to get ahead in this orchestra? A. "There is no point in it. As much is expected of you no matter where you sit. He [the conductor] might put his best men in back so [they] could watch the poor ones. It's more difficult to play [sitting in the back of the section because the conductor is further away.]"

In response to the same question an older second violin player had this to say: "Not particularly. I sit midway. I've sat back and forth. I prefer to sit in the middle of things. I've not tried for extra responsibility or asked for extra money. I think I'm capable of my job.... I'm older now and not ambitious any more. I never was much. Actually there's no "aheadedness" to it. There's very little difference in money except for the actual principals. "

A somewhat abused and buffetted cello player expresses the ultimate rationalization. "I feel my position is something like the first cellist, being as I sort of pull the section along from the rear. "

Some mention should be made here of the possibility of

leaving the system and finding career satisfactions in related
spheres. Specifically, enumeration of soloist[4] status, chamber
groups (primarily string quartets), a few opera and ballet orchestras, and the popular music field exhausts such avenues. For the
string player, opportunities in the popular field are few, and the
real chances of becoming a soloist or full-time member of a quartet that pays its own way are fewer. There are probably no more
than 10 string players successfully making a living as soloists in
the United States. For wind players, on the other hand, the situation is different. There are always jobs available and most symphony wind players augment their incomes substantially by playing
in popular orchestras, jazz bands, combos, etc. Of course, these
opportunities vary somewhat according to the demand for different
wind instruments.

In terms of the scope of employment opportunities, then, the
strings and winds find themselves in significantly different situations.
The string player experiences a relatively great "job confinement"
while the wind man has the vast field of popular music in which he
can work. While there are other important dimensions on which
the experience of string and wind players differ,[5] it is this one of
job confinement which must be kept primarily in mind as the context in which we shall examine the dynamics of occupational identification and aspiration as they shift over the course of a career and
have consequences for other facets of the musician's work life.[6]
Our main concern will therefore be with the string players, who
constitute about 70 percent of any symphony orchestra.

Mobility Mechanisms

In order for men to make claims on higher status positions
there must be modes of selection to get them in these positions.
Positions are distributed as opportunities for reward and perquisites
by conductors who select through auditions[7] the best players for the
jobs. Several features of this mechanism are of importance.

First of all, the top orchestras generally make a practice of
hiring only men under the age of 35. This means that for the vast
majority of musicians success must come early if it is to come at
all. If a man has not attained a high status position by the time
he is 35, or at the latest, 40, it is almost certain that he will
never attain it.

A second factor of importance, which contributes greatly to
the geographic mobility of the musician, is the principle in accordance with which principals and first men are selected. Replace-
ments of principals and first men are seldom made from sections
within the orchestra in which the position must be filled. The
manifest function of this practice is to control the "informal" features of a relationship that is, nominally at least, one of authority
--in this fashion the potentially disorganizing effects of formerly
egalitarian relationships are circumvented; but its significance extends beyond this--it also has the latent consequence of encouraging

and increasing inter-orchestra mobility.   The fact that, in the orchestra studied, 5 of 14 principals and 1st men were up from the
ranks, is probably primarily reflective of a poorly developed authority system at the level of principals and 1st men, for the conductor
exercises many leadership functions that in other orchestras are
delegated to section leaders.   Unfortunately, no comparative data
from other orchestras were available on this point.

    The fact that being selected for better jobs is rare for mu-
sicians over 35 means that their career changes are effectively
settled by that age; thus they must move fast.   The criteria of
principal and 1st man selection, taken together with the prestige
grading of orchestras described earlier, means that the musician's
potential career opportunities are structured in the following ways:
(1) a limited range within the orchestra, up to but probably not including the 1st chair jobs; (2) positions in higher ranking orchestras, with certain exceptions--section principals would seldom accept section jobs in higher ranked orchestras; (3) in some cases,
higher status positions in lower ranked orchestras--this almost always would mean a section man accepting a principalship or soloist
job in the lower ranked orchestra.   Since the number of orchestras
that at any given time are relevant for a musician's mobility
chances is never large, knowledge of potential openings tends to be
encyclopedic, though this varies by the size of the aspirant's section.   Whereas trumpet sections usually have five or six men,
first and second violin sections taken together normally have at
least five times as many.   Mobile musicians will probably know the
approximate ages, professional history, and ability of most of the
incumbents of what, from their perspective, are desirable jobs,
and perhaps even in some cases whether there is an inclination to
quit, and the character of relations with the conductor.   Thus, each
musician is, in a sense, his own employment agency, compiling an
inventory of probable and possible jobs.   Such knowledge serves
the function of preparing the musician for opportunities that "come
like a flash, are there for a moment, and then are gone."   The
career of the symphony musician is not one of steady advancement
through a series of finely graded positions with predictable promotions based mainly on presentation of credentials of service and
tenure, but rather, one of watchfully awaiting the opportunity that
may appear but once in a lifetime.

Occupational Identification, Aspiration, and the Career

    Extraordinarily long training periods and intense study pro-
duce musicians whose occupational identification is of the strongest
sort.   A complex of factors accounts for this.

    The training of the musician, particularly the string musi-
cian, begins at an early age in the form of private lessons (usually)
and long practice sessions.   Some musicians actually begin their
training at the age of three or four.   The fact that intense training
begins so early means two things: (1) that other experiences, particularly work experiences, are considerably circumscribed, and

(2) such an early investment of time, money, and effort typically creates a firm basis for a strong occupational commitment while the potential professional is yet a child.   Consequently, other identities have little chance to develop.   And it is not by chance that those who remain in the profession have such long histories of study.   Competence on stringed instruments particularly depends on years of arduous practice: one cannot begin late and hope for success.

Isolation from other occupational experiences, toward which the musician is predisposed by early training, is perpetuated by two institutional features characteristic of his late youth and early adulthood: the conservatory, and his great social and geographic mobility.   Of the musicians interviewed, 77 percent attended at least one conservatory, and many attended two or more.   Periods of attendance ranged up to 14 years.   The curriculum of a music conservatory is not calculated to give the student a rounded education.   It is clear that he is there for one purpose--to become a polished musician.   This means that opportunities to develop knowledge of and interest in other areas of endeavor tend to remain minimal.   Then, as a young man just on the job market, the true professional must maximize a potential for mobility.   Since his career orientation forces him to face upward toward better jobs in other orchestras-- and thus outward from the community he is, at the moment, in, but not of--his social life is typically restricted to a culture flourishing on the periphery of his work life, a culture participated in by others like himself, stopping for a year or two, then going on. Extreme involvement with colleagues off, as well as on the job, means that the musician's professional identity, developed over long years of training, is constantly being buttressed and reinforced, holding to a minimum the possibilities of pursuit, or even consideration, of other possible ways of life.

This intense occupational identification so characteristic of the young symphony musician, taken together with the reward features of the system--which, in orchestras roughly below the top 10 practically fail to provide even a subsistence level of existence[8]--tend to inculcate in him the strongest aspirations.   Now we do not wish to assert as an empirical generalization that either the level or the strength of aspiration necessarily co-varies with the strength of occupational identification; only that in the case of the symphony musician, strong occupational identification, conjoined with the pattern of reward and status distribution, produces high aspirations of considerable intensity (at least in the early work years). [9]   Let us look now at the dynamics of occupational aspiration and identification over the course of the career characterized by great job confinement.

The highest aspiration a string musician can have is to some day become a self-employed soloist.   This ambition was expressed by many young violinists particularly,[10] in the subject orchestra of the study.   For any young man roughly between 25 and 30 to be a player in the orchestra means that at this point in his career he is successful.   Ambitions of such musicians are typically big: a

24-year old second violin player had this to say. "This is the beginning of my career and what I would like to do eventually is to
be on my own and become a soloist. "

Such men, in their first professional experiences, are intensely motivated toward unrealistically high goals. This strong
motivation is in part the product of success experience in moving
through relatively low echelon orchestras up to a point where, for
most, a personal plateau is reached. The orchestra studied was
such a plateau for many. After a few years without noticeable progress, aspirations tend to become scaled down. In the following
exerpt from an interview, a 32-year old violin player expresses
the inner struggle typical of string players beginning to sense that
their career aspirations may never be realized.

> My problem is that I always have ambition to be a solo-
> ist, but that's your ideal point of view. You always have
> to make adjustments to live life or you drive yourself to
> destruction. You have to keep your ideal and make ad-
> justments. I wanted to be a soloist but I know now there
> is not enough space for that. So I chose the orchestra
> and I'm pretty happy about playing in it. But I have am-
> bitions to become a soloist some day. Playing in the
> orchestra is just as valuable because of the experience,
> and is of more value musically, but when I play a solo I
> think it counts more because I have all the responsibility
> on me. I have to ... do my best to become a first-rate
> player. In the orchestra you can do all those things but
> you can't reach that level to get that reward. You can
> get some satisfaction playing in the orchestra: you can
> see the standard of a solo piece is higher. You can hear
> yourself--you are more of an individual. You have it dif-
> ficult and more to give than in the orchestra.

In later years the process of persistent thwarting of aspirations often touches the musician's very identity as a talented and
schooled artist performing the work he esteems, making great music come alive in the concert hall. A 47-year old first violin player quite well-placed in the section answers the question, What do
you expect to be doing five years from now? "That's a hard question. If I can still be playing I'll be playing in an orchestra. If
I can get decent commercial work the year round I'd rather do
that.... I've done cabaret work. I'd rather play in any cabaret
in the country than the symphony orchestra. " This is typical of
the older strings: many want to get out. Some have tried; few
have succeeded.

The years complete the process of effacement of the occupational identity. As the player grows older, into and beyond the
50's, his talent begins to erode and his value to the organization
diminishes, particularly in terms of his future potential. A number
of string players (and a few of the winds) report having been
"pushed back" in the section. Here, a 54-year old second violinist
who had once played in the 1st violins comments.

Q. What are some of things you like best about being a musician? A. "I don't like any part of it. As a matter of fact, all
the time I've had several experiences in the business world, but
they failed and I had to come back. But as a professional musician I've never liked it.... The first chance to get out I will. I
still am looking. [Later] ... by the time you reach an age where
you should be independent, it's just the opposite. As you grow older you get less desirable, less valuable. It's not like other
things.... "

The material and status rewards offered the symphony musician, particularly the string players, in the circumscribed world
of symphonic music are structured such that only a relatively few
jobs, those in top orchestras plus a number of section principal-
ships and first man jobs, can satisfy the demands created by years
of study and an idealized self-image. When the aspirations emerging from these factors fail in fulfillment they begin to erode, and
before too long the idealized occupational identity upon which they
are in good part founded becomes, over the years, progressively
more rent and torn, in many cases ultimately undergoing near-com-
plete effacement. [11]

For the young musician, bringing to the job an idealization
of the musician's role and a sense of personal musical integrity,
contact with such disillusioned older musicians can be a rather bewildering experience, and in some cases was the fountainhead of
considerable hostility directed toward them: such encounters scarcely engender confirmation of the artistic image of the symphony musician. A 27-year-old cello player says: "Most people in the orchestra don't want a conductor who will make them play well.
They don't want to be pushed. They want to just sit back--they
aren't interested in playing well. In general, the younger fellows
are more conscientious, more interested in making music. "

Or a second violin player of the same age: "But you're not
playing with virtuoso musicians. Young people are ambitious, want
to play energetically. These people simply do not do it. "

The erosion of a man's occupational identification means a
concomitant resignation from the struggle for organizational and occupational values. In the case of the symphony musician such a
resignation means two things: first, that the individual now regards
his job as permanent rather than as a stepping stone to better
things. He "settles down. " While the younger set is "on the
move, " older musicians become psychologically estranged from
formerly held mobility aspirations. Decisions such as buying a
home, and even getting married, become symbolic of withdrawal
from the activities peripheral to the work life that are so significant to the younger musician. In such a situation it is possible to
develop a widening range of social experience and involvement not
important for someone here today but gone tomorrow. The social
life of the musician still riding a career is an extension of professional colleagueship, while the man who stays enmeshes himself,

in diverse ways, in the life of the community as he withdraws from
the society of the young and mobile.

Second, and closely related to the point made above, there
exists a widening gap of communication and values between the two
groups. The younger group, focusing on work and cut off from
main streams of community life, create a situation where great
meaning is placed upon certain rather stereotyped activities in-
dulged in somewhat compulsively. The best illustration of this is
undoubtedly the extent to which chamber music is performed. Almost all young string players spend many hours weekly in this
"leisure" activity. [12]

Since this is the most significant activity of the musician off
the job in terms of time spent and meaning involved we shall use it
to demonstrate the second point made above. The string population
of the orchestra (except those not interviewed) was broken into four
age groupings; grouping I, ages 20-32 (15 cases); grouping II, ages
33-38 (11 cases); grouping III, ages 41-50 (10 cases); and grouping
IV, ages 54-63 (5 cases). Each respondent was presented with the
following question:

> Which of the following jobs would you prefer? Rate the
> most desirable, '1, ' the next most desirable, '2, ' etc.
>
>   Player in a small chamber group
>   Virtuoso performer
>   Conductor of a symphony orchestra
>   Member of a popular band or orchestra
>   Section player in a good symphony orchestra
>   Teacher in the public schools

Proceeding from the younger grouping toward the older, the choice,
"player in a small chamber group, " received a progressively lower
mean rating. The mean rating for grouping I was 1. 60; for grouping II, 1. 91; for grouping III, 2. 00; and for grouping IV, 2. 60.

The difference between the mean scores for grouping I and
grouping IV becomes more significant when we understand that most
of the respondents injected a "reality" dimension as a condition of
their responses, exemplified best by a strong rejection on the part
of many of the choice, "virtuoso performer. " On the basis of the
interview material this cannot be taken seriously. But the same
holds true of "conductor of a symphony orchestra. " Few musicians
can imagine themselves in this role. "Member of a popular band
or orchestra, " is unrealistic on other grounds: few such organizations hire string players (apart from string bass players, and then
the instrument is almost always plucked rather than bowed). So the
item makes little sense. Keeping these matters in mind, then the
differences loom as considerable.

The older settled and withdrawn musician does not value the
activities most significant to the mobile young. The result, in the

orchestra here studied, was a fairly well-developed schism created
from factors outlined earlier. The younger musicians, living in
quasi-bohemian style become, in the eyes of the settled, community-
involved man, "characters," and "queers"--he wants no part of
them. The older men, on the other hand, are apt to be defined by
the younger as defectors from artistic and professional values.
And this they find incomprehensible.

1. The higher up in the hierarchy the more permanent becomes
    the organization. The yearly rate of membership turnover
    would provide an index of permanency. Though at the time
    of the study the personnel records of other orchestras were
    not available for inspection, it is probably safe to assert
    that any significant shift in this rate would be accompanied
    by a shift in the prestige of the orchestra relative to other
    orchestras. This is because the relative permanence of an
    orchestra is an index of the degree to which values are
    satisfied. Theoretically, orchestras offering greater value
    satisfactions, i. e. material and status rewards, will also
    be "better" in terms of aesthetic "efficiency," or perform-
    ance norms.

2. A stand is composed of two players. There were 8 stands in
    the first violin section of the orchestra studied; thus, 16
    players.

3. Hiring of string players for whatever outside jobs are to be
    had is effected through a long-time member of the orches-
    tra who acts as a one-man employment agency for estab-
    lishments or individuals who wish to hire. The basis for
    selection is universalistic: he starts with the players at
    the front of the sections and works toward the back until
    the supply of jobs is exhausted.

4. This term as used here means a self-employed, entrepreneur-
    ing free agent, not to the first men of the wind sections,
    who are also referred to as soloists. Such names as
    Menuhin, Heifetz, Serkin, and Rubinstein come immediately
    to mind.

5. The most prominent of these is visibility by both colleague and
    concert hall audiences. Since most wind players are solo-
    ists, in the sense of playing a great many passages with
    the rest of the orchestra as a background, the condition
    for a "performance anxiety" is built into their jobs. While
    string players need only "blend" with the rest of the sec-
    tion (and it is therefore practically impossible to ascertain
    whether they are playing well or badly, indeed, whether
    they are playing at all), a great many of the sounds pro-
    duced by the wind player are audible to all, and these of
    course, include his mistakes.

6. The perquisites of a position are by no means inconsiderable.
    For instance, the first men and section principals monopo-
    lized most of the better teaching opportunities in the area,
    bringing them an income of substantial proportions.

7. The audition is a test of competence everyone must pass prior
    to admission into the orchestra. It is usually administered
    by the conductor (occasionally by the concertmaster), and
    is, for most, fraught with anxiety. Some argue that it is
    not a true test of ability to play in a symphony orchestra,
    i. e. to "blend" in with the total sound.

8. In the orchestra studied the weekly base pay (set by union con-
    tract was over $100 per week, with the possibility of indi-
    vidual bargaining with management for $5 or $10 more.
    Therefore no one could make over about $3200 in one year,
    because the season lasted through only a portion of it.

9. The strength of an aspiration and the level aspired to are ob-
    viously not the same thing. Neither are they necessarily
    in constant relation. A son of a laborer may aspire
    strongly to the rather modest occupational status of, say,
    barber, while the aspiration of a middleclass child for at-
    tainment of a much higher occupational status may be of
    considerably less strength.

10. Other than violinists and pianists there are hardly any instru-
    mentalists making a living in the concert hall as soloists.

11. Note certain parallels with the automobile worker as presented
    in Ely Chinoy, Automobile Workers and the American
    Dream (New York: Doubleday, 1955).

12. To speculate a bit: just as early morning jam sessions often
    held by dance musicians can be interpreted as ritual puri-
    fication acts carried out after the sacrifice of artistic
    standards and integrity necessary for commercial jobs con-
    trolled by a lay audience, so the playing of chamber music
    in this rather compulsive manner by symphony musicians
    seems to express the artistic spirit that chafes under such
    a close control as that of the conductor.

THE STRING SHORTAGE*

Max Kaplan

The most serious error this conference could make would be
to treat the issue as a fact that extends only into and through

*From American String Teacher, vol. 15, no. 2 (spring 1965).
Copyright 1965 by the American String Teachers Association. Reprinted by permission.

musical life.   On the contrary, the theme has variations in major
and minor keys that can be developed from numerous motifs of social change since the First World War and the ceasing of large-
scale immigration.

Even to conceptualize the phrase--"shortage of strings"--
suggests many relationships to the whole range of American life.   Do
we, in fact, have a shortage of strings in respect to a well-anticipated
minimum that was established by some consensus a decade or two ago?
Is there, rather than a shortage of strings, an unexpected surge of demand, brought about by the expansion of musical life; and if so, should
a minor dirge not be a chorus of national celebration?

There is no point in dwelling on history, for a yearning for
the simple past cannot void the complexity of the present.   Yet I
would point out that many of us, now in our forties and fifties,
grew up as violinists because this was, to our energetic parents,
a symbol of Americanization.   We were sent to private teachers,
and worked through Kreutzer, Fiorillo, Rode and, of course, the
Mendelssohn, as Mother kept the windows open to impress the neighbors with us and us with a rising aspiration in life.   Against our
will and sense of decent manhood before the judgment of our street
peers, we even learned to like this music, and a new world did
enter those open windows--a world that took us far from the one
familiar to our parents.   But aside from the parental needling that
kept the bow rosined and a memorized piece on tap for the relatives, we had no TV sets to attract us, almost no radios, no cars,
few telephones, and only a few nickels in our pockets.

This, I say, cannot be brought back, for the changes in the
time of our children and grandchildren have been profound and irrevocable.   Vast megalopolitan areas have been sprawled out.   Wars have
been suffered.   Men and machines have been hurled through space
and to the moon.   Education for the masses has reached its apogee
in the multi-university.   Affluence has become commonplace.   Government, business and labor have turned into giants.   Minority
groups became assimilated, often to lose sight of their pluralistic
values; their sons became lawyers, doctors, businessmen and professors.   And the average American home that in our youth hardly
afforded the phone now has enough electronic gadgets to equal the
muscular energy of ninety male servants.

It is not a wild observation to say that all this contributed
to the shortage of strings, just as it did to higher divorce rates,
more crime, more working women, international tensions, personal
"alienation," the growth of suburbs, or the singing commercial.

Nor can a conference seeking solutions or approaches to the
supply of string instrumentalists be a significant occasion unless the
future is put into the agenda.   Permit a few projections that may
be pertinent to the discussion.   Even now, in 1964, about 40,000
workers are losing jobs because of automation every week.   Whatever the presidential candidates may want to say, or be permitted

to say in the general climate of opinion, our welfare, public works, and federal aid to work retraining and general adult education, to the arts and to other meaningful uses of nonwork time will expand in the next decade. The naked fact is that our new technology is now not only capable of killing faster than we can give birth, it can also eliminate jobs faster than new work can be created.

The ever-longer bulks of leisure time, especially for the unionized industrial worker, will crystallize and pinpoint the kinds of experiences he seeks; more community and commercial alternatives will be opened to him; and by A. D. 2000, the average family will have over $14,000 a year to spend (based on prices of the present). In the St. Louis area, for example, the projection is that such activities as fishing, picnicking and travel will expand by fifty times, as the workers of that area will have a quarter of a year more free time than they have now. In a recent conference of the Missouri Arts Council, I raised the questions, first, whether we in the arts have thought into the future as carefully as have the experts in outdoor recreation, and second, whether we are making the same systematic preparations as they are to meet the needs and goals of a creative mass culture.

The art world has a stake in that future. For the mass culture, in spite of the epithets that are now fashionably hurled at it by Dwight McDonald, Pitirim Sorokin, Louis Kronenberger, T. S. Eliot, and others, has provided an accessibility to the finest of the arts by a new, broad social base. It would be naive to overlook the justifiable concern over the vulgarity, mediocrity, conformity, "mid-cult," and "waist-high" culture that are widely in evidence and will continue; it is equally short-sighted to downgrade the enormous vitality that is evident in all parts of the country in the schools, in the communities, in literary discussions, in festivals and workshops, in foundation thinking, in new art centers, arts councils, governmental participation and international exchange. Their interest indicates a realistic confrontation with the mass culture of our times, alongside the subjective celebration in some camps and the criticism in others. The confrontation, for our immediate purpose here, must advance from several guiding principles that build on the strength of the current scene, then move into concrete proposals.

The first principle is one that is technically important from an aesthetic view but also provides a continuity from the past to the future, namely, that the goal of a string movement must be toward the cause of chamber music. This would rectify the fundamental mistake of public school music. Its political origins, dating from Boston in 1838, emphasized music for every child; it is a gross distortion to assume that this should mean either music for large groups, or every child on the stage, or a band on every football field. Only now, after a long period in which school directors felt impelled to be miniature Goldmans and Leinsdorfs, is there a feeling that band and orchestra, however valuable and necessary they may be in the formative years, must be supplemented, indeed, preceded, by the discipline and aesthetic nourishment that only chamber music making can provide.   This has been my advice recently to the Canadian music teachers, to begin their instrumental movement with the goal that our own institutions are just approaching.   We will obtain better string players by raising standards in the school, not by involving more students.   And string quartet or ensemble coaching, whatever other values it has, will demand better musicians, for then they cannot hide behind the baton or in a dilution of tunes from <u>South Pacific.</u>

The second principle is that our sights must go beyond the needs of the professional, major symphony orchestra in planning for the strings.   No more can the destiny of the professional and the dedicated, skilled amateur be neatly distinguished.   A large proportion of the more than 1200 symphony orchestras now contain both.   Indeed, even these familiar terms are long overdue for radical reconsideration embracing psychological, social, and aesthetic factors as well as the purely economic.

Third, we must continue the growing harmonious relationship between the professional musical community and the schools, but all resources of the community must be re-examined for their potential usefulness in reaching both young people and adults.   By providing adult programs in the strings, we develop a family and neighborhood climate without which the young person is estranged.   But even on the level of children and youth, the public schools do not exhaust the vehicles open to an imaginative program.

Fourth, there is need for a massive string program to reach children who are "culturally deprived," whose parents cannot afford musical training, whose homes lack many basic necessities of life, whose aspirations are stunted by ghetto and slum conditions, and whose schools are ill-equipped or inadequate.   This refers especially, but not alone, to Negroes.   Among these groups we have a vast and almost entirely untouched reserve of creative talent.   Although the civil rights struggle is necessarily dominated now by the implementation of the laws and by the change of attitudes toward work, housing, and political rights, it is essential that planning also go on for the content, the substance and fulfillment of a large segment of persons who must, by law and by democratic ethos, soon find themselves in the mainstream of aesthetic life as well. We have a possibility of a significant contribution, to music as well as to the dignity of man.

Finally the approach to the shortage of strings must move in many directions: there is no one formula or solution.

With these introductory comments as a base, I move to more concrete programs.   If we itemize a chronology of elements that enter into the production of a good string player from childhood to maturity, we have:

1. The interest of parents.

2. The early interest of the child.

3. The commitment of school officials.

4. Good teachers and teaching programs.

5. Maintenance of the student's interest through late adolescence.

6. The student's choice of career.

7. The university or conservatory training.

8. Training orchestras and musical experiences between the school and professional activity.

9. The family situation of the mature musician.

10. Steps involved in professional admittance and membership.

All of these items are important and need close attention. Here I select only a few for direct comment.

(Item 1) The interest of parents, especially of younger parents now found in many suburbs, may best be obtained by involving them directly in making music. Family performance groups can be established by cooperation between schools, adult centers, recreational departments, and community or settlement music centers. These might be centered on the playing of recorders, on combinations of instruments, or on singing. Suzuki has demonstrated this point with violin lessons for mothers. The increased nonwork time among adults is a favorable factor. The recreation movement is itself looking for a philosophy and technique to use more of the arts. Since one characteristic of many large housing projects is the development of self-governing educational and cultural units, urban renewal and housing leaders are open to ideas. Television, private as well as educational, should be approached for special courses or programs on family music making.

(Item 3) The interest of school officials is directly affected by an expression of interest from parents--for string instruction as well as for science and other areas. But parental action must be organized. Musical associations have published fine statements, but they have not moved on the grass-roots level through the local power structure based on parental conviction and action.

(Item 4) The crucial matter of finding and using mature string players as teachers is related to the teacher training curriculum, of course, but also to strategies by which performers can be brought into the educational community over the "dead body" of excessive and often unrelated courses leading to college degrees.

For example, we need to devise a program to prepare musicians directly for college positions; there is no such curriculum now, according to the research of Dr. Lee Chrisman of Boston University. (In my own case, I spent a quarter of a century on university levels, never taught in other schools, but sat through courses on how to teach the rote song and the eighth note to primary grades.) Ways are needed to grant credit to the mature musician for his working experience, and to provide an individualized internship to qualify him for the teaching certificate.   Emanuel Amiran, Minister of Music for Israel, does precisely this, and allows no music to be taught, even in the early grades, except by musicians.   We need ways to utilize the services of good string teachers who do not fit into the academic environment, whether by personality, desire, or other commitments; one way to do this is to bring the talented students to the community music school.   Here, with fees based on ability to pay, we have a long established type of institution with high standards and which embraces private and class lessons, theory and history, and chamber music experience.   Public school administrators might be approached to release students during school time in order to attend these schools and to accept grades for such time if credit is given for music work.

Settlement or community music schools are often located in the underprivileged areas of the city, by virtue of their philosophy and history; they might therefore serve as central agencies in reaching Negroes and other minorities.   The local Urban League, Jewish Centers and YMCA are useful when no community school exists.   The Higher Horizons program of New York has lessons for other areas in the utilization of many community resources for the underprivileged.

(Item 5)   As students enter late adolescence, they become cognizant of the other sex, their mental horizon reaches out quickly, they rely increasingly on control through their peers, they wean themselves from parental authority.   Yet, my close association with the Greater Boston Youth Symphony Orchestra suggests that in such groups we have at once a musical instrumentality of the highest potential and also a social tool that satisfies the need for status, sociability, and excitement.   Marvin Rabin, since he brought to the Boston group an insistence on musical excellence as well as a sympathy and understanding of young people, has found no lack of talented and serious members.   Many such orchestras are to be found across the country.   They could, in many cases, use consultations, funds to commission new music, scholarships for private lessons, important instruments, festivals and summer sessions.   A journal has recently been started in California for youth orchestras.   There is now a need for a more general music journal designed for music students between the ages of twelve and eighteen.

Together with such moves there should be a bold program of survey, research, and publication.   First is needed a compilation of opinion and empirical projections into American society of the next several decades, such as have been done by agencies of the Congress, the National Commission on Goals for Americans, the Twentieth Century Fund, and other agencies. These broad documents need to be interpreted for their meaning to the arts. The forthcoming study by the Rockefeller Foundation and the Twentieth Century Fund on the economics of the arts may hold some clues.

We need to encourage sociologists who specialize in the professions to examine the career stages of the musician, especially to serve the purposes of guidance counselors.

We need careful case studies of successful school string programs; we need more experimental films on class violin instruction, such as begun by George Bornoff. Visual aids and tapes are needed for seeing and hearing how sample passages are played by leading artists, or the musical consequences of different fingerings and bowings, or the methods of teaching by masters in their own studios.

We could utilize the resources of a daring university training department and several bold high schools which would agree to start from scratch with music training methods and with establishing relationships with the community.

The next step, in my view, if this conference is to come to grips with the issue, is to bring together a working session of representatives from organizations already active in the string area, and including persons from the fields of education, the social sciences and the mass media. Their work would be to assess all the suggestions that come out of this conference and other sources, to affirm a philosophy, establish priorities for action, and establish a continuing liaison to implement the total program. The executive staff would in the course of time pinpoint gaps, refine procedures, work closely with specific agencies, call upon foundations, cooperate with Lincoln Center and with local and state arts councils, assess resources, evaluate results, and report back to a general Tanglewood conference.

In the largest sense, the string shortage, like all other aspects of musical creativity, stems from basic values and directions of American life on the whole. Thus, by moving ahead on this problem, we contribute to the aesthetic and cultural climate of that whole, creative America.

SYMPHONIES VIE
FOR TOP ORCHESTRAS' STRING PLAYERS*

Carl Apone

The Pittsburgh Symphony Orchestra gets stacks of letters from musicians who want to join its ranks. But of the some 500

*From The Pittsburgh Press, Sunday, April 25, 1971. Reprinted by permission.

letters received annually, only about 40 come from string players.
These cold figures--40 string players among 500 musicians--drama-
tically point up the serious string shortage confronting major orchestras.

Strings--violins, violas, cellos, basses--make up 70 per
cent of the orchestra, yet only 8 per cent of applicants play those
instruments. No wonder then that personnel directors of major orchestras believe the string player to be the vanishing American.
No wonder they are ready to fight to get youngsters to switch from
guitar, clarinet and trumpet to cello, violin, viola. If they don't,
the orchestra as we know it could go the way of the village black-
smith.

Sidney Cohen, personnel director of the Pittsburgh Symphony,
said the string shortage is so serious that "major orchestras steal
from each other. The most successful orchestra is often the biggest thief. "

It also helps if the "thief" has an outstanding conductor, high
pay scale and a long season. Last season the New York Philharmonic tried to steal a first violinist from the Pittsburgh Symphony
but the local orchestra would not release him from his contract until they found a suitable substitute. They never did find a suitable
replacement and he is still here.

According to Cohen, the "string situation has worsened in the
past ten years. In another ten to twenty years, it appears, the
problem will become intolerable. We will probably have to lower
standards to fill out our string sections. I am extremely pessimistic. I see nothing on the horizon to relieve the string shortage. "

Cohen maintains the conservatories produce few fine string
players.

The ones they do produce seem to prefer jobs in universities
where they get better pay, longer vacations and the opportunity to
perform in chamber music groups. However, with higher pay scales
now going to players in major orchestras, some of the university
musicians are drifting to orchestras.

Cohen traces the origin of string problems back to grade
school.

I believe a potential string player should start on the instrument in the fourth grade. Yet the youngster with the
fortitude and talent to play the instrument is rare. And
the good teacher with the talent and fortitude to teach instruments is rarer.

The blunt and unvarnished truth is that the teachers in
our schools are for the most part music educators rather

than players.   To earn a college degree they might study
each instrument for six months.   Yet a symphony player
is not certified to teach in grade or high school though he
can qualify to teach in universities.   As an example of
how ridiculous this can become, William Steinberg would
not be certified to teach in our grade or high schools.

When the Pittsburgh Symphony receives letters of application,
Cohen asks a committee from each section of the orchestra to help
screen candidates.   The players the committees believe are qualified are invited to audition.

Yet even the most vigorous and extensive auditions often fail
to turn up a qualified candidate.   This year the orchestra heard
some twenty players and didn't like any of them.   So they reviewed
the contract of the player who sought to leave and persuaded him to
stay.

Within the string section, the most serious shortage is violinists.   The local orchestra searched in vain for two years to find
a second violinist.   Finally they were able to persuade Teresa
Harth, a member of the Carnegie-Mellon University string quartet
and wife of Sidney Harth, head of the university's music department, to join the orchestra.   She will be the associate principal
second violinist next season.

Other players the orchestra has been able to lure here next
season in the battle of musical chairs, include: Marc Jeanneret,
Indianapolis Symphony violist; David Cowley, assistant principal
cellist of the Buffalo Philharmonic; Paula Page, second harp; and
James Gorton, an Eastman graduate who will come here as oboist.
He replaces David Weiss who is going to Washington's National
Symphony as first oboist.

Officials of local schools and universities are not as pessimistic as Cohen about the string shortage.   Dr. Gerald Keenan,
dean of Duquesne University music school, said there are many
string applicants for the fall semester, though scholarship money
is needed to aid some of them.   "And for the first time we seem
to have more school orchestras than ever in our Mideast Music
Conference which attracts student musicians from all over the
country.   This indicates the string shortage is lessening."

Chauncey Kelly, acting head of music at Carnegie-Mellon
while Harth is on a six-month sabbatical, said:

> We are encouraged by the performance level of string
> players applying for our master's programs, even though
> there are not many in number.
>
> The real difficulty is at the undergraduate level.   This is
> due primarily to the emphasis on band in school programs.
> It's much easier for a youngster to learn brass and wood-
> winds than a string instrument.

But when they see how few openings are available in orchestras, the pendulum will swing. The good student sees the high pay and long seasons in the major orchestras and will study strings as a means of reaching the orchestral ranks.

Stanley Levin, director of music in Pittsburgh public schools, has encouraged string players through programs for the musically talented, discovery and teaching programs, all-city grade and high school orchestras. He said over 2000 students are now studying string instruments in city grade schools.

So, if you have a violin stashed away in the attic, get it out and begin practicing. In this day of a serious shortage of string players you could still make it to the Pittsburgh Symphony Orchestra.

CAN BLACKS OVERCOME
THE CLASSICAL MUSIC ESTABLISHMENT?*

Herbert Russcol

With the exception of a few stars like Andre Watts and Leontyne Price--and, of course, the field of jazz and popular entertainment--music has been a whites-only stronghold. Lip service has been paid to equal opportunity for Blacks in concert music, but the fact is that discrimination--covert or open--still operates against the hiring of Blacks for symphonic ensembles. Among the most prestigious orchestras in the United States there is one Black in the New York Philharmonic, one with the Cleveland Orchestra, and three with the Pittsburgh Symphony. Stokowski's American Symphony Orchestra has eight.

Why? "An unfortunate shortage of qualified Negro players," I was told by a number of managers. "We have scoured the country," states Howard Harrington, manager of the Detroit Symphony. Peter Pastreich of the St. Louis Symphony says, "We're dying to get our hands on a Negro." Apparently the Boston Symphony is too--at least it has asked Benjamin Steinberg, director of the Negro-training Symphony of the New World (38 of its 90 players are blacks), to be on the lookout for a Negro percussionist. In one sense, of course, a shortage does exist. "It takes fifteen years to develop a classical musician," says recently appointed New Jersey Symphony conductor Henry Lewis, the first Negro permanent director of a major American orchestra; "how many young Negroes saw a future in classical music fifteen years ago?" The Ford Foundation's Douglas G. Pugh, author of a study on the Negro musician, adds, "The chance to play with a major orchestra depends on what kind of

*Abridged from High Fidelity/Musical America, August 1968. Reprinted by permission.

experience players get in the minor league. " (The Ford Foundation, by the way, withholds its considerable orchestral grants from any ensembles that have discriminatory hiring practices.) But the situation was, until recently, dismal. Now, there are a few Blacks who appear intermittently, at least, and managers seem to be bidding for them.

The theory of an "unfortunate shortage of Negro players" is emphatically denied by some sources close to the scene. Benjamin Steinberg, for instance, says, "It's hard to believe, when we can put thirty-eight Negroes on stage--and look at their credentials, listen to them play--that more Negroes shouldn't be playing in the smaller orchestras. "

What do Black musicians have to say about the paucity of Negroes auditioning for symphony positions? "Twenty years ago, " says violinist Sanford Allen, the sole Black in the New York Philharmonic, "Negro children did not see Negroes in major symphony orchestras. As a result, there was little incentive to study symphonic instruments, since there was no visible outlet for any talents thus developed. It's more than six years since I was hired. Where are the others? Only a small percentage of the symphony orchestras in this country are integrated, and the causes are being eradicated at an agonizingly slow pace. I'm still the only Black in the 'Big Three' orchestras. " Henry Lewis is one musician who takes a rather mellow, even optimistic view. 'The orchestras today are bending over backwards to get Negro players. In fact, if a Negro oboist and a white oboist audition for the same opening, the Negro has an edge on the job--things being as they are. "

From this we turn to Europe, where a remarkable colony of "Afro-American musicians" live and work. Black artists are scattered in Rome, Paris, Zurich, and all over Germany's music centers. The most noted of these expatriates is the conductor Dean Dixon, now General Director of the Frankfurt Opera. He left America for good in 1948, fed up with all the obstacles he ran into as a Black musician. The doors were closed to him then for a permanent post, and are probably still closed. Even in Europe, Dixon had to overcome what he calls 'prejudice against a black man in tails leading a hundred white musicians through a symphony. " Would he come back to America today? According to Ernest Dunbar's The Black Expatriates--A Study of American Negroes in Exile (Dutton), Dixon's attitude is "No no no no no. I kicked myself out of America, and even if I didn't nobody was interested in helping me. Because helping a Negro in my field, a field which requires a certain intellectual background, which requires a leadership ability, goes against what America says we Negroes don't possess. "

Dixon was permanent conductor of the Göteborg Symphony in Sweden before his recent Frankfurt appointment. Everett Lee is another Black conductor who settled successfully in Sweden after an abject time in America; he now leads the Nörrkoping Symphony there. Twenty years ago, Lee tried to form an interracial

"Cosmopolitan Little Symphony" in New York.   It was to be a training orchestra for talented Black musicians, who otherwise had no
place to get orchestra experience.   "I pleaded with them to come
in with me and keep practicing for that Big Day.   It was no use.
They were all too skeptical, the odds were too long.   Some of
them went into jazz, some of them are washing cars today. "

          Henry Lewis believes that education is all-important and that
the crucial age is 14 to 16.   "That's when the Negro boy drops out
to support himself, or to help his family.   That's the age when he
drops his big dream about being a concert musician. "   What is being done to help the talented young Black get a scholarship to a
music school, or lessons with a good teacher?   The Juilliard
School replied that there was no special program of aid, and they
had 'no idea how many Negroes attended Juilliard. "   The New England Conservatory of Music stated that they had no program to aid
Blacks, were aware of none in Boston.   It has some thirty Blacks
enrolled out of more than five hundred students.   The Chicago Symphony Orchestra does maintain a first-rate training orchestra,
which has several Blacks enrolled.   This admirable scheme seems
to be unique in America, sponsored and run by the Chicago orchestra itself, with its own endowment program.   St. Louis has a bust-
ling community orchestra, and is doing much to teach Blacks, with
aid from "Title Three" Federal funds.

          In Harlem, singer Dorothy Maynor directs a School of the
Arts "from the age of three, until the artist is ready to walk out
onto a concert stage. "   Special attention is devoted to string players; violin teacher Ivan Galamian organized their instruction program.   The experience of Benjamin Steinberg's Symphony of the
New World is more heartening.   Well-known white players teach
and sit in the first chairs, for token payment.   Steinberg got
$25,000 from the National Foundation of the Arts, $5000 from the
Martha Baird Rockefeller Fund for Music.   "We need more, " he
says.

          It's easy enough to say, "Where are the foundations, and all
the educators?"   But the conservatories, orchestras, philanthropies
are doing little or nothing to get these kids onto a serious-music
track.   Neither is the government.   Any accomplishment seems to
lie in the activities of concerned individuals of good will.   If we as
Americans are too selfish of our time, energy, and money to help
young Blacks, at least we as serious music lovers should be selfish
enough to help tap the musical resources of the black community.
We do need them more than they need us.

AN ABOUT FACE ON
BLACK MUSICIANS AT THE PHILHARMONIC*

Donal Henahan

There is, to quote a prophetic American folk song of the
fifties, "A Whole Lotta Shakin' Goin' On. " Last week we saw the
New York Stock Exchange electing the first Black director in its
180-year history--which sounds earthshaking even to one who is
quite vague about what, exactly, the New York Stock Exchange does.
In the same week, another pillar of the establishment, the New
York Philharmonic, agreed on a fair-employment program with the
city's Human Rights Commission after three years of debate.

Such seismic rumblings can only lift the hopes of those of
us who have listened in growing consternation while spokesmen both
black and white have advised us that the country's only future lies
in some homegrown variety of apartheid. The Philharmonic agreement is, in fact, a brilliant example of what should be an old saying: people always will do what is right, so long as someone insists on it. The Philharmonic now tacitly concedes that it was un-
wise in not getting started long ago on some plan for finding and
hiring Black musicians.

Ten years ago, the orchestra did engage a Black violinist
as a permanent member, but then, as if stunned by its own audac-
ity, stopped short. Now the old inertia has been overcome, so
that even before the commission officially ordered it to do so, the
Philharmonic had been starting to move. It is not unusual nowadays to look up and see Black instrumentalists working in the Philharmonic.

So far, progress has been limited to engaging substitutes and
extras, but the commission agreement also puts on pressure to insure that minority musicians will be considered for whatever permanent openings occur. Special effort is going into ambitious
training programs for potential orchestra players (just how ambitious will depend upon the amounts of money that can be raised).

The most tangible results so far came from last September's
Orchestra Repertoire Institute, financed half by the orchestra and
half by the New York State Council on the Arts, which brought 53
Black instrumentalists from 12 states and the Dominican Republic
to work side by side with the Philharmonic members for one week.
According to Helen M. Thompson, the Philharmonic's manager, who
stage-managed the affair, tremendous personal as well as professional involvement developed between students and orchestra members. Of the 53 students taking part, Philharmonic musicians found

10 qualified to be offered advanced study under a continuing program. Half a dozen finally entered that program.

It was only a start, but a start is always the hardest part. What the mere existence of such programs means to young Blacks in terms of incentive can hardly be calculated, but Mrs. Thompson has a touching file of letters that young players sent to Philharmonic members after the week of morning, noon and night coaching was over. One letter, fairly typical, reads: "I had given up all hope because I felt I was born too soon and in the wrong place and therefore would not have the chance to become a professional symphony musician. Now I am renewing my efforts."

At least as significant as anything that may result from the Philharmonic's own talent search is its plan for extending information about talented young instrumentalists to other American orchestras. Under the program accepted by the Human Rights Commission, reports on qualifications of the most advanced players are being made available to some 100 orchestras. "They're all looking for Black players," reports Mrs. Thompson. A long-range hope also lies in a scholarship project begun a few years ago and now shifting into higher gear: this year the Philharmonic gave out $37,000 to finance 61 such scholarships for young Black musicians.

Now there are even minority representatives on the Philharmonic's board of directors (three) and on the upper rungs of administration (two). Black faces appear in the orchestra with increasing regularity, and it seems inevitable that some will be finding their way into permanent membership before too long. Serious problems will have to be faced all along the way. Only the most implacable music-hater would wish to see quota systems applied, either voluntarily or by municipal decree, in a field where only the most talented, most thoroughly prepared specialists of any color should be considered.

Parallel with fair-hiring policies, ways have to be evolved to insure that artistic quality does not seriously suffer because of amateur meddling. But at the moment, the problems are different. With so brief a history of symphonic participation, the Black today finds himself constantly on the defensive and forced, like the Jew of previous centuries who was locked inside the pale, to be twice as good in order to succeed.

Chapter VII

WHAT THE FUTURE HOLDS

Introduction. The orchestra from its beginnings to the present day is not merely a musical instrument, but one which reflects and is an intrinsic part of the world we live in. The orchestra (and all other performing arts) must of necessity continue to be a part of our society--it must meet the wants and expectations of human beings in the future.

To say simply, "man does not live by bread alone," is not itself a reason for the being of an orchestra. Man as well does not live without developing an understanding of the fine and the performing arts, learning of careful uses for human and financial resources, and of course choosing inspiring performances of music of all kinds within his society. For their contribution to this end, orchestras justifiably are revered, and must continue to be so in the future.

An orchestral musician (Rafael Druian), the Rockefeller Brothers Fund Panel, an orchestra manager (Patrick Hayes), an economist (William J. Baumol), a critic (Harold C. Schonberg), and a composer-conductor (Leonard Bernstein) give their appraisals of today's problems and what the future holds.

ARTISTIC INTEGRITY IS THE FIRST THING TO GO
(Money talks but can it be taught to sing?)*

Rafael Druian

On January 1, 1948, at about 11:00 am, the Dallas Symphony assembled at the Dallas railroad station to start on a tour of several weeks. This was my first tour of my first season as concertmaster. The day stands out in my memory because of the events that followed.

*From Symphony News, vol. 25, no. 3 (June 1974). Copyright 1974 by the American Symphony Orchestra League. Reprinted by permission.

Our first concert of the tour, in Yoakum, Texas, was to have started at 8:30 pm. However, the train that was to take us to the bus that was to take us to Yoakum was about three or four hours late. The time seemed endless, for there were several high school bands serenading the arrival of players for a New Year's Day football encounter. In a station that was acoustically resonant beyond one's fondest hopes--these were the days of marble waiting rooms--the sound was quite overpowering. And remember, it was New Year's morning.

When the train finally arrived, we set out for Yoakum, arriving about 9:30 pm. The audience was seated, patiently waiting, and eventually the concert started at about 10:00 or 10:30. It finished at about midnight, and we climbed back on the buses to take us to the in-town hotel where we were to stay overnight. However, when our manager inspected the rooms in the hotel, which had seemed a bit suspicious from the outside, his fears were confirmed that this hotel was not fit to be our oasis. Patiently, we waited in the buses while our manager made many frantic phone calls, finally securing the required number of hotel rooms in Houston, where we arrived at approximately 3:15 am.

What I remember clearly is that, for the most part, this sequence of events was accepted in fairly good humor. There was a spirit of adventure and a "show must go on" attitude. While no one was enchanted with the way the day (night) turned out, everyone took it in stride and made the best of a very trying situation.

Now, as I finish my last few weeks as concertmaster of American orchestras, I can reflect on the many changes that have taken place during the 25 years I occupied this interesting and challenging chair. To name but a few: the expanded season, the salary increases, the many fringe benefits, and the musicians' greater role in making all these come into being. In the year I started, the present situation could not have been imagined. This was not a gradual development; it happened in the last ten years or so. And as a result of the speed and lack of planning, some undesirable things developed along with the welcome ones.

A serious problem I think is the credibility gap, as well as communication gap, that exists between many managements and the members of the orchestras. There are cases in which the lack of respect for a musical director is a serious drawback to the successful operation of the orchestra. Today in many instances, the morale is low and militancy on the rise more than ever. Why so much bad along with the good and where does the responsibility lie, if anywhere? It seems to me that there are several contributing factors to this situation. My observations of them are purely subjective and must be understood in that context.

A serious problem resulted by entering the 52-week season without sufficient preparation and research into its consequences. For example, the dramatic budget increase caused by year-round

employment forced management to create more outlets for performances.   To earn more income, more concerts were given.   But
no more services were provided for.   As a result, many concerts
were under-rehearsed and thrown together hastily.   This is de-
moralizing for the players and has the effect of making an orchestra career more of a job than a profession.

Certainly the highest possible musical standards cannot be
observed in these situations.   The artistic interests of the orchestra suffer, resulting in poor morale, disenchantment, and greater
intransigence at subsequent negotiations.   Often this results in the
need for more money to meet the new contract requirements.   And
the circle widens.

There is another factor that has had serious effects.   When
musicians realized that they were actually subsidizing their respective orchestras by working for wages that were intolerably low and
seasons that were much too short, they demanded that the local
union representatives remedy the situation.   In some cases, local
officials did not necessarily agree with the musicians' position and
did not take the initiative.   That's when the players began insisting
on doing their own bargaining.   Where this was permitted by the
union, the musicians made real gains.   Ratification became the
call of the orchestras, and the results, in regard to working conditions, salary increases, and so on, were dramatic.

But along with this came the negative aspect.   The musicians' preoccupation with the new duties they had assumed, that of
bargaining for a new contract and then policing it, brought on a
situation where their interest lay more in this direction than in
practicing their profession at the highest level.   When recognition
came to members of the orchestra for their work in labor matters, and when very little if any recognition was ever accorded the
members as players (other than some principals), it was not hard
to understand why the vital but nonetheless non-musical matters
preoccupied their time and attention.   Again, what suffered was the
performance.   Another reason for lack of musical fulfillment developed.

The matter of recognition I feel is a very pertinent one
psychologically to a person who is able to achieve enough stature
to join a first-class orchestra.   There are outmoded conventions,
such as seating (for the strings), that do much to accentuate this
problem.   The maintenance of a seating hierarchy contributes much
as an irritant.   When one considers that all the players in a section play the same notes all the time, it is really difficult to understand why it matters so much what chair one sits in to play
these same notes.   This problem needs serious thought and immediate attention, for it stratifies people without reason and creates
artificial and frustrating situations.   The whole concept of promotion by moving a stand closer to the conductor is absurd.

Great conductors are indeed far too few today, and as a

result, the title of music director often falls to a person not really qualified to handle such a complex and distinguished position.   The main criterion used by some boards of directors seems to be "can he sell tickets?", a talent one can hardly argue with, but not in itself enough to qualify an individual as the music director of a symphony orchestra.

In some cases, the appointed music director does not live up to his box office expectations, and the public does not respond to his performances.   Instead of examining the situation from a professional and musical standard, the management simply publicize the conductor more--making him a star--so that more tickets can be sold.

In order to do this, a great deal of money is spent.   But what then if the box office does not reflect the anticipated improvement?   And if the performances not only obviously do not improve but actually become worse?   The conductor is so busy being a personality that he does not have time to prepare his scores, and the audience is not fooled.

If the musicians of an orchestra call this kind of situation to management's attention, the response is often condescending and patronizing.   This apparent lack of concern with the professional level of a music director, not to mention the arbitrary lack of interest in seeking advice from musicians when selecting a leader, brings on an even greater cynicism on the part of the players, their position being "if they don't care, why should I?"   This again encourages concentration on the only means of expression that really exists between the members of an orchestra and its management, that of contract negotiations.   All the stored up resentments caused by such circumstances are parlayed into more money demands.   And the circle widens irrepressibly.

The cause again seems to be the lack of musical concern. There was a time in which one achieved a certain stature through work and diligence; recognition, respect, and fame eventually came, and one was indeed a leader of his profession.   Now, it appears, one becomes famous first, and then we are all kept dangling, waiting, to see if he will also become good.   Nowhere is this more true than in conducting, and no one is exploited more than young conductors.   And thereby the talent, which is extraordinary in some cases, is never allowed to take root and grow. What a pity.

Normally, an orchestra grows artistically when led by a distinguished musical director.   If one examines the history of our great orchestras, the efforts of one person always stand out.   It is through his musicianship and his concern that the orchestra attains eminence, for example, Koussevitzky and the Boston Symphony, Szell and the Cleveland Orchestra, Toscanini and the New York Philharmonic.

When there is no such leadership and the void is not filled, the resulting musical standard becomes a cause for concern for all. Until the situation can be remedied, performance will continue to suffer. The players will become more demoralized, and the audience, sensing this, will be unenthusiastic about supporting the organization.

There are very few tasks that require the kind of dedication, talent, leadership abilities and knowledge that conducting requires. And I will say that no one has more respect for great conductors than I do. I have been fortunate enough to have played with some that had these qualities and it always was an experience to learn from and to cherish. An orchestra needs a musical objective to guide its destiny. No other kind of objective can serve to sustain an orchestra's existence. If a conductor is not capable of doing this, then other means must be found to achieve this end.

In conclusion, I want to emphasize my disappointment with the attitude of many of my colleagues whose concern with matters non-musical exceeds their concern with their professional standards. I know full well that there may be reasons for their attitudes, but it is hard to find justification for it. Where the members of an orchestra filled the need in negotiating matters, they were not always as insistent on filling the need created in the artistic and professional area. While one might say that they were not invited to do so, neither were they invited to become negotiators. And in the same way, if they took it upon themselves to right one wrong, perhaps they should have taken equally positive action in the musical and artistic problems that arose.

The one underlying factor that is common to the situations I mentioned is the one of artistic integrity. This is the first thing that goes. And I feel if it does go, all else goes with it. For the orchestra is not there to pay musicians. The orchestra is not there to provide ego satisfaction for conductors. The orchestra is not there to be a property of its board of directors and its manager. The orchestra is there to make music. And only if that is its sole function and only if that function is carried out at the highest possible level of achievement, can answers be found for problems that develop in trying to achieve this end. For instance, if it is true in a specific situation that a distinguished musical director cannot be obtained to lead the orchestra at a specific time and to provide a high level of integrity and artistry, surely there must be amongst the orchestra members several musicians who together might be given the task of preserving the quality and standards of the orchestra.

I think if a real effort is made to identify the problems that arise as the orchestras develop, solutions can and will be found. But one must be ready to adjust or abandon many practices that were right in the past but were not able to encompass the changes brought on by the passing of time. If the objectives are simply to keep going somehow, I doubt that even massive Federal aid can be of much help. For the problem is not really money; money is the symptom. When the contributing factors to the problems of an orchestra are not identified and dealt with, they usually translate themselves into "more money. "

The musicians want "more money"; the association has to raise "more money"; the public is asked to contribute "more money"; and the tickets cost "more money. " No matter how much money is raised or paid in salaries, the sum will never be sufficient to eliminate the cause which necessitated raising the money in the first place. The preoccupation with money only creates the need to raise more money.

Along with reevaluating many values, the young musician of the emerging generation also questions the objectives of some of his older colleagues and does not rush to enter a situation in which the values are traded for money. I have personally known too many young people who will not join an orchestra because of some or all of the reasons I have mentioned. And if we cannot find qualified musicians to play, then the future of the orchestra is not hard to predict.

DEVELOPING PUBLIC INTEREST
IN THE PERFORMING ARTS*

Rockefeller Brothers Fund Panel

Perhaps the most important role of the university and the liberal arts college is, and has traditionally been, development of an appreciation and understanding of the arts as part of a broad general education in the humanities. Many educators still believe this is the university's only legitimate function in the arts.

Responsiveness to the performing arts is created through knowledge and attendance, and educational institutions have consequently had an enormous influence on the development of discerning audiences. An important factor in the growing interest in the arts in America has been the expanding audience coming from the increasingly higher proportion of the population with college degrees.

But the humanities generally are at a disadvantage compared to the physical sciences in our universities, and the imbalance appears to be growing. Special aid from the federal government is available for science programs in universities. This in turn attracts matching funds from other sources, putting the humanities at

*Pages 181-182 from The Performing Arts: Problems and Prospects, by a Rockefeller Brothers Fund panel; New York: The Fund, 1965. Copyright 1965 by Rockefeller Brothers Fund, Inc. Reprinted by permission.

a still further disadvantage.   This long-range trend in American
education can only have an adverse effect on audience development
for the arts.   The panel believes there is urgent need to redress
the existing imbalance in the financial support of the physical sciences and that of the arts and humanities in universities.

There are many techniques available for achieving this balance.   They range from the creation of new professional training
schools to the expansion of courses in the appreciation of the arts.
All universities cannot and should not attempt all of these things.
Each will have to consider the needs of its students and community
in determining what it should undertake.   But the university is one
of the natural homes for the arts, and it should be encouraged to
extend the range of its hospitality in the years to come.

THE NEED FOR MAJOR SUBSIDIES*

Patrick Hayes

Soon after Antal Dorati arrived in Washington to become
Music Director of the National Symphony Orchestra, he made a
speech at the National Press Club.   In response to a question about
his plans to introduce classical music to a wider public and to
establish a new relevancy in the spirit of the times, he replied that
he had no such plans, that his task was to make music, good music, the best music, for those who wished to come and hear it.
"We are an elite," he said.   "This music is not for everyone. "

A few in the audience gasped.   Here was an Old-World attitude, that art and the good things in life are only for the privileged
few; and such an attitude was being expressed in the 1970s by the
new leader of the symphony orchestra of the capital city of the
world's leading democracy, where any reference to or emphasis
on any project or movement as being "only for the few" was ana-
thema.   Mr. Dorati's brief comment in this direction was not
picked up, nor was much made of it.   Even if it had been, the
dialogue would have been healthy; for upon reflection, it can be
shown that he was both right and timely, and not undemocratic at
all.   His own personal feeling and assertion about an elite do, indeed, stem honestly from his European background, but the application of his assertion to the American scene has a different connotation than he might have imagined.

It has to do with the nature and character of "the few" for
whom classical music holds charm.   Usually an elite or "the few"

*From The Annals of the American Academy of Political and So-
cial Science, vol. 405 (January 1973), George Fox Mott, Special
Editor.   Reprinted by permission.   Mr. Hayes was Managing Director, Washington Performing Arts Society.

implies those at the top of a society, the well-to-do and privileged, and those with social and political power. But in the same way that there is an intellectual elite in American society which is not necessarily rich and privileged and is not privy to social and political power, there is also a musical elite, and it is found in a vertical column rather than a horizontal stratum of our society. The audience for classical music, for opera and ballet, for theatre, and those attending art galleries and museums in the United States include people from a wide span of economic and social levels whose appreciation of these arts makes them an elite for all their diversity of levels of affluence, education, family backgrounds, and individual lifestyles.

This understanding of the audience for the arts in America is essential to an appraisal of whether the American people may one day become a broadly cultivated society, Athenian in tone and Augustan in proportion. If appreciation and patronage of the arts were confined to an elite at the top of our society, it would be a question of their eventually trickling down to the lower levels where most of us are, and this would be a slow process of audience development.   As it is, then, we find the arts-elite already spread upward and downward in the social and economic scales, and they need only widen to embrace more people at each of the levels to increase the audience and bring to more people the cultural enrichment and personal pleasure which are the mission of the arts.

How wide is this vertical band today, and how far does it have to expand for Athenian and Augustan dreams to come true? All available figures add up to not more than 5 percent of the total U. S. population, and the study of Professors Baumol and Bowen of Princeton put the figure closer to 3 percent.   Lest those who read these paragraphs become discouraged at such a low percentage, let me promptly put it in positive perspective.   Three percent of America's once 200 million population is just over six million for the category of the arts-elite.   Not bad.   And 5 percent is ten million, an important constituency for any activity or national program.   However, at this juncture in our history the percentage of the population which identifies with the arts is smaller than it should be.   The reasons for the limitation are rooted in our history, dramatically forecast by John Adams in a letter to his wife--probably written from Philadelphia during the long dreary year leading up to the final agreement and signing of the Declaration of Independence.   Mr. Adams wrote:

"I must study politics and war, that my sons may have the liberty to study mathematics and philosophy.   My sons ought to study mathematics and philosophy, geography, natural history and naval architecture, navigation, commerce, and agriculture, in order to give their children a right to study painting, poetry, music, architecture. "

In a speech delivered at the American Federation of Arts in

April 1962, Arthur Schlesinger, Jr., quoted these words of Mr.
Adams and added: "The arts logically occupy a secondary place
in the priorities of national development. A nation must achieve
its independence and begin its economic take-off before it can begin to devote serious attention to the quality of its culture. We
have as a nation fulfilled these conditions. We have long since
secured our political identity and our economic momentum. We
have long since reached John Adams's third phase. "

If the arts in America may be referred to as a product,
they presume a market and a marketplace. Thus far in this article we have dwelt on the audience as the market for our arts.
What of the marketplace? The arts marketplace is a concert hall,
an opera house, a theatre--let us here agree to refer only to the
performing arts, with which the writer is identified, although the
reader may easily substitute "art gallery" or "museum" for reference to painting and sculpture. The United States in the 1970s
abounds in places to perform. The cultural real-estate boom of
the last decade has been of bullish proportions. Examples are the
Lincoln Center for the Performing Arts in New York City, the
Pavilion in Los Angeles, and the John F. Kennedy Center for the
Performing Arts in Washington, D. C. Many universities have
added substantially to the national total of performing arts buildings,
for example, the University of Illinois with its Krainert Center,
Butler University in Indianapolis with the Crowe Auditorium, Dart-
mouth's Hopkins complex, and the University of Michigan's new
Power Theatre.

These concert halls and theatres, by their mere presence,
attract attention and serve as a magnet for action. Actors want to
act, singers want to sing, dancers to dance, and producers are
quick to seize upon all opportunities to bring these forces together
into performances for the public. The well-publicized growth of
ballet and modern dance in the United States during the last 15
years and the spread of regional theatre, decentralized away from
Broadway, are two evidences of this fact, not to mention the phenomenal growth in the number and quality of America's symphony
orchestras, with nearly 30 of them rated high in excellence by
world standards. When a fine arts activity building is built, there
is a natural inclination to use it--it is not a question of the chicken
or the egg--for while the artist indeed always comes first, he
must have a place to perform; he can exist without a place to perform, but this would be mere life-existence, not artistic fulfillment. It is a matter of good fortune and rejoicing that in these
times our artists have performing arts centers to turn to with a
supporting network of university auditoriums to supplement the opera
houses and concert halls of the major cities for well-planned tours.
In our Adam's third phase, the arts-housing problem can be said
to be well solved.

In Hamlet act 2, scene 2, Shakespeare reveals his own understanding of the actor as an artist. After greeting the itinerant
players, Hamlet charges Polonius with their care, saying: "Will

you see the players well bestowed? Do you hear, let them be well used; for they are the abstract and brief chronicles of the time: after your death you were better to have a bad epitaph than their ill report while you live. " During the nearly 400 years since these lines were written, the artist as a brief chronicle of his time has not always been well bestowed or appreciated or understood.   The artist is a distinctive member of society.   He has every attribute of other human beings of the time, plus artistic talent.   He enjoys the blessing of a gene, the seed word of "genius, " that comes down through generations of his family.   How else to account for a Mozart, a Beethoven, a Shakespeare, a latter day Heifetz and Rubinstein?   Recently a critic observed about Rudolf Serkin that "he came out of the womb playing a piano. " Born talent is what usually sets artists apart from their fellow men, and the degree of born talent is what sorts them out among themselves.

Another paragraph from Mr. Schlesinger's speech on Government and the Arts says it well: "The first point to understand is that the source of art is the artist.   This sounds obvious enough. Yet in a day when patrons of the arts sometimes seem to act as if the source of art were an institution--a university, say, or a foundation--it is no wonder that some go on to suppose that in the future the source of art might be the government itself.   Universities and foundations are splendid institutions and so too is government.   But art results from the confrontation of experience by a disciplined, sensitive and passionate individual, possessed of an intense interior vision and capable of rendering that vision in ways which heighten and deepen the sensibility of others; and it is this individual--the artist--who must always remain in the forefront of our consideration. "

Emergence of American Artists

American artists have come into their own in this century, especially in the last 25 years.   European artists still hold a special place in our esteem and affection as do the European countries themselves, and they are warmly welcome in our annual programs of concert presentations.   But it had to happen, as John Adams' third phase had to come, that our own country would produce its own artists.   Today we see American names in the opera lists, where Italian and German names dominated 30 to 50 years ago-- Richard Tucker, Roberta Peters, Leontyne Price, Jess Thomas, James MacCracken.   Russian names such as Rachmaninoff, Horo- witz, Piatigorsky, and Milstein dominated the instrumental lists before World War II; now we see the names of Van Cliburn, Isaac Stern, Andre Watts, and an all-American Juilliard String Quartet. Among conductors we have Leonard Bernstein, Thomas Schippers, Michael Tilson Thomas, and the young James Levine, the newly appointed chief conductor of the Metropolitan Opera Company.   Our university fine arts departments and our conservatories turn out hundreds of well-equipped musicians every year, adding to the na- tional inventory of performers and teachers.   Herein lies a chal- lenge to the American society to accelerate the national audience growth rate so that all of our artists may be well used.

Thus far our growth in the arts has been sporadic, un-
planned, and without official encouragement. The tensile strength
of our artists themselves has brought us as far as we have come.
In contrast to our progress in the space program where all was
indeed planned, encouraged, and financed, the arts have had to
make progress on their own.

It is surely now time for a national thrust of public commitment and financial support commensurate with the levels of the
Arts Council of Great Britain and of the Canada Arts Council,
judged in per capita ratios. Present policy only implies a statement of national purpose with skeletal legislation establishing a
National Council on the Arts and the National Endowment for the
Arts and Humanities. We have the beginning of an intelligent
bureaucracy in the staff of the National Endowment for the Arts,
with Nancy Hanks as chairman. Appropriations for this endowment
are increasingly modestly year by year, to a present level of just
under forty million dollars, and there is a recent call from a
group known as "Partnership for the Arts" for a $200 million goal
of federal support for the arts in America by 1976.

Justification for Public Support

Although private in origin and development, as are universities and hospitals, the public service demands on arts organizations are extensive, so much so that the costs of rendering such
service outrun private capacity to pay for it. If service to music
itself were the sole question generation by generation, chamber
music in small places for a few people would serve the purpose--
as was the case prior to the first public musical events in 1672 in
London. But public music is the order of the day, and it carries
a high price tag which invokes a dilemma. If the costs of public
music were passed on to its consumers, ticket prices would be increased to a point beyond the reach of a majority of the members
of the vertical column of patrons. Attendance would drop, while
costs continued to rise.

"Ticket prices within the reach of all" has been our public
philosophy since at least 1881, when Henry Lee Higginson founded
the Boston Symphony Orchestra to perform concerts for a general
public. With ticket prices kept within general reach, ticket revenue,
like tuition revenue at a university, does not cover the total costs
of the arts presented to the public, and this leads to annual deficits
which must be covered. Private gifts and donations and general
sustaining funds no longer suffice. A point of no return has been
reached. The time for higher levels of government subsidy is at
hand.

As we move toward necessary full public support for the arts
in the form of federal funds, we must be on the alert to avoid any
semblance of political interference in artistic programs and activities. The American arts of today are preponderantly a product of
the private sector, and the independence inherent in the private

origin of our arts organizations, as well as the independence of
our artists themselves, must be maintained and held inviolate.
Governor Nelson Rockefeller cautioned his fellow governors in a
speech at their 59th annual meeting in October 1967, with these
words: "The politics of art are hazardous--yet an unalterable
axiom will eliminate all dangers: There must be no political interference in the arts by government. If the artistic community feels
it is being used or its freedom controlled by government, it will
react loudly and heatedly."

Care in the language of the act of Congress that established
the National Council on the Arts, and later the National Endowment
for the Arts and Humanities, has made possible a record of several
years of noninterference by government in artistic programs. The
grants of money from the endowment to arts organizations are on a
basis of no-political-strings-attached, only that there be strict and
complete accountability for the expenditure of the funds for the purpose stated in the application.

The end result of adequate financing of the arts in America
will be the full use of our artists, making it possible for them to
give their full measure toward improving the quality of life in our
society and to assist all of us in the pursuit of happiness. In his
speech to the nation's governors just referred to, Governor Rockefeller said: "The arts are a critical measure of 'the quality of
life'--a fact that historians, if not always politicians, have recognized for centuries. And as politicians and governors, we are
constantly faced with combating the negative, inherited problems
that have become too much for any other segment of society to
handle--drug addiction, crime and poverty to name a few. The
arts offer us the rare opportunity to further something that is posi-
tive--the expansion of human capacity and the pursuit of happiness--
which is, after all, not only the central element of the arts, but
of good government as well."

In sum, there is now underway a trend toward the arts in
our lives, consistent with John Adams's prediction. With each
generation more people become educated and cultivated and have
more leisure time. We have a splendid supply of artists in our
population. We have, today, a national awareness of the value of
the arts in our society. It remains for us to widen the base of
participation on the part of audiences and to provide for intelligent
and adequate public financing measures, and thus achieve a democracy of artistic appreciation.

PERFORMING ARTS: THE PERMANENT CRISIS*

William J. Baumol

At the end of a recent talk, a member of the audience

---

*See footnote next page.

asked me whether I thought that live performance is obsolete. This
is not an idle question; it is controversial on artistic as well as on
economic grounds.   Let me cite the opinions of two highly respected authorities.   The noted composer Milton Babbitt has suggested that listening to live performances is a peculiar and pre-
historic form of self-abuse.   What would happen, he said, to the
audience for the novel if its reading required people to assemble
in hot, uncomfortable, and crowded auditoriums in which the text
was rather badly projected on a screen.   On the other hand, many
feel just as strongly that live performance is the essence of artistic
experience.   Here again I cite an eminent authority, a man who
has made important contributions to music in a variety of roles,
and who has compared the experience of listening to a recording to
kissing one's sweetheart over the telephone.

   But my purpose is not to discuss the esthetic elements of
the controversy; my objective is to examine its financial implications.   And I intend to show that there is a startling difference between the economic structures of live and recorded performances,
a difference that has a great deal to suggest about their futures.

The Problem

   I will start with a paradox readily observed in the history
of the live performing arts, an observation that may be backed up
statistically.   First, figures going back to the middle of the 18th
century show that the salaries of performers increase more slowly
than salaries in the economy in general.   This, I am sure, comes
as a surprise to no one.   Second, we observe that in the live performing arts, salaries constitute the bulk of cost of operation.
(Typically, 70 to 80 per cent of the budget of a performing organization consists of payment to performers.)   Third--and here the
paradox arises--we observe that costs of production of live performance rise steadily and far more rapidly than production costs
in the economy as a whole.   Why, if costs in the performing arts
are composed of salaries and if these salaries rise more slowly
than those elsewhere in the economy, do the costs of live performance rise more rapidly than costs in the economy as a whole?

   (This relationship is paralleled in the economics of our institutions of higher education.   Those who are concerned with the
budgetary problems in educational institutions are constantly plagued
by precisely these three phenomena, and they are constantly in difficulty explaining to their sponsors how one resolves the fundamental paradox they represent.   The bulk of observations in this article on the economics of the performing arts apply directly to higher
education.)

   The remainder of my discussion will be devoted to a

*From Business Horizons, vol. 10, no. 3 (fall 1967).   Copyright
1967 by Foundation for the School of Business, Indiana University,
Bloomington.   Reprinted by permission.

resolution of this paradox. First, I want to emphasize that it is
no mere curiosity. To say that the future of live performance depends on these issues is not an exaggeration. Only if we understand these cost phenomena are we in a position to recognize the
magnitude and nature of the financial requirements for a viable
performing arts.

This paradox at once suggests that a number of the alleged
explanations of the financial difficulties of the performing arts
really are not at the heart of the matter. For example, one of
the standard phenomena cited as an explanation for the budgetary
problems of the arts is the pressure of inflation. Clearly, if inflation were the primary cause, the cost of performing arts would
go up, but the cost per performance would rise no more rapidly
than the cost of manufacturing in the economy as a whole. Yet,
while costs in the economy as a whole rise on the order of 1.5
per cent a year, costs of live performance characteristically rise
at a cumulative compounded rate on the order of magnitude of 3 to
6 per cent compounded. (These figures are for the period since
World War II.)

Those who are familiar with compound interest calculations
will recognize immediately how terrifying a rate of increase this
represents. This extremely rapid rate of increase far exceeds,
for example, any known rate of increase of ticket prices. Though
we complain about how much ticket prices have gone up for Broadway shows and the Metropolitan Opera, a comparison of the figures
with those of the 1920's shows that these prices have increased
roughly at the same rate as the price level. Thus, in purchasing
power, it costs virtually no more today than it did in 1926 to buy
the most expensive seat at a Broadway musical.

The threat to all performing institutions is obvious and constitutes what I term a "permanent crisis." Such a crisis exists
if this cumulative increase in costs is not an accidental phenomenon,
not a fortuitous historical event. If, on the one hand, resistance
to increases in ticket prices continues, while, on the other, the
costs continue to compound at their current rates, then in the long
run, the year-to-year deficits and shortfalls about which we read
in the newspapers will be magnified. And the dangers to our arts
institutions (both the public institutions in their relationship to the
legislature, and private institutions in their relationship to private
donors) are perfectly clear.

The Explanation

My objective, however, is not merely to cite these facts,
startling though they may be, but to explain them in order to determine whether they represent an accidental relationship or whether,
in fact, they result from something inherent in the nature of the
operations.

This process requires us to turn briefly to abstract theory

to show precisely what is going on. I shall argue that the explanation is inherent in the very technology of the living arts. Let me
explain our theoretical analysis by dealing for a moment with a
world in which only two types of economic activities exist--activi-
ties that we may characterize as the technologically progressive
and the non-progressive. In one of these, productivity per man-
hour rises constantly; in the other, the output of each man is exactly the same year after year. There will be a difference in the
history of these two types of industry. In the progressive industry
where productivity rises perhaps 3 per cent a year, workers and
their unions will soon recognize that output per man also rises at
that rate; it will not be long before their wage demands will go up
accordingly. At the same time, in the nonprogressive industry, in
which productivity per man-hour remains constant, one of two alternatives may occur. First, wages may remain unchanged, in
which case, in relative terms, the workers in those industries become progressively poorer and poorer. Or, second, some adaptation may result--perhaps workers may leave the nonprogressive sector
and enter the progressive industry and, for this reason or as a consequence of public sympathy, the nonprogressive sector's labor force
will demand and receive increases in wages.

     Assume that wages in the nonprogressive sector rise not by
3 per cent, but 2 per cent a year. Now, let's take stock of what
has happened. In the progressive sector wages and productivity
have gone up by 3 per cent; the two offset one another precisely,
and, therefore, the labor costs per unit of output have remained
precisely unchanged. In the nonprogressive sector, however, wages
have gone up only 2 per cent. But what has happened to productivity? Productivity has remained constant and, therefore, labor
costs per unit of output rise every year by 2 per cent. A technological difference then accounts for the disparity in cost behavior,
and no efficiency expert, no amount of enthusiasm, and no degree
of determination can do more than provide temporary relief. In
the long run these trends are nearly immutable.

     We have one step further to go--to explain the inherent dif-
ference between the technologies of the two sectors. From what
has been said so far, it might still be a historical accident that
one sector is progressive and the other is not. To see why the
difference is not simply fortuitous, we must be a little more specific about the nature of the two industries. Suppose we have only
two commodities in the world--the performance of Schubert lieder
and the manufacture of pinball machines. As one would expect,
the production of pinball machines will turn out to be the progressive sector. The very nature of these two operations dictates a
difference in the role of labor. In the one case, labor is the end
product, whereas in the other, labor is only a means. The player
of a pinball machine neither knows nor cares how many hours of
craftsmanship went into its production. Given two pinball machines
of identical quality--one produced with three hours of labor, one
produced with one hour of labor--the amount of labor does not influence one's choice of machines. The choice depends on a variety

of other considerations, such as which machine is more attractive or which is more conveniently located to refreshments.   In the case of the Schubert lieder, however, if we are dealing with a song cycle that was written to be performed in approximately 38 minutes, it may be that by heroic effort and superb training and practice the singer may manage to complete it in 27 minutes, thus increasing the output per man-hour.   The quality of the performance, however, will suffer.   It is inherent in the technology of the product that just so many man-hours are required for its performance.   No matter how brilliant the engineers or efficiency experts, relatively little can be done to increase the output per man-hour of the lieder singer, but there are no similar barriers preventing an increase, year after year, in the pinball machine output.

All the evidence that we have suggests that the world has behaved precisely in accord with these observations.   That is to say, all the statistics suggest that manufacturing productivity per man-hour (including the manufacturing of the electronic media), has, year in, year out, gone up with astonishing consistency at about 2.5 per cent per year compounded.   This figure holds true from the beginning of the century.   Compounded productivity per hour has gone up as a result of technological change, capital accumulation, and a variety of other such aids.

In education and live performance, it is an exaggeration to say that no increase has occurred in productivity per man-hour. The picture is not as black and white as my abstract model would suggest.   For example, the jet has increased the productivity per man-hour of the Boston Symphony by reducing the total number of man-hours necessary to get its members from performance to performance.   There is some room for improvement in productivity in the live performing arts, but obviously that area is narrow and highly limited.   The evidence, again is that increases in productivity per man-hour, while they have occurred, have been far more sporadic and far smaller in magnitude than those in manufacturing.   The consequence is clear.   We do have in our economy a progressive sector and a nonprogressive sector.   Although no sharp line divides the two, certain industries fall without any question into the one or the other.   The one activity that falls most obviously and clearly into the nonprogressive sector of the economy is the live performing arts.

Implications

I have shown that as productivity in the progressive sector continues to rise, cost of live performance per member of the audience must continue to rise steadily and cumulatively.   But recorded performance can benefit from all the advantages of technology, and so its relative cost advantage over the living arts can be expected to increase.

The implications for the financing of <u>live</u> performance (and live education) are clear cut. Unless ticket prices, tuition costs, or other direct levies on the recipient of these outputs are to rise at a rate far faster than has ever been experienced, the amounts supplied by government and private donors must rise and must continue to rise indefinitely. What is sufficient today must be inadequate tomorrow. What is enough for tomorrow will be insufficient the day after. This is the nature of the social commitment: cumulatively rising responsibility. It is a hard lesson, but a lesson that will have to be taught to those who propose to finance such operations. It is easy to evade the issue and say to donors, "Just give us this additional amount--just enough to cover the great deficit that we have today, and all will be well tomorrow." Although this strategy may help in the short run, I think in the long run it will leave us to reap the whirlwind.

Already the private universities are finding this out. In many of the nation's colleges and universities, contributions have gone up at the phenomenal rate, for one period at least, of 15 per cent a year compounded. Institutions have just concluded fantastically successful capital campaigns netting them, in a number of cases, well over $100 million per institution. On the average, these institutions have raised tuitions seven times since the 1920's, and yet they find that at the conclusion of all this, once again, they are in difficulties. How can they go back to those who have just supplied them with money and tell them they face another crisis? This suggests how important it is to recognize the underlying problems and their technological antecedents and to make these matters clear to the legislatures, to the governments, and to the private supporters who must undertake the funding that will assure to the arts their long-run viability.

This is a hard lesson, but, though it may sound so at first, the outlook it suggests is not as pessimistic as it first appears. When viewed in another way, the resolution of the paradox with which I began is seen to lie not in the growing absolute costs of the arts or of education, but rather in the accumulatively declining costs of manufacturers whose labor becomes constantly more efficient. This means in turn that the phenomenon arises not from the impoverishment of society but from its growing wealth. This difficulty, the cumulative rises in the cost of live performance, is a result of the growing productivity of labor, and the rise in cost becomes more serious the faster productivity rises. The arts become more expensive the more rapidly we accumulate the means with which we can pay for them.

Thus, if society chooses to meet its responsibilities, by the very nature of the problem, it will have the means to do so. And, clearly, if society is not to lose its living arts, an ever-growing volume of financial support is the obligation and the nature of the challenge. Nothing less will suffice.

PRESENT AND FUTURE*

Harold C. Schonberg

After World War II nothing much happened except the most convulsive scientific, social and cultural upheaval in history. Naturally music was affected in general, and the symphony orchestra in particular. Completely new attitudes came into being. Culture, which had been a dirty word in the tobacco-chewing, rural-dominated legislatures of the United States, suddenly became a way of life. This may have resulted from competition with Russia. If Russia could send its great musicians and dancers around the world, to its own infinite credit, the United States could do the same. It did. But there was more to it than that. Something was in the air; and legislators, who previously would not have bothered to send in a single marine had all the orchestras of the country been against a wall faced by a firing squad, began to vie with one another to create arts councils and cultural centers. Culture was Cinderella, and the little lady needed a coach-and-four and a nice, new palace in which to live.

Musicians, especially those who played in orchestras, demanded an equivalent change in their economic status. For the first time, the possibility of full employment and a satisfactory wage scale came within their grasp. Not without fighting for it; there were strikes and cancellations of part or all of a season. But an extraordinary amount of money--government, foundation, industrial and private--was being poured into the American symphony orchestra by the middle 1960s, and the musicians were determined to share in the general prosperity. The Big Five of American orchestras (Boston, New York, Philadelphia, Cleveland and Chicago) actually negotiated contracts that called for full employment. In smaller cities, negotiations resulted in longer seasons and a wage scale that gave more than the miserable pittance prevalent until then.

The esthetic side saw as much of an upheaval as the cultural. Composers immersed themselves in a new kind of music that seemed incomprehensible to all but a few other composers. The schism between avant-garde musician and audiences seemed complete. Another upheaval was the dominance of musicological research, which began to color the viewpoints of all performing musicians, especially when it came to early music. By trying to eradicate certain traditions of romantic performance practice, musicology helped cement a general anti-romantic attitude that had been becoming more and more general since the 1920s.

All this, and more, after World War II.

Efforts were made to meet the new problems. But there
were those who seemed to think it a waste of time. For suddenly,
in the middle 1960s, began to be heard the cry that the orchestra
was dying, and such eminent figures as Leonard Bernstein took to
print worrying about the future.

At the basis of their argument was the fact that, as far as
the repertoire of the symphony orchestra was concerned, music
was no longer a living art. The active repertoire began with Bach
and continued through Strauss and Mahler, with a tapering-off at
Prokofieff and early Stravinsky. Conductors therefore were muse-
um-like custodians of the past. Composers were no longer writing
for the symphony orchestra, on the whole. When they did, the
public refused to listen. Tonality was dead, and the public had no
interest in atonal music. So ran the argument. In any case, electronic music was around the corner, and this medium did away
with the orchestra entirely. As David Burrows wrote in the July
1966 Musical Quarterly:

> ... only in this century has music found a technology to
> compete with what had long been taken for granted in the
> other arts; if so, it does qualify as the cultural Spätling
> [late arrival] that Nietzsche called it. Electronic media
> have put the composer in the position of the painter and
> the poet, not only by giving him complete control over
> the final result, but also by making his tradition continu-
> ously and directly available to him in recordings.   'Pre-
> electronic' may one day have the meaning in music that
> 'pre-literate' does now in literature.

The thought had occurred to some who had attended, in the
early 1960s, the first concert of electronic music sponsored by the
Columbia-Princeton laboratory. When the curtain went up, it revealed some half-dozen loudspeakers on stage in addition to those
placed throughout the auditorium. The audiences, after a startled
gasp, applauded the speakers. (The speakers did not applaud back.)
Throughout the entire evening, not one human being was seen on
stage. Science had finally done it: abolished the performer and
his nasty little ego. Now the composer (and his nasty little ego?)
could rule supreme. Every composer from Mozart on had always
been complaining about the virtuoso and his ego. The complaints
rose to such a crescendo after World War II that today most performers would no sooner change or even modify a composer's
score than a theologian would alter the meaning of the Sermon on
the Mount. But now, after millennia, electronic music had arrived, and the composer could snap his fingers at the world. He
could, literally, create his own tonal universe, assemble the results on tape with appropriate instructions for copying, and the one
performance, the definitive and only performance, unchanging, permanent, could be duplicated anywhere in the world for all time to
come.

Electronic music, together with much avant-garde music, are

but a reflection of the new set of problems that are changing the lives of everybody, and music along with it.   Every generation sees a change in musical philosophy, but never in history has there been the kind of accelerated movement that began with the atomic age following World War II.   It is the end result of a process of disintegration that has been going on since 1900:   an appropriate date, for 1900 saw the formulation of Max Planck's quantum theory, upon which all modern physics is based.   The first decade of the 20th century saw the breakup of classical physics with the work of Planck and Einstein.   The first decade of the 20th century also saw the breakup of representational art with the abstractions of Kandinsky.   The first decade of the 20th century saw the breakup of tonality with the music of Arnold Schoenberg. All within ten years!   Seldom has the <u>Zeitgeist</u> functioned so obligingly and so convincingly.

But if life and thought started to undergo traumatic change shortly after 1900, the accelerated movement of the period after World War II is frightening.   We are faced with the shards of thought that represent the smashup of centuries of accumulated learning, and nobody as yet knows how to put the shards together again.   Very little seems anchored.   Why should not theologians discuss the death of God if Heisenberg is right and molecular movement is merely a set of statistical probabilities?   What happens to causality?   Scientists are busy questioning, and even disproving, assumptions that had been held basic since Euclid.   Existentialism has taken hold of a sizable segment of postwar philosophical thought and has even become a quasi-popular philosophy. Outer space is being explored, and the planets are within our reach: the planets, when the basic problems of humanity are as far from salvation as ever, when modern weaponry can mean the end of the world, when the threat of the population explosion is a prophecy of still another kind of end.   It is an age of psychic unrest, and creators reflect it in their several ways.

Musicians of the avant-garde reflect it by composing a kind of music that is pointillistic, atonal, athematic, rhythmically complicated, resembling nothing so much as atoms in a cloud chamber. Musicians even call upon modern mathematical thought to support their compositions.   Thus Yannis Xenakis in 1957 composed a work named "Pithoprakta," and he explains it by citing "discontinuity ... dense clouds of sound-atoms....   Use is made of the law of large numbers: the normal curve of Gauss, of Maxwell, of Poisson, of continual probabilities, etc., with the criteria of Pearson, Fisher, etc."   Connoisseurs of the new argot dote on those etceteras.

The new music has led to a split between composer and audience.   Today there is much talk about the "crisis in composition," meaning that the avant-garde produces music that only a tiny percentage of the public wants to hear.   A more or less straight line has been broken, and this total rupture between composer and

public is new in the musical scheme of things. In previous generations, roughly to the beginning of this century, there was no
problem. The avant-garde, starting with Mozart (who was considered quite a dangerous radical in some quarters), always saw its
music played. Audiences expected new music. In the 18th century, indeed, brand-new music was the only music in the repertoire. Audiences wanted to hear the very latest; and if they were
disturbed by Mozart or the young Beethoven, there always were
more comforting composers like Salieri or the great Paisiello to
satisfy them. In the 19th century, new music never had to wait
very long for a hearing. If anything, it was old music that had to
wait. When Mendelssohn decided to give a series of programs devoted to Bach, Handel, Mozart and Beethoven, he did so with much
preparation and apology, calling them "Historical Concerts. " Berlioz, Liszt, Schumann and Wagner may have been controversial
figures, to be damned by such important conservative critics as
Chorley and Hanslick; but their music was played, discussed, argued about, constantly analyzed in the newspapers and magazines.
And, again as in the 18th century, there always was a bulwark of
new music that was less controversial. It was supplied by such
composers as Raff, Rubinstein, Parry, Gade: all part of the then
active repertoire, all big men in their day.

    Today there are few big men, in the sense that the previous
avant-garde composers were. Of the manifestations since World
War II--serialism, full atonality, aleatory, Dada, third-stream
jazz--the public will have none of them, even from Stravinsky.
Electronic music is attracting many young composers, but, again,
not the public. Many musicians themselves are baffled. The new
music is immensely hard to play, demanding new ideas about
rhythm, color and, even, basic instrumental technique. Its notation frequently is meaningful only to a relatively few specialists,
and it displays an unheard-of complexity. It is so difficult, poses
so many problems, scares so many performers, that some composers of the avant-garde have been pleading for a return to common sense, saying that matters have gotten out of hand.

    Orchestral musicians on the whole like this music as little
as the public does. The conductors of the older generation find it
meaningless; the conductors of the younger generation avoid it for
reasons: active dislike, in some cases; fear that their orchestras
are not equipped to play it; fear that their audiences will be alien-
atedated. Avant-garde music thus has had to be conducted by
young, dedicated men, none of whom is an international podium
star: men like Pierre Boulez, Gunther Schuller, Robert Craft,
Bruno Bartoletti and Lukas Foss. (Two exceptions were Hermann
Scherchen and Hans Rosbaud, both 19th-century men who managed
to accommodate to the new thought of the 20th.) The problems of
conducting, rehearsing and playing avant-garde music are of such
fantastic complexity that only full-time specialists can handle it.
The New York Philharmonic discovered that during its avant-garde
series in 1963. Its players could not play the music; and more,
they fought it, laughed at it, resented it. Perhaps the next

generation will see musicians who are able to play this music. At
the Berkshire Music Festival, the student orchestra conducted by
Schuller can play avant-garde material with much more authority,
technique and style than their opposite numbers in the Boston Symphony. When the new supply of musicians enters the symphony orchestra the problem may be solved. Until then, there will exist a
breakdown in musical communication between the avant-garde creator and his audience. Right now there is a sort of backlash, in
which the public actively resents the new music and goes out of its
way to avoid it. It is all very well to say that all creators of the
avant-garde have had to fight and wait until their work was accepted. This is true. But the cultural lag until the 20th century
never extended much beyond twenty years or so. In its present
phase it has run over a half century, if such a pivotal score as
Pierrot Lunaire is taken into account. And, considering avant-
garde music after World War II, never in music has there been
the kind of universal loathing that has been created. Which leads
to some hard questions. Is this lack of rapport and communication
necessarily the public's fault? Has the composer failed in his
function? Or has the language of music itself been exhausted?

It is an interesting speculation whether or not the general
retreat from the new music has caused a different post-World War
II phenomenon, the baroque revival. Up to 1948 baroque music
was something for the history books. But, thanks to the long-
playing record, baroque music suddenly became a potent force.
Vivaldi, Corelli, Zelenka, Fasch, Schütz, Geminiani--their music
became the rage. They stepped from the pages of the history
books, bowing and saying hello, very much alive. There was
something in the ordered and logical patterns of much of their music, something in their objective approach, with which modern intellectual life could, and did, identify. But who was going to play
their music? Certainly not Furtwängler or Toscanini. And that
is where musicology stepped in, to correct the abuses of romanticism and show a new generation how this music should be performed.

To the romantic interpreter of the 19th century, life and
music were relatively simple. The romantic period had created
the concept of the Virtuoso-as-Hero. With the arrival of Paganini
and Liszt, and the great singers of the 1830s, and the emergence
of Wagner and his Bayreuth school of conductors, a performance
style for the entire century was formed. It was a style in which
strict textual fidelity did not exist, any more than it had existed in
previous centuries. It goes without saying that romantic performers were completely at home in romantic music. When it came to
earlier music, they were not troubled by the kind of questions that
so agitate today's performers. They merely used their own romantic conventions in the earlier music. Their instinct and intuition
were their sole guide.

Today those practices are frowned upon. It is felt that instinct and intuition are not enough; that a specific set of tools is

needed in addition. In any age dominated by science, the prevailing attitude is objective, and it is an attitude that involves enormous respect for the findings of the specialist. Music is not exempt, and it is part of the Zeitgeist that the findings of musicology have, in recent years, done so much to shape musical thought. Musicology has supplied the tools.

Musicology, one of the newest of the scholarly disciplines, has been conditioning all performers and critics to a greater or lesser degree since World War II. For the past fifty years, musicologists have been attempting to codify musical thought and performance practice of the past, and in the last twenty years a tremendous amount of material has been published. Instead of superimposing artificial, arbitrary and obviously incorrect notions upon early music, said the musicologists, why not try as closely as possible to duplicate the actual practices of the 17th and 18th centuries? To do so, certain questions had to be answered. How big was Bach's orchestra? Mozart's? How were the instruments distributed? Exactly how are the ornaments to be played and the figured basses to be realized? How is a trill executed? How did the execution of the ornaments vary from period to period and country to country? Just how corrupt were the editions of early music commonly used by performers? (Very corrupt, it often turned out.) What was pitch 250 years ago? Tempo?

Conductors with their roots in the 19th century--Walter, Beecham, Furtwängler, Toscanini--never worried much about those problems. Nor did younger conductors, for their training was in a romantic tradition. In any case, the problems were largely immaterial. Aside from a few pieces by Bach and Handel (who was known almost exclusively by one work, his Messiah), and some ten symphonies by Haydn and Mozart (who composed 145 between them), the repertoire up to the end of World War II was an overwhelmingly 19th-century one, Stravinsky, Bartók, Shostakovich and Prokofieff notwithstanding. Then came the LP disc, and for some inexplicable reason there arose an unprecedented demand for baroque music. The law of supply and demand immediately went into effect, and with it the emergence of a new kind of podium specialist--a conductor who devoted himself almost exclusively to pre-Beethoven music, often working closely with musicologists, anxious to present early music with maximum authenticity. Such conductors as Karl Münchinger, Karl Richter, Mogens Wøldike, Frederic Waldman, Antonio Janigro, Safford Cape, Rudolf Baumgartner, Thurston Dart, Noah Greenberg, Karl Haas, Denis Stevens, Newell Jenkins and August Wenzinger came into prominence after World War II as scholar-conductors who knew much more about performance practice in early music than any of the international stars.

Europe and the United States were inundated by the baroque. But there was a curious by-product. Popular as it is--many record companies have been kept alive specializing in it--baroque music has made very little impression on the international symphony orchestra, which, by and large, plays much the same music it did fifty years ago. Therefore, small orchestras had to be created to take care of early music; their big brothers could not be less interested. In addition, small performing groups sprang up. A close study of the New York recital scene shows a formidable number of concerts devoted to baroque and Renaissance music. Some are well publicized and fill the major concert halls; many are intimate affairs played by little-publicized musicians in the smaller halls. This interest in the baroque is one of the phenomena of the postwar period, and it is not the antithesis of the other phenomenon --the international serial language of the avant-garde--that one might imagine. Like serial music, the preponderance of baroque music is objective, dealing more with workmanship than with striking ideas, bearing its own built-in academism.

One other striking aspect of the period following World War II should be mentioned, and it involves the newer conductors. Two of them are Oriental--Zubin Mehta, from India, and Seiji Ozawa, from Japan--and they are the first two in history to impress one as altogether major talents. But take a look at some of the other prominent young conductors: Lorin Maazel (United States), Bernard Haitink (Holland), Colin Davis (England), Istvan Kertesz (Hungary), Claudio Abbado (Italy). Each of these is a candidate for greatness, and it is interesting to note that there is not a German or Austrian on the list. Can it be that the great Austro-German tradition of conducting is in the process of being broken up? For some two hundred years it has been the most potent force in the history of conducting, but Wolfgang Sawallisch and Herbert von Karajan seem to be the last major conductors of that school, and they can no longer be considered young conductors.

What we have, all over the world in every aspect of music, is something that can be described as The New Eclecticism. A few exceptions to the contrary, it is hard to tell the difference between a young American and a young English or Hungarian conductor, just as it is getting harder and harder to distinguish national styles in piano playing or composition. Even symphony orchestras are beginning to sound alike, no matter where their point of origin.

The chances are that--barring a universal disaster--future years will see less and less of a national school of conducting or, indeed, of any kind of nationalistic music making. Slowly the one-world idea is becoming more than mere idea. Intellectual life today has become highly international. Ideas are disseminated with, quite literally, the speed of light, and there has been since World War II a kind of cross-pollination that is making provincialism and nationalism a thing of the past. Even physical bodies are transported so quickly and efficiently that there has been a smoothing-out in human contact. It has come to the point where regional accents have all but been eliminated, even in Russia, where once-forbidden ideas are now openly discussed, and where there are active schools of ultra-modern music and painting. A sort of musical lingua franca will be the end result. As human beings,

musicians, of course, will respond individually to the various
stimuli they encounter and absorb; but the stimuli are beginning to
be much the same everywhere, thanks to radio, television, Tel-
star, the jet plane, the tape recorder and LP records, the breakdown of social classes and the generally higher educational background. Interpreters of music will continue to be individuals in
that they are individuals; but they also will be representatives of
international rather than local thought. While none of us will live
to see the Schiller-Beethoven ideal--Alle Menschen werden Brüder--
it is inevitable in the progress of music, just as it is inevitable
in the progress of mankind.

AN OPEN LETTER*

Leonard Bernstein

My dear and gentle Reader:

        Everyone says that this is a critical moment in the history
of music. I agree, but double in spades: it is a scary moment.
The famous gulf between composer and audience is not only wider
than ever: it has become an ocean. What is more, it has frozen
over; and it shows no immediate signs of either narrowing or thaw-
ing.

        It has been claimed that the abovementioned gulf first ap-
peared as a tiny fissure the moment a composer first set down his
personal message, conceived in his own unconscious rather than in
the collective unconscious of the sacred/secular community. This
may well be; and, if true, makes our gulf hundreds of years old.
But throughout this period--even in the wildest years of Roman-
ticism--there has always been some relation between composer and
public, a symbiotic interaction that has fed both. The composer
has been the manipulator of musical dynamics, responsible for
change and growth, creating the public taste and then satisfying it
with the appropriate nutriment; while the public, quid pro quo, has
nourished him by simply being interested. Any new opera, by
Monteverdi, Rossini, Wagner or Puccini has in its time invariably
been an occasion for curiosity, speculation and excitement. Likewise a new symphony of Haydn or Brahms, a new sonata of Scar-
latti or Chopin.

        This is no longer true, nor has it been true in our century.
The First World War seemed to mark a full stop: Debussy, Mahler, Strauss, and the early Stravinsky barely made the finish line;

*From The Infinite Variety of Music, by Leonard Bernstein; New
York: Simon & Schuster, 1966. Copyright 1962, 1965, 1966 by
Leonard Bernstein; copyright 1966 by the Leonard Bernstein
Foundation. Reprinted by permission of Simon and Schuster.

they were the last names in that long era of mutually dependent composer and public. From then on it became a hassle: composer versus public. For fifty years now audiences have been primarily interested in music of the past; even now they (you) are just catching up with Vivaldi, Bellini, Buxtehude, Ives. The controversy backs and fills about Wagner, as though he were Stockhausen. We (you) are still discovering Haydn symphonies, Handel operas. And it still requires a monumental effort of concentration for the average concert-goer to absorb the "Eroica" as a full, continuous formal experience. To say nothing of "Elektra," "Pelleas," or Mahler's "Seventh." Gentle Reader, be frank and admit it.

What this means is that for fifty years the public has not anticipated with delight the première of a single symphonic or operatic work. If this seems too strong a statement, then fight back; remind me of the glaring exceptions: Porgy and Bess (can show tunes make an opera?); Shostakovitch's "Seventh Symphony" (a wartime enthusiasm inflated to hysteria by the competition of broadcasting networks); Mahagonny (a local quasi-political phenomenon).... The list could go on; but these works were all exceptions, and their delights anticipated chiefly for nonmusical reasons. The hideous fact remains that composer and public are an ocean apart and have been for half a century. Can you think of any other fifty-year period since the Renaissance when such a situation obtained? I can't. And if this is true, it signifies a dramatic qualitative change in our musical society: namely, that for the first time we are living a musical life that is not based on the composition of our time. This is purely a 20th-century phenomenon; it has never been true before.

We could conceivably look at this drastic change with equanimity, form a quasi-scientific opinion about its causes, and even project an objective theory as to its probable future course--if it were not for the fact that we are simultaneously living with such an incredible boom in musical activity. Statistics are soaring: more people are listening to more music than ever before. And it is the intersection of these two phenomena--the public's enormous new interest in music, plus their total lack of interest in new music, the musical bang plus the musical whimper--that has created this scary moment.

I am a fanatic music lover. I can't live one day without hearing music, playing it, studying it, or thinking about it. And all this is quite apart from my professional role as musician; I am a fan, a committed member of the musical public. And in this role (which I presume is not too different from yours, gentle Reader), in this role of simple music lover, I confess, freely though unhappily, that at this moment, as of this writing, God forgive me, I have far more pleasure in following the musical adventures of Simon & Garfunkel or of The Association singing "Along Comes Mary" than I have in most of what is being written now by the whole community of "avant-garde" composers. This may not be true a year from now, or even by the time these words appear in

print; but right now, on the 21st of June, 1966, that is how I feel.
Pop music seems to be the only area where there is to be found
unabashed vitality, the fun of invention, the feeling of fresh air.
Everything else suddenly seems old-fashioned: electronic music,
serialism, chance music--they have already acquired the musty
odor of academicism.   Even jazz seems to have ground to a painful halt.   And tonal music lies in abeyance, dormant.

And right here, dear Reader (if you are still with me and
have your wits about you), you will put me up short.   How can
you, as you have, contend (you will ask, I hope) that there is infinite variety, hence untold aspects of beauty, still to be revealed,
if this change is qualitative?   How do you reconcile the gulf with
the hope?   I have two answers.   The first is simple, reverse
logic: if I believed in the permanence of that gulf I would have to
disbelieve in the validity of musical communication, of our psychic
speech; and I would then no longer wish to live in this world.   But
I do want to continue living in this world, and therefore musical
communication (warmth, understanding, revelation) must be valid.
I wish there were a better word for communication; I mean by it
the tenderness we feel when we recognize and share with another
human being a deep, unnameable, elusive emotional shape or shade.
That is really what a composer is saying in his music: has this
ever happened to you?   Haven't you experienced this same tone,
insight, shock, anxiety, release?   And when you react to ("like")
a piece of music, you are simply replying to the composer, yes.

My second answer is simpler still, although it may take a
little longer to say it.   The gulf is temporary; the change, though
qualitative, is transitional.   The critical moment through which
we are living, extended though it may be into an era, cannot define
music in terms of its future.   It is a moment of waiting, of flux.

Having said that I believe this musical crisis to be transi-
tory in nature, I must now say where the transition may be leading, and why.   I think that the key is to be found in the nature of
music itself.   It is an art so distinct, so utterly different from all
other arts, that we must be careful not to assign to it values and
dynamics it does not have.   This is the mistake so many people
make who follow the arts as a whole and try to deduce generalizations about them.   What works in other arts does not necessarily
work in music.   Let us, for the sake of argument, try for a generalization.   What is the nature of this crisis in all the arts today?   We are constantly hearing negative phrases: anti-art, anti-
play, anti-novel, anti-hero, non-picture, non-poem.   We hear that
art has become, perforce, art-commentary; we fear that techniques
have swallowed up what used to be known as content.   All this is
reputed to be lamentable, a poor show, a sad state.   And yet look
at how many works of art, conceived in something like these
terms, prosper, attract a large following, and even succeed in
moving us deeply.   There must be something good in all this nega-
tivism.

And there is. For what these works are doing is simply
moving constantly toward more poetic fields of relevance. Let us
now be specific: Waiting for Godot is a mightily moving and com-
passionate non-play. La Dolce Vita, which deals with emptiness
and tawdriness, is a curiously invigorating film, even an inspiring
one. Nabokov's non-novel Pale Fire is a thrilling masterpiece, and
its hero, Charles Kinbote, is a pure non-hero. Balanchine's most
abstract and esoteric ballets are his prize smash hits. De Koon-
ing's pictures can be wonderfully decorative, suggestive, stimulating and very expensive. This could become a very long list indeed; but there is one thing that it could not include--a piece of
serious anti-music. Music cannot prosper as a non-art, because
it is basically and radically an abstract art, whereas all the other
arts deal basically with real images--words, shapes, stories, the
human body. And when a great artist takes a real image and ab-
stracts it, or joins it to another real image that seems irrelevant,
or combines them in an illogical way, he is poeticizing. In this
sense Joyce is more poetical than Zola, Balanchine more than
Petipa, Nabokov more than Tolstoy, Fellini more than Griffith.
But John Cage is not more poetical than Mahler, nor is Boulez
more so than Debussy.

Why must music be excluded from this very prosperous
tendency in the arts? Because it is abstract to start with; it deals
directly with the emotions, through a transparent medium of tones
which are unrelated to any representational aspects of living. The
only "reality" these tones can have is form--that is, the precise
way in which these tones interconnect. And by form I mean the
shape of a two-note motive as well as of a phrase, or of the whole
second act of Tristan. One cannot "abstract" musical tones; on the
contrary they have to be given their reality through form: up-and-
down, long-and-short, loud-and-soft.

And so to the inescapable conclusion. All forms that we
have ever known--plain chant, motet, fugue, or sonata--have always been conceived in tonality, that is, in the sense of a tonal
magnetic center, with subsidiary tonal relationships. This sense,
I believe, is built into the human organism; we cannot hear two
isolated tones, even devoid of any context, without immediately im-
puting a tonal meaning to them. We may differ from one another
in the tonal meaning we infer, but we infer it nonetheless. We
are stuck with this, and always will be. And the moment a composer tries to "abstract" musical tones by denying them their tonal
implications, he has left the world of communication. In fact, it
is all but impossible to do (although Heaven knows how hard composers have been trying for fifty years)--as witness the increasingly desperate means being resorted to--chance-music, electronic
sounds, noteless "instructions," the manipulation of noise, whatnot.

It has occasionally occurred to me that music could conceivably exist, some distant day, ultimately detached from tonality. I
can't hear such music in my head, but I am willing to grant the
possibility. Only that distant day would have to have seen a

fundamental change in our physical laws, possibly through man's detaching himself from this planet. Perhaps he has already begun, in his spacechase, the long road to that New Consciousness, that Omega point. Perhaps we are some day to be freed from the tyranny of time, the dictatorship of the harmonic series. Perhaps. But meanwhile we are still earth-based, earth-bound, far from any Omega point, caught up in such old-fashioned things as human relationships, ideological, international, and interracial strife. We are not by any stretch of the imagination planet-free, the wish dreams of our cosmologists notwithstanding. How can we speak of reaching the Omega point when we are still playing such backyard games as Vietnam?

No, we are still earth creatures, still needful of human warmth and the need to communicate among ourselves. For which the Lord be praised. And as long as there is reaching out of one of us to another, there will be the healing comfort of tonal response. It can be no mere coincidence that after half a century of radical experiment the best and best-loved works in atonal or 12-tone or serial idioms are those works which seem to have preserved, against all odds, some backdrop of tonality--those works which are richest in tonal implications. I think offhand of Schoenberg's Third Quartet, his Violin Concerto, his two Chamber Symphonies; almost all of Berg's music; Stravinsky in "Agon" or "Threni"; even Webern in his Symphony or in his second Cantata-- in all of these works there are continuous and assertive specters of tonality that haunt you as you listen. And the more you listen, the more you are haunted. And in the haunting you feel the agony of longing for tonality, the violent wrench away from it, and the blind need to recapture it.

We will recapture it. That is the meaning of our transition, our crisis. But we will come back to it in a new relationship, renewed by the catharsis of our agony. I cannot resist drawing a parallel between the much-proclaimed Death of Tonality and the equally trumpeted Death of God. Curious, isn't it, that Nietzsche issued that particular proclamation in 1883, the same year that Wagner died, supposedly taking tonality to the grave with him? Dear Reader, I humbly submit to you the proposition that neither death is true; all that has died is our own outworn conceptions. The crisis in faith through which we are living is not unlike the musical crisis; we will, if we are lucky, come out of them both with new and freer concepts, more personal perhaps--or even less personal: who is to say?--but in any case with a new idea of God, a new idea of tonality. And music will survive.

SELECTED BIBLIOGRAPHY
(Books and Periodicals)

American Federation of Musicians of the United States and Canada. International Musician. Newark, N. J. , 1901- monthly.

American String Teachers Association. The American String Teacher. Wantagh, N. Y. , 1950- quarterly.

American Symphony Orchestra League. Economic Conditions of Symphony Orchestras and Their Musicians. Charleston, W. Va. : American Symphony Orchestra League, 1961.

_____ . Newsletter. Vienna, Va. , 1950- bi-monthly (became Symphony News in 1972).

_____ . Symphony News (formerly Newsletter, q. v.).

Antek, Samuel. This Was Toscanini. New York: Vanguard Press, 1963.

Arian, Edward. Bach, Beethoven, and Bureaucracy. University: University of Alabama Press, 1971.

Austin, William W. Music in the Twentieth Century. New York: Norton, 1966.

Babitz, Sol. The Violin: Views and Reviews. Urbana, Ill. : American String Teachers Assoc. , 1959.

Backus, John. The Acoustical Foundations of Music. New York: Norton, 1969.

Baines, Anthony, ed. Musical Instruments Through the Ages. Baltimore: Penguin Books, 1961.

Bamberger, Carl, ed. The Conductor 's Art. New York: Mc-Graw-Hill, 1965.

Barzun, Jacques. Music in American Life. Garden City, N. Y. : Doubleday, 1956.

Bate, Philip. The Flute. New York: Norton, 1969.

Baumol, William J. and Bowen, William G. Performing Arts:
    The Economic Dilemma. New York: Twentieth Century
    Fund, 1966.

Bekker, Paul. The Orchestra. New York: Norton, 1936.

Benade, Arthur H. Horns, Strings and Harmony. Garden City,
    N. Y. : Doubleday, 1960.

Beranek, Leo. Music Acoustics and Architecture. New York:
    Wiley, 1962.

Berlioz, Hector. A Treatise on Modern Instrumentation and Or-
    chestration. Translated by Mary Cowden Clark. London:
    Novello and Co. , 1858.

Bernstein, Leonard. The Infinite Variety of Music. New York:
    Simon & Schuster, 1966.

Billboard Publications, Inc. High Fidelity/Musical America. New
    York, 1965- monthly (plus Dec. directory issue).

Blades, James. Orchestral Percussion Technique. London and
    New York: Oxford University Press, 1961.

Blaukopf, Kurt. Mahler. New York: Praeger, 1973.

Boult, Adrian C. Thoughts on Conducting. London: Phoenix
    House, 1963.

Business Committee for the Arts. Arts Business. New York,
    1972--monthly.

Carpenter, Paul S. Music: An Art and a Business. Norman:
    University of Oklahoma Press, 1950.

Carse, Adam. The History of Orchestration (1925). reprinted
    New York: Dover Publications, 1964.

_____. The Orchestra from Beethoven to Berlioz. Cambridge,
    Eng. : W. Heffer & Sons, 1948.

_____. The Orchestra in the XVIII Century. Cambridge, Eng. :
    W. Heffer & Sons, 1940.

_____. Orchestral Conducting. London: Augener, 1935.

Chagy, Gideon. The New Patrons of the Arts. New York: Ab-
    rams, 1973.

_____, ed. The State of the Arts and Corporate Support. New
    York: Paul S. Eriksson, 1971.

Chase, Gilbert. America's Music: From the Pilgrims to the Present. New York: McGraw-Hill, 1966.

Chotzinoff, Samuel. Toscanini: An Intimate Portrait. New York: Knopf, 1956.

Coar, Richard. The French Horn. Ann Arbor, Mich. : Edwards Brothers, 1947.

Cumming, Robert, ed. They Talk About Music. Rockville Centre, N. Y. : Belwin/Mills Pub. Corp. , 1971. 2 vols.

Dickson, Harry Ellis. Gentlemen, More Dolce Please! Boston: Beacon Press, 1969.

Dorian, Frederick. Commitment to Culture. Pittsburgh: University of Pittsburgh Press, 1964.

_____. The History of Music in Performance. New York: Norton, 1942.

Eells, Richard. The Corporation and the Arts. New York: Macmillan, 1967.

Erskine, John. The Philharmonic-Symphony Society of New York: Its First Hundred Years. New York: Macmillan, 1943.

Etzkorn, K. Peter, ed. Music and Society. New York: Wiley, 1973.

Ewen, David. Dictators of the Baton. Chicago: Alliance Book Corp. , 1943.

Farga, Franz. Violins and Violinists. New York: Praeger, 1969.

Farnsworth, Paul R. The Social Psychology of Music. Ames: Iowa State University Press, 1968.

Flesch, Carl. The Art of Violin Playing. English text by Frederick H. Martens. New York: C. Fischer, 1924-1930.

Ford Foundation. Activities in the Creative and Performing Arts: Support in the Musical Arts, 1957-1970. New York, 1971.

_____. The Finances of the Performing Arts, Vols. I & II. New York, 1974.

Fuchs, Peter Paul. The Psychology of Conducting. New York: MCA Music, 1969.

Furlong, William Barry. Season with Solti: A Year in the Life of the Chicago Symphony. New York: Macmillan, 1974.

Geiringer, Karl. Musical Instruments. London and New York: Oxford University Press, 1945.

Gingrich, Arnold. Business and the Arts. New York: Paul S. Eriksson, 1969.

Goldbeck, Frederick. The Perfect Conductor. New York: Pellegrini and Cudahy, 1951.

Goldin, Milton. The Music Merchants. New York: Macmillan, 1969.

Goulden, Joseph C. The Money Givers. New York: Random House, 1971.

Grant, Margaret S. and Hettinger, Herman S. America's Symphony Orchestras. New York: Norton, 1940.

Gregory, Robin. The Horn. New York: Praeger, 1969.

Grout, Donald Jay. A History of Western Music. New York: Norton, 1960.

Hart, Philip. Orpheus in the New World. New York: Norton, 1973.

Hatterer, Lawrence J. The Artist in Society. New York: Grove Press, 1965.

Hines, Robert Stephan, ed. The Orchestral Composer's Point of View. Norman: University of Oklahoma Press, 1969.

Howard, John Tasker. Our American Music. New York: Crowell, 1946.

Howe, M. A. DeWolf. The Boston Symphony Orchestra 1881-1931. Boston: Houghton Mifflin, 1931.

Hughes, Charles W. The Human Side of Music. New York: Philosophical Library, 1948.

Hurok, Solomon. Impresario. New York: Random House, 1960.

Instrumentalist Co. The Instrumentalist: A Magazine for School and College Band and Orchestra Directors.... Evanston, Ill., 1946- monthly (except July).

International Conference of Symphony and Opera Musicians. Senza Sordino. Cincinnati, 1962--bi-monthly.

Jackson, Gerald. First Flute. London: J. M. Dent, 1968.

Johnson, H. Earle. Symphony Hall. Boston: Little, Brown, 1950.

Kaplan, Max. "The Musician in America: A Study of His Social Roles. " Unpublished dissertation. Ann Arbor, Mich. : University Microfilms, 1951.

Kennedy, Michael. Barbirolli, Conductor Laureate. London: MacGibbon and Kee, 1971.

Kniebusch, Carol. Analysis of Major Orchestra Master Contracts. Vienna, Va. : American Symphony Orchestra League, 1972.

_____. Analysis of Metropolitan Orchestra Master Contracts. Vienna, Va. : American Symphony Orchestra League, 1972.

Krehbiel, Henry Edward. The Philharmonic Society of New York. New York and London: Novello, Ewer and Co. , 1892.

Krell, John. Kincaidiana. Culver City, Calif. : Trio Associates, 1973.

Krueger, Karl. The Way of the Conductor. New York: Scribner's, 1969.

Kupferberg, Herbert. Those Fabulous Philadelphians. New York: Scribner's, 1969.

Lang, Paul Henry. Music in Western Civilization. New York: Norton, 1941.

_____, ed. The Symphony; 1800-1900. New York: Norton, 1969.

Langenus, Gustave. Six Articles for Woodwind Players. New York: C. Fischer, 1923.

Langwell, Lyndesay G. The Bassoon and Double Bassoon. London: Hinrichsen Edition, n. d.

LeBlond, Jr. Richard Emmett. "Professionalization and Bureaucratization of the Performance of Serious Music in the United States. " Unpublished dissertation. Ann Arbor, Mich. : University Microfilms, 1968.

Leichtentritt, Hugo. Serge Koussevitzky: The Boston Symphony Orchestra and the New American Music. Cambridge, Mass. : Harvard University Press, 1946.

Leiter, Robert D. The Musicians and Petrillo. New York: Bookman Associates, 1953.

Levant, Oscar. A Smattering of Ignorance. New York: Doubleday, Dorman, 1940.

Levy, Alan. The Culture Vultures. New York: Putnam, 1968.

Marsh, Robert C. The Cleveland Orchestra. Cleveland: World,
    1967.

Mayer, Martin. Bricks, Mortar and the Performing Arts. New
    York: Twentieth Century Fund, 1970.

Mayer, Robert M. Essentials of Oboe Playing. Des Plaines, Ill. :
    Karnes Music Co. , 1969.

Mellers, Wilfrid. Music and Society. New York: Roy Publish-
    ers, 1950.

Meyer, Leonard B. Emotion and Meaning in Music. Chicago:
    University of Chicago Press, 1956.

_____. Music, the Arts, and Ideas. Chicago: University of
    Chicago Press, 1967.

Midwest Research Institute. An Evaluation of the Performing Arts:
    The Symphony. Kansas City, 1969.

Morison, Bradley and Fliehr, Kay. In Search of an Audience.
    New York: Pitman, 1968.

Moskow, Michael H. Labor Relations in the Performing Arts: A
    Preliminary Survey. New York: Associated Councils of the
    Arts, 1969.

Mozart, Leopold. A Treatise on the Fundamental Principles of
    Violin Playing. Translated by Editha Knocker. London and
    New York: Oxford University Press, 1948.

Mueller, John H. The American Symphony Orchestra. Blooming-
    ton: Indiana University Press, 1951.

Mueller, Kate Hevner. Twenty-Seven Major American Symphony
    Orchestras. Bloomington: Indiana University Press, 1973.

Munch, Charles. I Am a Conductor. Translated by Leonard Bur-
    kat. London and New York: Oxford University Press, 1955.

Music Journal Inc. Music Journal; Educational Music Magazine.
    New York, 1943- monthly (Sept. -June).

Musselman, Joseph A. Music in the Cultured Generation. Evan-
    ston, Ill. : Northwestern University Press, 1971.

National Research Center of the Arts. Americans and the Arts.
    New York: Associated Councils of the Arts, 1974.

Nelson, Sheila. The Violin and Viola. New York: Norton, 1972.

Ostransky, Leroy, ed. The World of Music. Englewood Cliffs, N. J. : Prentice-Hall, 1969.

Otis, Philo A. The Chicago Symphony Orchestra: Its Organization, Growth and Development. Chicago: Clayton F. Summy, 1924.

Pavlakis, Christopher. The American Music Handbook. New York: Free Press, 1974.

Piatigorsky, Gregor. Cellist. Garden City, N. Y. : Doubleday, 1965.

Prieve, E. Arthur and Allen, Ira W. Administration in the Arts: An Annotated Bibliography of Selected References. Madison: Center for Arts Administration, Graduate School of Business, University of Wisconsin, 1973.

Reed, H. Owen and Leach, Joel T. Scoring for Percussion. Englewood Cliffs, N. J. : Prentice-Hall, 1969.

Reid, Charles. John Barbirolli. New York: Taplinger, 1971.

Reiss, Alvin H. The Arts Management Handbook. New York: Laws-Arts Publishers, 1970.

_____. Culture and Company. New York: Twayne, 1972.

Rendall, Francis Geoffrey. The Clarinet. New York: Norton, 1971.

Rensch, Rosalyn. The Harp. New York: Philosophical Library, 1950.

Rich, Allen. Careers and Opportunities in Music. New York: Dutton, 1964.

Rockefeller Brothers Fund. The Performing Arts: Problems and Prospects. A Rockefeller Panel Report. New York: Mc-Graw-Hill, 1965.

Rockefeller Foundation. R F Illustrated. New York, 1972-- quarterly.

Rothwell, Evelyn. Oboe Technique. London and New York: Oxford University Press, 1953.

Roussel, Hubert. The Houston Symphony Orchestra, 1913-1971. Austin: University of Texas Press, 1972.

Rudolf, Max. The Grammar of Conducting. New York: G. Schirmer, 1950.

Russcol, Herbert and Banai, Margalit. Philharmonic. New York: Coward McCann and Geoghegan, 1970.

Russell, Charles Edward. The American Orchestra and Theodore Thomas. Garden City, N. Y. : Doubleday, Page, 1927.

Sachs, Curt. The History of Musical Instruments. New York: Norton, 1940.

_____. Our Musical Heritage. New York: Prentice-Hall, 1955.

Scherchen, Hermann. Handbook of Conducting. London and New York: Oxford University Press, 1942.

Schlesinger, Janet. Challenge to the Urban Orchestra--The Case of the Pittsburgh Symphony. N. p. , n. p. , 1971.

Schonberg, Harold C. The Great Conductors. New York: Simon & Schuster, 1967.

Schroeder, Carl. Handbook of Conducting. Translated and edited by J. Matthews. London: Augener, 1889.

Seligson, Sureva. Economic Aspects of the Performing Arts: A Portrait in Figures. Washington, D. C. : Government Printing Office, 1971.

Shanet, Howard. Philharmonic: A History of New York's Orchestra. New York: Doubleday, 1975.

Shemel, Sidney and Krasilovsky, M. William. This Business of Music. New York: Billboard Pub. Co. , 1964.

Shore, Bernard. The Orchestra Speaks. London: Longmans, Green, 1938.

Silbermann, Alphons. The Sociology of Music. Translated by Corbet Stewart. London: Routledge and Kegan Paul, 1963.

Smith, Moses. Koussevitsky. New York: Allen, Towne and Heath, 1947.

Stoddard, Hope. Subsidy Makes Sense. Newark: American Federation of Musicians, n. d.

Stokowski, Leopold. Music for All of Us. New York: Simon & Schuster, 1943.

Swift-Door Publications, Inc. Brass and Percussion. Oneonta, N. Y. , 1973--Feb. , April, June, Sept. , Dec.

_____. Woodwind World. Oneonta, N. Y. , 1957--Feb. , April, June, Sept. , Dec.

Swoboda, Henry, ed. The American Symphony Orchestra. New
    York: Basic Books, 1967.

Szigeti, Joseph. Szigeti on the Violin. New York: Praeger, 1970.

_____. With Strings Attached. New York: Knopf, 1947.

Tandler, Adolph. The Orchestral Manual for Orchestral Players.
    Los Angeles: Tandler, 1946.

Taubman, Howard. Music on My Beat. New York: Simon &
    Schuster, 1943.

_____. The Symphony Orchestra Abroad. Vienna, Va. : Amer-
    ican Symphony Orchestra League, 1970.

Temianka, Henri. Facing the Music. New York: David McKay,
    1973.

Terry, Charles Sanford. Bach's Orchestra. London and New
    York: Oxford University Press, 1932.

Thompson, Helen M. Report of Study on Governing Boards of
    Symphony Orchestras. Charleston, W. Va. : American Sym-
    phony Orchestra League, 1958.

Thomson, Virgil. The State of Music. New York: Morrow, 1939.

Toffler, Alvin. The Culture Consumers. New York: St. Martin's
    Press, 1964.

Toobin, Jerome. Agitato. New York: Viking Press, 1975.

Twentieth Century Fund. How Collective Bargaining Works. New
    York, 1942.

Upton, George P. , ed. Theodore Thomas. Chicago: A. C. Mc-
    Clurg, 1905. 2 vols.

Walter, Bruno. Of Music and Music-Making. New York: Norton,
    1961.

Williams, Raymond. Culture and Society. Garden City, N. Y. :
    Doubleday Anchor Books, 1960.

Willis, Thomas. The Chicago Symphony Orchestra. Chicago:
    Rand McNally, 1974.

Woodwind Anthology. Evanston, Ill. : Instrumentalist Co. , 1972.

Wooldridge, David. Conductor's World. New York: Praeger, 1970.

Yates, Peter. Twentieth Century Music. New York: Pantheon,
     1967.

Ziff-Davis Pub. Co. Stereo Review (formerly HiFi Stereo Review).
     New York, 1958- monthly.

INDEX

461